Business in Action

An Introduction to Business

Second Edition

LESTER R. BITTEL
Professor of Management
School of Business
James Madison University

RONALD S. BURKE
Adjunct Professor
Lord Fairfax Community College

R. LAWRENCE LaFORGE
Associate Professor of Management
College of Commerce and Industry
Clemson University

Gregg Division/McGraw-Hill Book Company
New York   Atlanta   Dallas   St. Louis   San Francisco
Auckland   Bogotá   Guatemala   Hamburg   Johannesburg   Lisbon
London   Madrid   Mexico   Montreal   New Delhi   Panama   Paris
San Juan   São Paulo   Singapore   Sydney   Tokyo   Toronto

Sponsoring Editor: Lawrence H. Wexler
Editing Supervisor: Sharon E. Kaufman
Design and Art Supervisor/Cover and Interior
   Design: Karen Tureck
Production Supervisor: Frank P. Bellantoni

Cover Art: Iversen Associates
Pictograph Artist: David R. Thurston
Charts and Graphs: Steve Burnett Inc.

**LIBRARY OF CONGRESS CATALOGING IN
PUBLICATION DATA**

Bittel, Lester R.
   Business in action.

   Includes index.
   1. Business enterprises—United States.
2. Industrial management—United States.
I. Burke, Ronald S.   II. LaForge, R.
Lawrence.   III. Title.
HF5343.B57   1984   658   83-18687
ISBN 0-07-005515-7

Contents

PREFACE vii

TO THE STUDENT xi

ACKNOWLEDGMENTS xiii

CHAPTER 1   **THE BUSINESS SYSTEM IN THE UNITED STATES 2**

1 The Business Enterprise 4   2 Values 6   3 The Business Process 8   4 Kinds of Businesses 9   5 The Dynamics of Business 11   6 American Business History 14

CHAPTER 2   **THE AMERICAN ECONOMIC SYSTEM 18**

1 Features Common to All Systems 20   2 The Law of Supply and Demand 22   3 The Private Enterprise System 24   4 Modified Capitalism 27   5 Socialism and Communism 28   6 Economic Measurements 30

CHAPTER 3   **THE AMERICAN BUSINESS ENVIRONMENT 38**

1 Systems and the Environment 40   2 The Economic Environment 41   3 The Legal-Political Environment 43   4 The Social-Cultural Environment 45   5 The Physical Environment 49

Unit 1 The Nature of American Business 1

CHAPTER 4   **THE LEGAL FORMS OF BUSINESS OWNERSHIP 54**

1 Private Versus Public Ownership 56   2 Forms of Business Ownership 56   3 Sole Proprietorship 58   4 General Partnership 60   5 Corporation 61   6 Choice of Ownership Form 64   7 Other Forms of Business 65

CHAPTER 5   **MANAGERIAL FUNCTIONS IN A BUSINESS 74**

1 Management Defined 76   2 Management as Art and Science 77   3 Approaches to Management 78   4 Management Functions 79   5 Characteristics of Good Managers 83

CHAPTER 6   **INTERNAL STRUCTURE OF BUSINESS ORGANIZATIONS 88**

1 Organization Defined 90   2 Formal and Informal Organization 90   3 Allocation of Work 91   4 Delegation 92   5 Principles of Organization 94   6 Typical Organization Structures 96

Unit 2 The Form and Structure of American Business 53

CHAPTER 7   MARKETS AND MARKETING 106

1 The Marketing Concept 108   2 Marketing Elements 108   3 Markets 109   4 Product Planning 114   5 Product Pricing 115   6 Functions of Marketing Managers 117   7 Marketing Segmentation and Market Research 120

CHAPTER 8   MARKETING DISTRIBUTION SYSTEMS 124

1 Purpose of Distribution Systems 126   2 Distribution Channels 127   3 Wholesalers 131   4 Retailers 132   5 Physical Distribution Strategies 134   6 Modes of Transportation 135

CHAPTER 9   MARKETING PROMOTION 142

1 The Function of Marketing Promotion 144   2 Promotion Objectives 145   3 Personal Selling 147   4 Advertising Principles 149   5 Advertising Media and Selection 152   6 Sales Promotion 154   7 Advertising and the Public 155

**Unit 3
Basic Business Operations—
Marketing 105**

CHAPTER 10   LOCATION, LAYOUT, AND MANAGEMENT OF FACILITIES 162

1 Location of Facilities 165   2 Kinds of Business Processes 167   3 Equipment and Technology 171   4 Physical Layout of Processing 173   5 Management of Production or Operations 174

CHAPTER 11   PRODUCTION MATERIALS MANAGEMENT 182

1 Purpose and Scope 184   2 Production Planning and Control 185   3 Industrial Purchasing 190   4 Inventory Control 193   5 Materials Movement and Handling 195

CHAPTER 12   OPERATING A SMALL BUSINESS 198

1 Small Firms Do Everything Large Firms Do 200   2 A Special Kind of Individual Prevails 202   3 Each Kind of Operation Has Its Distinct Challenge 204   4 Financial Literacy Is Essential 208   5 The Government Tries to Help 212

**Unit 4
Basic Business Operations—
Production and Small Business 161**

CHAPTER 13   FINANCIAL MANAGEMENT AND FUNDING 218

1 Financial Planning for Businesses 220   2 Sources of Funds for Business 223   3 Equity Versus Debt Financing 224   4 Short-Term Debt Financing 225   5 Long-Term Debt Financing 228   6 Long-Term Equity Financing 232

**Unit 5
Basic Business Operations—
Finance 217**

CHAPTER 14 MONEY SUPPLY AND FINANCIAL INSTITUTIONS 240

1 Money: The Basic Means of Exchange 242   2 The American Banking System 246   3 Buying and Selling Securities 252   4 Financial News Reports 257   5 Regulation of Stock and Bond Sales 259

CHAPTER 15 RISK, INSURANCE, AND CREDIT MANAGEMENT 264

1 Risk 266   2 Risk Management 269   3 Insurance 270   4 Types of Insurance Coverage 271   5 Credit Management 279

CHAPTER 16 PERSONNEL MANAGEMENT 286

1 Work Force Planning 288   2 Managing the Employment Process 291   3 Training and Developing Personnel 293   4 Coordinating and Recording Job Changes 296   5 Assuring Safety and Health Maintenance 297   6 Designing and Supervising Compensation Programs 299   7 Administering Employee Benefits 302

CHAPTER 17 HUMAN RELATIONS IN BUSINESS 306

1 Humanizing Forces in the Environment 308   2 Needs, Motivation, and Human Behavior 311   3 Managers and Motivation 313   4 Managers and Leadership 314   5 The Effect of the Work Itself 316   6 Communication With Employees 320

CHAPTER 18 LABOR-MANAGEMENT RELATIONS 324

1 Makeup of the Labor Force 327   2 History of U.S. Organized Labor 329   3 Types of Labor Unions 330   4 The Collective Bargaining Process 331   5 Labor Disputes and Their Settlement 335   6 Landmarks of Labor-Management Legislation 339

CHAPTER 19 INFORMATION SYSTEMS, DECISION MAKING, AND PLANNING 344

1 Management Information Systems (MIS) 346   2 Data Processing Systems 348   3 Managerial Decision Making 349   4 Decision-Making Techniques 351   5 Business Planning 354   6 Plans and the Planning Process 355

CHAPTER 20 ACCOUNTING FOR MANAGERIAL AND FINANCIAL CONTROL 360

1 The Accounting Process 362   2 Uses of Accounting Information 364   3 Accounting Principles 364   4 Cost Accounting Practices 368   5 Balance Sheet 371   6 Income Statement 373   7 Statement of Changes in Financial Position 375   8 Interpretation of Financial Statements 375

Unit 6

Basic Business Operations— Human Resources 285

Unit 7

Basic Business Operations— Information and Controls 343

CHAPTER 21 BUSINESS FORECASTS AND BUDGETS 382

1 Business Forecasts 384   2 Forecasting Techniques 387   3 Budgets 389   4 Types of Budgets 390   5 Fixed or Flexible Budgets 394   6 Budget Variance Reports 396

Unit 8

Advanced

Business

Operations 399

CHAPTER 22 FORMATION AND MANAGEMENT OF CORPORATIONS 400

1 The Corporate Form of Business 402   2 Formation of Corporations 403   3 Going Public 405   4 Stockholders and the Corporation 406   5 Growth of Large Corporations 408   6 Are Big Corporations Good for the United States? 412

CHAPTER 23 INTERNATIONAL BUSINESS 418

1 What Makes Business International? 420
2 Influences on a Nation's Ability to Trade 422
3 How Companies Trade and Operate Internationally 424   4 Obstacles to International Business 426   5 Multinational Companies 430
6 International Cooperation in Trade 431

CHAPTER 24 USE OF TECHNOLOGY, STATISTICS, AND COMPUTERS IN BUSINESS 436

1 Technology 438   2 Statistics in Business 440
3 Descriptive Statistics 441   4 Inferential Statistics and Other Quantitative Methods 444   5 Computer Systems 447   6 Computer Applications 453

CHAPTER 25 GOVERNMENT REGULATION, TAXATION, AND LAW 460

1 Government Regulation of Business 462
2 Taxation 467   3 Business Law 470   4 General Relationships 477

Unit 9

Societal

Influences on

Business 459

CHAPTER 26 ETHICAL BEHAVIOR AND SOCIAL RESPONSIBILITY 482

1 Ethical Behavior 484   2 Attitudes and Expectations 485   3 Power Groups 488   4 Business Response 489   5 Current and Continuing Problems 491

APPENDIX EXPLORING CAREERS IN BUSINESS 499

1 Transition Into Business 499   2 A Choice of Two Directions 500   3 Getting a Job 505   4 Holding a Job 507

GLOSSARY 510

INDEX 520

Preface

The second edition of *Business in Action* introduces the subject of business to the student by creating a learning system that includes a clearly written text organized to make it easier for students to grasp basic business concepts and *the option* of a unique simulation/workbook supplement that gives students the opportunity to apply theory to practice by becoming involved in a simulated model of a business and its interrelated economic, social, and legal-political environment.

Significant changes are introduced with the second edition of the text and its ancillary components:

■ The textbook is fully comprehensive. It presents a complete and up-to-date picture of today's business world.

■ A new functional and colorful design assists students in their study of business. A color-coding system (explained later in this Preface) reinforces the self-outlining heading structure of the text, making it easier for students to identify the key points in their reading.

The new business magazine look and format of the text, with its modern three-dimensional diagrams, charts, and graphs, is designed to engross students in the study of contemporary business and absorb them in the learning process.

■ The treatment of basic economic concepts has been expanded and there is a new chapter on "Operating a Small Business."

■ Many of the "Action Briefs," which are examples of business practices, are new, as are nearly all the "Issues & Highlights" readings, which focus on thought-provoking, business-related issues.

■ Each chapter contains two case studies, called "Case Critiques." These supplement a rich and varied assortment of end-of-chapter materials.

■ The pedagogical design and program format give instructors greater flexibility in choosing a method and approach to teaching the introductory business course.

■ New computer software, which capitalizes on the natural interest and curiosity of students in franchising, is now available.

A Flexible Teaching-Learning System

The *Business in Action* program offers a flexible, adaptive approach to the study of business.

The textbook can now be used alone as an independent study resource. It can also be used with the student supplement, the *SSweetco: Business Model and Activity File for Business in Action*, Second Edition. (SSweetco is the tradename of an imaginary, but realistic company, the Shenandoah Sweets Company, which is the core element of the student supplement.)

The uniquely designed textbook is especially easy to read and comprehend. Each chapter systematically enumerates and links together its vital highlights, learning objectives, and major descriptive sections in an easy to follow self-outlining structure. Extensive business examples, case studies, and end-of-chapter review questions, make this textbook, by itself, a complete and well-rounded teaching-learning resource.

Many instructors, however, choose to supplement text instruction with the *SSweetco: Business Model and Activity File*. The SSweetco supplement provides an opportunity for students to extend and reinforce their study. The assignments and activities in *SSweetco*, alone, provide a rich variety of problems and projects to test student comprehension of terminology and concepts. However, when the *SSweetco* material is used as a simulated model of a business, it enriches student learning by enabling students to carry out the tasks of a number of career role models in fields such as marketing, management, finance, accounting, data processing, and the like. This gives students a more realistic picture of business activity and the career paths open to them.

An extensive *Course Management Guide and Instructional Resource* clearly shows how the text can be used independently or how the text and the student supplement can be combined by the instructor to create a unified and mutually supportive learning system. The resultant course design is thus highly flexible and uniquely appropriate to the instructor's professional skills and his or her course objectives.

A Business Point of View

Business is good for the United States, just as the United States has been good for business. The textbook emphasizes how business operates in the American environment. With minimal editorializing, the text presents facts for the student to examine. Business is shown for what it is and how it functions, without apology or censure.

The text is comprehensive in its coverage. A broad range of areas has been treated, as the contents and index bear out. The literature of business has been carefully researched and distilled. Subject topics are presented in logical sequence. The functions of marketing, production, and finance precede the discussion of accounting controls and other more specific, complex, or advanced business activities. A new chapter on "Operating a Small Business" is introduced midway in the text. It provides operational insights into those activities that must receive immediate attention from small business operators. The instructor may, of course, introduce the small business chapter earlier in the course, immediately following Chapter 4 on "The Legal Forms of Business Ownership." In any event, small business is given thorough attention, and numerous examples of small businesses in action are integrated throughout.

The text also has a fundamentally practical orientation. It presumes that students need to know, and want to improve their understanding of, how business in the United States really works. Approaches that have worked well in business operations and those that have not are examined. To aid students who wish to prepare for the best kind of employment they can find in the business world, an updated Appendix, "Exploring Careers in Business," and other materials are included. These materials give students a fair picture of business career options, pointing out both the areas of opportunity and the less promising aspects of business.

Textbook Features

Each chapter of the textbook integrates a set of learning devices that promote an understanding of how business operates.

Pictographs. Pictographs are previews, or advance summaries, of the chapter presented in pictures and words. They are used to simplify and speed up the absorption of complex ideas. Similar illustrations are widely used in news magazines, such as *U.S. News and World Report*, to convey ideas readily and save readers precious time.

Key Terms. Significant terms are highlighted in boldface italic at their point of definition in the textbook. They are also listed at the end of each chapter with convenient cross-references to the pages where they are defined.

Tables and Figures. Tables presenting arrays of data and figures that illustrate concepts and ideas are widely used throughout the text.

Action Briefs. Short anecdotes are interspersed in the margins of the text, providing a representative sampling of business practices, commendable or otherwise. There are over 100 Action Briefs throughout the text; most are new to this edition.

Issues & Highlights. These readings, which occur in each chapter, are based mainly on current events. They focus primarily on thought-provoking, business-related social issues and aim to stimulate students to form their own opinions about those issues.

Key Concepts. At the end of each chapter, the ideas presented in the pictographs and main headings are summarized. Here again, the concepts are keyed by number to the pictographs, objectives, and the major text headings—a system that helps link all the learning elements together.

Review Questions. Each chapter concludes with a list of questions testing students' understanding of text material.

Case Critiques. Each chapter is supplemented with two documented and/or hypothetical case studies illustrating practical applications of key concepts and key terms. These case studies are designed to encourage students to develop critical judgments in assessing business actions.

Following a step-by-step procedure recommended in the student study guidelines (see page xi), and making maximum of the textbook's unique "three-part linked learning system" (also described in the study guidelines), students can utilize these features in a systematic and coordinated way to more easily learn the basic concepts presented.

The Optional SSweetco: Business Model and Activity File Supplement

SSweetco: Business Model and Activity File forms the second—and optional—component of the *Business in Action* teaching-learning system.

The first part of this component is a business model. This is an integrated set of data about a typical business: the Shenandoah Sweets Company (SSweetco), its industry, and its environment. The action takes place in Valleyville, a typical American business community, where a dozen businesses and over twice as many public figures and businesspersons interact daily. However, the action focuses primarily on the creation, operation, and growth of SSweetco, a candy manufacturing and retailing company. The action extends from SSweetco to other businesses in Valleyville—manufacturers, wholesalers, vendors, and the like.

The businesses in Valleyville range in size from an insurance agency owned and operated by one individual and small proprietorships to a fledgling partnership and a large corporation. Students participate in the problems and situations arising from the growth of SSweetco into a corporation (SSWEETCORP) with national and international business aspirations.

Through this business model, students meet 32 personalities carrying out typical business functions. They also observe representatives of federal and local government agencies and consumer and public interest groups as they monitor the business community.

Immediately following the business model is the second part of the SSweetco supplement: student activities and exercises that correspond to each chapter of the textbook. These assignments are based on the integrated set of data provided by the business model. They provide a specific, practical way for students to check their understanding of the principles presented in the text. At the first level of achievement (application), students are challenged with specific problems requiring calculations, selection of appropriate terminology, completion of typical business forms, and manipulation of data. At the second level of achievement (analysis and interpretation), students actually assume the roles of one of 32 career models. They solve both routine and complex problems and participate in realistic case studies in dozens of settings involving many kinds of businesses.

A third and new part of the SSweetco supplement is a special section, "The Donut Franchise: A Microcomputer Simulation," with student materials for an easy-to-use microcomputer simulation. These student materials can be used in conjunction with available software (a floppy disk) to further extend student involvement and simulate real world business experiences in the classroom.

Consequently, instructors who choose to adopt the *SSweetco: Business Model and Activity File* may use its learning resources in three possible ways:

■ It may be used as a workbook and study guide for selected problems and projects.

■ It may be used as a comprehensive experiential model for maximum student involvement in the learning process and identification with work in the business world.

■ At the instructor's option, a special section can be used in combination with disk software as a vehicle for creating a microcomputer simulation, which can provide an added dimension of "reality" to the classroom study of business.

The Donut Franchise: A Microcomputer Simulation

This software has been created by Chad T. Lewis and Philip C. Lewis. The setting for the simulation is a chain of donut shops, which SSweetco has acquired and franchised at a point when the firm becomes SSWEETCORP and is in the process of diversifying its product line. Students make key decisions in the following areas for the donut shops they operate: marketing (advertising/pricing), ordering, equipment purchases, financial, and personnel. The story of SSWEETCORP's acquisition of the donut shop franchise, the directions for student play, and the planning and decision forms that they need to organize and input data for microcomputer processing are to be found beginning on page A-1 of *SSweetco*.

Through this short simulation, groups of students can compete against one another (and even against the instructor operating a company-owned, rather than a franchised, donut shop) to return the largest profit to the parent company. Results of their decisions, including information about profitability, are fed back to students in the form of financial statements for their evaluation and help in further decision making.

For easy classroom management, the microcomputer simulation is instructor-administered and contains self-correcting features. The instructor can therefore control the pacing of the simulation and when and how it is used for instruction. For example, it can be used after select units of the text to reinforce specific topics and concepts covered in those units. Or, if the instructor chooses, it can be used as a culminating activity for the entire course to illustrate how marketing, production and operations, financial, and personnel decisions have an interrelated impact upon business activity.

Operation of the microcomputer requires the separate order of a single floppy disk. An accompanying user's guide provides step-by-step instructions for class management and procedures for running the software. Versions of the software are compatible with a number of popular microcomputer machines.

Course Management Guide and Instructional Resource

The *Course Management Guide and Instructional Resource* provides all the resources that an instructor needs to successfully implement the *Business in Action* program. Included are:

■ General course management suggestions.
■ Time schedules for courses of varying length.
■ Detailed lesson management strategies for each chapter.
■ An audiovisual guide.
■ Readings for student enrichment.
■ Additional recommended student projects and assignments.
■ Two tests banks with 1,500 objective-type items to choose from.
■ Transparency masters.
■ Keys to all textbook exercises, *SSweetco* activities, and test questions.

This softbound manual, organized in a convenient chapter-by-chapter format, is among the most useful of the instructional support materials available for any introductory business course.

Lester R. Bittel
Ronald S. Burke
R. Lawrence LaForge

The following steps constitute an effective way to study the materials in each chapter. *The key to effective study is making maximum use of the numbers that identify each pictograph, objective, major text heading, and key concept.* If you are not already familiar with these features, you should read the discussion of "Textbook Features" starting on page viii of the Preface.

Step 1: Study the pictograph. Spend two or three minutes to be sure you get the whole picture. Then read the learning objectives that precede each chapter.

Step 2: Now skim through the entire chapter reading only the main headings and subheadings. They should be easy for you to pick out. The main headings are underscored by a blue rule; the subheadings by a green rule.

These headings provide a self-outlining structure for each chapter. They reinforce and extend the ideas presented in the pictograph. (These headings also may be used as your outline framework for any notetaking from the text.)

Step 3: Read the Key Concept summaries and glance at the list of key terms at the end of the chapter. Be alert for definitions of these terms as you read the chapter.

These first three steps, which make up a "three-part linked learning system," will help you quickly summarize the basic concepts in a chapter by skimming it in about 10 to 15 minutes. You are now prepared to read the chapter for details that will help you flesh out the Key Concepts.

Step 4: Read the chapter carefully for detail. Keep notes of important facts. Write down the definition of any terms that are necessary for understanding the topics under discussion. Key terms are in boldface italic for ease of identification.

As you read each chapter for detail, be certain to study each table and figure to be sure of its meaning. Also read the "Action Briefs" in the margins of the text to get a feel for what actually occurs in business as opposed to what ought to happen. Read each "Issues & Highlights" feature as it occurs, then form an opinion by answering the questions that follow the reading.

Step 5: Answer the Review Questions. It is a good idea to make a note of the pages on which the answer appears.

Step 6: Read each of the Case Critiques. Try to make a connection between what has occurred in the cases and what you have just read in the text. Answer the questions associated with each case.

Continue with the next two steps only if your instructor has assigned material from the student supplement, SSweetco: Business Model and Activity File for Business in Action, *Second Edition.*

Step 7: If your instructor has included the *SSweetco* supplement in your course materials, move to the corresponding chapter in the activities section of *SSweetco: Business Model and Activity File.* Read the performance objectives that precede the two levels of achievement. Then answer the exercises and activities for the first level of achievement, the "Application Level."

Step 8:   Proceed to the next, higher level of achievement, "Analysis and Interpretation," by completing the decision-making and case problem assignments.

Rigorous follow-through on these study procedures will lead to good study habits that should have a positive effect on what you learn in this introductory business course.

Acknowledgments

The authors would like to offer thanks and acknowledgment to the following individuals in the academic ranks who served as reviewers or consultants either for the first edition or this revision. Their ideas and suggestions have profoundly shaped the pedagogy, format, features, and content of the text and the varied components of the Business in Action teaching-learning system.

Special thanks are extended to Pavey L. Hoke, director of the learning laboratory of Lord Fairfax Community College, and Gwendolyn L. Smith, assistant professor of business administration at Norfolk State University. Professor Hoke prepared the original glossary for the textbook. Professor Smith offered her expertise in refining the assignment materials in the SSweetco: Business Model and Activity File and made some significant contributions to the development of the Course Management Guide and Instructional Resource.

Finally, the authors would be remiss if they did not recognize the creative efforts of Philip C. Lewis and Chad T. Lewis, developers of "The Donut Franchise: A Microcomputer Simulation." Their materials correlate with, and help to reinforce, many of the basic concepts presented in the Business in Action program.

Patricia G. Bounds
James H. Faulkner State Junior College

Lloyd Brooks
Memphis State University

Clifford Butje
Suffolk Community College

Archibald B. Carroll
University of Georgia

Andrea Colangelo
The Berkeley School

Lydia C. Conklin
The Heald Colleges

Richard Crowe
Hazard Community College

Les R. Dlabay
Lake Forest College

Carol Eakle
Katherine Gibbs School

Robert M. Fishco
Middlesex County (New Jersey) College

Philip E. Gover
Spoon River College

Roberta Greene
Central Piedmont Community College

David E. Greenrich
Waukesha Technical Institute

Pavey L. Hoke
Lord Fairfax Community College

David A. Huddleston
Lurleen B. Wallace State Junior College

Edwin D. Johnson
Parkersburg Community College

Van Johnson
Midland (Texas) College

William Jordan
Community College of Allegheny County (Boyce Campus)

Judy Khaner
Sawyer Business College

Bernard M. Kaplan
J. Sargeant Reynolds Community College

Carole Kaplan
The Berkeley School

Allen D. Kartchner
Utah State University (Logan)

Timothy R. Keeley
Tacoma Community College

George Kelley
State University of New York (Erie Campus)

Phyliss Kennedy
Highline Community College

Charles H. LaClair
Cochise College

Jerre J. Lewis
Kirtland Community College

Mason Linkous
National Business College

Connie B. Morrow
Midstate (Illinois) College

Paul Miller
Somerset Community College

Howard Newhouse
The Berkeley School

John D. Reck
Mt. San Antonio College

Douglas Richardson
Eastfield (Texas) College

Wallace J. Richardson
Lehigh University

Karl C. Rutkowski
Pierce Junior College

Rafael Santos
Imperial Valley College

Gwendolyn L. Smith
Norfolk State University

James N. Smith
Wallace Community College

Margaret E. Sprencz
Lorain County Community College

Val Stauffer
Dixie College

Elizabeth Strenkowski
The Bradford School

Richard P. Swanson
Phillips College

Maryann S. Taliaferro
Elizabeth Brant School

Michael P. Viollt
Robert Morris College

Geraldine Weissman
Monroe Business Institute

Charles Wetzel
Milwaukee Area Technical College

Harvey P. Wiley
Midstate (Illinois) College

Unit 1
The Nature of American Business

Unit 1 establishes what American business is all about. It lays the groundwork for understanding how an idea or a concept can be translated into a viable product or service for sale in the marketplace.

Business is a creative, competitive activity that has always played an important part in shaping American society. By satisfying needs and wants people cannot satisfy themselves, business improves the quality of their lives.

The purpose of business is to combine resources such as land, labor, and capital in a way that will make them more valuable. Operating in a political and economic climate that supports individual rights, American business has as its guiding principle the right to private ownership and profit.

Business today faces the challenge of adapting itself to the rapid changes occurring in both our social and physical environments.

Chapter 1

The Business System in the United States

1 DEFINITION

Business is an activity that satisfies human needs and wants by providing goods and services for private profit.

2 VALUES

Business provides individuals and society with . . .

Means of exchange
Wealth
Employment

3 PROCESS

Business processes convert input resources—by creating or adding utility of form, place, time, or possession—into more valuable outputs or end products.

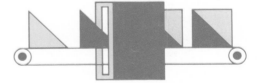

4 VARIETY

Businesses occur in a variety of sizes and classifications.

Production:
Manufacturing of consumer and industrial goods

Distribution:
Transportation, storage, and retailing

Services:
Personal, professional, financial, and communications

5 DYNAMICS

The business environment is characterized by:

Risk/Uncertainty   Gain/Loss
Success/Failure   Stagnation/Growth
Change/Opportunity

6 HISTORY

American business has gradually shifted its emphasis:

Agriculture
Transportation
Communications
Banking
Industry
Production
Services
Marketing

1770s

TODAY

Learning Objectives

The purpose of this chapter is to define business in the United States, describe its characteristics and the conditions under which it operates, and summarize its development.

After studying Chapter 1, you should be able to:

1. Define a business enterprise and distinguish among private, nonprofit, and public enterprises.
2. Discuss the three major functions of business in society.
3. Explain the process of converting resources and adding utility.
4. Recognize the threefold classification of business enterprises by type and activity, and identify the groupings under the Standard Industrial Classification system (SIC).
5. Explain the meaning of risk and uncertainty in business.
6. Recall the major stages in the development of modern American business.

If your class is using SSweetco: Business Model and Activity File for Business in Action, see Chapter 1 in that book after you complete this chapter. There you will find exercises and activities to help you apply your learning to typical business situations.

When Calvin Coolidge said, "The business of America is business," he was echoing the thoughts of a great many Americans both then and now. Coolidge's statement is far more complex than it seems when the interactions between business and government, business and labor unions, business and consumers, and business and society as a whole are considered. Still there can be no doubt that in the United States business is an extremely powerful force, utilizing the nation's resources to supply the material needs of society.

1   THE BUSINESS ENTERPRISE

A private, profit-motivated means of satisfying human needs

An activity that satisfies human needs and wants by providing goods or services for private profit is called a **business enterprise.** From a cookie-vending cart to General Motors, every business (a) satisfies needs, (b) provides goods and services, and (c) does so with the intention of making a profit. A fundamental characteristic of American business is that it uses private money and resources, or capital, to pay for the costs of setting up and running commercial enterprises. The willingness of private investors to risk their capital in the hope of gaining profit distinguishes the American system from those in which the government supplies the resources.

SATISFYING NEEDS AND WANTS

The guiding principle

All human beings have certain basic needs—things that they must have in order to survive. In addition to these basic needs, there are many things that people want to make their lives more comfortable or satisfying. A business must provide its customers—whether they are individuals, other companies, or the government—with something that they need or want. Otherwise, the business will have no sales, no income, and no profit and will be forced to close its doors. The idea that success in business depends on fulfilling consumer needs and wants is fundamental to the American business system.

Human needs and wants shift with the advance of civilization. Yesterday's demand for horse collars and horse carriages has been replaced today by an even greater demand for automobiles and motorcycles. Specific consumer demands change constantly, but there will always be a wide range of human wants and needs to encourage business to operate, whatever the circumstances.

GOODS AND SERVICES

The means to satisfy human needs and wants

In meeting human needs and desires, businesses provide goods and services to consumers. *Goods* are physical products and include both necessities like food and shelter and luxuries like television sets and motor boats. **Services** are activities that help people or organizations without directly creating a physical product. Services can be classified as personal, professional, or financial. In the modern world, services range from home and office maintenance and repair to financial operations and highly complex communications and research activities. Thousands of different kinds of services make up this rapidly growing business segment.

There are additional subcategories of goods and services. Goods made and sold to meet the needs and wants of manufacturers are called industrial goods. They normally undergo a process of conversion as they are utilized in the fabrication of the final product. Goods made and sold to meet the needs and wants of consumers are known as consumer goods and do not require processing by their ultimate users. Services may also be subdivided into those that are business-oriented, such as office maintenance, and those that are consumer-oriented, such as hairstyling. Non-profit organizations also provide services, usually related to education, health care, and social welfare.

PRIVATE PROFIT

The payoff for satisfying needs

The primary goal of business is to make money. In a sense, it is the businessperson's payoff for satisfying human needs and wants. In simplest terms, **profit** is the amount of money left from income made by selling goods and services after all costs of producing, marketing, and distributing the goods and services have been paid. See Table 1-1. Obviously, sometimes there is no money left over, or costs turn out to be higher than income, and the business either breaks even or takes a loss. The intention in business, however, is to operate in such a way that profits will be as high as possible, consistent with social responsibility. The incentive to make money is called the **profit motive.**

TABLE 1-1 Profit or Loss?	
How One Company Makes a Profit	
Company A adds up the revenues each year from sales of its products or services (like this).	$100,000
It deducts the costs each year for its materials, labor, rent, utilities, etc.	− 90,000
What's left is its *profit*.	$ 10,000
How Another Company Doesn't Make a Profit	
Company B adds up its revenues for the year (like this).	$100,000
It deducts its expenses for the year (like this).	−105,000
And it ends up with a *loss* (like this).	− $5,000
Moral	
To make a profit, a business must generate revenues that are greater than its expenses.	

The profit motive is that which most clearly distinguishes business from other kinds of enterprises in the United States. There are other organizations that also meet some of the wants and needs of people. They provide goods and, particularly, services. These enterprises differ from business in several ways, but the principal difference is that they do not seek a profit. The most important kinds of enterprises of this kind are private nonprofit enterprises and public enterprises.

NONPROFIT ENTERPRISES

Voluntary contributions or taxes provide capital

Private Nonprofit Enterprises *Private nonprofit organizations* are financed, established, and operated in much the same way as business. However, their goal is not to make a profit, but to meet needs that are not or cannot be effectively or fully satisfied by business. Among private nonprofit enterprises are hospitals, museums, research and charitable organizations, colleges and universities, and professional associations. Financing for these organizations is provided by voluntary contributions from individuals, businesses, and, in part, the government.

Public Enterprises *Public enterprises,* organizations operated by units of government and financed with taxes or service charges to the public, are increasingly important in American society. Many of these organizations, like highway departments, public health services, local sewage disposal plants, and water systems, are operated just as if they were businesses. They have the same management problems, the same kinds of budgets, similar physical plants and personnel, and often the same concerns with income and costs. The difference is that a public enterprise is not financed with private capital and does not expect to make a profit. Funds to establish public enterprises usually come from taxes. The enterprises generally are operated so that income and expenses will be equal. If a profit does occasionally result, this surplus belongs to the sponsoring government body rather than to private investors.

2   VALUES

Business contributes certain values to society

Although the main motivation for establishing and operating a business is to make a profit for investors, business serves important social functions beyond this. It provides individuals and society as a whole with a means of exchange, with wealth, and with employment. It is not the only institution in the United States that makes such contributions to society, but it is probably the most important.

MEANS OF EXCHANGE

Buying and selling

Few societies have ever endured where each individual or family produced all of the essentials of life for private use. Even in early cultures,

---

specialization existed in the production of tools and weapons, household implements, and certain other goods, including agricultural products. The fact that certain people and groups had goods that others needed and did not or could not produce for themselves created a need for trade. The trade of goods and services is a basic function of business. In a highly technical, specialized society such as ours, this aspect of business predominates. A modern family directly produces virtually none of the necessities of life. Food, clothing, shelter, and the means of transportation and communication are all supplied by the buying and selling processes that are part of business.

WEALTH
More than money

Business creates wealth that would not otherwise exist. Although *wealth* is commonly interpreted to mean the possession of a super-abundance of money, the term embraces everything that money can buy as well. More specifically, wealth also includes material goods, services, and leisure, all of which have been made available to us by business. Consider again a family attempting to produce everything for its own needs. One or two people working with handmade tools can produce only the most rudimentary goods—and barely enough of them to fill even the family's needs. No matter how skilled these people may be, the demands made on their time are enormous. They must, for example, grow and preserve food, build and maintain shelter, deal with medical problems, and find fuel. Such diverse activity does not leave them free to accumulate wealth of any kind. Business allows the accumulation of wealth by providing economical manufacturing and efficient distribution of goods and services. This is not possible in a subsistence society.

Most people seem to strive for a life that is more than a hand-to-mouth existence, but not everyone pursues wealth with equal fervor. The business system in America serves the ambitious as well as the satisfied, but it tends to encourage earning and spending.

EMPLOYMENT
Rewarding occupations

One of the greatest social contributions of business is to provide employment. An obvious benefit of employment is that it gives people the money needed to buy goods and services in a business-oriented society. Employment serves a greater function, however. In today's society, jobs and careers can be among the most important paths to personal satisfaction. Useful, productive, and rewarding employment can give meaning to people's lives by providing them with a sense of purpose, a feeling of accomplishment, and an outlet for creativity. In a relatively free and open business environment such as ours, the opportunity to advance as the result of improved skills and abilities is a great incentive to personal growth. As a society is the sum of its citizens, personal growth contributes to social and economic growth.

3 THE BUSINESS PROCESS

Converts resources to useful goods and services

Business performs its many functions mainly by converting available resources into products or services for which there is a demand. The **conversion process** creates or adds value or usefulness to resources. This is achieved by giving resources utility of form, place, time, or possession—or of some combination of these.

CONVERTING RESOURCES

Transforms input into output

Of the **resources** used by business, the most familiar may be the physical raw materials used in manufacturing. The conversion of iron ore and other materials into steel and of steel into farm implements are clear examples of creating a useful product from a raw material of little apparent value. Soil and seeds are familiar resources too. The farmer combines them in the agricultural process to produce vegetables, grains, and fruit. Resources may themselves be manufactured goods as they are for retail camera or clothing stores. Human skills or knowledge, particularly in the modern world, may also be considered as business resources. For an advertising agency, a newspaper, or a research organization, human abilities and creativity are the chief resources.

Conversion of resources takes place on a far broader plane than the manufacture of shoes and sunglasses. It is inherent in every business. Banks convert money into loans and interest. Department stores convert goods into sales. Movie theaters convert film into entertainment. Restaurants convert foodstuffs into meals. Insurance companies convert premium payments into protection. Motels convert furniture and fixtures into shelter for travelers. Construction firms convert concrete into highways. Airlines convert fuel and planes into transportation. A doctor converts the knowledge of medicine into health.

In summary, the business process converts **inputs,** resources that go into a production or operation process, into **outputs,** end products or services which have value and utility. See Figure 1-1.

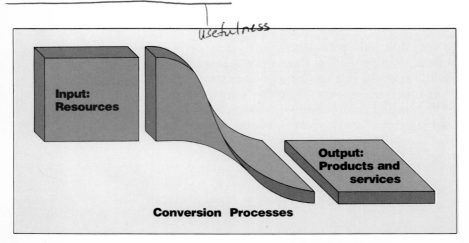

Conversion Processes

Figure 1-1
How businesses add value to resources.

ADDING UTILITY
Makes output more useful than input

Businesses change their resources in some way to make them more useful or desirable to consumers. A business may give these resources **utility of form** by physically changing them in a way that increases their value. A sheet of plastic, for example, is shaped into a Frisbee. **Utility of place** is given to resources by moving them into a location where they are available for immediate use by customers. In this way, a transportation company creates utility of place by conveying goods and raw materials to where they are needed. For instance, fuel oil stored at the refinery cannot be used by consumers; the oil is valuable for heating a house only after it has been delivered there. **Utility of time** is given to a resource or product by making it available to consumers without delay. Thus retailers who invest their money to maintain a stock of goods that is always available on their shelves provide their customers with utility of time. These stocked goods are more valuable to consumers because they can be readily obtained. **Utility of possession** is created by advertising and promotion. These activities increase the value of goods and services by increasing public demand for them. Since advertising and promotion stimulate the feeling or awareness of desire to possess and use, they are essential aspects of the American business system. Utility of possession, place, and time are closely related to marketing activity, as you will see in Unit 3, for the major goal of marketing is to get products to those who need them, in places where they are needed, at the time of such need.

ACTION BRIEF

Psst! Wanna Buy a Business! *Of the 14 million businesses in the United States, nearly one out of four changes hands each year. And there are some 17,000 small business brokers who will try to sell you anything from a liquor store to a pawnshop near an Atlantic City gambling casino—or even a casket company. Why a casket company? Burials take place in good times and bad. They provide a recession-proof business with a history of steady profits.*

Source: *John A. Byrne, "The Up-and-Comers", Forbes, December 21, 1981, p. 96.*

4 KINDS OF BUSINESSES
An endless variety

The many functions of business and the endless possibilities for carrying out the processes just described have resulted in remarkable diversity in American business, from single-owner welding shops to multinational manufacturing companies like General Electric, employing hundreds of thousands of people. Products range from electrical circuit systems nearly too small to see with the naked eye to an entire steel mill prefabricated for export. Businesses can be classified by type: production, distribution, or services. Businesses may also be grouped into standard industry classifications.

PRODUCTION ENTERPRISES
Emphasize physical conversion

Companies that manufacture materials or goods are engaged in **production.** The production may be on a basic level, such as mining, farming, or forestry (often called the extractive industries), or it may use already manufactured materials to produce higher-level goods. The final manufacture of a television set, for example, is the end result of a long chain of processes usually performed by many different companies.

DISTRIBUTION ENTERPRISES

Emphasize transportation and selling

The process of moving goods from their point of production to consumers is called *distribution.* The most obvious example of distribution is physical transportation: railroads, shipping and trucking companies, and airlines. Packaging and grading operations (of foods, for example) belong to this category, as do companies that store goods and wholesale and retail merchants.

SERVICE ENTERPRISES

Provide assistance rather than goods

Service enterprises comprise a rapidly growing area of business activity which includes firms that do not directly create or distribute goods. The communications industry, including the press, radio and television, and the telephone and telegraph system, is a service industry. Services to individual consumers, such as repair and maintenance, are also included, as are hotels and restaurants, barbers and hairdressers, private educators, doctors and dentists, and hospitals. Financial institutions, such as banks, savings and loan companies, and insurance companies, also provide services and are included in this classification.

CLASSIFICATION BY INDUSTRY

Federal designations

A somewhat more detailed breakdown of businesses by type is often used by trade organizations and by the government for reporting and analyzing statistical data on business. Individual businesses are grouped into large industry types. Thus an *industry* is a collection of all businesses that perform similar operations to provide the same general kinds of goods or services. All companies producing steel make up the steel industry.

The *Standard Industrial Classification (SIC)* is a numerical system devised by the U.S. Office of Management and the Budget. SIC places specific industries into even more comprehensive categories. This system is shown in Table 1-2.

TABLE 1-2 Standard Industrial Classification System (SIC)
Major Classification Divisions*
A. Agriculture, Forestry, and Fisheries
B. Mining
C. Contract Construction
D. Manufacturing
E. Transportation, Communication, Electric, Gas, and Sanitary Services
F. Wholesale and Retail Trade
G. Finance, Insurance, and Real Estate
H. Services (Hotels, Amusements, Auto Repairs, Medical, Legal, and Educational)
I. Government
J. Nonclassifiable Establishments

*Each major division is further broken down into subclassifications indicated by numbers, for example, 2521 for manufacturing of wooden office furniture. There are 99 major groups in all, with Manufacturing having nearly 450 individual (or four-digit) classifications.

Source: *Standard Industrial Classification Manual,* Executive Office of the President, Office of Management and the Budget, U.S. Government Printing Office, 1972.

5   THE DYNAMICS OF BUSINESS

Business is dominated by uncertainty and change

The activities of business take place in a turbulent, dynamic environment. Business itself changes as social and economic conditions change. Forecasting the overall performance of business is difficult; precisely determining the outlook for any individual business is nearly impossible. Uncertainty underlies all business activity. It is this uncertainty, coupled with the element of change, that creates an environment of risk for business while at the same time presenting business with major opportunities for reward and success.

RISK

A basic feature of American enterprise

Risk is a fundamental feature of American business. People are free to invest their capital and make a profit, but at the same time, they must face the possibility of loss. This is the risk that they take. The expectation of gain is the major driving force of business, but there is always the chance that a decrease in the demand for products, ineffective management, government regulation, social change, or dozens of other factors may cause a loss. If this loss is only temporary, a business may recover. If, however, the expenses of the business continually exceed its income, the business will be insolvent, no longer able to pay its debts. Though the possibility of loss and failure is a problem, it is also a great incentive to careful management and aggressive competition.

GROWTH, STABILITY, OR STAGNATION

Describes the level of economic activity at a given time

A certain amount of inertia enters into every human enterprise. Although growth appears to be the healthiest state for people, businesses, and the economy in general, periods of stagnation have always interrupted this process. Stability is an intermediate stage that seems only to be maintained by the promise of future growth. The government has attempted to counteract national economic stagnation, and good business managers make a concerted effort to prevent slumps in their company or industry, but performance uncertainty continues.

OPPORTUNITY AND CHANGE

An impetus for growth

The continual change in the business world creates conditions ripe for opportunity. Risk of loss and failure may threaten survival in the business world. Without the freedom that results in risk, however, opportunity is lost. Shifting markets, management and personnel problems, and a changing social environment all present the manager with opportunities to implement new practices and operations. It is only through the exploitation of opportunities presented by change that growth and profits occur.

ACTION BRIEF

Fly No-Frills Now; Fail Later.   *Probably the major transportation fiasco of the 1980s was the failure of Laker Airways, the airline that pioneered in low-fares, no-frills flying. Laker's move triggered a price war among airlines. Along with the recession, devastating competition sucked up the company's money faster than it came in, and Laker was forced into bankruptcy within five years. However, Freddie Laker, like many another entrepreneur, was back in business within a short period of time with another discount flying scheme.*

Source: *"The Laker Legacy,"* The Economist, *February 13, 1982, p. 15.*

They Don't
Build Houses
Like They
Used to

On the heels of the back-to-nature trend of the last decade, Tom Huth, a young reporter for The Washington Post, *traveled West one year, and this is what he told his friends back East:*

"When the West was still raw and untamed, a house was of the earth on which it stood. It was built from the skins of animals who chanced to live nearby or from the trees which were cleared to make way for it or from the ancient sod itself.

"Now look at how we do it. At the mass-housing development here where I worked for the last three months, we used lumber trucked in from Idaho, windows prehung in Virginia, bathtubs sent from Kilgore, Texas, closet rods from Taylorsville, Mississippi, furnace ducts made in Indiana, and that wasn't the half of it.

"The light switches came from New York, the light sockets from New Bedford, the circuit breakers from St. Paul, and the fuses from St. Louis.

"The baseboard heaters came from Tennessee, the water heaters from Kankakee.

"An all-American house indeed. The door locks came from Anaheim and the scaffolding from Berkeley. The fiberglass insulation came from Valley Forge.

"The tiny plugs of putty in the nail holes . . . those came from Dayton.

"Our job site lay at the foot of the front range of the great Rocky Mountains, and yet the pine trees were imported from a nursery in Nebraska. The silver maples came from Oklahoma. The peat moss came all the way from Banff, Alberta. And the fertilizer, believe it or not, was shipped over here from Marysville, Ohio.

"Such are the inexplicable ways of mass production. We are told it is the most efficient system of manufacture in the history of the world.

"They were handsome semidetached homes, with open ceilings and skylights and rugged beams and cedar siding—like the houses being built in many similar developments across the country.

"Bulldozers shoved the land around to fit the plan. All rocks were seized from the soil to become retaining walls. The earth was being bullied into rearrangement. Working there was like putting together an incredible model train layout.

"And the work was being done, for the most part, not by your sturdy career artisans of yesteryear, but by a motley variety of dropouts, deserters, drifters, and dreamers, who had also come from all over creation."

Source: Tom Huth, "They Don't Build Houses Like They Used to . . .," The Washington Post, July 3, 1977, p. C1.

What does this tell you about the interdependency of the American business system? Is this mass production? Is it good or bad for the country to substitute unskilled labor assisted by machinery for old-time artisans?

6 AMERICAN BUSINESS HISTORY

From exploitation to regulation

In the beginning, the business of America was mainly farming. Most manufactured goods were imported from Europe. As the population migrated westward, however, the need arose for an efficient means of transporting goods between cities. Railroads were built by business speculators in the 1800s to fill this need. In turn, the railroads spurred the growth of business beyond the pioneers' wildest dreams. It also made possible telegraph lines along the rights of way. This fast new method of communication linked buyers and sellers across great distances, creating a network of business markets across the nation. Banks, then run by unregulated groups of investors, supported these flourishing markets by supplying capital. Population growth was stimulated by an influx of immigrants attracted by expanding employment opportunities in the growing American economy.

RAPID INDUSTRIAL GROWTH

From agriculture to industry

The vastness of American resources—land and minerals, a cohesive transportation and communication system, capital, and an eager labor force—gradually shifted the focus of business from agriculture to industry. Small shops were incorporated into large factories. Product parts were standardized so that the unskilled labor market could be tapped. New sources of power—steam and electricity—turned the wheels and did the work faster. Business growth spurted ahead in the late 1800s. This was a period of rapid industrialization that caused business to run rampant in its haste to make profits. Lack of restraints resulted in capricious, often unfair business practices.

Workers were exploited. Labor unions were pushed aside. The little investors were duped. The interests of the general public were ignored. As a response to this exploitation, there began a trend in 1889 and 1890 that continues to some extent today. The public called upon its government to pass laws regulating and limiting business operations. Chief among these laws were the Interstate Commerce Act, which is a law to regulate transportation, and the Sherman Antitrust Act, which is a law designed to discourage anticompetitive business practices. (These, as well as other important regulatory laws, will be discussed in more detail in later chapters.)

TOWARD A SERVICE ECONOMY

From products to services

Nothing held back the growth of business for long. American business soon took worldwide leadership in production capabilities. By the middle of the twentieth century, however, a subtle shift took place in consumer demand. The public, with its newfound leisure, began to demand services as well as products. These purchased services came in the form of hotel and motel rooms, meals served in restaurants, extensive health care, vacation trips to faraway places, and entertainment of all kinds. The business entrepreneur proved to be just as eager to provide services as goods, as long as there was a possibility of profit.

MARKETING EMPHASIS

From production to marketing

In the rush to produce either goods or services, business had a tendency to make something available first, and then to sell it. When the public displayed indifference toward these products and services, this practice often led to great waste. Goods were sold at a loss and services went begging. To avoid this outcome, the emphasis in American business has swung since World War II from production to marketing. Successful business firms now first try to assess what the market wants—or will buy—and then try to match their production efforts to that demand.

THE MODERN OUTLOOK

A balanced approach

Maintaining a balance between what is good for business and what is good for the public at large is a major concern in America. Each decade, of course, introduces new problems. Today, we are concerned with such matters as decent wages and rising prices, industrial pollution and protection of the environment, the need to create more jobs and to make jobs more satisfying, equal employment opportunities, and business ethics. The American approach is to seek resolution of these issues two ways—in the marketplace and in the legislature. Business generally will do everything in its power to make a profit; consumers usually will do their best to buy only what they feel is a bargain. When the marketplace fails to provide mutual satisfaction, both parties are likely to seek government aid.

Key Concepts

1. Business is an enterprise that satisfies the needs and wants of consumers by providing goods and services to make a profit.
2. Business serves important social functions by providing wealth, employment, and a means of exchange.
3. a. Business operates by converting resources into more valuable end products.
   b. Business makes resources more valuable by giving them utility of form, place, time, or possession.
4. The many varied businesses in the United States are often classified by their type of operation: production, distribution, or services.

5. Risk, growth or stagnation, change and opportunity characterize the business environment.
6. The development of the business system in the United States demonstrates:
   a. Its basic dependence on transportation, communications, and banking services.
   b. Its need for some regulation and control to protect the public interest from the business abuses of the few.
   c. Its emergence from an industrial preoccupation with products and production to an emphasis on services and marketing.

Review Questions

1. Define, identify, or explain each of the following key terms and phrases found on the pages indicated.

    business enterprise   (p. 4)
    conversion process   (p. 8)
    distribution   (p. 10)
    goods   (p. 4)
    industry   (p. 10)
    inputs   (p. 8)
    outputs   (p. 8)
    private nonprofit organization   (p. 6)
    production   (p. 9)
    profit   (p. 5)
    profit motive   (p. 5)
    public enterprise   (p. 6)
    resources   (p. 8)
    service enterprise   (p. 10)
    services   (p. 5)
    Standard Industrial Classification   (p. 10)
    utility of form   (p. 9)
    utility of place   (p. 9)
    utility of possession   (p. 9)
    utility of time   (p. 9)
    wealth   (p. 7)

2. Show how a specific business meets the definition of a business enterprise.
3. Name the three types of enterprises discussed in the text. How do the three differ in their sources of financing, reasons for operating, and goals?

4. How does business contribute to society other than providing profits to investors?
5. Describe and give examples of some of the resources that business uses in creating its end products for sale. Is it likely that new resources will be exploited in the future? Why or why not?
6. What is meant by giving resources utility of form, place, time and possession? Give an example of a type of business that increases or creates each kind of utility.
7. The simplest classification of business types uses only three categories. Name the three categories, and give examples of companies in each.
8. Why is risk a basic fact of any business undertaking in the United States. Is this good or bad? Why?
9. Why was the railroad such an important contributor to business growth in the United States?
10. What four conditions does the text identify as helping to shift the focus of business from agriculture to industry? Can you think of others?
11. What role did labor unions and government regulation play in the development of American business as we know it today?
12. Give some examples of the modern approach of balancing what is good for business and what is good for the public at large. In your opinion, is the modern approach working?

Case Critique 1-1
Staying Alive and Well

DuMont invented the first television set. For the ten years following World War II, people clamored to own that product. Duryea introduced the first automobile. It was a knockout; for years it was the best of dozens of competitors. Hurley introduced the first automatic washing machine about one hundred years ago. Few people can remember back to when his product was the popular one to have. The businesses that make Du-Mont television sets, Duryea autos, and Hurley

washing machines are no longer in existence. Yet, people buy millions of television sets, automobiles, and washing machines each year.

On the other hand, virtually everyone knows the Xerox Corporation. That's the company that makes the famous copying machine. The modern copying process was invented by Xerox's founder. Chester Carlson, an amateur physicist, perfected the process in a small laboratory in 1937, but 20 companies to whom he turned for backing (including RCA) turned him down. They didn't want to take a chance on his untried idea. Finally, in 1947 Carlson made a deal with a small, upstate New York firm, Haloid, to develop his "electro-photography" machine. That company's president, Joe Wilson, perfected Carlson's machine and created a market for it. Stenographers, clerks, and secretaries all over the world discovered that they had been waiting for something to take the pain out of making copies of letters and records with carbon paper. Carlson became so rich that he could give away $100 million to charity. The Xerox company now generates sales of nearly $9 billion a year and makes a profit of $500 or more million. Its seemingly miraculous machines have drawn competitors like flies. Some of these competitors, like IBM and Kodak, are even bigger than Xerox. Others are located in foreign lands. But Xerox stays alive and keeps on growing. It prides itself for regularly introducing copying machines that can do more and better things than the ones

the company introduced a year or two before. Xerox says about itself: "We became the DuMont of our business by inventing the business. We became the Xerox of our business by going on and reinventing it year after year."

1. What kind of need did the first copying machine satisfy?
2. What would appear to have been a principal motive of the Haloid Company in agreeing to develop an "electrophotography" machine?
3. What sort of utility did the Xerox machine create?
4. What kind of enterprise does the Xerox Corporation represent?
5. Why did Chester Carlson have difficulty in finding financial backers?
6. Why is Xerox still in business today while companies with other great products like Du-Mont and Duryea have disappeared?

Case Critique 1-2
Blue Suede Shoes

Hush Puppies, those marvelous sueded, pig-skin shoes, were big money makers in the late 1950s and early 1960s during Elvis Presley's hey-day. What they lacked in style they had in comfort. The company that produced them, Wolverine World Wide, Inc., was earning its owners $1.04 a share in 1968. Gradually, however, the people to whom Hush Puppies had their greatest appeal grew older. Younger people wanted something more fashionable. By 1972 the average customer's age was 50. Earnings per share for the owners dropped to 2 cents. Then Wolverine decided to do something about the changing market environment. It brought in a stylist who redesigned its line of Hush Puppies to appeal to younger people. It took on a line of hiking boots, handsewn moc-

casins, and boating shoes. Soon, the age of the average customer had dropped to 30. Sales picked up dramatically, and profits began rolling in again.

1. What resources does Wolverine convert into products, and what kind of utility does the company add by so doing?
2. What kind of utility do the retailers add who carry the Hush Puppy line?
3. What changes in the environment threatened the success of the Hush Puppy line? What did Wolverine do to counteract those changes?

Source: "How Seven Firms Have Bucked the Tide," *U.S. News & World Report*, November 23, 1981, p. 59

Chapter 2

The American Economic System

1 FEATURES IN COMMON

These economic resources are common to all economic systems:

Land

Labor

Capital

Technology

2 LAW OF SUPPLY AND DEMAND

Economic systems try to balance

Supply   **Demand**

3 PRIVATE ENTERPRISE: THE MARKET SYSTEM

A private enterprise system is an unplanned, demand, market economy which adds entrepreneurship to other economic resources and is called "pure capitalism," when characterized by . . .

Private ownership

Private profit

Free markets and Free choice

Free competition without monopoly or oligopoly

4 MODIFIED CAPITALISM: THE AMERICAN WAY

In the United States there is modified capitalism because the system includes limited government regulation.

5 SOCIALISM AND COMMUNISM

Other economic systems are planned, command economies.

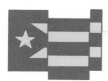

Socialism:
Centralized planning
Extensive government regulation
Government ownership of basic industries

Communism:
Centralized planning
Extensive government regulation
Total government ownership

6 ECONOMIC MEASUREMENTS

These are measurements of the effectiveness and growth of an economic system:

Standard of living
Disposable income
Personal spending

Gross national product (GNP)

Capital supply
Inflation

Productivity
Employment
Quality of life

Learning Objectives

The purpose of this chapter is to outline the resources common to all economic systems, define capitalism as it operates in the United States, and provide an understanding of other economic systems so that you may compare their effectiveness.

After studying Chapter 2, you should be able to:

1. Identify the four features that are common to all economic systems and distinguish between producers and consumers.
2. Relate the concept of supply and demand to a business situation.
3. Recognize the elements of a private enterprise system and the presence of a monopoly or an oligopoly.
4. Understand the role of government regulation in modified capitalism.
5. Compare and contrast socialism, communism, and capitalism.
6. Outline the various kinds of measurements for gauging the effectiveness of these economic systems.

If your class is using SSweetco: Business Model and Activity File for Business in Action, see Chapter 2 in that book after you complete this chapter. There you will find exercises and activities to help you apply your learning to typical business situations.

Society has a basic problem. On the one hand, it has a population that requires basic necessities like food, shelter, and protection from injury and that desires many other goods and services. On the other hand, the society has access to limited amounts of resources—land, plant and animal life, minerals, air, and water. The problem is how to manage the use of these limited resources to meet people's needs and wants. An economic system has as its primary challenge the resolution of this problem.

Different societies have developed widely varying solutions. They vary, for example, as to who has access to resources, who decides what goods and services to provide, and who allocates the products made from the resources. An examination of these differences in some of the world's major economic systems will point up the distinctive nature of the system of modified private enterprise as practiced in the United States.

1 FEATURES COMMON TO ALL SYSTEMS

Limited resources and unlimited needs

Every economic system operates under two constraints: (a) the limitations of its economic resources and (b) the counteracting forces of supply and demand.

ECONOMIC RESOURCES

These are always limited

4 Basic Resources

All economic systems begin with the same basic resources: land, labor, capital, and technology. These are limited in extent at any given time, both in the world at large and in a specific country. Using these limited resources for the good of society is the chief task of any economic system.

Land All real property is a basic economic resource. *Land* includes the open fields used by farmers, urban factory sites, and backyards. The oceans, also a resource, are considered part of the land. The physical raw materials used by manufacturers, such as iron ore and petroleum, are products of the land. The basic industries of agriculture, forestry, and fishing depend directly on the land. Land as a resource is clearly limited in extent and in the amount of raw materials it contains.

Labor All of the men and women who are available to do work of any kind make up the country's *labor force.* The hundreds of millions of people worldwide who are employed by business organizations are part of the labor force, as are the self-employed. The president of a corporation is as much a part of labor as a materials handler on the loading dock.

Capital Wealth that is available to support the activities of producing goods and services is *capital.* Capital may be cash that has been accumulated to start a business, to cite a simple example. A woman who has saved $10,000 from her salary managing a retail store might use it to buy equipment and merchandise to open her own store. The $10,000 is capital. Capital may be in any form; it may be money, material goods, or talent. Any kind of wealth qualifies if it is used to create more wealth.

Technology   *Technology* refers to the methods used in producing goods and services. Although technology is usually thought of as involving machines and electronics, it is the applied science or knowledge behind the machines and is a most important and useful economic resource.

PRODUCERS AND CONSUMERS

Makers and takers

In every type of economy there are two sets of people—or enterprises—that make the system work. These are producers and consumers.

Producers   Producers are the people who perform the work that provides goods and services for society. This group includes not only those people who work with their hands, but also those who start up and/or manage a business. It also includes the investors who supply the money to initiate and sustain a business. Producers, taken as a whole, supply the products and services that are demanded by consumers.

Consumers   Consumers are the people (often the same people who are producers, only now wearing different hats) who buy the products and services provided by the producers. Consumers are made up of individuals, families and households, businesses, and also government purchasers. Consumers play an important role in most societies since they decide what they will buy, where they will buy it, when, and from whom. Their decisions about how they will spend their incomes greatly affects what the producers will supply.

A SYSTEM OF EXCHANGE

In one pocket and out the other

Oddly enough, almost all producers are also consumers. That is, a person who works in a factory making shoelaces is a producer; when that same person spends the money received for working to buy food, he or she is a consumer. Similarly, the factory that produces shoelaces is also a consumer—of yarn for the laces and metal for the tips. In a way, the continual exchange of money between producer and consumer is what makes an economy function, as is shown in Figure 2-1.

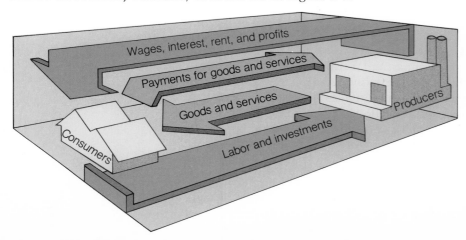

Figure 2-1
Circular flow of income between producers and consumers.

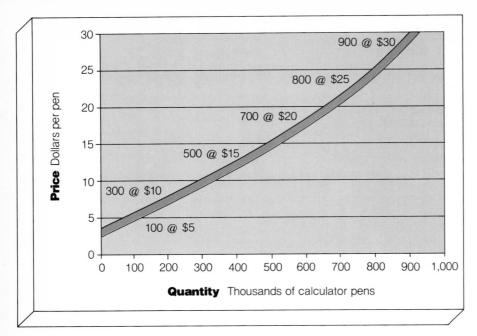

Figure 2-2
Simplified producer supply curve for calculator pens showing the number of pens that will be made available by manufacturers at each given price.

2   THE LAW OF SUPPLY AND DEMAND

It is a perpetual balancing act

The central function of every economic system is to allocate its limited resources to satisfy the needs and desires of its people. The amount of goods produced depends upon the amount of resources available and on many other factors. At the same time, the people in a society have a great variety of needs and wants. Some of these, such as the need for food and shelter, always exist. Others, such as the desire to own a particular style of clothing, continually change. Economies generally try to maintain a balance between the goods and services available from their producers (the supply) and the needs and wants of their consumers (the demand).

Supply and demand also have more precise meanings. These meanings are essential to an understanding of economic systems.

Supply   *Supply* may be defined as the quantity of an economic good that is made available for sale by all the producers of that particular product or service. Figure 2-2 shows, for example, what the supply of digital-calculator pens might be at a particular time. In its simplified format, it shows that producers are ready to provide only 100,000 pens at a price of $5 each. They are willing to make increasingly larger quantities available at higher prices, however. For $10 each, the quantity would be another 200,000 pens, or 300,000 in all. And so on up to a price of $30, where 900,000 would be available. In other words, producers are likely to make more goods available at higher prices and fewer at lower prices.

Demand   *Demand* may be defined as the quantity of an economic good that consumers will buy at a specific price. Figure 2-3 shows, for example, what the overall demand for pens might be at a particular time. Consumers are ready to purchase only 100,000 pens at $30 each. But they

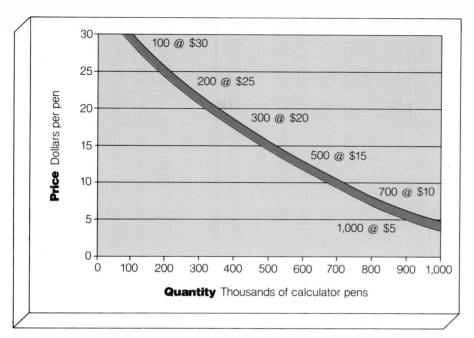

stand ready to purchase increasing amounts at lower prices. Their viewpoint toward prices is in direct contrast with that of the producers.

Law of Supply and Demand   The conditions of (*a*) supply and (*b*) demand for a particular good, like the calculator pen, at a particular time work together to determine the price of the good and the amount that will be exchanged. This relationship is called the ***law of supply and demand.*** It is best illustrated by placing the demand curve (from Figure 2-3) on top of the supply curve (from Figure 2-2) as shown in Figure 2-4. The point

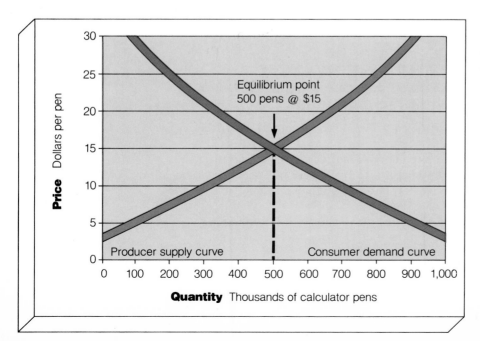

Figure 2-4
How supply and demand conditions determine price and quantity sold.

where the two curves intersect determines for both producers and consumers what quantity of goods will be produced and what price they will sell for. In the case of the pens at this particular time, 500,000 will be available at $15 each. This point of intersection is sometimes called the *equilibrium point,* or *equilibrium price.* This is an ideal condition. It does not always work out this way in practice. It does represent, however, the kind of thinking on the part of producers and consumers that enables them (collectively) to arrive at a point of exchange that will satisfy the greatest majority of both.

Conditions of supply and/or demand change constantly. As a consequence, the supply curve of Figure 2-2 may move to the right or the left on the price versus quantity chart, according to many factors that may affect producers' attitudes, motivations, and ability to compete. When this happens, the supply curve will intersect the demand curve at a different point. As a result, the quantity available and its price at that particular time will change. Similarly, the demand curve (or condition) shown in Figure 2-3 may shift to the right or left, according to factors that affect consumers as a whole, such as the amount of money they have to spend. When this happens, the demand curve will intersect the supply curve at a different point, with a resultant change in the quantity and price of goods available and purchased.

GOVERNMENT'S ROLE

Arbitrating of supply and demand

How to supply goods and services to meet demand is a fundamental question facing all economies. The manner in which the question is resolved, serves as a basis for distinguishing between different economic systems. Systems can also be distinguished by the role of the government, by those who control capital and the means of production, by the amount of central planning, and by other factors. The U.S. economy is based on the principles of private enterprise and modified capitalism.

3   THE PRIVATE ENTERPRISE SYSTEM

Depends upon demand in the marketplace

Private enterprise allows businesses to pursue their operations without repressive central government planning or control. It depends on stimulating and satisfying consumer demand rather than on planning supplies and then trying to control demand. Control over how resources are used and what goods and services are produced is determined by the operation of a free market.

A *free market* exists whenever one person wishes to sell something, another wishes to buy it, and they determine the price of sale by negotiation without outside interference. This concept of a marketplace is central to a private enterprise economy. It describes the free behavior of buyers and sellers even in a very complex society where there are many sellers with the same or similar goods and many buyers with different amounts of money and motivation. Thus a **market economy** can be regarded as a system in which buyers and sellers exchange goods and services at prices mutually agreed upon.

The marketplace controls a private enterprise economy by automatically allocating resources to meet consumer demands. Goods that consumers do not want or need will not sell and will not continue to be produced. Goods for which there is a great demand will sell well, and producers will increase the supply. The free market operates on all transactions in a true private enterprise system. It not only affects the cost and supply of goods and services produced by businesses; it applies equally to wages paid to employees, costs of factories and production equipment, interest on borrowed money, and every other transaction between individuals or companies.

The main distinguishing features of the private enterprise system, then, can be summarized in three terms: (a) it is *unplanned* because government controls neither the supply nor demand of goods and services, (b) it is a *demand economy* because the wants and needs of consumers determine the allocations of resources, and (c) it is a *market economy* because it responds to the effects of supply and demand operating in a free market.

THE ENTREPRENEURIAL SPIRIT

Individual, private initiative

To the four basic economic resources, private enterprise adds a factor that must be considered in itself—the entrepreneurial spirit. An ***entrepreneur*** is someone who uses personal initiative to organize a new business. The entrepreneurial spirit shows itself in the creativity and willingness to take risks displayed by those men and women who have made the free market system work. New consumer demands would remain unsatisfied if entrepreneurs did not recognize them and assemble the capital and organize businesses to provide the wanted products or services.

Most of the famous names of American business have been entrepreneurs: Rockefeller, Carnegie, Ford, Morgan, Mellon, and countless others. All those thousands of people who go into business for themselves to provide services on a local level are entrepreneurs, too.

PURE CAPITALISM

Unrestrained freedom to buy, sell, and compete

The system of true private enterprise is often called ***pure capitalism.*** It is based on the private ownership of business capital. Consumers and producers have a free choice of what to buy and what to sell. Profits from business operations go directly back to the people who invested their capital. Competition is free and is allowed to operate and evolve without regulation.

Private Ownership   The ability to produce, buy, and sell goods for a profit is rooted in private ownership of property. Under capitalism, land and buildings, machinery, furniture, works of art, inventions, mineral and water rights, and all other kinds of property are privately owned.

The profit motive is based on this right to own and to dispose of property. Since individuals can use things they own as they see fit, they are free to use them for their own private gain, if they so choose. Also, any profits they make will be their private property as well, and they are motivated to make as much profit as possible.

Free Choice   Pure capitalism implies free choice for both consumers and producers. Consumers may decide to buy or not to buy a product and may buy it from any supplier they choose. Manufacturers and distributors are also free to produce or sell the goods they believe will be most profitable. This freedom of choice is an essential feature of a free market system.

Individual freedom extends further. Under pure capitalism, people are free to pursue any occupation they choose. They are free to become entrepreneurs and produce their own goods or services for their own use or for sale. They are free to work for any person or company they choose or to work for no one at all.

Private Profit   The hope of making private profit and of creating more personal wealth is the main reason businesses are started and continue to operate. Without private profit, entrepreneurs would not be encouraged to use their skill and creativity to meet consumer demands. Without private profit, investors would not take the sometimes substantial risk of providing the capital needed for business. Without private profit, buying and selling in a free marketplace would not take place. Capitalism depends on profit for its motive force.

Free Competition   In an economic system with freedom of choice, competition will develop among producers of the same or similar products. If someone in town processes dairy products, an entrepreneur is free to open a similar plant and to attempt to sell the same kinds of goods to the same customers. This is direct competition. In pure capitalism, all buyers and sellers operate in competition with other buyers and sellers of the same goods and services.

Free competition has many advantages. Competitive enterprises usually sell at lower prices. If one firm tries to create maximum profits by selling goods at a very high price, another firm is very likely to gain a competitive edge by selling the same goods at a lower price. In a competitive situation, companies often try to attract customers by offering better service, warranties, financing, and other benefits. Competition encourages business managers to produce a better product for the same price. It also leads to efficiency in production and management because improvement in these areas will increase profits without driving customers to other firms. All of these benefits help individual consumers and, at the same time, improve the productivity of the whole economy. They help to produce the most and best goods and services for the least investment in capital, labor, and other resources.

In some cases, free competition is self-limiting, and this may be disadvantageous. Companies may compete so successfully, ethically or unethically, that they are able to eliminate other companies that sell the same goods and services. A company that operates with no competition in producing or marketing particular goods is a *monopoly.* If such a company

ACTION BRIEF

Success Draws a Crowd.   In 1970, Levi Strauss Co. produced half of all the blue jeans sold in the world. The demand for jeans kept on growing, from $2 billion in 1970 to over $4 billion in 1980. But Levi Strauss discovered that along the way lots of other producers had gotten into the act. In fact, a survey made one day in a New York City elementary school showed that of 217 students wearing jeans, there were 43 different brands! No wonder that the original jeans maker's share of the market dropped from 50 percent to 30 percent during the decade.

Sources: "Jeans: The Name of the Game," Pennypower, February/March 1982, p. 8. Jennifer Pendleton, "Can Levi's Get Back into Jeans Saddle?" Advertising Age, February 15, 1982, p. 4.

makes a product that is in high demand, it can charge unreasonably high prices and act in other ways that are harmful to society.

An *oligopoly* exists when there are only a few competitors supplying the same goods or services to the same market. This is a common situation in the United States today whether one looks at automobile manufacturers or at the florist shops in a small town. Oligopolies are not usually strongly competitive because managers are aware that all the competing firms can sell at higher prices to their mutual benefit. This can happen when a company is very familiar with its competitors' business practices and prices, even without deliberate price fixing (companies conspiring to set abnormally high prices industrywide).

Problems such as those caused by monopolies have resulted in changes in the private enterprise system in the United States. Most of these changes involve increased government regulation of business practices. Because of these changes, the U.S. economic system today may best be called modified capitalism.

4   MODIFIED CAPITALISM

Imposes some government regulation

Our economic system was founded on the principles of private enterprise. The basic rights of capitalism—private property, freedom to buy and sell, private profit, and competition—are protected. Today, however, the government takes a much more active role in economic issues, mainly to protect individual consumers and society as a whole from abuses by business.

GOVERNMENT REGULATION

Laws protect the powerless

Many kinds of business activity today are regulated by legislation. In many cases, it is illegal to knowingly sell products that are harmful to the public. Safety devices and special materials are required for many products. Fraudulent marketing practices are generally outlawed. Laws protect society from dangerous manufacturing processes and waste products. Other laws attempt to protect the environment from long-term destruction.

Unfair business practices, such as creating monopolies and price fixing, are prevented by regulation. Companies are required to provide their workers with safe working conditions, and most employers are required to pay a minimum wage. Activities of organized labor are controlled to some extent; certain restrictions on strikes are available to protect the national interest, for instance.

Government regulation of business in the United States is limited. Its intention is to allow private enterprise to operate to the greatest extent possible, while protecting the safety, health, property, and rights of individuals.

Other Government Intervention   Government intervention manifests itself in other ways besides direct regulation. In recent years, there has been a growing acceptance of the belief that the government should try to protect citizens from the effects of business cycles. Historically, the economy has passed through periods of high production with full employment and increasing wages, followed by periods of recession accompanied by unemployment and falling output. Through various means and with varying success, the government has tried to stabilize the economy, restraining growth on the peaks and stimulating business in the valleys.

Even this kind of intervention in the free operation of business is very limited compared to that of other economic systems. Two systems of particular interest today—socialism and communism—are distinguished from modified capitalism by their strong reliance on government planning and control, as well as by other factors.

5   SOCIALISM AND COMMUNISM

Alternative economic command systems

Most other economic systems differ from private enterprise in their stress on government planning of economic activity. (See Table 2-1, "Comparisons Between Capitalism, Socialism, and Communism.") In other systems, government planners assess resources and social needs and then direct the manufacturing and distribution facilities in their country toward certain goals. Since economic activity is controlled by government command or edict, these are called *command economies.* Socialism and communism will be considered here only in their economic aspects. The political and philosophical backgrounds of the systems are not essential to a general understanding of their functioning.

SOCIALISM

Government ownership of key industries

Socialism is an economic system in which the major production and distribution industries are owned and operated by the government. Officials directly manage some or all of the extraction of raw materials, manufacturing, communications, and transportation. Government also plays a heavy regulative role in all other business activity. Some of the freedoms of capitalism, however, exist in modified form. Private ownership of small businesses, residences, and personal property is allowed. People are generally free to work where they wish, although the government encourages workers to enter industries where they are needed. A limited amount of private profit is available to small businesses, but most profits end up in government hands because of high taxation. Limited competition among some businesses is permitted, but every effort is made to eliminate competition in major industries. Proponents of socialism claim that the absence of large-scale competition results in increased efficiency. They believe that the presence of many small competitors in the same market causes duplication of effort and wastes resources.

In control of the major production facilities, socialist governments are able to plan the kinds and quantities of goods to be produced. The

TABLE 2-1
Comparisons Between Capitalism, Socialism, and Communism

Factor	American Capitalism	Socialism	Communism
Ownership of land and other productive assets	Private ownership with certain guaranteed rights as to ownership of its output.	State owns and operates certain basic industries such as utilities, transportation, and steel.	State owns all productive land and assets.
Incentives	Wages and profits directly related to one's ability to serve in the market.	Wages related to a judgment of the value of each person's contribution to society.	Publicly announced work standards with incentives in the form of patriotism, public recognition, status, and awards.
Labor	Freedom to work where and at whatever job one chooses.	Free choice of work, but state encourages some and discourages other forms of employment.	Workers have some choice of occupation, but state prescribes the place of work and is the only employer.
Capital	Provided primarily by private investors and lending institutions.	Provided by individuals' investment in state's bonds and by prices paid for goods.	Provided by the state from taxes generated by production.
Risk and loss	The responsibility of private individuals, owners, investors, and creditors, with little or no help from the government.	Risk and losses of state-owned industries borne by citizens either through higher taxes or higher prices.	Government and, in turn, the people accept all risks; losses generally absorbed by a lower standard of living.
Technology	Generated privately and stimulated by government funding of research.	Stimulated largely by government intervention and funding.	Generated almost exclusively by state actions and funding.
Competition	Free choice to compete encouraged, protected, and regulated to some extent by law.	State-owned facilities operate according to master plan; private businesses may compete, but must accommodate themselves to the master plan.	Generally prohibited and counter to dominant economic and political philosophy; under rigidly enforced state economic and political restrictions.
Government influence	Stimulates private and individual initiative and regulates business actions that are legally deemed to be not in the public interest.	State prepares master plan specifying most economic activity, including regulation.	State owns and operates virtually all productive assets in accordance with economic and political plans.
Products and services	Determined largely by consumer demand and profit potential for private business enterprise.	Basic products and services determined largely by central planning; other products by profit potential.	Commanded entirely by state economic and political plans.
Consumer choice	Extremely broad, and generally unrestricted except by an individual's income.	Generally unrestricted except by consumers' income.	Limited to planned supply and restricted by individuals' incomes.

governments usually intend to use this power to distribute the goods and services of the economy more equally to the citizens. In theory, basic services like health care, employment, education, good housing, and transportation are available to everyone.

The economies of countries such as Sweden, Denmark, France, Great Britain, and many African and South American states are socialist to varying degrees. The long-term success or failure of these economies has yet to be determined, but problems have emerged. Government-run production facilities tend to develop large, nonproductive managerial bureaucracies resulting in less efficient provision of goods and services. Individual incentive to produce appears to wither under socialism. Creativity and initiative are not always rewarded, and socialist economies easily fall into stagnation because they imitate rather than innovate.

COMMUNISM

State ownership and operation of all resources

Communism replaces the operation of a free market almost entirely with central government planning and control. Most of the rights enjoyed in a capitalist system are denied. Private ownership of business property is usually prohibited; the state owns resources and production and distribution facilities. Decisions about what goods and services will be available are made by state planners rather than by consumers in a free market. Individuals are not allowed to establish business enterprises. Private profit is not permitted. Citizens are expected to contribute their best for the good of the state and receive in return only what they need for a modest life. Competition has been almost eliminated.

Justifications for such a system are similar to those for socialism. Supporters believe that the wealth of the society can be more equitably distributed and that central planning and the lack of competition result in more efficient production.

The Soviet Union, the People's Republic of China, and Cuba have communist economies. In the Soviet Union, particularly, a considerable evolution from pure communism has begun to take place. Incentives for increased worker performance are now more common, and wealth is being distributed to some degree according to the abilities and contributions of the individual.

None of these economic systems exist in pure form. Just as capitalism allows government regulation and control of the economy, socialism and communism often introduce features of private enterprise. These adjustments are efforts to improve the functioning of these economies.

6 ECONOMIC MEASUREMENTS

How well people live under a system

In determining the effectiveness of an economy, a variety of measures are available. These center on how well people are able to live (standard of living, amount and type of employment, and access to the good things in life), the total production of goods and services, the efficiency of that production (gross national product and productivity), and the financial status of the economy. These measures contribute to an understanding of an individual economy and help us to compare economies.

STANDARD OF LIVING
Basics plus amenities

A *standard of living* is the extent to which members of society are able to satisfy their basic needs such as food, adequate clothing, and shelter and are able to acquire the other goods and services that make life more comfortable and more enjoyable. Two specific measurements are (a) *disposable income,* the amount of income left to be spent after taxes have been withheld, and (b) *personal spending,* the amount of income actually spent and how it is spent. In some economies, workers are unable to obtain the necessities of life even after spending their entire income. In advanced economies, ordinary employees may have as much as 50 to 60 percent of their income left after attending to basic necessities.

GROSS NATIONAL PRODUCT
The sum of all economic output

The *gross national product* (GNP) is the total market price of all the goods and services created by an economy. It is calculated over a year and reflects the total output of production facilities. The GNP in the United States has been increasing at a rapid rate: from $504 billion in 1960 to over $3,000 billion in 1983. The per capita gross national product is often used in comparing the economies of different countries. It is calculated by dividing the GNP by the country's total population. The per capita GNP for several nations is shown in Table 2-2.

CAPITAL SUPPLY
Assets available for business and production

The supply of capital in use and available for use by business can be estimated as an indication of present and potential business activity. Without adequate capital for business operations, other resources cannot be utilized to produce goods, resulting in a stagnating economy. Heavy capital investment in plant and production equipment, on the other hand, is a sign of a growing economy since it creates conditions for increased production.

TABLE 2-2
Gross National Product* per Capita in 14 Nations

U.S. Dollars*	Nation
14,034	Switzerland
10,910	West Germany
10,814	Sweden
9,869	United States
9,127	France
8,901	Japan
8,674	Canada
5,625	England
4,402	Soviet Union
1,677	Brazil
1,481	Mexico
831	Nigeria
433	People's Republic of China
103	Bangladesh

*Figures are for 1979 and are stated in constant 1978 dollars.

Source: Table No. 1524, "Gross National Product, in Current and Constant (1978) Dollars per Capita, 1970 to 1979". *Statistical Abstract of the United States, 1982–83,* 103d ed., U.S. Department of Commerce, Bureau of the Census, 1982, p. 865.

Capital supply is also greatly affected by inflation. Inflation is an increase in the amount of money in circulation or available as bank credit. This causes a decrease in the value of money and a general increase in prices. Consumers' dollars become worth less than before. Investors hesitate to put money in new ventures. Producers, too, pay more for the products and services (such as labor and materials) that they consume. In turn, the producers raise prices. Such step-by-step raising of prices and wages has been dubbed "the wage-price spiral." Inflation is damaging to an economy and its people. In most countries of the world, including the United States, inflation has become a major problem with no easy or apparent solution.

PRODUCTIVITY

A measure of an economy's efficiency

The amount and value of the goods and services produced from a given input of resources is a measure of *productivity.* The higher the relative productivity of an economy, the better that economy is judged to be. A business, or a nation, can improve productivity in two ways: (a) by producing more and better goods from the same amount of resources, or (b) by producing the same quantity and quality of goods from fewer resources. This concept is illustrated in Figure 2-5. In 1900, for example, it may have taken a cobbler 1 week to make a pair of boots. Today, the same cobbler, assisted by modern machinery acquired through the investment of capital, might produce 50 pairs of boots. The quantity and value of the cobbler's output (productivity) would have increased 50 times. The cost and value of the inputs, however, would also have risen because of the higher tool costs. Productivity improvement, like inflation, has become a major problem of most economies. The United States was once the indisputable leader in the world's productivity, but it has now fallen behind such nations as Japan, West Germany, France, and Canada.

Figure 2-5
Productivity compares output with input.

EMPLOYMENT

How many share in the economy's fruits

The number of people in a society who are employed or unemployed is a useful measure of the economy's success. A high unemployment rate means that many people are being excluded from at least some economic benefits. It also means that one of the basic economic resources—labor—is being underutilized and the output of the economy is not at its maximum.

The quality of employment is also an indicator of how well the economy is functioning and the extent to which economic benefits are

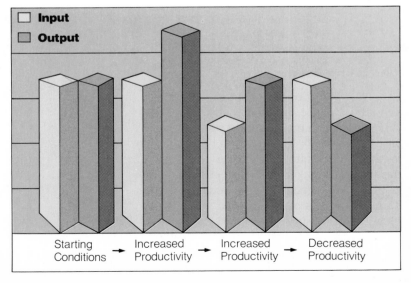

Issues & Highlights

Here is today's box score on productivity (compared with 1978, when the United States set the level at 100.0): United States, 101.4, West Germany, 100.6, Canada, 100.5, France, 99.2, and Japan, 77.2. Obviously, we are neck and neck with our competitors, but they are gaining on us. Productivity growth rates stack up like this: Japan, + 4.5 percent; West Germany, + 4.0 percent; France, + 4.0 percent; Canada, + 2.0 percent; and the Unied States, last in this race with + 1.5 percent. The productivity of labor, the most commonly used measure, has been at a standstill in America since the mid-1970s. Meanwhile our major industrial competitors continue to increase their annual GNP and their citizens' personal income. The Japanese have set their sights on the U.S. semiconductor industry. The U.S. steel and auto industries are floundering.

What's the problem? Is the American worker goofing off? Have American investors failed to put up the capital needed to make our plants more efficient? Is American management at fault for not finding ways to utilize our vast resources? Are American citizens to blame for not saving enough money so as to create capital? Or does the United States tax laws discourage savers and investors all along the line?

Source: Mike Hogan, "Productivity: Capitalization Is Not Our Only Problem," California Business Review, May 1981, p. 107.

From what you know from your own experience, where do you think the blame lies? What measures do you think Americans should take to improve productivity?

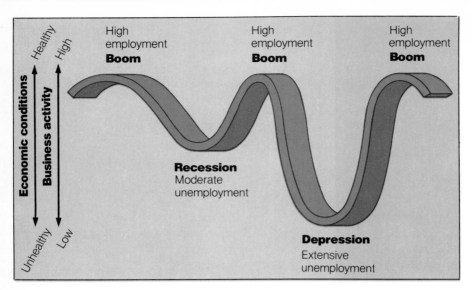

Figure 2-6
Employment and the
business cycle.

being enjoyed. Societies in the early stages of growth have more workers performing basic production activities and relatively few managers and professional workers. As economies advance, more and more workers perform work other than basic production, such as services.

More importantly, healthy economies tend to create jobs. Unhealthy economies tend to suffer from unemployment. It is typical of modified capitalism that its economic health varies over a period of years from healthy to unhealthy and back again. These variations occur in varying degrees of intensity. When the economy is in very good condition, it is said to be "booming." When it is in only moderately poor health, it is said to be in a recession, and employment falls off. When the economy is very poor, it is in a depression and unemployment is high. Such variations in economic health create the **business cycle,** as shown in Figure 2-6, where business activity and general employment alternately rise and fall. The duration of a business cycle from boom to boom may be as little as 5 years or more than 15 years.

QUALITY OF LIFE

Nonmaterial benefits

A final indication of economic success is the quality of life of the society's population. Although this is more difficult to measure, it may be the ultimate test, since the fundamental purpose of an economic system is to satisfy as many wants and needs as possible with its available resources. Leisure time, recreational and cultural facilities, adequate health care, physical safety, attractive surroundings, social cooperation, and thousands of other factors contribute to a worthwhile life. Providing this kind of life appears to be the highest challenge of an economic and social system. It is a challenge that is now being confronted by advanced nations such as the United States but that may, unfortunately, remain far beyond many other nations.

Key Concepts

1. All economic systems have four basic resources for producing goods and services: land, labor, capital, and technology. They also have producers and consumers and some system of exchange between them.
2. Economic systems try to balance the supply of resources with the demand for them.
3. A private enterprise sytem is an unplanned, demand economy, controlled by a free market. It is based on private ownership, free choice, private profit, and free competition.
4. The U.S. economic system is called modified capitalism because it is rooted in private enterprise but permits limited government control to protect society from harmful business practices.
5. Other systems have highly planned command economies. Under socialism, the government owns some or all of the main production and distribution facilities, and competition is limited. In a communist system, most property is in government hands, and individual economic freedom and competition are at a minimum.
6. A number of economic measures show how well citizens live, how many and how efficiently goods and services are produced, and how well economies function. These measures include the standard of living, gross national product, capital supply, level of productivity, level and distribution of employment, and the quality of life.

Review Questions

1. Define, identify, or explain the following key terms and phrases found on the pages indicated.

   business cycle   (p. 34)
   capital   (p. 20)
   command economies   (p. 28)
   communism   (p. 30)
   demand   (p. 22)
   disposable income   (p. 31)
   entrepreneur   (p. 25)
   equilibrium point (equilibrium price)   (p. 24)
   free market   (p. 24)
   gross national product   (p. 31)
   labor force   (p. 20)
   land   (p. 20)
   law of supply and demand   (p. 23)
   market economy   (p. 24)
   monopoly   (p. 26)
   oligopoly   (p. 27)
   personal spending   (p. 31)
   private enterprise   (p. 24)
   productivity   (p. 32)
   pure capitalism   (p. 25)
   socialism   (p. 28)
   standard of living   (p. 31)
   supply   (p. 22)
   technology   (p. 21)

2. Distinguish between a producer and a consumer. In what ways are they similar?
3. What is the law of supply and demand? Give an example of a product or service for which the price has changed due to shifts in supply or demand.
4. What is the difference between a demand economy and a command economy? Which economic systems fall into these two categories?
5. Why is the economic system in the United States called modified capitalism?
6. What are some of the goals and purposes of government intervention in economic and business affairs in the United States?
7. How do private ownership and competition work under capitalism, socialism, and communism?
8. What is meant by gross national product? If productivity were to increase, but all other aspects of the U.S. economy remained unchanged, what would be the effect on the GNP? What effect do you think such a situation would have on the price of individual goods and services?

Case Critique 2-1
Office Space for Rent

In 1982, office space was a glut on the market. All over the United States, space in downtown office buildings was going begging. In Dallas alone, 45 new buildings were opening their doors with 9.5 million square feet of space newly available. "All of a sudden, we've got all kinds of space coming on board and not enough tenants," said the vice president of one of the largest investors in office buildings. "As the general economy slows down and there are fewer relocations of corporate headquarters, the space will not be absorbed." One immediate reaction was for the real estate companies that underwrite the construction of these buildings to call a halt to the construction of new facilities. A second reaction came from the banks and insurance companies that lend money to these real estate developers. They asked for much higher down payments on their mortgages. Taken as a whole, the situation put the owners of office buildings in an economic squeeze.

1. If you were the owner of a building with vacant space, what might you do to attract tenants?
2. If you were a company looking for office space, would you pay whatever the asking price was for rent? Why?

3. In looking at all the office space in the country, what would you say has happened to the supply? Has it increased or decreased? At a given price, say of $25 per square foot, would you think there is now more or less space available for rent?
4. In looking at all the people in the country who might want to rent office space, what would you say has probably happened to their overall demand for space? Has it increased or decreased? From the point of view of the landlords who own the existing office space, what effect would this change in demand have upon the number of potential renters at a particular price? Would there be more or fewer renters?
5. Suppose the demand for space had in fact remained exactly as it was, and only the supply had changed as you decided in question 3. Will the changed supply curve intersect the unchanged demand curve (refer to Figure 2-4 again) at (a) a higher or lower rental price, and (b) at a higher or lower quantity of units, or space, available for rent?

Source: "An Office-Space Boom Screeches to a Halt," *Business Week*, March 22, 1982, p. 25.

Case Critique 2-2
High Wages, Cheap Gasoline, and a Productivity Problem

As painful as it felt then in 1981, when automobile owners in the United States were paying $1.45 a gallon for gasoline, owners in West Germany were paying $2.46. In England, the price was $2.78 a gallon, in Italy, $3.06, in Uruguay, $4.64. Prices were comparatively high in Japan, too. At the same time, automobile workers in the United States were receiving, on average, a grand total of $18.60 an hour; their counterparts in Japan, now the biggest automobile producer, were getting $10.78.

Surprisingly, in light of these figures, productivity in West Germany and Japan, for instance, was rising faster than in the United States. Con-

sumers here were increasingly buying goods made overseas, not only because of their high quality, but because they were cheaper than the ones made at home. The General Electric Company (GE) had been feeling this pinch on the sale of its products. Overseas competitors were a serious threat. Accordingly, in 1979 GE began a drive to improve productivity in its factories. Over the next two years, GE spent $1.26 billion for machines and equipment that helped its employees to create a greater output from the inputs made to the conversion process.

Meanwhile, another company, a machine tool company in Massachusetts, was also running into productivity problems. It kept paying its employees higher wages and benefits, a total of $13.14 an hour in 1981. But productivity in the plant fell by 10 percent from 1976 to 1981. On the other hand, the company had invested practically no money in new machinery during that period. Competition from lower-priced products became a major headache. Because of the low productivity in that plant, the company decided to shut it down completely.

1. For both the General Electric Company and the machine tool company, what economic factors seemed to have the biggest impact upon their productivity?
2. The well-being of both GE and the machine tool company were threatened by goods made by other companies. What characteristics of pure capitalism are represented by this situation?

3. Despite higher productivity in some countries abroad, what would you conclude about the standard of living in the United States compared with other countries, based upon the data provided in the case?
4. What economic factor that affects productivity has the machine tool company failed to provide as an input to its conversion process?
5. If goods made overseas can be sold at lower prices than those made in the United States, should the United States government intervene to reduce wages or insist that companies invest more in new equipment, for example, so that goods made domestically can compete more effectively? Why?

Sources: "Investment Becomes a Strike Issue," *Business Week*, July 5, 1982, p. 23. "Tale of the Pay Envelope," *Forbes*, November 23, 1981, p. 40. *General Electric Investor*, Summer 1980, p. 13.

Chapter 3

The American
Business
Environment

1 THE BUSINESS FIRM
is a "system" which exists within
and interacts with interdependent
environments.

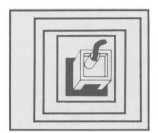

**2 THE ECONOMIC
ENVIRONMENT**
includes such factors as risk, market
dynamics, the money supply, and
economic growth and stagnation.

**3 THE LEGAL-POLITICAL
ENVIRONMENT**
embraces political and public policies,
government regulation and control,
government assistance to business,
and taxation.

4 THE SOCIAL-CULTURAL ENVIRONMENT

considers social values, social protection, and demands for corporate citizenship.

5 THE PHYSICAL ENVIRONMENT

encompasses energy supplies, natural resources, environmental pollution, and the ecological outlook.

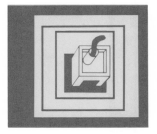

Learning Objectives

The purpose of this chapter is to show how business is affected by the complex environment in which it must operate and to identify some of the interrelated economic, legal-political, social-cultural, and physical forces that affect business operations in the United States.

After studying Chapter 3, you should be able to:

1. Recognize the elements of a business system and the environments that influence it.
2. Determine how the economic environment affects a business.
3. Identify factors in the legal-political environment that influence business enterprises.
4. Analyze and discuss the social-cultural environment, and describe how business may be influenced by its own sense of social responsibility, social values, and demands for social protection.
5. Describe the major factors in the physical environment that have an impact on business operations.

If your class is using SSweetco: Business Model and Activity File for Business in Action, see Chapter 3 in that book after you complete this chapter. There you will find exercises and activities to help you apply your learning to typical business situations.

In its day-to-day operations, business has constant interactions with the outside world. This chapter describes some of these interactions that set the framework within which business functions and that affect management decisions.

The **business environment** is the collection of the physical and cultural factors outside of the business system itself that influence the activities of business. The environment determines what businesses can do and has a shaping and channeling influence on their development.

1   SYSTEMS AND THE ENVIRONMENT

Business interacts with other systems to shape the total environment

The nature of the interplay between business and its environment will be easier to understand if the concept of a system is examined in more detail. A *system* is a group of related parts that work together in an organized way for some specific purpose or purposes. Figure 2-1 in the previous chapter illustrates the exchange system between producers and consumers. An individual business firm is a system. It has related parts: management, production workers, machinery, the physical plant, and

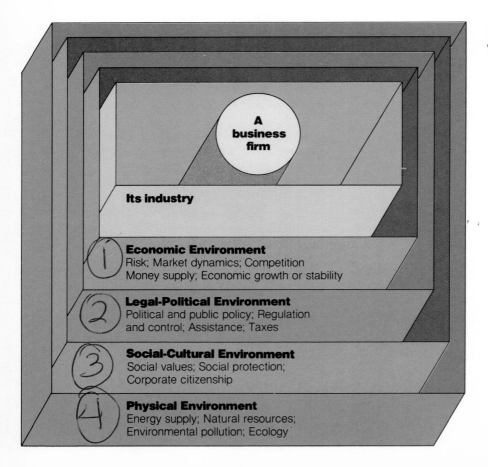

Figure 3-1
Four environments surround a firm and its industry.

A business firm

Its industry

1. **Economic Environment**
Risk; Market dynamics; Competition
Money supply; Economic growth or stability

2. **Legal-Political Environment**
Political and public policy; Regulation
and control; Assistance; Taxes

3. **Social-Cultural Environment**
Social values; Social protection;
Corporate citizenship

4. **Physical Environment**
Energy supply; Natural resources;
Environmental pollution; Ecology

often hundreds more. The parts are organized into a system so that they can work together to convert resources into valuable end products.

Just as the shipping room may be a working part of an individual business firm, the firm is itself a working part of an industry. An *industry* may be viewed as a collection of related businesses that all work together to supply the total demand for a particular kind of product or service. A small metal foundry may produce machine castings by organizing people and equipment for the purpose of buying and storing raw materials, building forms and molds, producing molten metal, making castings, and handling inventory, shipping, recordkeeping, sales, advertising, and financial and general management. In turn, all the metal foundries work together, using common materials and methods, exploiting new research findings, supporting suppliers, and selling to the same general market.

Businesses and industries play various roles in a number of larger settings. Overlapping systems that are part of society include the business system as one of their working parts. These systems, or environments, interact with and influence business at every level. They may be grouped into four environments: economic, legal-political, social-cultural, and physical. Figure 3-1 illustrates the way a firm and its industry are surrounded by their four environments. Although each is discussed separately, the four systems always work together to shape the total environment that impacts on a business and its operations.

2   THE ECONOMIC ENVIRONMENT

Provides the basic setting

The *economic environment* sets the basic rules by which business operates. In the United States, the economic setting is guided by the principles of modified capitalism. Business functions in an environment where entrepreneurs are free to risk capital with the hope of creating profits and where a free market has the ultimate control over business decisions. The supply of money available in the economy is part of the environment and profoundly affects operations. Periods of economic growth and recession also affect business operations.

RISK

An opportunity to fail

Every investor or manager in business faces possible loss. Risk is involved not only when capital is invested to start a business, but also during ongoing operations. Products must be developed and new management techniques must be tried, but the costs of these may be lost if the product does not sell or the new method does not work.

MARKET DYNAMICS

Changing needs and fashions

Although a completely free market does not exist in the United States, supply and demand still determine what goods and services will be sold, in what quantities, and at what prices. Managers must grapple with shifting supplies and prices of the goods and raw materials they buy. The unpredictable demands for products they sell require decisions about sales prices, production quantities, and product development.

The environment of the marketplace has become increasingly changeable in recent years as styles and fashions have begun to affect the sale of a wider range of goods. Consumer tastes in clothing have continually shifted for centuries, for example. The changes have accelerated in recent decades to the point where a particular style of men's jacket or women's skirt may be popular for only a year or less. The same patterns of consumer demand extend to automobiles, electronic equipment, garden supplies, foods, and other goods.

MONEY SUPPLY
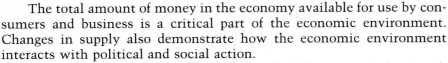
Affects growth and prices

The total amount of money in the economy available for use by consumers and business is a critical part of the economic environment. Changes in supply also demonstrate how the economic environment interacts with political and social action.

Businesses need money to operate. Much of the money is borrowed. When interest rates are low, businesses are encouraged to expand their facilities because the total cost will be lower. Low interest rates also encourage consumers to borrow money to buy the things they want. Business expansion and heavy consumer buying may rapidly increase the total demand for goods and services, surpassing the economy's capacity to supply them. The result is rapidly rising prices and inflation. In this situation, the government may raise the interest rates on money it lends to banks. The increase is passed on to borrowers and makes borrowing more expensive and less attractive. The total supply of money available for immediate spending then decreases, placing restraints on both inflation and economic expansion.

PROFITS
A compelling incentive

A belief fundamental to American business is that private capital may be used to create private profit. Prevailing economic and social environments place limits on the pursuit of private profit, however. Most investors would agree that it is the *responsibility* of a business to make a profit, but *not* through unethical means or dangerous or undesirable practices. Socially responsible profit seeking is still the main incentive to business and the main source of capital to support long-term growth.

ECONOMIC STABILITY AND GROWTH
A cyclical pattern

General economic growth or stagnation has an important influence on business. Hundreds of factors can affect economic conditions: wars, new inventions and techniques, political assassinations, the discovery of new physical resources, labor negotiations, government action, and many others. When the economy is strong and demand is high, without outstripping production capabilities, business can prosper. Challenges still remain in competing with other firms for scarce raw materials and labor, however. When a business cycle is down and unemployment is high (as shown in Figure 2-6 in the previous chapter), consumer demand usually falls off and products are harder to sell. Without great care, profits may suffer enough to endanger the existence of many companies. Every business owner or manager is confronted with the problems that result from general economic conditions.

3   THE LEGAL-POLITICAL ENVIRONMENT

The regulatory framework

The *legal-political environment* in which business functions has become incredibly complex. It is shaped by the interactions between business and government at the federal, state, and local levels. The main job of government has traditionally been to protect the property rights and civil rights of its citizens. In performing this role, governments have maintained police protection, a judicial system, and a national defense system. Government activities in regulating private and business activities and in enforcing contracts stem from this central purpose.

Increasingly, the government is also an important purchaser and supplier of goods and services. Today, over 20 percent of the gross national product (GNP) of the United States results from government spending. Taxation policies and public support of business development have also had significant influence on business operations in this country.

POLITICAL AND PUBLIC POLICY

For the greatest good of all

Government actions are based on public policies and goals controlled by political forces. Business interests are only one of many factors considered when determining public policies. Government usually tries to protect and regulate every kind of enterprise for the greatest good of the society. Many decisions having little or nothing to do with business may profoundly affect individual businesses or the entire business system.

REGULATION AND CONTROL

Protection for all the publics

The government regulates business activities in the United States for a number of reasons. It promotes free competition and protects consumers from harmful products and practices. It tries to reduce the effects of inflation and business cycles. It protects the ownership of patents and trademarks. It sets minimum standards for the operation of certain businesses that deal directly with public health and safety.

Promoting Free Competition   The earliest government regulations resulted from the growth of powerful monopolies in the second half of the last century. Some of these companies forced smaller competitors out of business through unethical means and then raised prices to create large profits. The Sherman Antitrust Act of 1890 was the first of a number of laws that prohibit contracts or conspiracies which limit free trade and competition. Certain firms, such as telephone and power companies, are sometimes allowed to operate as monopolies; they are, however, regulated in other ways.

Through the years, many products have been sold that were harmful or even fatal to users. Our government has acted repeatedly to outlaw such products and to protect consumers from false advertising and other fraudulent marketing practices. Regulation has been widely publicized in recent years with frequent public discussion of actions by the Federal Trade Commission and the Food and Drug Administration.

Price Controls   At various times, spurred by fear of economic decline caused by inflation, the federal government has stepped in to control directly the prices of goods and services in the market. The most notable examples occurred during World War II and during the Nixon Administration in the early 1970s. In contrary moves, the petroleum, trucking, and airline companies were *de*regulated in the past few years. The value of such actions in controlling inflation is the subject of much debate, and while some progress on this front has been registered by the Reagan Administration's *de*regulatory efforts, the permanence of these gains remains to be tested.

Patent Protection   Other kinds of government regulation have been less controversial because they are regarded by many as being more direct expressions of government's central purpose. Numerous laws exist to protect the ownership of **intangible property.** Intangible property is something of value that is not a physical resource or product. Such property is particularly important to businesses. An invention is a new way of doing something and is protected by **patents.** A **trademark** (or brand name, and sometimes a logo) is valuable because it makes products recognizably different. Trademarks are protected by registration. A particular way of putting musical notes and words together to make a song is protected by **copyright,** as are books, articles, poems, and other written material.

Health and Safety   Government regulations also control many practitioners and businesses that directly affect the public's health or safety. These rules apply to people like pharmacists and opticians (who must be licensed to practice) and to companies that operate taxicabs, buses, and many other transportation services. Legislation now requires minimum health and safety standards for all businesses to protect workers and the general public from danger.

GOVERNMENT AID TO BUSINESS

A stimulating force

It is far from true that the only government role in business activity is that of regulation and control. Many government actions are designed to encourage business growth and prosperity. Some kinds of production, notably agriculture, receive subsidies. A **subsidy** is direct financial aid from the government for use in business operations. The Department of Agriculture, the Small Business Administration, and other agencies have many loan and grant programs to assist businesses. Some of the facilities that businesses depend on, such as highways and airports, are directly

ACTION BRIEF

Lemonless Lemonade.   A major consumer organization, the national advertising division of the Council of Better Business Bureaus, was asked to settle a dispute between two makers of lemonade. Coca-Cola, maker of Minute Maid Lemonade Crystals, implied in its advertising that General Foods (GF) put no lemons at all in its Country Time drink. That's not true, replied General Foods. Our product contains lemon oil derived from lemon peels. And besides, said GF, in one of its ads, "In a recent test, people agreed that Country Time tastes better than Minute Maid." Coca-Cola bristled back that only 55 percent of those people in GF's survey had expressed a preference. The council ordered both companies to clean up their advertising act.

Source: "NAD Moderates Sour Lemonade Battle," Advertising Age, February 15, 1982, p. 10.

maintained by governments. The Department of Commerce provides information and promotional assistance to help businesses and, cooperating with other agencies, attracts foreign investment to this country. Federal international tariffs help protect American business from foreign competition. A _tariff_ is a special tax on imported goods, that protects domestic producers from lower-priced foreign products. Import quotas are sometimes set on certain goods for the same purpose. Governments also assist businesses by operating general and vocational schools that train thousands of skilled workers every year.

TAXES
The price of doing business

Businesses must pay taxes on their profits. The level and type of taxation imposed by federal, state, and local governments have a significant impact on business operations. In general, high taxation reduces the amount of private profit that can be made from a given amount of capital. The tax system may also be used to provide incentives, however. Many local governments grant temporary relief from property taxes to encourage industries to locate in their jurisdiction. The federal government sometimes reduces taxes on money used for certain purposes, such as exploration for oil or the development of new production facilities.

4   THE SOCIAL-CULTURAL ENVIRONMENT
The people's way of living

Culture is usually defined by social scientists as the total collection of beliefs and ways of living that develop within a given society. Clearly, culture is an important part of the environment that surrounds business. Business itself is part of the _social-cultural environment_ in the United States.

SOCIAL VALUES
Materialism and human rights

The economic and governmental environments in the United States reflect values widely held by a majority of the people. The belief in the importance of physical goods and in the desirability of accumulating wealth, called _materialism,_ is the basis of capitalism. If people did not desire wealth, there would be no profit motive. Hard work, frugality, and efficiency are considered great values in our society. Some Americans even believe that leisure time should not be wasted but should instead be filled with active recreation. These beliefs have contributed greatly to the enormous growth of business in the United States.

Business, in turn, influences values. The marketing emphasis in business, for instance, has changed the ordinary person's concept of necessities. Advertising and promotion have stimulated the demand for products that, once considered luxuries, are now accepted as being desirable and valuable. Such beliefs become part of the culture and have a long-term effect on values.

Giving

Business

a Break

Most observers agree that so far as government regulations go, the 1960s and 1970s were rough on business. It was the time of the enactment or intensified enforcement of a number of laws that some business people found harassing. Among them were the Occupational Safety and Health Act (OSHA), the Equal Employment Opportunity (EEO) sections of the Civil Rights Act, affirmative action programs, the Employment Retirement Income Security Act (ERISA), Truth-in-Lending laws, Clean Water and Clean Air acts, and the Drug Regulation Reform Act.

As the 1980s progresses, however, the public attitude toward business has begun to soften. Many people who had vigorously disagreed with former General Motors chairperson Charles M. Wilson when he said, "What is good for GM is good for the country," were beginning to wonder whether or not Mr. Wilson's point had at least some merit. They reason that if Federal regulation stifles and discourages business, perhaps it is time to let up a bit. As a result, there are a growing number of people who favor business over labor when they contest one another about wage rates. Other people believe that the United States should raise barriers against imports, which would tend to hold domestic prices, free from foreign competition, at a higher level. Business supporters among the public observe that business, when unfettered, was able to constantly raise our standard of living. These people say, in effect, don't try to make business bear a bigger burden of restrictive legislation than it can carry. Maybe, they say, the United States cannot really afford many of the social benefits that are related to business regulation.

Source: **Suggested by Robert J. Samuelson, "Softening Attitudes Toward Business," The Washington Post, November 28, 1978, p. E1.**

Do you think that the public should allow business greater freedom? Why? What social benefits (like cleaner air and water, more information on the label of a jar of skin cream, or less double talk on a loan agreement) would you be willing to give up if it meant that business would prosper as a result?

Certain values may conflict with others. The completely unrestrained right to make a private profit may frequently cause severe harm to other people. In recent years, there have been various efforts to balance certain human rights with the freedoms basic to capitalism, resulting in changes which, in many cases, have posed difficult challenges to business.

SOCIAL PROTECTION

A demand for more safeguards

A persistent and potent social force is emerging today to try to protect individuals from low quality or unsafe merchandise and from unreasonably high prices and other unfair business practices. Since it is largely made up of consumers to protect their own interests, the movement is called **consumerism.** Much of the government regulation in recent years has come about through consumerism. Changes have also been brought about through public education and organized actions such as product boycotts, the effort to convince consumers not to buy certain goods and services. Unit pricing, for example, is now required by many states. **Unit pricing** specifies that the price of a grocery item, like a package of cereal, must be converted to a standard unit weight. For instance, a 12-ounce box of corn flakes that sells for $1.20 must be marked to show that its unit price is $1.60 a pound.

Another area where social forces have brought change is in supporting the rights and opportunities of groups in society that have been discriminated against in the past. Today in America, strong social pressure is placed on businesses to give equal opportunities to the poor, to minorities, and to women. Businesses are beginning to respond, some voluntarily, some only as the result of government action.

Forces for social protection have influenced business in other ways, either directly or indirectly, by prompting government regulation. Efforts to assure the health, safety, and chances for improvement of every citizen are probably greater in the United States today than in all but a few other countries such as Sweden and West Germany. These efforts continually force changes in the outlook of the business sector.

CORPORATE CITIZENSHIP

An enlightened viewpoint

Business policies today reflect the need to consider the interests of consumers and of society as well as those of business. A small local business is in direct contact with consumers and cannot survive for long if it ignores their concerns and wishes. As large centralized corporations developed in the United States during the nineteenth and twentieth centuries, however, communication between business management and consumers became far less direct. This distance and lack of contact often leads managers to ignore general social interests. People today are demanding more responsiveness to human needs on the part of business. Business organizations, as a result, are finding that it is good business to think and act like responsible citizens.

ACTION BRIEF

Sorry, We Don't Need You Anymore.   For over 13 years, John Bigler ran a first-rate service station that he leased from giant Gulf Oil Corporation. He doubled the business his first year and contributed thousands of dollars in sales thereafter. When his lease ran out in 1980, however, Gulf chose to shut down the operation. The company agreed that Bigler had done a good job for its products, but it was no longer interested in his service-oriented location. Gasoline marketing methods had changed, and Gulf was setting out in a new direction. As an independent operator, Bigler was left out in the cold to try to start all over again.

Source: Post-Gazette (Harrisburg, Pennsylvania), November 20, 1980, p. 4.

5 THE PHYSICAL ENVIRONMENT

Nature's boundaries

The interdependence of business and its various environments is further demonstrated by its relationship with the *physical environment.* Many of the resources used to create products come from the physical environment—from the land and seas. The use of these resources is a legitimate concern of the economic system, of government, and of the entire society. Some of the gravest problems faced by business have arisen from conflicting interests in the use of natural resources and from the depletion of raw materials.

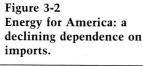

ENERGY SUPPLY

A dwindling reserve

All production requires energy. Manufacturing, transportation, farming, mining, communications, and all other business activities are impossible without a reliable source of power. Over the years, energy in the United States has become more and more dependent on petroleum products like oil and natural gas. Now, business and society are beginning to realize that the amount of petroleum remaining in the ground in the United States is not sufficient to meet our long-term needs. (See Figure 3-2.) Having to rely on oil produced in other countries is a serious problem because the demand for oil is increasing all over the world with the spread of industry. Besides sending oil prices up (except for periodic declines during recent recessionary periods), this gives oil-rich countries the option of cutting off supplies for political reasons. Recognizing this problem, some countries, such as the United States, have begun to reduce their dependence on foreign energy sources through conservation and other means.

Obviously we need to reduce our dependence on petroleum products, especially since foreign supplies are also limited. However, there are problems connected with the other sources of power, too. For example, the United States is well supplied with coal, but burning coal causes undesirable air pollution unless expensive devices or processes are used to avoid it, and nuclear power plants pose problems of safety.

While the energy shortage is a severe challenge, it also can be seen as creating an unprecedented opportunity for business to supply an enormous market for alternative energy sources. First, these alternatives have to be found, so capital is now being risked for developing solar power, wind, and other possible energy sources.

**Figure 3-2
Energy for America: a declining dependence on imports.**

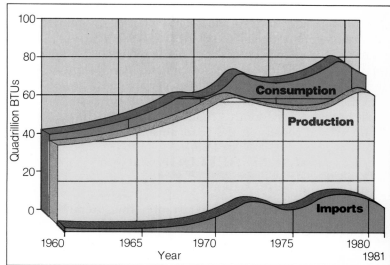

Source: Table 972, "Energy Supply and Disposition, By Type of Fuel: 1960 to 1981," *Statistical Abstract of the United States, 1982-83,* 103d ed., U.S. Department of Commerce, Bureau of the Census.

NATURAL RESOURCES

A need for conservation

In the United States, many other natural resources that once seemed inexhaustibly abundant are in danger of depletion. We are facing shortages of iron, copper, and other minerals, as well as of petroleum, an essential raw material and source of energy. Reforestation programs have not kept up with the demand for timber. Water, which is essential for irrigation, manufacturing, and domestic use, is in short supply in many areas. And there is not enough land to meet the demand for residential and commercial development.

The challenge business must confront is to find ways of making production more efficient and less wasteful of scarce and increasingly expensive raw materials. Recycling of paper products and reprocessing of water for industry are examples of more efficient use of resources. Another challenge is to find alternative raw materials that can be regenerated naturally, such as the sun's action on plant material.

ENVIRONMENTAL POLLUTION

A costly trade-off for growth

Any efforts to solve the shortages of energy and raw materials have to be evaluated in terms of their potential effect on the environment. Often, there is a high price to be paid in terms of polluting the air, soil, or water, or permanently damaging the land. On the other hand, efforts to safeguard the environment can involve an even greater expenditure of energy, as exemplified by automobile air pollution controls, which cut down on gasoline mileage.

Not all environmental pollution is caused by businesses. Municipal governments with inadequate sewage treatment and trash disposal systems are major offenders, as are careless individuals. Business, however, has been in the public eye, and much of the social pressure to control pollution has been directed against it. The pressure has had an effect. Efforts are under way to control the chemical, biological, and thermal quality of water returned to streams. Gases emitted into the air and solid wastes dumped onto the land are being reduced in quantity or changed to nontoxic forms. Noise reduction programs are common. Matters of taste and beauty in construction and land use are receiving more attention than ever. Before pollution can be controlled, however, billions of dollars more must be spent. Raising this money will be a challenge for business, government, and society in the years ahead.

ECOLOGICAL OUTLOOK

Toward a better balance

Ecology is the science that studies the interaction between living organisms and their environment. Ecologists generally view the natural world as a complex, interrelated system in which the actions and behavior of every part affect every other part. A concern for ecology on the part of business is being stimulated by all of its environments—the economic system, the government, social and cultural forces, and the physical world. It has become increasingly important to consider all of the possible results of business decisions, good and bad. Maturity, it is said, is reached when a person understands and accepts the consequences of his or her actions. The same appears true of business.

Key Concepts

1. Business functions in a complex environment, influenced by interdependent economic, legal-political, social-cultural, and physical forces.
2. Businesses continually interact with an economic environment made up of the markets in which they buy and sell goods and services, the external supply of money, and an overall economy subject to growth and recession.
3. The legal-political environment (a) allows business to operate by protecting property and enforcing contracts while, at the same time, (b) it limits its freedom by outlawing dangerous and undesirable practices.

4. Basic social values, such as materialism, encourage the growth of business. Society's need to protect the rights and safety of individuals and groups is now forcing businesses to become more aware of the social consequences of their actions.
5. The physical environment presents a challenge to business and society because energy and raw material sources are being depleted. Air, water, and other kinds of pollution caused by industrialization are giving rise to further problems.

Review Questions

1. Define, identify, or explain each of the following key terms or phrases found on the pages indicated.

   business environment   (p. 40)
   consumerism   (p. 48)
   copyright   (p. 44)
   culture   (p. 45)
   ecology   (p. 50)
   economic environment   (p. 41)
   industry   (p. 41)
   intangible property   (p. 44)
   legal-political environment   (p. 43)
   materialism   (p. 45)
   patent   (p. 44)
   physical environment   (p. 49)
   social-cultural environment   (p. 45)
   subsidy   (p. 44)
   system   (p. 40)
   tariff   (p. 45)
   trademark   (p. 44)
   unit pricing   (p. 48)

2. Name the four business environments. What is the relationship among the four? Are any of the environments subordinate to any of the others?
3. What is a system? Give an example to show that small systems are themselves organized into larger systems for more generalized purposes.
4. Name two main ways that market dynamics affect a business manager's decisions?
5. How are interest rates used to shape the economy?
6. What are the five main purposes of government regulation?
7. How does the government protect intangible property? Why is such protection important?
8. How does materialism affect the growth of business?
9. What is the relationship between the energy shortage and efforts to reduce pollution?
10. What is meant by "corporate citizenship"? Give examples of corporate citizenship.

Case Critique 3-1
Pity This Poor Giant

It may be hard to feel sorry for a company that does $5 billion a year in sales. But, today, even the behemoths can have problems. The Georgia-Pacific Corporation (G-P) is the giant of building materials and plywood, and no small factor in paper bags and chemicals. As an investment, however, you might do better by putting your money in the bank. Here are some of the problems that have plagued the big company in the last dozen years. First, the federal government thought G-P was about to operate a monopoly, and forced the company to sell many of its wood operations to create an independent competitor, Louisiana Pacific. At the same time, the government also forbade G-P from buying timber tracts in the South.

Then there is the nature of the paper business. It creates some of the most noxious effluents. To comply with federal regulations, G-P had to spend hundreds of millions of dollars to lessen air and water pollution at its plants. The environmentalists also get into the act. They don't like timber cutting in the first place, and so G-P regularly has to fight off pressure from people who think that forests ought to remain in public hands.

The building products business is also very cyclical. When the general economy is booming, people build homes and buy plywood and other building products. When the economy slumps, G-P finds itself sitting on huge inventories of materials. Finally, the paper business takes a lot of capital. G-P borrows a great deal of money. What with exceedingly high interest rates, a good part of the company's potential profits are used to pay interest on its loans.

1. What parts of the economic environment affect Georgia-Pacific adversely?
2. What features of the legal-political environment have affected the company's operations?
3. What features of the social-cultural environment have affected the company adversely?

Source: Kathleen K. Wiegner, "Georgia-Pacific in Middle Age," *Forbes*, August 17, 1981, p. 42.

Case Critique 3-2
Why Is It Happening to Me?

All Patricia Price wanted to do was to operate her own dress shop. It would be attuned to the tastes of the people with modest incomes who lived nearby. Price rented a nice, small store just off Main Street. She stocked her racks with attractive, but inexpensive, merchandise. She opened her doors and waited for the business to roll in.

Business did roll in. Price had a good sense of what the women in the neighborhood liked. Sales increased every month, and at the end of her first year, Price was making a nice profit. Then, a number of unexpected things happened. A chain merchandiser of discounted name-brand fashions opened on Main Street. Next, the city road department decided that the street that the shop was on needed repair. It ripped up the asphalt right in the middle of the Easter season. Even Price's regular customers had to go out of their way to reach her shop. Then there was the matter of taxes. The city, in order to raise revenues, enacted legislation that assessed Price with a 2 percent annual tax on her equipment and the inventories she kept in stock. At this point, Price was ready to pull her hair out. "Why," she said, "is all this happening to me?"

1. What environmental factors have caused Price to become so frustrated?
2. If you were Price, would you continue in business or not? Why?
3. What sort of corrective action might Price take to improve her environment?

Unit 2

The Form and Structure of American Business

Unit 2 shows how a business gets started in the United States. It outlines the various legal forms of enterprise, explains the functions of managers, and describes alternate ways of structuring a business's internal organization. All of these determine the success or failure of a business.

Businesses can take many different forms, each with its built-in advantages and disadvantages. The way a business is managed is another factor that governs its prosperity. Those companies that plan realistically and follow through with sound organization, direction, and control have the best chance of succeeding. The fate of a company is also determined by the people involved and the logic and quality of their relationships. It is critical, therefore, that the internal structure of the company be appropriate to its goals, plans, and resources, especially its human resources.

Chapter 4

The Legal Forms of Business Ownership

1 BUSINESS OWNERSHIP IMPLIES PRIVATE OWNERSHIP

2 THERE ARE THREE COMMON FORMS OF OWNERSHIP

They depend on the number of owners and the extent to which the owners share in the risks, liabilities, and profits of the business.

3 PROPRIETORSHIP

(Ownership by one individual)

4 PARTNERSHIP

(Ownership by two or more individuals)

5 CORPORATION

(Ownership by the shareholders)

Key Concepts

1. Nearly all business facilities and resources in the United States are privately owned. The ownership may take a number of legal forms.

2. The most common forms of ownership are sole proprietorships, general partnerships, and corporations. Most businesses (about 76 percent) are proprietorships, but most revenues (about 88 percent) are generated by corporations. Partnerships are the least common form of business organization, making up about 8 percent of the total of all business organizations in the United States.

3. In a proprietorship, assets and profits are owned by one individual who has unlimited liability for the legal and financial obligations of the business.

4. In a general partnership, assets and profits are owned by two or more persons who each have unlimited liability for business debts.

5. Stockholders own the assets and share the profits of a corporation. Their risk and liability are limited to the amount of their investment. Corporate enterprises enjoy many important advantages, including the ability to raise large amounts of capital, continuous existence, ease of investing and withdrawing an investment, and specialized management.

6. The choice of the best type of ownership for a business is based on the nature of the business, the financial effects on operations, and the attitudes of the owners.

7. In addition to the three common forms of ownership, there are five alternative forms which can provide special solutions to special business problems and needs. These alternate forms include the limited partnership, the joint venture, the joint stock company, the cooperative, and the franchise. Franchising in particular has been a very popular and rapidly growing form of business organization in recent years.

Review Questions

1. Define, identify, or explain each of the following key terms and phrases, found on the pages indicated.

   assets (p. 58)
   cooperative (p. 66)
   corporation (p. 61)
   franchise (p. 66)
   franchisee (p. 68)
   franchisor (p. 68)
   general partnership (p. 60)
   joint stock company (p. 66)
   joint venture (p. 66)
   limited liability (p. 62)
   limited partnership (p. 66)
   sole proprietorship (p. 58)
   Subchapter S corporation (p. 63)
   unlimited liability (p. 58)

2. Why is such a large part of business revenue in the United States earned by corporations when the great majority of businesses are proprietorships?

3. What is the difference between unlimited and limited liability? Which of the three main forms of ownership have limited liability and which have unlimited liability?

4. Assuming a proprietorship, a general partnership and a corporation were all the same size, which do you think would pay more taxes on earnings? Which would probably have the highest credit standing? Explain the reasons for your answer.

5. Like proprietorships, partnerships are easy to start, have a good credit standing, and result in tax savings. In what ways are partnerships superior to proprietorships?

6. What are the main points of the definition of a corporation?
7. What are the five important advantages of the corporation form of ownership?
8. How is a limited partnership different from a general partnership? How is a joint venture different from other partnerships?

9. Why do small producers sometimes form cooperatives? How are profits distributed in a cooperative? In what industries might one find cooperatives in operation?
10. What are some of the advantages and disadvantages of franchising to the franchisor and the franchisee?

Case Critique 4-1
Pet Potatoes?

Potatoes are very big in Idaho. The record size is 7 pounds, 2 ounces. A few years ago, someone got the idea that shipped potatoes might also be big elsewhere in the United States. The reasoning went like this: If you can package oranges from Florida as gifts, what could be more appropriate than a gift box of potatoes? The race in Idaho for this special market was on. Bill Ricktor and three others put together a partnership to market Awsome Potatoes. These are 8-inch long, hand-picked, 18-ounce, No. 1 Idaho potatoes. Awsome packs four of them in a handmade mahogany box and ships them anywhere in the United States for $9.95 plus postage. Says Ricktor, "They're better than Pet Rocks." Roger Jones, an independent proprietor, will ship a baker's dozen of 13 choice potatoes from his farm for only $7, including shipping costs. Dozens of other potato growers in the state will ship a 25-pound case for $8 plus ship-

ping charges. Some of these farmers are small, family-owned corporations. Others operate together in local cooperatives. The total crop of potatoes shipped from Idaho, mostly in carload or truckloads, comes to $1 billion each year. Most of the big shippers are corporations or large co-ops.

1. What advantage do Mr. Ricktor and his friends have over Mr. Rogers?
2. What disadvantages do Mr. Ricktor and his friends have over Mr. Rogers?
3. Why would some farmers form a small, family-owned corporation instead of a single proprietorship? What is such a corporation called?
4. Why would some farmers form a cooperative to market their potatoes rather than do it themselves?

Source: William E. Schmidt, "Idaho Potatoes Packed as Gifts," *The New York Times,* May 12, 1982, p. 25.

Case Critique 4-2
$150 Million Down the Drain

One of the great corporate collapses of the last decade was the failure of AM International. Once known as Addressograph-Multigraph Corporation, this manufacturer of old-fashioned duplicators and addressing machines had been marginally

profitable for over 50 years. With the advent of copying machines, its technology became rapidly obsolete. The company changed its name to AM International and went all out to develop the new technology of word processing.

For a while, in the late 1970s and early 1980s, it looked as if the company would fly very high again. Hundreds of thousands of investors purchased over 10 million shares of its stock. They paid prices ranging from $9 to $21 a share. Then, suddenly, everything went wrong for AM. In 1981, it lost $245 million on sales of $857 million. This means that for every dollar the company took in, it lost 29 cents! A close look at the way the company was being run showed that its managers were careless and inefficient. By early 1982, the company was $250 million in debt to banks and suppliers. Its net worth to the stockholders dropped to a paltry $14 million, or about $1.40 per share.

The company kept losing money so fast that its creditors pressed the company into bankruptcy. The stockholders, who had invested over $150 million in the company, were left holding a company whose principal assets were owed to its creditors. AM's stockholders were unhappy, of course. But, unlike the company's creditors who were still clamoring to be paid, the stockholders' losses were limited to exactly what they had invested in the corporation. There was no legal way the creditors could collect any money from the shareholders. If there was not enough money left after the sale of the company's plants and equipment to pay all the creditors, that was no concern of the stockholders.

1. Under corporate law, what privilege did AM's stockholders enjoy when the company failed? What is the significance of this privilege in the corporate form of business organization?
2. What was the advantage to AM International, in the first place, of forming a corporation rather than a single proprietorship?
3. How much control did AM's owners (stockholders) have over the way the company was managed?
4. In spite of its ultimate collapse, AM, under one name or another, had stayed in business for over 50 years. What corporate feature does this longevity stem from?

Source: "AM International: When Technology Was Not Enough," *Business Week*, January 25, 1982, p. 62.

Chapter 5

Managerial Functions in a Business

1 MANAGEMENT

Management is the process of planning, organizing, directing, and controlling the use of a firm's resources so as to attain its objectives effectively and economically.

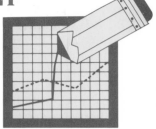

2 MANAGEMENT IS BOTH AN ART AND A SCIENCE

3 APPROACHES TO MANAGEMENT

Management may be approached from a variety of standpoints:

Classical (Rational)

Behavioral (Human Relations)

Quantitative

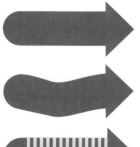

4 THE FOUR KEY FUNCTIONS OF MANAGEMENT

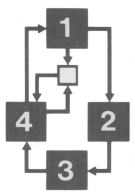

1 Planning
  ☐ Objectives
  ☐ Strategic plans
  ☐ Operating plans

2 Organizing resources, activities, and people

3 Directing and coordinating

4 Evaluating and controlling

5 CHARACTERISTICS OF GOOD MANAGERS

An effective manager must develop and apply these qualities and skills:

Innovation	✔
Decision making	✔
Leadership	✔
Communication	✔
Motivation	✔

Learning Objectives

The purpose of this chapter is to define the nature and purpose of management and explain three widely accepted approaches to management, describe the four key functions that managers perform, and outline some of the qualities and skills needed by professional managers.

After studying Chapter 5, you should be able to:

1. Define management and managers in general terms.
2. Differentiate between management as an art and as a science.
3. Distinguish between the classical, behavioral, and quantitative approaches to management.
4. Identify and be able to apply the four functions of the management process: planning, organizing, directing, and controlling.
5. Identify and assess the value of certain characteristics of professional managers.

If your class is using SSweetco: Business Model and Activity File for Business in Action, see Chapter 5 in that book after you complete this chapter. There you will find exercises and activities to help you apply your learning to typical business situations.

Nothing gets done without management. In our daily lives, we have to see that the bills get paid on time, that food is bought, that the house or apartment is taken care of, that taxes and insurance are paid, that gas is put in the car, and that hundreds of other details are attended to. Business management deals with the same general kinds of activities but differs in two principal ways: (*a*) it handles resources and activities on a larger scale than most of us are accustomed to in our personal lives and (*b*) it accomplishes work through other people.

1 MANAGEMENT DEFINED

Attaining results with the help of others

The process of planning, organizing, directing, and controlling the use of a firm's resources to effectively and economically attain its objectives is called *management.* A business can be viewed as a system: a group of related parts organized to work together for some purpose. Management is the function that integrates the parts of this system and makes sure that they work together toward a desired purpose. *Administration* is another term with nearly the same meaning, though it is more often used to refer to the management of institutions, such as schools or hospitals. It may, however, also be applied to business firms, particularly to the functions of higher-level management.

MANAGERS

Perform common duties although exact roles differ

Manager   A person who performs the unique work of management is called a manager. That is, a *manager* plans, organizes, directs, and controls a company's business.

An important characteristic of managers is that they do their jobs by working with and through *other people.* If the manager of a furniture plant wishes to manufacture a thousand coffee tables, he or she does not go to the plant and start producing them. The manager directs other employees to do the work. When directly creating products, a manager is not performing the management function.

In many small businesses, managers work only part-time at management. They then devote the rest of their time to selling, production, or some other business function. A carpenter who heads a crew of workers for a construction company has a similar role. Half of the carpenter's time may be spent actually using the tools of the trade, while the remainder of the time may be spent telling others what to do and in checking the quality of their work. The latter exemplify the true management functions.

Types and Levels of Management   Small businesses usually have one or two managers who are responsible for the diverse management duties needed to keep the business running. Typically, the owners of a small company are the direct managers. The range of a manager's function extends from deciding to buy new stationery for $30 to deciding to buy a new store for $500,000. Large companies, on the other hand, have staffs of professional managers who specialize in particular facets of the overall operation. One person may be responsible for production, another for sales, another for advertising, and so forth. All of these functions must then be integrated and evaluated by top management. Typically, managers in larger companies are ranked according to their level within the company, as shown in Figure 5-1. Managers at the highest levels are usually called executives. They may also carry titles like president, chairperson, vice president, or general manager. Managers at the lowest levels are usually called supervisors. In between the highest and the lowest levels, managers are usually called managers, although their titles may also bear a prefix (like *sales, production,* or *accounting*) to show what type of managers they are. All managers, however, regardless of the size of the company or their level within it, try to achieve the same thing: to work effectively with people so that the business achieves its objectives.

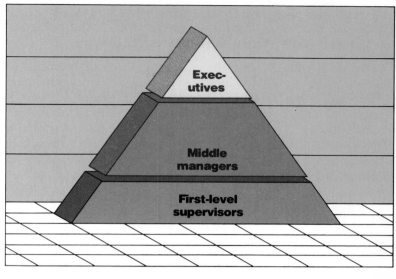

Figure 5-1
Levels of management.

2 MANAGEMENT AS ART AND SCIENCE

A combination of instinct and logic

The goal of management is to integrate the diverse elements of a business—people, machinery, money, buildings, and raw materials—and direct them toward a common purpose. To do this well, a manager must combine the intuitive abilities of art with the rational methods of science.

Nearly everything a manager does is accomplished through other people. Although psychology and sociology are making progress in describing human behavior scientifically, most facets of personal interactions remain unclear. Basically, successful personal interactions in a business setting are dependent on the sensitivity of the manager. Intuition and sensitivity are also useful in the many business decisions that must be made with incomplete data. If an executive must decide whether to introduce a new product, he or she will have a variety of data and the opinions of others. Nevertheless, much, even most, of the relevant data will not be available. In order to make such decisions, experienced executives must have a feel for the market and for the behavior of consumers.

Rational and quantitative approaches are becoming ever more common and successful in business. These scientific aspects of management stress the use of data gathered and measured according to certain orderly principles. These methods are widely used not only in production and distribution, but also in the people-oriented management functions, such as supervision and sales. In spite of the growing importance of these techniques, however, management will probably continue to function as both an art and a science.

3 APPROACHES TO MANAGEMENT

Three prevailing schools of thought

It has been clear from the emergence of modern business that effective management will produce higher profits. Accordingly, managers have been highly motivated to understand the nature of their job and to improve their performance. From the last half of the nineteenth century to the present, three theories of management have achieved popularity. These are the classical, the behavioral, and the quantitative approaches to management. Today, management combines features of all of these in a balanced approach.

CLASSICAL APPROACH

Features rational analysis

The central belief of the *classical school of management* is that by applying rational analysis to the production and management functions of a business, worker and equipment productivity can be increased, resulting in higher profits. This idea was first introduced around the turn of the century by Frederick W. Taylor, in the United States, and Henri Fayol, in France, among others. They put forth the view that a logical study of procedures was required in order to improve the efficiency of the increasingly complex businesses that had begun to spring up in their time. Fayol divided the manager's job into specific functions in the belief that this systematic breakdown of responsibilities would promote effectiveness. Taylor was particularly interested in what is now called industrial engineering. His time-and-motion studies, as well as other job studies in the 1880s and 1890s, prepared the way for the mass production and assembly line system of today.

BEHAVIORAL APPROACH

Emphasizes human relations

The classical, rational approach to management tended to ignore the human element. Its originators, especially Taylor, believed that higher productivity would permit higher wages and salaries. They made little allowance, however, for other human needs. In the 1930s, there arose a new approach to management stressing the human factors in business. This approach became known as the *behavioral,* or *human relations, school.* Its adherents believed that an organization's goals could be met only by first understanding and then consciously dealing with human needs and interactions. Great emphasis was placed on human motivations and on group dynamics. In more extreme expressions of this view, managers were expected to act as psychological counselors for their workers.

QUANTITATIVE APPROACH

Stresses numbers and systems

In the 1960s, another emphasis in the study of management began to emerge. A *quantitative approach* stressing the use of numbers and derived largely from systems theory began to be applied to business management and its associated activities. *Systems theory* is a group of verbal and mathematical principles that describes how the related parts of a system may be organized. Such an arrangement permits management to predict how changes in one part will affect the other parts. This approach allows the use of statistical studies of groups of workers, consumers, or managers for making certain decisions. Mathematical models are often constructed to predict the results of alternative management actions. A new field of study, *operations research,* analyzes the methods by which business activities are carried out and proposes changes for increased efficiency. The difference between this kind of analysis and the classical approach is that the quantitative method emphasizes (*a*) the overall system in which work is being done and (*b*) the statistical study of groups of operations rather than a close analysis of a particular worker or job.

TODAY'S APPROACH

Toward optimization and balance

The main effort among managers today is to take the best of these approaches and use each where it will do the most good. Some call this the **contingency,** or **situational, approach.** The functional analysis of the classical school is still useful in improving efficiency and in organizing management tasks. The human relations school is influential in many personnel decisions and contributes greatly to the understanding of leadership, motivation, and other human characteristics. The quantitative tools of systems theory and operations research are only now beginning to be used confidently by large numbers of managers to improve decision making. These various approaches to management, combined with intuitive ability and with common sense and experience, help to make modern business management increasingly effective, humane, and flexible.

4 MANAGEMENT FUNCTIONS

Managers have four basic responsibilities

Managers typically perform four key functions for their businesses: (*a*) planning, (*b*) organizing and staffing, (*c*) directing and coordinating, and (*d*) evaluating and controlling. Each of these functions is continuous and all are interrelated, as shown in Figure 5-2. The functions can be seen as a process continuously repeated in a cycle. Managers make plans to solve the problems and to take advantage of the opportunities presented to their companies. People

Figure 5-2
Management functions.

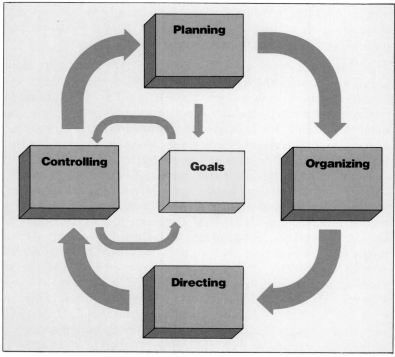
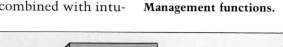

are recruited to carry out the plans. Some kind of organization indicating who works for whom and what each person's responsibilities are is set up. The manager oversees the operation of this organization. He or she directs and coordinates the activities of those who work in it. Evaluations of how well the organization is working toward its goals partially determine plans for future operations.

These managerial functions overlap and affect one another. While one plan or group of plans is being carried out, other plans are being made. The results of one effort influence the results of others. The evaluation of results leads to control, which influences other functions.

PLANNING

Setting goals and establishing procedures

Planning is the backbone of every management effort. A *plan*, to a business manager, is an explicit statement of the business's future objectives combined with a step-by-step description of the actions that will be necessary to reach those objectives. The planning process centers on satisfying the two main requirements of this definition: clear goals and specific actions to meet them.

Goals and Objectives   The terms *goals* and *objectives* can be used interchangeably. They represent the targets, or endpoints, toward which business efforts are directed. At a given time, a company may have hundreds of overlapping objectives. Some are general and long-range, such as maintaining an acceptable profit and rate of company growth. Others are more specific, usually devised to contribute to the general goals. Some specific objectives might be to gain a large share of the market by introducing an improved product, to make the inventory control system more efficient, to reduce shipping costs, to attract more customers to a particular product line, or to improve morale among production workers. All of these are goals in themselves, and in turn, contribute to the general goals of profit making and expansion.

Planning Process   The first important part of the *planning process* is to set forth the important objectives of the company and to make them explicit. The other steps in planning follow naturally from this beginning. An executive of a company that manufactures marine products may notice, for example, in monitoring daily operations, that the costs of warehousing stock and filling customer orders have been increasing faster than other costs in the past two years. On investigation, the executive learns that the extra costs result from the storage space and worker time needed to handle two new electric starters for outboard engines with their complicated subassemblies. The parts for the starters can be ordered separately. The manager's goal is to reduce the costs of selling the product. The manager then considers several alternative solutions: (a) discontinuing the starters, (b) establishing a minimum order size, or (c) installing expensive new conveyor systems to aid order filling. Finally, the manager may decide to make it a company policy to sell the starters only in assembled form. The firm will discontinue sales of the component parts, even though this will cause a slight loss of revenue.

This manager has carefully followed every step needed for good planning. A specific action was taken after identifying an objective, consider-

ACTION BRIEF

"Take-Charge" Strategies Get the Nod. *"Managers should be proactive,"* says B. Dean Liles, vice president for administration of Zale Corp., a large jewelry retailer in Dallas, Texas. *"This requires taking charge and developing strategies and plans before people come to you with problems."* In a national survey, Liles, like other middle managers and upper-level executives, said their jobs required them to be 50 percent or more proactive—concerned with planning—as opposed to being merely reactive—carrying out jobs originated in other departments of their companies.

Source: "More Planning Urged," Management Information Systems Week, July 19, 1981, p. 6.

ing alternative solutions, and evaluating the alternatives. The same kind of process must be applied to all planning and at every level of management. The resulting plans for attaining the overall, long-term goals of a company are called *strategic plans.* The plans and procedures for reaching goals that are only a week, or month, or year away—those plans that involve what must be done from day to day—are *operating plans.*

ORGANIZING

Arranging resources, activities, and people

Plans specify the actions to be taken; the way in which these actions will be carried out is determined by the organizing function of management. *Organizing* is the process of setting up the structure and rules to control the way resources—workers, material, machinery, and money— work together to reach objectives. Organizing determines what authority each employee has, who will do what job, what methods and equipment will be used, and other specific rules which determine how the work will be done. Chapter 6 describes the organizing function of management in greater detail.

DIRECTING

Putting plans and people in motion

Outstanding plans and an excellent organization will accomplish nothing unless people are actually put to work, doing the right job and doing it correctly. *Directing* is the process of guiding and motivating people in the organization to do the work needed to accomplish the company's goals. It includes telling and showing subordinates what jobs to do and how to do them and detecting errors and seeing that they are corrected. Effective directing requires the kind of sensitivity and leadership that will motivate subordinates and fellow workers.

Another aspect of directing an organization is the coordination of effort that all good managers try to achieve. In management, *coordinating* is largely a process of assuring communication between parts of the organization—individuals, departments, and levels of management—to make sure that they are working together on appropriate efforts toward mutual goals. Coordination attempts to avoid duplication of effort or omission of some essential activity. It insures that various parts of a total effort will take place at the right time and in proper sequence.

Directing requires the ability to influence other people so that they will work toward the goals of the company. It requires the ability to motivate others to do their best work. It requires the ability and willingness to communicate and to get others to communicate. For further discussion see the section entitled "Characteristics of Good Managers" later in this chapter.

CONTROLLING

Evaluating and correcting performance

The final function of management is *controlling.* It requires evaluating the performance of the firm and its parts and making changes to improve operations. This function is clearly related to all of the other things management does, but it is most intimately connected with planning. The evaluations that are made as part of controlling the business operation serve to determine whether plans are being carried out and objectives met. This information is, in turn, used to formulate new plans so that there is a constant interaction between the two functions.

Controlling compares actual results of operations—sales, production output, costs, product quality, and employee performance—with performance goals or standards. (See Figure 5-3.) These **standards** describe what will be considered desirable results. They should be established as the first step in control. Ideally, the standard should be set as part of the planning process.

In the controlling process, the results of current operations are measured in some way, quantitatively if possible. Statistical reports for product quality control, sales reports showing quantities of goods or services sold, budget variance reports showing costs of operations, and numerous other statistics on clerical activity, inventory, plant maintenance, and personnel provide a great deal of the information necessary for effective control.

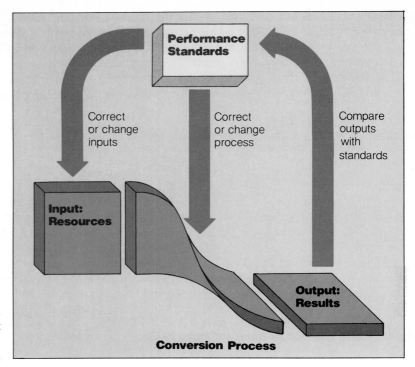

**Figure 5-3
Management controlling process.**

This operating data is then compared with performance standards, and variances are identified. Investigation is necessary at this point. Many factors may cause variances between performance and standards. The standards themselves may be out of line and need adjustment. Faults in the way a company or department is organized may contribute; for example, directing and coordinating efforts may have been inadequate. Factors in the business environment—such as an economic slump, a drop in consumer confidence, or government action—may also account for unexpected results.

After identifying the problems and contributing causes, management must take action to correct them. The control function then gives way to the planning function. Control procedures may show that product quality is slipping so that new machinery or better supervision may be needed. Costs may be too high in certain departments so that more efficient procedures or restriction of operations may be called for. Sales for a certain product may not be as high as expected so that sales commission rates may have to be increased or more advertising and promotion or product improvements may be required. All of these questions, in the typically successful business, will begin yet another turn of the continuing management cycle or system of planning, organizing, directing, and controlling.

5 CHARACTERISTICS OF GOOD MANAGERS

Good managers are hard to find

Clearly, management is a difficult job. All of the functions a manager must perform require dedication, perseverance, intelligence, an ability to deal with concepts as well as details, and the willingness to accept stress and responsibility. Particularly in the modern world, where business operations are becoming increasingly complex, a manager must consciously develop his or her personal qualities, professional skills, and business knowledge to become and remain effective. Business management is developing into a profession. It encompasses a body of related knowledge which must be intelligently and creatively applied to practical problems. Some of the important skills and activities a manager must bring to the job are innovation, decision making, leadership, communication, and motivation.

INNOVATION

Finding better ways to get the job done

Managers must strive to find new and better ways to accomplish the work of their business. Many management decisions are extremely complex. Gains resulting from a course of action may be offset by losses resulting from the same action. Such situations require a high level of **innovation,** or creativity to devise new techniques, products, and approaches to business problems.

DECISION MAKING

Managers must take risks to solve problems

The capacity for **decision making,** often with data that is incomplete or of doubtful accuracy, is a prime requirement for a manager. Particularly in the planning function, managers must make decisions that may commit their company to the expenditure of large amounts of money and time and that could result in failure or loss of prestige for themselves and their company. This kind of decision making requires the willingness to take risks. Even more, it requires the high level of analytic and integrative ability that will allow such decisions to be made with reasonable confidence.

LEADERSHIP

Binding the organization together

Business managers can tell their subordinates what work to do and how to do it because they are given that authority by their companies. A subordinate, in theory, agrees to take direction from his or her superiors as one of the conditions of employment. In addition to authority, a manager must also use leadership to produce a truly effective organization. **Leadership** may be defined as the ability to influence the attitudes and behavior of others through skill in personal relations and without the use of force. Many have held that leaders must be born with these skills, but

ACTION BRIEF

A Supervisor's Long-Day Journey. *Ray R. Meyers, area supervisor for a Texaco, Inc., pumping station in Louisiana, is responsible for the proper operation of 97 miles of oil pipelines. Ray (called "Papa" by his associates) directs the work of 11 specialized mechanics who are spread over 215 miles of marshland. Their daily goal is to get 35,000 barrels of crude oil pumped from 279 wells along the Louisiana coast to the next collecting station some 42 miles north of them. Not only does the oil make a long journey each day. So does Ray Meyer as he traverses the lines to see that all is going according to plan.*

Source: *James F. Robertson, "The Long Journey." The Texaco Star, Vol. LXVIII, No. 1, 1981, p. 4.*

Issues & Highlights

Lord Mountbatten, who was one of Britain's greatest leaders, described himself as "the most conceited man I know." After all, he said, "if you want to be a leader of men, you can't go around like a shrinking violet." On the other hand, overconfidence did in Joseph R. Hyde III, president of a major grocery warehouse chain (Malone & Hyde) in the southeastern United States. "Overconfidence became a self-inflicted wound," says Hyde. The company tried to grow too fast and almost fell on its face. "We were too eager for sales," says Hyde, "and we should have looked before we leaped."

Another view about leadership is voiced by David C. Mollen, senior staff member of IBM's Research Institute in New York. "Politics is needed," he says, "It is the recognition that, to get things done, you have to deal with and motivate people as they are, rather than as you think they should be." Arjay Miller, once one of Ford Motor Co.'s most prestigious managers, takes a middle ground: "The two essentials of successful leadership are (1) the capacity to perceive what should be done and (2) the ability to influence other people to achieve results."

Sources: Dorrine A. Turecamo, "Developing Leadership Style," Phi Kappa Phi Journal, Spring 1982, p. 38. Thomas Jaffe, "A Self-Inflicted Wound," Forbes, February 1, 1982, p. 81. Josh Martin, "Choosing a Management Style," Computer Decisions, December 1981, p. 81.

Which sort of leadership would you prefer to serve under? Which sort of leadership most closely resembles your own style? Which do you think is best under most circumstances? Why?

modern practice views leadership as resulting from a combination of talent, training, and experience.

COMMUNICATION

Promoting exchange of information

Nearly all of a manager's time is spent reading, writing or dictating, and talking and listening, on the telephone or in person. All of this is behavior that involves **communication**—the exchange of information, ideas, and feelings between people. Communication is the fundamental activity that allows organizations to work. Plans, work orders, and even products are worthless if the manager is unable to communicate with coworkers in the company, and if the company is unable to communicate with the outside world.

Communication is so important that companies of any substantial size usually establish formal networks for written messages to insure that all employees get the information they need. Group meetings and training sessions are other formal means of communication used by businesses. Informal communications also take place between workers and can be very valuable when they concern work-related matters. An important personal attribute of managers is the willingness to encourage accurate and complete two-way communications. Managers, like anyone else, do not enjoy hearing bad news, but without all the facts, good and bad, effective management is impossible.

MOTIVATION

Adding incentive and meaning to work

An ability to motivate others to give their best efforts toward company goals is an important aspect of leadership. Self-motivation is also an essential requirement for a successful manager. Traditionally, **motivation** centered almost exclusively on money (wages, raises, etc.) as a motivating factor. As time went by, however, it was realized that external rewards (or even punishments) were not as effective in improving performance as were the satisfaction of other less obvious psychological needs.

Abraham H. Maslow proposed a principle to explain this: the hierarchy of needs. As human needs lower in the hierarchy are satisfied, they lose their motivating force and people will then be motivated only by opportunities to meet higher level needs. Maslow's hierarchy includes (*a*) physiological needs, such as hunger and thirst, (*b*) safety needs, such as personal security and freedom from danger, (*c*) needs for social belonging and love, (*d*) needs for esteem and recognition, and (*e*) the need to make oneself the best and most valuable person possible, the need for knowledge, and the need for beauty and aesthetic satisfaction. (See Figure 17-2 in Chapter 17.) Maslow suggested that the lowest-level unfulfilled need *at a given time* would be the main motivating need. Someone who had only managed to satisfy physiological needs would be immediately motivated to achieve personal safety. Someone who had food and drink, safety, love, and esteem would mainly be motivated by opportunities for self-fulfillment.

This scheme has become popular for managers because it has proved itself useful in motivating employees. It is limited in its applications, of course, and it is challenged in many quarters. Work, however, is so impor-

ACTION BRIEF

Middle-Manager Coordinators. David Querbach started out after college as a night desk clerk at the Woodlands Inn and Country Club in California. Today he is the director of its massive conference center. In between, he headed up Woodland's promotions, audiovisuals, and conference coordinating departments. "Involvement in all the Center's operations is the secret of my success," he says. Donna Davidson, events coordinator of the Monterey Conference Center, also in California, has a managerial responsibility similar to Querbach's. Davidson, however, emphasizes the need for communications with other departments. "Good communications is the foundation of successful interaction with all involved," she says. Querbach was named the No. 2 World's Best Convention Services Manager in 1981; Davidson was No. 1.

Source: "World's Best Convention Services Manager," Successful Meetings, *December 1981, p. 42.*

tant to Americans that they look to their jobs as the most likely source of satisfaction for many of their needs. That managers are coming to understand this is reflected in the modern emphasis on providing meaningful employment with greater opportunities for self-expression and creativity, along with reasonable security and monetary rewards.

Key Concepts

1. Management is the process of planning, organizing, directing, and controlling the use of a business's resources so as to effectively and economically attain the business' objectives.
2. Effective management requires a combination of the intuition and sensitivity characteristic of art and the rationality typical of science.
3. Modern managers usually try to use the best features of the classical, behavioral, and quantitative approaches to management.
4. The major management functions are (a) planning specific actions to meet future objectives,

(b) organizing people and other resources to accomplish the actions, (c) directing members of the organization in performing their jobs, and (d) evaluating results and exercising control by making needed improvements.
5. Management is evolving into a profession that creatively employs a body of knowledge and techniques to solve practical problems. In order to perform effectively, a manager must develop skills in innovation, decision making, leadership, communication, and motivation.

Review Questions

1. Define, identify, or explain each of the following key terms and phrases found on the pages indicated.

   administration   (p. 76)
   behavioral (human relations) school   (p. 78)
   classical school of management   (p. 78)
   communication   (p. 85)
   contingency (situational) approach   (p. 79)
   controlling   (p. 81)
   coordinating   (p. 81)
   decision making   (p. 83)
   directing   (p. 81)
   goals   (p. 80)
   innovation   (p. 83)
   leadership   (p. 83)
   management   (p. 76)
   manager   (p. 76)
   motivation   (p. 85)
   objectives   (p. 80)
   operating plans   (p. 81)
   operations research   (p. 79)
   organizing   (p. 81)
   plan   (p. 80)
   planning   (p. 80)

   planning process   (p. 80)
   quantitative approach   (p. 78)
   standards   (p. 82)
   strategic plans   (p. 81)
   systems theory   (p. 79)

2. What is the main contribution of management to a business?
3. Distinguish between management and managers.
4. Modern managers usually combine features or three main schools of thought in their management approach. What are the three, and what is the main emphasis of each?
5. The four basic functions of the management process are referred to as a cycle. What are the four functions, and why are they a cycle?
6. Why are plans vital to business operations?
7. How are plans, goals, and standards related?
8. What element links controlling to planning?
9. Why is communication so important to the directing function of management?
10. What practical application could Maslow's hierarchy of needs have for managers? Why?

Case Critique 5-1
A Long Wait for *Heaven's Gate*

One of the worst movie flops of all time occurred in 1981. It was *Heaven's Gate,* produced for United Artists' Corporation by Michael Cimino. Estimated originally to cost $12 million, the film cost almost triple that figure. Then it turned out to be box office poison. *Heaven's Gate* was only the most dramatic boo-boo by United Artists. Of ten films produced in 1980, seven cost twice as much as they drew from rentals. Experts in the industry criticized United for not having the "expertise to select, coordinate, and monitor difficult film projects." United, unlike other film companies, did not have a full staff of production-liaison executives closely monitoring costs as a film was being shot. In fact, most films were not planned with a specific cost limit in mind.

United Artists at the time was a company owned by another giant corporation, Transamerica Corporation. (Later Transamerica sold United Artists to Metro-Goldwyn-Mayer.) Insiders in the industry said that Transamerica's management was never aware of how bad the situation was with *Heaven's Gate.* Otherwise, they would have cut off funds early on.

1. What management function was most lacking in this case?
2. In order to have a target so that the cost of films would not be too high, what should United Artists have done for each film?
3. What was a key missing ingredient between the management of United Artists and its then parent company, Transamerica Corporation?

Source: "How UA Became a Grade B Film Company," *Business Week,* June 22, 1981, p. 100.

Case Critique 5-2
King of the Scallops

Bill Lambert is a throwback to an earlier kind of manager. He believes that profits are the result of productivity. His approach is one of hard-headed logic, always trying to get more done in less time. Lambert built his own pulpwood company, retired at 42, and then created another completely unrelated business. Today, he is the owner and operator of the largest scallop shucking (shell removal) company in the world, a company that annually shucks and sells about a million gallons of "calico" scallops.

After Lambert retired from his pulpwood business, he hung around the fishing docks. He was disturbed to see the crude way in which the scallop meat was shucked from the shells. The shucking rate was about 25 gallons an hour. Lambert went back to his shop and designed and patented a shucking machine that would handle 100 gallons an hour. Then he studied the slow way in which scallops were hand-shoveled off the deck of fishing boats into bushel baskets. He borrowed a cranelike tool from the pulpwood industry, fitted it with a scoop, and soon his employees could unload in one hour what it took ten people to do in

eight. "I took that cherry-picker out of the woods," Lambert says, "and adapted it to scallops."

When a scallop fishing ground dries up, Lambert doesn't stand around waiting for the bed to renew itself. He moves his crews to where the new fishing grounds are. The crews bring along with them mobile processing plants built into tractor-trailer beds. They are ready to roll anywhere scallops are being landed.

Scallop fishing wasn't much of an industry until Lambert got into it. Now it's a $40 million a year business, and most everybody does it his way. He's known as The "King of the Scallops."

1. What managerial approach (or school) would you say that Lambert represents? Why?
2. What characteristic of a good manager does Lambert's borrowing of the cherry-picker from the pulpwood industry to use in handling scallops represent?
3. What qualities make Lambert a good manager?

Source: Neil Caudle, "Of Lions, Pulpwood, and the Scallop King," *Coastwatch,* April 1982, p. 8.

Chapter 6

Internal
Structure
of Business
Organizations

1 INTERNAL ORGANIZATION

It prescribes the tasks and activities to be carried out, establishes the relationship between them, and assigns each individual certain roles in order to meet planned objectives.

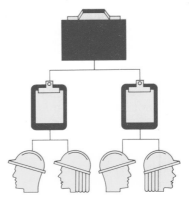

2 TYPES OF ORGANIZATION

Organization may be formal or informal.

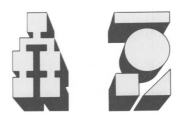

3 DIVISION OF LABOR

The organizing process involves the division of tasks and activities among individuals and departments.

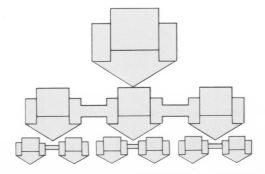

4 DELEGATION OF AUTHORITY

Distribution of authority along with responsibility assures that tasks and activities are carried out.

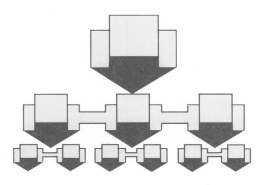

5 PRINCIPLES OF ORGANIZATION

An organization should be set up in accordance with well-established principles.

Service of planned objectives	✔
Form to fit size and function	✔
Clearly defined duties	✔
Limited number of subordinates	✔

6 TYPICAL ORGANIZATION STRUCTURES

Three forms predominate.

Line organization	Line-and-staff organization	Functional organization

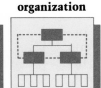

Learning Objectives

The purpose of this chapter is to define the internal organizational structure of business and the organizing process, delineate the principles of good organization, and identify the predominant organizational structures of business enterprise.

After studying Chapter 6, you should be able to:

1. Differentiate between organizing and organization.
2. Distinguish between formal and informal organizations.
3. Explain the principle of division of labor and how tasks and activities are typically divided up into departments within a business organization.
4. Define authority and responsibility, and explain the importance of delegating each.
5. Understand and apply the four principles of good organization.
6. Recognize the three basic organization structures.

If your class is using SSweetco: Business Model and Activity File for Business in Action, see Chapter 6 in that book after you complete this chapter. There you will find exercises and activities to help you apply your learning to typical business situations.

Whenever individuals come together for a common purpose, their separate activities must be coordinated to achieve maximum effectiveness. A professional football team, for instance, is divided up into three groups—offense, defense, and special teams. The responsibility for the actions of each group rests with an assistant coach or group captain. The combined actions of all three groups are coordinated under the direction of the head coach. The same principle operates in business. The work performed in a restaurant, for example, is divided among three functions—food purchasing, food preparation, and food service. Each group of employees that performs these functions has its own supervisor or manager. The efforts of all three groups are coordinated under the direction of a general manager or owner.

1   ORGANIZATION DEFINED

Organizing is the process; organization is the structure

The term "organization" has come to acquire a number of meanings. An organization of people who meet and have some sort of formal relationship, such as a civic club, a political party, or an athletic team, may be called an organization. A business enterprise, with all its resources, personnel, equipment, and methods of production and distribution, is typically called an organization. The term "organization," however, has its most proper meaning in a managerial context when it refers to the outcome of the organizing function described in Chapter 5.

In the *organizing process,* management sets up the structure and rules that control the way a company's resources will interact to reach objectives. The resulting internal structure is the *organization:* this structure prescribes the tasks and activities to be carried out, the relationship between these activities, and the role each individual in the company will play in meeting planned objectives. Thus management is responsible for the organizing function or process and the organization itself. The organization forms the framework within which all other activities take place. A poor organization causes confusion, waste, and dissatisfaction. A good organization allows employees to do their best work in meeting company goals.

2   FORMAL AND INFORMAL ORGANIZATION

One is planned; the other occurs mainly as a matter of course

Organizational relationships within a business may be formal or informal. *Formal organizations* are consciously planned. They are arranged according to rational principles which are usually set down in writing. *Informal organizations* exist without specific planning. Small businesses, especially proprietorships, usually have a minimum of formal organization. Decisions about what work will be done and by whom are generally made by the owner. Large companies, however, almost always have complex and detailed formal organization plans. These describe exactly the jobs to be done. They define each employee's responsibilities and the rights and powers employees have in carrying out their work. The purpose of these formal organizations is to control the routine activities and decisions that keep the company running.

Awareness of Informal Organization   Even in large companies with comprehensive formal organization, informal relationships exist and remain important. This informal organization develops from the social likes and dislikes of employees. Much of the communication in a business takes place within this informal organization, as workers tell each other things they have heard and done. Many employees have special know-how skills in persuasion; such employees can affect the way work is done even though they are not given the formal authority. These spheres of influence overlap the formal structure and can either reinforce it or work against it. Personal friendships and conflicts are another force in the informal organization. People will usually try to work with other people they like and will try to avoid those they dislike. These patterns can have a significant influence on the way projects are actually executed, regardless of the specifications of the formal organization.

Emphasis on Formal Organization   Although managers must be aware of the existence and influence of informal relationships in their firm, their main concern is supervising the process of formal organization. The process involves defining and allocating the work to be done and establishing the responsibilities and authority associated with each job.

3 ALLOCATION OF WORK

Dividing up tasks and responsibilities

One of the manager's first tasks, when organizing, is to divide up all the activities involved in operating the business into specific jobs and departments. This is called the *division of labor.* It is based upon the premise of all formal organizations that every employee should have a clearly defined job with specific activities and duties to perform. Ideally, a particular routine of activities should always be done by the same person or job classification. All of the specific jobs are then grouped, for management purposes, into sections, departments, or divisions, or some other designation. The process of creating such groupings is called *departmentalization.*

Departmentalization   The distribution of jobs and activities into departments may be based on many factors.

■ *By function.* Most companies define jobs and departments by function: shipping, purchasing, accounting, selling, advertising, maintaining machinery, and so forth. Managers generally believe that it is best for a single job to lie wholly within one functional area whenever possible. Jobs within a larger department or division may be grouped by the requirement for certain skills or by the use of similar working methods. In a department responsible for maintaining the machinery in a large plant, there might be sections or individuals specializing in caring for fluid systems or making electrical repairs.

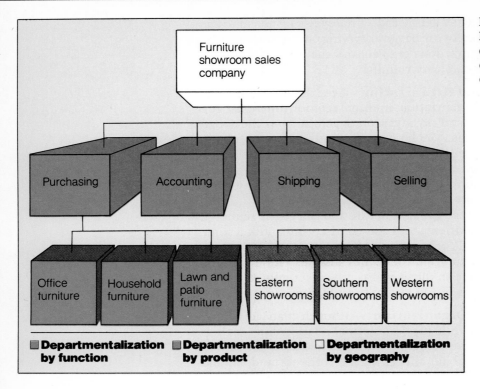

Figure 6-1
Different methods of departmentalization combined in the same company.

■ *By geography*. Some companies split activities along geographical lines. A large retailing company may have four sales managers performing nearly the same job in different regions of the country.

■ *By product or customer*. Departments or individual jobs may also be established to deal with particular products or to sell to special customers, such as the government.

Many large companies combine these methods of allocating work and responsibility, as shown in Figure 6-1.

4   DELEGATION

Distribution of responsibility and authority

The division of labor creates individual jobs with particular, defined responsibilities—along with certain rights and restrictions.

Responsibility   The responsibilities of a job are the duties an employee is obligated to fulfill while performing the job. ***Responsibilities*** are prescribed by the activities to be performed combined with standards for correct performance. For example, a production worker may have the responsibility of installing the control panel frame on an electric stove, using the right number and size of bolts, and adequately tightening the bolts without damage to surrounding parts. An advertising manager might be responsible for supervising a staff of people and planning and carrying out advertising campaigns for a wide range of markets within a specific budget. The president of a corporation is usually responsible for the smooth operation of the entire company, for making an adequate profit now and in the future, for planning and managing expansion, and for avoiding internal developments that may harm the company.

Authority   When accepting a job, an employee is obligated to meet its responsibilities. To do this, employees at any level must have adequate authority. *Authority* has two main aspects: (a) the right to take certain actions, such as spending company funds or sending out news releases, in the performance of a job and (b) the right to require subordinates to perform duties they are assigned. Authority allows employees to make decisions and take actions needed to carry out their jobs. Authority involves the right to commit company resources to meet goals. A production worker might have the authority to use expensive machinery, to reject faulty assemblies, or to stop operations if a malfunction or dangerous situation arises. Higher level jobs in the organization have increased levels of authority, extending to the right to commit millions of dollars to a new product or to company expansion. It is essential that responsibility and authority be equitable, or balanced, as shown in Figure 6-2. That is, there should be neither too little nor too much authority assigned to the job to be done.

The authority to direct the work of others is basic to the operation of a formal organization. If the division of labor in a company is to function smoothly, managers must have the authority to require their subordinates to perform the work specified in the organization plan and to work according to planned standards. This does not eliminate the likelihood that subordinates will have considerable influence on the decisions and activities of their managers. But without ultimate authority of supervisors over subordinates, most organized companies could not remain that way.

Delegation   Authority is said to be "delegated" within an organization. *Delegation,* in this sense, means assigning specific responsibilities along with related rights and authority to individuals and groups. The chief executive officer of a corporation, with the concurrence (approval) of the board of directors, usually has broad responsibilities and the authority to make decisions and direct others in the company. It is not possible, however, for the president or chairperson to personally attend to all management issues. The chief executive delegates some tasks to others. They perform certain duties and make specific kinds of decisions. They, in turn, will delegate responsibilities and related authority to others, down to the lowest level of workers in the firm. The belief that clear-cut lines of authority should be established to connect the top to the bottom of the organization is called the *scalar principle.*

One other aspect of the delegation of authority and responsibility deserves consideration. A manager

**Figure 6-2
Responsibilities balanced with authority.**

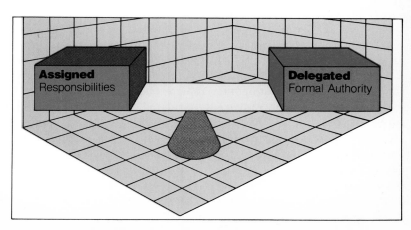

may delegate responsibility to a subordinate—and grant him or her sufficient authority to carry it out—but the manager never escapes the *accountability* for the proper completion of the task that has been delegated. If things go wrong, the superior is the one who is held to be at fault, not the person to whom the task was delegated.

5   PRINCIPLES OF ORGANIZATION

Four guidelines help to create a sound internal structure

Every business firm has its unique organization requirements. There are, however, certain principles that help to establish a sound internal structure. By following these principles, management creates an organization that is planned, suitable to its purpose, well-defined, and as uncomplicated as possible.

ORGANIZATION FOLLOWS PLANNING

Structuring the organization to meet company objectives

The organization process should always follow the planning process. In the management cycle described in Chapter 5, organization is described as one of the steps used to meet objectives set in the planning process. An important measure of the effectiveness of an organization is the extent to which it allows and helps its members to work for the goals of the company. Therefore, a clear definition of the goals is essential to setting up a good organization. Planning should also provide the performance standards and evaluation methods needed to make improvements in the organization. The close relationship between planning and organization also implies that an organization must be flexible. Through the planning process, new objectives will be generated as problems and opportunities arise. An organization must have the capacity to adjust itself to these new objectives. A manager who imposes a completely rigid organization on a company's operations is not making the best use of the company's resources.

STRUCTURE FITS SIZE AND FUNCTION

Determining whether a complex or simple structure is most suitable

The organization must deliberately be made suitable to the size and function of a company. A proprietorship with two or three employees requires little formal organization. A large manufacturing firm with thousands of workers cannot operate at all without a formal and sophisticated organization plan. Imposing a sophisticated organization on a small company, however, is inefficient. The functions a company performs must also partly determine the best kind of organization. Manufacturing firms need complex structures to manage the intricacies of production, while a department store needs a different structure to generate income by stocking and selling goods. Companies with many unskilled workers need different supervisory patterns from firms with highly trained professional or technical personnel.

ACTION BRIEF

A Whirlwind Reorganization.   When the nation's oldest airline found itself in financial trouble late in 1981, its president at that time acted very quickly to save it from failure. His objective was to streamline the organization so that it might compete more effectively in the deregulated skies of the 1980s. Within four months, Neil G. Bergt of Western Airlines, had gotten rid of 19 of the company's 33 corporate executives. The jobs of three others were also dropped to a lower level in the hierarchy. The executive decision makers who were retained were fewer and younger than before. Overall, the effect was to restructure the company's organization in order to remain competitive.

Source: Carole Shifrin, "Western Airlines, Nation's Oldest, Struggles to Escape Turbulence," The Washington Post, April 11, 1982, p. G-1.

DUTIES AND RELATIONSHIPS ARE CLEARLY DEFINED AND SPECIFIED

Clarifying and unifying the chain of command

The flow of delegated responsibility and authority and channels of communication should take place in a carefully specified *chain of command.* The chain of command is directly related to the scalar principle, which establishes who reports to whom from the bottom to the top of the organization. This requires that every job be clearly positioned in the organizational structure with a specified superior and subordinates, if there are any. As a consequence, every person will know exactly what his or her duties are as well as have the authority to perform them. Additionally, the principle of *unity of command* advises that every employee should have only one superior. Such unity avoids conflicting commands and instructions and confusing divisions of authority.

As another general rule, it makes sense to keep the number of levels of authority at a minimum. Unnecessarily long chains of command slow down the communications and the decision making processes.

NUMBER OF SUBORDINATES IS LIMITED

Restricting the span of control to promote effective supervision and coordination

The *span of control* (also called the span of management), or the number of employees directly supervised by one person, must be restricted. Supervision mainly involves assigning work, stimulating motivation, locating errors and inadequate work, and seeing that corrections are made. Effective supervision requires involvement with subordinates; this limits the number of direct subordinates a supervisor should be assigned. Six to eight direct subordinates is a frequently mentioned maximum. Actually, the number of subordinates will depend on the type of work they do, the amount of authority given to them, and other factors. In certain kinds of activities, like an automobile assembly line for example, 50 employees under a single supervisor is not unusual.

Centralization Versus Decentralization   Organizations can also vary in the extent to which authority is distributed down the chain of command to middle and lower levels of management. A *centralized organization* is one in which almost all of the authority is concentrated in a few positions at the top. In a company with centralized organization, nearly all important operating decisions will be made by top management. The main task of those below is to carry out their decisions efficiently. A *decentralized organization* delegates much more authority to the managers who are closer to actual operations. First-level supervisors and department heads have maximum responsibility and authority to make decisions concerning their work. Top management devotes its attention to general company goals and policies and to monitoring and handling exceptional conditions that arise.

Centralized organizations usually give managers a limited but tighter span of control, with each manager having fewer subordinates. This often adds additional—and cumbersome—levels of authority, which creates a taller organizational structure as shown in Figure 6-3. Managers in decentralized organizations often have a larger span of control (creating a flatter organizational structure) since subordinates are given more authority and freedom to act and may receive less direct supervision from above.

6   TYPICAL ORGANIZATION STRUCTURES

Three types predominate

In the long history of business management, three major kinds of internal structures have evolved: line,

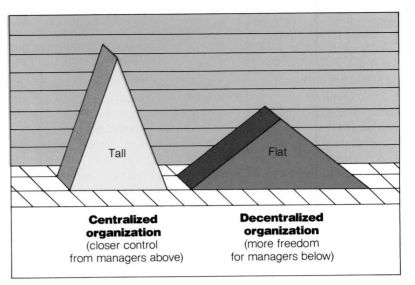

Centralized organization
(closer control from managers above)

Decentralized organization
(more freedom for managers below)

**Figure 6-3
Differences in organization structures according to degree of centralization.**

line-and-staff, and functional. Most companies use one or more of these forms today. All of these structures are ways of delegating authority and assigning responsibility to achieve a manageable division of labor. Patterns of delegation differ in each case.

Managers view some positions in a company as line positions and others as staff positions. Line positions are the direct chain of command that carries out the company's business. Production, sales, financing, and all of the other jobs directly related to generating income for the company are usually considered line positions. Positions that assist the line employees with specialized abilities and activities, such as an attorney, a market researcher, and a public relations specialist, are called staff positions. The different functions of the positions result in differences in their authority relationships. Line positions have a direct supervisor-subordinate relationship; the supervisor is authorized to direct the work of the subordinate, and the subordinate is obliged to accept the direction. Staff positions usually have an advisory relationship with other managers and workers in the company. As advisors, they may offer expert guidance and analysis for any level of management but their recommendations do not usually have the force of authority.

LINE ORGANIZATION

Simple and direct

An internal business structure in which every employee is a member of a direct chain of command from the top executives down through the levels of management is called a *line organization,* illustrated in Figure 6-4. In this structure, every person is directly responsible to a single supervisor who is superior in the organization. It is called a line organization because authority flows in a direct line from the top of the organization to any individual worker at any level. A production worker may report directly to a supervisor, the supervisor to a plant superintendent, the plant superintendent to a production manager, the production manager to a general manager, and so on. Each department or division is relatively independent of other departments or divisions and concentrates on its own role.

The line organization has a distinct advantage in its simplicity; every employee can understand the organization and know where he or she stands. Line organization affords clear and distinct distribution of authority and allows every employee to answer directly to only one supervisor. The direct supervisor-subordinate relationship makes it easier to maintain discipline and quality of work. The direct line relationship also aids faster decision making and makes individuals more accountable for their actions.

A great disadvantage of the line organization is that it is sometimes not capable of handling the complex management and technical needs of a large, modern company. For this reason, relatively "pure" examples of this structure are generally found in smaller companies. Another disadvantage is that there are often insufficient formal means for communication and coordination between departments. Also, since managers are responsible for all of the work of their subordinates, they are often burdened with decisions about details.

LINE-AND-STAFF ORGANIZATION

Adds specialists

As the complexity and size of a company increase, managers usually find it necessary to modify the line organization by adding staff specialists to handle certain specific duties. This is called *line-and-staff organization* and is illustrated in Figure 6-5. It is the most common internal structure today, especially for large companies. The staff specialists perform technical services and provide expert guidance to line managers. They may also assume part of the planning and communicating functions of

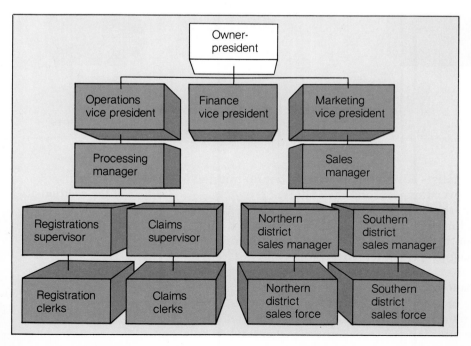

Figure 6-4
Example of basic line organization in an insurance company.

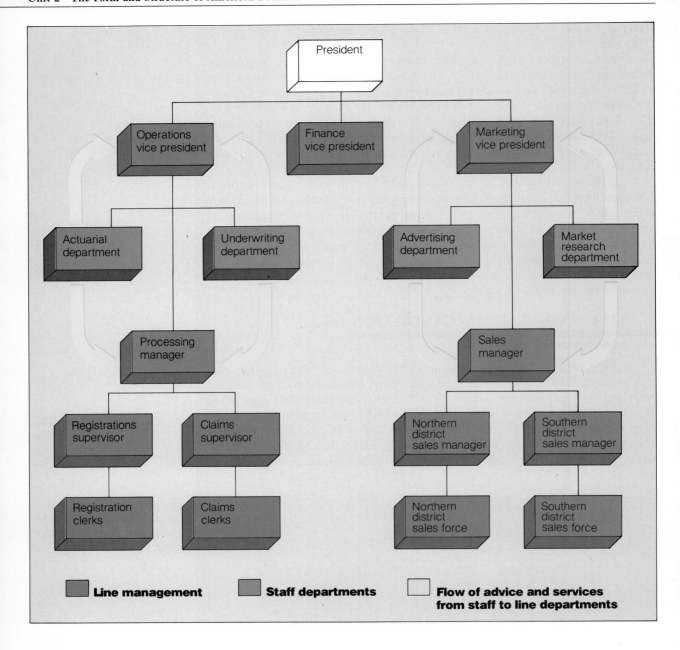

Line management   **Staff departments**   **Flow of advice and services from staff to line departments**

line managers. The staff specialists advise line managers but do not normally have direct authority over the positions they advise.

The great advantage of the line-and-staff organizations is that it allows specialists to handle highly technical or complex functions while the company retains many of the benefits of line organization. Many typical staff functions—purchasing, personnel, data processing, and engineering and design work, for example—can be performed by experts in these areas while the company continues to maintain the clear chain of responsibility and authority of a line organization.

The disadvantage of a line-and-staff organization is that conflict often arises between line positions and staff positions. Line managers and work-

Figure 6-5
Example of the addition of staff departments to form a line-and-staff organization structure.

Our economic growth has been based on specialization. A prime example of production specialization is the division of labor which is the very foundation of the factory system.

Adam Smith describes in The Wealth of Nations, *published in 1776, a British pin factory:*

One man draws out the wire, another straightens it, a third cuts it, a fourth points it, a fifth grinds it at the top for receiving the head; to make the head requires two or three distinct operations; to put it on is a peculiar business, to whiten the pins is another; it is even a trade by itself to put them into the paper; and the important business of making a pin is, in this manner, divided into about eighteen distinct operations. . . . I have seen a small manufactory of this kind where ten men only were employed. . . . Those ten persons . . . could make . . . upwards of forty-eight thousand pins in a day. . . . But if they had all wrought [worked] separately and independently . . . they certainly could not each of them have made twenty, perhaps not one pin in a day.

The goal of establishing the internal structure of a business is to create just this smoothly coordinated division of effort. The work of every part of the organization—management, sales, production, warehousing, and all the rest—is broken down into subordinated units. The many units are then connected together with a flow of materials and information.

Source: Adam Smith, The Wealth of Nations, *Modern Library, New York, 1937, pp. 3–4.*

Has the division of labor really increased the productive ability of people? What are some of the disadvantages of division of labor?

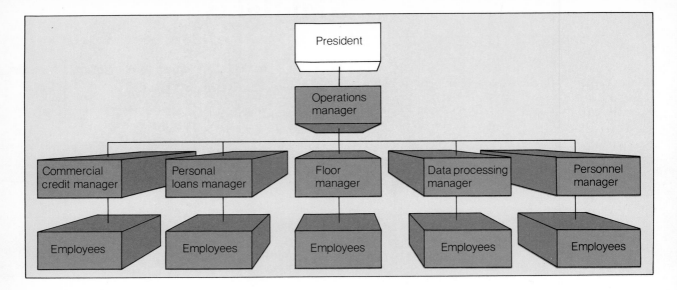

Figure 6-6
**Example of functional
organization in a bank.**

ers may consider staff specialists as expensive extra baggage. Staff workers may resent managers who do not take their advice. Staff workers may try to exert authority over line operations. The cost of staff specialists increases the company's overhead for management as well. Line personnel may come to rely too heavily on the services of staff experts. Thus decisiveness may be sacrificed and authority diluted.

Line employees and staff employees may be organized in many combinations. For example, a company may set up separate divisions to handle different products, different customers, or different geographical regions. Each division may be organized as a line-and-staff structure, and the overall organization of the company may also reflect this structure.

FUNCTIONAL ORGANIZATION

Specialization dominates

An alternative way to organize a business is to assign managers the responsibility for all activities and decisions in certain defined functional areas of operations. This is called *functional organization,* and is illustrated in Figure 6-6. This structure, for example, might have five managers supervising the workers in a manufacturing plant. The personnel manager would directly handle all personnel matters, including hiring and firing, rather than advise and assist other managers as in the line-and-staff organization. The production manager would concentrate exclusively on production and would not be expected to make any personnel decisions.

The main advantage of functional organization is that it allows managers to specialize in one particular area of operations. Their expert guidance becomes directly available to all workers without an intervening line manager. The fact that each worker has more than one supervisor is a great disadvantage of functional organization, however. This can cause conflicting commands and loss of discipline and can make it difficult to pin down the responsibility for decisions. For this reason, most businesses that choose a functional organization try to clearly restrict the degree of authority certain functions can exercise over other functions.

MATRIX ORGANIZATIONS

Dual authority for special projects

A fourth kind of organization is used by firms that must manage a number of one-time projects—such as road, dam, or bridge building, construction of large aircraft or space exploration vehicles, or of research investigations. These firms use a *matrix organization,* which allows a project manager to exercise temporary authority over a number of specialists who also must report to different line managers for supervision in their specialties. This enables specialists to be assigned to projects where they are needed, as shown in Figure 6-7. It has the disadvantage, however, of asking an employee to report to two different bosses.

Figure 6-7
Example of a matrix organization.

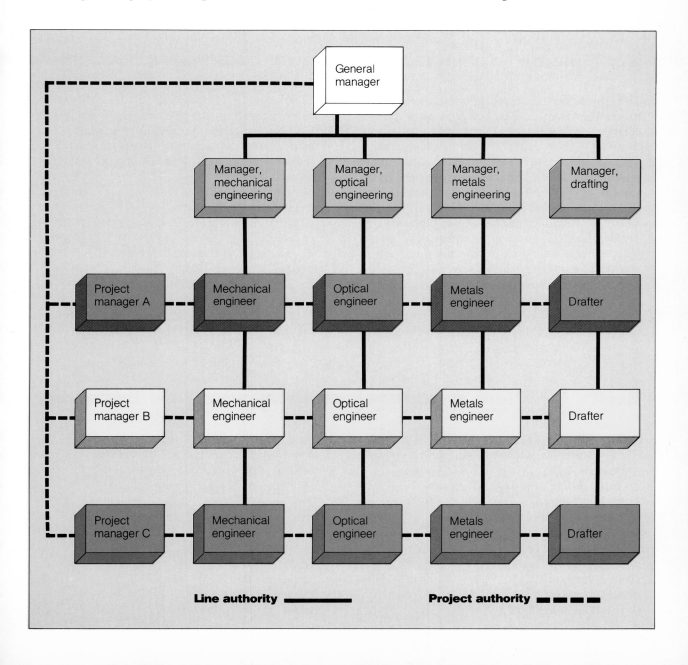

COMMITTEES

Combine varied viewpoints and expertise

When a group of people are assigned to discuss, or to deal directly with, a well-defined matter, this group is called a **committee.** A committee's role may be strictly advisory, as when a cost reduction committee makes suggestions to a production manager as to where costs might best be reduced. Or a committee may be given power to act directly, as when a bank's loan committee decides whether or not to grant a large loan to a credit applicant. Committees have the advantage of bringing together many viewpoints to bear on a problem. They also have the disadvantage of tending to arrive at ineffective compromises so as to satisfy everyone.

Key Concepts

1. The internal structure of a business determines the relationships between a company's activities and personnel, and it controls how they interact to achieve planned objectives.
2. Organization may be formal, consciously planned according to rational principles, or informal, occurring on the basis of personal influence and social likes and dislikes.
3. The first task in the organizing process is to divide all of the company's internal activities into defined jobs and to group these jobs in appropriate departments.
4. Every job in a business has certain duties or responsibilities that employees are obligated to perform. Authority, the right to make specific kinds of decisions and to direct the work

of subordinates, is delegated to employees to allow them to meet their responsibilities.
5. Certain principles help managers establish organizations that are well planned, suitable to their purpose, well defined, and as simple as possible:
   a. The organization should be structured to meet company objectives.
   b. Structure should fit the size and function of a company.
   c. Duties and relationships should be clearly defined and specified.
   d. The number of subordinates should be limited.
6. The most common organizational structures are line, line-and-staff, and functional.

Review Questions

1. Define, identify, or explain each of the following key terms or phrases, found on the pages indicated.
   accountability (p. 94)
   authority (p. 93)
   centralized organization (p. 95)
   chain of command (p. 95)
   committee (p. 102)
   decentralized organization (p. 95)
   delegation (p. 93)
   departmentalization (p. 91)
   division of labor (p. 91)

   formal organization (p. 90)
   functional organization (p. 100)
   informal organization (p. 90)
   line-and-staff organization (p. 97)
   line organization (p. 96)
   matrix organization (p. 101)
   organization (p. 90)
   organizing process (p. 90)
   responsibility (p. 92)
   scalar principle (p. 93)
   span of control (p. 95)
   unity of command (p. 95)

2. What is meant by the internal organization of a business?

3. How does formal organization differ from informal organization?

4. One of a manager's first concerns, when establishing an organization, is with dividing up a company's activities into specific jobs and departments. What are some of the bases on which work activities can be divided?

5. What is authority, and why must it be delegated within an organization?

6. What are some of the principles of organization mentioned in the chapter?

7. What is the difference between a centralized and a decentralized organization?

8. What is the main advantage of a line-and-staff organization over a line organization?

9. What is the main disadvantage of a functional organization?

10. From what two superiors is a person employed in a matrix organization likely to receive orders or instructions?

Case Critique 6-1
Loosening the Reins

When Tom Barrea, chief executive officer, set up an organization structure for his company, he did it all by the book. The Thomas National Group would provide data processing services to other companies for a fee. The company would be relatively small, with about 100 employees. As chairperson, Tom had three vice presidents reporting to him. Each was in charge of a separate function—marketing, programming, and data processing. In turn, each of these vice presidents had a number of specialized managers reporting to them. Under this system, when someone down the line had a problem, the employee would bring it to his or her manager for an answer. If it couldn't be resolved at that point, the problem would be relayed up the line to the next level for solution. Work had been delegated so that each person knew the limits of responsibility and authority and who his or her boss was.

Problems began, however, when this vertical system kept the company's relatively small staff of people from communicating with one another across functions. If a programmer got an idea, for example, it would have to pass up the line to the president before getting the benefit of the thinking in, say, the data processing department. The company was also adding new services to be offered to its customers. Under the original organization system, there would have to be a specialist for the new service in each department. Gradually, communications in the company broke down. Problems took forever to be solved. Management was increasingly indecisive.

Finally, Barrea changed the company's organization structure. Instead of a narrow, vertical pattern, he created a broader, horizontal one. Now Barrea has not only the three functional vice presidents reporting to him, he also has an executive vice president to coordinate administrative affairs and three vice presidents who head up the new special services. Each vice president has been given greater authority to deal with problems in his or her area. Barrea is in constant touch with all seven vice presidents. He encourages communications between departments. And even the lowest-ranking person in the organization has only a level or two to get to the top.

1. What is the name of the reporting system that the chief executive officer of the Thomas National Group originally set up for the organization? What were some of its shortcomings?

2. What was the form of departmentalization originally chosen? What were some of its limitations?

3. What new form of departmentalization was added to the old structure?

4. Is the new organization structure more centralized or decentralized than before? What are its advantages and disadvantages?

Source: Thomas Barrea, "I Unchained My Chain of Command," *INC.*, October 1981, p. 129.

Case Critique 6-2
Decisions by Committee

While Sears, Roebuck and Co., K-Mart, and other major retailers were staggering around during the early 1980s, J. C. Penney Company was on the move, especially in making profits. The company, which employs more than 180,000 people, attributed its success to the extensive use of committee judgments. Penney has a 14-person management committee. Its purpose is only partly advisory. It also makes decisions and often implements them. No major problem that the company faces is resolved without having the committee take a look at it. Penney's management committee is divided into several subcommittees that watch over special areas like personnel, merchandising, long-range strategy, operating plans, and the company's economic welfare. Penney's president concedes that committees often lead to group decision making. In fact, he says that he encourages it, "You get a mixture of people who are knowledgeable on a subject and others who can lend a broader view." In one instance, Penney's president had just about made up his mind to concentrate on the company's major stores and let the 1,065 smaller stores gradually wither away. The management committee, however, looked at the picture from the viewpoint of real estate, construction, and overall company development. They disagreed with the president's conclusion. Their solution was to assign special merchandising and marketing teams to find ways of making the small stores more competitive and profitable.

1. What is a major drawback of the use of committees in an organization?
2. What distinguished Penney's management committee from many other committees?
3. What sort of problems might Penney's committee cause for the company's line and staff departments?

Source: "Teamwork Pays Off at Penney's," *Business Week*, April 12, 1982, p. 107.

Unit 3

Basic Business Operations— Marketing

Unit 3 explains why marketing is so vital to business and outlines the factors that make up a marketing mix. It describes the flow of goods and services to consumers and selling and advertising techniques for the promotion of goods and services.

The vastness and diversity of the consumer population have given rise to the marketing concept. Part of the marketing process involves deciding which goods or services to offer and how to develop a price strategy. Research programs for determining the classification of products and the segmentation of consumer groups aid business in these matters. The next problem is distributing products in the best way possible to markets with the most profit potential. Advertising and promotion is the final step. Businesses have come to rely more and more on this method of stimulating market demand and are faced with important questions about the effects of these sales techniques on society at large.

Chapter 7

Markets and Marketing

1 THE MARKETING CONCEPT
emphasizes profits derived from customer satisfaction.

2 THE MARKETING MIX
has four main ingredients:

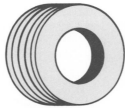

Products or services planned to satisfy consumer needs.

Pricing according to consumer habits and purchasing power.

Placement in the market for distribution.

Promotion for sale and consumption.

3 TWO MARKETS PREDOMINATE

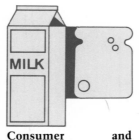

Consumer market   and   Industrial market

4 PRODUCT PLANNING
has three key concerns:

| Product lines | Brand names | Product life cycles |

5 PROFITABLE PRICING
depends upon three factors:

| Pricing strategies | Pricing techniques | Government regulations |

6 MARKETING FUNCTIONS

are many and varied.

Buying	Bearing risks
Selling	Standardizing
Transporting	Grading and labeling
Storing	Financing

| Information gathering |

7 SCIENTIFIC METHODS
assist marketers.

 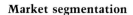 

| Market segmentation | Market research |

Learning Objectives

The purpose of this chapter is to explain the marketing concept and the marketing mix and their importance to business, distinguish among markets, identify some common marketing practices, and outline the functions performed by marketing managers.

After studying Chapter 7, you should be able to:

1. *Define the marketing concept.*
2. *Identify the four ingredients of the marketing mix.*
3. *Differentiate between the consumer market and the industrial market and recognize specific buying motives.*
4. *Understand the importance of product planning, explain three methods of product identification, and identify the four stages of the product life cycle.*
5. *Describe four common techniques for setting prices.*
6. *Recognize the nine functions performed by marketing management.*
7. *Understand and apply the concept of market segmentation and define the objectives of market research.*

If your class is using SSweetco: Business Model and Activity File for Business in Action, see Chapter 7 in that book after you complete this chapter. There you will find exercises and activities to help you apply your learning to typical business situations.

Two hundred years ago, it was common for every producer of goods to know his or her customers personally and to hand deliver products or wait for people to come into the workshop where the goods were made. Today, the practice of making products by hand for local customers has all but disappeared. It has been replaced by an extremely complex marketing system that moves goods and services of all types to diverse markets all over the country and the world.

Producers today are usually separated from consumers by a complicated chain of brokers, wholesalers, agents, and retail stores. Producers must make an effort to find out what kind of products consumers want and to create and offer these products for sale. They also must make efforts—through advertising and other means—to inform consumers about the goods and services that are available. Product designs, pricing, and advertising all depend on knowing markets.

1   THE MARKETING CONCEPT

The marketing concept builds profits from corporate concern for consumer needs and interests

In Chapter 1, it was mentioned that early in this century most companies emphasized production efficiency as the means of creating and increasing profits. This may be called the *production concept.* At the time, the manufacturing capabilities of industry were so limited compared with the large demand, that any useful goods produced could usually be sold with little difficulty. As the years went by, however, production capacities increased faster than the population. Managers came to see that positive sales efforts would be needed if production and profits were to be maintained at a high level. Companies began to use sophisticated and expensive advertising methods and employed staffs of trained salespeople. This is typical of the *selling concept.*

In the last twenty-five to thirty-five years, business has been influenced by the *marketing concept.* This concept rests on the belief that profits can be maximized by concentrating on the needs and wants of consumers and by creating products for which there is a known demand. One result of this belief is that more companies are using research to find out what kinds of goods and services consumers want before developing new products. The marketing concept has not eliminated earlier concerns with production efficiency or with selling, but has added to them. Most managers today believe that the evaluation of consumer desires for goods and services is as necessary to long-term success as are high-quality, low-cost production and persuasive selling techniques.

2   MARKETING ELEMENTS

Marketing requires a mix of four p's: product development, pricing, placement, and promotion

Marketing systematizes business activities that (*a*) plan products or services to satisfy actual needs and wants of consumers, (*b*) price the products so they will suit the buying habits and purchasing power of potential customers, (c) place the products in the market for distribution, and (d) promote the products' sale to and use by consumers.

These four activities, taken together, make up a **marketing mix.**

Product planning concentrates on learning which goods and services consumers want and then designing products to meet these desires. Pricing is a critical decision because it ultimately determines whether a product will be bought and, if so, whether it will be profitable. **Product placement** and **product distribution** involve decisions about warehousing and transportation and about whether to sell directly to the public or through various chains of intermediaries. **Product promotion** is an important function that includes personal selling, advertising, and direct sales promotion, such as free samples, point-of-purchase displays, and discount coupons.

All of these functions must be pursued on a continuing basis to improve sales. Marketing operations are especially apparent when new products are introduced. A good example is the successful marketing of L'eggs pantyhose. The product was made of modern synthetic materials and was designed to sell at prices below those prevailing in the women's hosiery market. The lower price, combined with distinctive and convenient packaging (the hose are sold in a plastic egg-shaped container) and with an innovative distribution method, resulted in an immediately successful product. The distribution, in particular, contributed to success. L'eggs are sold from display racks in supermarkets, drugstores, and other outlets not specializing in women's apparel. The marketers created a large demand by making their product a convenience item for many women. The product, price, and distribution system were reinforced by an advertising campaign designed to create recognition of the unusual name and motivate impulse buying.

In the case of L'eggs, the marketers were able to create the right marketing mix, the right combination of product type, price, distribution, and promotion to tap strong consumer demand. Their efforts demonstrate the modern approach to management which uses the marketing concept to increase company profits.

3   MARKETS

Markets: where the buyers are

Effective marketing focuses on an understanding of markets. A market has been defined as a means by which buyers and sellers exchange goods at a price they agree upon. Marketers concentrate on buyers: people with needs and wants that will cause them to buy products. To constitute a market, the people must have money to spend on goods and services and the willingness to spend it. To a marketing manager with a product to sell, the market also includes other sellers with products that compete for the satisfaction of the same consumer demands.

In the broadest terms, all goods and services are sold either to the consumer market or to the industrial market. **Consumer goods** are bought and used by individuals and families without any further processing. **Industrial goods** are used to make other products or in the general operations of a business or institution. Both markets have their own characteristics, but both are shaped by the ability and willingness of their members to spend money to satisfy their needs and wants.

The federal government also identifies certain very large concentrations of population as markets. If an urban area has a city or county with 50,000 people or more, it is designated a *Standard Metropolitan Statistical Area* (SMSA). There are 323 SMSAs in the United States and Puerto Rico. Many companies plan their marketing programs around these large markets.

THE CONSUMER MARKET

Consumers buy for themselves and their families

People who purchase goods and services for their own or their family's use make up the consumer market. Numerous factors affect what people buy, in what quantities, and where. The most important of these are the nature of individual needs, buying habits, motivation, and purchasing power. These correspond almost directly to the needs, willingness to buy, and ability to buy that characterize every market.

They Buy for Primary Needs as Well as Selective Satisfaction Every consumer requires the necessities of life: food, clothing, shelter, and some medical care. These are called *primary needs.* Consumers also want other kinds of goods and services based on their interests, goals, and individual characteristics. When they buy goods and services for this reason, this is called *selective purchasing.* The wish to buy a piece of jewelry, an antique pistol, a rare coin, or a trip to the Bahamas does not result from primary needs for sustenance and protection. Instead, it stems from higher level needs such as esteem, mental stimulation, or physical attractiveness. Such needs operate in people of all economic classes. The Kaiser automobile, which had a very short market life, is a good example. As George Romney, an auto company executive explained: "The Henry J. (Kaiser) failed because they stripped it to make a car for the poor people, and the poor people didn't want a car made for poor people."

Since everyone must meet primary needs, marketing efforts in this area generally focus on inducing consumers to buy one particular brand rather than another. For the consumer, there is no choice as to whether to buy food or not, but there is a huge variety of competing brands and stores. Marketing efforts for selective purchases try to make the product itself attractive—and then call attention to the attributes of a particular brand or supplier.

They Choose Particular Products for Three Compelling Reasons Consumer motives for choosing to buy certain products and rejecting others may be rational or emotional. *Rational motives* involve reasoned judgments about the desirability of a product based on its value or quality compared with competing products. Choices based on cost—buying lower cost goods of similar quality or buying at sales—usually result from rational motives. Buying one brand of lawn mower rather than another because of known facts about its good service record, or its ease of starting, is rational. Rational motives lead consumers to make a purchase only if the product is needed for a specific practical use.

Emotional motives spring from feelings. The emotions usually motivate purchases of products bought to provide physical pleasure: foods that taste good but have little nutritive value, phonograph records, art, and furniture that is expensive but attractive to look at. Consumers may be motivated to buy a certain kind of car or house or clothing because they feel these goods will boost their status or self-esteem. Pride in ownership is a powerful motive. The desire for personal attractiveness to others, socially and sexually, affects the selection of hundreds of products, from cosmetics to yachts. Fear—of financial loss, physical harm, or ill health— is a common motive for buying insurance, health care aids, safety devices, and similar products.

Consumers are influenced as to *where* they buy by **patronage motives.** These result from a complex of rational and emotional factors that make a particular store appear more desirable than another. The services offered by a store, such as delivery, extended credit, refunds, and exchanges, may make it more attractive to customers. A convenient location, adequate parking, ease of access, protection from weather, and other similar factors may make one store seem more desirable than another. A reputation for providing high-quality merchandise or service is a powerful draw for many customers.

Buying a particular product at a particular store usually results from a combination of rational, emotional, and patronage motives. Reasons for buying sports equipment, for instance, may be largely emotional, but usually also include some rational concern for fitness and health. Selecting a particular set of golf clubs almost always includes judgments about quality versus cost combined with emotional factors such as the desire to emulate expert golfers.

Customers Need the Wherewithal to Buy   Besides the desire to buy, consumers must have the ability to buy before they can be considered part of a market. This ability to buy goods and services is called **purchasing power.** Purchasing power for some products depends on disposable income and for other products on discretionary income. **Disposable income** has already been defined (Chapter 2) as the amount of money left after federal, state, and local taxes and other fixed deductions have been withheld; it is the same as take-home pay. Disposable income has a direct effect on the type of housing, clothes, food, and other necessities a family can afford. Producers of those kinds of goods judge consumer purchasing power by disposable income. **Discretionary income** is the amount of money that is left after the basic needs of life have been obtained. It determines purchasing power for the thousands of products that may or may not be bought, at the consumer's discretion. Purchases made with discretionary income have received great attention from business in the last 50 years.

CLASSIFICATIONS OF CONSUMER GOODS

Consumer goods fall into three classes

Consumer goods are bought by individuals or families to satisfy their own needs and desires. Goods and services for consumers include thousands of different products manufactured and distributed by numerous firms. These products are divided into three types based on the buying

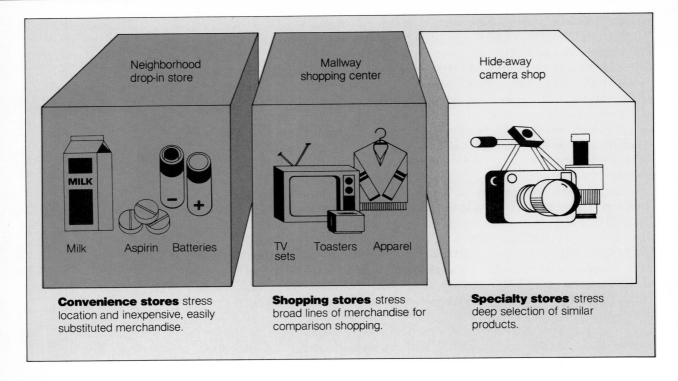

Neighborhood
drop-in store

Mallway
shopping center

Hide-away
camera shop

MILK

Milk   Aspirin   Batteries

TV   Toasters   Apparel
sets

Convenience stores stress
location and inexpensive, easily
substituted merchandise.

Shopping stores stress
broad lines of merchandise for
comparison shopping.

Specialty stores stress
deep selection of similar
products.

habits of consumers: convenience, shopping, and specialty goods. (See
Figure 7-1.)

**Figure 7-1
Classifications of consumer
goods puts them into three
kinds of stores.**

Convenience Goods   *Convenience goods* include products and
services that are selected because they are readily available, rather than
because they compare favorably with other products. Consumers are
familiar with these products and are usually willing to accept substitutes
or pay a slightly higher price rather than go to another store. Consumers
usually buy convenience goods at retail outlets near their homes. Unit
prices are generally low. Products that are used frequently in the home are
convenience goods: orange juice, milk, razor blades, cleaning products,
nonprescription drugs, and flashlight batteries, for example.

Shopping Goods   The most important characteristic of *shopping
goods* is that consumers not only buy them regularly, but consider it
worthwhile to devote effort to comparing prices, brands, and dependabil-
ity. Shopping goods are almost always more expensive items than convenience goods, and buyers are often willing to do considerable shopping
around before making a selection. Some examples of shopping goods are
furniture, most home appliances, apparel, television sets, and automobiles.

Specialty Goods   *Specialty goods* have unique characteristics not
shared by competing goods that make consumers willing to exert considerable effort to locate and buy them. Buyers normally will not accept a
substitute for a specialty product; they want a particular brand and no
other. Consumers are familiar with the distinctive qualities of different
brands of specialty goods, sometimes even to the extent of having sophis-

ticated technical knowledge of them. This is often true of purchasers of stereophonic sound equipment, for instance. Many specialty goods have relatively high unit prices, but this is not always true. Many people will not accept substitutes for a particular brand of soft drink or cigarette. For them, these products are specialty goods. Other more typical examples are automobiles, high-priced clothing, cameras, sports equipment, and some kinds of home furnishings.

The automobile is an example of a product that is both a shopping and a specialty good. Different shoppers may view products in different ways. Most people buy television sets as shopping goods; whenever they want to buy a new set, they will consider a number of competitors and then make a selection. Some people, however, consider a television set a specialty item and would be willing to drive to another town, if necessary, to buy a particular brand. Services vary in the same way. Many people consider having the oil changed in their car a convenience service and will have it done at the nearest gas station even at a slightly higher price. Others will compare the prices and services of a number of shops.

THE INDUSTRIAL MARKET

Industrial buyers: fewer in number, but they usually make bigger, more rational purchases

Industrial goods are used to produce other goods or services or are consumed in the operations of a business or other organization. *Raw materials* are unprocessed natural resources such as the products sold by mines, farms, and forestry operations that are bought by other businesses for use in their manufacturing processes. Many companies process raw materials into intermediate materials that are usable by consumers only after further processing. Sheet metal and leather are two examples. The manufacture of *component parts* for sale to a manufacturer is a major industry. Many companies produce machinery and equipment to be used by other companies. Expendable supplies, such as paper and typewriter ribbons, are bought for use in daily operations. All of these are examples of goods sold to the industrial market.

The industrial market differs in a number of ways from the consumer market. Demand fluctuates more in the industrial market. This is partly because there are usually fewer potential customers for a particular industrial product and partly because industrial buyers are more aware of and more quickly influenced by general economic changes. Industrial purchases are made to meet clearly defined needs; goods are rarely bought when not needed. Thus, demand for industrial goods is relatively stable; it does not vary much as the price of products changes.

Industrial orders are usually much larger than individual consumer purchases. This, combined with the fact that industrial buyers are typically more rationally motivated and better informed about the products they buy, creates selling patterns different from those in the consumer market. An exchange of considerable technical information between buyer and seller is often needed. Sales representatives for the industrial market often have broad technical training and skills. Extended periods of negotiation and revision of specifications are also common.

4   PRODUCT PLANNING

Marketers must create products for the market

Of the four general marketing functions—product planning, pricing, distribution, and promotion—*product planning* is surely one that is indispensable. Business income depends entirely on the sale of products, whether they be goods or services. Successful companies must develop and introduce new products continually as markets, economic conditions, competition, and company goals change. A study of 700 companies, conducted in 1981, showed that over a five year period a total of 13,311 items were introduced, or an annual average of about four per company. Half of these products, however, were modifications of existing products and only 27 percent were completely new. Only approximately one out of four of these new products survived in the market for five years.

PRODUCT DEVELOPMENT

Successful products emerge from expert knowledge of the market to be served

The main role of marketing managers in this process is to try to insure that the goods and services that are developed can be sold. This role often involves conceiving the products by using expert knowledge of the market and of consumers' wants and buying habits. It almost always includes helping to design the specifications of a product, including its precise function and quality. A soft drink company, for instance, might wish to develop new products to replace an existing unprofitable one. Top management expects its marketing department to outline the general characteristics of the products for which consumer demand is believed to exist. The marketers might use their knowledge of the market to propose a drink with a new flavor, one made from all-natural ingredients, or one that contains no caffeine. Marketing personnel would certainly have a major influence on the packaging of the new drink, since packaging is an integral part of products today. They might be asked to make a judgment about the desired quality of the product, since a lower-priced drink might sell better, even if it were lower quality.

An important consideration in planning a new product is differentiating it from other similar products. Packaging and the general presentation of products helps to do this, but specific features must often be built into the goods or services themselves for the purpose of differentiation.

Another concern in product planning is seeing that new products fit into an existing or future product line. A *product line* is a group of similar or related products that can be sold using the same distribution and promotion methods. Efficiency is increased by using the same means of transportation, sales representatives, wholesalers, and advertising techniques to sell the whole group rather than just a single product.

BRANDS AND TRADEMARKS

Brands help to identify products

A trademark or brand is an important tool in differentiating products and creating buyer loyalty. A *brand* is some combination of words or symbols that identifies the goods or services of a specific producer and distinguishes them from the products of other manufacturers. ***Trademark*** has essentially the same meaning except that it refers to brands that are protected by law. The government prohibits the use of a trademark except with the permission of the company that registered it. Brands are important in marketing because they make it easy for consumers to tell one product from another. Buyers feel confident buying certain brands because they can be assured of consistent quality. Advertising depends on brands. Even if consumers were convinced about buying a company's product, they would not be able to identify it without a brand.

PRODUCT LIFE CYCLE

The four phases in a product's life

The main reason companies must continually develop new products is because products have a life cycle. The four stages in the **product life cycle** are introduction, growth, maturity, and decline. (Their effects on sales and profits are shown in Figure 7-2.)

When a product is first introduced, there will have been no sales yet and there will be an accumulated loss resulting from development costs. Initial promotion efforts must expose the product to consumers and publicize its unique features and value. If the introduction is successful and if there is a potential demand, the product will enter a period of growth, when sales increase, sometimes at a very rapid rate. It is generally during this phase that a product first becomes profitable. At this stage, other companies recognize the success of the product. They begin to compete by producing their own version of it. Maturity follows with sales growth reaching a plateau as the market demand becomes satisfied. Profits may remain satisfactory at the beginning of this stage, but they often dwindle as the increasing efforts of competitors begin to be felt. At some point in the maturity stage or even earlier, a new product aimed at the same market will probably have been introduced and the original product will enter the decline stage. Profits will fall rapidly because of intense competition, and eventually sales will fall to a low level as the product is succeeded by a new and better one. The Action Brief on page 116 concerns a product in decline.

Figure 7-2
Stages in a product life cycle.

5 PRODUCT PRICING

The price is not set by the marketer alone

Setting the right price for products is absolutely critical for their success. The main factors that affect ***product pricing***, even in our economy where there are many other influences, are demand and competition. As explained in Chapter 2, demand is closely linked with price. If the supply of a product is constant, greater demand will allow higher

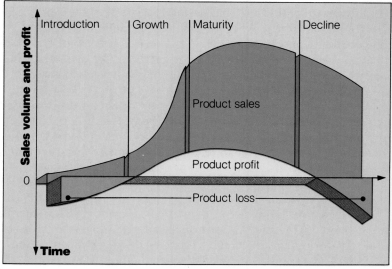

prices to be charged without affecting sales volume. At the same time, however, significantly higher prices will tend to reduce demand.

Competition also counteracts the freedom to raise prices. Free competition tends to drive prices down for two reasons. First, the entrance of a competitor into the market will increase the supply of a product. This works against high prices because the immediate scarcity is reduced. Additionally, new competitors often purposely sell at a lower price in an effort to cut into the sales of an established producer or supplier.

PRICING STRATEGIES

Prices are chosen to maximize profits

The practical result of this is that marketers have a choice to make when pricing products. They can establish high prices with the expectation of selling fewer units but with a greater profit on each unit. The other alternative is to set low prices in an effort to achieve volume sales even though the profit on each unit may be small. The typical response to this choice is to try to find exactly the right price that will maximize profits by balancing sales volume with profit per unit.

PRICING PRACTICES

Prices are set in four ways

Specific methods for setting prices usually depend on development costs, manufacturing costs, demand estimates, existing and potential competition, promotion and distribution plans, expected length of the product's life cycle, and other factors. Many of these pricing methods are complex. There are, however, certain general pricing practices that demonstrate the approaches that companies use. The four major methods are cost-plus, follow-the-leader, penetration, and skimming.

Probably the single most common pricing method is to set prices that are very close to those already established for similar products of competing firms. A major company in the industry, called a price leader, may determine what the new prices will be. Other producers usually adjust their prices to stay in line. This may be called *follow-the-leader pricing.* The advantage of this practice is that it limits excessive price competition that might result in lower profits for everyone. It also simplifies the pricing process. Companies do not have to perform all of the research and analysis involved with other pricing methods. At the same time, companies that use this kind of pricing do not have the assurance that they really are selling at the optimum price.

Penetration pricing is sometimes used when introducing new products. It involves setting as low a price as possible, considering manufacturing and other costs, with the expectation of achieving volume sales. Its main advantage is that it can result in high profits if market penetration is sufficient. It also discourages competitors from entering the field because a substantial part of the demand will already be met and because the profit margin on each unit will be slim.

A third alternative is to set the highest price consumers are likely to accept when the product is introduced and plan to lower prices later when competition makes itself felt. This is called *skimming.* The intention behind skimming is to recover the development costs of a product while

ACTION BRIEF

Disappearing Landmarks. *A couple of decades ago, motorists knew they were approaching town by the glow of neon lights on the horizon. Every commercial enterprise on the strip, from all-night hotdog stands to sleepy-time motels, blazed their messages in orange-red neon tubes. Since the 1950s, however, the neon light has passed into the last stages of its product life cycle. In 1946, there were 3,500 tube benders. Today, as the demand for these lights rapidly declines, there are fewer than 500 craftspeople practicing the art.*

Source: "Neon Signs: Disappearing Landmarks," Daily News-Record (Harrisonburg, Virginia), March 19, 1979, p. 21.

the field is still relatively noncompetitive. This approach is more common with products that have a novelty value and for which there is a strong demand and few competitive suppliers.

Cost-plus pricing simply adds an arbitrary markup to the cost of producing the goods or service. The percent of the markup, however, must often be determined by one of the techniques described above.

A proper determination of price is also aided by breakeven analysis. This technique is based upon finding the point at which sales revenues exactly cover costs, as described in Chapter 12.

GOVERNMENT AND PRICES

The government watches and regulates prices

Federal and state governments have passed laws that influence pricing decisions. **Fair-trade laws** prohibit retailers from selling goods at a price lower than that set by the producer. These laws, which still exist in a few states, are supposed to protect small retailers from the competition of large stores that can afford to set lower prices because of their volume sales. Jewelry, some sporting goods, drugs, and tobacco products are examples of goods that are often priced according to fair-trade laws.

Certain federal provisions also affect pricing. The Robinson-Patman Act states that purchasers of the same quality and type of goods from one manufacturer or distributor must be charged the same price unless different prices do not restrict competition or are clearly justified by cost differences. Its intent was to eliminate price discrimination. Government efforts to establish the practice of unit pricing in retail stores also may have an effect on pricing decisions. **Unit pricing** helps consumers compare the prices of similar items by giving the price in a standard unit such as an ounce or a pound. It is much easier to compare a 10-ounce can at 45 cents with a 12-ounce can at 50 cents if the unit price is 4.5 cents an ounce on the first can and 4.2 cents an ounce on the second.

6   FUNCTIONS OF MARKETING MANAGERS

Marketing management requires more than just buying and selling

The marketing process includes a wide range of specific activities and duties. The relative importance of each may vary with different companies, but nearly every business firm is concerned with buying, selling, transporting, storing, risk-bearing, standardizing, grading and labeling, financing, and gathering and using information. (See Figure 7-3.)

Buying   Buying is an extremely critical concern for wholesale and retail companies. The success of these firms is very directly dependent on their purchasing agents' ability to anticipate consumer demand for particular goods. They must also be able to locate the best sources of supply for goods and to negotiate favorable terms in price and quality.

Selling   Selling is often seen as the core of the marketing function. All the other marketing activities ultimately aim at selling goods and services to produce income. Personal selling, sales promotion, advertis-

ACTION BRIEF

So Much for the Cost Factor.   *According to one study, product pricing has more to do with psychology than with cost analysis. A few examples cited: J. C. Penney prices its "plain pockets" jeans $4 less than the ones with the leather emblem; likewise, it sells its fox-embroidered leisure shirt for $5 less than the one with an alligator. Penney's pricing strategy: quality look-alikes at bargain prices. Proctor-Silex marks up its most expensive fabric iron $5 more than its nearest competitor, even though the cost hardly justifies it. Says the marketing manager: "There is a significant segment of the market that wants to buy the best, despite the cost." F. B. Rogers division of National Silver Industries, Inc., has established a reputation for quality. As a result, says the sales manager, "You can take any silver item, put 'Rogers' on it, and get $2 more for it."*

Source: Jeffrey H. Birnbaum, "Pricing of Products Is Still an Art," The Wall Street Journal, November 25, 1981, p. 29.

Figure 7-3
**Functions of marketing
management.**

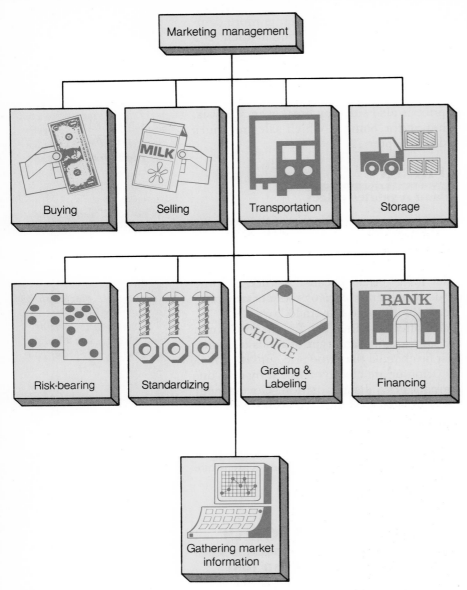

ing, demonstrations, and displays all contribute to this goal, as will be seen in Chapter 9.

Transportation Goods cannot be sold without transporting them to the point of sale and then to the ultimate consumer. Careful management of the transportation of products can bring significant savings in the cost of selling them. The vast network of transportation systems in the United States enables many firms to centralize their manufacturing facilities. This helps them to achieve economies of scale while still reaching customers in remote areas.

Storage Storage is required to keep goods until they are made available to consumers. Some goods, such as agricultural produce, must be stored because they are produced seasonally. Many wholesalers and

Issues & Highlights

Most consumers feel that life is difficult enough without faulty, irksome product packaging to add to their woes. What about bothersome things like the tiny toothpaste cap that drops down the sink? Or the aspirin tin that doesn't snap open when you "press the red dots"? Or the cereal that gets stale because the inner bag tears and won't reseal properly? Producers tend to ignore these problems if they believe that the package has the proper level of appeal to induce you to buy the product in the first place. A study of consumers, however, by Consumer Network, Inc., showed great dissatisfaction with the packaging of—among other items—luncheon meats, bacon, ice cream, snack chips, and nail polish. Another survey conducted by the Package Designers Council found that what consumers wanted most in packaging were storage life of unused portions, easy recognition of the package contents, and ease of resealing and storage. Manufacturers do not quickly change the packages to suit your interests because of the costs involved in new molds, dies, and handling equipment.

*Source: **Bill Abrams, "Packaging Often Irks Buyers But Firms Are Slow to Change,"** The Wall Street Journal, **January 28, 1981, p. 29.***

There are several steps open to dissatisfied consumers. Among them: complaint letters to retailers and manufacturers, return of the merchandise, collective consumer boycotts, legal action, or simply not to repurchase. Which action appeals most to you? Why?

retailers store goods near final buyers in order to avoid delays caused by transportation from the point of manufacture.

Risk-Bearing   Whenever goods are produced or bought to be sold, there is the risk that they cannot be sold profitably. Risk-bearing, then, is an inevitable function in any marketing activity. Efficient management, including careful market and cost analysis, will reduce but not eliminate this risk. Other risks, such as fire and theft, can be reduced through insurance.

Standardizing   The modern system of producing goods in one location to be sold to buyers in a wide area requires that products be standardized. This way, customers know what to expect from a product wherever they buy it. Safety razors, for instances, have their heads all made the same size so that when customers buy razor blades they know that the blades will fit.

Grading and Labeling   Grading and labeling have a similar purpose, allowing buyers to know the quality of goods without inspecting them. Meat that is graded "U.S. Choice" by government inspectors will have nearly the same quality and characteristics regardless of which producer it comes from.

Financing   Most companies must pay for the production or purchase of goods before they receive payment from customers. This requires financing. Money is often borrowed to pay for raw materials, transportation, or inventory. The loans are then repaid from income when the goods are resold to consumers. This system of financing production and inventory stabilizes the market, making goods available on a steadier basis.

Gathering Market Information   This is important to the management of all the other marketing activities. It may involve: (a) sophisticated research on the desires and buying habits of consumers, (b) automated systems giving frequent sales and inventory information, or (c) informal information gathering through contact with suppliers, dealers, and buyers. Without some means of gathering information, other marketing decisions cannot be made with any confidence.

7   MARKET SEGMENTATION AND MARKET RESEARCH

Dividing, simplifying, and understanding a diverse market

The marketing concept stresses tailoring products and marketing efforts to consumers—but consumers are a diverse group. To deal with this diversity, a technique called *market segmentation* has been developed which divides a market into smaller groups whose members are similar to each other (homogeneous) in one or more important ways. Once the market has been segmented—into the teenage, middle-income, or sports-minded market, for example—promotion and distribution methods and even new products may be tailored specifically to the different segments. (See Figure 7-4.)

As an aid in segmenting markets and understanding the effect of buyer diversity on product sales, managers often emphasize the study of demography and market research. **Demography** is the study of population statistics and subgroups within the population. It gives marketers data about the size of the population and its characteristics (age and sex composition, geographic location, personal income, spending patterns, and other factors) that affect buying patterns. **Market research** uses such methods as questionnaire surveys, consumer test panels, and observation of shopper behavior in stores to identify and characterize markets. A questionnaire survey uses a standardized set of questions to ask people about their preferences or their buying habits. A **consumer test panel** is a group of people gathered (by mail, by telephone, or in person) to get their reactions to new products and new product ideas. Such techniques give information about what kind of products will sell, what kinds of advertising and packaging are effective, and what influence price has on buying decisions.

Market research may also be used to forecast future trends in markets, but information for this purpose typically comes from studying data and trends in the national economy and analyzing the past and present performance of a particular industry or firm.

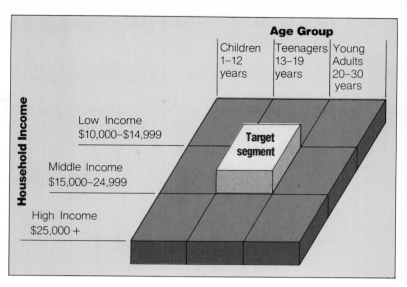

Figure 7-4
Example of market segmentation **showing a segment for TV-computer games targeted at teen-agers from middle-income homes.**

Key Concepts

1. The marketing concept rests on the belief that profits can be maximized by concentrating on the wants and needs of consumers and by marketing products for which there is a known demand.
2. The marketing mix involves the business functions that carry out the planning, pricing, distribution, and promotion of products.
3. A market exists when people have wants and needs combined with the willingness and ability to spend money to satisfy them. The general market for goods and services includes the consumer market and the industrial market.
    a.   The consumer market consists of people who buy products for their own use. The purchasing behavior of this market is affected by buying habits, motivation, and purchasing power. Products for the consumer market are traditionally divided into convenience goods, shopping goods, and specialty goods.
    b.   The industrial market consists of people and firms who buy goods and services that will be used to produce other products or in the daily operation of a business or institution.
4. Product planning is concerned with devising goods and services for which there is an anticipated demand.
5. Product pricing strategies are influenced by demand, competition, and government regulation. Typical practices are follow-the-leader, penetration, skimming, and cost-plus.
6. The responsibilities of marketing managers are to buy, sell, transport, store, bear risk, standardize, grade and label, finance, and gather and use marketing information.
7. Market segmentation involves splitting the to-

tal market into subgroups that are homogeneous in some way, while market research helps identify and characterize markets and forecast their future behavior. These activities help match products and marketing methods to consumer demands.

Review Questions

1. Define, identify, or explain each of the following key terms or phrases found on the pages indicated.

   brand   (p. 114)
   component parts   (p. 113)
   consumer goods   (p. 109)
   consumer test panel   (p. 121)
   convenience goods   (p. 112)
   cost-plus pricing   (p. 117)
   demography   (p. 121)
   discretionary income   (p. 111)
   disposable income   (p. 111)
   emotional motives   (p. 111)
   fair-trade laws   (p. 117)
   follow-the-leader pricing   (p. 116)
   industrial goods   (p. 109)
   market research   (p. 121)
   market segmentation   (p. 120)
   marketing concept   (p. 108)
   marketing mix   (p. 109)
   patronage motives   (p. 111)
   penetration pricing   (p. 116)
   primary needs   (p. 110)
   product distribution   (p. 109)
   product life cycle   (p. 115)
   product line   (p. 114)
   product placement   (p. 109)
   product planning   (p. 109)
   product pricing   (p. 115)
   product promotion   (p. 109)
   production concept   (p. 108)
   purchasing power   (p. 111)
   rational motives   (p. 110)
   raw materials   (p. 113)
   selective purchasing   (p. 110)
   selling concept   (p. 108)
   shopping goods   (p. 112)
   skimming   (p. 116)
   specialty goods   (p. 112)
   Standard Metropolitan Statistical Area
      (p. 110)
   trademark   (p. 115)
   unit pricing   (p. 117)

2. How does the marketing concept differ from earlier approaches to creating profits?
3. Describe the four major functions carried out in the marketing mix.
4. In the context of marketing strategy, what are the three main requirements that must be met for a market to exist?
5. How does the industrial market differ from the consumer market?
6. List three factors that marketing managers take into account when planning products.
7. At what stage of the product life cycle would you say that TV-computer games are now? Why?
8. Demand and competition are the strongest determinants of prices in our economy. How do they affect a marketer's pricing decisions?
9. What are fair-trade laws and what is the purpose of these laws?
10. What is the value and purpose of market segmentation and market research?

Case Critique 7-1
Pickle Power for Weight Watchers

When H. J. Heinz acquired Weight Watchers International, the pickle people decided to begin its marketing planning "at ground zero." Company researchers spent more than a year trying to revamp the frozen dinners line in order to make them tasty as well as low in calories. It re-examined its other related products as well, like its low-calorie dressings and sauces. To do so, it tried out many different recipes with a variety of customers. Then, Heinz studied the motivation of the potential buyers of low-calorie foods. Research showed that 67 percent of all Americans are "weight conscious." Many of these people "want to eat without feeling guilty." A significant portion of this population (38 percent) are "serious dieters." A smaller part (15 percent) are "cosmetic dieters." These are typically college-educated females, between 24 and 44 years old and especially concerned about their figures.

Based upon its research, Heinz decided to target its advertising differently to each part of the market, using a different appeal for the weight conscious, the serious dieters, and the cosmetic dieters. Next, the company took a hard look at the packaging of its products, its pricing policies, and its distribution system. Overseas, Heinz decided to use Schweppes to distribute its Weight Watch-

ers' diet sodas and Nabisco to distribute its Weight Watchers' breakfast cereals.

1. In what ways does this case illustrate the marketing concept and the marketing mix?
2. In dividing up its market into three classes of potential buyers, what marketing technique was the company using? Can you think of ways in which the advertising appeals might be effective without being different?
3. Heinz researchers studied how the low-calorie market was divided up in the United States and also how people responded to the taste of its products. Which aspect of marketing did this research focus on? Where would a consumer test panel have been most useful?

Source: Thomas Petzinger, Jr., "Heinz Tries to Reshape Demand for Weight Watchers' Products," *The Wall Street Journal,* July 17, 1980, p. 23.

Case Critique 7-2
The Shoes That Go "Swoosh"

What company sells more running shoes than anyone else? Nike, Inc. What company sells more athletic shoes than anyone else? Adidas. In a market that spends $1.5 billion on all kinds of athletic shoes in the United States and millions of dollars in Europe and Japan, you can't tell the leader without first determining what kinds of shoes you are talking about.

Nike transformed itself from a tiny importer of Japanese-made running shoes in 1970 to a major factor in all kinds of athletic shoes by 1980. Since then, it has tried to extend its leadership in running shoes to basketball, tennis, and even soccer shoes. To continue to grow, however, Nike has broadened its product line even further. It now makes children's shoes, work shoes, nonathletic leisure shoes, and sports' clothing.

To help launch its newer products, Nike continues to keep its name widely displayed. In the past, it had forged ties with professionals by asking them to help design the shoes and had also

signed great numbers of them to exclusive promotional contracts. It gives its shoes to many of the top college athletic teams and sponsors running clinics, amateur athletic events, and a women's professional tennis circuit. Nike's "Swoosh" trademark has made its moderately priced running shoes the "thing" for students to wear from grade school through college.

1. What is your reaction to the breadth of the Nike product line? Is it too broad, or not broad enough?
2. How would you classify Nike's athletic shoes as a consumer good? Why?
3. Which buying motive do you think is more powerful when people buy a pair of athletic shoes, the rational motive or the emotional motive?

Source: "Fitting the World in Sports' Shoes," *Business Week,* January 25, 1982, p. 73.

Chapter 8

Marketing Distribution Systems

1 DISTRIBUTION SYSTEMS PLACE PRODUCTS IN MARKETS

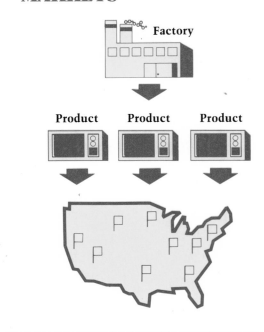

2 PRODUCTS FLOW THROUGH DISTRIBUTION CHANNELS

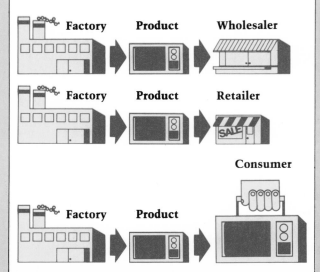

3 WHOLESALERS OPERATE BETWEEN PRODUCERS AND RETAILERS

Wholesaler

4 RETAILERS OPERATE BETWEEN WHOLESALERS AND CONSUMERS

Retailer

5 PHYSICAL DISTRIBUTION

Resolves storage, handling, and moving problems and places warehouses in optimum locations between producers and consumers.

6 DIFFERENT MODES OF TRANSPORTATION

Trucking   Rail

Pipeline   Water   Air

Learning Objectives

The purpose of this chapter is to explain the function of the marketing distribution process, and discuss the role of wholesalers and retailers, physical distribution strategies, and modes of transportation in this process.

As evidence of general comprehension, after completing this chapter you should be able to:

1. Relate the purpose of the marketing distribution system.
2. Recognize and explain the various distribution channels.
3. Distinguish between wholesalers and retailers and identify the various kinds of wholesaling operations.
4. Identify the various ways by which retailing ownership and operations can be classified.
5. Explain physical distribution strategy as it applies to warehousing costs.
6. Identify various modes of transportation and explain the advantages and disadvantages of each mode.

If your class is using SSweetco: Business Model and Activity File for Business in Action, see Chapter 8 in that book after you complete this chapter. There you will find exercises and activities to help you apply your learning to typical business situations.

Everything you buy when you go shopping has been made available through distribution systems. The sporting goods store that sells your tennis shoes may have bought them from a wholesaler 300 miles away. The wholesaler, in turn, may have bought thousands of similar pairs from the manufacturer in Boston or Los Angeles, or from an importer who got them in Italy or Korea. The couple with the craft store down the street sells their leather products directly to the public, but the leather they decorate and finish comes from an agent outside Chicago. Milk at the supermarket may have been produced by a dairy cooperative that buys it from a number of local farms, processes it, and then distributes it to stores in your part of the state.

You could not have bought the tennis shoes, the belt, or the milk without distribution systems. These systems include the wholesalers, distributors, agents, and retailers who buy and sell goods to make them available to consumers. These agencies are coordinated with the transportation companies—truckers, railroads, and others—that physically move goods to the market. Factors such as the type of product to be shipped and other matters, including the speed, cost, and accessibility of shipping modes, are considered in determining which particular method of physical transportation will be used. Product distribution, including physical transportation, is a marketing function that is fundamental to the functioning of business and to the economic well being of the country.

1 PURPOSE OF DISTRIBUTION SYSTEMS

Distribution systems make manufactured products available for purchase

Businesses set up distribution systems to make their products available to consumers. Almost everything that people buy is made by a company that specializes in producing a limited range of similar products. Distribution systems physically move these products from the producer to the buyer. Thus they enable stores to stock many kinds of specialized products for convenient purchase.

Product distribution requires distribution channels and physical transportation. **Distribution channels** are the means producers use to put their goods on the market. This may be done through wholesalers, retailers, or by selling directly to consumers. Transportation systems determine how goods are to be stored and transported to where they will be sold and ultimately used.

Product distribution adds value to goods by creating utility of place. To a person with a blowout, a new tire is worthless in the manufacturer's warehouse. It becomes valuable only after it has been brought to where it is accessible to the consumer. Product distribution makes goods more valuable by placing them where they can be bought and used by people who need them. As a consequence, each intermediate person or firm who handles a product also expects to retain a portion of the sales price, which increases at each exchange, as a profit for his or her efforts. These profits come from the price increase that takes place at each exchange. These price increases—or markups—vary at each stage of exchange and also from product to product, as shown in Figure 8-1.

2   DISTRIBUTION CHANNELS

Distribution channels: routes that products follow on the way to consumers

Distribution channels are the routes products follow as they are bought and sold on their way to final buyers. Many goods, especially those for the consumer market, are sold by the producer to intermediaries. *Intermediaries* are companies that perform the marketing functions of storing and selling in return for discounts from the producer or potential profits from markups when they resell the goods. These intermediaries perform an indispensable service for today's businesses. A manufacturer in Ohio may wish to sell shoelaces to shoe stores, shoe repair shops, grocery stores, sporting goods shops, department stores, and variety stores across the country. The shoelace maker probably could not profitably sell to, supply, and bill each of these stores individually, as the cost of maintaining an account is very high. The solution to this problem is for the manufacturer to sell to intermediaries. The manufacturer's marketers might sell to one wholesaler who supplies shoe stores nationwide. Sporting goods distributors might buy and resell to local shops. Chain stores might buy large quantities to reship to their many local outlets. All of these intermediaries take over some of the burden of marketing from the original producer. The specific channels that a producer might choose depend on the type of product and on the size and kind of market, as illustrated in Figure 8-2.

CONSUMER CHANNELS

Intermediaries dominate consumer channels

The most common channel for distributing consumer goods is the traditional path from manufacturer to wholesaler to retailer to consumer. This is called *indirect distribution* because intermediaries move the goods from producer to consumer. Some companies use *direct distribu-*

Figure 8-1
How intermediaries share the dollars consumers spend on food.

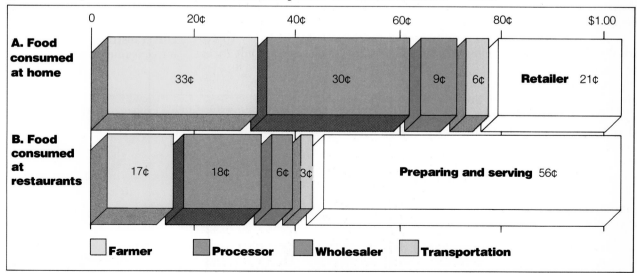

Source: "Food Marketing," *Agricultural Outlook*, U.S. Department of Agriculture, March 1983, p. 14.

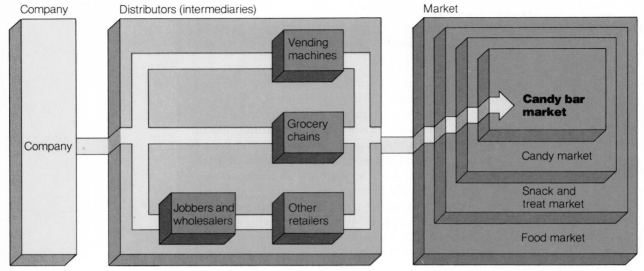

Source: Philip Kotler, *Marketing Management: Analysis, Planning, and Control,* 2d ed., Prentice-Hall, Inc., Englewood Cliffs, New Jersey, 1972, p. 32. Reprinted by permission.

Figure 8-2
Example of distribution channels selected by a candy company to deliver goods to the candy bar market.

tion channels, selling their products to ultimate buyers with no intermediaries involved. This approach is less common for consumer goods than it is for industrial goods, but many companies combine it with traditional indirect distribution to reach specific market segments.

Direct Distribution   The form of direct distribution most familiar to consumers is *direct mail.* Consumer goods are shipped directly to the customer's home. Sales are solicited either through the mail, television, telephone, or through coupon advertisements in magazines. Books and records, in particular, have been successfully sold using this method. Selling and distribution costs are generally very high, however.

Door-to-door personal selling is another means of direct distribution that has been used for products like cosmetics and encyclopedias. The goods may either be delivered by salespeople or shipped after an order has been taken. Sales costs are high with this method as well.

Some manufacturers maintain retail stores that sell directly to customers. These are called *manufacturer's outlets.* They have the advantage of returning retail profits to the manufacturer and may sometimes generate a large volume of business. The disadvantages of these outlets are that they require a large capital investment, compared with other distribution methods, and they involve the manufacturer in the specialized management problems of retailing. Figure 8-3 shows direct channels for distributing consumer goods.

Figure 8-3
Direct distribution channels for consumer goods.

Indirect Distribution   Some producers sell goods to retail stores that resell them to consumers. Automobile and home appliance manu-

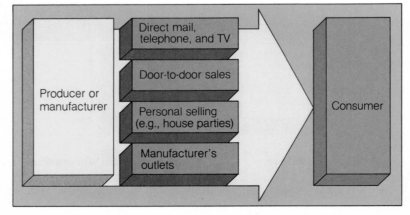

facturers are good examples. This practice gives the manufacturer more control over the marketing of products, often provides faster distribution of new models or styles, and helps to insure that the goods will be aggressively promoted. It also requires the manufacturer to deal directly with a large number of individual stores.

Important advantages of the manufacturer-wholesaler-retailer-consumer distribution channel account for its widespread use. The *wholesaler* saves both manufacturers and retailers the complications and expenses of dealing with large numbers of accounts. Wholesalers buy a variety of goods in substantial quantities from different manufacturers. They then resell smaller quantities of different goods to individual retailers. As a result, manufacturers deal directly with fewer points of sale, and retailers work with fewer points of purchase. Wholesalers take up some of the marketing functions of manufacturers, and retailers can keep a smaller stock of goods since resupply from wholesalers is convenient and rapid.

Distribution through chain stores or buyer's *cooperatives* works in a similar way and has some of the same advantages. The chain provides central purchasing facilities and curtails expenses by buying in large quantities. Most chains have their own warehouses and sometimes their own transportation facilities.

The various indirect distribution channels for consumer goods are illustrated in Figure 8-4.

ACTION BRIEF

Co-op's No Turkey in the Straw.   *To city folks, the farmers' cooperative brings an "aw-shucks" vision of Pete, Hiram, and Chloe working together for the common good. The picture may, in part, be true. But today the co-op is very big business. And the biggest of them all is Farmland Industries. It operates in 15 midwestern states, has 2,300 local co-ops, with about 500,000 farmers and ranchers participating. Sales each year come to more than $3 billion. Farmland not only purchases basic supplies, hardware, and the like for resale to its members, it also helps them sell their produce to firms that resell assembled crops to the big food processors like General Mills, Central Soya, and General Foods.*

Source: *Cynthia E. Hardie, "Co-op Effort Binds Farmers," Advertising Age, December 3, 1979, p. S–10.*

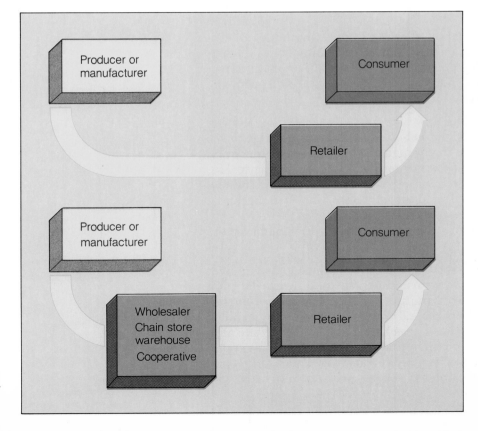

**Figure 8-4
Common indirect
distribution channels for
consumer goods.**

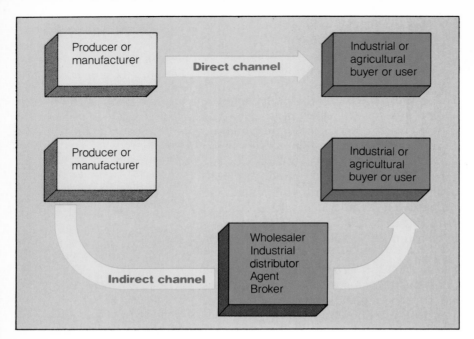

Figure 8-5
Distribution channels for goods sold to the industrial and agricultural markets.

INDUSTRIAL CHANNELS

Direct selling predominates

Goods for the industrial market also have direct and indirect distribution channels. Direct selling and distribution predominate in this market, however. Figure 8-5 shows the most often used direct and indirect channels for products for the industrial market. (It also illustrates the direct and indirect channels used for agricultural products.)

Direct Distribution   The flow of technical information between buyer and seller in the industrial market often makes it impossible to use a wholesaler. The high price of many industrial goods—machinery and large quantities of raw materials, for example—also makes it practical for producers to devote more of their own staff's time to selling to individual accounts. Producers of industrial goods usually have a smaller number of potential customers. This makes it easier to deal with them without intermediaries. For these reasons direct distribution is popular in the industrial market.

Indirect Distribution   Some industrial suppliers do use indirect distribution. Expendable supplies, such as paper, business forms, data processing supplies, as well as office furniture—are sold through wholesalers. Tools, small parts, and electrical and plumbing supplies are handled by industrial distributors. The advantages for buyers and sellers are similar to those for consumer goods. Other kinds of intermediaries also operate in the industrial market. Brokers, agents, and manufacturers' representatives may perform various roles for buyers and sellers in setting up the final exchange of goods.

DISTRIBUTION OF AGRICULTURAL PRODUCTS

Specialized intermediaries prevail

Farm products often have complex distribution channels. Farmers sometimes sell directly to consumers at "pick-your-own" orchards or roadside stands. More often, however, farm produce must be processed before it is used by consumers. Farmers sell to an intermediary such as a granary, dairy or fruit cooperative, or livestock buyer. The intermediaries then resell the goods to processors. The output of the processing of food is then distributed much as other consumer goods. Brokers and agents often play the same roles in the distribution of agricultural produce as in the industrial market. (See Figure 8-5.)

3   WHOLESALERS

Wholesalers link producers and retailers

Distribution for many companies is often wholly dependent upon the use of wholesalers and retailers. These two kinds of intermediaries are distinguished mainly by how their customers will use the goods they buy. Wholesalers sell to companies or individuals who will either directly resell the products or process them further and then resell them. Retailers, on the other hand, sell their goods almost entirely to the ultimate consumers. Wholesale and retail operations both can take a variety of forms. The wholesaling function is performed by merchant wholesalers, agents and brokers, assemblers, chain store warehouses, and cooperative wholesalers. They perform for the producer many of the marketing management functions described earlier in Chapter 7 under "Functions of Marketing Managers."

MERCHANT WHOLESALERS

They take ownership before reselling

Merchant wholesalers may best represent the true wholesaling process. They buy goods in quantity from many different manufacturers and generally resell them in different quantities at a profit to other wholesalers, to retailers, or to other companies. They simplify selling for the producer and buying for the retailer. Merchant wholesalers are often divided into categories according to the types of services they offer. *Full-service wholesalers* usually have a regular sales program, allow credit purchases, assist with transportation, and perform most of the other marketing functions, whereas *limited-function wholesalers* perform few functions besides buying and reselling products. They may provide a specialized or limited range of goods on a cash-and-carry basis.

AGENTS AND BROKERS

They operate on commissions

Agents and brokers differ from merchant wholesalers in that agents and brokers do not actually purchase the goods they sell. They facilitate

ACTION BRIEF

Wholesalers Think Big, Very Big.   *When queried about grocery marketing trends, wholesale executives gave their most enthusiastic votes for large-format merchandising. That is, they saw convenience stores (30,000 plus outlets in the United States), warehouse stores (products displayed in their shipping containers), and superstores (100,000 square feet interiors, about double the size of the largest conventional supermarkets) as having the most promise for the future. The executives were less impressed, by far, with conventional supermarkets. Wholesalers gave an 18 to 20 percent rating of excellent prospects to each of the first three formats, only 5 percent to the typical supermarket. Obviously, the opportunity to make big shipments to one chain or to a single location appeals to the wholesalers.*

Source: *Theodore J. Gage, "Inventory of Formats,"* Advertising Age, *April 27, 1981, p. S–2.*

sales by personal selling. Agents and brokers help develop specifications, assist in negotiations, and sometimes set up transportation and financing. *Selling agents* handle nearly the entire marketing function for a company and sell its entire output. *Manufacturer's agents* sell only part of a company's output and engage in direct selling efforts while the company handles other marketing functions, including advertising, shipping, and billing. *Brokers* may represent either buyers or sellers. Their main function is as an intermediary in specialized or complex marketing situations. Brokers usually receive a commission for their services.

OTHER KINDS OF WHOLESALERS
Each serves a special purpose

Wholesalers who specialize in buying produce from individual farmers and putting together large quantities for processing and distribution are called *assemblers.* They make it possible for a cheese manufacturer, for example, to collect all of the milk needed for production without having to deal with hundreds of individual farmers. Assemblers also deal with forest products and certain other goods.

Many chain stores perform the wholesaling function for themselves by maintaining centralized warehouses. They save money by buying goods in quantity directly from the producer and then redistributing them in smaller quantities to the chain's retail outlets. To gain this kind of advantage for themselves, independent retailers sometimes band together to set up a wholesaling cooperative. As the member-owners of this cooperative, which functions much like the chain store warehouses, the retailers are said to be part of a *cooperative chain.*

4   RETAILERS

Retailers sell directly to consumers

The type of intermediary most familiar to consumers is the *retailer.* These are companies or individuals who buy products for resale to ultimate consumers. Retail outlets range in size from sidewalk stands to ten-story department stores and sell everything from candy bars to cabin cruisers. Retail outlets also sell services. Many deliver goods, allow purchases on credit, and give information and advice. For some retail businesses, such as restaurants, the service component—cooking and serving food—may be a very significant part of the retailer's contribution. The great diversity of retail outlets may be organized in several ways: by types of ownership, by types of operation, and by types of goods and services provided.

TYPES OF OWNERSHIP
Most are independent proprietorships

Most retail stores are sole proprietorships or partnerships that operate independently. They buy goods from wholesalers or manufacturers and resell them, providing whatever goods and services they believe will be profitable. A second important class of retail outlets is *chain stores.* These are companies, often corporations, with a number of retail stores at different locations. The central management of a chain store usually handles some or all of the purchasing for all of the outlets and manages storage and transportation of goods. Individual stores have varying degrees of independence in different chains. Retailers that function both as independent stores and chains are called **voluntary chains.** Independent stores may band together, or join an existing group of similar stores, to gain certain advantages of chains, such as volume buying, without giving up their individual ownership.

Franchising, as was discussed in Chapter 4 under "Other Forms of Business," has also become a major form of retail ownership.

TYPES OF OPERATION

Five types prevail

Perhaps the classic example of a retail store is the **general store,** so important during the early part of this century as a marketplace for consumer goods. Stores like this carried many different kinds of merchandise and served a local market. General stores still exist in many rural areas, but they have largely lost their economic importance. Stores that sell only one type of merchandise, such as food, hardware, books, and drugs, are called **single-line stores.** They usually have a wide selection within their particular line and often give extra services such as delivery and credit. A subcategory of the single-line store is the **specialty shop.** These are even more specialized and carry a narrow line of goods. Some stores, for instance, carry only knives but have a vast selection of hunting and camping knives, pocketknives, and all kinds of cutlery for the kitchen, often made by scores of different manufacturers. Other specialty stores may sell only denim clothes or hiking boots, citizens' band radios, or any of dozens of other specialized lines of goods. A **department store** may be viewed as a large version of the general store. Department stores try to carry a variety of different kinds of merchandise and offer many choices within each line. Most department stores stress service and offer a wide range of aids and conveniences to shoppers. **Variety stores** also offer a diverse range of goods. The selection, however, is not as great as in a department store. Variety stores often specialize in lower-priced merchandise.

Some retail outlets are not stores. **Mail-order houses** sell directly to consumers and are like retail stores except that orders are placed by mail and goods are sent or shipped by freight. Door-to-door and vending machine selling are other kinds of retail distribution that do not use a local store.

TYPES OF GOODS OR SERVICES

Classification by the U.S. Bureau of the Census

The U.S. Bureau of the Census further classifies retail outlets according to the kinds of goods they sell. The categories include food stores, eating and drinking establishments, general merchandise stores, clothing and accessories dealers, furniture and appliance stores, cars and automotive supplies dealers, gasoline service stations, sellers of building materials, hardware and farm equipment dealers, drug and proprietary stores, and other retail stores. Although the classification is based on the type of goods sold, these operations also differ significantly as to the kind and amount of service offered. A restaurant may buy seafood, meat, and vegetables for resale, but its most important contribution is cooking and serving the food. A gas station often also gives a great deal of service beyond buying and selling gas, oil, and other automotive products.

TRENDS IN RETAILING

High volume, minimum service, and low prices

Just as the local general store is being replaced by other kinds of retail outlets, new patterns of retail selling are also emerging today. One of the most noticeable trends has been the move toward offering less service in exchange for lower prices on goods. Food and drug supermarkets and self-service variety stores are good examples. Discount houses operate on the same principle, usually selling more expensive items such as home appliances. Warehouse showrooms for furniture and similar goods are another example of the same trend. These retailers try to sell at the lowest possible price by reducing overhead (such as costs for attractive stores, large, trained staffs, delivery, and allowing purchases on credit) and often by serving as their own wholesaler. Catalog stores that specialize in appliances and related products operate in a similar fashion.

Another trend is the increasing popularity of shopping centers. These are collections of separately owned stores in one location. The largest shopping centers offer a wide selection of convenience, shopping, and specialty goods in a variety of stores that range in size from low-service discount outlets to full-service department stores. The recent growth of vending machine sales must also be considered a trend. Mechanical vending devices are being designed for ever wider lines of products.

5   PHYSICAL DISTRIBUTION STRATEGIES

Problems with storage, handling, and movement

A knowledge of wholesale and retail intermediaries, their operations, and the costs that they charge is essential to developing a workable marketing distribution system. Just as important is the design and maintenance of a system for the economical and efficient physical distribution of goods and services to customers. It is the physical distribution manager who has the responsibility for devising and implementing strategies that provide for the orderly physical flow of goods and services to consumers. A physical distribution manager must resolve questions like:

■ Where will *inventory* (goods awaiting sale) be stored and in what quantity?

■ How will goods be shipped to the points of production, storage facilities, and points of purchase?

■ How will they be loaded, unloaded, and moved within the plant or storage locations?

■ How will control be maintained over how much inventory is on hand and where it is located?

The first two issues are the most important in establishing a physical distribution system. Loading, unloading, and moving goods within the plant is called **materials handling.** Careful planning and management of this function can be important in reducing costs and avoiding breakage and delay. Controlling inventory is critical to the financial position of the firm. It also contributes greatly to customer satisfaction by avoiding delays and unfilled orders. These latter functions are discussed in detail in Chapter 11.

STORAGE OF INVENTORIES

Minimum inventory with maximum availability is the goal

The first task involved in physical distribution is deciding where goods are to be stored while they are awaiting sale. Some will be held at intermediaries' storage facilities, some at the manufacturer's warehouse, and some at the point of manufacture. The distribution manager's goal is to maintain inventory levels as low as possible without causing unfilled orders or delay to customers (see Figure 8-6). Inventory represents money that has been spent (by purchasing from the manufacturer) and not yet re-earned (by selling the goods). One important aspect of inventory control is warehouse location.

Warehouse Location   Managers have several alternatives when establishing a warehousing system. They may own and operate their own warehouses at any number of locations, they may use public warehouses operated by other companies for profit, or they may use a combination of the two. The location of warehouses and the amount of inventory to be kept in each is important. Managers must try to balance the costs of maintaining a high inventory with the costs of running out of goods and being unable to fill orders. Products must be stored at locations that will reduce delays caused by shipping. At the same time, marketers must avoid establishing so many distribution points that they become inefficient and difficult to manage.

**Figure 8-6
Three factors that must be balanced in inventory decisions by the physical distribution system.**

6   MODES OF TRANSPORTATION

Efficient transportation can cut costs

Many business managers today believe that the transportation of goods is one major area in which operating efficiency can be significantly improved. Decades of emphasis on increasing production while lowering costs may have pushed improvements in manufacturing efficiency nearly as far as possible with present technology. Physical distribution ac-

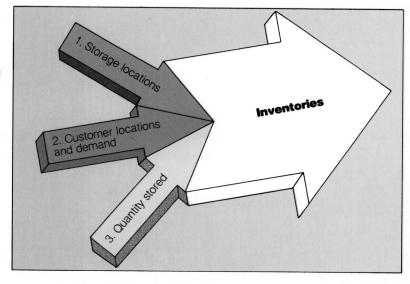

Issues & Highlights

Telephone marketing in the 1980s became the darling of the direct marketers. It was stimulated by the ubiquitous Watts lines, collect calling, toll-free 800 numbers, and credit cards. Most consumers enjoy the convenience of placing such calls themselves. It is a different story, however, when a consumer is disturbed—and then pressured—by a salesperson using the telephone marketing channel. Direct mail is pretty inoffensive. The garbage can is only an arm's length away. But the telephone, when used by a persistent huckster, can be a real nuisance. To this end, a bill was put before Congress to curtail the use of the telephone for direct marketing. One provision was to insist that the telephone companies give their customers a year to express a preference not to receive unsolicited commercial calls. However, this bill was never enacted into law.

Source: **Theodore J. Gage, "Telephone Rings in the Last Frontier,"** Advertising Age, *January 21, 1980, p. S-20.*

Is telephone usage of this sort a right of free speech or an invasion of a citizen's right to privacy? How do you feel about this issue?

counts for as much as 10 to 40 percent of the total sales price of common goods. Savings in transportation costs can, therefore, have a significant effect on prices and profits.

SELECTION OF MODES

Advantages and disadvantages of each method

Products can be transported by many means: rail, air, truck, pipeline, steamship, and barge. Table 8-1 summarizes some of the general advantages and disadvantages of different transportation modes. Decisions about how to ship goods are influenced by a number of important factors. The type of product is a basic determinant. Iron ore is too heavy and is needed in quantities that are too large to be shipped by air. Television sets cannot be transported by pipeline. Speed is often important because it

TABLE 8-1
Advantages and Disadvantages of Major Modes of Transportation

Mode of Transportation	Advantages	Disadvantages
Railroad	Low cost shipment of heavy goods over long distances. Reliable schedules. Little damage to goods.	Access to terminals sometimes difficult. No service in many small towns. Less suitable for small shipments and short distances.
Motor trucks	Provide door-to-door delivery. Can ship to and from nearly any point. Frequent service. Little damage to goods.	Less suitable for shipping very large quantities and for some bulky or large goods. More affected by weather than railroads.
Water transportation	Low cost. Can handle very large quantities.	Slow speed. Infrequent service. Not available in many places. Damaged goods more likely.
Airlines	High speed. Frequent service. Little damage to goods.	High cost. Access to terminals sometimes difficult. Not available in many small towns. Schedules affected by weather.
Pipeline	Low cost. Continual delivery. Not affected by weather.	Only suitable for liquids or gases. Slow delivery.

reduces delays and may allow companies to keep a smaller inventory. The cost of shipping has a direct effect on selling price and on profits. A shipping method that has reliable schedules and nearby terminal facilities is desirable.

An important consideration is how well a mode of transportation suits other features of a product's distribution system. A company that ships goods to only two or three intermediaries has far different requirements from one that ships directly to hundreds of individual retail stores in towns and cities. Even a feature so basic as transportation costs must be considered only as a part of the whole. A number of companies have found that the extra cost of shipping by air was justified by its speed. Rapid deliveries by air allows the elimination of many warehouses close to markets and means that total inventory on hand can be reduced.

FREIGHT RATES

Weight and distance determine rates

Rates for shipping goods by any method are usually based on the weight of the goods and how far they are to be shipped. Other charges, such as loading, unloading, and insurance, must be added to determine the total cost. Railroad freight rates vary for different kinds of goods. Different shipments may be charged class rates, exception rates, or commodity rates. In setting some rates, goods are grouped into classes based on their size, weight, value, perishability, and other characteristics. Goods that fall into one of these classes are charged the *class rate.* For various reasons, particularly the desire to compete with other shipping modes, railroads offer lower rates for certain goods. These are called *exception rates.* Certain other basic goods that are regularly shipped in large quantities, such as grain and coal, are given *commodity rates.*

SHIPPING TERMINOLOGY

It pays to know who pays the freight

When price quotations are given for goods, it is common to specify who must pay shipping costs. *FOB factory,* or FOB city of origin, means that the buyer must pay shipping costs, but the seller will load the goods at their point of origin. FOB stands for "free on board." *FOB destination* means that the seller will pay transportation costs except for unloading at the destination.

GOVERNMENT REGULATION OF TRANSPORTATION

Regulation is intense and complex

Governments have assumed the right of regulating transportation companies from early times. States usually have bureaus to oversee *intrastate transportation*—transportation within their borders. They often delegate some of their authority to local governments. Most towns and cities directly regulate local bus lines and taxi companies. The federal government has regulatory authority over transportation and commerce that crosses state borders. The Interstate Commerce Commission, created in 1877, is one of the most important federal regulatory agencies. It has the power to affect rates, schedules, service, safety features, mergers, and other decisions of transportation companies that engage in interstate commerce. It also has legal authority over trucks and buses, railroads, pipelines, ships, and barges, whenever they move across state borders.

The Civil Aeronautics Board (CAB) and the Federal Aviation Agency (FAA) regulate air travel, and the Federal Maritime Board and the Maritime Administration regulate oceangoing shipping vessels. The Federal Power Commission has authority over natural gas mains and the interstate transmission of electricity. The complex regulations of these and other agencies must always be considered when making physical transportation decisions, as these regulations affect shippers as well as transportation companies.

During the period from 1976 to 1980, Congress enacted legislation that greatly relaxed the regulation of air transportation and also restricted the power of the CAB. Similarly, the Motor Carrier Act of 1981 sharply reduced federal regulation of trucking operations.

Key Concepts

1. Marketing distribution systems make products available to buyers by using distribution channels and various modes of transportation. Product distribution adds value to goods by giving them utility of place.

2. Distribution channels are the paths that goods follow on their way to markets. The channels are said to be direct when the goods pass straight from the producer to the ultimate consumer. The channels are said to be indirect when products pass through various intermediaries. Intermediaries may be wholesalers or retailers.

3. Wholesalers distribute goods to buyers who are not the final consumers, such as retailers, other wholesalers, and companies that will further process the goods.

4. Retailers buy goods to resell in the consumer market. Retail outlets differ in types of ownership, types of operation, and types of goods and services provided.

5. Physical distribution controls the way goods are stored and moved from producer to points of sale. Managers try to balance warehouse locations, inventory size, and transportation methods to provide the best service at the lowest cost.

6. Choice of transportation methods depends on the type of product to be shipped and on other factors such as speed, cost, and accessibility of shipping modes. All of these must be considered in relation to other distribution elements like the number of wholesalers or retailers, the number and location of warehouses, and so forth.

Review Questions

1. Define, explain, or identify each of the following key terms and phrases found on the pages indicated.

   assembler (p. 132)
   broker (p. 132)
   chain store (p. 132)

   class rate (p. 138)
   commodity rate (p. 138)
   cooperatives (p. 129)
   cooperative chain (p. 132)
   department store (p. 133)
   direct distribution (p. 127)
   direct mail (p. 128)

distribution channels (p. 126)
exception rate (p. 138)
FOB destination (p. 138)
FOB factory (p. 138)
full-service wholesaler (p. 131)
general store (p. 133)
indirect distribution (p. 127)
intermediary (p. 127)
intrastate transportation (p. 138)
inventory (p. 134)
limited-function wholesaler (p. 131)
mail-order house (p. 133)
manufacturer's agent (p. 132)
manufacturer's outlets (p. 128)
materials handling (p. 135)
retailer (p. 132)
selling agent (p. 132)
single-line store (p. 133)
specialty shop (p. 133)
variety store (p. 133)
voluntary chains (p. 133)
wholesaler (p. 129)

2. What are the two main decisions a marketing manager makes in setting up a distribution system?
3. What is the difference between a direct distribution channel and an indirect one?
4. Describe a typical distribution channel from farm to corner grocery store for a common product like packaged frozen corn.
5. How do wholesalers help producers and retailers with distribution channels?
6. What is the difference between a merchant wholesaler and a manufacturer's agent?
7. In what ways is a department store like a general store? A variety shop?
8. Describe some local examples of the trend of retailers toward obtaining a high volume of sales at low prices.
9. What is the general goal of marketers when deciding where to store inventories and what amount to keep at each location?
10. Compare the advantages and disadvantages of shipping by rail with shipping by truck.

Case Critique 8-1
One-Stop Fashion Merchandising

When apparel manufacturers, especially those in the fashion trades, want to get their goods to market, they usually sell first to a retailer. Typically, manufacturers display their designs at a fashion show. Retailers from all over the country attend the show and select the merchandise they wish to purchase. When the purchase is consummated, the manufacturer ships directly to the retailer, who in turn sells the clothing to the ultimate consumer.

It is a common practice also for manufacturers to use the services of another type of intermediary—wholesalers, agents, or brokers—to get goods to the market.

To facilitate the work of the manufacturer's own salespeople as well as wholesalers and other intermediaries, some very large cities, like New York and Chicago, provide special facilities, such as a merchandise market. A good example is the gigantic one in Dallas, called The Apparel Mart. It is a six-story building that covers four city blocks (larger than 37 football fields). Inside, there is an immense showroom filled with display booths and a theater where fashions are modeled. Representatives of some 10,000 lines of clothing, western wear, and accessories for men, women, and children are typically on duty during a seasonal show. At shows, as many as 100,000 buyers from retail stores see the latest fashions, talk to designers, representatives of manufacturers, and wholesalers. Firms that exhibit or "write business" at the mart pay rent for their display space. All merchandise is shipped, as usual, from the manufacturer, either directly to a retailer or through a wholesaler to the retailer.

1. The Apparel Mart is part of a channel of indirect distribution. What service does it perform that makes it worth the cost of space rental by the manufacturer or wholesaler?
2. Why would a retail store buyer travel to a merchandise mart to make a purchase when it might be assumed that a manufacturer's salesperson should call on the retail store?

3. How does a person who buys his or her clothing at a retail shop benefit from the function performed by the merchandise mart?

Source: Thomas W. Lippman, "Dallas Has Own 'Garment District' in Texas-Size Apparel Mart," *The Washington Post,* June 1, 1982, p. D–1.

Case Critique 8-2
Do You Know the Muffin Man?

A hundred years ago, the distribution of Thomas' English Muffins was a very simple business. Sam Thomas baked the muffins in the basement of his home and then sold them to a muffin vendor. The muffin vendor would, in turn, sell them to people as he or she walked down the street. Later on, Thomas opened a retail bake shop on the first floor of his home and also delivered his muffins by horse-cart to local restaurants.

Today, Thomas' sells $100 million of baked goods each year. It no longer operates a retail bake shop. It does, however, still deliver its muffins by truck to retail stores, mainly supermarkets, directly from its manufacturing bakeries. The muffins now come in cornmeal, sourdough, or whole wheat and are as frequently eaten as a hamburger roll or pizza base as for breakfast.

With few exceptions, Thomas' does not use wholesalers. Its plants are in New Jersey, Maryland, and California. This poses a problem since shelf life of the muffins is only about 10 days, and the company believes that its bakeries can be no more than 1,000 miles from its farthest customer.

1. Why might it not be a good idea for Thomas' to set up a network of wholesalers with intermediate warehouses to handle its products?
2. Why would Thomas' use trucks for delivering its products rather than train or air service?
3. What changes will Thomas' have to make if it is to extend its markets broadly throughout the United States?

Source: Cecelia Lentini, "S. B. Thomas Samples New Muffin Markets," *Advertising Age,* April 7, 1981, p. S-29.

Chapter 9
Marketing
Promotion

1 THE FUNCTION OF MARKETING PROMOTION

is to push products

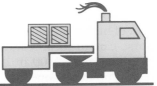

and/or pull products through distribution channels

2 THE PROMOTIONAL MIX

● Advertising

■ Selling

▲ Sales Promotion

3 PERSONAL SELLING

4 ADVERTISING
supports personal selling and influences buyers

5 ADVERTISING MEDIA
stimulates in many forms

Radio, television, billboards, print, etc.

6 SALES PROMOTION
complements personal selling and advertising

**Samples,
Contests,
Coupons,
Etc.**

7 SOCIETY REGULATES AND CHALLENGES THE VALUE OF ADVERTISING

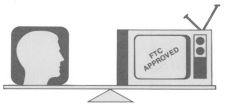

Learning Objectives

The purpose of this chapter is to explain the function and the objectives of marketing promotion, describe the role of personal selling, sales management, and advertising in promotion, and outline some of the methods and techniques employed in sales promotion.

As evidence of general comprehension, after studying this chapter you should be able to:

1. *Define the promotional mix and distinguish between pushing and pulling strategies.*
2. *Recognize the factors that influence promotion objectives and strategies.*
3. *Distinguish between selling and nonselling functions in the selling profession, and describe the nature of various sales jobs and positions.*
4. *Outline the five classes of advertising.*
5. *Recognize the factors that influence the selection of advertising media.*
6. *Explain six specific techniques utilized in sales promotion.*
7. *Identify the major government agency that regulates advertising and debate the value of advertising for the economy and for society in general.*

If your class is using SSweetco: Business Model and Activity File for Business in Action, see Chapter 9 in that book after you complete this chapter. There you will find exercises and activities to help you apply your learning to typical business situations.

If a club you belong to were to put you in charge of promoting an amateur variety show it is presenting, you would face a challenge. First, no one except the club members would know that the show is to be held. Second, even though people usually enjoy locally produced shows, they need persuasion to buy tickets. Several coordinated efforts would probably be necessary to approach the problem. You might send news releases or make personal visits to newspapers and radio and television stations in your area. These media might consider your event newsworthy, especially if it benefits a charity. They might also publish or broadcast general announcements of community events. You might place paid advertisements in the same media to inform people about the show and interest them in buying tickets. Advertising and publicity alone would sell some tickets through your ticket offices, but you would probably need to do some direct selling as well. Club members could sell tickets on downtown streets, at shopping centers, and door-to-door. Advertising would reinforce these personal selling efforts and make them more successful. You might also decide that door prizes would generate more interest or that offering free tickets as prizes on a radio contest would produce free publicity.

These efforts at promoting your club's variety show demonstrate the elements of promotion: selling, advertising, and sales promotion. Almost all formal organizations use some kind of promotion in their activities. Promotion is one of the essential marketing functions that allow businesses to operate.

1   THE FUNCTION OF MARKETING PROMOTION

Promotion uses a three-part mix to move products through distribution channels

As in the example of the amateur variety show, professional marketers try to establish the right mix of promotion efforts to sell their products. There are three major promotion tools:

- *Personal selling,* which involves presenting goods or services to potential customers on a person-to-person basis.
- *Advertising,* which is a sales presentation delivered through communications vehicles known as the *media.*
- *Sales promotion,* which includes specialized techniques used to back up selling and advertising: such as contests and store displays.

THE PUSH-PULL EFFECT

Promotion pushes and/or pulls

The promotion techniques described above may be combined in different ways for different products and markets. Two common strategies are to push goods through distribution channels and/or to pull them through.

In the *pushing strategy,* products are promoted strongly to wholesalers and retailers in an effort to persuade them to sell the products aggres-

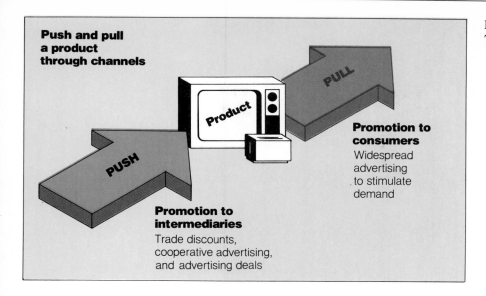

Figure 9-1
Tandem promotion strategy.

sively in the market. This approach stresses personal selling to intermediaries. Producers give trade discounts, help to pay for advertising (they give **cooperative advertising allowances**), and often provide selling materials, such as brochures, posters, and so forth. Selling to intermediaries is emphasized so as to insure that the products will be widely available to consumers.

The **pulling strategy** attempts to stimulate a strong consumer demand which will, in turn, influence intermediaries to distribute products widely. This approach emphasizes advertising more than personal selling. The idea behind this strategy is that if direct consumer advertising convinces people that they want to buy a specific product, they will ask for it in stores. The stores will then order it from wholesalers to meet the demand. Products are thus pulled through distribution channels by strong consumer demand.

Most marketers use both strategies for common consumer goods. (See Figure 9-1.) They may, however, emphasize either pushing or pulling for a particular item. The pushing strategy, with its personal approach, is more common in promoting products to the industrial market.

2 PROMOTION OBJECTIVES

Promotion campaigns require a unified strategy

To be successful, promotion efforts must be integrated. Advertising, selling, and sales promotion must work together and reinforce one another. The entire coordinated promotion effort for a product or group of products is called a **promotion campaign.** Campaigns try to maintain the right promotion mix for every product. In setting up campaigns, marketers use planning and analysis to suit promotion activities to the nature of the product and company. They specify objectives and devise promotion strategies to meet them.

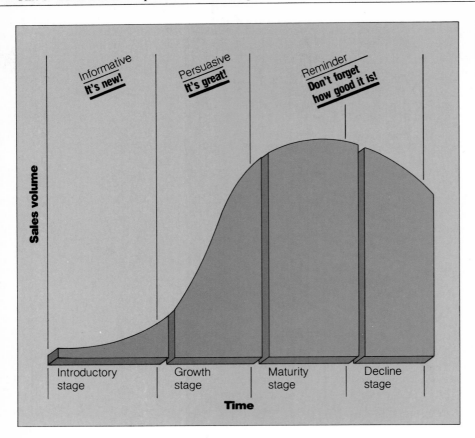

Figure 9-2
Different kinds of advertising
for different stages of the
product life cycle.

INFLUENCING FACTORS

The product, its life cycle, and costs are determinants

The kind of product and the market to which it will be sold are important in choosing a promotion strategy. Generally, advertising rather than personal selling is used to promote consumer products, while the reverse is the case for the industrial market. Goods and services for the industrial market typically have promotion campaigns that emphasize personal selling. They use advertising and sales promotion only for support. Even for consumer goods, companies that produce high-priced goods often stress personal selling or use an expensive combination of selling and extensive advertising.

The present stage of a product in its life cycle also affects promotion needs. (See Figure 9-2.) The introduction of a product is usually accompanied by **informative advertising.** Its purpose is to generate an initial demand by describing the features of the product and making it recognizable to consumers. As a product reaches the growth and maturity stages, **persuasive advertising** may be used to improve its position relative to increasing competition. Persuasive advertising often compares a product with its competitors, and points out superior features of the advertised product. In their late maturity and decline phase, products are often given **reminder advertising.** This is intended to keep well-established products fresh in the minds of consumers. Products' life cycles affect personal selling and sales promotion the same way as they affect advertising.

The amount of money available for promotion limits a sales campaign. Advertising and personal selling are both very expensive, especially when carried on through a long campaign. This is one reason companies try to develop product lines. Promotion dollars can then be spread over a group of related products instead of on a single one.

STRATEGIC OBJECTIVES

Promotion must inform, tempt, and differentiate

Whichever promotional strategy is chosen, it will almost always have one or more of these goals:

■ Promotion tries to inform and educate the public about a company or its products. This kind of informational promotion may range from letting potential buyers know about the availability of products to sophisticated campaigns that present a company or industry in a favorable light.

■ Promotion attempts to increase or maintain sales volume or share of market. Increasing product sales and thus revenue is, of course, the fundamental purpose of promotion. Maintaining a stable sales pattern can also be important, however. A constant, predictable minimum sales volume can improve planning, budgeting, and distribution. Careful promotion can help achieve this.

■ Promotion helps to position products in the market and to differentiate them from competitors. *Positioning* refers to aiming a product at specific market segments which would be most likely to buy it. *Differentiation* means pointing out the unique features of a product that would make it appeal to the market segments chosen. Positioning and differentiation take place in all kinds of promotion. They are especially prevalent in the automotive industry. Some cars are promoted for their luxurious appearance, even though they may be costly to operate because of low gas mileage. Others are clearly differentiated as having good gas mileage, unusual safety features, a good service record, or other features that would appeal to certain segments of the total market. Figure 9-3 illustrates how differentiation qualities in two toothpaste products can be used to position a third.

Figure 9-3
How product differentiation is used to position toothpastes.

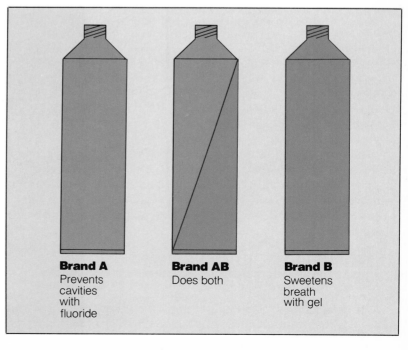

Brand A
Prevents cavities with fluoride

Brand AB
Does both

Brand B
Sweetens breath with gel

3 PERSONAL SELLING

Person-to-person contact is essential

Personal selling uses person-to-person contact to make a sales presentation to a potential customer. It *informs* potential buyers of the characteristics of a product and *persuades* them to buy. Personal selling includes the actual selling process and a number of nonselling activities that support company relations with customers. This support may range in complexity from clerical order-taking to sophisticated technical consulting.

THE SALES PROCESS
Locating, presenting, and closing

All good salespeople engage in a process of communication with prospective customers. The purpose of the communication is to describe the product, stress its desirable qualities, and influence the prospect to buy.

Personal selling efforts may be divided into three progressive steps.

■ *Locating prospects.* It is useless and wasteful to make a sales presentation to someone who is not genuinely a potential customer. The main requirements for prospects is that they have a need or desire for the type of product being sold, that they have the money to buy it with, and that they have the authority to buy it.

■ *Making the sales presentation.* Many salespersons divide the presentation into (a) getting the prospect's attention, (b) stimulating the desire to buy and (c) meeting objections. The presentation must include making a good initial impression, describing the product and its advantages, and answering questions.

■ *Closing* occurs when the salesperson actually asks for an order or a purchase. Closing techniques range from making a direct request to starting to write the order as if the customer had already agreed to the sale.

NONSELLING FUNCTIONS
Salespeople do much more than sell

Sales personnel provide many services to customers. Wholesalers' representatives, for example, sell almost exclusively to intermediaries. Besides selling, they may help to arrange store and window displays, help to train retail clerks, handle adjustments and returns, help their customers to price goods for resale, and help to set up delivery schedules and methods. Retail salespeople handle complaints and returns and often give information unrelated to selling.

Salespeople also have a number of nonselling duties to perform for their company. They may be required to attend sales meetings and training sessions, help to train other salespeople, locate new customers or prospects, and collect credit information. Some retail clerks help to count inventory and stock display shelves. Most sales representatives and retail clerks must also keep sales records.

THE SELLING PROFESSION
Jobs range from the straightforward to the subtle

Specific jobs in personal selling vary greatly in their complexity, skills required, and salaries. Many sales jobs, particularly at the retail

---

ACTION BRIEF

Saving Salespeople's Shoe Leather.   The time salespeople spend traveling from one customer to another makes no money for them or their company. In many instances, however, the possible choices of sales routes from customer to customer are so great as to defy the human mind. Thankfully, such an analysis is not beyond the scope of a computer program. Many companies now use a computerized time log to pick the best route. Based upon this kind of analysis, one company, U.S. Shoe Corp., maps out the most efficient sales trip each week for its salespeople. This schedule adds 20 to 30 percent to the time that salespeople are face-to-face with customers. It not only saves a lot of shoe leather, it also generates more sales for the company and bonuses for the sales force.

Source: *Michele Weldon, "Computer Helps Shoe Salesmen Hoof It,"* Management Information Systems Week, *January 20, 1982, p. 23.*

level, are mainly clerical. They involve completing sales slips, making change, and recording credit purchases. Route salespeople, such as those who supply dairy and bakery goods to grocery stores, also mainly take orders and supply goods, without doing much actual selling. House-to-house salespeople spend most of their time actually making sales presentations or traveling, but they work in an environment where the percentage of successful presentations is rather low. Engineering and industrial sales require substantial technical ability and high-level creative selling skills.

Some salespeople concentrate almost entirely on opening new accounts, maintaining good will, and helping customers make good use of the products after purchase. The activities are called **missionary selling** and are very important in dealing with technical products like computers and manufacturing machinery.

Generally, intangible products are harder to sell than physical goods. Selling life insurance requires considerable skill in financial planning, for instance. Selling a product such as advertising space in a magazine or a service like management consulting, requires subtle control of selling techniques, sensitivity to other people, and a command of technical knowledge.

4   ADVERTISING PRINCIPLES

Media, not people, persuade

Advertising is a type of promotion that does not use personal contact. Advertising presents informative and persuasive sales messages through communications media such as newspapers and television. Advertising stimulates interest in and demand for specific products, and thus supports sales promotion and personal selling. It is also often used to generate a favorable public attitude toward a company, industry, or other institution.

OBJECTIVES OF ADVERTISING

Advertising supports selling

The main purpose of advertising is to help sell goods and services. Specific advertisements or advertising campaigns may try to meet this goal in different ways:

■ Advertising supports personal selling. At every stage of a distribution channel, products are more readily accepted if advertising has already informed the potential buyer of a product's features and has encouraged a favorable attitude towards it.

■ Advertising reaches people sales personnel cannot. It is rarely possible to have a sales force large enough to reach every potential customer. Effective advertising can motivate people to seek out salespeople or retail outlets on their own.

■ Advertising improves relationships with dealers. Retailers and wholesalers know that products that are advertised will be in greater demand and have a larger sales volume. A manufacturing company that

ACTION BRIEF

Where There's a Coke, There's a Slogan. Makers of the most popular soft drink of all time never seem to be satisfied. Since 1886, Coca-Cola has had dozens of ad themes. At the start, it was simply "Drink Coca-Cola." Here's a sampling of the slogans Coke has used over the years: 1905, "Coca-Cola revives and sustains;" 1906, "The great national temperance beverage;" 1922, "Thirst knows no season;" 1925, "Six million a day;" 1927, "Around the corner from everywhere;" 1929, "The pause that refreshes;" 1938, "The best friend that thirst ever had;" 1948, "Where there's Coke there's hospitality;" 1949, "Along the highway to everywhere;" 1952, "What you want is a Coke;" 1956, "Makes good things taste better;" 1957, "Sign of good taste;" 1968, "The cold, crisp taste of Coke;" 1963, "Things go better with Coke;" 1970, "It's the real thing;" 1971, "I'd like to buy the world a Coke;" 1976, "Coke adds life;" and 1979, "Have a Coke and a smile."

In 1982, Coke kicked off still another slogan: "Coke is it!" It was conceived by the man who thought up the "Pepsi generation" campaign for Coke's major competitor.

Source: John Huey, "Lots of Hoopla About Three Little Words," The Wall Street Journal, February 5, 1982, p. 29.

advertises will not only increase its own sales, but also sales for wholesalers and retailers who stock the producer's goods. Such results and the hope of sales encourage intermediaries to stock the producer's goods so that they are available when consumers want to buy them.

■ Advertising helps open new territories, tapping potential markets. When a company is trying to expand its sales territory, advertising can create the product and company recognition that will allow its sales force to start generating sales.

■ Advertising creates an initial demand for new products. When a new product or service is introduced, no demand exists because potential buyers do not even know the product is available. Advertising is usually the best way to inform enough people about new products.

■ Advertising increases sales volume. Keeping consumers constantly aware of a particular brand of product will make them more likely to buy it. Advertising can increase sales by popularizing goods or services among segments of the market that have not used them in the past. It can point out less familiar features to people who already use particular kinds of products.

■ Advertising can promote goodwill. Many advertising campaigns portray a company as being reliable, interested in the public good, and a good citizen. These advertisements focus on the company or organization itself rather than on a specific product. Advertisers benefit by creating public acceptance. Sales may increase if the company creates an image of providing good service or reliable products. Goodwill toward a company or industry may make higher prices more acceptable. Some companies have even tried to influence upcoming legislation that may affect them by presenting their case to the public through advertising.

CLASSES OF ADVERTISING

Advertising has five dimensions

All advertising is intended to present an informative and persuasive message that will in some way help the advertiser to meet his or her goals. Within this general framework, however, advertising varies greatly. Types of advertising are usually classified by general objectives, content, intended market, geography, and media as illustrated in Figure 9-4.

General Objectives   Advertisements are classified generally by whether they are indirect or direct. Most advertising is *indirect,* as it does not attempt to close sales or directly generate orders. Instead, the intention is to increase product acceptance and preference in order to bring about more sales in the future. Some advertising is *direct,* however. It aims at getting people to actually place orders directly by mail or telephone. Familiar examples are advertisements for records on late-night television, and mail and coupon advertisements for magazine subscriptions.

Content   *Product advertising* is designed to increase sales of specific goods or services. All of the familiar advertisements for television sets, automobiles, hair sprays, restaurants and motels, drugs and cosmetics, and hundreds of other products are meant to persuade people to buy

---

ACTION BRIEF

Hey, Big Buddy! Ads *that appeared on Volkswagon "Beetleboards" a few years ago were considered a novelty. Now the mobile billboard has become a full-fledged business. Truck'N Display (Phoenix, Arizona) will put your ad on the panel of an 18-wheel truck, if you'd like. It offers a national network of hundreds of huge, semitrailers, giant vehicles that travel regular routes over the interstate highway system. The company estimates that each ad is seen by 2.5 million travelers each month. At that rate of exposure, an ad would cost less than 75 cents per 1,000 viewers.*

Source: *"75¢ CPM," a brochure distributed by Truck'N Display, Phoenix, Arizona, 1982.*

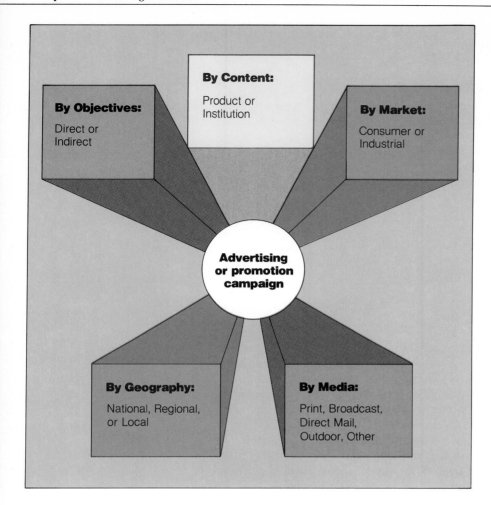

Figure 9-4
Different classifications of
advertising are used to create
an advertising or promotion
campaign.

the goods and services advertised. ***Institutional advertising*** presents the
messages of a company, a group of companies, or other institutions without the intention of selling specific products. Companies often use institutional advertising to promote their reputation for providing good service or for showing concern for social interests. Industry organizations
often advertise specific kinds of goods and services supplied by many individual companies. The wool, cotton, and railroad industries, for example,
have used this approach. The federal government is another outstanding
example of an institutional advertiser. Measured by total advertising
expenditures, the government is one of the largest advertisers in the
United States. The government spent nearly $190 million on advertising
in 1982. Advertising done by institutions in general constitutes a growing
segment of this country's total advertising expenditures.

Advertising to Markets   Advertising must be aimed at specific
markets and can be classified that way. The largest general categories are
consumer, trade, industrial, and professional markets. Of these, advertising to consumers is the most important type. Trade advertising is directed
toward wholesalers and retailers; professional advertising is aimed at law-

yers, doctors, and dentists; and industrial advertising promotes products for industrial use.

Geographical Classification Advertising is often divided into national and local components. Many media, such as television networks and national magazines, can present sales messages nationwide. Others, such as local radio stations and newspapers, reach only a local audience. Major advertisers often combine the two kinds of exposure to reach the market segments they are aiming at. Businesses with local markets normally use only local media.

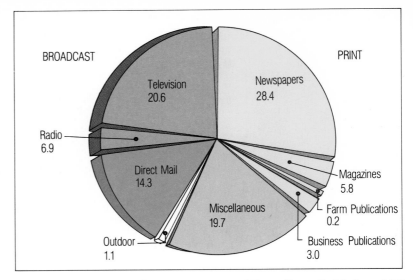

Source: Table 963, "Advertising—Estimated Expenditures By Medium, 1960 to 1981," *Statistical Abstract of the United States, 1982–83,* U.S. Department of Commerce, Bureau of the Census, p. 566.

**Figure 9-5
Estimated advertising volume by media.**

Advertising Media Print, electronic broadcast, direct mail, and outdoor billboards, are the most commonly used media for presenting advertising messages. Newspapers account for nearly a third of total advertising revenues. Television is second, followed by direct mail, radio, magazines, and miscellaneous media. The large miscellaneous category is a collection of advertisements on public transportation, floor racks, window signs, matchbooks, and pens, to name a few examples. Although television is now in second place in advertising revenues, it is growing in importance. Magazines are capturing smaller shares of advertising revenues now than they did in the past. The percentage of total volume of advertising carried by different media is illustrated in Figure 9-5.

5 ADVERTISING MEDIA AND SELECTION

The options are numerous

Success in advertising requires using the best media for presenting sales messages. Monthly magazines have different readers than do tabloid newspapers. Television advertisements reach different people at a different cost than do billboards on the expressways. An advertisement on the local radio station makes a different impression from one received in the mail. Many factors have to be considered in choosing a medium for any given purpose. The most important are the audience to be reached, cost, timing, and flexibility.

For an advertisement to be successful, it must reach enough people, and it must reach the right people. Media vary tremendously in the size of their audience or readership. A rural newspaper may be read by fewer than 5,000 people. Some network television events may be viewed by 50 million people. Media also differ as to the market segments that have exposure to advertisements. Some magazines, for instance, are read almost exclusively by affluent, well-educated urban and suburban readers. These usually contain many advertisements for restaurants, jewelry, and expensive home furnishings. Discount houses or manufacturers of low-priced goods prefer to advertise in some other medium that would reach more lower-income people.

Costs for advertising must be considered in relation to the size and type of audience reached. Most newspapers, magazines, radio and television stations give potential advertisers estimates of the cost per thousand readers or listeners. This information can be used in comparing costs among the different media.

Media also differ in timing. Some magazines present a company's sales message only once a month, while radio stations can air sales messages every half hour. Timing also affects the preparation of advertisements and the extent to which they can be kept up-to-date. A complex filmed message for network television will have to be written, filmed, and scheduled months in advance and cannot easily be changed if the advertiser's plans change. A single advertisement for a newspaper can be revised up until the day before publication, and sometimes up until a few hours before the paper is printed. Magazine advertisements must usually be in final form by four weeks to two months before printing. Radio advertisements are normally fairly easy to keep up-to-date if they are locally produced.

Table 9-1, which appears on the following page, outlines some of the major advantages and disadvantages of the most important advertising media.

ADVERTISING AGENCIES
They produce the words and music

Advertising agencies are companies that plan, produce, and place advertisements in the media. Business enterprises that perform these services are called agencies because they were once viewed as manufacturers' agents for newspapers and magazines, radio and television stations, and other advertising media. Agencies advise advertisers on their total marketing programs and help decide what part advertising will play. They write the advertising copy and produce artwork, films, songs, and other material. They then serve as contracting agents and buy newspaper and magazine space or broadcast time needed to display or present the advertisements. The work of an advertising agency is complex. It requires a wide range of different technical and creative skills combined with careful business and financial management.

Agencies are paid through a combination of commissions based on media billings and reimbursement for direct costs. An agency that prepares a series of newspaper advertisements for a department store, for example, will charge the store for costs of preparing artwork, typesetting, and other similar direct costs. Their main revenue, however, will come from a commission deducted from the price of the newspaper space used in running the advertisements. The agency bills the department store for the full cost of the space. It then deducts its commission (usually 15 percent) and pays the remainder to the newspaper.

ACTION BRIEF

Help Wanted! by Television. Newspapers carry nearly $5 billion in classified ads each year. These ads range from extensive "Help Wanted" columns to tiny items to sell a pet gerbil. They make up about one-third of all newspaper advertising. This total is so great that now the electronic media is trying to get a piece of the action. There is no good reason, say the experts, that timely ads could not be carried on television; a sort of "yellow pages" of the screen. Obviously, many newspapers don't much like the idea— unless they can find a way to share in the profits. The federal government, too, is worried about the impact of electronic media in this field. Nevertheless, it isn't a matter of whether or not classified ads will appear on TV. The question is when and under whose sponsorship. For as one marketing research manager has said: Electronic media is a "natural" for classified ads.

Source: Cindy Ris, "Electronic Newspapers Could Alter Shape of the $4.6 Billion Classified Ad Market," The Wall Street Journal, August 11, 1980, p. 16.

TABLE 9-1
Advantages and Disadvantages of the Major Advertising Media

Media	Advantages	Disadvantages
Newspapers	Reach very large proportions of local markets. Cost per thousand people reached often relatively low. Advertisements may be revised until day before publication. Special interest sections may be able to reach market segments.	Read quickly. Some pages or sections are often skipped. Difficult to reach national audiences. Market segmentation is not as precise as with some other media.
Magazines	Suitable for reaching national market. Can provide very precise market segmentation. Read more carefully than newspapers and advertisements are more prominent.	Advertisements must be prepared up to three months in advance and cannot easily be changed afterwards. Cannot reach specific local markets as easily as newspapers. Do not reach as large a national market as television networks. Advertisements are only published once a week or once a month.
Television	Advertisements can be lively and persuasive. Network television reaches a large national market. Local stations reach specific local markets. Advertisements can be repeated frequently.	Costs may be too high for small advertisers. Advertisements must be prepared far in advance and are difficult and expensive to change. Precise market segmentation usually cannot be achieved.
Radio	Similar to television. Costs may be lower. Exposure to local markets is often very good.	Advertisements are easily lost in program content. Network radio does not reach the large national market of television networks.
Direct mail	Directly solicits orders. Precise market segments can be reached. Can be used locally, regionally, or nationally. Can be used by any size and type of business.	Cost-per-sale can be high. Maintaining current and accurate mailing lists is difficult. Expensive to project high-quality image.
Outdoor	In areas of high traffic, billboards can effectively repeat simple sales messages. Total cost is competitive.	Not suitable for many products. Some objections on the ground of taste. Difficult to keep messages up-to-date.

6   SALES PROMOTION

Everything that is not selling or advertising

Sales promotion is the third type of promotion complementing personal selling and advertising. It includes a number of specific sales tools:

■ *Point-of-purchase advertising* (POP) includes any kind of sales message presented at the place where goods are actually bought, especially in retail stores. These include store displays, in-store sales posters, and similar promotional devices intended to stimulate sales immediately.

■ *Specialty advertising* refers to sales messages presented on small gift items such as matchbooks, pens, ashtrays, coasters, key rings, and balloons.

■ *Trade shows* give producers the opportunity to show and sell their goods, mainly to intermediaries. Manufacturers or service companies present displays at trade shows that are attended by wholesalers, retailers, agents, or sometimes by the general public. This relatively low-cost promotion method is often a major pushing strategy.

■ *Samples* are useful in getting consumers to try new products or different brands. Distribution of free samples is commonly integrated with advertising campaigns when new products are introduced.

■ Premiums and coupons are used similarly to samples. *Premiums* are small gifts offered with a purchase of the product being promoted. *Coupons* give buyers a discount when buying promoted goods. Both may make a product attractive enough for trial use by consumers.

■ *Promotional contests* offer prizes to participants in conjunction with the promotion of products. They sometimes help generate word-of-mouth advertising. Great care and specialized knowledge is needed for their use because of legal restrictions and high costs.

7   ADVERTISING AND THE PUBLIC

Society regulates it and challenges its value

Most marketers make a good case for advertising. It helps to bring new ideas and comforts to many people who otherwise would not enjoy them. Economically, advertisers claim that the costs of distribution are lowered and mass production is made possible. The public at large has its doubts about these conclusions. Accordingly, society has seen fit to enact legislation regulating advertising in the United States and to engage in inconclusive debates about its social worth.

REGULATION OF ADVERTISING

The FTC holds the whip

Because of the effects of advertising on consumer buying habits, and because advertising clearly has the ability to deceive, the government has taken considerable interest in regulating advertising practices. The most general legal tool has been the Wheeler-Lea Bill of 1938. This gave the Federal Trade Commission (FTC) the responsibility of monitoring advertisements that fall under federal jurisdiction. The FTC goal is to eliminate advertisements that deceive the public about the nature of products or services advertised. The FTC tries to get advertisers to tell the whole truth about their products.

Getting Hooked

by Bait

and Switch

"Terrific buy! Name brand Stereo now 25 percent below wholesale cost!" That ad sounds attractive, doesn't it? But how often have you dashed into the store that displays it only to find that this "terrific" buy "was just sold out"? Or, upon examination, you discovered that the "name" brand was not the one you were led to believe it was? If an ad like that were run by a legitimate merchant and the item were out of stock, you would probably be offered a rain check. But for some dealers who operate on the shady side of the street, the ad is simply "bait" to bring you into the store. A "switch" takes place when the salesperson tries to get you to buy a more expensive model. The bait-and-switch scheme is against the law, but every day hundreds of innocent people fall for it to their sorrow.

Source: Carol Krucoff, "Money: Bait, Switch, and Other Schemes," The Washington Post, May 5, 1981, p. B5.

What can a buyer do to avoid getting taken in by such deceptive, unethical, and illegal advertisements?

A number of federal laws also affect the labeling and advertising of certain products. The Wool Products Labeling Act, the Flammable Fabrics Act, and Truth-in-Packaging Act are examples. Many states also have similar statutes aimed at specific industries or practices. Industry self-regulation through such organizations as the Association of National Advertisers and the American Association of Advertising Agencies also attempts to limit deceptive advertising.

IMPLICATIONS FOR SOCIETY

Its social value is challenged

The social value of advertising in the United States is controversial, but few would argue with its economic importance. Over $50 billion were spent on advertising in 1982, and the total has been increasing annually. Table 9-2 shows the top 15 national advertisers arranged by industry. It is clear that for many large companies, advertising their products is a major undertaking. Procter & Gamble Co. spent $672 million and General

TABLE 9-2
Leading Advertisers

Company by Rank	Advertising Expenditure*	Percent of Sales Revenue Spent for Advertising	Product Line
1. Procter & Gamble Co.	$671,800,000	5.6	Soaps and cleansers
2. Sears, Roebuck & Co.	544,100,000	2.0	Retail chain, insurance
3. General Foods Corp.	456,800,000	5.5	Food products
4. Phillip Morris Inc.	433,000,000	4.0	Tobacco, beer, soft drinks
5. General Motors Corp.	401,000,000	0.6	Automobiles
6. K mart Corp.	349,600,000	2.1	Retail chain
7. Nabisco Brands	341,000,000	5.9	Food Products
8. R. J. Reynolds Industries	321,300,000	2.7	Tobacco, food products
9. American Telephone & Telegraph	297,000,000	0.5	Communications
10. Mobil Corp.	293,100,000	4.3	Oil, retail chain
11. Ford Motor Co.	286,700,000	0.7	Automobiles
12. Warner–Lambert Co.	270,000,000	8.0	Drugs and cosmetics
13. Colgate–Palmolive Co.	260,000,000	4.9	Soaps and cleansers
14. PepsiCo Inc.	260,000,000	3.7	Soft drinks, fast foods, snacks
15. McDonald's Corp.	230,200,000	3.2	Fast food restaurants

*Ranked by expenditures in 1981.

Source: Reprinted with permission from the September 9, 1982, issue of *Advertising Age.* Copyright 1982 by Crain Communications Inc.

Motors Corp. spent $401 million in one year. Certain industries, especially those heavily aimed at consumers, such as cosmetics and cleaning products manufacturers, spend significant portions of their total revenues on advertising. For example, Noxell Corp. in the early 1980s spent about 20 percent of its revenues for advertising.

There is little doubt, then, that advertising has a significant economic impact. But what does it accomplish? Does it really contribute to the good of society? There is widespread disagreement on these questions.

Proponents of advertising point out its benefits to business and society. Business gains from advertising because it helps sell products. It supports other promotion efforts, especially personal selling. It helps increase the strength of whole industries, as when railroad lines advertise as a group to improve their competitive position with respect to other modes of transportation. Advertising increases demand, both for the goods and services of particular companies and for products in general, thus benefiting business by increasing market size. It may also benefit society. Higher production creates more jobs and a higher standard of living. Extensive demand allows economical mass production so that goods can be manufactured at a lower unit cost. Advertising also helps to spread new ideas and innovations.

Nevertheless, many people are doubtful about the social value of advertising. The most common objection is that even if advertising has potential benefits for consumers, the benefits are not enjoyed by them. Manufacturers, they say, use mass production to make goods at a lower unit price but do not pass the savings on to consumers. Advertising may also interfere with free competition. Instead of competing on the basis of price or product quality, some companies are able to maintain and increase market shares merely by advertising more heavily. Some brands may be so strongly advertised as to gain a near monopoly in some segments of the market. Advertising may make these products almost immune to competition, even from a better product. In spite of government regulation, some advertising is deceptive. Even without making clearly false statements, advertising can mislead by implication. A man in a white laboratory coat promoting a pain remedy on television may suggest to viewers that doctors support the product even if they do not.

A fundamental objection to advertising that is often voiced is that advertising promotes materialism by constantly stressing the value of buying goods. According to this view, advertising encourages people to change their attitudes and ideas about life merely so that businesses can sell their products. Supporters of advertising reply that strong product promotion does not create materialism but merely operates within a society that was materialistic long before advertising gained its present importance.

Key Concepts

1. Marketing promotion uses a combination of personal selling, advertising, and sales promotion to push or pull products through distribution channels.

2. Promotion campaigns establish a unified promotion effort appropriate to the product, company, and market and are designed to achieve planned objectives.

3. Personal selling is a major type of promotion using personally presented sale messages to persuade prospects to buy goods or services.

4. Advertising uses communications media to support personal selling and to stimulate buyers' interest in and demand for products or to promote goodwill. It may be classified by its objectives, content, market, geography, and media.

5. The best media for specific advertising campaigns and messages must be chosen on the basis of costs, type and size of audience, timing, and flexibility. Advertising agencies specialize in coordinating campaign design and media selection.

6. Sales promotion complements personal selling and advertising with a variety of techniques such as point-of-purchase displays, speciality advertising, trade shows, samples, coupons, and contests.

7. The government, and in particular the Federal Trade Commission, regulates advertising to help prevent deceptive practices. Nevertheless, the public still has concerns about the value of advertising for society and the economy.

Review Questions

1. Define, explain, or identify each of the following key terms or phrases found on the pages indicated.

   advertising   (p. 144)
   advertising agencies   (p. 153)
   cooperative advertising allowances   (p. 145)
   coupons   (p. 155)
   differentiation   (p. 147)
   direct advertising   (p. 150)
   indirect advertising   (p. 150)
   informative advertising   (p. 146)
   institutional advertising   (p. 151)
   media   (p. 144)
   missionary selling   (p. 149)
   personal selling   (p. 144)
   persuasive advertising   (p. 146)
   point-of-purchase advertising   (p. 155)
   positioning   (p. 147)
   premiums   (p. 155)
   product advertising   (p. 150)
   promotion campaign   (p. 145)
   promotional contests   (p. 155)
   pulling strategy   (p. 145)
   pushing strategy   (p. 144)
   reminder advertising   (p. 146)
   sales promotion   (p. 144)
   samples   (p. 155)
   specialty advertising   (p. 155)
   trade shows   (p. 155)

2. What are the three main kinds of promotion efforts and how do they work together in a campaign?

3. How is promotion related to a product's life cycle? What type of promotion is needed when a product is first introduced? In growth and early maturity? In late maturity and decline?

4. What are the important functions that must be performed as part of the personal selling process?

5. What are some of the most important objectives of advertising?

6. Give examples of product and institutional advertising.

7. What kinds of advertising media reach the largest national audiences? What kind of media directly solicit orders?

8. Cite some commonly seen examples of sales promotion techniques.

9. What are some of the arguments used to defend the value of advertising, and what are some used to challenge it?

10. What major federal agency regulates advertising? Describe the kinds of advertising you find most deceptive and/or most objectionable.

Case Critique 9-1
Extending the Co-op Ad Dollar

Cooperative (co-op) advertising simply means that a company's supplier shares a portion of the cost of advertising its products locally. A typical arrangement might call for manufacturer PQ to contribute to retail store WX's advertising of PQ's products in local media according to the following formula: 100 percent of the ad bill, limited to 5 percent of the total cost of merchandise purchased from PQ. For instance, if WX buys $5,000 of merchandise from PQ, then PQ will pay WX for advertising costing up to $250. Companies like American Greeting Cards and Bic Pens offer such agreements.

A home improvement store, for example, carried two different but comparable brands of paint. The retailer asked each manufacturer about its cooperative advertising policy. One supplier offered 100 percent on 5 percent of total sales. The other supplier offered no cooperative advertising program.

1. Would the difference in policies toward cooperative advertising influence your purchases if you were the store owner? Why?
2. Why might one company offer a co-op advertising program and another not do so?
3. Which kind of advertising has the greatest influence on your purchasing practices—national television or ads in your local newspaper or on your local radio station?

Source: Elyse Sommer, "Tapping Into Hidden Advertising Dollars," *In Business*, Autumn 1981, p. 60.

Case Critique 9-2
Heating Up a Hunger for Soup

An occasional marketer captures not only the lion's share of the market, but the market itself. Campbell Soup Co. is one of the rare producers who has done just about that. It sells about 80 percent of the $1.2 billion of condensed (water added later) soup sold in the United States. Campbell is satisfied with its market share, but not with the size of the market. Soup buying has slowed down to a walk in recent years; it grows only 1 percent a year. Now Campbell would like to see the market grow faster. It wants more people to buy soup—from anyone—and the people who already buy soup to buy more of it. Campbell's promotion strategy in the past has emphasized ease of preparation. And its campaign was placed mainly in newspaper food sections, women's magazines, and daytime TV shows. Now Campbell has shifted its campaign to stress nutrition ("Soup is good food"), and it spends the bulk of its $23 million ad budget in newsmagazines, regular news sections of newspapers, and prime-time television.

1. Why would a nutrition campaign be more effective today than it might have been a generation ago?
2. What do you suppose made Campbell shift its ads from media oriented primarily toward women and homemakers to media more likely to reach a general audience?
3. Many people think Campbell is justified in using advertising to create a larger market for a nutritional food product. Would they be just as supportive toward a company trying to create a larger market for a purely luxury item? Why?

Source: Bill Abrams, "Campbell's New Ad Strategy: Make Folks Hungrier for Soup," *The Wall Street Journal*, September 24, 1981, p. 33.

Unit 4

Basic Business Operations— Production and Small Business

Unit 4 deals with the heart of the American business process— the conversion of resources into useful goods and services. It shows how operating sites are chosen and how production processes are laid out and managed so as to contribute value to a business.

Expertise in industrial production has made the United States a great power. But what were once exclusively manufacturing techniques are now utilized by every kind of business operation, from banks to fast-food restaurants, from retailing to home building.

The acquisition, movement, and storage of materials and finished goods has become a major function in many businesses. Accordingly, a number of specialties have evolved, including production planning, purchasing management, inventory control, and materials handling.

Operation of small businesses, while similar in many ways to that of larger ones, takes on a unique character of its own. As a result, its managers must be generalists, capable of operating every function and facet of the business.

Chapter 10

Location, Layout, and Management of Facilities

1 LOCATION OF FACILITIES
must take into account five factors:

Markets
Resources
Utilities
Community
Process

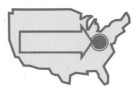

2 BUSINESS PROCESSES
fall into two categories:

Industrial/Manufacturing
(those that produce goods)

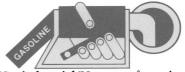

Nonindustrial/Nonmanufacturing
(those that provide services)

3 EQUIPMENT AND TECHNOLOGY
(computers, automation, standardization, and miniaturization) are powerful forces of change.

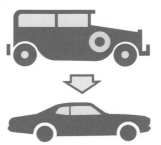

4 PHYSICAL LAYOUT

determines operational efficiency through orderly flow, minimum handling, and maximum space utilization.

5 PRODUCTION OPERATIONS MANAGEMENT

involves five activities:

Product design and development

Production materials management

Inspection and quality control

Work methods selection and improvement

Maintenance, safety, and housekeeping

Learning Objectives

The purpose of this chapter is to illustrate the main factors that influence the location of a business establishment and the nature of the process it carries out, delineate the basic principles of facilities layout, and explain the major aspects of production/operations management.

As evidence of general comprehension, after studying this chapter you should be able to:

1. Evaluate the various factors that influence the location of a business.
2. Classify various processes or operations as either manufacturing/ industrial or nonmanufacturing/ nonindustrial.
3. Recognize the influence of equipment and technology on a production or operations process.
4. Explain the major principles of facilities layout.
5. Outline the five major aspects of production/operations management.

If your class is using SSweetco: Business Model and Activity File for Business in Action, see Chapter 10 in that book after you complete this chapter. There you will find exercises and activities to help you apply your learning to typical business situations.

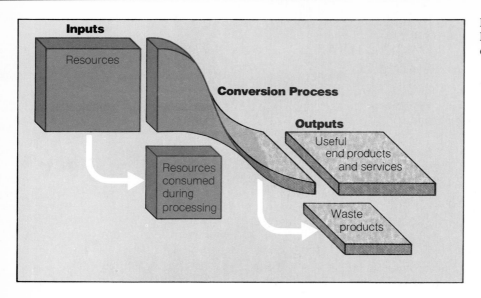

Figure 10-1
Inputs and outputs from the
conversion process.

As described in Chapter 1, all companies transform resources of some kind into an end product with increased value. Manufacturing companies transform physical resources, like raw materials or component parts, into useful products. Service companies transform materials and human skills and labor into useful services. In the conversion process, other resources, chiefly fuel, power, and supplies, such as lubricants and abrasives, are used up without being incorporated into the product. Starting materials, consumable resources, labor, and all the other resources that go into a production or operation process may be called input. The result of the process is output. (See Figure 10-1.) The output is of two general types: valuable products and wastes. The valuable products are sold to produce revenue. The wastes must be disposed of somehow. Wastes range from the used paper in trashcans to huge quantities of chemical-laden water or solids.

From the Stone Age up to the period before the Industrial Revolution, relatively little conscious effort was applied to the management of the conversion process. Stone Age toolmakers did what came naturally. They operated wherever appropriate materials were found. Typically, one person would perform the entire production process from collecting raw materials to distributing or using finished goods. Even in the agricultural societies of sixteenth and seventeenth century Europe, distribution channels were short and mobility was limited. Business decisions could safely be based on tradition more than on purposeful analysis.

Business managers today, however, face many possibilities and complexities. They must balance numerous factors in the environment—markets, resources, civic attitudes, and legal restraints—in choosing a location for business facilities. Modern technology and operation methods have made office and plant layout a complicated function. Managing the operations, once under way, requires continuing attention to the development of new products, control of the supply and use of materials, maintenance of product quality, selection and improvement of work methods, and keeping offices, plants, and equipment in good shape. These and other factors contribute to the successful management of production and other operations.

1   LOCATION OF FACILITIES

Locations must optimize several factors

Modern transportation and communication systems have broadened the range of potential business sites. At one time, it was nearly impossible to produce iron at any distance from ore deposits and charcoal sources because means of moving materials in any quantity did not exist. Today, many such barriers can be overcome if there is sufficient reason to do so. In selecting a location for facilities now, managers must balance a number of sometimes conflicting needs. The major considerations are the availability of markets, resources, utilities and reasonably priced building sites, and an encouraging social and political setting.

MARKETS

Vital for retailers

Nearness to markets has long had an important influence on the location of facilities. Areas with high concentrations of people, such as the corridor between New York City and Chicago and the areas around San Francisco and Los Angeles, continue to attract many companies. This is because of the many buyers who can be reached with low shipping costs. The southern and southwestern regions of the U.S. have seen striking business growth in recent years due to the increased size of their markets, which resulted in part from population growth.

Moving close to markets is particularly important for manufacturers of products that are difficult and expensive to ship. Goods that require a significant amount of service, like electronic computers, must either be produced close to markets or a separate facility must be maintained to provide the service. Businesses that provide services almost always select locations mainly on the basis of nearness to markets.

RESOURCES

Labor and materials

The availability of the resources a business uses often affects the choice of the facilities' location. Being close to the sources of raw materials is important for many industries. Those that use bulky and heavy materials or perishable farm produce are especially affected. Some industries use huge amounts of water and must establish their operations in areas where it is available. Companies that use partially processed materials, such as lumber, sheet metal, or component parts in their operations may benefit by locating near these sources.

Labor is another resource that affects the location of facilities. Companies that provide services often need highly skilled workers who are hard to find except in areas with concentrated populations. The same is true of many manufacturing processes that require laborers with highly developed skills. Companies that use workers with skills that are easily taught are often attracted to areas with low average pay scales. This was another reason for the growth of industry in the South and Southwest.

UTILITIES

Increasingly important

Most industries today rely on tremendous amounts of power for their operations. If coal or oil are used, it may be beneficial for companies to locate near their sources. Prices are usually lower there because transportation costs are minimal. Electric power purchased from utility companies also varies in price from place to place.

Some companies need unusual capacities for the disposal of solid or liquid wastes. Some communities have public facilities capable of handling these problems. In other cases, a natural resource, such as a large body of water, may be needed for the disposal of treated liquid waste. Transportation is important to most companies. The availability of major highways, waterways, airstrips, or other transportation facilities plays a role in business location. Communications facilities are also important, but they are becoming so widespread that their impact on location is diminishing.

COMMUNITY INFLUENCES

Attitudes and amenities

The overall attitude of a community influences whether businesses locate there. Many towns and cities give temporary preferential tax rates or other incentives to new businesses. Local ordinances on land use and other aspects of development often affect companies' decisions. Some companies are attracted to communities with no zoning restrictions, while others believe that communities with strong zoning restrictions are preferable. Zoning is the practice of restricting the use of certain areas for specific purposes, such as residential, commercial, agricultural, and industrial uses.

A community's attitude toward education and other public services influences company location decisions as well. A good educational system produces people who are generally more capable workers. Adequate fire and police protection and other local services, such as hospitals, make some places more desirable for workers to live in than others. And since workers are an important resource, communities that attract the best potential employees are the most attractive to business.

SITE AVAILABILITY

Room to grow at the right price

The final requirement of a good location is the availability and suitability of an appropriate building or site. A good site must be large enough for the proposed operations. Room for parking and future expansion must be considered. The land itself should be suitable for building—neither so soft as to require deep pilings for support nor so rocky as to require blasting. The property must be zoned to permit the kind of operations intended. Finally, the price must be affordable.

TYPE OF BUSINESS

Sensitivity varies

The relative importance of different influences on facilities location will vary with the type of operations a company engages in. Manufacturing companies often must give nearly equal weight to all factors. However, some manufacturers of goods that are easily shipped find it less important to be near markets. Warehousing operations may give first consideration to the availability of transportation facilities. Distributors may need a location that has access to several different means of transport. Nearness to markets is usually more important to their operations than it is to manufacturers. The prime consideration for a retail business is easy access to its markets. Retailers must try to locate in a market area that is sufficiently large and will generate demand for the products they sell. Expensive furs will not sell well in a low-income neighborhood, for instance. Companies that provide services—banks and restaurants, for example—usually emphasize easy access to markets in their location decisions. Table 10-1 on page 168 lists the variety of factors that different types of businesses might consider in locating their facilities.

2   KINDS OF BUSINESS PROCESSES

Processes fall into two broad classes

Many of the decisions about how a business is run depend on the nature of the process to be performed. All business processes may be divided into the broad categories of industrial, or manufacturing, and nonindustrial, or nonmanufacturing. All processes that create goods or services may be called production. The term *production,* however, is commonly used only for processes where the physical form of materials is changed. Thus manufacturing processes are production processes. Other business processes that do not create physical goods are called *operations.*

INDUSTRIAL AND MANUFACTURING PROCESSES

These produce goods

Industrial and manufacturing processes are distinguished from other processes in that manufacturing, mining, or construction changes the physical form of materials. It adds value to starting materials by reshaping, combining, or transforming them. This value is called utility of form. The different industrial processes may be described as extractive, analytical, fabrication, synthesis, and assembly.

Extractive processes take physical resources from the earth, sea, or air for use in further manufacturing or directly by consumers. Pumping crude oil from the ground, digging out copper ore, growing and harvesting vegetables, fishing, and chopping timber are all examples of extraction. While extraction usually provides starting materials for further manufacturing processes, some extracted products, such as vegetables and shellfish, may be sold directly to consumers.

TABLE 10-1
How Different Businesses Are Influenced by Site Location Factors

Location Factor	Kinds of Businesses Most Concerned
Markets and customers	Producers of perishable products, such as bakeries; producers of products that are expensive to transport, such as road surfacing tars, asphalt, and concrete; or businesses that depend upon consumer traffic, such as banks and retail stores.
Transportation	Producers of goods that are relatively heavy in weight and low in price, such as bricks and roofing shingles; or costly to ship in relation to their value, such as beer cans and soft drink bottles.
Labor supply	Businesses that require a highly educated and/or skilled work force such as electronic design systems and research and development laboratories.
Raw materials	Businesses that depend largely upon raw materials that are costly to ship, like cement and steel plants; or whose raw materials are perishable, like food packing plants.
Taxes	Businesses that have great investments in facilities and other fixed assets such as chemical plants and real estate developments.
Community attitudes	Businesses operating processes that are likely to pollute, like chemicals and bleaching plants; whose products are dangerous, like insecticides and explosives; or whose products have an odor, like rayon, paper, and rubber.
Land	Businesses that need large acreages of land for cultivation, such as growers of large crops of tomatoes, lettuce, onions, and so on; and paper and forest products; or for processing operations, like steel mills and petroleum plants.
Climate	Businesses that require optimum conditions of temperature, humidity, and rainfall, such as farming or aircraft manufacturing.
Utilities	Businesses that require large amounts of power or water, like aluminum and paper plants.

Analytical processes break materials down into new and more useful forms. An analytical process separates iron ore into iron and waste rock. Copper and other ores must be treated in the same way. Raw petroleum is separated into useful components such as gasoline, heating oil, asphalt, and polymers. Threshing wheat separates the useful grain from the worthless chaff.

Fabrication processes change the size or shape of materials and may join them together in various ways to create new products. Fabricating may involve cutting parts from sheet metal and stamping them into shape, cutting fabric and making it into clothes, cutting and shaping wood into pieces and gluing them together to make furniture. The construction industry fabricates when putting up bridges and buildings. Fabrication may produce finished products for sale to final buyers, or it may create component parts to be used in further manufacturing.

Synthetic processes create new materials by chemically or physically combining and changing other materials. The original materials are no longer distinguishable. Plastics, for example, are synthetics made from binders such as cellulose or synthetic resin and other materials. Many fibers for cloth are made in a similar way. Steel is created from iron and other substances.

Assembly processes create products by joining together component parts without changing their shape or composition. A bicycle can be made by screwing and bolting together the proper frame, hubs, spokes, brake parts, and so forth. A new product has been created, but all of the component parts have retained their original physical form. They have merely been attached to one another. The final manufacturing process for many goods, from automobiles to pocketknives, is assembly. The component parts have been produced by previous manufacturing processes from extraction through subassembly.

NONINDUSTRIAL AND NONMANUFACTURING PROCESSES

These perform services

Nonmanufacturing processes perform operations other than changing the physical form of materials. Some of the important processes are warehousing, wholesaling and retailing, transportation and communications, and a variety of direct service operations.

Warehousing includes a number of activities in addition to the simple storing of goods. Grading, sorting, packing, and contracting for shipping contribute to making goods more valuable by making them available when and where they are needed. These activities contribute utility of time and place.

Wholesaling and *retailing* also add utility of time and place to goods. The process includes buying goods for which there is an anticipated demand, keeping them on hand until buyers want them, and then reselling these goods at a profit. Food service and furnishing hotel or motel accomodations are important forms of retailing that also resemble manufacturing in that they convert materials into useful products—prepared meals and comfortable resting places.

Transportation services add utility of place. By moving goods from their place of origin to where they will actually be used, the goods become more valuable. Although this process usually includes only loading, moving, and unloading, the management decisions can be complex. Scheduling, equipment use, and maintenance of aircraft, for example, is critical to airlines operations. Communications—such as telephone, radio, and television—is also a form of transportation, in that sounds or images are transported from one place to another. The products in these instances are information and entertainment; the service provided involves their creation (or manufacture) and distribution.

Direct service operations covers a multitude of activities. Typically, however, these services provide labor, skill, methods, or facilities to aid individuals or organizations. Various kinds of utility may be created indirectly as a result. A bank is one example. Its operations deal with recording, storing, and distribution of information as it processes deposits, withdrawals, and checks. The bank may also earn money by lending it to others and pay interest to those who have placed money in the bank's keeping. The bank itself contributes the equipment, methods, and personnel to handle these processes.

There are also a great many other direct service operations, such as dry cleaning of clothing, repairing of automobiles and appliances, issuing insurance protection, caring for hair, painting and papering homes, lawn mowing, removing trash, providing security, fixing teeth, and burying the dead.

Increasingly, the processing of paperwork for insurance, purchase and sale of stocks and bonds, and financial transactions of every kind has created massive operating problems. The handling of this process is known in many circles as "back-office operations," and represents a challenge to those who provide these and other similar direct services.

PROCESS TERMINOLOGY
Key to production planning

All processes may be continuous or intermittent. **Continuous processes** run for long periods of time with few pauses or changes. Chemical plants, steel mills, and auto assembly lines usually operate around the clock for months with no essential changes in their production activities. **Intermittent processes** operate for shorter periods, in batches and often only for an hour or two, and are easier to change. Commercial printers, for instance, often use a different setup for every job.

Continuous processes produce **standard products.** A great quantity of the output is produced to the same specifications. Standard products are usually made in advance of sale to unknown customers. Toothpaste, for example, is made in huge quantities without the producer knowing specifically who will buy it or when. Similarly, certain services are available continuously, like telephone service and television entertainment. Intermittent processes are suited to **custom products** or services. Custom goods, for example, are not made until an order is placed; the customer usually has some latitude in determining the specifications of the product. A custom-made suit, for instance, will be cut to the buyer's measurements and made of material that the buyer selects.

Processes differ in the amounts of labor and capital they require. **Capital-intensive processes** use expensive equipment or materials and are less dependent on the activities of workers. Petroleum refining and electrical power generation are capital-intensive processes. They use expensive plants and relatively few workers, compared with the quantity and value of output. In **labor-intensive processes,** workers make a significant contribution to the value of the output. The production of hand-carved furniture is an example. The relatively inexpensive starting materials are converted into high-priced products through the skill of workers. Many repair services, like automobile repair, television repair, or plumbing, are labor intensive also.

3 EQUIPMENT AND TECHNOLOGY

Forces of change in business

Industry in the United States has stressed mechanization almost from its beginnings. Recent years have seen the continuing development of mechanical and electronic aids to production and operations.

EQUIPMENT TRENDS

Toward automation and robotics

Mechanization replaces the labor of humans with work done by machines. At one time, garden shovels were made using the methods of the blacksmith: they were hammered out by hand. Today, machinery powered by steam or electricity can stamp out millions of shovel blades with little hand labor involved. Mechanization has greatly reduced the number of workers needed to produce a given amount of goods. At the same time, it has greatly increased the amount of capital needed for equipment.

One result of mechanization has been the increasing standardization of goods. A worker making products by hand can make each one to different specifications. For most machines to be efficient, they must make a large number of identical products. Frequent retooling of manufacturing machinery to new specifications is simply too expensive.

A modern extension of mechanization is automation. **Automation** is a collection of methods for controlling machinery and production processes by automatic means, usually with electronic equipment. Automation requires a device that is capable of two-way communication with the machinery it is controlling. The control device must be able to send messages to the machine instructing it to perform certain operations. The machine returns **feedback** to the controller communicating the results of the operations.

An increasingly popular form of automation is **robotics.** This is the use of mechanical devices that duplicate the motion of the human hand. They are especially good for dirty, dull, repetitive, and precise work. In 1983, there were more than 10,000 robots employed in the United States (far fewer than in Japan) and the prediction is for there to be 120,000 in place by 1990.

Broad Applications   Many modern operation aids are examples of the move toward automation in all areas of business. Some complex warehousing and shipping problems have been nearly eliminated by automatic stockpicking systems. An order to a large distributor may require a shipment of two crates of one item, three boxes of another, and so on, down through hundreds of different items. The cost of assembling such an order by hand can be high. It is now possible to install machinery that will select specified quantities of many different items and move them to some central point for shipping by automatic control.

Retailing is beginning to introduce automatic price calculators at checkout stands. An optical reader identifies items by scanning a series of parallel lines printed on cans, magazines, meat packages, and other goods.

ACTION BRIEF

Thousands of Transistors on the Head of a Pin. The vacuum tube all but disappeared with the invention of the transistor. Today, these microscopic electronic devices are so tiny that 5,000 of them can be put on a silicon chip smaller than a child's fingernail. They made the pocket calculator possible. Researchers didn't stop there. Next, they put 20,000 of them into the same space, and the microprocessor (heart of the microcomputer) was born. And when they put 100,000 transistors on one chip and 60,000 each on two others, they created a microcomputer that can do what only the room-sized, mainframe computers could do a few years ago. Compact size was not the only payoff. Since the cost of the chip doesn't change much as more and more transistors are put on it, the price of computers doesn't change much either. Between 1960 and 1980, the cost of making computer memories decreased by a factor of 320,000!

Source: William J. Cromie and Harold A. Rodgers, "The Big Squeeze," Technology Illustrated, *February/March 1982, p. 55.*

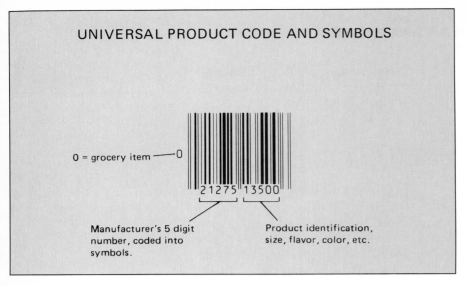

UNIVERSAL PRODUCT CODE AND SYMBOLS

0 = grocery item

Manufacturer's 5 digit number, coded into symbols.

Product identification, size, flavor, color, etc.

Figure 10-2
Universal Product Code (UPC). Optical scanning devices in supermarkets automatically read the information printed on product labels. The UPC uses the first five figures to designate the manufacturer and the last to specify the product. The lines above the numbers can be read by the scanning device at the checkout counter which instantly transfers the price to the cash register and prints the type of product and its price on the customer's receipt and records the purchase on a stock control and reorder system.

(See Figure 10-2.) A computer then looks up the price of each item and computes a total price. The system eliminates expensive training of checkout personnel and is expected to be faster and more accurate.

Computers have nearly revolutionized office services. In areas such as billing, inventory control, accounting, and credit, computers have greatly increased the volume of information a single clerk handles. Frequent and detailed reports and complex data summaries that would have been nearly impossible to produce by hand are now available for use by managers.

TRENDS IN TECHNOLOGY

Toward computers and miniaturization

Technological trends in production and operations are now affecting all phases of business. Computer assistance, for example, is being applied to virtually every area of business. The use of computers for analyzing and summarizing large volumes of numerical data has already become commonplace. Today, their functions are being expanded to include data gathering and problem solving. One example is the systems that monitor the climate inside buildings, controlling heat, air conditioning, and power. Another example is the systems that help to diagnose medical ailments and auto engine malfunctions.

The increase of computer use on the front lines has been made possible partly by the development of microcomputers that are small enough and sophisticated enough to take on the new assignments. Microcomputers, in turn, are part of a general trend toward miniaturization, especially in electronic equipment. More complex control and computing functions can now be fitted into smaller spaces. This has led to the use of computerlike control devices (originally called numerical control) in sewing machines, automobile engines, and other consumer goods. Automation and numerical control are becoming the rule rather than the exception in more and more production and service operations.

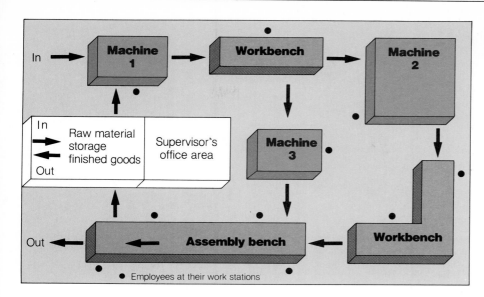

Figure 10-3
Layout for a manufacturing operation.

4 PHYSICAL LAYOUT OF PROCESSING

Work flow determines efficiency

The efficiency of business processes depends partly on how well the physical components are arranged. Designers of production facilities, stores, and offices strive to create a physical setting that will allow work to be done with minimum congestion, backtracking, and interference of one activity with another. For any kind of process, a simple arrangement or layout is usually best. Designs that result in the least amount of paperwork and handling of materials usually result in less wasted effort.

Layouts also attempt to make maximum use of the space available. Office, store, and plant floor space is expensive, and wasted space reduces profits. Most layouts for production processes arrange workers and machines in a line so that the placement of equipment physically matches the production sequence. If wood must be cut to size before shaping, the saws will be placed in front of the shapers. The lines may be straight, L-shaped, or U-shaped, depending on the building used.

A U-shaped layout for a production process is shown in Figure 10-3. Machines and work stations are arranged to follow the sequence of fabrication. Methods of moving materials and the location of storage areas for intermediate assemblies are arranged to insure the smooth flow of materials as they move through the fabrication and assembly lines.

Layout of office and clerical operations is equally important. As shown in Figure 10-4, an office in a high-rise building will concentrate its frequently used activities in a service core. The various clerical operations will be distributed in a U-shape around the core. And at the circumference will be the administrative offices of specialized personnel and the executives and administrative assistants. Such an arrangement saves steps and simplifies communications.

Retail stores are also designed to have a smooth flow of customer traffic while displaying as many goods as possible to potential buyers.

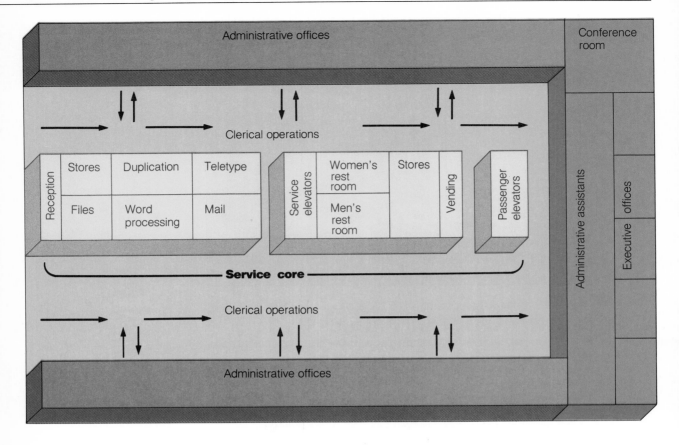

Frequently purchased merchandise is placed so that customers must pass other displays on their way to it. Items that might be bought on impulse are placed in high traffic areas, especially at checkout counters where customers often must stand and wait. The standard retail grocery store layout shown in Figure 12-2 in Chapter 12 demonstrates some of these considerations.

Figure 10-4
Office layout in high-rise building.

5 MANAGEMENT OF PRODUCTION OR OPERATIONS

The goal is efficient conversion

Managing a business's production or operations processes is central to its success. These processes create the useful goods and services that the business provides. If Procter & Gamble could not efficiently make good quality soaps and NBC did not produce television shows that attracted audiences, their central functions as businesses would be lost.

The management of business processes that create physical goods is called ***production management.*** Management of processes that mainly create services may be called ***operations management.*** Both production and operations management are concerned with product or service design, inspection and quality control, the selection and improvement of work methods, and the maintenance of facilities. Production management must, in addition, find effective ways to plan and control the use of physical materials converted in the manufacturing process. Many of the concerns of nonmanufacturing operations, such as retail stores, however, are similar to those of manufacturers. McDonald's fast food chain is a good example. It establishes a number of measurable standards for the quality of its hamburgers, carefully details every processing method in their preparation, and judges its success by how efficiently it converts its raw materials into a finished product.

PRODUCT DESIGN AND DEVELOPMENT

Products must be producible and profitable

One of the most important decisions to be made when establishing a new company is determining what products will be sold. Nearly all products have a life cycle and enter a decline in sales and profitability after a period of time. (See Figure 7-2 in Chapter 7.) Designing and introducing new products and services must, therefore, be a continuing concern of successful businesses. Developing new products is almost always a team effort. It combines marketing, financial, production, scientific, and engineering skills. Production management must play an especially important role, however. If a new product cannot be efficiently produced at an acceptable price, development of that product should be halted.

When a new product is proposed, market studies are usually made early in the development process to determine potential demand. The demand for several different variations of a basic product may be tested to decide on the most desirable design. At the same time, design engineers study the possible characteristics of the product based on available materials and production methods. After the data gathered from these two types of studies has been applied to the design and development process, the result should be a product that can be made and sold.

Early in the development process, engineers or managers must establish the process by which the goods or services will be provided. If it is a manufactured product, every step and procedure in the manufacturing process must be worked out. If the product is a service, exact methods and procedures for providing it must be set. The equipment needed by the process must also be established. For example, will manufacturing be accomplished with full, or partly, automated machinery? Or, for a bank, will the check sorting be done by magnetic scanning or by hand? Once all the production or operations process has been planned, cost estimates for materials, power and fuel, and workers can be made. At this point, the product and process will be fully specified and be ready for production.

PRODUCTION MATERIALS MANAGEMENT

Planning, scheduling, and moving materials

The purchase, movement, use, and storage of production materials are fundamental management concerns in any manufacturing process. The basic task of production materials management is to determine at what rate and in what sequence workers and equipment will be used to

ACTION BRIEF

An Inside Bookmobile. The Library of Congress of the United States consists of three huge buildings. Moving books back and forth between them used to require a gigantic, time-consuming effort. Now, books are moved automatically on trays (carts) through a system of conveyorized tunnels. Library assistants put the books onto the trays, but the trays are dispatched through the complex by a series of 18 load and unload stations. To dispatch a tray of books, the assistant brings the tray to a loading station, keys its destination on a device mounted on the tray, and then pushes the proper destination button. The tray is automatically transferred to the first empty trolley car that passes the loading station and conveyed to the unloading station where it is discharged automatically. Human hands pick up the trays at that point, roll them into the stacks, and place the books on the shelves.

Source: "Largest Mobile Filing System Scores 80 Percent Space Savings," Modern Office Procedures, December 1981, p. 66.

convert materials into goods to fill sales orders. Production managers try to make the best use of facilities and money through careful scheduling of the sequence and timing of work and through the efficient control of buying, using, and storing materials.

The most commonly recognized functions in production materials management are (a) planning and scheduling of the production function, (b) purchasing materials, equipment, and supplies, (c) controlling the inventory of materials and finished goods, and (d) moving and storing materials and finished products within the production plant. The broader issue of production materials management and especially of these four functions will be considered in more detail in Chapter 11.

The acquisition of materials for wholesaling, and especially retailing, operations has a different focus than purchasing and managing materials for production. As a consequence, the purchasing of materials for resale in retail stores is called merchandise buying. It will be discussed in detail in Chapter 12.

INSPECTION AND QUALITY CONTROL

The consumer's ultimate protectors

The main goal of inspection and quality control is to insure that products going out to consumers meet specifications. With physical goods, *quality control* tries to make sure that products conform to established standards for size, shape, weight, durability and strength, color, texture, taste, or any other characteristics that are important to the product's function. As an aid to operators and inspectors, some companies provide a *trouble code list,* like that shown in Table 10-2. Mounted at each work station, a trouble code alerts workers to potential trouble spots and also provides them with a simple, uniform way for describing and reporting quality defects as they occur. Similar quality controls for service operations focus on effectiveness, timeliness, errors, and other indications of acceptable performance.

TABLE 10-2
Trouble Code List for a Motor-Driven Pump*

Code No.	Trouble or Defect	Code No.	Trouble or Defect
01	Shaft improperly aligned	20	Shorted or grounded
02	Gears stick or bind	30	Loose or leaking
03	Housing not secure	40	Bent or warped
04	Packing leaks	50	Broken or damaged
05	Mounting holes not threaded	60	Dirty or corroded
06	Rusty interior chamber	70	Incorrect or missing
07	Exterior finish scratched	80	Alignment wrong
08	Lubrication fitting missing	90	Needs adjustment
09	Motor insulation damaged		
10	Shipping plugs missing		

*Code nos. 01 to 10 represent specific troubles most likely to be found with a particular part or expected function. Code nos. 20 to 90 represent general types of troubles or defects that might be found with any kind of part or function.

Issues & Highlights

Companies mechanize or automate processes because they hope to save money, either in the short or long run. Holiday Inns, Inc. is a case in point. Its Judy K. Watkins was declared 1980s "Word Processing Executive of the Year" for her efforts to develop and promote automatic word processing systems at the motel chain's headquarters in Memphis, Tennessee. Watkins, who is director of office services, attained remarkable results that year. Typing productivity, for example, as measured in lines an hour per employee increased 387 percent. That, and other associated activities of her program, netted the company a savings of $973,000 a year. Where did the savings actually come from? By reducing the number of people on the payroll. No one on the 2,700 employee payroll was dismissed at that time. Normal attrition took care of the reductions over a period of time. As employees routinely quit or retired, they were not replaced. Many of those who remained found their jobs upgraded as a result of the program.

Source: *"1980 WP Executive; Blending Technologies and Cost Savings,"* Modern Office Procedures, *June 1980, p. 50.*

If it were your own business, would you automate operations to save money, even if it meant that some employees would lose their jobs as a result? Why? What's good and what's bad about allowing the reduction in the labor force to depend upon attrition?

Although quality control procedures first attempt to identify and reject substandard products, they must also be set up to identify the source and cause of inferior quality. The comparison of output with standards in most cases is only an indication that some corrective action must be taken. The adjustment or repair of faulty machinery, the improvement of work methods, or the substitution of better materials may be needed to keep production up to standards.

Quality control is based on the inspection of materials and products. Inspection, which can occur at numerous points in the production process, may involve something as simple as visual observation. It may also require measurements of size, weight, and other characteristics or various kinds of tests to check the product's performance.

In recent years, many companies have come to believe that improvement in quality depends greatly upon the attitudes and training of employees. This has led to two different quality control approaches, each of which have been very effective. *Zero defects* is a concept, popularized when the United States was trying to put a person on the moon. It emphasizes a commitment by everyone in the organization, from top executive to least-skilled worker, to not making errors. *Quality circles* is a concept that has been perfected by the Japanese. It emphasizes the mutual dependence of everyone in an organization and the belief that workers themselves will identify and remove obstacles to good quality if they are given the opportunity to present their ideas to management.

WORK METHODS SELECTION AND IMPROVEMENT

Higher productivity and lower costs

One way to increase profits is to produce more goods or services by using facilities and workers as efficiently as possible. For this reason, much thought has been given to how workers and machinery can be made more productive. Three major approaches have been used:

■ *Job design and redesign* concentrates on getting the most out of the work that people do. It tries to minimize the effort and time needed to perform a certain activity. Work effectiveness has often been improved as a results of *time-and-motion studies.* These studies record every physical movement made by a production worker when doing a job and the length of time taken by each movement. This information is then used to choose the best layout for the work facility and to train workers to eliminate wasted effort.

■ *Process redesign* concentrates more on the methods and equipment used than on the activities of workers. Its goal is to increase production efficiency by studying and improving the conversion process. This is usually the concern of manufacturing or industrial engineers or, in service operations, of systems and procedures analysts. They might change the sequence in which operations are carried out, substitute a different kind of machine for one presently used, move storage areas, change the physical layout of the production line, introduce new equipment for moving materials between machines, or make other changes that would improve production.

ACTION BRIEF

De-batching Refrigerator Production.   The most efficient refrigerator manufacturing plant is not in the United States. It is in Mexico. It owes its efficiency, not to cheap labor, but to the continuous nature of its fabrication and assembly operation. Most large-appliance plants build refrigerators on a batch basis. That method averages 3½ to 4 worker-hours a unit as opposed to less than 3½ hours in the Mexican plant. The key to the continuous process system is a unique material handling system designed by a United States firm (Acco Industries). It reduces the time needed to change over the line from one model to another from four hours in a batch system to ten minutes on the continuous line!

Source: "Continuous vs. Batch Operation Ups Efficiency," Production, April, 1982, p. 51.

■ *Work simplification* employs both job and process redesign to make work methods as orderly and simple as possible. An important foundation for job simplification is the establishment of standard procedures to handle routine operations. Standard procedures reduce the effort needed for day-to-day activities, allow personnel to devote more time and energy to handling exceptional situations effectively, and make job training easier.

MAINTENANCE AND HOUSEKEEPING

Focus on repairs, safety, and sanitation

A well-managed operation must have standard provisions for still another production management function: maintenance and housekeeping. In a highly mechanized manufacturing facility, inadequate equipment maintenance can have disastrous results. Lost production, wasted materials, low-quality products, and even dangerous working conditions may result. Maintaining modern equipment is a complex specialty of plant engineering. Thorough maintenance usually has three requirements: (*a*) timely and reliable repair procedures must be available, (*b*) routine preventive maintenance schedules must be established and followed to minimize equipment failure, and (*c*) backup or substitute equipment should be kept ready for critical operations.

Routine housekeeping and sanitation is important to any kind of business operation. It not only helps to create safe and pleasant working conditions, but also can contribute to the quality of products. In a foundry, for instance, unwanted materials, dirt, and other residue mixed in with molten metal can severely damage the quality of castings. Food and dairy operations and pharmaceutical manufacturers must have extremely high standards of cleanliness. Even some very delicate mechanical and electronic products are fabricated and assembled in special rooms that are sealed to maintain a nearly dust-free environment.

ACTION BRIEF

The Cost-Savings Frontier. *Materials and contracts for maintenance and repairs account for 20 percent of all items purchased for production. One expert observed: "If you look at some maintenance operations, you find they are as large as many independent companies. They are a $10 million a year operation. For that reason, plant maintenance should be managed like a business. It must have the necessary tools to exercise tighter and more productive controls over costs and efficiency. In particular, maintenance management must have an appropriate data collection, analysis, and reporting system."*

Source: *Ed Hoeffer, "Buyers Explore the Last Cost-Savings Frontier,"* Purchasing, *November 25, 1981, p. 60.*

Key Concepts

1. The location of business facilities should provide the most advantageous balance of nearness to markets, availability of resources, utilities and services, and favorable civic and legal conditions.

2. Production management decisions must be suitable to the business process being carried on. The industrial processes are extractive, analytical, fabrication, synthesis, and assembly. Some nonmanufacturing processes are warehousing, retailing and wholesaling, transportation, communications, and direct service operations.

3. Discoveries in physics, chemistry, and other sciences are allowing a rapid increase in the sophistication of production and service facilities. Miniaturization, computer assistance, numerical control, and other modern techniques are finding applications in every kind of business activity.

4. The physical layout of business facilities must be designed to promote the orderly flow of materials and activities and to aid in the smooth interaction of different parts of the business process.

5. Management of production and operations includes product design, production materials management, inspection and quality control, work methods selection and improvement, and maintenance and housekeeping.

Review Questions

1. Define, explain, or identify each of the following key terms of phrases found on the pages indicated.

    analytical processes   (p. 168)
    assembly processes   (p. 169)
    automation   (p. 171)
    capital-intensive processes   (p. 170)
    continuous processes   (p. 170)
    custom products   (p. 170)
    direct service operations   (p. 169)
    extractive processes   (p. 167)
    fabrication processes   (p. 168)
    feedback   (p. 171)
    intermittent processes   (p. 170)
    job design and redesign   (p. 178)
    labor-intensive processes   (p. 170)
    operations   (p. 167)
    operations management   (p. 174)
    process redesign   (p. 178)
    production   (p. 167)
    production management   (p. 174)
    quality circles   (p. 178)
    quality control   (p. 176)
    robotics   (p. 171)
    standard products   (p. 170)
    synthetic processes   (p. 169)
    time-and-motion studies   (p. 178)
    trouble code list   (p. 176)
    warehousing   (p. 169)
    work simplification   (p. 179)
    zero defects   (p. 178)

2. For a manufacturer of straight pins, would nearness to markets likely be the most important factor in choosing a plant location? Why?

3. Would a plant that produced canned corn, lima beans, and tomatoes be more likely to locate near its sources of raw materials or near its markets? What about a bread manufacturer? Why?

4. What are two main differences between standard products and custom-made products?

5. Name the five manufacturing processes and give an example of each.

6. Why do product standardization and mechanization usually develop together?

7. What is the chief goal when designing the physical layout of facilities?

8. What are the two main influences that must be balanced when developing new products?

9. In what ways are quality control efforts and inspection related? How might zero defects or quality circles improve product or service quality?

10. What are the three major approaches used to increase worker and equipment productivity?

Case Critique 10-1
Farm It Out Versus Do It Yourself

Many companies routinely farm out—or subcontract—a portion of their production operations. They do so for two reasons. A subcontractor who specializes in making gaskets, for example, can probably make them better and cheaper than the firm that makes the pumps into which the gaskets will be assembled. Other firms typically farm out a portion of their work during peak periods when there is too much for their regular employees to handle. For example, a dress manufacturer might farm out some of its work before the spring holidays when people increase their clothing purchases. Or a manufacturer of CB radios might subcontract work during a boom period for a year or two, expecting the demand for its products to subside when the fad passes.

Workers don't always approve of these practices. They see themselves as pawns in a process that is threatening to them. In 1982, for example, thousands of striking workers sealed off all gates to a General Electric plant in Schenectady, New York. The workers insisted that they were suffering from layoffs and shortened workweeks because of GE's subcontracting policies. The company conceded that it routinely farmed out work, but it claimed that the reason for the layoffs was slack business conditions, not subcontracting. Neither the employees nor the labor union representing them was satisfied with the company's explanation.

1. What advantages are there to a company that limits the number of its full-time workers by subcontracting out work?

2. What disadvantages are employees likely to see in a company's farming-out practices?
3. Where do you stand on this issue? If you were running your own company, what kind of policies would you follow in subcontracting work?

Source: "GE Strikers Seal Off Plant," *The Washington Post,* April 19, 1982, p. C12.

Case Critique 10-2
Bigger or Better?

Since Henry Ford started automakers off on a mass-production binge, the automobile industry has believed in economies of scale. Now, the industry is beginning to have some doubts. Take the Ford Motor Co. engine plant in Flat Rock, Michigan. It is very, very big. It cost $200 million to build in 1971, is four stories high, and could hold 72 football fields. It was designed exclusively to manufacture engine blocks and to do so at the rate of 500,000 tons of blocks a year. The problem is that the plant was designed for continuous fabrication. If demand for autos slows down, the plant has to shut down for a while. Furthermore, the plant can make only one product, engine blocks, and is very inflexible at making new types and different sizes of engines. And this is increasingly required because newer cars have less cast iron in them to reduce weight and to save fuel.

In contrast, Ford has discovered that its 30-year old engine plant in Cleveland is far more efficient for today's manufacturing requirements. It has ten separate lines instead of one big one. The smaller lines are slower than the ones in the big plant, but they are far more flexible and they can be adjusted to make a variety of products. After Ford compared the operating costs between the two plants, it decided to put the newer, bigger plant in mothballs and to keep the older, smaller plant on stream.

1. What kinds of market conditions and technology changes affected the usefulness of the bigger plant?
2. How did product design changes affect production requirements for these two plants?
3. Which is more important for efficient production—high speed processes that can handle a great volume of output at least cost *or* a flexible, but slower process that can handle a greater variety of products?

Source: John Koten, "Ford Decides Bigness Isn't a Better Idea," *The Wall Street Journal,* September 19, 1981, p. 29.

Chapter 11

Production Materials Management

1 MATERIALS MANAGEMENT

is concerned with the cost of materials and their transfer.

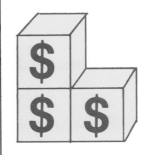 

2 PRODUCTION PLANNING AND CONTROL

decides what to make and how much, how to make it and in what sequence, and when to make it.

3 INDUSTRIAL PURCHASING

involves buying for conversion rather than resale.

4 INVENTORY CONTROL

balances the acquisition and storage of inventories with the demand for them.

5 MATERIALS MOVEMENT

combines internal handling with transport.

Learning Objectives

The purpose of this chapter is to define production materials management, showing how it fits into the total business and management system and to explain the major aspects of materials management, including product planning and control, industrial purchasing, inventory control, and materials movement and handling.

As evidence of general comprehension, after studying this chapter you should be able to:

1. *Define materials management and justify its importance.*
2. *Explain the scope of production planning and control, including the purpose of the Gantt chart and the PERT chart.*
3. *Explain the process of industrial purchasing and certain standard forms, records, and techniques, including make-or-buy decisions and value analysis.*
4. *Describe the inventory cycle and identify various inventory control techniques.*
5. *Differentiate between internal and external material movement and handling.*

If your class is using SSweetco: Business Model and Activity File for Business in Action, see Chapter 11 in that book after you complete this chapter. There you will find exercises and activities to help you apply your learning to typical business situations.

A weaver who makes fabrics for sale has the same production control problems as General Motors. Fabrics designed must suit the market. The weaver must plan the order of production and the amount, style, and color of each fabric to be made. Appropriate quantities of yarn and other supplies must be on hand for producing each kind of fabric. Total production quantities must suit market demands, or large stocks of cloth will remain unsold. Supplies and inventory must be moved, stored, and protected, and finished products must be transferred to retail outlets.

Production materials management involves itself with these concerns. Once a salable manufactured product has been designed, every step in its production—from the acquisition of starting materials to shipping the finished product—must be carefully managed. The effectiveness of this management will partly determine the success and quality of the product and will affect the manufacturer's profits.

1   PURPOSE AND SCOPE

Materials management minimizes the cost of materials and their transfer

Materials management is closely identified with manufacturing processes. These processes have the most complex requirements for the pur-

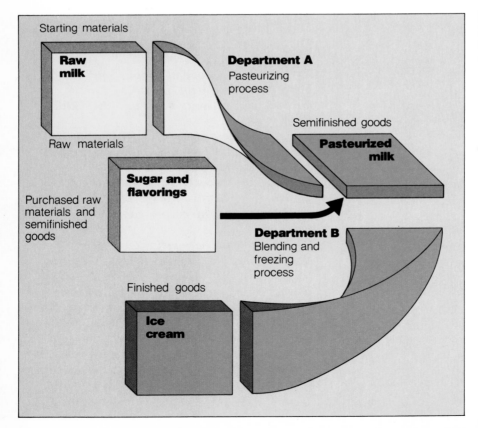

Figure 11-1
Materials that must be managed in converting raw milk into ice cream.

chase, use, storage, and movement of physical materials. The concerns of materials management—especially buying goods and controlling inventory—are vital to wholesaling, retailing, and other businesses.

Production materials management plans and controls the ongoing process of turning starting materials into finished products as shown in Figure 11-1. **Starting materials** are the physical goods that are transformed into more valuable end products. Starting materials may be of two general types:

■ **Raw materials** are physical substances that have been extracted, but have not been processed. Iron ore is a raw material, as is timber and unprocessed milk.

■ **Semifinished goods** are materials that have undergone some processing, but that must be processed still further before being used by final consumers. For example, iron is a semifinished product used in the making of steel, another semifinished product.

Finished goods are products that are ready to be used by consumers and undergo no further processing. However, the term is applied to the output of any manufacturing process, even if that output is to be further processed. A company that makes television components will thus call a glass screen shield a finished product, even though it is of no use to consumers until another company installs it on a television set.

Materials management concentrates on the management of four main areas: (a) production planning and control, (b) purchasing, (c) inventory control, and (d) materials movement.

2   PRODUCTION PLANNING AND CONTROL

Provides the plans for materials conversion

The need for production planning and control exists when a company has both production capabilities (workers and other resources) and customer orders for products. The role of production planning is to decide how the production capacity is to be used to fill the orders. Production managers control the quantities of specific products produced. They determine when production of a particular item begins and ends. They set the sequence in which different products are made. They try to balance the capacity of their production facilities with existing or projected customer orders. The result of this effort should be detailed production plans and schedules showing how workers, machines, and materials are used on a day-to-day basis.

In balancing production with customer demand, production managers must decide whether to make goods only for existing orders or to produce for stock. Producing for current orders has the lowest immediate cost. No goods are produced that are not immediately sold. It has its disadvantages, however. If a large, unexpected order arrives, it cannot be filled without delay. Disruptions may result from trying to increase production too rapidly. If schedules should be interrupted for some reason, no orders may be filled at all. A producer of custom goods has no choice but to produce for current orders.

The alternative—producing for stock—results in a greater quantity of items than may be needed for current orders. The excess is kept in stock for future orders. Producing for stock tends to smooth out the production flow. A more stable quantity of goods is produced, regardless of immediate orders. Fewer problems result if unexpected orders come in because the goods in storage can be used to satisfy them. Producing for stock has disadvantages as well, however. The greatest disadvantage is that the unsold goods tie up significant amounts of money spent on the materials and labor used in producing them.

In establishing how production facilities are to be used, managers try to make production runs as long as possible. Long production runs are efficient because setup time can be distributed over a larger number of items. Workers also tend to work more smoothly and effectively when they have been on a specific job for a longer time.

The goal of production planning and control is to use production facilities as efficiently as possible in order to produce goods needed to satisfy current or future customer orders. There are five steps that must be taken to reach this goal: planning, routing, scheduling, dispatching, and controlling.

STEP 1: PLANNING

What to make and how to make it

The first concern of production planning is to decide what to make and how much to make. Some companies make only one product. If a firm produces glass jars in only one size, no decision on what to make will be necessary. Many companies, however, even small ones, produce a range of products. A manufacturer of bicycle chains may make five different sizes in each of two different materials. The production manager must decide how many of each of these ten products to manufacture. These decisions will be based partly on known customer orders and partly on overall company plans and objectives. In recent years, marketing managers have been helpful in making production decisions because of the increasing accuracy of market projections.

Another major activity in production planning is determining what resources will be needed to make the designated product. All resources must be considered: How much equipment time will be needed? Are all the necessary tools available? How much labor time is needed? Will extra workers be required? How much material will be needed? Is the material already on hand or must it be ordered?

The last two questions are answered by preparing a bill of materials and comparing it with the materials inventory. A *bill of materials* lists all the raw materials or semifinished goods needed for a production run and specifies the quantities needed. Typically, some of the materials are on hand and some are not. By comparing the bill of materials with an inventory of materials on hand, managers can decide on what must be ordered from outside suppliers and in what quantities. These requirements point to an important fact about planning: production runs must be planned well in advance. It takes time to gather needed resources, unless large quantities of expensive materials are kept on hand.

STEP 2: ROUTING

Prescribes the work sequence

Routing and scheduling are specialized continuations of the planning already begun. *Routing* determines the exact path materials follow through the production facilities for a particular production run. It decides which machines are to be used and in what order. Look at Figure 10-3 in Chapter 10 for an example of the routes the materials might follow in a manufacturing operation. Routing sets job assignments for workers and determines how workers will use tools and machines to perform the specific steps of a production process.

STEP 3: SCHEDULING

Fits jobs and times together

Scheduling a production facility is a two-part task. Its first function is to fit entire production runs into a span of time when facilities are available. This function might decide that a 6-week run of 18-inch aluminum lamp bases would be turned on the lathes beginning April 1 and that another 4-week run of 24-inch bases could be placed on the lathes on April 15. This kind of scheduling views jobs as blocks of work and fits them together in a way that will make the best use of the facilities.

The second scheduling function deals with the details of job steps within a single production run. Just as routing sets the sequence in which operations will be performed, scheduling sets the amount of time allowed for individual tasks and decides when each begins and ends. For processes with many different steps, each taking different amounts of time and resources, this detailed scheduling can be a complex undertaking. A number of scheduling techniques have been worked out to help. One particularly useful, yet simple, aid is the Gantt chart.

Gantt Charts   In 1917, Henry L. Gantt devised a method for planning and controlling production schedules of shells for World War I. It is still widely used for scheduling manufacturing processes, marketing campaigns, and many other service-oriented business activities. A *Gantt chart* plots on the horizontal axis the time a specific work step takes. The machines, workers, or departments involved in performing the work are indicated on the vertical axis. The vertical axis may also be used for different jobs, customer orders, or production runs if the technique is used for overall scheduling rather than for scheduling the work steps of a single job.

Figure 11-2 shows how a Gantt chart was used to schedule orders in a machine stop so as to load each machine most productively. Gantt Chart B shows how the production planner has juggled the orders. Order Number 105 starts on Machine B, while Number 102 begins on Machine C, and Number 101 begins on Machine A. By overlapping the jobs, all five orders that were logged in can be finished by Friday. If they had merely been run in sequence as they arrived, as in Chart A, even Order Number 103 would not have been completed by then. Furthermore, Gantt Chart B used, through Wednesday 75 percent of Machine A's time, 92 percent of Machine B's time, and 100 percent of Machine C's available time.

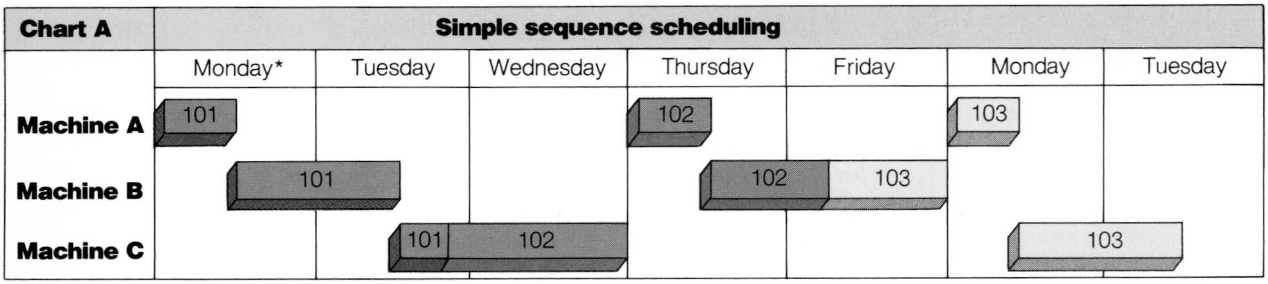

Chart A	Simple sequence scheduling						
	Monday*	Tuesday	Wednesday	Thursday	Friday	Monday	Tuesday
Machine A	101			102		103	
Machine B	101			102	103		
Machine C		101	102			103	

Log of orders for Charts A and B															
Order number	101 (mask)			102 (knob)			103 (optic)			104 (pan)			105 (quoit)		
Operation sequence	1	2	3	1	2	3	1	2	3	1	2	3	1	2	3
Machine number	A	B	C	C	A	B	B	A	C	A	C	B	B	C	A
Machine time (hours)	4	8	2	10	4	6	6	4	8	4	10	12	4	2	6

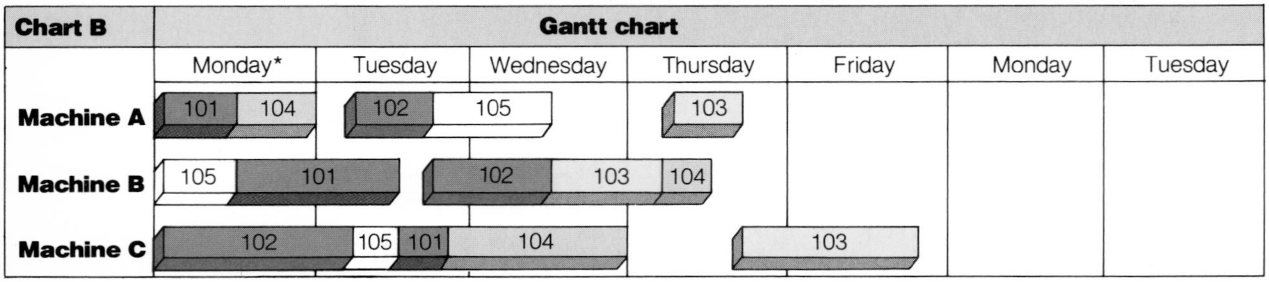

Chart B	Gantt chart						
	Monday*	Tuesday	Wednesday	Thursday	Friday	Monday	Tuesday
Machine A	101 104	102 105		103			
Machine B	105 101		102 103 104				
Machine C	102	105 101 104			103		

*Each day represents eight hours.

PERT Networks   PERT is especially useful for one-of-a-kind projects such as the construction of a bridge or the building of a ship. *PERT* was first developed in the late 1950s by the Special Projects Office of the U.S. Navy to launch the Polaris missile. The initials stand for Program Evaluation and Review Technique. Its purpose is to schedule activities and allocate resources in a way that will help complete complex projects in a minimum amount of time.

The PERT network for building a house shown in Figure 11-3 demonstrates features of this technique. PERT deals with the relationships between events and activities. *Events* refer to the times at which activities begin or end. *Activities* refer to segments of work that make up the total process. In building a house, installing the floor is an activity that is bounded by two events: a beginning and an end. The most important consideration in this network is whether one activity has to follow another or whether two or more can be done at the same time. In Figure 11-3, activities leading up to Events 1, 2, 3, and 4 must be done sequentially. The floor deck cannot be built until the foundation is complete, for example. Activities leading to Events 5, 6, 7, and 8 can all be done at once.

An important use of a PERT network is to find out which activities set the lower limit on the time needed to complete the whole project. This is done by locating the longest path of activities that have to be performed

Figure 11-2
Development of a Gantt chart from a series of production orders. Chart A shows jobs lined up in sequence as they were received. Chart B shows jobs rearranged (overlapped for maximum machine loading, with the prescribed sequence of operations for each job maintained).

sequentially. This **critical path** defines the activities that have to be managed most carefully. If any of the tasks on the critical path take longer than expected, the total project cannot be completed on time. Activities on other paths have slack time. Delays in some activities can be accepted without affecting the projected completion date.

STEP 4: DISPATCHING

Sends work and materials into movement

Dispatching involves issuing orders for production activities to begin. A dispatcher issues work orders that actually bring together all of

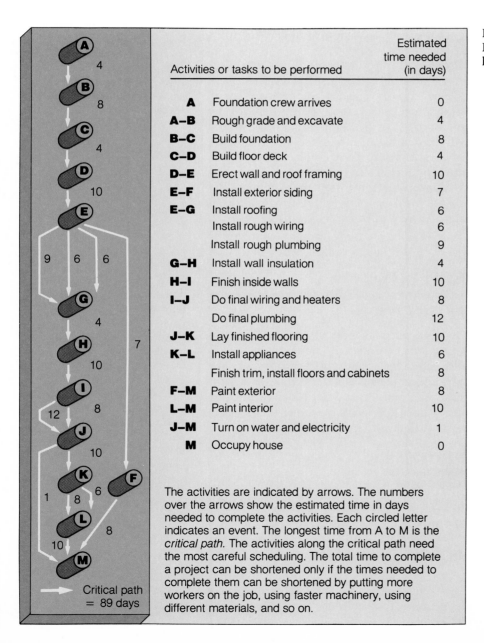

Activities or tasks to be performed		Estimated time needed (in days)
A	Foundation crew arrives	0
A–B	Rough grade and excavate	4
B–C	Build foundation	8
C–D	Build floor deck	4
D–E	Erect wall and roof framing	10
E–F	Install exterior siding	7
E–G	Install roofing	6
	Install rough wiring	6
	Install rough plumbing	9
G–H	Install wall insulation	4
H–I	Finish inside walls	10
I–J	Do final wiring and heaters	8
	Do final plumbing	12
J–K	Lay finished flooring	10
K–L	Install appliances	6
	Finish trim, install floors and cabinets	8
F–M	Paint exterior	8
L–M	Paint interior	10
J–M	Turn on water and electricity	1
M	Occupy house	0

The activities are indicated by arrows. The numbers over the arrows show the estimated time in days needed to complete the activities. Each circled letter indicates an event. The longest time from A to M is the *critical path*. The activities along the critical path need the most careful scheduling. The total time to complete a project can be shortened only if the times needed to complete them can be shortened by putting more workers on the job, using faster machinery, using different materials, and so on.

Figure 11-3
PERT Chart for planning a house construction project.

the planned resources and put them into operation. Orders will be sent to move materials from stores and place them where they will be used. Orders may be needed to set up equipment or to gather needed tools. Other orders will tell workers what their particular job assignment is in the scheduled production process.

STEP 5: CONTROLLING
Monitors work progress

Controlling has the same general goal in production management as in other areas of management. It compares actual results with plans and tries to correct any deficiencies. In spite of good planning, routing, and scheduling, many things go wrong in production processes. Needed materials are sometimes unexpectedly found to be unusable. Machines break down. Workers are absent.

Schedule performance reports are used to determine how well production activities are kept within their established time limits. Any problem in keeping on schedule must be explained and made up for. This is accomplished either by allocating more workers or equipment or by delaying later production. *Scrap reports,* for example, show how many items in process have had to be discarded because of defects. This allows corrections to be made if faulty work or equipment can be identified. It also may be a signal to extend the production run to make more goods to replace the faulty ones. It also calls to the attention of management the fact that some starting materials are not being converted into end products as planned. Additional materials may need to be obtained.

3   INDUSTRIAL PURCHASING
Buying for conversion, not resale

Most companies make extensive purchases of goods and services from outside suppliers. Manufacturing companies have to buy raw materials and semifinished goods, supplies, machinery, equipment, and services. This buying for use in manufacturing is called *industrial purchasing.* It is different from the buying done by a wholesaler or retailer. These commercial companies buy goods for resale without further processing. This kind of purchasing is called *mercantile buying.*

THE PURCHASING PROCESS
Requisitions, orders, and receipts

The main function of industrial purchasing is to decide how much to buy, at what price, from whom, and when. These decisions are part of a purchasing process that uses a flow of information among the company departments that will use the goods bought, the purchasing department, and outside suppliers.

Initiating Purchases   The decision to buy goods and services usually originates within the department that is to use them. One of the

ACTION BRIEF

Crackdown on Early Deliveries.   *Vendors are typically eager to unload their goods on customers so that they can get paid. On the other hand, customers, like Onan Industries, don't like shipments to arrive until they are ready to use them. Inventories of raw materials take up storage space, and they cost money to keep. Says Onan's purchasing director, "If we said March 15, we might get a shipment in January. That way we had inventory we didn't need but had to pay for. We like liquid assets, money in hand, rather than inventories." To control this problem Onan initiated a three-point plan: (1) Explain to vendors the importance of the specified delivery date, (2) check to see that supplies ordered in advance aren't shipped until needed, and (3) verify dates when shipments arrive on the receiving dock. "We accept shipments within a day or two of the specified date," says the purchasing director, "but otherwise we ship them back."*

Source: Margaret Nelson, "Rigid Shipment Dates Help Onan to Run 'Lean and Mean'," Purchasing, April 3, 1982, p. 15.

tasks of production planning is to determine what starting materials must be bought. Other departments determine their need for supplies, equipment, and services in their own planning processes. The initiating department will also decide on the most desirable specifications of the goods or services to be bought. The required specifications are formally communicated to the purchasing department on a **purchase requisition.** This is a written request to obtain the goods or services described.

In practice, the exact specifications of purchases are often negotiable. Similar goods not exactly meeting the requesting department's specifications may serve the intended purpose as well or better. If these can be found at a lower price or from a more reliable supplier, exceptions may be made to the specifications.

Purchasing Activity   When a requisition has been received, actual purchasing activity begins. The main steps are to locate potential suppliers, determine prices, and issue a purchase order. For goods that are bought routinely and frequently, there may be no question about who the supplier will be or even about the price. For many purchases, however, an extensive search may have to be made to find suppliers capable of meeting required specifications. Purchasing agents rely heavily on experience and personal contacts to maintain a current stock of knowledge about the capabilities and reputations of suppliers. Prices may be accepted after a simple quotation, or they may require lengthy negotiation or multiple bids from different suppliers. Prices of some commodities, like vegetable oil, cocoa, or soybeans, change sharply from day to day. Purchasers who buy products like these must stay in constant contact with the trading places when prices are set.

When the supplier and price have been set, the purchasing agent issues a **purchase order.** This is a formal request for an outside supplier to provide goods or services. It is, in effect, a legal document setting forth the terms of the purchase: specifications, price, quantities, shipping instructions, delivery date, and any other specifications agreed on between the purchaser and supplier.

Follow-Up   After a purchase order is issued, it is important for the purchasing agent to follow up on the order. Many goods, especially expensive production materials, may be ordered so that they arrive close to the time they are needed. This reduces storage costs and investment in inventory. If the materials do not arrive on time, however, serious production problems can result. Usually a formal follow-up procedure is used in this case. The purchasing department checks with suppliers periodically to make sure promised delivery dates are maintained.

When goods are received, they must be checked against the purchase order to make sure that specifications have been met. Many incoming goods must be inspected for quality. Even if these inspections are under the control of another department—typically quality control or the production or receiving department—it is important for the purchasing department to know the results. A **receiving report** is usually made showing that the goods have arrived and whether they have met specifications. When there is some discrepancy in quality or quantity, the purchasing agent has to renegotiate the terms of the purchase.

Issues &
Highlights

One effective way for scheduling service operations, like maintenance and clerical work, is called short-interval scheduling. Using this system, a supervisor issues the work piecemeal to each employee, along with a deadline for early completion. For example, a maintenance supervisor might assign a pipefitter to replace a broken water valve along with the advice that the job should be completed in one hour (or by 9:45 a.m.). When the pipefitter had completed that job, she would be assigned another job with another short-interval deadline (from 15 minutes to a maximum of 2 hours). Similarly, an office manager might give a batch of three letters to a typist and ask that they be finished within 45 minutes, and then repeat this process all day long.

Source: Lester R. Bittel, What Every Supervisor Should Know, 4th ed., McGraw-Hill Book Company, New York, 1980, pp. 483–485.

What sort of advantages and disadvantages for the company do you see with the short-interval scheduling approach? Would you like to work under this system, or would you rather be assigned a whole day's work and be allowed to set your own pace?

MAKE-OR-BUY DECISIONS

Compares total costs

A manufacturing company usually has the option of buying semifinished goods for some of their processes or of making the goods itself. This **make-or-buy decision** is usually made by top management as part of overall planning for company operations. Cost is a frequent determining factor. Managers compare the quoted cost of buying from outside suppliers with the estimated cost of making the goods in-house. Full costs, including such items as training employees and buying and maintaining equipment, must be considered. In some cases, materials or parts may not even be available for purchase and must be made by the user. Many companies have secret product designs that give them a competitive advantage. To avoid the risk of exposing their secret design to others, these companies do not order materials or subassemblies from outside suppliers.

VALUE ANALYSIS

Focuses on function

The importance of good communications between the purchasing department and operating departments of a company is clearly demonstrated in a procedure called **value analysis.** Its purpose is to reduce production costs—mainly of materials—for products while maintaining or increasing the quality of the products. The analysis focuses on a product's function. Engineers and purchasing agents work together to examine every part of the product to see if less expensive substitutes can be used without impairing function. If even very small cost reductions can be achieved, the effect will be substantial over a long production run.

4   INVENTORY CONTROL

Juggles materials cost and availability

Managers responsible for inventory control are faced with the problem of having enough, but not too much, of everything. This applies to materials used in production and to goods that result from production.

The **materials inventory** includes all of the starting materials and supplies used in a manufacturing process. If the stock is not sufficient to keep up with production, operations will be disrupted. If too much is kept in storage, money that could be used more profitably in other ways will be tied up in materials.

The **finished products inventory** is a list of the stock of finished goods awaiting sale. An adequate stock must be maintained so that customer orders can be filled with minimum delay. However, the stock must still be small enough to minimize investment and storage costs.

A similar inventory problem faces managers and buyers in retailing and wholesaling establishments. The **merchandise inventory** is the stock of goods that a wholesaler or retailer has purchased for resale. Managers of these companies must constantly balance the need to meet customer orders quickly with the high cost of keeping a large stock of goods. Thus

ACTION BRIEF

Boxed-In by Wood. *For years, Bundy, the world's largest maker of small-diameter steel tubing, shipped its bundled rods in wooden crates. Cost of the wood alone was $8. Labor for assembling the crate added another $3.70. These costs got the attention of the value analysis team at Bundy. Was wood really necessary, they asked. So they tried substituting corrugated cardboard cartons and found they did the job as well as wood. Cost of the knock-down cartons is only $5.45, and they assemble easily at a labor cost for packing of $2.21. Total cost for the corrugated box is less than the cost of the wood alone. And, since the wooden box weighed 45 pounds as compared with 16 pounds for the corrugated container, there is also a significant savings in freight charges.*

Source: *"Value Analysis '82: Corrugated Gives Wood a Simple Boxing Lesson,"* Purchasing, *March 25, 1982, p. 154.*

they seek the highest turnover of inventory. ***Inventory turnover*** measures the average number of times a year stock must be replaced. Whether for production or retailing, the better the management, the higher the turnover.

Purchasing, production, and inventory control must be coordinated to have any chance of achieving the balances needed. Inventory levels for both materials and finished goods constantly fluctuate as materials are purchased and goods are produced,

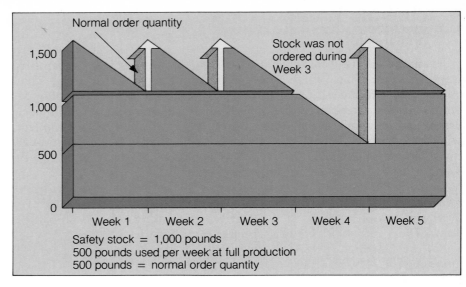

and as materials are used and goods are sold. These changes in inventory levels make up the ***inventory cycle.***

Figure 11-4
Example of an inventory cycle.

INVENTORY CYCLE

From minimum to maximum levels

For any kind of inventory, managers try to control the minimum and maximum levels as the stock on hand fluctuates with receipts, use, production, or sale. Figure 11-4 shows the inventory cycle for a material used in a manufacturing process. Every week five hundred pounds of the material are used. The manufacturer wishes to keep a 2-week supply, or ***safety stock,*** on hand in case regular deliveries of the material are delayed. During the normal cycle, 500 pounds of the material are received and used in a week's time. This allows normal inventory to fluctuate between 1,000 and 1,500 pounds. In the fourth week, normal supply does not arrive and part of the safety stock is used. The delayed shipment and the normal shipment for the fifth week are received at the same time, and inventory returns to its maximum of 1,500 pounds.

This kind of inventory cycle determines how purchases are made. Purchasing managers must take into account the desired safety stock, the daily or weekly use of material, and the ***lead time,*** the length of time between the placement of an order and the receipt of the goods. Only by considering all three factors can purchasing managers be reasonably assured that a constant supply of materials will arrive in time to continue uninterrupted production.

ECONOMIC ORDER QUANTITY

Optimizes costs of ordering and stocking

When deciding how much stock to order at a time and how often to order it, purchasing agents must be guided by a number of considerations. Placing very large orders infrequently might allow goods to be bought at a lower unit cost. The danger of running out of stock on materials or goods also makes buyers favor large orders. If the sources of supply are not reliable, large orders may be necessary to insure the availability of goods when they are needed. Even the cost of negotiating prices and placing orders is considerable and would lead purchasers to try to make orders as infrequently as possible.

At the same time, however, the practice of placing large, infrequent orders ties up capital, uses expensive storage space, and may cause loss or damage to goods in storage. Managers try to determine exactly the costs associated with different-sized orders and pick an order size and frequency that results in the greatest advantages at the least cost. Formulas developed as an aid in this decision are widely used.

PERPETUAL INVENTORY CONTROL
Maintains a running record of stock on hand

Most companies periodically take an exact count or measure of the amount of all the inventory on hand. In this way, inventory may be checked annually or more often. Between these exact assessments of inventory, or *periodic inventories,* managers must have some way of knowing on a continuous basis how much stock is on hand. A *perpetual inventory* provides this information. This is a frequent, often daily, tabulation of how much has entered inventory and how much has left. If an accurate beginning count is used, it is possible to figure an approximate daily or weekly inventory balance by adding to the starting amount all receipts and subtracting all quantities used. The figure is only approximate because there is usually some unrecorded damage or loss of goods in inventory.

5   MATERIALS MOVEMENT AND HANDLING
An internal expense that does not add value

Much of the cost of production processes arises from the need to move materials and goods continually. Starting materials, work in process, and finished goods have to be moved among machines and storage areas within a manufacturer's plant. Materials and supplies have to be transported to processing facilities and finished goods to warehouses or points of purchase.

INTERNAL MOVEMENT
Pickup and laydown handling

Materials must be moved from the area where they are stored to the starting points of the production process. They must then be moved from machine to machine and work station to work station as they are processed. Finished goods must then be transported to temporary storage facilities where they await sale or further transfer.

Substantial amounts of labor can be used for this internal movement and handling. Particularly in recent years, great attention has been given to these costs. Solutions to the high costs have come mainly from the development of new equipment and from greater care in designing the

ACTION BRIEF

Phantom Warehouses.   It started with the Japanese. First, Toyota Motor Co. cut down on the size of its storage areas for incoming parts and supplies. It did so by requiring their vendors to deliver only enough components to build exactly the number of cars scheduled to be built during a given week. Then Toyota cut the lead-time to one day. Factories of Japan's YKK (the world's largest zipper manufacturer, with giant plants in the United States) introduced the ultimate variation, called the "just-in-time" system. This not only cut down on warehouses for incoming materials, it virtually eliminated warehouses on the shipping end. As soon as YKK manufactures a day's production, it ships it directly from the production line to its distributors without an intermediate stop in a warehouse. Ford, General Motors, and Firestone soon saw the advantages of phantom warehouses and adopted their own variation of the system.

Source: Christopher Byron, "Getting Control of Inventories," Time, May 10, 1982, p. 93.

layout of production processes. Mechanical loaders, conveyor belts, chutes, gravity-powered feed systems, and other mechanical devices have helped eliminate repetitive loading and unloading, crosshauling, and handling. The advanced design of manufacturing processes has often minimized handling, making physical operations as continuous as possible by designing machine layouts to follow work sequence.

EXTERNAL MOVEMENT

Shipping and receiving

External movement transports goods from producer to warehouses, between warehouses, from warehouses to points of sale, from points of sale to users, and to any other places where they are needed. The *traffic manager* controls the complex transportation requirements of a business. A traffic manager is usually in charge of packing and loading goods, deciding on the best shipping methods, negotiating freight rates, and taking care of routing, insurance, and recordkeeping. Shipping costs are an important part of total costs, especially for some goods. Efficient management of these activities can reduce costs and increase profits.

Key Concepts

1. Production materials management plans and controls the purchase, use, storage, and transfer of goods in the production process.
2. Production planning and control determines how production facilities are used to make products so that customer orders can be filled. It is concerned with planning, routing, scheduling, dispatching, and controlling.
3. Manufacturing companies buy starting materials, machinery, equipment, supplies, and services through industrial purchasing.
4. Inventory control manages the inputs and outputs of production processes. It maintains adequate stocks of materials to allow uninterrupted production. It also maintains a stock of finished goods to insure that customer orders can be filled without delay.
5. The movement of materials within and outside of production facilities contributes significantly to the cost of making goods. Improvements brought about by the use of materials handling equipment, by careful design of production processes, and by efficient use of transportation facilities can reduce these costs.

Review Questions

1. Define, explain, or identify each of the following key terms or expressions found on the pages indicated.

bill of materials (p. 186)
critical path (p. 189)
dispatching (p. 189)
finished goods (p. 185)
finished products inventory (p. 193)
Gantt chart (p. 187)
industrial purchasing (p. 190)
inventory cycle (p. 194)

inventory turnover (p. 194)
lead time (p. 194)
make-or-buy decisions (p. 193)
materials inventory (p. 193)
materials management (p. 185)
mercantile buying (p. 190)
merchandise inventory (p. 193)
periodic inventory (p. 195)
perpetual inventory (p. 195)
PERT (p. 188)
purchase order (p. 191)
purchase requisition (p. 191)

raw materials (p. 185)
receiving report (p. 191)
routing (p. 187)
safety stock (p. 194)
schedule performance reports (p. 190)
scheduling (p. 187)
scrap report (p. 190)
semifinished goods (p. 185)
starting materials (p. 185)
traffic manager (p. 196)
value analysis (p. 193)

2. What kinds of materials and goods must be managed in a manufacturing process?
3. What is the major objective of production materials management?
4. What is the purpose of a bill of materials?
5. Briefly describe the five activities involved in production planning and control.
6. What is the difference between industrial purchasing and mercantile buying?
7. What are the three factors a purchasing agent must consider in deciding when to place orders to insure an adequate stock of starting materials?
8. How does lead time affect inventory cycle?

Case Critique 11-1
Scheduling the "Moon-Man"

The OK Toy Company has been having trouble with planning and scheduling. Right now, its managers face two critical problems. Today is May 1, and the company's designer has just developed an electronically driven "Moon-Man." The company wants to make sure that special tools and materials are purchased, the production presses set up, and employees trained so that the new toy can be shipped to retailers by November 15 for the Christmas rush. The second problem involves scheduling of OK's five plastic molding presses. The company makes more than two dozen different plastic toys on these presses. The quantity of each toy made at a particular time depends greatly upon how many customers' orders are in the shop at one time. The way the presses are scheduled now is troublesome and costly. Sometimes, two or three presses are idle at once. Other times, the same presses have to be worked overtime for days on end. The plant manager is seeking a solution to both problems.

1. Which problem can best be solved by using a Gantt chart? Why?
2. Which problem can best be solved by using a PERT chart? Why?
3. Why wouldn't it be wise to settle on just one scheduling technique to solve both problems?

Case Critique 11-2
The Out-of-Stock Tape-Reel Labels

"We're out of tape-reel labels again!" exclaimed Bill Becket, administrative assistant at the Miracle Data Processing Center. "I checked on them a couple of weeks ago, and we had more than 5,000 of them. Someone must be pilfering them for labeling packages at home."

"I don't think that 5,000 labels is an awful lot, the way that we use them," observed Mary Jo McGuire, the Center's processing supervisor. "My guess is that we use more than 500 a day. What with spoilage and the like, we probably used up that batch of 5,000 in the last ten days."

"Well," said Bill, "I'm going to set up some sort of inventory control system so that this doesn't happen again." Then Mary Jo asked what system he would use.

"It's going to be very simple. I'm going to mark my calendar for the last day of each month. Then, on those days, I'm going to make a count to see how many labels are on hand. Whenever I see fewer than 5,000 labels, I'll place a purchase requisition to build up our inventory again."

1. What do you think of Bill's inventory control system? What is such a system usually called? What are some of the possible flaws in it?
2. What better kind of inventory control system could you suggest?

Chapter 12

Operating
a Small
Business

1 SMALL FIRMS MUST DO EVERYTHING THAT BIG FIRMS DO . . .

but with fewer resources.

2 INDIVIDUALISTS PREVAIL

Energetic, innovative, freedom loving, and broad-gauged.

.3 DIFFERENT KINDS OF OPERATIONS PRESENT SPECIAL CHALLENGES

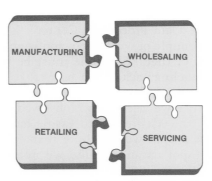

MANUFACTURING

WHOLESALING

RETAILING

SERVICING

4 FINANCIAL LITERACY IS ESSENTIAL

Ignorance of basic money matters is a major stumbling block.

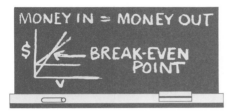

5 THE GOVERNMENT TRIES TO HELP

through various agencies.

Learning Objectives

The purpose of this chapter is to emphasize the similarities and differences between small and large business operations and to discuss the various factors needed to make a small business succeed.

As evidence of general comprehension, after completing this chapter you should be able to:

1. *Define a small business and comprehend the difficulty of operating one.*
2. *Recognize the kinds of people who create small businesses and explain the advantages and disadvantages of their operations.*
3. *Compare the ease of entry into capital-intensive and labor-intensive businesses and recognize the ways in which operating emphasis differs among such businesses.*
4. *Explain the value to a business of having sales revenues exceed operating expenses and know how to find a break-even point.*
5. *Identify various agencies of the federal government that aid small business and describe the services they provide.*

If your class is using SSweetco: Business Model and Activity File for Business in Action, see Chapter 12 in that book after you complete this chapter. There you will find exercises and activities to help you apply your learning to typical business situations.

It is the dream of many job-locked individuals that some day they will break the bonds and open their own small businesses. Thousands do each year. And thousands fail. The opportunity glows like a rainbow, nevertheless. Liz will start up her own tailor shop. Joe, Frank, and Marian will form a partnership for a balloon business. Sybil's idea for a diet center will start on a shoestring and mushroom 20 years later into 1,300 franchises. Anthony will form his Spaghetti Pot, not to serve meals to sit-down customers, but as a take-out service. David grows his own grapes and operates a marginally profitable winery. John and his family incorporate to sell the flowers they grow at a roadside stand. In Alabama alone, 500 small business people are growing Christmas trees for sale. Elsa and Peter run a unisex hairstyling parlor. Linda operates a small firm that provides accounting services for other small businesses. Charlie mowed lawns in high school; his incorporated firm now performs contract gardening for over 200 homeowners, restaurants, banks, and shopping malls. What does it take to run a small business profitably? Five areas of expertise predominate: an ability to operate on limited resources, personal energy and initiative, an ability to apply different skills in different businesses, financial awareness, and a little bit of help from the government.

1   SMALL FIRMS DO EVERYTHING LARGE FIRMS DO

And they must do it with less

When it comes to business, size is relative. About 99 out of every 100 United States' firms have annual sales of less than $1 million. The great majority of businesses do far less than that and are very, very tiny by comparison. The gigantic companies get the attention. More than 500 of them do more than $1 billion in sales each year. These are companies like Aetna Life & Casualty, Bank of America, Campbell Soup, and Du Pont. Down a notch in sales revenues are another 1,000 firms that seem small only when compared with giants. These firms, although their names and brands may be nationally known, number their sales only in the tens of millions of dollars. Companies with brands like Wham-O, Crayola, and Tobasco, are examples.

Below these 1,500 to 2,000 companies, lies the large mass of small businesses. For example, 8 out of 10 of the more than 11 million businesses in the United States take in less than $100,000 a year. That means that nearly 9 million companies are so small that they can support only two or three adult owners or employees. They can do that only under the most favorable conditions. Most small businesses do not do nearly so well. And most small businesses remain small; only a few grow up to be big businesses.

WHERE THE MONEY GOES

Only a little left for the owner

To get a better sense of the challenge to small business operations, consider a business that has sales at the top of the range, or about

ACTION BRIEF

From the Rag Business to Riches.   On Seventh Avenue in New York City, the apparel trade is known as "the rag business." Many of the people who work there, however, dream of becoming millionaires. A couple of years ago, it happened big for one such dreamer. Liz Claiborne, a fashion designer, broke away on her own to style and manufacture her own moderately priced clothing. Under the Liz Claiborne label, her skirts and blouses compete favorably with those from the top design houses. Claiborne's firm "went public" in 1980. At that point, she pulled $2.7 million out of the business as a reward for her efforts as a small business operator. Today, Claiborne is president of the corporation, which does in excess of $100 million a year.

Source: John Byrne, "Faces Behind the Figures: Liz, Tailor," Forbes, January 4, 1982, p. 286.

$100,000 a year. That figure sounds like a lot, doesn't it? A closer examination of the numbers, however, is revealing.

- Most businesses spend 20 to 50 cents of their sales dollars for materials and supplies. Let's be generous and earmark only $20,000 for this expense. (That leaves $80,000.)
- Businesses typically spend another 20 percent for rent, heat, light, telephone, insurance, and taxes. We will earmark $20,000 for these. (That leaves $60,000.)
- It is a rare firm that does not incur 20 to 50 percent for labor costs. We will use the lower figure and take away only $20,000. (That leaves $40,000.) We are not through yet.
- Many companies need an auto or truck for transportation, buy advertising, and pay commissions to salespeople or distributors. This eats up another 10 percent, or $10,000. (That leaves $30,000 for the owner-operator—before taxes—to compensate for the risk involved and his or her own labor.)

A profit of $30,000 a year on $100,000 sales is exceptional. In the great majority of cases, the profit figure is much lower than that—more nearly $10,000 or less. Why do owners choose to stay in business under these circumstances? The answer is often quite simple. The major portion of their labor costs is paid not as wages to outsiders, but to the owners themselves, or to employees who are members of their families.

DEFINITION OF SMALL

It is a relative term

Agencies of the federal government have taken pains to try to define "small business." The purpose of their definitions is to guide the government in its efforts to provide support and encouragement to small business operators. These definitions of *small business* can be summarized as follows:

1. It is small relative to other firms in its industry.
2. It is independently owned.
3. Its operations are typically local in nature.
4. Its owners are likely to be its operators.
5. For federal interest and support purposes, certain upper limits have been set on size according to the nature of the class of business: At their largest, (a) a small retailing firm will have less than $1 million in annual receipts, (b) a wholesaling firm less than $9.5 million, (c) a service firm less than $2 million, and (d) a manufacturing firm fewer than 250 employees.

As you can see, "small" can be quite large, even under the federal specifications. In this chapter, however, the focus of the discussion is on the 9 million or so firms whose businesses fall far below the federal limits.

Finally, ownership of small businesses can, and do, take any form of legal ownership. Small businesses are mainly single proprietorships, but they may also be partnerships. A great many are in the form of small, family-style or closely-held, corporations.

SMALL VERSUS LARGE OPERATIONS

They differ in scale and resources

It is true that the operation of a small business is fundamentally the same as a large one. Regardless of size, every business has to perform the same managerial and operational functions. Every business must find a way of competing in the social, political, physical, and economic environment. Nevertheless, there are significant differences, and they are mainly a matter of scale and resources.

The scale of operations in a small business is often crude and in miniature. The owner of a small manufacturing company, for example, must plan production (although it may be done on the back of an envelope), engage in research and development (if only in the backroom over a hot-plate), arrange for operating materials and supplies (perhaps picking them up in the trunk of a car), and exercise control (such as checking accounts on the kitchen table at midnight).

It is legendary, too, that managers of small businesses wear a number of hats as they fulfill various functions. Their businesses are not large enough to afford the hiring of specialists. The heart of the matter is that small businesses operate without the resources of larger ones. To begin with, they do not have as much money. And it is money that provides the financial support needed to obtain all the other essential operating resources of a business—facilities, equipment, materials, and labor. In spite of this, small business operators can find a way to survive and succeed. They do so by cutting everything down to size and by applying their limited resources to the most pressing, immediate problems. Rarely, however, are the resources of a small business ample enough so that it can afford to take the long view of its operations.

2   A SPECIAL KIND OF INDIVIDUAL PREVAILS

Energetic, innovative, freedom-loving, and broad-gauged

Some people like the security that employment in a large business can offer. Wage rates are often higher and in large organizations the physical environment more attractive. Procedures and relationships are more carefully prescribed so that managers and employees alike know where they stand and what is expected of them. On the other hand, many other people are attracted to small business operations. They like the informality and the potential breadth of daily assignments, as opposed to more narrowly specialized work in large companies. People who work in small companies often feel that they are closer to, and more involved in, the important action of the business.

ENTREPRENEURS AND FREEDOM SEEKERS

They enjoy a keener sense of involvement

Many people can start up or join a small business. Those who start them up, however, are characterized by unusual initiative, energy, and the

ACTION BRIEF

So You Want to Open a Restaurant! New York City is the Mecca for people who would like to start a restaurant. Some 3,000 people respond to that urge each year but many don't make it. Why? There are three main causes: squabbling among the operators, not enough startup money, and inexperience in selling food for profit. Says one expert: "People who have been super in their kitchens at home don't do so well when they have to cook for 200 people a day rather than 20. Some open a place and expect a big, delightful dinner party every night. They find out that it's a life of dirty dishes and no night life." Costs, too, surprise many who start up a place for the first time. A glass of water served with a meal, for example, may cost 12 cents when all the overhead is prorated. Just to equip a 40-seat restaurant, for example, $30,000 is common. Added to that are rent, utilities, telephone, insurance, and laundry, and these can easily run to $40,000 a year. Fees and permits in a city like New York add up quickly to another $10,000. Payroll for such a restaurant (paying union scale) adds still another $80,000 a year.

Source: Paul Tharp, "So You Want to Open a Restaurant." New York, February 18, 1980, p. 37.

willingness to take risks. Typically, these entrepreneurs see an opportunity that has been overlooked by, or that is too small to attract, a larger business. A major construction firm, for example, may not want to take on small jobs, like renovating an old house or putting in a dormer window. To entrepreneurs, jobs like these represent opportunity. They are willing to risk their capital and their jobs to take advantage of them. (See Table A-1 in the Appendix.)

Many entrepreneurs seek independence. They have a maverick streak in them that urges them to try to go their own way. They like freedom of choosing their own work methods and setting their own work hours. Often, these small business operators find out that such independence is illusionary. They discover that instead of having to knuckle under to a boss in a large corporation, they must accommodate the whims and demands of their customers. In general, hours of employment for operators of small businesses tend to be very long. Sixty-hour weeks are not unusual.

Many people like to work for smaller firms because jobs there offer a higher degree of involvement. Even the lowest-level employee is given a chance to interact with high-level managers and with customers and vendors. The work itself seems more relevant because employees can see how the business operates from beginning to end. A clerk in a large insurance company, for example, may know only what happens in the specialized, data-recording department. A clerk in a local independent insurance agency gets a fuller picture of the meaning of her routines. She sits at a desk near the owner, meets clients regularly, and feels a personal impact when fire or accident strikes a client. On the other hand, advancement opportunities in small businesses are greatly restricted. The sheer number of jobs in larger companies creates many more chances for an employee's upward movement.

SMALL BUSINESS ADVANTAGES

Faster response and lower overheads

People who operate small business often find that they have several advantages over larger ones. If a business succeeds, an owner may find himself or herself deriving far more income from profits than he or she might earn otherwise as an employee of a larger company. It is a fact that hundreds of people become millionaires each year by starting up their own businesses.

Small firms can act faster than larger firms. They are like small motor boats that can turn quickly in the water to avoid a collision. A large ocean liner may take a mile or more to alter its course.

Decisions are made more rapidly in small firms because there are fewer people whose opinions must be considered. There are fewer levels of bureaucracy and considerably less red tape. A local retail store, for example, can detect the appeal of the latest clothing fad and put that merchandise on its shelves, while the potential for that fad is still being discussed in product committee meetings of a large department store chain.

Finally, overhead is far less than in larger companies. *Overhead* is the term applied to the expenses incurred by activities that do not add visible value during the conversion process. A large manufacturing firm, for example, may employ a full-time nurse to take care of employees' minor ailments. While this may be a desirable service to the employees and to the organization, a smaller firm may not offer the same kind of service. As a consequence, it spends less money on medical care and many other desirable, but not indispensable, overhead activities.

PITFALLS OF SMALL BUSINESSES

Weak, narrow-gauge management is a problem

Dun & Bradstreet is a firm that specializes in examining the credit-worthiness and financial strengths of businesses. It regularly reports that the major cause of failure in small businesses lies in the weakness of its management. Men and women who start up a business often excel in one specialized line of work. It may be in design, or production, or marketing. Unless these people can broaden their skills to include all the major functions of operations, they may find themselves in trouble. Then, too, each function of a business requires its own particular know-how and skill. At the minimum, these include marketing, production and operations, finance, accounting, and personnel. Successful small business operation requires the capability of covering all these functions effectively.

Successful management, in small as well as large businesses, requires the ability to plan, organize, direct, and control. Unfortunately, a great many entrepreneurs lack such general competence.

It is not enough for the owner to wear many hats. He or she must also be able to carry on effectively the functions that these hats signify. If he or she cannot, then such skills must be added to the staff, or acquired through contracting the service from others.

3 EACH KIND OF OPERATION HAS ITS DISTINCT CHALLENGE

Labor is often more vital than capital

Small businesses are usually those that require relatively little money to start up. This means that they are not capital-intensive. They are more likely to be labor-intensive, in that labor, usually the owner's, is the prime resource. Inner-city people who start their own businesses often describe the assets they build this way, from their own labor, as "sweat equity." Businesses that require little in the way of capital, equipment, and facilities to begin are described by economists as having *ease of entry*. Capital intensive and labor intensive businesses, however, have their own special problems, as shown in Figure 12-1.

FOUR COMMON FIELDS ATTRACT

Each presents its own particular challenge

Certain kinds of industries attract small business because of their relatively low capital requirements and their ease of entry.

Retailing All that is required in the way of facilities is a rented store and some shelving. Merchandise may often be bought on credit.

ACTION BRIEF

A Back-Breaking Romance. David Lett's Eyrie Vineyards bottle over 2,000 cases of wine each year, for a net sales of about $100,000. The company, however, doesn't make a profit: it is still hoping to break even. "I'm not in the winemaking business to make money. I'm in it to make wine," says Lett. To keep the business afloat financially, Lett has sold college textbooks during the winter and worked his vineyard during the summer. "Everyone gets into this business for the romance of it," observes Lett, who at age 42 has found his beard turning white. "It looks like a wonderful way of making a living, but it's a lot of back-breaking work."

Source: Sanford L. Jacobs, "Business Realities Can Ruin Romance of Small Vineyard," The Wall Street Journal, September 21, 1981, p. 37.

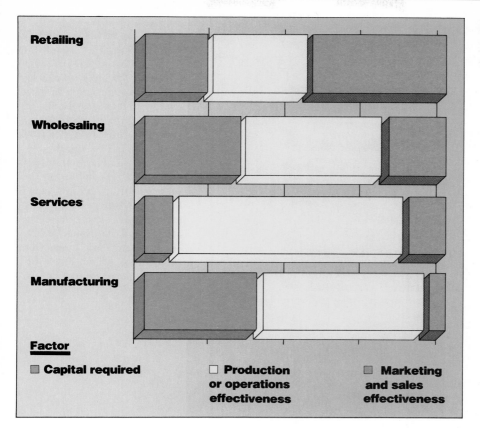

Figure 12-1
Relative importance of various factors to small business operations.

Location, however, is critically important, and rent for good locations, such as at a shopping mall, can run as high as $3,000 per month for a 20- to 30-foot store. Retailing is intensely competitive, and the markup margins for profit very slim. *Markup* is the difference between what the retailer pays for the merchandise and the price a customer is charged. Markup can be calculated a number of different ways. One simple way is to divide (a) the difference between the cost and the selling price by (b) the selling price and express this as a percentage. For example, if a retailer pays $10 for a man's shirt and sells it for $20, the markup would be $10 ÷ $20, or 50 percent. This markup may seem a lot, but by the time other expenses of operating are paid, the amount left for profit is very small. Grocery retailing is a case in point. The most successful supermarkets average less than 3 percent net profit on sales, even though their markups may typically range from 20 to 40 percent on each item sold.

Merchandising sense is particularly critical to retailing. Store layouts, for example, can be cleverly arranged to steer customers to high-markup items, as shown in Figure 12-2. In recent years, a sensitivity to local consumer needs has helped small, independent supermarket operators to succeed in many instances where a supermarket giant has failed.

Wholesaling   Despite the criticism that "middlemen" or "intermediaries" occasionally attract from consumers, the United States' economy would not survive without them. There always seems to be a place

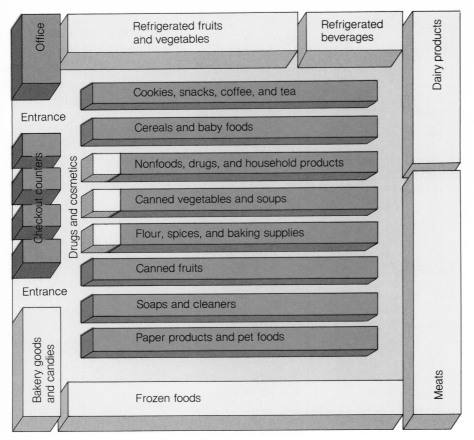

Figure 12-2
Typical layout for a small supermarket. The layout of merchandise in a retail shop is often critical to its success. Layouts are designed to direct customer flow past high profit and impulse products and make the customer work harder to find low profit staple items. Here, frequently purchased perishables are placed at the sides and rear to divert customers from the center aisles where staples are located. Nonfood items, such as drugs and cosmetics are displayed near checkout counters to promote impulse buying.

for the entrepreneur who is willing to assume the burden of helping to distribute someone else's products. The wholesaler does this by either (*a*) buying from a manufacturer and reselling to retailers or industrial users or (*b*) acting in some way or another as a go-between. Wholesaling markups are almost always less than retailing markups. The profit a wholesaler makes depends greatly upon the value the manufacturer and the retailers, or industrial users, place on the service that is rendered. As a consequence, wholesalers often find themselves in a profit squeeze between the two.

Services   Here, again, small businesses may provide services directly to consumers or to other firms. The firms that buy this service may be other small businesses or very large ones. Opportunities to create a small service business are everywhere. To begin with, there are those services that are relatively capital-intensive, like dry cleaning, self-service laundries, and photofinishing, of course. There are a greater number of services that are labor-intensive, however. These include accounting and tax preparation, hairdressing and barbering, window washing and floor waxing, lawnmowing and gardening, painting and carpentering. Many of these small businesses exist by performing for a fee a portion of the work (*subcontracting*) of a larger firm. This helps to lessen the need for marketing skills, since the larger firm often obtains the business through its own sales force or advertising programs before passing a portion along to the small subcontractor.

Manufacturing   Small business operators look for manufacturing opportunities that are relatively low in capital requirements. As a result, many small manufacturing companies use secondhand equipment or engage in labor-intensive operations. Leather working, silversmithing, weaving, and other small craft operations have been especially popular in the last decade. Small manufacturers often keep their capital needs low by purchasing semifinished components rather than by acquiring expensive equipment to make the parts themselves. Small manufacturers also do a great deal of subcontracting work for larger firms so as to minimize marketing expenses.

THREE POPULAR FORMS OF OPERATION
Provide a fast start and low overhead

As indicated earlier in the chapter, small businesses can and do choose any legal form they wish. Within these options, three methods of operation have become increasingly popular. These are discussed below.

Franchising   The skills required in starting a business from scratch are so varied that the opportunity to purchase a franchise appeals to many entrepreneurs. As discussed in detail on pages 66 to 70 in Chapter 4, the franchisor provides all the financial, production, and market planning for the business, along with a location and the equipment needed to start up. The franchisee pays a flat sum of money for this comprehensive head start (called a *turnkey arrangement*, as shown in Figure 12-3). Typically, the franchisee also continues to pay the franchisor a percentage of sales revenues so long as the franchise exists. The advantages of obtaining the varied know-how and assistance is often offset by the fees charged by the franchisor. Franchise operation, like most small businesses, usually requires hard work and long hours from the owners with no guarantee of success.

Subcontracting   This approach enables a small business to get a share of a job that it could not afford to finance or handle by itself. A couple of individuals working together as a roofing partnership might never be able to manage the building of a complete house. Subcontracting that portion of a larger contractor's business is attractive to them. Their financial investment is minimal. They have little marketing to do. They get paid quickly for their efforts, since they do not have to wait for the house to be sold. On the other hand, they may be forced to take on work that has only minimal profitability, since the house builder also expects to make a profit from the subcontractor's work.

Direct Mail   In the last several years, many a person has started a

Figure 12-3
Turnkey arrangements provided by some franchisors are designed to get the franchisee off to a comprehensive headstart in operating a business. The wherewithal and services provided by the franchisor, in effect, allow the franchisee to simply "turn the key" to open the door of his or her business and begin immediate operations on a fairly sound basis.

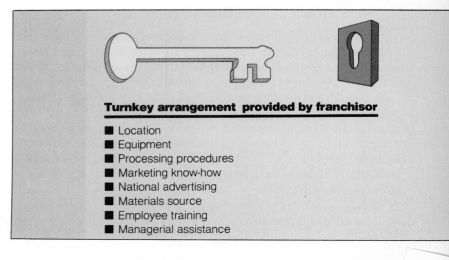

Turnkey arrangement provided by franchisor

- Location
- Equipment
- Processing procedures
- Marketing know-how
- National advertising
- Materials source
- Employee training
- Managerial assistance

part-time business based upon direct mail operation. Direct mail is the solicitation of customer orders by mail (telephone, television, or magazine advertisements may also be used) and fulfillment of these orders by postal or commercial delivery. This is a special form of retailing, of course. It has the advantage of enabling a business to be begun on a very small base. The business, if it succeeds, can be built little by little. Direct mail is very risky, however. To be profitable, 2 out of every 100 mailings must be converted to sales. This takes unique marketing and cost control efforts. Postal rates keep rising. Catalogs and mailing pieces are increasingly expensive. In its early stages, direct mail operation is very labor intensive. It requires a great deal of careful record keeping and market analysis.

Inventory costs for direct mail operations can be minimized through the use of **drop shipments.** Using this method, the direct-mail operator does not stock the items that are promoted. In effect, he or she acts like a manufacturer's agent. When a customer makes a purchase, the direct-mail operator notifies the manufacturer, distributor, or retailer who, for a fee, ships the product directly from its inventory.

4   FINANCIAL LITERACY IS ESSENTIAL

Naiveté in money matters is a major stumbling block

Small business operators have been notorious for their ignorance of two basic financial truths. These are two concerns that are crucial to every enterprise: (a) the need for incoming revenues to match or exceed outgoing expenditures and (b) the knowledge of the exact point at which this can occur. The former principle is enlarged upon later on in Chapter 20. It has proven to be such a stumbling block to small businesses, however, that it will be outlined briefly in this section. The second principle will be discussed here in full.

THE NEED FOR A POSITIVE CASH FLOW

More money coming in than going out

For a business to survive, it is essential that—over an extended period of time, such as a year—the money flowing into the business from sales equals or exceeds the money that flows out to pay its bills. Said another way, small business operators cannot (for long) spend more money than is coming in through the cash register. For this reason, banks and other institutions that lend money to a small business usually insist that the operator develop a business plan. A **business plan** is simply a numerical projection of (a) how much money the business expects to generate through sales over the next year or two, and from what sources, and (b) how much money the business expects to spend, and for what, during the same period. A carefully planned, realistic business plan is the foundation of business success. It goes a long way toward identifying the main sources of risks and directing the operator to take steps to minimize them.

Issues & Highlights

When Helen Wacey's husband died and left her with a little capital and four children, she had an idea. She and a friend wanted to open a retail craft center, which would be called Scarborough Fair. Ultimately, they would employ a staff of seven people to sell a unique line of pottery, jewelry, and gourmet cookware. At the time, however, Wacey's lawyer listened to her idea and advised her to get a steady job instead. She didn't agree. "Why should I throw myself into the job market, where women earn only 60 percent of what men do when I can go into business for myself and create more money?" She got help from a small government project aimed at assisting women who wanted to start their own businesses. The American Women's Economic Development Corporation (AWED), a pilot unit of the Small Business Administration, sponsored Wacey's notion by training her for a year. Wacey got her business going, and it succeeded very well. In fact, of the 266 women assisted by AWED, only 2 went bankrupt. That compares exceptionally well with the four out of five new businesses that fail within the first five years.

Source: Reynolds Dodson, "Capitalist Tools for Women," Parade, October 28, 1979, p. 21.

Should the government continue to give special assistance to would-be owners and owners of small businesses who are women or members of a disadvantaged minority group? Or should everyone, regardless, have equal access to such assistance?

KNOWLEDGE OF THE BREAK-EVEN POINT

The sales volume at which profits begin

All pricing decisions and production plans for a business must be based on the knowledge of the business's **break-even point.** This is the point at which the volume of goods sold at a chosen price will exactly equal the total cost of producing these goods. Below that sales volume, a company will lose money. Sales above that point will return a profit to the company.

In figuring the cost of making products for sale, companies must consider two different kinds of costs. Some costs are directly associated with the production of a specific item. A wooden table, for instance, may contain $12 worth of wood, glue, screws, and finishing materials and take $14 worth of labor to construct. These costs are directly related to the number of tables made. One table will need $26 worth of materials and labor. One thousand tables will need $26,000 worth. (For the sake of simplicity, quantity discounts on materials are ignored.) Since these costs vary with the amount of output, they are called **variable costs.**

Other costs do not vary so directly with the amount of goods produced but remain relatively stable. These **fixed costs** include such items as rent, heat, light, insurance, and other overhead costs. They cannot be associated with any particular unit of output. It should be noted that fixed costs are not, in fact, entirely fixed. For instance, a machine that is used heavily on long production runs may need more repairs and replacements than one that is rarely used. More heat will be needed when a plant has full employment than when it is partly idle. Fixed costs are the general costs of keeping a business running. They do, nevertheless, affect the total costs of producing goods. In break-even calculations, they are considered fixed regardless of the amounts produced.

The break-even point is the quantity of goods or services that must be sold at a chosen price so that the total revenue from these sales will exactly equal the total costs (variable as well as fixed) incurred by the company for making that quantity of goods or services. The calculation of this point is done in three steps, as shown graphically in Figure 12-4.

Step 1 Is to Find the Total Cost of Producing the Goods The graph in Part 1 of Figure 12-4 assumes that the fixed cost of operating this particular company is $1,000. A straight line (the fixed-

Figure 12-4
How a break-even point is determined.

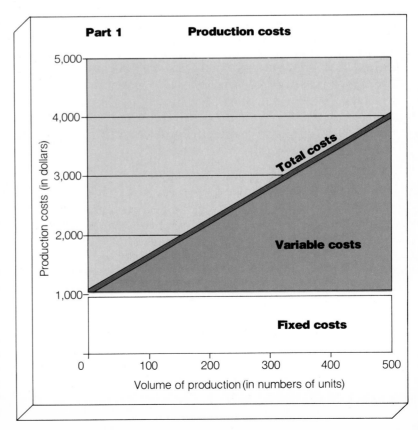

cost line) is drawn at the $1,000 cost level, indicating that the company will have to spend that amount regardless of whether it makes no widgets or 500 of them. The variable cost for making this particular widget is known to be $6 each, to cover the cost of materials and labor. If the company makes 100 widgets, the variable cost will be $600 (100 × $6); if it makes 200, the variable cost will be $1,200; if it makes 300, the variable cost will be $1,800, and so on. The trick now is to find the total cost. This is done by adding the variable costs in each instance to the fixed costs. Thus, for 100 widgets, the total cost is $1,600 ($600 + $1,000); for 200, $2,200 ($1,200 + $1,000); for 300, $2,800 ($1,800 + $1,000); and so on. The graph shows the total cost by plotting 0 production at $1,000, 100 at $1,600, 200 at $2,200, and 300 at $2,800, and connecting the points.

Step 2 in Calculating the Break-Even Point Is to Find the Total Revenue for Any Level of Sales   Here, the assumption is that the company will sell its widgets at $10 each. If it sells none, its revenue will be zero. That is the first point on the graph, shown on Part 2 of Figure 12-4. If it sells 100, the revenue will be $1,000 (100 × $10); if it sells 200, the total revenue will be $2,000 (200 × $10); if it sells 300, it will be $3,000 (300 × $10), and so on. These points are plotted on the sales revenue chart (Part 2 of Figure 12-4) and connected to form the total revenue line.

Step 3 Is to Put the Two Charts Together   The point at which the total sales revenue line intersects the total cost line is the break-even point (as shown in Part 3 of Figure 12-4). If you look closely, you can see that the company would lose money if it made and sold only

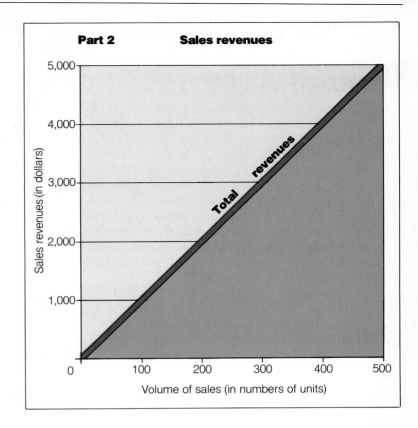

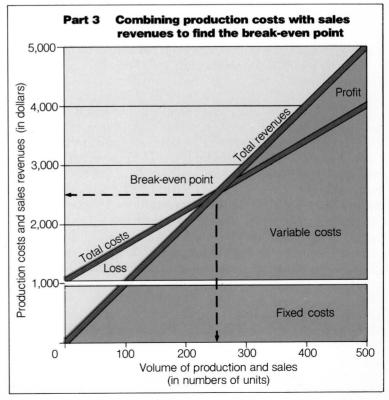

100 widgets (total revenue = $1,000; total cost = $1,600). Similarly, it would lose money at 200 widgets (total revenue = $2,000; total cost = $2,200). It will make a profit, however, if it makes and sells 300 widgets (total revenue = $3,000; total costs = $2,800). The point at which it will begin to make a profit, then, is somewhere between 200 and 300 widgets, the point at which the total revenue line crosses the total cost line. For this company, the break-even point is 250. (Total revenue for 250 widgets is $2,500 [250 × $10]; total costs for 250 widgets is $2,500 [250 × $6 + $1,000].)

The company in this example now knows that if it decides to make fewer than 250 widgets and sells them for $10 each, it will lose money even if it sells them all. If it decides to make more than 250 widgets, and is able to sell them all for $10, it will begin to make money. Based on this knowledge, a company can try to either raise its selling point or reduce its costs in order to lower its break-even point. In any event, the company will always know how many widgets it must sell to make a profit, regardless of how many it makes initially.

Service companies use the same principle in pricing and costing their units of service (such as the number of windows to be washed). Retailers and wholesalers apply the same analysis in determining how many units of merchandise must be sold at a given price to break even.

5   THE GOVERNMENT TRIES TO HELP

Federal agencies aid small business operators

There are several agencies of the federal government whose primary purpose is to offer support and guidance to small businesses. Principal among these is the *Small Business Administration (SBA)*, an agency created by the Small Business Act of 1953. The SBA has its headquarters in Washington, D.C., and it operates from 6 regional and nearly 100 field offices.

Specifically, the SBA provides guidance to small business operators in the form of special courses and workshops in management problems and skills. It publishes a number of booklets designed to show how to prepare a business plan, start up and operate dozens of popular kinds of small businesses. (See Table 12-1 for an example of the kind of information the SBA makes available to small retailers.) The SBA also helps small businesses obtain their fair share of government contracts.

Of particular interest to many small business owners and potential owners is the SBA's function in helping them to obtain loans for a broad range of business reasons, but especially the capital needed to start up and operate a business until it gets moving. While the SBA may not be able to provide nor guarantee the funds needed to start a business, the agency offices can be of assistance to small business people in finding venture capital. *Venture capital* is simply another name for the money that a person must find in order to start up a business and keep it in operation during the start-up period, which may last as long as three years. Venture capital is obtained from banks and other lending institutions. It may also come from individuals in a community who may be willing to risk their own capital in order to share in the business's ownership.

TABLE 12-1
Twenty-Six Danger Signals for Small Retail Operators

According to the Small Business Administration, certain signals of poor retail management pop up like red flags on expired parking meters. The SBA says that a small retail store is in trouble if:

1. Many customers walk out without buying.
2. Many old customers no longer visit the store.
3. The number of pedestrians and vehicles passing in front of the store has fallen off.
4. Customers are not urged to buy additional or more expensive items.
5. Sales are down for the month over the same month last year.
6. Sales for the year are down over the same period last year.
7. Display windows are not trimmed with new, exciting merchandise.
8. Display racks, shelves, and counters are dusty.
9. Some of the stock looks "shopworn."
10. Prices are not in line with those of competitors.
11. Money that can be spent for new stock is limited because the backroom is full of slow-moving items.
12. Markdowns on style items are not made quickly when customers begin to discard an old style for a new one.
13. More than a few seasonal items are carried over to next year.
14. Cash discounts are not taken on purchases.
15. Employees are slow in greeting customers.
16. Employees appear indifferent and make customers wait unnecessarily.
17. Personal appearance of employees is not neat.
18. Salespeople lack knowledge of the store's merchandise.
19. The owner-manager barely makes ends meet from month to month.
20. The owner-manager has trouble meeting payments on bank loans.
21. The owner-manager pays herself or himself more than is justified by the store's sales.
22. The bank is reluctant to lend the store money.
23. The owner-manager pays personal expenses out of the same checking account as his or her business expenses.
24. Credit customers are behind in their payments.
25. Stock turnover is slower than the average for the type of merchandise carried.
26. Gross profit is less than the average for the type of retail operation and the merchandise carried.

Source: "Watch Out! Trouble Is Brewing in a Small Retail Store If . . . ," *Atlanta Business Chronicle*, October 9, 1978, p. 16.

The **Small Business Institute (SBI),** sponsored by the SBA, functions at over 300 schools and colleges throughout the country. Senior and graduate students, under the supervision of faculty, offer consulting services to small businesses under this program. Firms that operate with SBA guaranteed loans often must utilize this service as a loan requirement.

Another federal agency, the *Office of Minority Business Enterprises (OMBE),* works alongside the SBA to provide special assistance to women, blacks, and other small business operators who are judged to be minorities in the United States' population. The *Committee for Economic Development (CED),* chartered by Congress and supported by federal funds, is also active in providing information and assistance to small businesses, especially those that operate in disadvantaged areas.

In the long run, however, most small businesses must start up and survive on their own. Informed operators, however, seek and accept every kind of assistance they can get from federal sources.

Key Concepts

1. Small firms must do everything that large firms do, although they have fewer resources and operate on a much smaller scale. As a consequence, small businesses are more likely to be preoccupied with current problems than long-term considerations.

2. People who operate small businesses derive advantages from their characteristic initiative, energy, and desire for independence. Decisions can be made more quickly, red tape is at a minimum, and overheads are low. On the other hand, operators must become generalists in management for the business to survive.

3. Each kind of business poses different kinds of startup and operating problems, according to how capital-intensive or labor-intensive it is. Emphasis in retailing and wholesaling is on marketing skills; in services and manufacturing, upon production and operations excellence.

4. Small business operators must comprehend the principle that income from sales revenues must regularly exceed outgoing expense. They must also know the exact point at which the sale of a certain quantity of goods or services at a chosen price will match the cost of producing these goods or services. Below that point, the firm loses money; above it, the firm makes a profit.

5. The federal government offers special assistance to small businesses in the form of information, management training, and loan guarantees through such agencies as the Small Business Administration, the Small Business Institute, and the Office of Minority Business Enterprises.

Review Questions

1. Define, explain, or identify, each of the following key terms or phrases found on the pages indicated.

   break-even point (p. 210)
   business plan (p. 208)
   Committee for Economic Development (p. 214)
   drop shipment (p. 208)
   ease of entry (p. 204)
   fixed costs (p. 210)
   markup (p. 205)
   Office of Minority Business Enterprises (p. 214)
   overhead (p. 203)
   small business (p. 201)
   Small Business Administration (p. 212)
   Small Business Institute (p. 213)
   turnkey arrangement (p. 207)
   variable costs (p. 210)
   venture capital (p. 212)

2. What four general classes of expenses must a small business be concerned with?

3. List at least three characteristics that define a small business.

4. Describe some advantages that small businesses have over larger ones.

5. What is the most common reason for failure of a small business? Explain why.

6. What is the difference between a company's markup and its profit?

7. Why might a person who wants to start up a small business choose to obtain a turnkey arrangement from a franchisor?

8. In what way can a business plan help a small business operator to avoid spending more money than the firm takes in?

9. List three specific kinds of information a businessperson must know in order to compute a break-even point.

10. What federal organizations are likely to be of most help to small businesses? Explain the reasons for your answer.

Case Critique 12-1
Disposing of the "Dogs"

Men's clothing shops have their own special kind of problems. To begin with, there isn't much margin to work with. Net profits average only about 5 percent of the sales dollar. Unlike grocery stores where the merchandise often turns over 40 or more times a year, the inventory of men's fashions turn over only about 2 times a year. For a family-owned store like Strouse & Bros. of Evansville, Indiana, this is only the tip of the iceberg. Like other independent clothiers, Strouse must place orders for its fall clothing line, for example, 90 or more days in advance. If a particular style doesn't sell, the company is stuck with the merchandise on its shelves. To get rid of an unpopular fashion, the company frequently has to "mark down," or cut its prices. Meanwhile, it has incurred the cost of stocking the inventory and passed up the chance to sell some other article of clothing from the same shelf space. Out of 100 fashions each year, the firm regularly finds that 10 become best-sellers and 10 turn out to be "dogs." One option that is open to men's clothing retailers is to buy fewer fashions in advance. Another is to wait until the season is on and buy manufacturers' closeouts at a special discount.

1. If you were running this store, would you place orders for more, or less, clothing in advance? Why?

2. What might you do to increase the chances of your selecting best sellers in advance rather than "dogs"?

3. How long would you wait before marking down a poor selling article so as to close it out of stock?

Source: "POS Data Collection, Computer Support Makes Better Fit for Clothier Retailer," *Data Management*, April 1981, p. 34.

Case Critique 12-2
Dreaming of an Evergreen Christmas

Nearly 300,000 families in Alabama want to have a Christmas tree in their living room when Santa Claus comes down the chimney. About 80 percent of these trees come, not from Alabama, but from the West and Midwest. This gave 500 Alabamans the idea that growing Christmas trees might be a good business. Some farmers chose to plant 1,000 trees, others as many as 10,000. Most of the planting and trimming was done by hand. About 980 trees can be planted per acre.

For many of the growers, it turned out to be a nightmare. While evergreens spring up faster in the South than elsewhere, they also attract more voracious insects. Weeds flourish in the South, too. To control these conditions, trees must be sprayed and the soil hoed. Both operations are costly. Even experienced farmers found out that shearing trees to get dense foliage took a critical know-how they didn't have. And then, there was the problem of how to sell the trees once they were ready for cutting. The choices were: (1) sell them to wholesalers who will pick them up at the site, (2) truck them to retailers for sale in bundles, or (3) invite homeowners out to the farm to cut their own.

1. Would you classify Christmas tree growing as a capital or labor-intensive business? Why?
2. How would you decide on how many trees to plant?
3. Which channel of marketing distribution would you choose? Why?

Source: Ken Copeland, "We Have the Edge on Growing Christmas Trees," *Progressive Farmer,* June 1982, p. B-1.

Unit 5
Basic
Business
Operations—
Finance

Unit 5 analyzes the financial needs of business and describes where and how funds are obtained. It also explores the ways in which businesses can reduce their financial risks and sets forth the principles of good credit management.

One of the goals of management is to obtain financing for such permanent assets as buildings and machinery and for current needs such as payrolls and purchases. These financing needs, which include both long-term and short-term funds, can be met either by selling a share in the ownership or by borrowing. The banking system, private and institutional investors, and the securities exchanges all play important roles in business financing.

To minimize risks, managers and owners of businesses must exercise caution, especially in credit matters. They must also take advantage of the protection that insurance can provide.

Chapter 13

Financial Management and Funding

1 FINANCIAL PLANNING
decides how much money a firm needs for how long and how the firm will use that money.

Acquiring a new plant
Hiring workers
Buying additional equipment

2 SOURCES OF FUNDS
are determined by the duration of a firm's needs.

Long-term need

Short-term need

3 EQUITY FINANCING
for business shares ownership and the possibility of profit or loss.

+$
−$

DEBT FINANCING
commits the borrower to payment.

10% DUE

4 SHORT-TERM DEBT FINANCING

comes from:

Trade credit	✔
Bank loans	✔
Factors	✔
Commercial paper	✔

5 LONG-TERM DEBT FINANCING

comes from:

Mortgages   Corporate bonds   Government

6 LONG-TERM EQUITY FINANCING

comes from the sale of preferred or common stock.

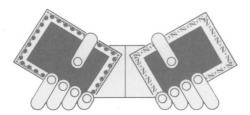

Learning Objectives

The purpose of this chapter is to describe the vital function and role of financial management in business, explain the various considerations that enter into financial planning, and distinguish between equity and debt financing.

As evidence of general comprehension, after studying this chapter you should be able to:

1. Distinguish between current and fixed assets, and show how financial management plans for the acquisition and use of funds out of current and fixed assets.
2. Explain why the source and method of financing depend on how long capital is needed.
3. Differentiate between equity financing and debt financing.
4. Identify the standard methods of short-term debt financing.
5. Identify the standard methods of long-term debt financing.
6. Recognize and explain the common methods of long-term equity financing.

If your class is using SSweetco: Business Model and Activity File for Business in Action, see Chapter 13 in that book after you finish this chapter. There you will find exercises and activities that will help you apply your learning to typical business situations.

In many parts of the country, people earn extra money by cutting and selling firewood. Even in a business as simple as this, good financial management soon proves its importance. The aspiring woodcutter cannot simply trespass on someone's property and raid the forest. The business needs capital before it can begin. The capital can come from a number of sources. The proprietor might have $900 in cash to pay for the right to cut timber for 6 months in someone else's woodlot. A local bank might lend the proprietor $3,200 for a used pickup truck to carry the wood out and deliver it to customers. A farm supply store might sell a $300 chain saw for a $100 down payment, with the balance due over a 3-month period. Once the business is set in motion, sales of firewood must produce income to pay for gas, advertising, and maintenance of the truck and saw. Income must also be sufficient to pay off the balance due on the saw, repay the bank loan plus interest, and pay for extending the woodcutting rights. If there is any money left after paying all the bills, the proprietor keeps it as profit.

These simple transactions for starting and running a part-time extractive business illustrate some of the concerns of financial management. **Financial management** plans what funds are needed for a business and where the money is to come from. It sets up the specific ways that revenues from the sale of goods or services are to be used to pay for the things the company needs. It tries to balance the flow of money into and out of the business so that the money is used efficiently and for its intended purpose.

1   FINANCIAL PLANNING FOR BUSINESSES

Financial management plans for the acquisition and use of funds

Financial planning must cover all aspects of how money is acquired and used in a business. Money for operating businesses is acquired from the personal assets of the owner or owners, by issuing and selling stocks, or by borrowing from other people or institutions that own capital. Money is used to pay for the resources needed to operate the business.

WHY BUSINESSES NEED MONEY

Capital is needed to pay for resources

Although land, labor, technology, and capital are all needed to keep businesses running, in practice, capital is the most fundamental resource. Capital is used to obtain the other three resources. The physical labor, skill, and knowledge of the women and men who work for businesses are purchased with wages, salaries, and other kinds of payment. The materials used in production processes—whether they be starting materials, supplies, or power sources—must be bought. Businesses buy (or rent) their facilities—buildings, equipment, and machines. When businesses borrow money, they must make payments—in the form of interest. **Interest** is a charge made by lenders for the use of their money.

CURRENT AND FIXED ASSETS

For short-term or long-term needs

All of the valuable resources that a business has gathered together for its use are called *assets.* Assets may be of two types: current assets and fixed assets.

Assets used to support the day-to-day operations of a company are *current assets,* or *working capital.* These assets normally can be converted into cash within a short time, usually a year or less. Current assets meet the short-term obligations of a company: employees' wages, paying bills, shipping goods to meet customer orders, and allowing credit purchases by customers. Current assets consist of cash or securities that can readily be converted to cash, inventories, and accounts receivable. Inventories are current assets because the company expects to sell them soon and recover the cash for other uses. *Accounts receivable* are the amounts owed to the company for goods or services provided to customers but not yet paid for. They are current assets because they represent the cash expected in a short time.

Fixed assets are relatively permanent goods or resources owned by a company. Most companies do not expect to turn their fixed assets into cash on a regular basis. Examples include land, factories, office buildings, durable equipment, and other long-lasting facilities of a business. The fixed assets of a company provide the long-term setting in which operations take place.

MOVEMENT OF FUNDS IN BUSINESS OPERATIONS

More money must flow in than out

For operations to continue, there must be a flow of money into and out of a business. Figure 13-1 on page 222 shows some of the specific forms the flow of funds may take.

The top drawing in the figure shows the sources of a business's financial input. Cash is received when customers pay for goods or services (**A**). This is called income or revenue. A sizeable portion of the money that flows into a business, however, does not come from sales revenue. Companies need money to buy their production facilities when they start operations and to replace and expand them later. Also, the original working capital has to come from somewhere. No current assets can be generated from sales until some goods or services are first produced. Companies need funds for this. This money can come either from borrowing or from investments by owners. Money that is borrowed by the business is called *debt financing* (**B**). Money that enters a business from its owners is called *equity financing* (**C**).

At the same time that money flows into a business, it is also expended in the form of cash to be paid out (**D**) to cover bills for materials, wages, rent, and so forth. The surplus, if there is any, is the profit (**E**) a business makes.

Some outflow of money results from a business's use of equity or debt financing. Owners who invest money will usually wish at some point to withdraw part of the profits. Companies that are publicly owned (corpo-

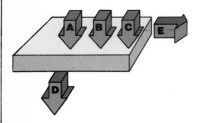

While a portion of a company's financial input is derived from **A** sales income, additional funds are acquired by the financial manager through **B** debt financing or **C** equity financing.

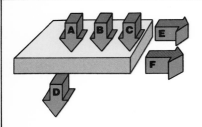

Money flows out of a firm's reserves in the form of **D** payment of bills. It is the responsibility of financial management to balance its input and its payments while trying to create **E** profits.

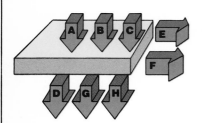

Financial management must see to it that a certain amount of the profits are paid out as **F** dividends to equity shareholders.

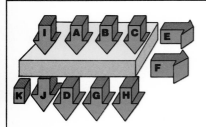

Financial management must plan for debt retirement. When the firm borrows money, it must be prepared to make **G** repayments and **H** interest payments.

Additional income is accrued from **I** interest on charge accounts. However, input is reduced as a result of **J** slow payments and **K** bad debts when income from sales comes from charge accounts and debtors are reluctant to pay. Financial management, thus, involves supervising credit and collections.

Figure 13-1
How the flow of funds into and out of a business affects the responsibilities of financial management.

rations) must pay out part of the profits in the form of dividends (**F**) to shareholders. Companies with debt financing must also make some provision to pay off, or retire, the debts (**G**). Although many companies maintain a long-term indebtedness, part of the debt must be retired periodically, even if new debts are incurred. Interest (**H**) must also be paid to the lender in return for the use of the borrowed money.

Cash flow is also affected by the ability of a business to supervise the credit it extends to its customers and its effectiveness in collecting payments. Though interest (**I**) is accrued by the company on charge accounts, the inflow of money is usually restricted to some extent by slow payments (**J**) by customers. Some customers will never pay. This money is lost to ***bad debts*** (**K**)—money not paid to the business even though goods or services have been provided.

Financial management must plan for and control all of these incoming and outgoing funds by trying to balance income from sales with the costs of operating. Equity and debt financing for facilities and working capital must be arranged. All money paid out to investors or lenders must be accounted for, all money owed to the company collected, and bad debts limited.

2   SOURCES OF FUNDS FOR BUSINESS

Duration of need dictates the source

Businesses need funds for different purposes. The specific use to which money will be put partly determines the best source for the money. Different uses for funds tie up money for different lengths of time. Money used for current assets is expected to be converted into cash within a year. Funds for fixed assets may be tied up for decades or even for centuries in some companies.

Financial needs for current assets vary. Many companies have significant changes in the levels of their current assets at different times of the year. Retail stores usually increase their merchandise inventory before Christmas, for example. A cannery might need large amounts of cash during the summer and fall to meet increased payroll and to buy fruits and vegetables. The money borrowed is expected to be recovered from sales within a short time. These are some examples of short-term requirements for funds.

There is a certain minimum level of current assets that must be maintained at all times, however. The retail store must have some merchandise inventory, and the cannery will have some inventory and accounts receivable throughout the year. These minimum current assets require funds for long periods. They may be financed differently from short-term current assets.

Long-term financing is needed for nearly every kind of fixed asset. Buildings, equipment, land, and other kinds of facilities tie up money for long periods. They must be bought with funds that are appropriate for this long-term use. Figure 13-2 illustrates the three types of funds needed for a retail store with a large increase of inventory for the Christmas season: short-term for current assets, long-term for current assets, and long-term for fixed assets.

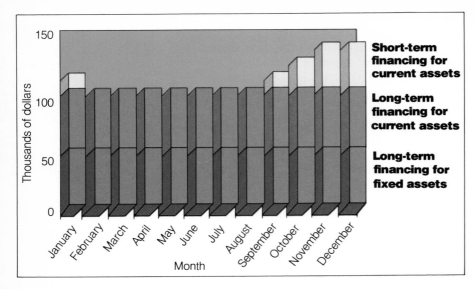

Figure 13-2
Analysis of financing needs for a retail store. The store builds merchandise inventories for the Christmas selling season and uses short-term debt sources to finance this temporary need.

3   EQUITY VERSUS DEBT FINANCING

Methods of obtaining outside funding

Most companies try to finance expansions at least in part by reinvesting—or plowing back—profits from ongoing operations. This use of **retained earnings** is a sound, stable method of growth for established companies. All businesses, however, must have financing from outside sources when they first begin operation, and most businesses need additional financing at certain points in their growth. These outside funds may come from equity financing or from debt financing. Financial management must decide what contribution each type will make to the total funds available to the business. See Figure 13-5 on page 234 for an example of how three major companies use different sources of funds to sustain their businesses.

EQUITY FINANCING

Equity shares ownership, risk, and profits

In equity financing, funds are raised by selling a portion of ownership, or equity, in the business, as by selling stock to shareholders. With this type of financing, the original owners of the business agree to share the ownership, risks, and profits of the firm with new owners or investors.

The major advantages of equity financing are:

■ No interest charges must be paid. This is a particular advantage in an economic slump when sales and revenues may be reduced.

■ Businesses with a high proportion of equity financing are generally more stable. Their solvency is less likely to be threatened by an inability to meet obligations to lenders.

■ Profits produced by a business financed by owners rather than lenders belong to the owners and are not reduced by loan payments.

The major disadvantages of equity financing are:

■ Capital needs of businesses vary over time. If requirements decrease, invested money may remain idle and not produce income.

■ A greater total investment by owners is required to maintain a given scope of operations when little or no borrowed money is used.

Equity financing has the major drawback of diluting ownership; in effect, the original owners sacrifice a portion of their control and profits.

DEBT FINANCING

Debt commits the borrower to payment

Debt financing is accomplished by borrowing funds. The borrowing may, for example, take the form of a loan from a bank or the sale of bonds. Some advantages of borrowing money for a business are:

■ Interest paid for the use of borrowed money is not taxed. This effectively reduces the cost of using the money.

■ Borrowing is convenient for short-term needs. It makes it unnecessary to keep large amounts of cash for peak needs.

■ Borrowed money provides additional capital without giving up any ownership or control of the business.

■ Owners who are able to borrow money and make profits on it can enjoy the increased profits without increasing their investment. The ability to create profits from the total capital, part of it owned and the rest borrowed, is called *leverage.*

Debt financing also has disadvantages:

■ Borrowed money is sometimes unavailable or can only be obtained at high interest rates. Companies that have come to rely on debt financing may encounter severe difficulties in this situation.

■ Companies that use borrowed money must meet interest payments regularly. This can be a burden—or even an impossibility—when revenues are down or the company is facing other financial difficulties.

Most companies today try to strike a balance between equity and debt financing. The ratio of borrowed assets to owned assets, or *debt ratio,* is another meaning of leverage. If a company's debt is $100,000 and its equity is $50,000, its debt ratio is 2:1, or 200 percent. Companies with high leverage are often believed to have a good profit potential—especially when interest rates are low. However, they are also believed to be more susceptible to failure in an economic slump.

4 SHORT-TERM DEBT FINANCING

This is the staple of finance

Companies that wish to use borrowed money for short-term needs have a variety of sources. Some of the terminology used in discussing these sources applies to almost all kinds of financing. An *instrument* is a

ACTION BRIEF

Overnight Financing. Back in 1971, Frederick W. Smith was only 27 years old and he had a great idea. He wanted to start a cargo air carrier that could promise overnight delivery of small packages all over the country. He had a very big problem, however. He would need to find $75 million to purchase a fleet of jets. By dint of both selling equity and borrowing, he found the money and formed Federal Express. Today, his company has a fleet of 75 jets, 6,800 employees, and delivers an average of 65,000 packages every night. The trick to financing Federal Express was this: about one-third of its funds came from a group of "venture capitalists" who bought shares of the proposed business; on the strength of that $25 million, Smith was able to borrow the remaining $50 million he needed. Eventually, Federal Express paid back the money it borrowed to the lenders. And the venture capitalists sold their shares to the general public in the successful corporation for about $170 million.

Source: Alan D. Hess, "Bonanza in Venture Capital," Kiwanis Magazine, June–July 1981, p. 23.

document that represents the terms of a financial transaction. A dollar bill is an instrument, as is an IOU, a stock certificate, or a government bond. *Collateral* is anything of value that a borrower promises to give the lender if the borrower is unable to repay a loan. When a bank lends money to an automobile buyer, the bank normally keeps the title to the car until the loan is paid off. The car is collateral and can be taken and sold by the bank if the borrower does not repay the loan. A loan for which collateral is held is *secured;* one with no collateral is *unsecured.*

The main types of short-term debt financing are trade credit, unsecured or secured direct loans, factoring, and commercial paper.

TRADE CREDIT
Suppliers furnish this free

The most common source of short-term borrowed funds is *trade credit,* or purchases made on credit from suppliers. Suppose that a company buys $10,000 worth of component parts from a supplier and is not required to pay for them until 30 days after they are received. This way, the purchaser is, in effect, borrowing $10,000 from the supplier for 30 days. The buyer enjoys the use of the goods for a month without having paid for them.

Companies try to reduce the amount of credit they extend to customers because giving large amounts of credit requires a large investment in current assets. Many firms allow a small discount if bills are paid quickly. Invoices may show terms such as 2/10, net/30. This means that 2 percent may be subtracted from the invoice amount if it is paid within 10 days, but that in any event the total (net) amount is due in 30 days. A bill for $800, for example, may be paid with $784 if this is done within 10 days; otherwise, the full amount must be paid. Increasingly, firms that extend trade credit apply an interest charge (typically of 1.5 percent a month) on the unpaid balance. This practice is similar to that used on consumer charge cards, such as VISA or MasterCard.

DIRECT SHORT-TERM LOANS
Banks are the primary source

Banks and other financial institutions lend money to businesses for short-term use. Numerous different instruments and borrowing methods are used. The loans may or may not require collateral.

Unsecured Loans   Unsecured loans for business use may be obtained from banks and other lending institutions, individuals, or other companies. The most common forms are promissory notes and lines of credit. A *promissory note* is one way of formalizing a direct loan. (See Figure 13-3.) It states that the borrower, who signs the note, will pay to the lender the money borrowed plus a certain interest rate at a specified future date. Most promissory notes specify periods of less than 6 months. These loans are generally used by businesses for short-term purposes such as harvesting crops or building inventory for a heavy sales season.

A *line of credit* is an agreement between a lender and a borrower that loans up to a specified maximum will be extended if needed. A retail

ACTION BRIEF

Don't Be Bashful When Borrowing.   Citibank's vice president Leonard Druger makes this observation about business borrowing: "In less than 5 percent of all applications does the businessperson ask for enough money at first. There are always cost overruns and expenses they have forgotten. Second, people who borrow want to pay the loan back too quickly. Half the time they want to borrow short to pay for a long-term asset that is not going to generate a lot of cash right away. On the other hand," advises Drugar, "the old saying that the loan shouldn't last longer than the asset is really true. Just as you don't want the payment period to be too short, you don't want to have a ten-year repayment for an asset that is only going to last five years."

Source: Edited by Paul B. Brown, "The Up-and-Comers: 'Ask for More,' " Forbes, March 1, 1982, p. 56.

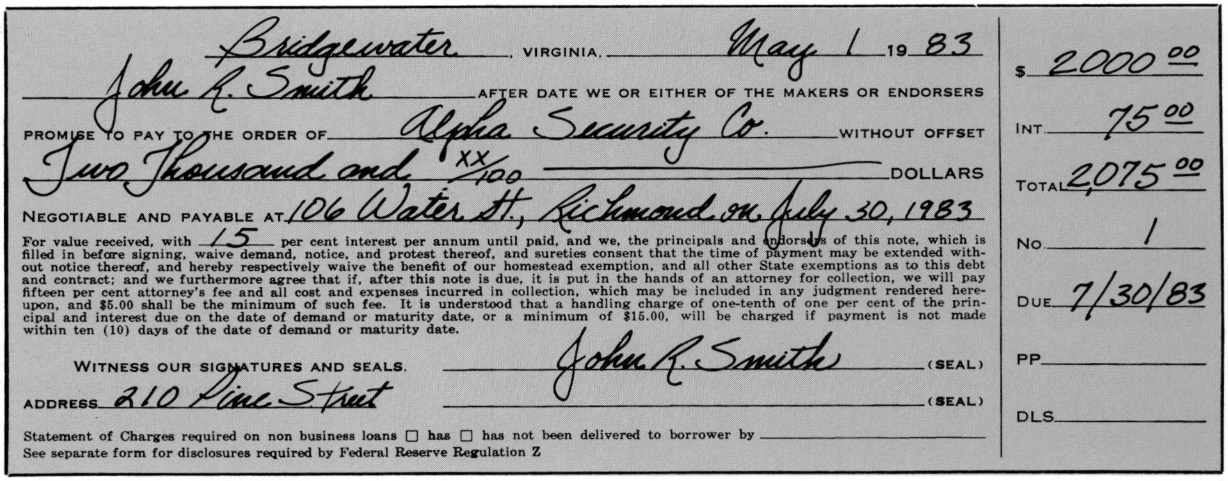

Bridgewater, VIRGINIA, *May 1* 19 83

_____ *John R. Smith* _____ AFTER DATE WE OR EITHER OF THE MAKERS OR ENDORSERS

PROMISE TO PAY TO THE ORDER OF *Alpha Security Co.* WITHOUT OFFSET

Two Thousand and XX/100 _____ DOLLARS

NEGOTIABLE AND PAYABLE AT *106 Water St., Richmond Va. July 30, 1983*

For value received, with __*15*__ per cent interest per annum until paid, and we, the principals and endorsers of this note, which is filled in before signing, waive demand, notice, and protest thereof, and sureties consent that the time of payment may be extended without notice thereof, and hereby respectively waive the benefit of our homestead exemption, and all other State exemptions as to this debt and contract; and we furthermore agree that if, after this note is due, it is put in the hands of an attorney for collection, we will pay fifteen per cent attorney's fee and all cost and expenses incurred in collection, which may be included in any judgment rendered hereupon, and $5.00 shall be the minimum of such fee. It is understood that a handling charge of one-tenth of one per cent of the principal and interest due on the date of demand or maturity date, or a minimum of $15.00, will be charged if payment is not made within ten (10) days of the date of demand or maturity date.

WITNESS OUR SIGNATURES AND SEALS.   _____ *John R. Smith* _____ (SEAL)

ADDRESS *210 Pine Street* _____ (SEAL)

Statement of Charges required on non business loans ☐ has ☐ has not been delivered to borrower by _____
See separate form for disclosures required by Federal Reserve Regulation Z

$ *2000 00*

INT. *75 00*

TOTAL *2,075 00*

No. *1*

DUE *7/30/83*

PP. _____

DLS. _____

No. 9 Rev. 7/70 (Time and Demand—Unsecured)

business might establish a line of credit for $50,000 with a commercial bank. The bank agrees to lend the store any amount up to the maximum during a specified period of time. Early in the summer, the store may not use any borrowed money. It may borrow $15,000 for the back-to-school season, repay $5,000 in October, and borrow $40,000 more in November for Christmas inventory. A line of credit is convenient for both lender and borrower because a number of loans can be made without separate credit investigations for each.

Secured Short-Term Loans   The amount of money that can be borrowed without collateral is limited, except for the largest companies. Small or recently formed companies may not be able to get unsecured loans at all. A wide variety of valuable property may be used to secure a loan. Equipment or other movable goods such as trucks and automobiles are commonly used as collateral. Other business facilities, such as buildings, may be used, although this is less usual for short-term loans. Inventories, whether of starting materials or of finished goods, are common collateral.

Accounts receivable—the money owed to a firm by its customers—may be pledged as collateral in some cases. The borrower may select a number of outstanding accounts and promise to pay the lender the proceeds from these accounts in return for a loan of 75 to 80 percent of their total value. The borrower retains responsibility for collecting money owed on the accounts and must make up the difference if any of the accounts cannot be collected. Lending money secured by proceeds of accounts receivable is called *discounting.* The term is used because the lender is paying out a smaller amount than is expected to be received from the collateral. The difference serves as interest on the borrowed money. For example, the ABC Manufacturing Company may obtain a loan of $8,000 on accounts receivables that are worth $10,000. When collected, the lender will receive the entire $10,000. The $2,000 difference represents the discounting of 20 percent of the value of the receivables.

Figure 13-3
Example of a promissory note.

FACTORS AND SALES FINANCE COMPANIES

They lend for accounts receivables

Factors and sales finance companies are businesses that provide money in return for accounts receivable. Factors may simply discount, or lend only a portion of the face value of, receivables and consider the accounts as collateral on a loan. *Factoring,* however, often involves buying the accounts outright. The factor pays whatever it thinks the accounts are worth and takes over responsibility for collecting them. Many companies that deal with customers who are not expected to make repeat purchases sell accounts receivable to factors. Factoring is common in the sale of lots in vacation housing developments, for instance.

A *sales finance company* is similar to a factor in that it buys accounts receivables or lends money with receivables as collateral. Sales finance companies usually specialize in accounts for installment plan purchases. Expensive consumer goods, like home appliances and cars, are often sold with an agreement that the buyer will make monthly payments for a period of one to three years. These installment sales tie up significant amounts of money for long periods. The seller is often glad to sell the accounts receivable to a finance company, even at a relatively heavy discount. The purchaser who is delinquent in payments may be surprised to find that it is the finance company that sends dunning collection letters rather than the store where the purchase was made.

COMMERCIAL PAPER

A source for large corporations

Some large companies have such an unquestionably high credit standing that they are able to borrow large sums of money simply by offering short-term promissory notes without any security. When a large company issues such notes, they are called **commercial paper.** They usually specify a repayment period of from three to six months. Companies with reputations good enough to have their commercial papers accepted by lenders prefer this method of short-term financing. Businesses often can borrow at a lower interest rate than that offered by a commercial bank for an ordinary loan. This preferred interest rate is called the prime rate and is described more fully in Chapter 14 on page 247.

5 LONG-TERM DEBT FINANCING

May be used for both current and fixed assets

Most companies have important long-term money needs. Fixed assets tie up money for long periods. Good financial management usually calls for a substantial portion of the current assets to be paid for with long-term financing also. Two sources for these funds are loans and bonds. Almost any successful company will qualify for some kinds of long-term direct loans. Bonds can usually be issued only by organizations like corporations and governments. Investors are willing to buy bonds from these enterprises because their continued operation is more certain than is the continued operation of proprietorships or partnerships.

How about this deal? In 1982, PepsiCo (the soft drink people) sold a batch of bonds worth $850 million dollars for only $54 million! There was a catch, of course. No one who bought these bonds could cash them in until 1988 at the earliest, 2012 at the latest. Meanwhile, PepsiCo won't pay any interest on these bonds. They are called zero-coupon bonds because there is no stated interest rate on them. If you were to put your pocket calculator to work, it would show that the average interest rate on these bonds was actually 13.4 percent. At the time that PepsiCo offered the bonds, the going rate for 30-year bonds was 15.5 percent. So, PepsiCo was actually saving money. As another example, the Bank of Virginia offered a series of zero-coupon bonds in these two deals: (1) pay $500 in 1982, collect $1,000 in 1987; (2) pay $250 in 1982, collect $1,000 in 1993.

Sources: **Subrata N. Ohrakravaty, "Things Won't Go Better With Pepsi,"** Forbes, May 24, 1982, p. 177; Ad in The Wall Street Journal, May 21, 1982, p. 44.

Which kind of bond would you prefer—one that paid interest every six months and could be sold at anytime at something like its face value or one that did not pay interest, but whose redeemable value kept on increasing to a maximum at its due date? What factors would influence your choice?

LONG-TERM LOANS

A secured mortgage is the most common

When funds are available, banks frequently make loans for periods of one to five years—and sometimes longer. These are called **bank term loans.** They often carry certain restrictions for the borrower, such as the requirement to get the lender's permission before assuming more debts. Other direct loans are available from insurance companies, savings and loan associations, trust companies, and the government.

The most common long-term loan is a **mortgage.** This is a loan secured by some kind of valuable property. Tangible property such as buildings, land, and equipment may be used as collateral, as may stocks and bonds, insurance policies, and other financial instruments.

CORPORATE BONDS

A mortgage-like pledge

A **bond** is a written pledge to lenders stating the borrower's intention to repay a loan. (See Figure 13-4 on page 232.) A bond specifies (a) the amount of money that has been borrowed, or the **principal,** (b) the date the principal will be repaid, or the **maturity date,** and (c) the rate of interest that will be paid periodically over the life of the bond. If a company wishes to borrow a million dollars, for example, it might issue a thousand bonds worth $1,000 each. An individual investor who buys one of the bonds gives the company $1,000 (usually through an agent). In return, the investor receives a bond certificate that may promise to pay the bondholder $1,000 in the year 2000 plus 12 percent interest every year up to maturity. Most individual bonds have a value of at least $1,000; some may run as high as $50,000. Maturity dates may extend to as much as 100 years and are rarely less than 10 years from date of issue.

When bonds are issued, the total amount borrowed may be very large, and individual bonds may be sold to many different investors. For these reasons, a **trustee** is appointed to deal with and protect the interests of bondholders. Trustees are usually banks or trust companies. Their job is to enforce all of the specific terms of the bond issue. These terms are spelled out in a written agreement called an **indenture.** Trustees may hold collateral, if any is called for. They oversee the payment of interest and the repayment of principal. If the company that issued the bond is unable to meet its required payments, the trustee must take action—including forcing the sale of collateral, if necessary—to protect the financial interests of bondholders.

Registered and Bearer Bonds   Issuers of bonds, or their trustees, may keep a record of all the people and organizations that buy individual bonds and send interest payments to them when due. Such bonds are **registered.** They are convenient and safe for bondholders but expensive to administer for the issuing company. Other bonds pay interest to whoever physically possesses them when interest is due. No record is kept of individual owners. These are called **coupon,** or **bearer, bonds.** When such bonds are printed, a series of coupons is made part of the certificate. To collect interest, bondholders must cut off a coupon and present it to the issuing company or its agent. Beginning in 1983, the federal government forbade the issuance of bearer bonds, although millions of these bonds will continue to exist until they mature.

Types of Corporate Bonds   Although many variations are in common use, three types of bonds are seen most frequently.

■   *Mortgage bonds* are secured by property owned by the issuer. Mortgage bonds are relatively safe investments because the collateral can be sold to satisfy the indebtedness if the issuing company is unable to make payments. A real estate mortgage bond is secured by property. A chattel mortgage bond is secured by movable goods like aircraft. Collateral trust bonds are secured by other stocks and bonds owned by the issuing company.

■   *Debenture bonds* are unsecured, except by the credit standing of the issuer. For this reason, their use is restricted to large, stable companies with long records of consistent earnings.

■   *Convertible bonds* can be exchanged for common stock at a rate specified in the indenture. This provision makes bonds more attractive to many investors. If a $1000 bond can be converted to 100 shares of stock, the value of the bond increases substantially if the value of a share of stock rises above $10.

Bond Retirement Methods   Companies use a variety of methods to retire bonds. Retirement means paying back the principal that was originally borrowed. Some companies issue *serial bonds.* Under this plan, a portion of the "issue" matures each year. The company continues interest payments on all outstanding bonds and repays the principal on part of the issue each year. These bonds carry serial numbers that are used to identify the year of maturity.

Companies may establish a *sinking fund* to accumulate the money to retire bonds. The company sets aside a given amount each year so that by the maturity date of the bond issue, the fund contains enough money to retire, or sink, the issue.

Indentures sometimes specify that bonds are *callable,* or *redeemable.* This allows the issuing company to retire the bonds before their maturity date, at the company's option. Management might wish to retire bonds early to reduce a corporation's leverage or in order to borrow money elsewhere at a lower interest rate.

NONCORPORATE BONDS

For governments and nonprofit organizations

Governments and nonprofit organizations also raise debt financing by issuing bonds. Local, state, and national governments use bonds for funds to build schools, libraries, and sewer and water treatment plants, for example. The interest received from many bonds issued by local and state governments is not subject to federal income tax. Some are also free from state and local taxes as well. This feature makes *tax-exempt municipal bonds* popular with investors who have high incomes and heavy tax burdens. (See Figure 13-4.)

The federal government issues a range of bonds to finance its operations. The most familiar are United States Savings Bonds. The U.S. Treasury also directly issues large bond offerings, and a variety of other notes, bills, and certificates are used to promise repayment of money borrowed by the government.

GOVERNMENT SOURCES OF BUSINESS FUNDS

Primarily for small businesses

The federal government has programs designed to make it easier for businesses to get long-term financing. Small businesses have especially benefited from these programs. The Small Business Administration makes direct loans or guarantees loans made by private lending institutions. These loans are available only to companies that cannot get financing at a reasonable rate from ordinary private sources. The Veterans Administration guarantees certain types of business loans for veterans, especially for purchasing business facilities. The Federal Housing Administration also provides some loans for buying business facilities.

6   LONG-TERM EQUITY FINANCING

This is a source of funds for corporations only

Proprietorships or partnerships raise no question about ownership; all of their equity financing comes from the assets of the proprietor or partners. A corporation, however, is owned by a group. Equity financing is gained by selling shares of ownership to investors. The shares are represented by a financial instrument called *stock*.

Courtesy of Wheat, First Securities

Figure 13-4
This is a tax-free, municipal, coupon (or bearer) bond. It has the same promissory elements as a corporate bond: face (or cash) value of $5,000; interest rate of 5.90 percent; issue date of February 1, 1970; and due date of 1980. Coupons are attached to the bond. They are redeemable on February 1 and August 1 of each year for $147.50 each. Bonds issued from July 1, 1983 on do not require the coupon feature. All new issues from that date on must be sold in registered (not bearer) form, so named because the issuer must keep a record of ownership. Knowing the identity of bondholders means that interest can be mailed directly to investors without their clipping coupons.

CORPORATE STOCK

A way of sharing ownership

The people and organizations that own corporate stock actually own shares of the assets of the corporation. This contrasts with bondholders who have only lent money to the company. Bondholders do not participate in ownership.

Par Value   Many stocks have a price assigned to them when they are issued. This price is called *par value,* but it has little relation to the actual value or selling price of the stock. If, however, investors buy a stock below par value, they may, in some cases, be charged an additional amount to bring the stock up to par value. This can happen only if the corporation becomes insolvent and needs the money to pay off creditors. Many companies issue *no-par-value stock.* No arbitrary value is shown on the certificate. The choice between par- or no-par-value stocks is usually based on the rules of incorporation in specific states.

Dividends   An important reason to acquire part ownership in a company is to share in its profits. Corporations divide surplus profits among stockholders by paying *dividends* on shares of stock. Rules about the distribution of profits make an important distinction between the two major types of stock: preferred and common.

PREFERRED STOCK

It shares in the profits first

Preferred stock receives preference over common stock in the payment of dividends, in receiving the proceeds of assets if the corporation fails, and in other ways. The specific ways in which a particular issue of stock receives preference is described on the stock certificate. Many variations are possible.

Preferred Stock Dividends   Owners of preferred stock almost always receive the first portion when profits are distributed. It often happens that, except when profits are unusually high, owners of preferred stock receive dividends and owners of common stock do not. Preferred stock certificates state a rate at which dividends will be paid, such as $8 per $100 face value. The stated dividend will only be paid, however, when the company has adequate profits to cover it. Interest on bonds and all other payments due creditors must be paid before a profit is computed. When a dividend is not paid because of inadequate profits, it is said to be *passed.*

Some stocks are made even more preferred by being cumulative. *Cumulative preferred stocks* require that any passed dividends must be made up before any profits can be distributed to owners of common stock. A company might, for example, pass the preferred dividend for the last quarter of one year because of low profits. If, in the next quarter, profits are high, the company must pay cumulative preferred stockholders the passed dividend and the new dividend before paying anything to holders of common stock. Noncumulative preferred stock does not have this provision. If a dividend is passed, it need not be made up.

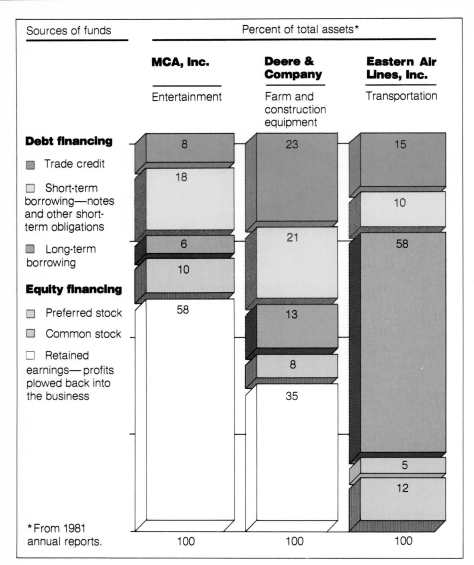

Sources of funds	Percent of total assets*		
	MCA, Inc.	**Deere & Company**	**Eastern Air Lines, Inc.**
	Entertainment	Farm and construction equipment	Transportation

Debt financing

- ■ Trade credit
- □ Short-term borrowing—notes and other short-term obligations
- ■ Long-term borrowing

Equity financing

- ■ Preferred stock
- ▨ Common stock
- □ Retained earnings— profits plowed back into the business

MCA, Inc.: 8, 18, 6, 10, 58 — 100

Deere & Company: 23, 21, 13, 8, 35 — 100

Eastern Air Lines, Inc.: 15, 10, 58, 5, 12 — 100

*From 1981 annual reports.

Figure 13-5
How sources of funds differ among three major companies.

Participating and Nonparticipating Stocks   Preferred stocks also vary in the extent to which they benefit from large profits. *Nonparticipating preferred stocks* are never paid a dividend larger than the rate shown on the certificate. *Participating preferred stocks* do receive a share of profits in addition to the stated dividend rate when such profits are available.

Voting and Nonvoting Stocks   Many preferred stocks do not carry the privilege of voting on company matters. Even though they represent ownership, these stocks do not give the stockholders active control of the corporation. Some preferred stockholders are given voting rights limited to matters that might affect the stocks preferred status, such as issuance of a large bond offering or merger with another company.

Callable or Redeemable Stocks   Preferred stocks may sometimes be made *callable* in the same way bonds are. The issuing corporation retains the right to buy back callable stocks at a stated price.

Convertible Stocks   Preferred stocks may share another feature with bonds: they may be *convertible.* Some stock issues state that a given number of shares of preferred stock may be exchanged for a given number of shares of common stock at the option of the stockholder. The purpose of this provision is the same as that of bonds. The preferred stock is made more attractive to investors because they can make a profit by converting it if the value of common stock increases.

COMMON STOCK

Greater risk, greater chance of gain

The shareholders of a corporation's common stock participate fully as owners of the corporation. The sale of *common stock* provides the day-to-day risk capital with which the company will try to make a profit. All corporations have common stock, though they may or may not have preferred stock or bonds. Preferred stock also represents ownership of a company, but it has safeguards and special protections which decrease the risk for investors. Owners of common stock participate fully in the risk of the business operation. They may also participate fully in the profits if the company is successful.

Common stock has no stated rate of return. The corporation is not bound to pay any dividends on common stock at all. When large profits are made, however, large distributions are sometimes made. Because holders of common stock share the ownership of a corporation, they are allowed to vote on important issues related to the company's management. Common stockholders, for example, elect the board of directors that is responsible for the operation of the company. It is possible to establish a class of common stockholders without voting rights, but this is far less usual than allowing all common stockholders to vote.

Since owners of common stock actually own the corporation, they receive any proceeds that are left over from the sale of assets if the company dissolves. As owners, however, they are responsible for paying off all of the company's obligations. For this reason, all agreements must be met with creditors, bondholders, and owners of preferred stock before any assets can be distributed to holders of common stock. If a corporation fails, however, and owes more than it owns, no stockholders—of either common or preferred stock—must make up the difference. Their liability, unlike that of a sole proprietorship or partnership, is limited to the price they paid for their shares of stock.

STOCK DIVIDENDS AND STOCK SPLITS

Mainly paper transactions

A corporation may wish to pay a dividend to stockholders. At the same time, however, it may wish to retain substantial portions of its profits for reinvestment. In this situation, corporations may issue a *stock dividend.* Some or all of the dividend will be paid in the form of new shares of stock rather than cash. The shares may be converted to cash if the stockholder chooses to sell them on the market, or the shares may be retained as a continuing investment.

One feature of common stocks that makes them attractive to investors is that they increase in value when a company is successful. A stock that is bought for $10 today may be worth $50 a number of years later. This increase in value may eventually make individual shares too expensive to attract small investors. Corporations may then declare a *stock split* to reduce the price of single shares. This procedure divides each share of existing stock into two or more new shares. Since the new shares represent smaller portions of ownership, they will be proportionately lower priced. If shares of common stock were selling for $210, the corporation might declare a three-for-one stock split. This would create three times the existing number of shares, with each share having an initial value of $70. The lower price per share might make the stock salable to a larger number of investors.

ISSUING AND TRADING STOCK

Intermediaries—bankers and brokers—prevail

A corporation originally issues stock to raise capital needed to begin and to carry on operations. It sells stock to individual investors or to other companies or financial institutions in return for cash to use in its operations. The first time the stock is sold is the only time the issuing company receives money from the stock.

Initial issues of stock are often sold in very large blocks to only a few buyers. Often a single investment bank may buy a whole issue. These original buyers may then resell shares in smaller lots to other investors. Even though a single share of stock may be sold and resold hundreds of times during the life of a corporation, the issuing company does not normally take part in these transactions. Stock shares are bought and sold through stockbrokers who simply inform the issuing corporation of the transaction and of the present owner. This is covered in greater detail in Chapter 14.

Key Concepts

1. Financial management plans and controls the acquisition and use of funds needed for business operations. Funds may be acquired either from investments or by borrowing. They are used to buy the facilities, materials, and other resources needed by a business.

2. The length of time for which funds will be needed affects the source from which they will be obtained. Some sources are best for short-term needs and some are best for long-term needs.

3. Business funds may be obtained from equity financing or from debt financing. Equity financing uses money invested by owners; debt financing uses borrowed money.

4. Some sources of short-term debt financing are trade credit, direct unsecured or secured loans, discounting, factoring, and commercial paper.

5. The most common sources of long-term debt financing are bank term loans, mortgages, and bonds. Bonds are secured or unsecured promises issued by an organization to repay prin-

cipal and interest in return for borrowed money.

6. Long-term equity financing results from the investments of proprietors or partners or from the sale of stock by corporations. Common stock represents basic shares of ownership in a corporation. Preferred stock also represents shares of ownership but receives priority in the payment of dividends and in other ways.

Review Questions

1. Define, explain, or identify each of the following key terms or phrases found on the pages indicated.

   accounts receivable (p. 221)
   assets (p. 221)
   bad debts (p. 223)
   bank term loans (p. 230)
   bond (p. 230)
   callable, or redeemable, bond (p. 231)
   callable, or redeemable, preferred stock
   (p. 235)
   collateral (p. 226)
   commercial paper (p. 228)
   common stock (p. 235)
   convertible bonds (p. 231)
   convertible stock (p. 235)
   coupon, or bearer, bonds (p. 230)
   cumulative preferred stock (p. 233)
   current assets (p. 221)
   debenture bonds (p. 231)
   debt financing (p. 221)
   debt ratio (p. 225)
   discounting (p. 227)
   dividend (p. 233)
   equity financing (p. 221)
   factoring (p. 228)
   financial management (p. 220)
   fixed assets (p. 221)
   indenture (p. 230)
   instrument (p. 225)
   interest (p. 220)
   leverage (p. 225)
   line of credit (p. 226)
   maturity date (p. 230)
   mortgage (p. 230)
   mortgage bonds (p. 231)
   nonparticipating preferred stock (p. 234)
   no-par-value stock (p. 233)
   participating preferred stock (p. 234)
   par value (p. 233)

   passed dividend (p. 233)
   preferred stock (p. 233)
   principal (p. 230)
   promissory note (p. 226)
   registered bonds (p. 230)
   retained earnings (p. 224)
   sales finance company (p. 228)
   secured loan (p. 226)
   serial bonds (p. 231)
   sinking fund (p. 231)
   stock (p. 232)
   stock dividend (p. 235)
   stock split (p. 236)
   tax-exempt municipal bonds (p. 231)
   trade credit (p. 226)
   trustee (p. 230)
   unsecured loan (p. 226)
   working capital (p. 221)

2. What are current assets? What three things of value usually make up current assets?

3. Why are current assets not usually paid with short-term funds? Give an example of when a need for short-term financing might arise.

4. What are some of the advantages of using borrowed money to finance business operations?

5. Why is trade credit considered debt financing?

6. What are two ways accounts receivable may be used to raise short-term financing?

7. Why are bonds usually issued by organizations like corporations and governments?

8. What is the main difference between bonds and preferred stocks?

9. How do common stocks differ from preferred stocks?

10. What is meant by the statement that "a company that issues stock receives payment for that stock only one time, no matter how many times it is resold thereafter"?

Case Critique 13-1
The High Cost of Current Assets

Peter and Mary Loring bought a country store in the ski country of Vermont for $87,500. They became the sole owners. The couple put up $42,500 in cash from their savings and got a mortgage on the building from a local bank for $45,000. The mortgage called for repayment at $700 a month. This left the Lorings with about $10,000 to buy inventories. The catch was that the business plan they developed projected a break-even point at about $91,000 in sales a year. They quickly discovered that the total cost of inventories needed to do this amount of business was $55,000. The question was: how can we finance these current assets? They did so by relying on a continuing series of high-cost small bank loans that had to be repaid every 90 days.

To top off their miseries, the first winter turned out to be warm with a resulting poor ski season and fewer sales than expected. The Lorings had earmarked $150 a week for personal subsistence—food and clothing and insurance. When the going got rough they cut this to about $115, and saved on operating costs by cutting 20 cords of wood instead of buying 2,000 gallons of heating fuel. After five years of belt tightening, however, the Lorings were comfortably in the black, but they attributed their success, not so much to financial foresight as to "sticking it out."

Both Mary and Peter appeared well qualified for the business. Mary had been a buyer for a large department store, and Peter had 15 years' experience in general management. Peter, however, commented, "I personally don't like to keep figures or ruffle papers, but you can avoid it for only so long. It's essential to have a good, easy accounting system from the very beginning. And a good financial advisor is worth the money."

1. What do you think of the Lorings' financial planning?
2. When the Lorings borrowed, what collateral did they offer to the lender?
3. What other sources of financing might the owners have tried to find, besides borrowing, to raise working capital?

Source: Kris Hundley, "Hard-Earned Growth in a Country Store," *In Business*, May-June, 1981, p. 25.

Case Critique 13-2
When the Bank Says No

Mary J.'s small dress shop was at a critical stage. Mary J. liked to say that she had started it on a shoestring three years ago. By that, she meant that she put up $10,000 of her own hard-earned savings to get a 3-month lease on a suitable store front and to purchase the first batch of merchandise for her shelves. Additionally, she got a couple of fledgling dress manufacturers to ship her some merchandise on credit. She stretched her financing a little more by getting a bank loan based upon what little success she could show and the amount of inventory she was holding. That was three years ago. Mary J.'s business had grown nicely in sales. Profits had not grown quite so fast. And, increasingly, Mary J. found that she needed cash to pay for large amounts of dress goods for the Easter and fall seasons.

Mary J. looked at her financial situation. She had a certain amount of equity in the business—an amount about equal to one-fifth of her annual sales. But she continued to need a great deal of money to stock up periodically. There were only two sources Mary J. could think of to tap for debt financing: her suppliers in the form of trade credit and her local bank in the form of short-term credit (or 30- to 90-day notes).

Mary J. soon found that her suppliers would not extend additional credit. So Mary J. turned to her bank. When she laid out her needs to the loan officer, he said, in effect, "Nothing doing."

Mary J. then showed how much inventory she was carrying. "That ought to be more than enough collateral to cover the loan I am asking for," she said. "If I go broke, you can sell it and get your money back."

"That's not how we view collateral," said the loan officer. "We are more interested in you as a continuing customer. We don't want to lend you so much money that you can't pay it back. Few banks would make a loan secured by a basket full of jewelry, for example, if they really thought they would have to sell the jewelry to get their money back. Banks are not pawn shops."

Mary J. told this story to a friend, who suggested that she try a commercial finance company. "They look at collateral differently," said the friend. "They are less likely to judge you by your chance of growing and prospering. As a consequence, the finance company may lend you money when a bank won't. But the finance company is likely to demand a higher amount of collateral and then charge you an interest rate four or five points higher than the going rate at the bank."

Mary J. thought this over and decided not to seek a loan from a commercial finance company.

Instead, she reviewed her inventory needs again and came up with a much more conservative plan for the next season. She then went back to her bank with a request for a much smaller loan. Her business would grow more slowly, Mary J. concluded, but it would be on a much sounder financial basis.

1. Do you think that Mary J. made the right decision? Why?
2. If, over a year's time, Mary J. borrowed and owed $40,000 while she used only $10,000 of her own money in her business, what is this kind of financial advantage called? What would her debt ratio be?
3. If Mary J. were to increase the rate of her borrowing, what kind of problems might that cause?
4. What would be the advantage to Mary J. if she were able to get the money she needed by selling stock in her company? What are the disadvantages?

Source: "When the Bank Says No," *INC.*, November 1981, p. 53.

Chapter 14

Money Supply and Financial Institutions

1 MONEY

is a medium of exchange. A given amount of money in hand is worth more today than in the future because it can be invested immediately and may increase in value.

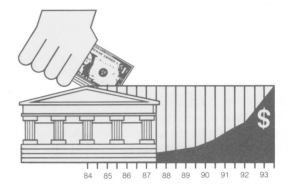

2 BANKS

provide a convenient, reliable source of money and facilitate its exchange. The Federal Reserve System, operating principally through its member banks, regulates the nation's credit and money supply.

3 SECURITIES EXCHANGES

aid in the buying and selling of long-term securities.

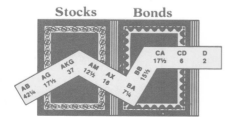

4 FINANCIAL NEWS REPORTS

list daily prices of securities and average price indexes.

5 REGULATION OF STOCK AND BOND SALES

is carried out principally by the Securities and Exchange Commission (SEC). Its goal is to protect investors and financial markets.

Learning Objectives

The purpose of this chapter is to define money and its function in business and society, show how the Federal Reserve System and other financial institutions operate, and describe the buying and selling of securities.

As evidence of general comprehension, after you study this chapter you should be able to:

1. Explain the function of money and understand how its supply and demand affect business conditions and vice versa. Calculate the effect of the time value of money on savings and investments.
2. Explain the objectives and basic functions of the Federal Reserve System. Distinguish between the services of a commercial bank and those of other lending institutions.
3. Identify key terms used in buying and selling securities.
4. Read and interpret stock and bond reports.
5. Outline the purpose of government regulations of the investment market and explain the role of the Securities and Exchange Commission in such regulation.

If your class is using SSweetco: Business Model and Activity File for Business in Action, see Chapter 14 in that book after you complete this chapter. There you will find exercises and activities that will help you apply your learning to typical business situations.

Markets are usually thought of as places where goods are bought and sold, but they also exist for other valuable forms of property, such as money and stocks and bonds. These markets are important to every business and individual. The manager of a graphic arts design company, for instance, makes financial transactions with cash and checking accounts. He or she may borrow money from banks or other sources for short-term or long-term needs and may invest some of the company's profits in the stocks and bonds of other companies. This businessperson may also use the financial markets for transacting personal business.

A complex financial system allows these transactions to be made conveniently and economically. The backbone of the system is our national currency and our network of commerical banks, supported and coordinated by the Federal Reserve System. Transactions in stocks and bonds take place in securities exchanges. Growth in business and industry would be nearly impossible without these trading places.

1   MONEY: THE BASIC MEANS OF EXCHANGE

Money makes the world go round

The use of money as a means of exchange developed early in most societies. It has many advantages over the **barter system** that it replaced, where specific kinds of goods or services are directly exchanged for other goods or services, as illustrated in Table 14-1. Because money can be exchanged for any kinds of goods or services, it is valuable to everyone. This universal acceptability makes trade much easier. Money is also divisible. An ax might be worth ten sacks of flour, but suppose the owner of the ax needs only one sack. While there is no way to divide an ax into ten parts, money can be divided into units as small as needed. These "units of account" enable money to measure the relative value of things.

Money makes commerce easier because it serves as a standard of value. The value of many different kinds of products can be expressed in a single standard: 20 yards of cloth may cost $50 and a box of nails $5. This is far more convenient than the barter system, where the cloth may be worth a single boot, a thousand buttons, or a tenth of a horse. Money also provides a convenient means of storing value. A person's or a company's income does not always match current needs for buying goods and services. A farmer may produce nearly all of the year's income at harvest season; the farm produce can be sold and thus converted to cash, which is kept for use throughout the year. Surplus income from a number of years can be accumulated for later use or for investment in enterprises requiring large amounts of capital. Such accumulation is difficult in a barter system.

MONEY SUPPLY AND DEMAND

The Federal Reserve System controls the supply

The chances are that when you think of money, you consider only the coins and paper money you can put in your pocket. These are called **currency**, but the basic money supply also includes **demand deposits**, which

TABLE 14-1
Desirable Characteristics of Money

- *Means of exchange* simpler and more flexible than the barter system.

- *Universal acceptability* as a *standard of value.*

- *Divisibility* that creates convenient *units of account,* such as pennies and dollars, enabling the relative value of things to be measured and the exchange of goods and services to be simplified.

- *Means of storing value* for the future so that surplus income can be accumulated for later use.

- *Durability* in handling and *difficulty in counterfeiting.*

is money kept in checking accounts. **Checks** are considered to be money because they can be used like cash and exchanged immediately for goods and services.

Deposits in savings accounts, if they are called **time deposits,** cannot be used directly in exchange for goods or services. Time deposits are considered investments and are not usually counted as part of the basic money supply. They are, however, considered when economists and the federal government take a broader look at money supply.

Money is supplied to the economy mainly by the Federal Reserve System (FRS, or sometimes the "Fed"). It issues new currency and gives credit to banks. Some commercial banks also supply money under the supervision of the Fed. The FRS also keeps track of the total supply of money according to four different classifications, as shown in Table 14-2.

TABLE 14-2
The Federal Reserve System's Four Classifications of Money

M1	Currency in circulation, traveler's checks, and demand deposits, including regular savings accounts from which withdrawals can be made without advance notice; plus certain other checking accounts, such as negotiable orders of withdrawal (NOW and Super NOW) accounts, which allow depositors to write checks on interest-bearing accounts; automatic transfer accounts (ATS); and "share drafts" which approximate checking accounts for credit unions.
M2	All of the above; *plus* savings and small-denomination time deposits; shares in money market mutual funds; money market fund accounts offered by savings institutions; and certain overnight commercial deposits.
M3	All of the above; *plus* large-denomination time deposits and long-term business borrowing arrangements; and balances of institutions-only money market mutual funds.
L	All of the above; *plus* other liquid assets such as certain monies (Eurodollars) held in foreign banks but owned by U.S. residents; commercial paper; and notes, bills, and other securities issued by the U.S. Treasury Department, including U.S. Savings Bonds.

The basic money supply (M1 in Table 14-2) consists of currency in circulation and a great variety of demand deposits, including those held in money market mutual funds, and NOW and Super NOW accounts. In early 1983, M1 was $491 billion, of which about 2 percent was in coins, 26 percent in paper money, and 72 percent in demand deposits. The grand total of all money counted by the FRS (M1 + M2 + M3 + L in Table 14-2) was about $2,428 billion.

With the introduction of plastic charge cards, like VISA and Master-Card which are so commonly used, the distinction between what is money and what is credit has become hard to make. Many consumers use their credit cards as a ready substitute for currency or checks, although ultimately their payments must be made in real money. Similarly, the use by banks of **electronic fund transfers (EFT)** from one person's or company's accounts to another's in payment for goods or services becomes a substitute for issuing of checks.

INFLATION AND DEFLATION

Related to money supply

The demand for money is created by individuals and organizations who want to use money as a means of exchange and for its storing and investing value. The effects on the economy of money supply and this demand for it are complex and not entirely understood. There are, however, two general effects that are widely recognized:

■ If the demand for money remains constant and the supply of money increases, the prices of goods and services increase. One interpretation of this effect is that an increase in the money supply leads to more buying. This increases the demand for goods and services and thus increases their prices. This increase in price is called *inflation.*

■ If the supply of money remains constant and demand increases, economic production decreases. Limits on the supply of money reduce purchasing power and limit the total amount of goods and services that can be sold and produced. If this brings about a drop in prices, it is called *deflation.*

INTEREST

The cost of borrowing money

The supply of and demand for money also affects and is affected by interest rates charged for borrowed money. *Interest rates* are usually expressed as a percentage to be applied as a charge over a specified period of time to the sum of money (principal) borrowed. For example, an interest rate of 12 percent a year on a loan of $1,000 means that the charge for the use of the borrowed money for one year would be $120. The borrower would be obliged, of course, to return the principal ($1,000) as well as the interest.

Among many complex interactions between interest rates, money supply, and demand for money, two are particularly noteworthy:

■ As interest rates rise, the demand for money decreases or at least lowers its rate of increase. High interest rates tend to encourage savings and discourage installment purchase of autos and homes.

■ When the demand for money remains constant and the supply increases, short-term interest rates usually decrease. Low interest rates tend to discourage savings and encourage purchases.

THE TIME VALUE OF MONEY

One dollar in hand is worth two in the future

Although money itself does not produce any income, it can be invested in ways that will produce income. This makes the value of money vary with the time when it is received. Money received next year is less valuable than money received today because today's money can be earning interest in the coming year.

For example, if a dollar can earn 5 percent interest in a savings account, the dollar is actually worth $1.05 if its owner is free to leave it in the account for a year. If the dollar is free to be invested for 15 years, it is worth about two dollars. Accumulated interest at 5 percent will about double the value of an account in that period.

The time value of money is especially important when managers or others wish to evaluate the true cost or return from an investment. Suppose, for example, a company was considering whether or not to purchase a labor-saving machine. The machine costs $100,000 and is expected to last 15 years. It would help the company to decide on this purchase if it also knew the true—or accumulated cost—of the machine over the full 15 years. The time value of the money to be invested ($100,000) becomes increasingly important as the interest rate rises. If, for example, at the time of purchase interest rates were 12 percent and were forecast to continue at that rate through the life of the machine, a calculation can be made to show what the $100,000 might have earned if it were in a bank drawing 12 percent interest all that time.

The true cost would be something like $457,000! It is computed by the principle of **compound interest.** This is done by applying the interest rate of 12 percent to the principal of $100,000 to find the value of the sum after one year: $112,000 ($100,000 + $100,000 × .12). The computation is repeated in that form for 14 more years, always applying the interest rate to the latest sum. For example, in the second year, the computation would be $112,000 + $112,000 × .12 = $112,000 + $13,440 = $125,440. In effect, the company must weigh the cost of investing $100,000 in the new machine against the possibility of putting the $100,000 in a compound-interest savings investment, which would accumulate another $357,000 over the 15-year period.

Ordinary citizens were made especially aware of the time value of money during 1981 when the federal government was urging them to invest in Individual Retirement Accounts (IRAs). The interest rates at that time were about 12 percent. The individual limit for investment in an IRA was $2,000. Banks were speculating that if a 30-year-old individual put $2,000 per year in a compounding IRA, and if the interest rates were to continue at 12 percent, the cash value of the IRA at age 65 would be $1,216,000!

The danger in estimating the future value of money is that it is directly dependent upon the interest rate that prevails each year. The lower the interest rate, the lower will be the future value of the money. Conversely, of course, the higher the interest rate, the higher the future value of the money. Predicting future interest rates is extremely difficult and uncertain, however. The most skilled economic forecasters are often wrong about future interest rates, even when the future is only a month or two away.

2   THE AMERICAN BANKING SYSTEM

The mainspring of the business system

Once money is used as a medium of exchange, a well-run banking system becomes a necessity. Banks provide a safe place for people to keep their money and facilitate its exchange through checking accounts, letters of credit, and other instruments. Banks also make loans to individuals, businesses, governments, and other organizations, and provide a method (savings accounts) for accumulating capital. In the United States, the banking system consists of the Federal Reserve System, commercial banks, and other kinds of financial institutions.

THE FEDERAL RESERVE SYSTEM

Its goals: stability and productivity

The Federal Reserve Act of 1913 created a partly governmental, partly private organization to improve the overall operation of the U.S. banking system. The organization, called the *Federal Reserve System,* consists of a seven-member board of governors, twelve Federal Reserve Banks, and thousands of privately owned banks throughout the country. Two top-level advisory groups are also part of this system. Each of the Federal Reserve Banks is responsible for certain banking activities within its region.

The goal of the Federal Reserve System is to regulate the supply of money and credit in order to promote a stable and productive economy. The board of governors maintains orderly economic growth by using information it has about the demand for money and credit and by using its ability to affect interest rates and to expand and contract the money supply.

The Federal Reserve System also (a) helps establish general banking procedures, (b) carries out transactions between banks, especially checking account transactions, (c) serves as a warehouse for cash belonging to banks, and (d) examines the records of member banks.

INFLUENCE ON MONEY SUPPLY AND CREDIT

The Federal Reserve System applies three techniques

The Federal Reserve has three main tools for performing its job of regulating the money and credit supply. It can (a) set the amount of cash reserves banks must keep, (b) buy and sell government securities to affect the money supply, and (c) affect interest rates by changing the amount it charges for loans to banks.

Control of Bank Reserves   Banks receive money from deposits to checking and savings accounts and lend part of the money to borrowers. A bank's profits depend on earning more interest on loans than is paid out to savings account depositors. For safe operations, a bank must keep on hand some of the money that is taken in. These *reserves* are used to cover day-to-day withdrawals and can never be lent out. The Federal Reserve specifies what proportion of deposits member banks must keep in reserves. If the reserve requirement is raised, banks will have less money to lend, and the total supply of money available to business and consumers is reduced. If the reserve requirement is lowered, more money is available for borrowing, and the money supply is increased.

Open Market Transactions   The Federal Reserve significantly affects the money supply by buying and selling government securities on the open market. *Securities* include all types of stocks and bonds and certain other financial instruments. When the Federal Reserve buys government bonds, it issues new money to pay for them. This increases the money supply. The money filters into the economy through government spending for goods and services. Also, when the Federal Reserve—rather than private investors—buys government bonds, private capital is still available for investment in other ways.

When the Federal Reserve sells bonds and keeps the proceeds, the money supply is reduced. The money received from the sale of bonds is actually taken out of circulation.

Control of the Discount Rate   Commercial banks lend large amounts of money, especially for business uses. They are able to lend more money than they take in through deposits because they are themselves able to borrow from the Federal Reserve. The Federal Reserve charges interest on the loans it makes to banks. The rate is called the *discount rate* because the transaction is similar to discounting accounts receivable or other accounts. When the Federal Reserve charges a high interest rate to banks, the banks must pass on the cost to their borrowers. This raises the general interest rate and makes borrowing less attractive. Changes in private interest rates are usually measured by the *prime rate,* or the interest charged by major banks for short-term loans to large commercial customers with the best credit standings.

COMMERCIAL BANKS

Privately owned, publicly regulated

Commercial banks in the United States are privately owned businesses that provide a variety of financial services to customers. They must obtain a government charter before they can begin operations. National banks are chartered by the federal government; state banks are chartered by individual states.

Commercial banks maintain savings accounts and pay interest on them. With the help of the Federal Reserve, they also handle checking accounts. Figure 14-1 shows how the system works when a check is sent from one city to another. Federal Reserve banks provide the communication between the local banks that maintain the accounts of the buyer and seller. No actual cash changes hands in the transaction. It involves only

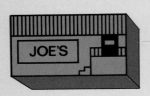

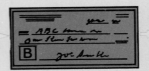

Joe, who runs a diner in Bixby, Nevada, buys a gas range made in Atlanta and sends his $1,250 check to the manufacturer.

ABC Mfg. Co. deposits the check in the Mobile Bank.

Joe receives the canceled check at the end of the month from the Bixby Bank.

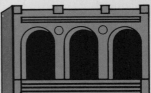

The Mobile Bank deposits the check for credit in its account at the Federal Reserve Bank of Atlanta.

The Federal Reserve Bank of San Francisco forwards the check to the Bixby Bank, which deducts $1,250 from Joe's account.

The Federal Reserve Bank of Atlanta sends the check to the Federal Reserve Bank of San Francisco for collection.

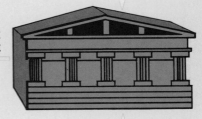

The Bixby Bank authorizes the San Francisco Federal Reserve Bank to deduct $1,250 from its deposit account with the reserve bank.

Funds are shifted from the San Francisco Reserve Bank to the Federal Reserve Bank of Atlanta. It credits the Mobile Bank's account, which, in turn, adds $1,250 to the account of the ABC Mfg. Co.

an addition to the balance of one account and a subtraction from the balance of the other.

Most of the profits of commercial banks come from the interest earned by making loans to businesses and individuals. Much of the short-term and long-term debt financing for business described in Chapter 13 comes from commercial banks. Such financing includes promissory notes, secured and unsecured bank term loans, mortgages, discounting, lines of credit, and others. A number of these loans are also available to individuals as personal installment loans for automobiles, home repairs, travel, and education. Banks also make short-term personal loans through certain credit cards that they manage.

Figure 14-1
How a check travels through the Federal Reserve System.

Commercial banks also offer a broad range of other financial services. They act as a depository for the stocks and bonds owned by their customers and give investment advice. They also give advice on taxes, estate planning, pension funds, and business investments. Many of the large banks hire specialists in the various business fields who can give business clients expert advice. Commercial banks have also taken full advantage of computers and now can perform such time-saving services as paying bills and preparing payrolls.

Commercial and other banks (see below) have progressively begun to see themselves as "retail bankers" also. Instead of assuming that depositors and borrowers must come to them, bankers now try to attract customers like other retail merchants. Such bankers are marketing oriented and typically offer their customers a wide variety of investing and borrowing options, as illustrated in Table 14-3.

ELECTRONIC BANKING

Changing the practice of banking

Use of computers, telephones, and other electronic devices appears to be changing the shape of banking everywhere. Electronic transfer of funds laid the groundwork for electronic banking on a broad scale, a development that will eventually draw many non-banking institutions into retail, as well as commercial, banking. This development is made possible by **automated teller machines (ATM)** In its simplest form, a customer obtains cash from one of them by inserting a proprietary "debit card"

TABLE 14-3
Sampling of Investment and Lending Services Offered by a Commercial Bank

■ "Earn interest on your checking with an automatic transfer of your money from savings to a checking account."

■ "The Express Statement: Our New Monthly Descriptive Statement."

■ "Introducing Future Fund. Now everyone with earned income can have an Individual Retirement Account."

■ "Put your house to work . . . with a second mortgage loan."

■ "Apply for Cash-A-Matic and give yourself pre-approved loans!"

■ "Statement Savings: no minimum deposit; 5¼% annual interest rate."

■ "Giant Bankbook: $100 initial deposit; 5¾% annual interest rate."

■ "Certificates of Deposit: receive interest either as regular income checks or as quarterly-compounded addition to the principal."

■ "2½–year Money Market Certificate; uses U.S. government securities as the basis for establishing interest rates."

■ "$10,000 minimum deposit, 6-month Money Market Certificate."

■ "Get low-cost insurance on your VISA/MasterCard balance."

Source: By permission of the First Virginia Banks, Inc. Falls Church, Virginia.

ACTION BRIEF

Shotgun Weddings for Ailing Banks. Savings and Loans, and banks that were heavily into mortgage loans for home ownership, found themselves in deep trouble in the 1980s. They were caught in a squeeze between laws that had restricted the interest rates they could charge for home mortgages and the skyrocketing interest rates they themselves had to pay for the money they loaned out. It was no wonder that so many went to the brink of failure. The FDIC and the FSLIC, however, regularly came to the rescue. In many cases, these federal insuring agencies stepped in and arranged a "shotgun marriage" between a failing institution and a healthy one. One of the largest such marriages involved the merging of New York City's Greenwich Savings Bank into Metropolitan Savings Bank. To make the merger possible, the FDIC assumed $465 million in losses. But had the FDIC waited until the Greenwich failed, the cost to the FDIC would have been much larger.
Source: *"The Cost of Saving Troubled Thrifts," Business Week, November 23, 1981, p. 44.*

issued by a bank for its own ATMs. By 1982 there were 2,500 ATMs. Since then, a number of networks have been formed by combinations of cooperating banks and private data processing firms. These networks allow a customer of one bank to use an ATM of any bank in the network.

Opportunities to combine electronic data processing with banking and investing are also growing. A recent development is the concept of cash management, which is offered by brokerage houses in connection with banking and credit institutions. One example is the Merrill Lynch Cash Management Account (CMA). (See Figure 14-2.) It requires an investor (private or commercial) to place a minimum of $20,000 at the broker's disposal. The broker immediately transfers this money to a money market fund (see below). The investor may, however, write checks on this account or use a VISA card in connection with it. Interest is compounded daily on the balance in the account. All transactions are made and reported electronically.

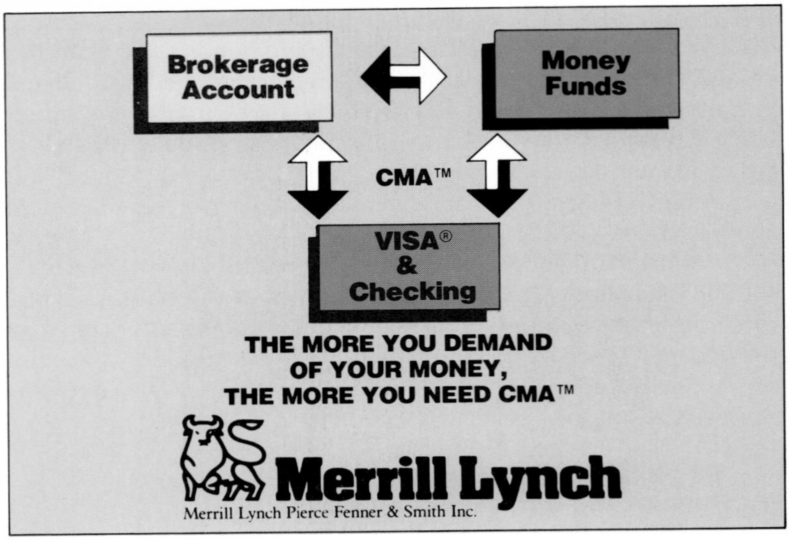

Figure 14-2
Example of electronic banking used to promote combination banking-credit-investment accounts by Merrill Lynch for its Cash Management Account.

OTHER BANKS AND FINANCIAL INSTITUTIONS

A wide variety of services

There are other kinds of financial organizations that perform some of the services of commercial banks or play other roles in transacting financial business.

Investment banks act as financial agents for businesses, governments, or other organizations wishing to raise money by selling stocks, bonds, or other securities. When a corporation, for example, wants to sell 1,000 bonds worth $1,000 each, it does not ordinarily go directly to individual investors. It arranges to sell the entire issue to one or more investment banks. The investment banks resell the issue to private investors and receive a commission from the issuing corporation.

Mutual savings banks maintain savings accounts for depositors and use part of the deposits for making mortgage loans and other investments. A unique feature of mutual savings banks is that they operate like a cooperative: all earnings are distributed to depositors as interest or are retained within the bank as reserves.

Savings and loan associations provide many of the same services as savings banks. Depositors maintain savings accounts on which regular dividends or interest are paid. A portion of the deposits is then lent out at interest for mortgages or other kinds of loans. In most states, the banking laws have been changed to allow mutual savings banks and savings and loan associations to handle demand deposits, and offer other investment opportunities such as insured money market funds, thus making them more competitive with commercial banks.

Credit unions are associations of members (usually employees of a private company or a government agency) who buy shares of ownership and make savings deposits in the union. Part of the money is then used to make loans to credit union members. Loans are usually small, but some of the larger organizations make real estate mortgage loans.

Money market mutual funds are viewed by many investors as a banking service, although technically they are speculative investments in securities that are not under the supervision of the Federal Reserve System. Investors buy shares in a money market mutual fund whose business is exclusively that of buying and selling commercial paper from very large borrowers (directly or from banks who have issued the paper) and from banks, U.S. Treasury bills,

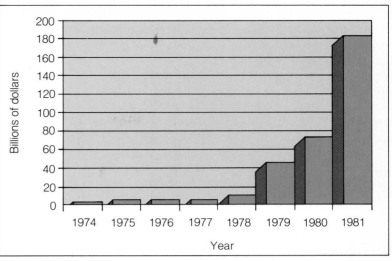

Source: Investment Company Institute, *The Washington Post*, p. K-1, March 7, 1982.

Figure 14-3
Growth of investments in money market mutual funds.

and other borrowing instruments of the Federal Government. Most money market funds require a minimum initial deposit (for example, $2,000 or more) and offer only limited checking services (such as requiring a check minimum of $500). The growth of these funds had been nothing short of spectacular, as can be seen from Figure 14-3. By 1982, over $200 billion was invested this way. With declining interest rates, the trend in money market funds has reversed itself, however. Banking institutions view the operators of money market funds as competitive, since a significant portion of the money invested in the funds represents transfers from commercial and savings banks. Not surprisingly, under a trend toward increasing deregulation, banks have now begun to offer services that combine the security of a banking deposit with those from the higher-paying interests from money market funds. The Merrill Lynch CMA mentioned above is one example of such a hybrid. The giant Chase Manhattan Bank, the nation's third largest, initiated its own hybrid, called The Chase One. It combined (in 1982) a 5.25 percent NOW account with investment in a 12 percent money market fund. When the two are blended together in a $15,000 deposit, the interest yield would be 8.63 percent.

Other important sources of loans are insurance companies and pension funds, which can accumulate sizable assets. ***Insurance companies*** are firms that share risks among members or clients by pooling their money, which is paid out to those who suffer a loss. ***Pension funds*** are monies set aside by firms, insurance companies, or trade unions to provide an income for retired employees.

GOVERNMENT REGULATION OF BANKING INSTITUTIONS

Actions affect banking and credit practices

Extensive government regulation controls and influences many of the practices and policies of banks. As already noted, the federal government—principally through the Federal Reserve System—has a major voice in determining interest rates, general banking practices, and business credit policies. The *Federal Deposit Insurance Corporation (FDIC)* insures savings up to a maximum balance per account in many national and state banks. This has made more investors willing to keep larger amounts of money in savings accounts. Since money that banks lend comes partly from invested savings, the FDIC has indirectly increased the amount of funds available for borrowing. *The Federal Savings and Loan Insurance Corporation (FSLIC)* has played a similar role for savings and loan associations.

Since the 1970s, the regulation of banking practices has been increasingly relaxed, both from the federal and state points of view. Most notable have been the legalization of branch banking (allowing a bank to set up local offices throughout a state) and the removal of the ceilings on bank interest rates on time deposits that mature in more than one year. This has induced a spate of new kinds of checking and savings options offered by banks and savings and loan institutions. Various money market accounts establish interest-paying individual investment accounts that allow for continuing additions and for demand withdrawals. Minimum initial deposits and balances (usually $2,500) are required. The investor may choose between insured savings accounts or checking (Super NOW) accounts. The former pays a higher interest rate but limits the number of checks that can be written a month. Even insurance companies benefit from the relaxing of regulations. Many of them offer a combined life insurance protection and financial investment plan (called Universal Life Insurance) with options similar to the money market accounts.

3   BUYING AND SELLING SECURITIES

The principal source of equity funds

Stocks and bonds are bought and sold just as other valuable possessions. An investor who owns 50 shares of one company's stock may wish to sell them and buy 75 shares of stock in another company. Speculators often buy large quantities of stocks with the expectation that prices of their stocks will rise rapidly so that they will be able to resell at a profit. They may buy a block of stock and resell it within a few weeks, or even within the same day. Individuals' interest in buying and selling stocks, bonds, and other securities is so lively that large formal marketplaces have been established to handle the trade. The purpose of these *securities exchanges* is to provide a means for buyers and sellers to contact each other. They also provide traders with up-to-date information on the current prices of securities.

The existence of securities exchanges actually makes the securities traded there more valuable. Bringing together a large number of buyers and sellers make the securities more liquid. *Liquidity* is the ease with which a possession can be sold, or turned into cash. The major exchanges make stocks a liquid investment because a buyer for them can always be found.

The securities exchanges also have a regulatory function. They establish rules of trading that make the exchange of securities safer for investors and more orderly for both buyers and sellers.

ACTION BRIEF

Handling Other People's Money. *Diners Card invented the idea of making money by acting as a guarantor and payment handler of credit purchases. American Express perfected the concept. Amex makes its money two ways: first by charging an annual fee to cardholders and then by discounting the bills that are forwarded to them by stores, hotels, restaurants, etc. That is, if you are charged $100 by a hotel, Amex is likely to take $4 or more as its cut for handling the transaction. By 1980, American Express had 10,283,000 cardholders worldwide compared with 3,000,000 for Diners and 800,000 for Carte Blanche. It was no wonder that the commercial banks realized what a good way this was to make money and rushed in with variations like VISA and MasterCard.*

Source: *Edited by Milton Moskowitz, Michael Katz, and Robert Levering, "Money Handlers," in* Everybody's Business: An Almanac, *Harper & Row, San Francisco, 1980, p. 481.*

Issues & Highlights

Unequal

Treatment

It used to be that when commercial firms borrowed money from a bank, they all were charged the same interest rate. That is no longer true. Today the prime rate (that charged to the companies with the most reliable pay-back) may be different for different firms. One reliable customer may pay one rate, while another equally creditworthy customer pays two or three percentage points more or less. It's not favoritism, say the banks: All loans are not equal. Two considerations other than the cost of money come into play. One; if a firm wants a standing commitment that a loan will be available, it must be ready to pay the prime rate plus an additional fee (in terms of interest points) for that assurance. Two; if supervision of the loan is time consuming, such as an auto dealer who pledges his inventory (or "floor plan"), then he should be expected to pay more, too. Obviously, this kind of reasoning usually results in larger, more affluent companies paying lower interest rates than smaller, less well-heeled companies, despite their record as prime credit risks.

Source: *Ben Weberman, "Cost-Plus Lending,"* Forbes, August 31, 1981, p. 46.

Is such cost-plus reasoning on the part of the banks justifiable? What action, if any, should the government take to regulate the interest rates charged to businesses that are large enough to shop around and find better deals?

STOCKBROKERS
The intermediaries of exchange

Millions of people and thousands of organizations in the United States own stocks and bonds. If all of these investors tried to deal directly with securities exchanges, the trading system would completely break down. A kind of intermediary—the stockbroker—channels the trading of securities into manageable trade routes. A *stockbroker* is a person or company that represents investors in the buying and selling of securities. If an investor wishes to buy 100 shares of stock, he or she will instruct a broker to make the purchase. In return for their services, brokers receive a commission based on the size of the order.

EXCHANGES
Where the securities are traded

Of the approximately fifteen formal stock exchanges in the country, the New York Stock Exchange is by far the largest. The American Stock Exchange is second in size, and a number of regional markets follow, varying in size and importance. Many stocks are not traded at a specific location but are exchanged through a network of brokers in different cities. These stocks and bonds are called over-the-counter securities. Exchanges in foreign countries also trade the securities of U.S. companies.

The New York Stock Exchange   The New York Stock Exchange (NYSE) serves as the major national securities market. The exchange is an association of brokers who have come together to establish a trading place. Members must buy "seats" on the exchange and must be approved by the governing board. Membership is limited to 1,366. The NYSE and other exchanges only carry on the trading of stocks and bonds for organizations listed with the exchange. This exchange currently lists about 1,600 stocks and 2,700 bonds. For a company to be listed on the NYSE, it must apply and be accepted by the board of governors. Listed companies must have (a) annual pretax earnings of at least $2.5 million, (b) 1 million shares publicly held, (c) 2,000 or more investors holding a minimum of 100 shares each, (d) a value of at least $8 million for outstanding shares of common stock, and (e) tangible assets of at least $16 million.

The American Stock Exchange   The American Stock Exchange (Amex) is also located in New York City and is also primarily a national exchange. Its listed companies are often, but not always, smaller than those on the NYSE. The American Stock Exchange lists about 1,000 companies.

Regional and Foreign Exchanges   A number of regional exchanges outside of New York are growing in importance. Examples are the Midwest Exchange in Chicago, the Pacific Exchange in Los Angeles and San Francisco, the Philadelphia-Baltimore-Washington Exchange and the Boston and Cincinnati city exchanges, as well as those in a number of other cities. These regional and local markets normally trade securities from local corporations and from some of the national companies listed on the NYSE or Amex.

Stock trading was carried on in foreign countries before the United States was founded. Important exchanges are located in London, Amsterdam, Paris, Tokyo, Zurich, Frankfurt, and a number of other cities. Some important American companies trade on these exchanges. Some foreign companies trade in the United States.

Over-the-Counter Trading   Many companies are not listed with a specific exchange. Their stocks and bonds are traded by a network of brokers who participate in *over-the-counter (OTC) trading.* The trading is similar to that on a city exchange except that no central location is established for the exchange. Brokers buy from and sell to other brokers across the country, making transactions by telephone or teletype. They deal in the securities of industrial firms, utility and insurance companies, in federal government bonds, and in municipal bonds. Some securities are listed with an exchange and also traded over the counter. Far more are traded exclusively over the counter. However, the greatest volume of trading, both in number of shares and in dollar value, is done by the large central exchanges. An independent group of brokers (National Association of Securities Dealers) provides a self-regulating body for OTC markets.

The Options Market   A form of investment that is highly speculative involves not the actual purchase of a share of stock but the *option,* or privilege, of buying it at a reduced price. The risk is that the purchaser of an option must predict either a specific *call* (rise) or *put* (fall) in the market price of a stock. Additionally, this change must take place within a stipulated period of time, usually three months. If the market price does not rise or fall as predicted, the investor loses his or her entire investment. If the *exercise price* (or price prediction) does come true, the purchaser wins the bet. Odds, as high as 10 times the purchase price, are paid at that time. The payment is provided by investors who, in effect, buy the option from the original holder so as to complete the actual stock purchase (or sale) at the price advantage provided by the option.

Options may be bought and sold on a number of exchanges, including the Chicago Board Options Exchange (CBOE), the American Stock Exchange, the Philadelphia Exchange, and the Pacific Exchange.

Mutual Fund Market   A *mutual fund* is an investment company in which individual investors, mainly small ones, pool their money to buy stocks, bonds, and other securities. Shares in these funds may be purchased directly from the company itself or through stockbrokers. Shares may be sold directly or through brokers. The advantage to the investor is that the company provides professional management of the purchase and sales of the securities it owns, something few individual investors are able to do effectively. Prices and sales charges are listed daily in financial papers such as *The Wall Street Journal* and are provided by the National Association of Securities Dealers.

Commodity Exchanges   Many processing and manufacturing firms, and other investors, regularly trade a variety of commonly used raw materials. These include grains like corn and wheat, livestock and meat, foods and fibers like coffee, cotton, and sugar, lumber, copper and gold, and currencies of various nations. A number of commodity exchanges exist for the purpose of such trading. Notable among these are the Chicago Board of Trade, the New York Mercantile Exchange, American Board of Trade, and the Kansas City Board of Trade. Trading may be done for immediate delivery—spot or cash trading—or for delivery at some future date—futures trading.

STOCK TRANSACTIONS

Take place in minutes

Stocks are sold in standard quantities of 100 shares, called a **round lot.** Any number of shares less than 100 is called an **odd lot.** Brokers charge commissions for handling the securities transactions of investors. Odd-lot transactions are more complicated to handle than round-lot transactions. Brokers must group together odd-lot orders from different investors to make up round lots. For this reason, they charge extra for trading odd lots. Current stock prices, or **quotations,** are available to brokers through several automatic telephone services or on a ticker tape, an electronic service that projects quotations for many important stocks on a lighted board. Many brokerage houses have a ticker tape in a public area for investors' use. Increasingly, quotations can be "called up" by a broker on a video display screen at his or her desk.

An NYSE Transaction   If someone in Texas wishes to buy 100 shares of CBS, Inc., stock, a complex chain of communication must take place before the certificates are actually delivered. The buyer calls or visits a broker, who has a local office, who places the order. The local office transmits the order to its firm's New York office by teletype. The New York office passes the order to its floor broker, who operates in the trading room of the NYSE where CBS stock is listed. The floor broker goes to a specific trading post where CBS stock is handled and bargains with other brokers there who have orders from their clients to sell CBS stock. If the Texas client placed a **market order,** the floor broker tries to get the best price possible immediately. If the client placed a **limit order,** the broker does not buy unless the stock can be gotten for the price specified in the order. Once the transaction is made on the trading floor, the New York brokerage office transmits details of the purchase, including price, to its Texas office and the broker there informs the client that the purchase has been made.

Over-the-Counter Transactions   Over-the-counter transactions are similar. Brokers negotiate prices by offering a certain price—the **bid price**—when they wish to buy, or asking a certain price—the **ask price**—when they want to sell. The ask price is normally higher than the bid price. The price of the final sale is usually a compromise between the ask price and the bid price. Many over-the-counter dealers keep their own inventory of stocks and make a profit by selling them at a higher price than they paid.

Bond Transactions   Bonds are also traded on exchanges, and their values change just as the values of stocks do. If a bond is issued with an 8 percent interest rate, the bond becomes more desirable to investors whenever interest rates for other investments fall below 8 percent. Investors would then be willing to pay a **premium;** they might pay $1,050 for a bond with $1,000 face value. If general interest rates (paid by banks, for example) rise above the rate paid by a particular bond, however, that bond will be less valuable to investors. In that case, the bonds are sold at a ***discount;*** for instance, a $1,000 bond might be sold for only $950.

4   FINANCIAL NEWS REPORTS

Information about where the action is

Most business managers and individual investors pay careful attention to financial news in magazines and newspapers. Many people in business invest in stocks and bonds and use financial news as a guide to investments and to follow current values of their holdings. Many facts and trends needed for management—such as the costs of borrowing money—are reported in financial news sections. Activities of the securities markets and related financial institutions reflect the general condition of the economy and help in decision making.

Some unfamiliar terms may be encountered in reading financial news. ***Bulls*** are people who think stock prices will rise within a fairly short time. ***Bears*** expect the market to fall. Speculators are often contrasted with investors. ***Speculators*** buy and sell securities to make profits from short-term swings in their prices. ***Investors*** buy securities for long-term growth or income; they generally act like real corporation owners participating in the growth of business.

A number of buying and selling strategies are especially used by speculators. It is possible to buy stock partly with borrowed money. The part of the purchase price that is paid in cash is called the ***margin.*** This practice allows buyers to take advantage of leverage. They can take all of the profits if the stock increases in value without having put up the full purchase price of the stock. If the stock goes down in price, however, they can lose both the money they invested and the money they borrowed. Even when a stock's price falls, a profit can be made. Speculators who ***sell short*** borrow shares of stock from their broker and sell them at the current market price. If the price of the stock then goes down significantly, they can buy shares at the new lower price to replace the borrowed shares. The difference between the price at which they sold and that at which they bought is left as a profit.

Institutional investors play a particularly important role in financial activities. These investors are organizations—trust fund administrators, foundations, investment funds, pension funds, insurance companies, banks, and others—that invest large amounts of money. Their buying and selling activities have a strong effect on the prices of securities.

STOCK AVERAGES AND INDEXES

Barometers of the financial market

Investors follow trends in stock prices by noting the changes in certain well-known averages of prices. The Dow-Jones Industrial Average is the most publicized. It is computed from 30 large, stable industrial corporations, such as United States Steel Corp., AT&T, General Electric Co., Texaco, Inc., and DuPont Co. Dow-Jones also publishes averages for 15

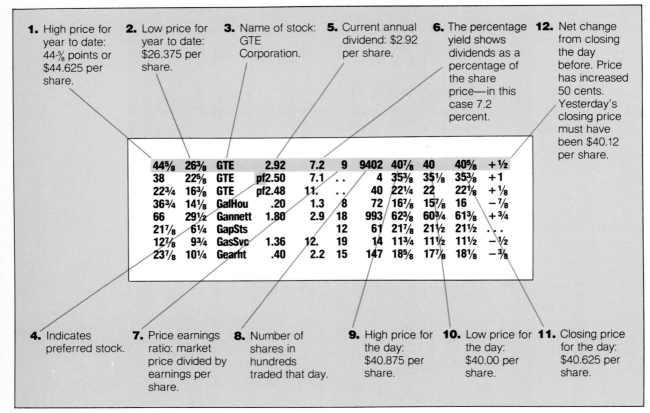

1. High price for year to date: 44-⅝ points or $44.625 per share.

2. Low price for year to date: $26.375 per share.

3. Name of stock: GTE Corporation.

5. Current annual dividend: $2.92 per share.

6. The percentage yield shows dividends as a percentage of the share price—in this case 7.2 percent.

12. Net change from closing the day before. Price has increased 50 cents. Yesterday's closing price must have been $40.12 per share.

4. Indicates preferred stock.

7. Price earnings ratio: market price divided by earnings per share.

8. Number of shares in hundreds traded that day.

9. High price for the day: $40.875 per share.

10. Low price for the day: $40.00 per share.

11. Closing price for the day: $40.625 per share.

Source: The Wall Street Journal, February 14, 1983, p. 34. Reprinted by permission of *The Wall Street Journal*, © Dow Jones & Company, Inc. 1983. All Rights Reserved.

Figure 14-4
How to read stock quotations reported in a newspaper.

utility companies, another for 20 transportation companies, and a composite average that combines all 65 of the industrial, utilities, and transportation companies. Standard & Poor's calculates a similar index based on 500 companies, mainly industrials but including a number of railroads and utilities.

The New York Stock Exchange and the American Stock Exchange both compute a stock value index, as do OTC (National Association of Securities Dealers Automated Quotation, the so-called Nasdaq index) and many other exchanges. The NYSE index is a good example of this type. It is based on all of the stocks traded, rather than on a small sample. It shows, among other figures, the increase or decrease in price of an average share of stock.

DAILY STOCK AND BOND REPORTS

The records of buying and selling, prices, and interest rates

Most newspapers give extensive coverage to daily trading activity on the major exchanges. Reports are printed of trading activity for the securities listed on the NYSE, Amex, and often regional and over-the-counter trading as well. Figure 14-4 shows a typical listing of these daily individual trading reports.

A number of bond averages are also watched carefully by investors and managers. The Dow-Jones bond averages are popular indexes. They

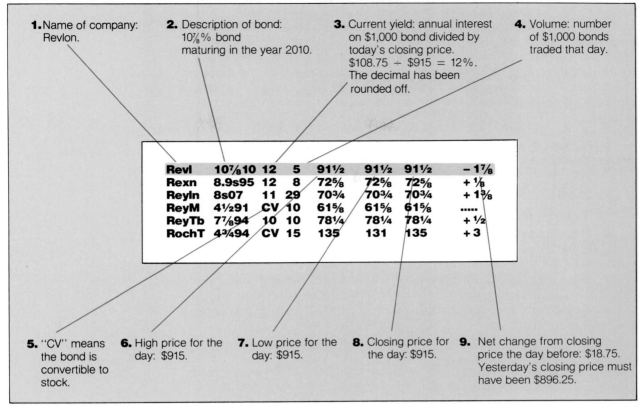

1. Name of company: Revlon.

2. Description of bond: 10⅞% bond maturing in the year 2010.

3. Current yield: annual interest on $1,000 bond divided by today's closing price. $108.75 ÷ $915 = 12%. The decimal has been rounded off.

4. Volume: number of $1,000 bonds traded that day.

Revl	10⅞10	12	5	91½	91½	91½	− 1⅞
Rexn	8.9s95	12	8	72⅝	72⅝	72⅝	+ ⅛
Reyln	8s07	11	29	70¾	70¾	70¾	+ 1⅜
ReyM	4½91	CV	10	61⅝	61⅝	61⅝	.....
ReyTb	7⅞94	10	10	78¼	78¼	78¼	+ ½
RochT	4¾94	CV	15	135	131	135	+ 3

5. "CV" means the bond is convertible to stock.

6. High price for the day: $915.

7. Low price for the day: $915.

8. Closing price for the day: $915.

9. Net change from closing price the day before: $18.75. Yesterday's closing price must have been $896.25.

Source: *The Wall Street Journal,* February 14, 1983, p. 30. Reprinted by permission of *The Wall Street Journal,* © Dow Jones & Company, Inc. 1983. All Rights Reserved.

Figure 14-5
How to read bond quotations reported in a newspaper.

show the average price for 10 bonds issued for industrial companies, 10 bonds from utility companies, and a composite. The averages show the price per $100 of bond face value. An average of 92.57 means that a typical $1,000 bond would cost $925.70 to buy. At that price, bonds are being sold with a discount. That is, they are selling for $74.30 below their face value. Daily bond transactions are also shown in many newspapers. A typical listing is explained in Figure 14-5.

5   REGULATION OF STOCK AND BOND SALES

Its goal: protection of investors and financial markets

Extensive government regulation controls and influences the selling and trading of stock and bonds. The objective of this regulation is to (a) insure that investors are protected from fraud, (b) maintain order in the financial markets, and (c) limit risk to the financial system by controlling the proportion of borrowed money that may be used in speculative investment. The Securities Act of 1933 and Securities Exchange Act of 1934 require that a corporation provide detailed information to investors before stock or bonds are first offered for sale. A summary of information is contained in a *prospectus* showing financial, legal, management, and operations data on the issuing corporation. The purpose of the prospectus is to inform potential buyers of facts about the company and the issues that affect its value. The *Securities and Exchange Commission* (*SEC*) establishes general policies and regulations for trading stocks and bonds. The Federal Reserve System, by raising or lowering margin requirements, regulates the practice of borrowing money to use for speculating in the stock market.

THE SECURITIES AND EXCHANGE COMMISSION

Watchdog of the investment markets

The SEC acts as the watchdog of the investment markets, exercising extensive regulatory powers. The most important of these are:

■ Requiring registration of new securities and disclosure of important information about stocks and bonds and about the issuing company pursuant to the various federal securities exchange laws.

■ Requiring that companies listed with exchanges register and disclose information even when they are not issuing new securities.

■ Registering and regulating investment trusts, investment companies, and investment advisors.

■ Regulating public utility holding companies.

Exercising its authority in these areas, the SEC has done much to reduce incidents of securities fraud. It has made the securities markets safer places for investment. The SEC cannot, however, protect investors from their own poor investment decisions. In that sense, the investors always assume some degree of risk whenever they invest in securities.

Key Concepts

1. Money serves as a means of exchange, as a standard of value, and as a medium for storing value. The supply of and demand for money have complex and important effects on prices and interest rates.

2. The U.S. banking system consists of the Federal Reserve System and thousands of private commercial banks. Together they provide (*a*) safe places to store money, (*b*) methods for making financial transactions, (*c*) sources of borrowed funds, and (*d*) means of accumulating capital. The Federal Reserve System influences the supply of money to promote economic stability and growth.

3. Organizations and methods for trading securities bring together buyers and sellers of stocks and bonds. The securities exchanges make it easier for businesses to raise capital. Stockbrokers act as agents for investors who wish to buy or sell securities on a formal exchange, such as the NYSE, Amex, or OTC.

4. Financial news reports give general information of use to managers, financial indexes, such as stock price averages, and daily trading results for individual securities.

5. The federal government regulates the securities and bond markets with the object of protecting investors from fraud, maintaining order in financial markets, and limiting risk to the financial system caused by speculative practices. The Securities and Exchange Commission (SEC) is the principal federal governmental agency involved in regulating the offering, trading, and selling of securities.

Review Questions

1. Define, explain, or identify each of the following key terms or phrases found on the pages indicated.

ask price   (p. 256)
automated teller machine   (p. 249)
barter system   (p. 242)
bears   (p. 257)
bid price   (p. 256)
bulls   (p. 257)
call   (p. 255)
checks   (p. 243)
commercial bank   (p. 247)
compound interest   (p. 245)
credit union   (p. 250)
currency   (p. 242)
deflation   (p. 244)
demand deposits   (p. 242)
discount   (p. 257)
discount rate   (p. 247)
electronic fund transfers   (p. 244)
exercise price   (p. 255)
Federal Deposit Insurance Corporation (p. 252)
Federal Reserve System   (p. 246)
Federal Savings and Loan Insurance Corporation   (p. 252)
inflation   (p. 244)
institutional investors   (p. 257)
insurance companies   (p. 251)
interest rates   (p. 244)
investment bank   (p. 250)
investors   (p. 257)
limit order   (p. 256)
liquidity   (p. 252)
margin   (p. 257)
market order   (p. 256)
money market mutual fund   (p. 251)
mutual fund   (p. 255)
mutual savings bank   (p. 250)

odd lot   (p. 256)
option   (p. 255)
over-the-counter trading   (p. 255)
pension funds   (p. 251)
premium   (p. 256)
prime rate   (p. 247)
prospectus   (p. 260)
put   (p. 255)
quotations   (p. 256)
reserves   (p. 247)
round lot   (p. 256)
savings and loan associations   (p. 250)
securities   (p. 247)
Securities and Exchange Commission (p. 260)
securities exchange   (p. 252)
selling short   (p. 257)
speculators   (p. 257)
stockbroker   (p. 254)
time deposit   (p. 243)

2. What are the three main ways that money is used in our economy?
3. Name the two most commonly accepted components of the money supply.
4. What are two likely effects when the money supply increases and the demand for money stays nearly constant?
5. How can a manager take into account the time value of money when deciding whether to invest in new equipment?
6. Name four important functions served by a banking system.
7. What is the main goal of the Federal Reserve System?
8. What is a stockbroker?
9. How is a profit made by selling short?
10. Why does the federal government regulate the selling and trading of stocks and bonds? What are four important powers of the Securities and Exchange Commission (SEC)?

Case Critique 14-1
The Overambitious Investor

Don had a good job. He was making nearly $20,000 a year and had prospects for advance-

ment. Of course, after income and social security taxes, and insurance deductions, the take-home pay was only about $15,000. His rent, telephone, and utilities, however, took over $7,000 a year. Meals and routine entertainment ate up another $3,000. Don had to have a car—a sports car at that—which cost him $2,500 a year in finance charges and $1,000 to operate. You can see that Don had only about $1,500 left each year for vacations and big weekends, when he dearly loved to swing. He had no savings account.

One day, when Don was broke and feeling blue, dreaming of his next big vacation fling—skiing in Colorado—a good friend made a suggestion. "Why don't you take a flyer on the stock market? I know of a number of nickel stocks where you can make a big killing for an investment of only a few hundred dollars."

"Nickel stocks!" said Don, "what kind of stocks can they be?"

"They are not really nickel stocks, but they do sell for less than $5 a share. You can buy 100 shares right now of one I know about that sells for $3 per share. This company has invented the most dynamic TV game that can be imagined. Its stock is so hot that when people catch on, it will go to $30 or more per share. For $300 now, you can probably make a cool $3,000 in two or three months."

Don thought this was a great idea. He took every last penny he could lay his hands on and bought 100 shares at $3. For a week, or two, he called his broker daily and was elated to find the stock climbing up to $4 and then $5. On the strength of his good fortune, Don put a down payment on a $1,500 stereo that he had been admiring. Then, something began to go wrong with the stock. Its price dropped back to the $3 that Don had paid for it. Then it continued to drop—as low as 25 cents—and there it stayed. If he were to sell it, he'd get less than $25. About that time, Don was hit with an unexpected repair bill of $250 for his car. And the payment for his stereo came through. Don looked at his checkbook. It was about to be overdrawn. And he didn't have enough money to pay the rent. Payday was still a week away. Don then set out to sell his sports car and his stereo for the amount still owed on them. He put an ad in the newspaper but got no response that week on the car and only what he considered a ridiculously low offer on the stereo.

1. When Don bought his stock, was he acting like an investor or a speculator?
2. Which of Don's purchases—the stock, the stereo, or the sports car—has the greatest liquidity?
3. If Don had wanted to be sure to make a profit from his $300, would it have been better for him to put his money into a checking account or a savings account?
4. Do you think Don was in a financial position that was sound enough for stock purchasing? Why?

Case Critique 14-2
Would You Lend This Man $300,000?

He had owned a small leathercraft business. Then he sold it to a larger company in return for some of its stock. He didn't like the way the larger company was being run so he organized a revolt among the stockholders and took over as president. His firm opened up a small chain of leathercraft shops and succeeded fairly well. Then he looked around for other opportunities. He spotted a near-bankrupt chain of Boston-based retail, radio-parts stores. They were already in debt to a Boston bank to the tune of $7 million. Our entrepreneur had little or no cash at the time. But he offered a deal to the chain owners and to the bank that was holding the loan.

"Let me take over 51 percent of the common stock of the company," he said to the owners. "I'll pay you $5,000 for this and take the debt off your hands, but I can't pay the $5,000 right away." To the bank, he said, "Lend me $300,000 to put this chain back on its feet. I'll pay you back in 24 months." While not every aspect of this arrangement is known, it is a fact that the owners and the bank accepted the no-down-payment, 24-months-to-pay offer from Charles Tandy, and he took over Radio Shack.

The rest of the story is history. He cleaned up the Radio Shack act by stripping down its product line, selling only items with a 50 percent or greater markup, and instituting strict inventory controls. He began opening up stores at the rate of one a day until there are now 8,500 of them. Sales zoomed to nearly $2 billion a year by 1982, and profit was rolling in at a far greater rate than at Sears or K-Mart. To top it off, Radio Shack's personal computer line was making even IBM sit up and take notice.

1. Why would a bank lend a large sum of money to put into a business that was already heavily in debt?

2. Why would the original owners of Radio Shack be more likely to sell their stock directly to Tandy rather than through brokers on a stock exchange?

3. What was there about Charles Tandy that made him a good risk for a bank loan?

Source: Howard Rudnitsky and Toni Mack, "Sometimes We Are Innovators, Sometimes We Are Not," *Forbes,* March 29, 1982, p. 66.

Chapter 15

Risk, Insurance,
and Credit
Management

1 RISK

is the possibility of loss or failure. There are two basic kinds of business risk:

Speculative (unavoidable) risk, which is inherent in the nature of the private enterprise system

Insurable (pure) risk, for which losses may be anticipated and shared

2 RISK MANAGEMENT

attempts to avoid or reduce the possibility of loss and lessen its impact when it occurs. A business can cope with risk through:

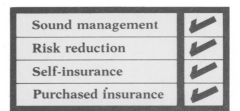

Sound management	✔
Risk reduction	✔
Self-insurance	✔
Purchased insurance	✔

3 INSURANCE

is a method of sharing risk protection.

POLICY

4 TYPES OF INSURANCE COVERAGE

include:

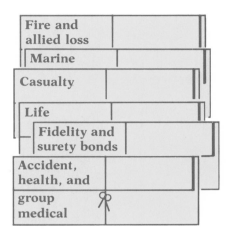

- Fire and allied loss
- Marine
- Casualty
- Life
- Fidelity and surety bonds
- Accident, health, and group medical

5 CREDIT MANAGEMENT

involves

Commercial credit:
Character
Capacity
Capital
Conditions

Consumer (retail) credit:
Fair Credit Reporting Act
Consumer Credit Protection Act

Learning Objectives

The purpose of this chapter is to relate the role and importance of risk, insurance, and credit management in the financial operations and financial planning of a business.

As evidence of general comprehension, after studying this chapter, you should be able to:

1. *Distinguish between speculative risk and insurable risk.*
2. *Outline and explain the four ways that business managers cope with risks.*
3. *Explain the key terms used in connection with insurance.*
4. *Identify and explain the principal kinds of insurance coverage.*
5. *Understand and apply the "four C's" of commercial credit, and analyze how truth-in-lending laws and various other consumer credit protection legislation affects credit management.*

If your class is using SSweetco: Business Model and Activity File for Business in Action, see Chapter 15 in that book after you complete this chapter. There you will find exercises and activities to help you apply your learning to typical business situations.

A company that imports cheese from France for resale in the United States operates under the basic risk that it may not be able to produce enough income to pay its bills. Owners risk losing some or all of the money they invested to start and operate the company. Beyond this, however, the company is subject to risks that have nothing to do with the usual shifts in the economy. A shipment of cheese may be damaged at the dock or may sink at sea. A warehouse may burn down, resulting in the destruction of large amounts of expensive inventory. A delivery truck may strike a pedestrian or a loading dockworker, resulting in a lawsuit against the company. The company's president may die from a heart attack, causing loss of income and affecting the management of the company.

These and other kinds of occurrences threaten the security of businesses. They cost money, and they may cause business failure. Through the years, various kinds of insurance have been developed to share these risks. Insurance protects businesses from many types of losses. For large corporations, the variety of insurable risks and the ways of dealing with them are so numerous that special departments are often established to handle risk management.

1   RISK

The possibility of loss or damage

For a business, **risk** is the possibility of the loss of invested money or the loss of or damage to other valuable possessions. Accordingly, there are two main classes of business risks: speculative and insurable.

SPECULATIVE RISK

The uninsurable chance of failure

Owners who invest money in a business are speculating on the outcome of the business operation. They hope that their investments will increase in value as the business grows and makes profits. They always face the possibility, however, that they may lose some or all of their investments if the business fails. **Speculative risks** are basic to the private enterprise system.

Managers must always use care in trying to reduce speculative risk. They must try to manage product development and quality, prices, distribution, and the availability and costs of materials to produce a sound and profitable business. They must juggle the constantly changing influences of market demand, interest rates, and government regulation. No matter how carefully managed, businesses cannot be immune to speculative risk as long as private capital is invested with the expectation of making a profit. There is always the possibility that a point may be reached where income is not sufficient to meet expenses and the business becomes **insolvent.** If that occurs, the firm may be declared—or declare itself—bankrupt. **Bankruptcy** is the legal condition where liabilities exceed assets with no hope of reversing this condition. When this happens, the courts will appoint a **receiver** to **liquidate** the firm, that is, to sell off its assets so as to pay the firm's creditors.

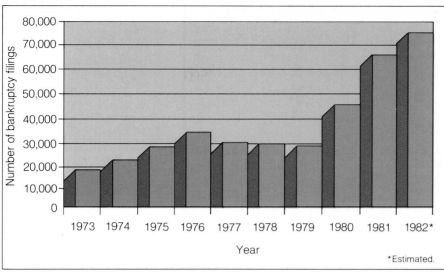

Figure 15-1
Business bankruptcy filings.

Source: Tables of Bankruptcy Statistics, Administrative Office of the United District Courts, Washington, D.C., annually.

Commercial Bankruptcy   In the last decade there have been spectacular business bankruptcies such as those that saw W. T. Grant (discount chain), A. M. International (formerly Addressograph-Multigraph office machines), and Braniff International (airlines) go under to the tune of several hundred millions of dollars. Big or small, however, the reason is the same: debt that is far larger than the company's assets and growing faster than it can possibly be paid off. Bankruptcy not only destroys the individual firm; it also does damage to its employees and suppliers in the form of unpaid wages and bills. It is not unusual for a sinking company to drag its suppliers down with it—those who risked their own business safety by continuing to extend trade credit when it was no longer prudent.

There is a sort of halfway house for firms on their way to complete bankruptcy. It is called *Chapter 11 bankruptcy* because Chapter 11 of the Federal Bankruptcy Law allows the receiver to try to reach an agreement with the firm's creditors short of liquidation so that the firm may reform its financial structure and recover. One way or another, however, the number of firms being compelled by their creditors to declare bankruptcy or who do so on their initiative has risen dramatically in recent years, as shown in Figure 15-1.

Personal Bankruptcy   Individuals may also go to federal court to declare themselves bankrupt. An increasing number of people do so: 452,730 in 1981 compared with 172,423 in 1978. They do so for the same reason that businesses do—because they owe far more than they can ever expect to pay back. Under a *Chapter 7 bankruptcy* as mandated by federal law, individuals who are declared bankrupt must allow the courts to sell their assets to pay their creditors as much as possible from the proceeds and cancel whatever debt is remaining. The law does permit the debtor to keep certain assets for survival purposes. This includes up to a $7,500 equity in his house and up to a $1,200 equity in a car, and a certain exemption for personal jewelry up to $500. Landlords, finance companies, department stores, and other creditors are understandably upset when individuals to whom they have loaned money or extended credit are forced to declare bankruptcy. This is a major reason why businesses and financial institutions are often so careful about extending consumer credit.

As a less drastic option, individuals are able to seek **Chapter 13 bankruptcy.** This provides for the debtor to pay all or part of his or her debts over a period of three years under a plan approved by the courts. Its impact is somewhat like that of a nonprofit *Consumer Credit Counseling Service (CCCS)* sponsored by banks, loan companies, retailers, and other companies that extend credit. The CCCS has 200 offices throughout the country and handles about 110,000 cases each year. Its method is to ask the insolvent debtor to give up all his credit cards and to promise not to do any further borrowing without the permission of CCCS. Then it works out a survival budget that enables the debtor to pay back part of the debt every month. At the same time CCCS gets the creditors to agree to wait for their money and also assumes responsibility for equitably dividing up whatever repayments there are.

INSURABLE RISK

The pure chance of accident or loss

Some risk is called **pure risk** because it can result only in loss and never in gain. This kind of risk consists of the chance hazards of nature such as fire, illness or injury, and many other kinds of damage to property or life. Speculative risk is different from pure risk because speculative risk carries the possibility of gain as well as loss and is accepted voluntarily by investors.

Insurance can be bought as protection against pure risk. Insurance companies make contracts with businesses, agreeing to pay the businesses for losses resulting from pure risk. The insured business makes regular payments, called **premiums,** into a pool maintained by the insurance company. The insurance company can afford to pay for losses suffered by their client companies because many companies pay into the pool, but relatively few have to be paid for losses at any one time.

Insurable risks, therefore, must meet several criteria:

■   The risk must be pure. It must be an accidental hazard and not a fundamental risk of doing business.
■   The extent of the potential loss from the risk must be measurable in some fairly accurate way.
■   The likelihood of any individual business suffering an immediate loss from a given risk must be slight.
■   There must be a very large number of companies subject to the risk. Many companies must contribute to the pool to provide enough money to pay for losses.

Accidental destruction of business property by fire is a good example of an insurable risk. It is a pure risk because it is not a basic risk of business investment. The value of the property can be determined accurately. An individual business is not likely to be destroyed by fire if precautions are observed. There is, however, enough risk to all business that large numbers are willing to pay premiums for protection.

2   RISK MANAGEMENT

Managers can and must guard against risk

Business managers can respond to risk in a number of ways. They can respond with sound management, risk reduction, self-insurance, and purchased insurance.

SOUND MANAGEMENT

Prudent finances and trained personnel

Sound management is clearly the best way to reduce speculative risk. Careful control of financing, product development and production, marketing and distribution, and other management concerns help insure that the result of speculative risk will be profits rather than loss and failure. Good credit management will reduce losses from bad debts and delayed payments. Good human relations management can reduce losses from strikes or other labor problems. Good general management polices also reduce pure risk. Well-trained personnel with good morale using modern equipment that is properly maintained are unlikely to have many accidents.

RISK REDUCTION

Precautions must be taken

Good managers take prudent steps to reduce insurable risks. Many companies specifically train employees in safe working procedures. Buildings may be built with fireproof materials. Sprinkler systems, adequate exits, and sources of water reduce losses if fire does occur. Plant and office security systems reduce theft and danger to employees. Machine designs and building layouts can also be made safer.

SELF-INSURANCE

Reserves cushion the losses

One sound way to deal with insurable risk is to remain financially prepared to accept a loss without damaging a business's strength. Small losses must be accepted as daily occurrences. Some materials and inventory will be damaged or lost. Machinery will break down. Windows will be broken. Roofs will leak. For most companies, these small losses are normal business expenses.

Some businesses also establish reserve funds to be used if a major loss occurs. This practice is called *self-insurance.* The advantage of self-insurance is that the money in the reserve can be earning interest for the company. Self-insurance, however, is usually practical only for large companies and for a limited range of risks. It is very difficult to keep a reserve large enough to cover all possible risks without tying up so much money that it harms normal business operations. Large corporations with numerous stores or plants in different locations, however, may be able to self-insure against fire since it is unlikely that more than one facility will burn at a time.

PURCHASED INSURANCE

Backstops all other measures

Nearly every company relies on purchased insurance to protect itself against pure risk. Despite good management, risk reduction efforts, and the ability to accept some losses, there will always be risks that threaten the company's strength. Insurance is usually the answer.

3   INSURANCE

A means of sharing risk protection

Providing insurance is a process whereby many people or organizations contribute regular payments to a fund. The fund is then used to reimburse a contributor who suffers a loss of a type specified in a contract, or *policy,* with the insurer. The effect of this arrangement is to share risk protection among a large group. In this way, each individual contributor to the fund is protected from major loss.

An insurance fund is based on the likelihood of specific losses occuring. For example, an established insurance company might decide to begin offering a new kind of coverage: protection for storefront plate glass windows. In researching the policy, they might find that on the average 170 of every 100,000 windows of the type they cover are broken each year. They may also find that the average loss from a single break is $1,000. They then compute their average payout a year to be about $170,000 (170 breakages × $1,000 a breakage) per 100,000 policyholders. They will establish premium rates to provide a fund of that size each year plus an additional amount to cover the expenses of administering the fund and handling claims. The portion of the fund waiting to be paid out is also available for investment by the insurance company.

Different kinds of organizations provide insurance. The federal and state governments are *public insurers.* The federal government provides a wide range of insurance: for bank deposits, home mortgages, life insurance for veterans, and others. State governments provide insurance against losses resulting from unemployment, for example. Nearly all commercial insurance in the United States, however, is provided by insuring organizations that are either stock companies or mutual companies. These are called *private insurers.*

STOCK COMPANIES

Profit-seeking corporations

An insurance company organized as a *stock company* is a normal business corporation. Stockholders invest money in the corporation with the hope of earning dividends. The corporation manages its operations in an attempt to make a profit. Except for life insurance, most private insurance is provided by stock companies.

MUTUAL COMPANIES
Policyholder cooperatives

Mutual insurance companies are owned exclusively by policyholders and not by stockholders. Their operation is similar to that of a cooperative. They are nonprofit and do not pay regular dividends. If a surplus accumulates, it is sometimes distributed to policyholders as a rebate.

Most mutuals collect full advance premiums. This means that they collect in advance the full premium needed to create a fund large enough to meet all likely payments for losses. Some smaller mutuals use an assessment system. They charge a lower premium and assess policyholders for an additional amount if and when it is needed to cover losses that are paid for.

4 TYPES OF INSURANCE COVERAGE
Pay your money and take your choice

Providers of insurance have originated hundreds of different kinds of policies covering scores of insurable risks in various combinations. The kinds of insurance a small business would carry probably include fire and burglary, public liability, workers' compensation and social security, business interruption, and, if appropriate, automobile insurance and fidelity and surety insurance. Large corporations usually hold a greater variety of policies.

FIRE AND ALLIED LOSS INSURANCE
Offers basic property protection

Loss resulting from destruction of property by fire, wind, water, and smoke damage and other hazards is covered by *fire and allied loss insurance.* Normally, coverage is purchased both for real property, such as factories, office buildings, and warehouses and for personal property, which includes inventory, furniture, machines and equipment, and other supplies. Premium rates for fire protection vary considerably. Much lower rates are charged for fire-resistant buildings located in areas with good fire protection than for frame buildings in an area with a poor water supply and limited fire-fighting capability.

Basic fire, wind, and water protection is *direct coverage.* It pays only part or all of the direct costs of replacing the damaged property. Many policies also cover specified *consequential losses* resulting indirectly from the damage. A business that is damaged by fire will often lose at least part of its income as a result and will have the added expenses of trying to operate while the damage is being repaired. Certain policies will pay some of these costs, such as rent on temporary business quarters. See Table 15-1 for the differences between direct and indirect damages.

TABLE 15-1
Insuring Against Direct and Indirect Damage to Commercial Property

Direct Damage

1. Damage resulting directly from fire, lightning, floods, high winds, vandalism, etc.
2. Leakage from sprinkler systems.
3. Water damage from fire fighting.
4. Damage done by demolition in connection with hazards removal.
5. Replacement cost of buildings and facilities.
6. Replacement cost of machinery, equipment, and furnishings.
7. Replacement cost of inventories.
8. Injury to employees and occupants.

Indirect Damage

1. Loss due to interruption of business.
2. Extra expenses during rehabilitation.
3. Loss of rents.
4. Rental of temporary operating space.
5. Loss of profits or commissions.
6. Loss of markup value of inventories.

A *business interruption policy* is an extension of this concept. This covers temporary loss of income from a variety of insurable causes. Interruption of operations by fire is the most common example, but coverage can also be obtained for power or fuel loss or other occurrences that cause loss of business income.

Most business fire policies include a *coinsurance provision.* This states that if property is insured for less than its total value and suffers only partial damage, the insurance company will pay for only a specified portion of the loss. The owner of the property must pay for the remainder as coinsurer. This clause is included because it has been a common practice for business managers to insure property for less than full value since losses from fire are usually not total. Carrying less insurance reduces the premium. Without the coinsurance provision, insurance companies would often be accepting lower premiums but still be paying the entire cost of a partial loss.

Coinsurance works this way. Suppose an industrial distributor has a warehouse building assessed at $100,000. The insurance company establishes a coinsurance clause stating that the building must be insured for 80 percent of its assessed, or market value. Suppose, then, that the industrial distributor decides to insure the warehouse for only $40,000 and subsequently the building is completely destroyed in a fire. The insurance company will pay only $20,000 or 50 percent of the insurance coverage on $40,000, because the industrial distributor insured the building for only half of the required amount. If the industrial distributor had taken out $60,000 in coverage, it would have received only $45,000 (since $60,000 is three quarters of the $80,000 coinsurance requirement). To get reimbursed for the full amount of coverage, the industrial distributor would have had to insure for $80,000.

MARINE INSURANCE
Covers ocean or land shipping

Marine insurance originated for protection against the risk of shipping goods at sea. It has now been extended to cover other kinds of shipping. The two major types are ocean and inland shipping.

Ocean marine insurance protects goods and ships while they are at sea and temporarily while they are in port. Although specific variations are possible, policies usually cover capsizing, sinking, fire and water damage, and vandalism, as well as other kinds of damage. Rates are based on estimates of the likelihood of loss.

The oldest ocean marine insurer is Lloyds of London, founded in 1779. This is a group of over 18,000 individuals who form syndicates under Lloyd's supervision to underwrite (or insure) just about every kind of high-risk venture, at sea or elsewhere. A ship's bell hangs in its chambers and, whenever an insured ship is lost at sea, the bell is rung.

Inland marine insurance covers the risks of shipping goods on inland waterways. It also covers other more widely used means of transportation—railroad lines, trucks, and airlines. Goods in transit are normally protected for loss or damage resulting from accidents such as train collisions, derailment, and road accidents. Coverage also usually includes damage from fire, wind, earthquakes, and other natural forces. Damage caused by people, such as theft or vandalism, may or may not be covered in a specific policy.

CASUALTY INSURANCE
Includes automobile, accident, and theft coverage

A number of different types of insurance are traditionally grouped under the heading *casualty insurance.* Casualty generally refers to death or injury in an accident, but for insurers it may apply to automobile; public liability; burglary, robbery, and theft; and worker's compensation insurance.

Automobile Insurance   *Automobile insurance* is important for business vehicles as well as for drivers' personal cars. Using an automobile is a considerable risk. Not only may the car itself be damaged or destroyed, but there is a danger of injuring other people or damaging their property. Causing injury to others can result in large losses from lawsuits. Basic automobile insurance coverage includes collision, fire, theft, and liability-bodily injury.

■ *Collision insurance* pays for damage to or destruction of the insured's car. Collision policies have a deductible clause. A *deductible provision* in any insurance policy means that the insured must pay a stated amount for the loss before the insurance company pays anything. If a collision policy has a $100 deductible, the insured must pay for all accidents causing less than $100 damage and must pay the first $100 for more serious accidents.

■ *Fire and theft coverage* pays for losses resulting from these causes. Other risks, such as windstorm, vandalism, and water, can also be included. The protection is then called *comprehensive coverage.*

■ *Liability-bodily injury coverage* pays for losses resulting from damage done by an automobile to other people or their property. Personal injury or property damage can result in expensive lawsuits. The person at fault may be asked to pay hundreds of thousands of dollars. Liability insurance, including both property damage and bodily injury done to others, could protect a small company from failure if a business vehicle is involved in a serious accident.

Public Liability Insurance   Damage or injury to others is not caused only by automobiles. A restaurant customer may become ill from eating spoiled food. A box in a warehouse may fall on a visitor. A dangerous stairway may cause a customer to fall and be injured. Damage may be caused to nearby buildings by construction work. A doctor or pharmacist may make an error that causes illness or death. All of these occurrences, and countless others, may result in a company's having to pay settlements to injured parties. *Public liability insurance* protects the insured from such losses up to a maximum value stated in the policy.

In addition to covering losses, insurance companies that sell liability policies provide many services that help protect the insured. The insurance company will thoroughly investigate the legal claims of the injured person or company. It will provide legal representation for the insured in court cases. It will usually advise the insured of ways to improve property or of procedures to avoid claims.

Burglary, Robbery, and Theft Insurance   Various policies are available to protect businesses from theft losses. *Burglary, robbery, and theft insurance* may cover payrolls, inventory, securities, contents of safes, or any other things of value. As with other types of insurance, rates vary according to the probability of loss, based on past experience with theft around the location of the protected property.

Federal Crime Insurance   Federal Crime Insurance is low-cost insurance that the federal government makes available to businesses in high crime areas where private insurance is normally not available. Often, business owners are unaware that they can obtain this.

Worker's Compensation Insurance   All 50 states require businesses to carry insurance to compensate employees for losses caused by physical injury suffered on the job. *Worker's compensation insurance* usually pays for medical expenses and for a portion of workers' salaries while they are unable to work. Worker's compensation (also called workmen's compensation in some states) also usually makes a payment to a worker's family if death results from a job-related accident.

Issues &
Highlights

Why is it that basically honest people are tempted to cheat when it comes to making insurance claims? Insurance premiums continue to rise, not only due to companies' operating costs or inefficiencies, but because so many people expect protection or redress for the most minor of damage or loss. Still other injured parties inflate their claims far beyond the true loss. There was the man, for instance, who slipped on a half-eaten tuna sandwich in New York's City Hall and sued the city for $1 million in damages. You might ask, "Whose fault was this—the city, the person who dropped the sandwich, or the man who slipped on it?" Some people, of course, are just plain dishonest, like the husband and wife who collected three times from three different insurers for a "theft" of jewelry that didn't even happen once. Still others are pushed into litigation that is costly for the insuror by lawyers who hope to get a fee for their efforts.

Down deep, however, many people pad their claims because they feel that getting something extra from a rich, greedy insurance company isn't stealing at all. But the net effect is to make insurance protection more expensive for others.

Source: Carol J. Loomis, "A Non-Boring Look at Insurance", Fortune, March 8, 1982, p. 105.

What do you think should be done—if anything—to reduce dishonest or unreasonable claims? If you were sitting in judgment during a trial for damages, whose side would you be on—the insurance company's or the person seeking damages? Would it make any difference to you if the person who was being sued had no insurance protection? Why?

FIDELITY AND SURETY BONDS

Pay for employee dishonesty

Businesses are subject to risk resulting from the possible dishonesty of their employees, especially those who have access to money. Insurance, in the form of a *fidelity bond,* can be purchased to make up for losses resulting from embezzlement, forgery, or outright theft by employees. Such bonds may be bought to cover specified employees, such as retail clerks, treasurers, salespeople, or others who handle money.

A company, government organization, or other organization may seek protection from losses that could result from a breach of contract. If a company with which a contract has been made fails to carry out the terms of the contract, that company may be required to purchase a *surety bond.* If, for instance, a school board hires a building contractor to build a school, the board may require a surety bond. Should the contractor fail to build the school adequately and in an acceptable time, the amount of the bond must be paid by the insurer to the school board.

Other bonds are available as protection from losses caused by contested title to real property. They are called *title insurance.* If a piece of land becomes less valuable because of unknown claims against it or if possession is lost because of a defective title, the insurer pays the amount specified in the policy. Bonds are also available to cover unexpected bad debts. These credit bonds pay a specified amount if a customer with a normally good credit rating fails to pay an obligation to the insured.

ACCIDENT AND HEALTH INSURANCE

Blue Cross/Blue Shield leads the way

Accident and health insurance policies usually provide one or more of three types of coverage: (a) it may pay some or all of the expenses of hospitalization, surgery, and other medical care resulting from accidents or illness, (b) it may pay the insured some or all of the income lost when illness or injury prevents working, or (c) it may make lump sum payments for loss of sight or limbs or for death resulting from an accident. Policies combine these benefits in different ways. Rapidly rising costs for medical care have made premium rates for high quality health insurance increase proportionately.

Another response to increasing health care costs has been the growing popularity of major medical insurance. These policies provide payment for the treatment of serious injuries resulting from accidents or major illnesses such as cancer and heart disease. Medical care for many conditions can run to tens of thousands of dollars. Consequently, major medical plans set a high maximum payment, often $50,000 or higher. They also usually have a high deductible—$1,000 is a common figure.

Some businesses provide health insurance for their employees. As an added benefit, many companies maintain a *group insurance* policy that provides payments to employees if they become sick or injured. The plans usually cover occurrences that are not covered by workers' compensation. Some companies pay the entire cost of the coverage. Others share the cost with employees. The total cost of the protection is usually lower than for an individual policy because it is less expensive for an insurance company to administer one policy for many people than many single policies.

LIFE INSURANCE

Repays survivors for lost income

In return for premiums, *life insurance* pays a sum to survivors if the insured dies while the policy is in effect. Many policies include provision for the accumulation of savings and other special features. Its basic purpose, however, is to repay survivors for some of the financial losses that result when a person dies. Medical and funeral expenses must be paid. Outstanding debts may be a burden. Loss of income formerly provided by the insured may greatly lower the standard of living of survivors.

Premiums   Life insurance differs in an important way from other kinds of insurance. Premiums for fire insurance, for instance, are based on an estimation of the likelihood that a fire will occur. In contrast, death is certain. The only unknown factors are the time and the cause. Insurance companies, therefore, use mortality tables that show the probability of death occurring at different ages in determining premium rates. If, for example, an insurance company has policies on 100,000 people 35 years of age, the tables show that 251 of these policyholders will be expected to die during the year. By combining these expectancies for all ages, the total amount likely to be paid out is estimated. Premiums can then be set to provide an adequate fund, considering variables such as the length of time policies will be in force, the type of policy, and others.

Types of Life Insurance   Life policies can generally be categorized as whole-life, endowment, or term.

Whole-life insurance may be considered the standard life insurance policy. The insured makes equal payments periodically from the purchase date until his death. When the insured dies, the face value of the policy is paid to his or her survivors or to other specified people or organizations. This type of insurance automatically includes a savings plan. As premiums are paid, over the years, the policy attains a *cash surrender value.* The policy may be traded at any time for its accumulated cash value or the cash value may be used as collateral for a loan.

On some policies, the insured person is required to pay premiums only for a certain period, for 20 or 30 years, for instance. Protection continues, however, for the rest of the insured's life. In this plan, premiums must be set higher.

Endowment life insurance policies stress the savings possibilities more than does whole-life. Higher premiums are charged so that the cash surrender value increases rapidly. Premiums are set so that in a specified number of years the cash value will have added up to the total value of the policy. Thus, the insured will have built up a savings fund equal to the face value of the policy and will have been insured during the period of saving.

Term life insurance provides payment if the insured dies within a certain number of years stated in the policy. A 10-year term policy, for example, requires the regular payment of premiums for ten years and pays the face value of the policy if the insured dies within that period. Term policies normally do not build up a cash surrender value. If the insured does not die during the specified term, all premiums remain the property of the insurer. Group life insurance coverage that companies offer employees is typically written as a term policy.

Each kind of life insurance policy has advantages and disadvantages and is best suited to particular situations. Term policies provide inexpensive protection for temporary periods. Their lack of cash value and increasing costs as the purchaser's age increases are limitations. Term policies are difficult and expensive for older people to buy. Whole life insurance is a compromise between term and endowment policies. It provides good protection at a reasonable cost. It is more expensive than term and does not have the extensive savings capabilities that endowment policies have. Endowment policies stress savings more than protection. Their premiums are the highest of the three types. The savings features of endowment policies can only be judged in comparison with other types of investment.

Specialized Life Insurance   Other kinds of life insurance policies are available for particular needs. Partnerships often maintain policies on each partner with the other partners named as beneficiaries. If one partner dies, the remaining partners can be sure of having adequate funds to buy the ownership share of the insured or to cope with other losses caused by the death. This, in effect, helps to insure the continued life of the partnership. A similar plan is sometimes used by corporations. They may buy "key employee" insurance to help cover losses caused by the death of an important manager or decision maker.

People who are making a large installment purchase or are seeking a mortgage loan on real estate often buy credit life insurance. These policies pay off the remaining part of the loan if the insured dies.

Life insurance is often provided by firms for their employees in the same way group health insurance is. The employer maintains a single policy covering some or all employees. Many such policies are renewable one-year term insurance. They provide a low-cost but valuable benefit that companies can offer, free or partially paid, to their employees.

CHARACTERISTICS OF INSURANCE POLICIES

Legal language predominates

The insurance policy is a legal contract. It sets down in writing a statement of the basic conditions under which it operates and then adds, according to the type of policy, a number of additional clauses that supplement or extend the basic coverage. In similar fashion, the contract also states what conditions are exempt from the policy and will not be covered by it.

Much of the language of insurance policies appears old-fashioned and hard to understand by consumers. One reason for this is that the real meaning of a policy, as with any contract, depends upon the way it is interpreted in court cases arising from it. When a particular clause or policy has had many legal decisions made about it, its meaning is clearly fixed. For that reason, insurers do not like to change to new language that might be interpreted in a different way by the courts. An historic example of such precise language that has lasted for over 200 years is part of the ocean marine policy of Lloyds of London. It was written in 1780 and still appears in today's policies:

> Touching The Adventures and Perils which we the Assurers are contented to bear and to take upon us in this Voyage, they are, of the Seas, Men-of-War,

Fire, Enemies, Pirates, Rovers, Thieves, Jetisons, Letters of Mart and Countermart, Surprisals, Taking at Sea, Arrests, Restraints and Detainments of all Kings, Princes and People, of what Nation, Condition, or Quality soever, Barratry of the Master and Mariners, and of all other like Perils, Losses and Misfortunes that have or shall come to the Hurt, Detriment, or Damage of the said Goods and Merchandise and Ship, etc., or any Part thereof.

In recent years, there has been consumer pressure for insurance companies to present their conditions in clearer language. Some insurers have responded by rewriting the principal clauses of policies or by providing the consumer with descriptive material about the policy that is written in nontechnical language.

5   CREDIT MANAGEMENT

Keeps a watch on credit customers

A potential source of loss that can be minimized by good management is bad debts resulting from credit sales. Nearly every business of any size sells a large portion of its goods or services on credit. When wholesalers buy from manufacturers, they almost always have at least 30 days to pay. Producers selling materials and equipment to each other offer credit terms. A substantial part of retail sales are made with some kind of deferred or extended (installment) payment plan. Deciding when to allow credit purchases and in what amounts is the basic job of credit management. Its goal for most companies is to allow credit to as many buyers as possible in order to increase sales while prohibiting credit purchases by bad credit risks to minimize losses from bad debts.

Good credit management is important to a firm's solvency. Most of the money a company uses to pay its bills comes from income produced by sales. If credit sales turn out to be uncollectible or if collection is long delayed, available working capital is seriously reduced.

COMMERCIAL CREDIT

Character, capacity, capital, and condition

Credit extended to other companies is usually called *commercial* (or *mercantile*) *credit*. The majority of commercial sales are made on credit, allowing payment to be delayed at least 30 days. Managers concerned with commercial credit must decide which firms will be allowed to buy on credit and what maximum amount of credit purchases will be allowed each customer. They attempt to determine the credit worthiness of each customer, often using the "four C's" of credit:

■ "Character" refers mainly to the buyer's reputation for meeting obligations in good faith. To many managers, customers' honesty and desire to pay are the fundamental requirements for credit.

■ "Capacity" is the basic financial ability of a customer to pay. Earning power can often be evaluated by considering the general business practices of a customer.

■ "Capital" is a measure of a customer's assets. If a credit customer's earning power fails, assets can be sold to pay off debts.

■ "Conditions" of the individual credit customer (how well the business is doing at a given time) and the economy in general, have an important effect on credit worthiness. Even a well-managed firm may have difficulty paying its debts on time when business conditions are very bad.

Credit management is so important to the financial condition of companies that a number of services have been developed to help rate customers for credit worthiness. Dun & Bradstreet, Inc., is probably the best known of these, but a number of trade organizations also maintain credit data. They often publish references giving credit ratings and prepare reports describing in detail the financial status of companies.

In deciding whether to give credit, managers sometimes conduct their own investigations. They may seek information from other companies that have extended credit to the company under investigation. They may also use financial statements, information from banks, and personal interviews. Table 15-2 illustrates the kind of information requested by lending institutions from commercial borrowers.

TABLE 15-2
Information Typically Required by Lenders From Commercial Borrowers and for Trade Credit

General Information About the Loan Request

Nature of the borrower's business

Amount and purpose of the loan

Repayment terms required

Security or collateral offered

Extent to which borrowers equity is affected by the loan (equity-debt ratio after loan)

Personal Information About Principal Owners

Credit references

Personal income tax statements

Personal net worth statements

Company Information

Business plan for one to three years, including break-even analysis

Casualty insurance coverage

Rental or leasing committments

Financial statements (profit and loss, assets, existing debt)

Cash inflow and outgo records for past two years or more

Detailed inventory status (materials, fixtures, equipment, licenses, permits, goodwill)

ACTION BRIEF

Dunning the Deadbeats. *When interest rates were soaring in the early 1980's, slow payers were the bane of many suppliers. A retail store that took 75 days to pay, instead of 30, had the use of the supplier's money for the additional 45 days. To keep that costly practice to a minimum, Intershoe, Inc., a shoe distributor, employed 15 of its 120 people for the sole purpose of pestering retailers who had fallen behind in their payments. The two keys to collections, says Intershoe, were (1) super-alert record-keeping to spot deadbeats, and (2) polite, but regular, telephone-dunning of past-due accounts. The telephoning was done by specialists who are adept in seeing through smoke screens, such as retailers who claimed the shipment never arrived, or who tried to avoid payment by returning shoes as defective long after they have gone out of style on the shop's shelves.*

Source: *Robert C. Wood, "Getting Cash From Slow Payers," INC., June 1982, p. 111.*

CONSUMER CREDIT

Government protection is increasing

Credit purchases by individuals is a characteristic of American life. Statistics, in fact, show that the use of credit by consumers has more than doubled in the past decade. A great many retail items are bought on some kind of credit plan. Most stores allow 30 days for payment, and many have longer-term installment plans for larger purchases. Items such as refrigerators, washing machines, and automobiles are routinely bought on an installment basis. In addition, one out of two families use credit cards to purchase anything from gasoline and clothing to hardware and airline tickets.

The fundamentals of credit management are the same for all businesses—for both retail sales and customers for commercial sales. A rule of thumb is to extend credit to as many customers as possible while eliminating those who are unwilling or unable to pay. Private, local, and national organizations maintain credit information on consumers and provide reports to businesses that wish to establish credit ratings for their customers.

Collecting bills from delinquent consumers, however, is a major problem, especially for retailers and the loan companies that finance many installment purchases. The problem is so great that there are about 5,000 agencies that specialize in collecting debts from consumers. These agencies are effective in collecting bills that the original seller has about given up on. They recover anywhere from 20 to 50 percent of what is owed, and they typically keep half of that amount. Collection agencies have often overstepped their legal position in the past. To correct this, the *Fair Debt Collection Practices Act* was passed in 1978. Among other things, the law forbids bill collectors to:

- Tell the debtor's employer, family, or neighbors about the debt.
- Telephone the debtor at home between 9 p.m. and 8 a.m.
- Use false identification as a lawyer or as any kind of official.
- Use obscene, profane, or abusive language.

Consumer Credit Protection Act   In an effort to help customers protect themselves in credit transactions, Congress passed the *Consumer Credit Protection Act (CCPA)* in the early 1960s. The Truth-in-Lending Law, as it is often called, requires many different kinds of businesses and organizations to disclose to customers the total interest and service charges on credit purchases and loans. The Credit Protection Act does not establish a maximum interest rate; it merely requires that buyers or borrowers be informed of how much interest they are paying for credit.

In April 1971 the Fair Credit Reporting Act (FCRA, Title VI Amendment of the Consumer Protection Act) became effective. This act specifically restricts the kind and amount of information that may be provided by one organization to another about an individual's credit worthiness. Restrictions are imposed on records of old bankruptcies, arrests, and/or convictions that occurred seven or more years ago. Furthermore, the act prohibits the distribution of listings of people who are believed to be poor credit risks, regardless of the list's validity. The act also requires that an individual being screened be made aware of the process and be told when

TABLE 15-3
Highlights of the Consumer Credit Protection Laws

1. Lenders must tell you the method used for calculating the finance charge and when your payments begin.

2. Credit advertising must be accurate and not misleading. "Only $2 down," for example, must also state that you will have to pay $10 a week for the next two years, if that is the case.

3. All credit applicants must start out on the same footing. Specifically, race, color, age, sex, or marital status may not be used to discriminate against you.

4. You may not be denied credit just because you or your family receive some sort of public assistance, including Social Security benefits.

5. If you are denied credit, you must be notified within 30 days after your application was completed. If you are dissatisfied, you may seek guidance from a number of federal enforcement agencies. As a starting point, contact your nearest Federal Reserve Bank.

6. The Law does not guarantee that you will be given a loan or obtain the credit you seek. Its purpose is to assure that your application will be treated fairly and equitably within the limitations prescribed by the law.

Source: *Consumer Handbook to Credit Protection Laws,* Board of Governors of the Federal Reserve System, Washington, D.C., December 1978.

his or her application has been denied on the basis of information furnished by credit reporting agencies. The provisions of the act do not apply, however, when commercial credit is being requested. In order to help consumers to more fully understand their rights under the law and to be more prudent in their assumption of debt, the Federal Reserve System publishes useful guidelines, some of which are illustrated above in Table 15-3.

Key Concepts

1. Every business is subject to two kinds of risks. Speculative risk results from investing money in a business with the hope of making a profit. Pure risk results from hazards that are not willingly undertaken by a business: fire, theft, and so forth. Businesses can protect themselves against pure risk with insurance.

2. Business managers cope with risk through good management, risk reduction, self-insurance, and purchased insurance.

3. Insurance is a process by which many people or organizations that are subject to similar types of risks contribute premiums to a central organization. These premiums are placed in a fund from which losses are reimbursed when damage occurs to a contributor.

4. The main types of coverage are fire; inland and ocean marine; auto; public liability; burglary, robbery, and theft; worker's compensation; fidelity and surety bonds; accident and health; and life.

5. Good credit management contributes to a company's solvency by helping to maintain adequate available working capital. Credit managers try to extend credit to customers to increase sales and avoid giving credit to customers who are unwilling or unable to pay.

Review Questions

1. Define, explain, or identify each of the following key terms and phrases found on the pages indicated.

   accident and health insurance   (p. 276)
   automobile insurance   (p. 273)
   bankruptcy   (p. 266)
   burglary, robbery, and theft insurance (p. 274)
   business interruption policy   (p. 272)
   cash surrender value   (p. 277)
   casualty insurance   (p. 273)
   Chapter 7 bankruptcy   (p. 267)
   Chapter 11 bankruptcy   (p. 267)
   Chapter 13 bankruptcy   (p. 268)
   coinsurance provision   (p. 272)
   collision insurance   (p. 274)
   commercial (mercantile) credit   (p. 279)
   comprehensive coverage   (p. 274)
   consequential loss   (p. 271)
   Consumer Credit Protection Act   (p. 281)
   deductible provision   (p. 274)
   direct coverage   (p. 271)
   endowment life insurance   (p. 277)
   Fair Debt Collection Practices Act   (p. 281)
   fidelity bond   (p. 276)
   fire and allied loss insurance   (p. 271)
   fire and theft coverage   (p. 274)
   group insurance   (p. 276)
   inland marine insurance   (p. 273)
   insolvent   (p. 266)
   insurance   (p. 268)
   liability-bodily injury coverage   (p. 274)
   life insurance   (p. 277)
   liquidate   (p. 266)
   mutual insurance company   (p. 271)

   ocean marine insurance   (p. 273)
   policy   (p. 270)
   premium   (p. 268)
   private insurer   (p. 270)
   public insurer   (p. 270)
   public liability insurance   (p. 274)
   pure risk   (p. 268)
   receiver   (p. 266)
   risk   (p. 266)
   self-insurance   (p. 269)
   speculative risk   (p. 266)
   stock company   (p. 270)
   surety bond   (p. 276)
   term life insurance   (p. 277)
   title insurance   (p. 276)
   whole-life insurance   (p. 277)
   worker's compensation insurance   (p. 274)

2. In what ways do Chapter 11 and Chapter 13 types of bankruptcy proceedings resemble each other?
3. What is the difference between speculative risk and pure risk? Can both risks be handled by management in the same way?
4. What are the four principal ways for a business to cope with risk?
5. What is the basic method by which an insurance company can provide repayment for losses suffered by its policyholders?
6. What is business interruption insurance? What kind of health insurance is it like?
7. What is the most important use of each of the three types of life insurance policies?
8. Describe each of the "four C's" of credit worthiness.

Case Critique 15-1
The Big Chance

Tom and Aretha, husband and wife, ran the best little coffee shop in Montana. Their red shack stood near the main highway and was frequented by tourists as well as "locals." They weren't getting rich, but, as Aretha said, "We're having a lot of fun." That was before a flash fire in the kitchen ductwork this summer put them out of business.

As Tom and Aretha looked back, they had some misgivings. Their fire insurance agent had visited the coffee shop in the spring of the year. He had advised that records showed that there was a terrible tendency for fires to start in kitchen ducts in which grease had built up. Tom and Aretha, he advised, could do two things so far as he was concerned. They could increase the amount of their fire insurance coverage to make sure that fire damage would be fully compensated. That would mean a much higher premium. Or, he said, they could install a sprinkling system in the ductwork. This would involve an initial cost on their part, but it would serve to add protection as well as reduce the insurance premium.

Tom's reaction was, "We don't need it. We run a very clean kitchen. Aretha scrubs up that ductwork regularly, and we keep a close eye on the grease filter to make sure it is clean."

"You two are the operators here," said the agent, "but, the way your coverage is right now, if your place burns down, your insurance would cover only about half of the restaurant's replacement cost. Do you have enough money set aside so that if you do have a fire, your savings will make up the difference between your coverage from us and what it might cost to rebuild?"

"We don't have that much money set aside,"

said Tom and Aretha. "We'll have to rely on the precautions we take to prevent a fire. For the time being, we'll just have to take our chances."

After the fire struck, Tom and Aretha found that they didn't have the money needed to rebuild. Like nearly half of all business establishments that are severely damaged by fire, the best little coffee shop in Montana never did reopen.

1. What risk management technique was implied both by the suggestion to install a sprinkler system and by Aretha's regular cleaning of the ductwork? What are some limitations on the effectiveness of this technique?
2. When Tom and Aretha decided to "take their chances," they were engaging in what other kind of risk management technique? What was its drawback?
3. What was the third kind of risk management technique that Tom and Aretha employed? What were its advantages and drawbacks?

Case Critique 15-2
The Quick and Easy Loan

ZIPetronics, a small manufacturer of plug-in switches used in TV-game assemblies, found itself in a bind one day just as its business was beginning to grow dramatically. That morning, it received a large order of switches from a major game company. When ZIP's production manager checked the inventories of copper wire and silver-plated connections needed for the switches, he found that they were far short of the amounts needed. To complete this order would require immediate shipment of materials. He talked the matter over with the company's finance chief. Together, they calculated that the firm would have to obtain a $25,000 loan for materials quickly, if the order were to be accepted and completed on time. Right away, the finance chief got on the telephone to the commercial loan officer of the local bank.

"Here's what we'd like to arrange," she said. "Instead of our usual line of credit of $10,000, we'd like to raise it immediately to $25,000."

"Why?" asked the loan officer.

"We've got a chance to do business with a major games manufacturer, who is new to us. But the size of the order is larger than we're stocked to handle. It's a great opportunity, but we must move fast."

"Let's see," said the loan officer, "we have your net-worth statement on hand, don't we?"

"Yes," said the financial chief, "it shows that we are in very good shape financially. Our profit picture gets better every day. This order will find us a little short on working capital, however, since we have so much tied up as fixed assets in our modern equipment. But we have very little debt outstanding. And the field we serve is going through the roof right now."

"I see," said the loan officer. "Our records also show that you've been maintaining a line of credit with us for over three years and your payments have always been very prompt."

"Well, what about it?," asked the finance chief.

"There's no problem," replied the loan officer. "We'll put the loan papers in the mail to you today and you should be able to start drawing upon the $25,000 by tomorrow."

1. Can you link up each of the "four C's" of commercial credit with something that is demonstrated in this case?
2. What might have been the loan officer's decision if ZIPetronics had a record of slow payment on its loans and was operating mostly on borrowed money? Why do you think so?

Unit 6

Basic Business Operations— Human Resources

Unit 6 sets forth some of the methods businesses use to assemble and manage a productive work force.

Human bodies and minds are needed by businesses to carry out their plans and to convert resources to valuable goods and services. The primary function of management is to select and develop a working staff.

The labor force in the United States today is a reservoir of great potential, much of it untapped. The expectations of the people who make up the labor force are very high. Management, therefore, must find ways to communicate effectively with employees and make their work more productive and meaningful. When conflict arises between management and labor, laws help to insure fair treatment of employees.

Chapter 16

Personnel Management

PERSONNEL MANAGEMENT IS CONCERNED WITH . . .

1 . . . PLANNING AND ESTIMATING EMPLOYMENT NEEDS . . .

JOB A.

TASK 1
TASK 2
TASK 3

Job analysis

Quantity

Legal restraints
(Equal Employment
Opportunity Commission)

2 . . . MANAGING THE EMPLOYMENT PROCESS . . .

Recruitment   Selection   Orientation

3 . . . TRAINING, DEVELOPING, AND APPRAISING PERSONNEL . . .

TRAINING

4 . . . COORDINATING AND RECORDING JOB CHANGES . . .

Transfers
Promotions
Separations

5 . . . ASSURING SAFETY AND HEALTH . . .

Accident prevention
Health protection
Legal compliance
(Occupational Safety
and Health
Administration)

6 . . . DESIGNING AND ADMINISTERING WAGE AND SALARY PROGRAMS. . .

Job evaluation
Job pricing
Compensation
systems
Legal compliance
(Fair Labor
Standards Act)

7 . . . DESIGNING AND ADMINISTERING EMPLOYEE BENEFITS AND SERVICE PROGRAMS . . . .

Group life
and health insurance
Pensions
and profit sharing
Nonfinancial
benefits and services

Learning Objectives

The purpose of this chapter is to show how all activities performed by the personnel administration function are essential to human resources management—from planning, recruiting, and developing the firm's work force to preparing paperwork, complying with health and safety requirements, and coordinating an effective compensation and benefits program.

As evidence of general comprehension, after studying this chapter, you should be able to:

1. *Explain the nature of human resources planning.*
2. *Describe the employment process and explain the role of recruitment, selection, and orientation and induction.*
3. *Distinguish between the three principal kinds of employee training.*
4. *Understand and explain the need to coordinate and record job changes and distinguish among transfers, promotions, and separations.*
5. *Identify some of the ways that personnel and business management try to insure safety and health maintenance.*
6. *Differentiate between the basic compensation plans.*
7. *Outline some of the employee benefits administered by personnel managers, and evaluate the impact and cost of such benefits to business in general.*

If your class is using SSweetco: Business Model and Activity File for Business in Action, see Chapter 16 in that book after you complete this chapter. There you will find exercises and activities to help you apply your learning to typical business situations.

At 6 a.m., most of the offices and stores and many of the manufacturing plants in any large city are dark and silent. Three hours later, they are filled with the tens of thousands of men and women who make American business work: typists, chief executives, machinists, salespeople, accountants, billing clerks, assembly line workers, receptionists, computer operators, and others. These people make up a basic part of businesses' production capacity. They all have certain skills and abilities. They all have personal and business problems. They all have interests and expectations. They all have jobs to do that require attention, perseverance, and care. Without workers at every level, business can accomplish nothing.

Personnel management (also known by many as human resources management) is concerned with selecting these people and finding ways to help them work to their best advantage and to the best advantage of the company. Personnel administration, in particular, recruits, hires, trains, evaluates, transfers, promotes, and terminates the work force needed by a company in order for it to meet its goals.

Up until the present century, little attention was given to personnel management or, as it was often then called, industrial relations. Workers were often hired arbitrarily, and harsh discipline—and the threat of extreme poverty if fired—were used to enforce work standards. Businesses today recognize the importance of a dedicated work force and pay more attention to hiring and training workers. Personnel administrators use careful testing and interviewing techniques when hiring. Many companies, even small ones, have formal training and development programs for employees. Great efforts are made to insure that surroundings and work procedures do not endanger employees. Salaries, wages, and other employment benefits are carefully studied and have reached very high levels compared with those of 25 years ago.

1   WORK FORCE PLANNING

Establishes the size and nature of the work force

A basic responsibility of personnel administration is estimating a company's personnel needs. Managers must know what qualifications and skills the company requires of its employees, and how many people are needed to perform functions in the company. These estimates become objectives for personnel planning. Plans for hiring, training, and the development of additional skills must be made to meet the objectives.

ESTIMATING QUALITIES NEEDED IN EMPLOYEES

Analyzing, describing, specifying

A tremendous range of personal qualities and abilities is needed for the thousands of jobs in business. Every job requires a different combination of physical, mental, creative, social, and personal knowledge and skills. The best way to decide which qualities employees should possess is through a careful analysis and definition of all the jobs that must be done.

The systematic study of the characteristics and activities required by specific jobs is called *job analysis.* These analyses try to find out exactly what a person in a given job does and what qualifications are needed to do the job. This information is summarized in a *job description* spelling out the activities and responsibilities of each job and the skills and other characteristics needed to do the job. A *job specification* is often used when actual hiring is done. It generally lists measurable information— years of schooling, length and type of experience, physical characteristics, and others—that would most likely describe an employee who would be suitable for a given job. Table 16-1 shows a typical job description and job specification combined.

ESTIMATING THE SIZE OF WORK FORCE

Planning around uncertainties

Companywide plans should always include specific targets for the quantity of goods and services to be produced. These can be used to make estimates of future work-force needs. In a company that has been in operation for some time, it is possible to estimate fairly accurately how much production can be expected from one person. With this information, the number of staff members needed to meet production goals can be projected.

A number of complicating factors make these projections more difficult in practice. Employee illnesses and absences may vary from time to time. The number of employees who leave work permanently and must be replaced (called *employee turnover*) should be considered. Promotions, dismissals, deaths, or retirements can all create openings and are often difficult to plan for. Sometimes changes in procedures, equipment or products that are on the drawing board create uncertainty about personnel needs. Normal growth will usually be reflected in production plans, but changing business conditions and unknown market factors can make actual growth considerably different.

For an example of how an electronics firm forecasts its human resources needs, see Table 16-2. It begins with (Column A) a list of existing position categories and the present number of staff incumbents. It adds to that list (Column B) all the new jobs that will be created to fulfill growth plans as well as anticipated cutbacks to provide a picture (Column C) of the future staff. An estimate is then made of how many of the present job incumbents will leave for one reason or another, including (Column D) promotions and transfers from that location, plus (Column E) unplanned quits and discharges, plus (Column F) planned retirements. The total number of open positions predicted for the future (Column G) will simply be the sum of those needed for growth plus those needed to replace employees who leave.

LEGAL INFLUENCES ON WORK-FORCE PLANNING

Equal employment opportunity is a major factor

Numerous laws and federal executive orders may affect a business' work-force planning. Most federal laws to eliminate discrimination are administered by the Equal Employment Opportunity Commission

TABLE 16-1
Sample Job Description

Position: Shipping Clerk   **Department:** Shipping and Receiving   **Location:** "C" Building Warehouse

Job Summary

Under general supervision of warehouse manager, processes shipments to customers in accordance with shipment authorization forms forwarded by the sales department. Together with other clerks and packers, removes goods from shelves by hand or by powered equipment and packs them in containers for shipment by truck, rail, air, or parcel post. Prepares and processes appropriate paperwork and maintains related files.

Education

High school graduate.

Experience

None required.

Duties Performed

1. The following represent 70 percent of working time:
   a. Removing stock from shelves and racks and packing into proper shipping containers.
   b. Weighing and labeling cartons for shipment by carrier designated on the shipping order.
   c. Assisting in loading carriers.
2. The following represent 15 percent of working time:
   a. Preparing and/or processing authorization forms (e.g., packing lists, shipping orders, and bills of lading).
   b. Maintaining shipment records by tally sheets or keypunch.
   c. Doing miscellaneous typing of forms and labels.
   d. Maintaining appropriate files.
3. The following represent the balance of working time:
   a. Driving company truck to post office or for an occasional local delivery.
   b. Assisting in taking inventory.
   c. Acting as checker for other shipping or receiving clerks.
   d. Keeping workplace clean and orderly.

Supervision Received

Except for general instructions and special problems, works mostly on his or her own.

Relationships

Works in close contact with packers, material handlers and other clerks. Has contact with truck drivers when loading. Has occasional contact with order department personnel.

Equipment

Operates mechanized stockpicker, powered conveyor belts, carton sealing machinery, keypunch recorder, and typewriter.

Working Conditions

Clean, well-lit, and heated. Requires normal standing, walking, climbing, and lifting. Subject to drafts when shipping doors are open.

TABLE 16-2
Human Resources Planning

COMPONENTS DIVISION	A	B	C	FORECAST PERIOD JAN.-DEC.			G
				D	E	F	
Position Categories	Present Staff Jan.	Planned Changes, Growth and Cutbacks	Future Staff Dec.	Attrition*			Net Openings
Managers							
Operations	30	+10	40	+3	+1	+2	+16
Sales	10	0	10	+1	0	+1	+2
Other	20	+5	25	+1	+1	+2	+9
Engineers	20	−5	15	0	+3	+2	0
Technicians	40	+10	50	0	+2	+2	+14
Clerical	80	−10	70	+5	+5	+3	+3
Hourly, skilled	300	+50	350	+20	+13	+13	+96
Hourly, other	500	+90	590	+20	+40	+25	+175
TOTAL	1,000	+150	1,150	+50	+65	+50	+315

*Attrition = **Column D** (Promotions and Transfers) + **Column E** (Unplanned Outs) + **Column F** (Planned Retirements).
Columns A + B = C Future staff size in December.
Columns B + D + E + F = G Net openings to be filled between January and December.

(EEOC). In general, the regulations bar employers from failing to hire or promote because of sex, age, race, religious beliefs, or for other similar reasons. Job specifications regarding age, sex, and other characteristics, as well as questions asked during recruiting interviews, are restricted to those that can be demonstrated to be undeniably relevant to job performance. This legal requirement is called a ***bona fide occupational qualification (BFOQ).***

Differences in salaries paid for equal work are also against the law. The regulations normally apply to companies with 15 or more employees, to most public institutions, such as local governments, to most labor unions, and to organizations with federal grants or contracts. Some organizations may be required to have ***affirmative action plans*** that not only rule out discrimination but also spell out positive steps to increase the hiring and promotion of minorities and other groups.

2   MANAGING THE EMPLOYMENT PROCESS

Creating an effective work force

Managers need systematic procedures for recruiting, selecting, hiring, and orienting new employees if personnel plans are to be met.

RECRUITING

Searching for the best candidates

When jobs are open, most organizations look first to their current employees to find possible candidates. Promoting someone from within to fill a vacancy has important advantages. A present employee will already be familiar with company operations and will usually need less orientation and training. The work habits, interests, and abilities of a current employee will also be well known to management. Promoting from within improves morale: workers will see that it is possible to progress in their work and will often remain more loyal to their employers. Moving a current employee into an opening also saves the time and expense of recruiting from outside the company.

In many cases, however, no current employee is really suitable for a position that is open. Organizations then are compelled to go outside to find candidates with the combination of skills, training, and experience the position requires. A variety of recruitment practices is commonly used:

■ Private or state employment agencies maintain records of many people who are seeking work. These agencies can do preliminary screening and refer candidates to the hiring company. Private agencies charge a fee to be paid by the employer or the employee. State agencies normally do not charge for their services.

■ Recruiting at colleges, universities, vocational schools, or trade schools has been successful for many companies. It is often possible to pick a candidate with exactly the training desired.

■ Most employers at some time must advertise in newspapers or in trade or professional association publications. These advertisements often draw a number of well-qualified candidates.

■ Many labor unions keep registers of members seeking work. In some fields, such as the construction trades, this is a major recruiting method.

■ Present managers or other employees will often be able to suggest friends or acquaintances for unfilled positions.

■ Most companies receive numerous unsolicited applications for employment. Some of these candidates may also be qualified for an opening.

SELECTION

Picking the most suitable people

Selection is the process of picking the one candidate thought to best match the job specification and to be the most likely to succeed in the job. A thorough selection procedure will typically include application, testing, interviews, investigation, and physical examination:

■ A written *application* form is an effective selection tool. By asking all candidates to describe their job interests, training, work history, and other experience and to provide business or personal references, employers can eliminate applicants who are clearly unsuited for a particular opening.

ACTION BRIEF

Handpicked for the Watchamacallit. When the Hershey Chocolate Company opened a new plant in Stuarts Draft, Virginia, it sorted through 800 job applicants to handpick 12 maintenance workers. These were the best qualified, said Hershey. The maintenance applicants were given special tests developed by the state's Department of Industrial Training at the local vocational school. The 12-employee crew works around the clock on the machines that make the Watchamacallit, a chocolate peanut bar. Since all 12 employees started work on the same day, their job seniority was established by drawing numbers from a hat. Seniority is important at Hershey in bidding for a preferred shift and in priority for vacations.

Source: Kay Frye, "Hershey Plans Innovative Management Here," Daily News Record (Harrisonburg, Virginia), April 12, 1982, p. 16.

■ *Testing* has a clear role in the selection process but its use must be carefully controlled to avoid unfairness. Some employment tests are clearly relevant to a candidate's ability to perform on the job. Asking an applicant for an office clerk job to type a sample report or an auto mechanic to rebuild a carburetor are examples. Personality, motivation, or intelligence tests may also be useful to companies that have had wide experience with them. They have been particularly effective in selecting salespeople and managers. A frequent problem with these tests, however, is that they generally reflect the values and interests of white, middle-class Americans and may unfairly penalize minorities who do not share that cultural background. For this reason, there is active pressure from many sources, including EEOC, to validate the usefulness of tests before using them for selection purposes.

■ The face-to-face job *interview* remains a central part of the selection process for most employers. Careful interviewers can learn important information about a candidate's attitudes, experience, interests, and aspirations. A disadvantage of interviews is that irrelevant facts, such as a style of dress or personal bias, may interfere with objective evaluation.

■ Most companies carry out at least a brief *investigation* of the information given by the applicant. The investigator may contact past employers, former teachers, or other people who know the candidate. One goal of the investigation is to check the accuracy of the information given on the application and to uncover any facts that might point to future problems with the applicant, such as a poor attendance record or dishonesty. Great care is needed by investigators to treat the applicant fairly.

■ Many companies require a *physical examination* before hiring. One purpose of this is to eliminate candidates who may be disabled in the near future because of an existing health problem.

INDUCTION AND ORIENTATION

Proper placement and initiation

The last step in the hiring process is getting the selected employee started on the job. This includes handling the record-keeping chores of putting the new worker on the payroll. It also includes instructing the employee about the work to be done, the people to work with, and company policies and rules. An explanation of a worker's responsibilities and rights at this stage can avoid many management problems later.

3   TRAINING AND DEVELOPING PERSONNEL

Improvement of knowledge, skills, and attitudes

One result of management's intensified interest in improving the effectiveness of employees is a new emphasis on training. Many companies and other organizations, large and small, have formal programs to teach new employees specific job skills or to retrain present workers to use new technology. Oftentimes, managers are also aware of the skills needed in their own jobs and have established development programs to produce better managers, now and in the future.

RANK-AND-FILE EMPLOYEE TRAINING

From simulated to actual experience

A number of approaches are used to teach specific job skills such as those used by production workers. Many kinds of work, such as machine operation and computer operation, can be effectively taught by the **vestibule method.** This training technique sets up a simulation of the work environment and allows trainees to perform the actual job activities in a classroom. To train a computer operator, for example, the actual console and equipment could be used for training. The student would receive simulated jobs to process and would be taught to use the equipment in the proper way. This method is useful when a large number of employees must be taught specific skills.

Actual **on-the-job training** is by far the most commonly used method for training employees in routine job competencies. This appoach, widely used during World War II, was known as Job Instruction Training, or simply J.I.T. Hundreds of thousands of shop and office supervisors were shown how to use this method. They were given, as a reminder, a little card upon which the following four-step training procedure was listed (although with slightly different wording):

Step 1: Prepare the worker to learn.
Step 2: Demonstrate how the job should be done.
Step 3: Try the worker out by letting him or her do the job.
Step 4: Put the worker on his or her own gradually and check back.

On-the-job training today follows much the same procedure. It takes advantage, of course, of modern technology such as audio-cassette and video-tape demonstrations. It still depends mainly, however, on the close attention of the employee's supervisor rather than a professional trainer or instructor.

Apprenticeship training normally combines on-the-job training with classroom work, which covers the theoretical aspects of the job being taught. It is a very effective training method if adequate time and resources are committed to it. Straight **classroom lecture and discussion training** is useful when verbal information has considerable use on the job. All of these methods have been used successfully for retraining present employees as well as for training new workers.

SUPERVISOR AND MANAGEMENT DEVELOPMENT

Insights and maturity are emphasized

Many organizations have formal development programs that help managers perform their duties more effectively. **Management development** programs use a variety of techniques:

■ Formal classroom training is often used, either at workshops or training sessions given by the company or at colleges and universities. These courses usually aim at teaching specific information and management techniques.

■ New methods requiring managers to act out various management roles in a training situation are widely used. This role-playing helps managers develop greater sensitivity to human expectations and interactions in organizations.

■ Coaching in actual work situations is still the most common management-development technique. Managers with more experience and responsibility usually make a conscious effort to advise, guide, and train younger managers.

■ Many companies give managers special assignments that will broaden their experience and skill. Some companies use job rotation, placing a manager trainee in a number of different jobs in succession to widen his or her experience. This can give the employee a broad perspective on company operations and, at the same time, teach many different management skills.

No matter which techniques are used, the goals of development programs are usually similar. They attempt to give managers the insight and maturity they need. They teach specific techniques of administration and organization. They try to provide thorough technical skills and knowledge in a manager's particular area of concern.

PERFORMANCE APPRAISALS

In transition from subjective to objective judgments

An important managerial and supervisory function is judging the quality of the work of others in order to maintain general productivity at as high a level as possible. *Performance appraisals* of subordinates are used in decisions about salary increases, training, promotions, assignment changes, and dismissals.

Most performance appraisals are guided by a form that lists several criteria against which the employee's performance will be judged. These criteria lend themselves to either objective or subjective judgments.

Objective judgements are those that can be readily counted or measured, like quantity of work output, work quality in terms of the number of errors made, and attendance in days absent or late. These judgments stress the results of an employee's efforts. When properly established, objective criteria also relate clearly to the company's goals and the extent to which an employee contributes toward their attainment.

Subjective criteria—no matter how important they may be—are difficult to describe and to measure. They suffer from distortions in human perceptions and from prejudice. As a consequence, the trend in business is toward appraisal criteria that are increasingly objective.

There are many variations of appraisal forms. Many of them include some sort of scoring system to simplify the summary of an employee's overall performance rating. Many such scoring systems also employ a *forced choice technique.* That is, the form lists a number of alternate gradings (such as unsatisfactory, acceptable, good, excellent, or superior.) The appraiser is forced to choose the term or phrase that best describes the employee's performance in that category. Table 16-3 illustrates a forced choice technique for rating aspects of an employee's personality. This particular form forces the appraiser to choose not only the most descriptive, but also the least descriptive, phrase.

Still another appraisal technique is the use of *critical incidents.* This approach was devised to encourage superiors to identify and record inci-

TABLE 16-3
Example of a Forced Choice Performance Appraisal Form

Describe the employee's personal characteristics. Which is most (**M**) and least (**L**) characteristic of the employee?

Group 1 Statements

a.	Always criticizes, never praises.	**M**	**L**
b.	Carries out orders by passing the buck.	**M**	**L**
c.	Knows the job and performs it well.	**M**	**L**
d.	Plays no favorites.	**M**	**L**

Group 2 Statements

a.	Commands respect by his or her actions.	**M**	**L**
b.	Cool-headed.	**M**	**L**
c.	Indifferent.	**M**	**L**
d.	Overbearing.	**M**	**L**

dents in an employee's performance that represent either exceptionally good or poor examples of behavior. It has the advantage of citing specific examples in support of an appraisal judgment rather than a general impression. It has the weakness, so common to most appraisals, of depending mainly upon the memory, impressions, and judgments of the superior.

The performance appraisal, in one form or another, is widely used in business and thought by many authorities to be an effective tool of personnel management. There are many critics of performance appraisals, however, who do not believe that the techniques can be used without bias or in an nonthreatening manner. For this reason, perhaps, the way in which performance appraisals are designed and conducted by a business are subject to challenge by the EEOC.

4 COORDINATING AND RECORDING JOB CHANGES

The recordkeeping task is enormous

In a large organization with well-defined jobs, enough employees move from job to job within the company that conscious management of job changes is needed. Changes normally result from transfers and promotions and from leaving the company for a variety of reasons. Managers must set up procedures for deciding on and administering these changes.

TRANSFERS

A sideways movement

A *transfer* is a move from one job to another within the organization without a significant change in salary or in the amount of responsibility or authority. Transfers sometimes are a consequence of job rotation. They often result from changing company needs. Transfers may also be made in order to take better advantage of an employee's abilities or interests.

PROMOTIONS

An upward movement

A change to a job at a higher level in an organization is a *promotion.* The employee who is promoted is given more responsibility and authority and usually receives a higher salary. Progressive companies try to tie promotions in closely with their employee appraisal system. Provision is often made in the appraisals to evaluate an employee's suitability for promotion. Evaluations based on merit are sometimes combined with, or replaced by, evaluations based on length of service with the firm or in a particular position. This basis for promotion or for salary increases is called *seniority.* It is a well-established practice in American culture, although it has been challenged by many companies and individuals.

SEPARATIONS

Layoffs and terminations

A *separation* occurs when a worker leaves a company. *Layoffs* are temporary separations. These occur when a certain number of employees are told not to come to work because the company wishes to reduce production because of declining demand. When sales increase, workers who have been laid off are given priority for rehiring.

Terminations are permanent separations from a firm. Voluntary termination has many causes. Workers may decide to leave a job expecting higher salaries, faster advancement, or greater benefits elsewhere. They may have lost interest in their present job or may have decided to change careers altogether. Each year, thousands of workers resign voluntarily.

Involuntary terminations also have various causes. Workers may have to be permanently let go if part of a business fails or if new procedures or products eliminate certain jobs. Poor attendance, dishonesty, or poor work performance may cause workers to be dismissed. Well-managed companies usually have a procedure for warning employees that performance is poor and giving them the opportunity to improve. If no improvement results, they are usually terminated.

5 ASSURING SAFETY AND HEALTH MAINTENANCE

For self-serving as well as social reasons

The protection of employees' health and the provision of safe working conditions is a prime concern of personnel management. It is an important social concern to provide a safe work environment. Careful health and safety management also helps to reduce insurance costs, protect against liability losses, and attract better workers.

ACCIDENT PREVENTION
Engineering plus education

An accident is any unplanned occurrence. Accidents may result in property damage, injury, or death, but they do not have to. Enlightened businesses try to take the same approach to accidents as do automobile designers. Automobile designers try to reduce accidents by building cars with better brakes or tires, for example. At the same time, they try to reduce the likelihood that injury will result if an accident does occur. Seat belts are one result of this effort. In a similar vein, managers and planners call upon designers and engineers to develop workplaces and surroundings that minimize the risk of accidents to employees.

Before accidents can be prevented, however, their causes and the causes of the resulting injuries must be determined. A careful, long-term record of accidents and their causes is essential to creating a safe working environment. Similar records for other companies and for whole industries can usually be obtained from the government or from industry trade associations. This information, combined with a thorough analysis of operations, will suggest changes for safer workplaces. Many companies have begun safety training programs for their employees, have redesigned machines, have placed guards over dangerous machine parts, have required hard hats in areas where tools or materials may fall from above, have started new traffic patterns, or have changed the whole layout of plants to make them safer.

EMPLOYEE HEALTH AND SANITATION
Safeguards are increasing

Manufacturing processes and plants present many hazards other than accidents. Dirt, chemicals, biological compounds, and noise may all endanger health. Management must use the same approach they use with accidents: they must locate sources of potential danger and find ways to eliminate it.

Reducing injuries and damage to health usually requires a formal management effort. Collecting information and devising solutions costs money. The expenditure is justified by a genuine regard for the welfare of workers. Profits can actually increase by avoiding the interruption of work and reducing insurance costs and liability claims.

OCCUPATIONAL SAFETY AND HEALTH ADMINISTRATION (OSHA)
OSHA makes safety and health a legal requirement

In recent years, employers have been required by law to provide safe working conditions. The Occupational Safety and Health Administration (OSHA) was created to administer a complex set of federal work safety regulations that went into effect in 1970. OSHA regulations apply to all workers except government employees and those covered by other safety

ACTION BRIEF

Thou Should (or Is It Shall) Not. *More than ten years after the enactment of the Occupational Safety and Health Act (OSHA) the government discovered that 194 of its standards were legally unenforceable because of the way that they were written. These provisions of the act use the word "should" rather than "shall." In legal terms, "shall" is considered mandatory and "should" only advisory. The problem originated because OSHA relied heavily upon standards developed by the American National Standards Association. ANSA is an association of private companies and their standards were intended only to be voluntary. When OSHA agencies went to court to insist that the standards be enforced, they were denied. In a mix-up late in 1982, OSHA had to first entirely rescind the original provisions and then have those portions of the law rewritten and re-enacted by Congress.*

Source: *Sandra Sugara, "OSHA Plans to Revoke 194 Rules," The Washington Post, June 2, 1982, p. A17.*

laws. They are especially aimed at industries with high injury rates, such as roofing, metalworking, construction, mining, and manufacturing of wood products.

OSHA requires businesses to avoid many specified work hazards and to take positive steps to create a safe workplace. Failure to comply can result in fines. Many businesses, especially small ones, have objected that compliance is expensive and complex. As experience with the regulations increases, however, companies are finding affordable ways to meet the intent of the law: to protect the health and lives of their workers.

6   DESIGNING AND SUPERVISING COMPENSATION PROGRAMS

Wages and salaries form the basis of employee motivation

Although for many people the rewards of working go beyond monetary values, salary and wages are extremely significant to most employees. They are especially important as a means of attracting and holding good workers. Only on this basis can other efforts to stimulate morale and motivate good performance be effective. Great care is therefore necessary in setting up and administering compensation programs. *Compensation* includes everything of monetary value that employees receive in return for work. It includes salary, wages, bonuses, and many other benefits.

JOB EVALUATION

Measures difficulty and importance

The basis of a rational compensation policy is often a formal job evaluation. By using existing job descriptions, personnel specialists are able to analyze every job to determine its responsibilities and its requirements for skills and training. These analyses are then used to rank jobs in order of their difficulty and their contribution to the objectives of the organization. The job levels thus established are then assigned a monetary pay range. Table 16-4 illustrates one approach to evaluating jobs using a scale of points for various job factors.

Like many human resources management techniques, job evaluation has its flaws, both technical and human. Because of the proliferation in some industries of jobs that were in the past evaluated as "men's" or "women's" or "black's" or "white's," job evaluation plan design and implementation is open to scrutiny by the EEOC.

JOB PRICING

Determines how much a job is worth

Setting the pay scale for each level and type of job is called *job pricing.* A number of factors combine to influence job pricing decisions. The general prices of goods and services have a double effect. A company that receives high prices for its goods and services is financially able to pay higher wages as long as sales remain good. High prices for consumer goods

TABLE 16-4
Points Assigned to Factors in a Job Evaluation Plan*

Factor	First Degree	Second Degree	Third Degree	Fourth Degree	Fifth Degree
Skill					
Education	14	28	42	56	70
Experience	22	44	66	88	110
Initiative and ingenuity	14	28	42	56	70
Effort					
Physical demand	10	20	30	40	50
Mental or visual demand	5	10	15	20	25
Responsibility					
Equipment or process	5	10	15	20	25
Material or product	5	10	15	20	25
Safety of others	5	10	15	20	25
Work of others	5	. . .	15	. . .	25
Job Conditions					
Working conditions	10	20	30	40	50
Unavoidable hazards	5	10	15	20	25

*Points vary for each factor according to the degree of job demand for that factor. For example, if the physical effort required on a job is low, it may rate only 10 points (first degree), but if it is a very demanding job it may rate 50 points (fifth degree).

also cause workers to demand higher pay in order to maintain their standard of living.

Surveys of prevailing pay rates within an industry are almost always a strong influence on the salaries and wages paid by individual companies. Variable production costs also affect a company's ability to pay wages. General economic conditions have the same kind of effect. Supply and demand in the labor market are important considerations. A skill that is in short supply will usually justify higher pay than one that is common among large numbers of workers. The existence of labor unions in a particular industry or company will influence pay rates. Collective bargaining by labor unions with management sets wage levels through negotiation. The effect of collective bargaining, in a particular company or in an entire industry, is thus a major consideration in setting pay scales.

METHODS OF COMPENSATION

From straight salary to incentives

Compensation for work done by employees can be paid in one or more different ways:

■ Straight *salaries* pay a set amount at regular intervals. Salaried workers are usually paid weekly, semimonthly, or monthly. Their pay is not based directly on the number of hours worked or on the amount produced. Management, white-collar, and professional employees are usually paid salaries.

Issues & Highlights

Fifty years ago, few people would have quarreled with the idea that employees who work harder or perform better than their peers should also be paid more. Piece rates, wage incentives, and bonus pay systems were all geared to pay employees in some sort of relationship to their productivity. Since many employees worked at jobs for which productivity was hard to measure, the concept of merit pay was introduced. The "merit" of an employee's efforts was judged by the employee's boss. Wage incentives and bonus systems (especially for salespeople) are still common. The practice of granting merit pay, however, has all but disappeared except among white-collar workers in nonunionized companies. Typically, employees there are periodically rated by their bosses. Their work may be judged as outstanding, superior, good, or acceptable. Employees rated as outstanding and superior will receive pay increases that place them in the higher levels of pay for a particular job. The good employee may be paid at the mid-point of a salary range, and the acceptable performers paid only the minimum rate for the job.

Source: **Bruce Ellig, "The Mysteries of Employee Pricing Solved,"** Supervisory **Management, January 1981, p. 16.**

What do you think of the practice of paying above-average performers more than average or below-average performers? What advantage do wage incentive systems have over merit rating systems? What is a major drawback of merit rating systems? Why might labor unions oppose either system of wage payment?

■ Time *wages* are directly based on the amount of time worked within a pay period. Each wage position has a pay rate that is multiplied by the number of hours worked to calculate the amount to be paid. Time wages are usually paid blue-collar workers for production work and for direct labor jobs as in construction or mining.

■ *Piece rates* base pay on the number of units produced by an employee without regard to the number of hours worked. Piece rates are common in certain skilled and semiskilled manufacturing jobs, such as garment making. They are also commonly paid in conjunction with, or as a supplement to, wages. When this method is used, piece rates are called *wage incentives.*

■ *Bonuses* are often paid in addition to a regular wage or salary as compensation for outstanding performance or unusually high production. These extra payments are usually thought of as incentives for better performance.

■ *Commissions* are paid to certain kinds of workers, especially sales personnel, as a variation on piecework rates. Salespeople often receive a percentage of their gross sales as their pay. Pay is thus based directly on productivity. As an incentive, commissions are sometimes paid in addition to a regular salary.

LEGAL REGULATION OF COMPENSATION

Wages and Hours Law sets standards

As with most other areas of management, legal restraints affect compensation programs. The most important is the requirement that no employee be paid less than a minimum wage established by state or federal law. The Federal Wages and Hours Law (Fair Labor Standards Act) requires most companies to adhere to established policies concerning overtime pay. According to this law, a higher wage rate (1½ times the base hourly wage) must be paid for any hours over 40 worked in one week. The Walsh-Healy Public Contracts Act requires companies on government contracts to pay overtime for all work over 8 hours a day.

7   ADMINISTERING EMPLOYEE BENEFITS

Fringe benefits add up to major employment costs

Employee benefits, sometimes called *fringe benefits,* include the things of value given to employees in addition to their pay. Benefits are often not paid in money, but may have some present or future monetary value. Employee benefits are an important form of payment for workers and an important source of expense for employers. Benefits often cost 30 to 40 percent or more of the amount paid for basic compensation.

LIFE AND HEALTH INSURANCE

Group insurance is an American way

Among the most common benefits are life and health insurance. They are valuable because they protect workers from possible future losses. Employers normally are able to buy group policies and can provide high quality insurance at a lower cost than is available to individual purchasers. Health insurance has the added benefit of encouraging employees to seek medical care early when they suspect illness. Without insurance, employees might put off checkups or treatment because of lack of money. This widespread practice contributes to better medical care for employees who are covered and may possibly result in a generally healthier population in the United States.

PENSIONS AND PROFIT SHARING

Supplement social security

A *pension* is a payment made at regular intervals to a retired employee or, in some cases, to his or her family after the worker's death. Payments are made from pension funds built up from regular contributions while the employee is working. Sometimes, the employer makes the entire contribution; sometimes it is shared by the employee.

Profit sharing is an increasingly popular benefit which distributes part of a company's profits to employees even when they do not share ownership in the company. Profit sharing is thought of as an incentive. If workers increase productivity, profits will usually rise and more will be available for sharing.

OTHER BENEFITS

From holidays to family picnics

Supplementary unemployment benefits are important, especially in industries where layoffs are common. They pay a compensation in addition to unemployment insurance to help employees maintain their standard of living during a layoff.

A guaranteed annual wage is offered by some companies and is a popular union demand in contract negotiations. This offers almost complete protection for workers from layoffs as it provides a minimum salary or wage to be paid should a layoff occur.

Many other benefits are available in different combinations. These include sick-leave pay, recreation programs, company-paid doctors and nurses, credit unions, holidays, vacations, paid rest periods, severance pay, free meals, educational assistance to workers and their families, workers' compensation and unemployment insurance, parties and picnics, stock and bond purchase plans, discounts on purchases, and others.

Key Concepts

1. Personnel management must estimate the number and kinds of employees that will be needed by a company in the future and make plans for hiring and developing the workers to meet those projected needs.
2. Managing the employment process requires procedures for recruiting and selecting employees and orienting them to their new work.

A thorough selection process includes a written application, testing, one or more interviews, investigation, and a physical examination.
3. A variety of methods are used to train and develop workers and managers. Job instruction, on-the-job, and apprenticeship training are commonly used for rank-and-file employees.

Most management development programs teach specific administration and organization techniques. Performance appraisals serve as guides for training and work improvement.

4. Personnel management must establish procedures for coordinating job changes. These include transfers, promotions, and separations.

5. Maintaining the safety and health of employees is an important social concern of personnel administration. It also lowers insurance rates, reduces work interruptions, and helps to avoid liability claims.

6. Compensation programs must evaluate jobs in order to rank them, assign monetary ranges, and decide on compensation methods for each type and level of job.

7. Employee benefits—including life and health insurance, pensions and profit sharing, and many others—are an important source of reward to employees and an important expense to organizations.

Review Questions

1. Define, explain, or identify each of the following key terms and phrases found on the pages indicated.

   affirmative action plans (p. 291)
   apprenticeship training (p. 294)
   bona fide occupational qualifications (p. 291)
   bonus (p. 302)
   classroom lecture and discussion training (p. 294)
   commission (p. 302)
   compensation (p. 299)
   critical incidents (p. 295)
   employee turnover (p. 289)
   forced choice technique (p. 295)
   fringe benefits (p. 302)
   job analysis (p. 289)
   job description (p. 289)
   job pricing (p. 299)
   job specification (p. 289)
   layoffs (p. 297)
   management development (p. 294)
   on-the-job training (p. 294)
   pension (p. 303)
   performance appraisal (p. 295)
   piece rate (p. 302)
   profit sharing (p. 303)
   promotion (p. 297)
   salary (p. 300)
   selection (p. 292)
   seniority (p. 297)
   separation (p. 297)
   termination (p. 297)
   transfer (p. 297)
   vestibule method (p. 294)
   wage (p. 302)
   wage incentives (p. 302)

2. Describe the basic steps in estimating future work-force needs.

3. What are some of the sources for recruiting new employees when openings exist?

4. Most supervisor and management development programs have at least one of three goals. What are the three goals?

5. Distinguish between objective and subjective criteria for performance appraisal.

6. Define the three kinds of job changes personnel administrators must deal with.

7. Give some examples of steps companies can take to reduce on-the-job accidents.

8. Differentiate between job evaluation and job pricing.

9. What steps are used in determining the salary or wages a particular job is worth?

10. Name some of the benefits that many workers receive in addition to their wages or salary.

Case Critique 16-1
The Aging Receptionist

The Jocular Advertising Agency was about to hire a receptionist. Jocular's office manager was certain that the job required someone who was personable, neat in appearance, and well spoken.

"Is that all the job requires?" asked the personnel director. "That covers the most important aspects of the job," said the office manager.

After interviewing a dozen people, both men and women, a middle aged individual, Teresa Lyle, was hired. She was personable and neat, although no one would ever accuse her of dressing fashionably. Her approach to people was friendly and her manner of speech was folksy.

When the office manager got a look at Ms. Lyle, she complained to the personnel manager. "Couldn't you have found someone under 50 years old? We want to project a youthful image for this agency. And, besides, we're not interested in having someone who dresses like her greeting clients!" The personnel director shrugged her shoulders and said that Teresa Lyle was the best person she could find.

Real trouble began when the office manager brought out a short report for Ms. Lyle to type. "I'll try," said Ms. Lyle, "but I'm just a hunt-and-peck typist." It took Ms. Lyle all afternoon to get the report typed, and it was full of errors and strikeovers.

The office manager stormed into the personnel director's office. "The new receptionist has got to go," she announced. "First, Ms. Lyle's an older person who looks like something out of the past. And now it turns out she can't even type."

"This is the first I've heard that typing is a requirement of the receptionist's job," replied the personnel director. "You should have made that clear before we began recruiting. As to Ms. Lyle's age and appearance, I don't think we can let her go for those reasons."

1. What was a main shortcoming in the plans to recruit a receptionist?
2. Why would the personnel director say that the agency could not let Ms. Lyle go because of her age and appearance?
3. If the office manager wished to hire a young person, what would she have had to first establish about that requirement of the job?

Case Critique 16-2
The Appraisal Disagreement

Jack O'Connor was glaring at his boss, Mr. Plum. The two were in the midst of a semiannual performance appraisal session. Jack, the assistant manager of a fast-food chain outlet, felt that his hard work was not sufficiently recognized. Mr. Plum was just as sure that Jack's work was anything but satisfactory.

"First of all," said Mr. Plum, "your job is to make sure that the deep-fry tanks are cleaned each night. You agree to that. But I've spot-checked them a half dozen times in the last 6 months and found that this is not being done with any degree of regularity."

"That's possible," said Jack, "but if you were to see how tired the fry-crew is at the end of the shift, you'd not want to push them too hard on something that can be postponed occasionally."

"Second," said Mr. Plum, "the records clearly show that the so-called spoilage on the cherry pies has been running at 5 percent as compared with the specified 2 percent. You're responsible for seeing that these pies are not damaged nor eaten by the staff."

"I can't keep track of everything," said Jack. "I'm working a 10-hour day, 6 days a week. I doubt if any of the assistant managers, here, or in the other outlets put in the time that I do."

"Hard work is commendable," said Mr. Plum, "and I give you a good rating for your efforts and dedication, but in the long run it is results that count. On 6 out of the 10 performance criteria set for your job, I can see something, touch something, or measure something that is below par. On the other 4 criteria, it's a matter of judgment as to how good you are. And even on these, you and I don't agree."

1. Upon what kind of judgments of Jack's performance does Mr. Plum's appraisal depend?
2. Upon what kinds of criteria would Jack prefer to be appraised?
3. If you were Jack, what might you try to do to get more recognition from Mr. Plum for outstanding performance in the areas you think are important?

Chapter 17

Human Relations in Business

ALL MANAGERS HAVE THE RESPONSIBILITY TO MAXIMIZE THE EFFECTIVENESS OF HUMAN RESOURCES. THEY MUST TRY TO . . .

1 . . . REACT TO THE HUMANIZING FORCES IN THE ENVIRONMENT . . .

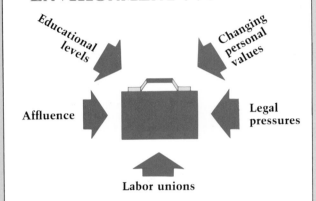

Educational levels

Changing personal values

Affluence

Legal pressures

Labor unions

2 . . . INTERPRET HUMAN BEHAVIOR AS AN EXPRESSION OF EACH PERSON'S NEEDS AND MOTIVATIONS . . .

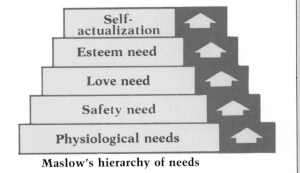

Self-actualization

Esteem need

Love need

Safety need

Physiological needs

Maslow's hierarchy of needs

3 . . .ANTICIPATE THE RANGE OF EMPLOYEES' RESPONSES TO MOTIVATIONAL FACTORS

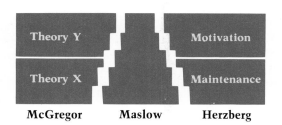

| Theory Y | Motivation |
| Theory X | Maintenance |

McGregor   Maslow   Herzberg

4 . . . PRACTICE CONSISTENT LEADERSHIP STYLES . . .

Authoritative   Participative

5 . . .RECOGNIZE THE IMPACT OF JOB DESIGN ON EMPLOYEE PRODUCTIVITY . . .

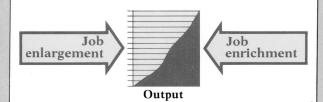

Job enlargement   Job enrichment

Output

6 . . . COMMUNICATE JOB INFORMATION AND ORGANIZATIONAL INFORMATION TO EMPLOYEES

MEMO

Learning Objectives

The purpose of this chapter is to demonstrate the increasingly important role of human resources management in business and specifically to discuss some of the forces that have humanized business's attitudes toward human resources, as well as certain theories and practices regarding human resources management.

As evidence of general comprehension, after studying this chapter, you should be able to:

1. *Suggest and discuss how environmental factors encourage better human relations in business.*
2. *Explain group dynamics, morale, and Maslow's hierarchy of needs.*
3. *Show the similarities among McGregor's Theories X and Y, Herzberg's Two-Factor Theory, Likert's System 4, and Maslow's hierarchy.*
4. *Distinguish between authoritative leadership and participative leadership and recognize the characteristics of these styles.*
5. *Explain and apply the techniques of job enlargement and job enrichment.*
6. *Analyze the value of effective communications in human resources management and explain two techniques of communicating job and company information to employees.*

If your class is using SSweetco: Business Model and Activity File for Business in Action, see Chapter 17 in that book after you complete this chapter. There you will find exercises and activities to help you apply your learning to typical business situations.

A business resource is anything that contributes to the production process. Crude oil, iron ore, timber, and other unprocessed materials are natural resources. Money used to build plants and offices and to buy materials is a financial resource. The transportation and communications systems form part of the society's economic resources. These resources have received careful attention and management so that the most valuable production is achieved for the lowest possible cost.

Only in recent decades has appropriate attention been paid to the management of human resources. In the long run, the contributions of people—from the hands-on production worker to top executives—are of the greatest value to business and to society as a whole. The discovery of a large deposit of iron ore or the accumulation of a large amount of capital definitely affect the economy and individual lives. However, a single idea, such as the invention of the transistor, can have far vaster effects on the population and on business. A careful production worker making high quality goods, a diligent salesperson presenting the goods to the widest possible market, a dedicated manager using intelligence, tact, and effort to meet company objectives—these make business work.

Some authorities believe so strongly in the critical value of human resources to a business that a technique has been created called **human resources accounting.** Using this system, a business lists on its financial statements the dollar value of its human assets. Several professional athletic organizations have calculated play-development costs and purchased-contract costs and placed these legally on their financial records. The value of human resources seems virtually unquestionable when sports are concerned. While less dramatic in business, the care and use of human beings is equally important there.

All business managers, regardless of their particular assignment, are responsible for developing and effectively using the human resources available to their companies. They must recognize their employees for what they are—human beings, not production machinery. They must find ways to meet the goals of their organizations and, at the same time, help organization members to meet their own personal goals. These are the responsibilities of human resource management.

1   HUMANIZING FORCES IN THE ENVIRONMENT

Change has been blowing in the wind

Many business, social, economic, and political changes have contributed to an increased interest in human resources management. Among the most important has been managers' interest in developing their supervisory skills. In their systematic examination of ways to do their own jobs better, they have repeatedly been made aware of the importance of human relations in the business world. Legal pressures, the development of labor unions, and changes in human outlook and behavior have prompted this concern.

LABOR UNIONS AND LEGAL PRESSURES

Enforced awareness

The development of organized labor has forced managers to focus on working conditions, training, fair treatment of employees, and on the many factors that affect employee morale. Union efforts, especially in the last ten to fifteen years, have reflected workers' growing expectations of what work should provide. Workers desire more respect, varied and interesting jobs, and other nonmonetary rewards. Some labor unions have begun to present these attitudes to management in an assertive way, even while a few unions, particularly in the troubled automobile and steel industries, recently have made concessions to management—through so-called "givebacks"—on matters concerning monetary and other types of rewards.

Certain legal regulations have also obliged businesses to increase their awareness of how their human resources are handled. The Occupational Safety and Health Act, to cite one example, has required managers to become deeply involved in efforts to create and maintain a safe workplace. The Equal Employment Opportunity Act has led many companies to begin thorough employee training and development programs. Frequently, when forced by law to have wider contact with minorities and women, managers and workers have in fact reduced their prejudices and preconceptions.

CHANGES IN HUMAN OUTLOOK AND BEHAVIOR

Greater affluence, but less materialism

The expectations and goals of American workers have changed a great deal over the years. Compulsory education together with an increasingly democratic attitude about which individuals ought to receive higher educations have created a highly-trained work force in the United States. The sophistication that gives workers the capability to handle today's technical jobs also leads them to expect greater rewards. Higher wages have also allowed individual workers to build up their own financial resources. This protection from financial disaster and the overall affluence of our society have caused workers to demand fair treatment and more rewarding jobs.

Just as individual workers have partially changed their focus from wages to a desire for broader fulfillment on the job, so business managers are also changing their values. Many managers feel a real sense of social responsibility and concern for the welfare of the people within and outside of their organization. This has helped to make positive human relations a desirable end in itself, rather than just a tool for increasing human productivity.

To make sure that they understand the changes that are taking place in our society, managers have turned to the work of psychologists, sociologists, anthropologists, and others who study human behavior. Many of the approaches and goals of human resources management have developed from the scientific study of social interactions, group behavior, motivation, leadership, communication, and other aspects of human relations.

ACTION BRIEF

All the Comforts of Home. In the furniture manufacturing plant of Herman Miller, Inc. in Roswell, Georgia, every employee has a clear view of the scenery outside. That was a design requirement. Most of the lighting inside comes from natural sources, too. So does the ventilation, which depends upon a special, red metallic wing suspended above the window walls. It acts both as a sunscreen and a device for channeling breezes throughout the factory. The objective of this unique architecture is to provide pleasant, comfortable surroundings which, the company believes, goes hand-in-hand with productivity and profitability.

Source: *John Maynard, "Building a Factory Workers Can Love," Atlanta Constitution, May 18, 1982, p. D–1.*

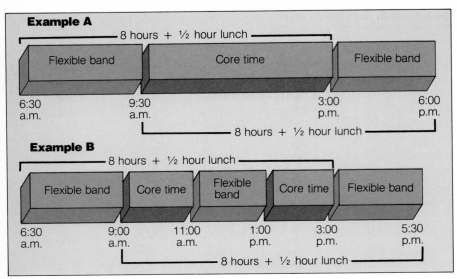

Figure 17-1
Two ways of designing
flexitime schedules.

Source: Barbara L. Fiss, *Flexitime—A Guide,* U.S. Civil Service Commission, May 15, 1974.

MORE DEMANDING LIFESTYLES

Requires flexibility at the workplace

Three changes in American lifestyle have greatly affected the routine operation of a business: (*a*) the greater participation of women in the work force, (*b*) the rapid growth of married couples with both partners working, and (*c*) the value placed by individuals upon their leisure, or nonworking, hours. These changes have had a most dramatic impact upon the traditional 8-hour workday.

In 1982, more than half of all women of working age were either employed or looking for work. This was up 20 percent from 1970 and was forecast to keep rising at that rate until 1990.

By 1982, 52 percent of all married couples had both partners at work. This was up 12 percent from 1970 and was forecast to keep rising at that rate until 1990.

The net effect of these two trends is to increase pressure for greater work-hour flexibility so that parents can stagger their sharing of child care, manipulate their commuting arrangements to save time and expense, and find ways to share their leisure time together. The existence of dual-income families, in itself, often makes leisure-time activities more affordable, which adds to the demand for work-hour flexibility.

Employers' response to this demand has been the creation of flexible work hours, or *flexitime.* By 1980, the U.S. Labor Department reported that 7.5 million full-time workers were on flexitime. Another 1.8 million full-time workers were on schedules of 4.5 days or less. Under a typical flexitime arrangement (see Figure 17-1), employees must be on the job during a certain core period, say 9:30 a.m. to 3:00 p.m. They then work the balance of their 40 hours before or after that core period. Flexitime schedules cause problems where there is a need for one employee to communicate with another working a different schedule. In some instances, however, this is offset by having scarce space or equipment better utilized by the extension of the overall workday.

2   NEEDS, MOTIVATION, AND HUMAN BEHAVIOR

A complex, conflicting, dynamic individuality

To be successful in human relations, a manager ought to have some conception of why people behave the way they do when they become members of an organization. Managers must consider what causes, or motivates, people to work effectively. They must understand something about how people interact in groups. They must also be sensitive to what it is that leads employees to feel satisfied or dissatisfied with their work.

Figure 17-2
The hierarchy of human needs proposed by Abraham Maslow. Lower level needs normally receive priority over higher level needs.

INDIVIDUAL MOTIVATION

A priority of needs

Although many theories exist about what causes people to work effectively, the *hierarchy of human needs* proposed by Abraham H. Maslow has been especially popular among business managers. The theory is important because it predicts that rewards such as wages, bonuses, and salary increases are not the only considerations that motivate workers. Threat of punishment, such as demotion or dismissal, may also be ineffective. Employees will work best when their jobs satisfy their personal needs. These needs may be more complex than was widely believed before Maslow's time.

Maslow's hierarchy summarizes human needs that must be satisfied in order to achieve fulfillment. The five needs he identified are described in Figure 17-2. Maslow arranges human needs in a hierarchy because he believes that they operate on a priority system. A person's lower-level needs almost always have priority over higher-level needs. Only when a person has adequate food, water, shelter, for example, is he or she free to be concerned with higher needs like love or esteem.

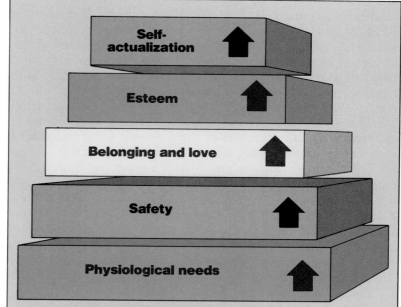

Self-actualization: The need to fully realize one's potential, to be the best person one is capable of being, and to do work that is really suited to one's skills and interests.

Esteem: The need for self-respect and for the esteem and respect of others and the desire for recognition as a skilled and useful human being.

Belonging and love: The need to be truly accepted by one's peers, the desire to be liked and loved, and the desire to give love and affection to others.

Safety: The need to be safe from physical danger and to be assured of emotional security.

Physiological needs: The need for satisfying bodily functions, such as needs for food and drink, shelter, warmth, rest, and sex.

Maslow's priority system has an important practical consequence. Once a person's need is satisfied, it no longer motivates him or her. This means that, with today's high wages, insurance, and other benefits, an individual's desire to satisfy higher-level needs, such as esteem, respect, praise, or self-actualization, becomes more important. Most people who work already will have achieved considerable satisfaction of their low-level needs.

GROUP DYNAMICS

Interactions among people

The study of human groups involves some very complex and subtle questions. People are different, and the way they react to and influence other people varies greatly. Groups are also different. Some work together with minimal friction. Others develop factions that interfere with group action. Also, most groups change over time.

Groups are made up of individuals who interact with each other. The members of a group talk, help one another, use gestures, stand, sit, express feelings, ideas, beliefs, and desires to each other. All of the interactions among the members are embraced by the term *group dynamics.* The dynamics of a particular group at a particular time may be positive or negative. If positive, they bind the group together to make it cohesive. If negative, they may cause the group to dissolve and may interfere with effective cooperation. Negative dynamics may be caused by excessive competitiveness, by personality conflicts, by lack of direction, by unequal treatment of group members by those outside the group, such as supervisors, or by scores of other factors operating together.

When an individual is a member of a group, his or her behavior will be partially controlled by the group. The amount of influence a group has on a person's behavior depends on (a) how cohesive the group is, (b) how forceful the members' individual personalities are, and (c) how different the group's goals, motivations, and behaviors are from those of the individual members. Some people are more likely to be strongly influenced by groups because their needs for love, esteem, and acceptance are strong. They are often willing to give up the satisfaction of other desires in order to gain acceptance.

Some understanding of group behavior is important to managers because it points to some practical steps that make groups work better. Cooperation within work groups and the adjustment of individuals to groups is almost always better when the group's manager (a) helps establish clear goals, (b) treats group members fairly and consistently, (c) encourages communication, and (d) does not treat individuals so poorly that they seek all of their rewards solely from the group rather than from both their work and the people they work with.

MORALE

A sense of mission

Individual and group *morale* is usually thought of as a satisfaction with and enthusiasm for work. Morale cannot be easily evaluated because it is largely emotional. Morale, however, does show itself in a number of ways. Workers with high morale will usually be cooperative, committed to their work and to mutual goals, loyal to the organization, confident, and self-motivated. Low morale will, sooner or later, cause a change in these behaviors.

A number of studies of morale among American workers have conflicting conclusions. In general, however, it seems that morale is fairly high. About two-thirds of the work force express considerable job satisfaction. One interesting point that some of the studies bring to light is that the causes of low morale are not usually related to low wages or salaries. Problems with the work itself, the lack of responsibility, the lack of opportunity to use initiative, and the lack of fulfillment in the type of work done, are cited as frequent causes of dissatisfaction.

3 MANAGERS AND MOTIVATION

The toughest managerial task of all

Managers make conscious efforts to motivate their employees to do their best work. They motivate indirectly by trying to create the kind of physical and emotional environment that encourages workers. They motivate directly through authority, discipline, and rewards. A number of different approaches to this task are popular today.

McGREGOR'S THEORY X AND THEORY Y

An insight into managerial beliefs

How managers try to motivate others is determined partly by their attitudes toward people. Douglas McGregor has described two common views, calling them Theory X and Theory Y. Some managers hold the view that the average human being has an inherent dislike for work, that he or she must be pushed into it, prefers to be directed by others, and wishes to avoid responsibility. This is *Theory X.* Managers who uphold *Theory Y* believe that mental and physical work is as natural as play or rest, that employees commit themselves to goals that satisfy their need for self-respect and personal fulfillment, and that they readily accept responsibility for such work, disciplining themselves as they strive to achieve these goals.

Managers who hold one or the other view use different methods to motivate employees. Theory X managers usually stress material rewards and job security: wages, salary increases, and employee benefits. When these fail as motivators, they may rely on strict discipline, threats of job loss, suspensions, demotions, and other punishments. Theory Y managers usually try to create work conditions that will bring more fulfillment to workers. They will often be more democratic and encourage workers to participate more in planning and management.

HERZBERG'S TWO-FACTOR THEORY

Maintenance or motivation?

Frederick Herzberg has devised a useful system for organizing motivating forces. According to Herzberg, two general factors influence motivation: (*a*) the need for survival, physical well-being, and comfort, and (*b*) the need for self-development, responsibility, and expression.

He calls the first group **maintenance,** or **hygiene, factors** because they relate to the maintenance of life and health. These probably have little effect on American workers today because the needs are adequately satisfied for a majority of them. These hygiene factors can only cause dissatisfaction when they are not present. When they are satisfied, they are ignored.

The second group are positive **motivating,** or **satisfying, factors.** Their presence brings actual satisfaction and fulfillment to humans. The positive motivators Herzberg lists include:

■   Opportunities to achieve something important: reaching a difficult goal.
■   Recognition for achievement: honest praise for goals attained.
■   The nature of the work itself: how interesting and challenging the work is.
■   The extent of responsibility an individual has.

LIKERT'S SYSTEM 4

Stresses employee participation

Rensis Likert, in his extensive studies of managers and management styles, has identified an approach to management that ought to provide employees with positive motivators. He calls it **System 4,** or participative management, contrasting it with three other systems: exploitive-authoritative, benevolent-authoritative, and consultive. System 4 stresses the active participation of employees for the management process. This gives workers greater opportunities in achievement, recognition, interesting work assignments, and responsibility. Likert's studies indicate that these factors really are motivating. He found greater group loyalty and more cooperation, along with higher outputs, better quality work, and lower costs, under System 4 management.

RELATIONSHIPS AMONG THE THEORIES

An underlying consistency

Although these different approaches to management and motivation were arrived at independently, they all have a common base. The needs and rewards of the lower levels of Maslow's hierarchy are generally the same as Herzberg's hygiene factors. These are the kinds of rewards Theory X managers usually offer as motivators. The higher-level needs in Maslow's hierarchy generally correspond to the factors Herzberg identifies as genuine motivators. These motivators are employed by Theory Y managers and those who follow Likert's System 4 management style.

4   MANAGERS AND LEADERSHIP

Not necessarily a natural ability

Motivating others is important in leadership, but it is only part of a complex ability. To be an effective leader, a manager must use complex intellectual and social skills to deal with different kinds of people in a wide variety of situations. An effective manager must be able to adapt his or her style and approach to many different situations.

PERSONAL TRAITS OF LEADERS

A standard to emulate

A successful leader in business usually has thorough technical knowledge, experience in his or her field, and appropriate training in necessary job skills. In addition to these, certain personal traits are often found in good leaders:

■ Being a leader requires dealing with other people. *Human relations skills* are essential. A leader must be sensitive to the needs and feelings of others and must genuinely respect those feelings. Effective leaders know how to communicate and how to encourage others to communicate.

■ Leaders must have *emotional and social maturity*. They must accept their own feelings and control their own behavior. They must remain rational when angry and not be defeated by frustration and stress. They must be able to accept diversity and disagreement in others.

■ Good leaders must be *intelligent*. They must be able to analyze complex situations and discover relationships, causes, effects, and solutions.

■ Good leaders need *self-motivation*. In the position of leader, men and women will be subjected to stress and anxiety; rewards may be intangible or delayed. Only a strong inner determination to succeed allows people to function well in this role.

It should be emphasized, however, that leadership is not simply a matter of having certain traits. Many who have desirable leadership traits do not succeed at it. Many others, who do not bear the outward signs of leadership, have proven to be effective leaders. While some individuals possess an instinctive insight into what it takes to make others respond willingly to their directions, many other individuals have learned how to acquire effective leadership skills.

SITUATIONS AND LEADERSHIP

Circumstances often determine style

Managers need great flexibility to be good leaders. They must be able to alter their leadership behavior to suit different situations, despite what certain theories say about one management style being more effective than others.

Management styles range from autocratic to participative. The **autocratic manager** makes decisions and imposes them on subordinates. Employees are required to obey. If they do, they will be rewarded, usually with money; if they do not, they will be punished. **Participative managers** invite employees to take part in the decision-making process. They encourage initiative and self-direction in others. They try to provide their subordinates with positive motivators, such as opportunities to satisfy their need for achievement.

ACTION BRIEF

A Quiet Leader. The owners of professional baseball clubs have been characterized by wild behavior. They have been known to throw tantrums in the locker rooms, treat their players like chattel, and go on national television to criticize their own teams. Peter O'Malley isn't a bit like that. Most baseball fans have never heard of him. Yet, for the past decade his Los Angeles Dodgers has been one of the best performing clubs in baseball. And it has been, by far, the most profitable.

O'Malley sets clear-cut objectives, develops a sound set of plans, and allows his 225 subordinates (Tom Lasorda is his coach) to follow their own judgment in carrying them out. O'Malley has a strong sense of obligation to people who work for him. This quiet approach to leadership shows up in a remarkably low rate of turnover among employees—even on the ball club itself, where a have-bat, will-travel attitude might be expected to prevail.

Source: John Merwon, "The Most Valuable Executive in Either League," Sports Illustrated, April 12, 1982, p. 129.

In practice, the best managers must be flexible enough to shift from the autocratic to the participative role as required in specific situations. Fred Fiedler has proposed a consistent relationship between management situations and the most effective leadership style. His studies show that in extreme situations, either very favorable or very unfavorable, a more autocratic management style is most successful. In moderately favorable or unfavorable situations—which are far more common in the real world—a participative or democratic style is most successful. This agrees with the commonsense observation that in emergencies, where much is at stake and rapid decisions are needed, as on a battlefield or when fighting a fire, autocratic leadership may be most appropriate. In normal management situations, where long-term relationships occur and individuals must continually develop new skills, participative management seems to be most effective.

MANAGEMENT BY OBJECTIVES

Emphasis on self-direction

Many companies rely upon an employee's knowledge of what is expected from him or her to furnish the necessary motivation. In essence, the objectives set for the individual provide the leadership. Generally speaking, this technique, called *management by objectives* (*MBO*), is used only with higher-level employees, usually middle and upper-level managers.

When MBO is used, a company's ongoing activities are planned and evaluated at periodic intervals, typically on a yearly basis. At the beginning of each period, a manager sits down with a subordinate and together they work out the subordinate's objectives for the coming period. They also mutually agree upon what measures will be used to tell whether and how well the subordinate has achieved these objectives. Performance is judged by the results that are attained rather than by what the subordinate does to achieve them. Management by objectives helps employees to concentrate on what is really important: what must be accomplished. It improves motivation both because clear objectives are easier to work toward than fuzzy ones and because subordinates are consulted about goals and allowed greater freedom in choosing the methods they will use to reach them. A weakness of MBO is that a manager may depend entirely upon the program to provide the leadership, when in fact, subordinates will still need and expect direction and encouragement.

5   THE EFFECT OF THE WORK ITSELF

Shaping jobs for people

Despite management efforts, many jobs remain boring and uninspiring. The simplest solution to the low morale that may result from these jobs may be to make changes in the jobs themselves. While continuing to require certain basic activities, jobs can often be redesigned to make them more satisfying and challenging.

End to

Pyramid

Power

The business world is looking more now to the individual rather than depending upon work organized according to the traditional military model. That's an opinion expressed in a report entitled "The Future World of Work," sponsored by the United Way. "There were clear lines of authority," says the report, "and the ideal organizational chart looked like a pyramid, with decisions being made at the top and flowing down to subordinates for execution. In the future," the report says, "organization charts will more likely resemble spider webs." The changing authority structure will come about because young people "possess a strong, positive self-image and a very definite view about what it wants to put into and get out of work and the work environment. . . . Above all, American workers want a very much greater say in all aspects of work decisions and will reject any and all vestiges of rigid authoritarianism."

Source: **James T. Yenckel, "Work: The End of Pyramid Power?," The Washington Post, September 7, 1981, p. C–1.**

Is this the way you feel about authority? Can you be relied upon to take initiative rather than simply wait to follow orders? How greatly do you want to be involved in the decision-making process on your job?

JOB ENLARGEMENT
Stretching jobs heightens interest

One way to make a job more interesting is to increase its scope and variety. Increasing the number and kinds of activities performed by a single worker is called **job enlargement.** It can give employees more personal responsibility, more opportunity for achievement and recognition, and more of a feeling of making a real contribution. At IBM, for instance, managers redesigned jobs so that machine operators do their own set-up work and actually deliver finished goods to the next work station. Some machinist jobs are extended to include preparing specifications, sharpening tools, and doing some machine maintenance. American Telephone & Telegraph Co. enlarged jobs for their keypunch operators by assigning full responsibility for complete batches of work. Each operator would punch, verify, record error rates, and take responsibility for the quality of a whole job, rather than being assigned a small, arbitrary job step.

JOB ENRICHMENT
Involvement makes work meaningful

Job enrichment makes work more satisfying by increasing the depth of employee involvement. Taking the time to show how an individual job contributes to the entire production process is important. Allowing workers a choice of methods or encouraging employees to make improvements in work methods also humanizes work. Texas Instruments Inc., for instance, trains employees in the principles of work simplification and then encourages them to make changes to improve their own jobs. Managers there also meet regularly with employees to ask directly for their help in solving department and company problems. Jobs can include activities that provide recognition for employees. General Motors' Rochester Products Division, for example, uses hourly workers to train other hourly workers and includes the training assignment as a recognized part of the job. Acknowledging that a worker has the ability to train someone else is clearly a form of praise.

QUALITY OF WORK LIFE
Upgrading the psychological environment

As the 1980s began, it was increasingly evident that Americans were caught on the horns of a dilemma. Productivity in the United States was slipping behind that of other major nations while at the same time American workers were becoming disenchanted with the demands of the traditional work environment. Their complaints were not about the physical aspects so much as about work that was endlessly repetitive, boring, and seemingly without meaning. Technical approaches for improving productivity were taken for granted. Those approaches, however, tended to make work even more meaningless and demeaning to some people, and were often resisted. A search by management to improve the quality of work life while at the same time improving the productivity of the work force led to a number of innovative approaches. Most of these were character-

ACTION BRIEF

Island Hideaways. *Years ago, it was considered good practice in factories to cluster assembly workers into unstructured work groups. This practice was made obsolete by the advent of mass production and the highly structured assembly line. Now, history appears to be repeating itself. At the huge Siemens' electronics plant in Germany, employees no longer perform simple tasks over and over again—as they did a year ago—spending less than one minute on each unit as it moved along a conveyor belt. Instead, employees now work in groups of from three to seven at well-designed "work islands." This way, they can avoid boredom by rotating jobs and socializing among themselves. And the assembly cycle for each unit has been lengthened to 20 minutes. Such concern for humanizing the work place is common in Europe. This concern is increasingly finding its way into America, too.*

Source: *"Moving Beyond Assembly Lines,"* Business Week, July 27, 1981, p. 87.

TABLE 17-1
Examples of Participatory Approaches Used to Improve Quality of Work Life and Productivity

Joint Labor-Management Committees

This is the core of many Quality of Work Life efforts. Both union and management representatives form a committee to talk over mutual problems. They may launch problem-solving activities to give workers more control over some aspects of local work areas.

"Semiautonomous" or "Self-Managed" Work Teams

A team of workers is given responsibility for turning out the whole product or task and can make their own decisions about division of labor. Members police themselves, and may elect their own team leader; in some situations, they may hire and fire.

"Quality Circles"

Modeled after the Japanese system, this mechanism gives workers responsibility for taking their own steps to monitor quality and improve productivity, based on group meetings and other forms of cooperation. Theoretically, it is strictly voluntary.

Problem-Solving Task Forces or Committees

This creates involvement of a group in making recommendations and sometimes decisions. They may be investigatory, fact-finding, or advisory. They may set their own agenda, but usually the agenda is defined. Temporary and ad hoc, they may be broadly representative but more often members are drawn from management ranks.

Communication Councils

These are diagonal slices through the organization that represent clusters of employees and serve as a forum for communication. They may be elected but are more often appointed. Membership may rotate, and there is usually no decision-making authority.

"Team Building"

This is a highly variable, local, sporadic, occasional process. It may involve a work unit in airing concerns, discussing goals, clarifying roles and responsibilities, recommending changes. More often than not, it is focused too heavily on feelings and relationships and not enough on tasks and content.

Source: Rosabeth Moss Kantor, "Dilemmas of Participation," *National Forum: Phi Kappa Phi Journal*, Spring 1982, p. 17.

ized by greater involvement by employees in the problem-solving and decision-making processes of business. As with job enlargement and job enrichment, these approaches included a large measure of participatory management. Some of these participatory approaches are not widely used in business to meet the dual objectives of improving the quality of work life and improving productivity. Table 17-1 explains a number of these.

6   COMMUNICATION WITH EMPLOYEES

A cohesive force in organizations

One of the most threatening positions human beings can face in ordinary life is to be shut off from information that affects them. One of the reasons for this is that people are social beings and depend on communication with others to orient themselves in the world. Another reason—and this is particularly true on the job—is that people need specific instructions and data to carry out their activities. It is the job of business managers to make sure employees get the information they need to do the job that is expected and to provide general information about developments that are important to workers' plans and security.

JOB INFORMATION

Knowledge improves skills

Managers must be absolutely sure that employees are given enough information to do their jobs properly. This must include information about work methods, exact work assignments, managers' expectations about the quality and quantity of output, priority of activities, what to do if something goes wrong, and other specific guidance. A one-to-one personal discussion of these matters is usually best. Questions and suggestions should be strongly encouraged. A group meeting may be appropriate when information concerns a number of people or is specifically related to group efforts or interactions. Demonstrations for groups are useful when new methods are introduced. Written communications may be used to back up individual or group meetings and, in some cases, may be useful by themselves. For extremely technical information, a presentation in writing gives employees a chance to study and think about the material. Bulletin boards and memorandums may provide effective communication if they are used carefully. The important point managers must keep in mind is to consciously decide to communicate and to stick to that decision, regardless of which method is used.

ORGANIZATIONAL INFORMATION

Provides a sense of belonging

Employees have a right and a need to know certain information that is not directly related to the performance of their jobs. Employees feel more secure and have higher morale when they are made aware of important developments in their company, such as significant gains or losses in sales, upcoming changes in production methods, new products, or changes in internal organization. This does not require the disclosure of confidential information. Managers should, however, try to keep employees informed of important nonconfidential information. Workers who are kept uninformed often feel they are not respected by management. Also, rumors are often substituted for real information.

Restricted Versus Open Communications   In simplest terms, a communications network describes who talks to whom. Often, depending on their attitudes toward employees, managers will enforce a

ACTION BRIEF

Erecting the Sound Barrier.   *In many an office or shop, unwanted noise disturbs the communications process. Privacy of speech becomes a valued condition. A certain level of sound, say the acoustical experts, creates a healthy, productive environment and provides a rhythm or tempo of work into which people fall easily. Too much sound disrupts concentration. Soundlessness tends to stifle initiative. Offices can be described as "lively" or "dead" according to the way they transmit airborne and structure-borne sounds. Conversational privacy, by definition, occurs when only five percent of the spoken words can be understood in adjacent work areas. What we want, apparently, are shops and offices where the conversation is lively enough to give us a sense of being where the action is, but just dead enough to allow us to communicate clearly and easily.*

Source: Archie Kaplan, "The Ergonomics of Office Economics," Modern Office Procedures, *May 1982, p. 51.*

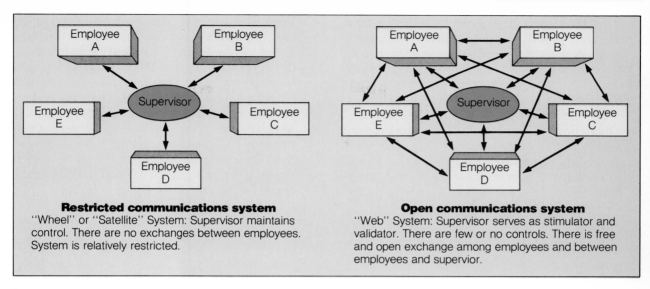

Source: Lester R. Bittel, *Improving Supervisory Performance*, McGraw-Hill Book Company, New York, 1976, p. 202.

Figure 17-3
Two approaches to organizational communications.

particular communications network whether they realize it or not. The network can significantly affect the success of communications. Figure 17-3 shows schematic representations of two kinds of networks—restricted, or satellite, and open, or web—which demonstrate some of these effects.

In a **restricted,** or **satellite, network,** the manager is at the center and directly communicates with each member of the work group. Employees are not encouraged to communicate among themselves. This system allows the manager to keep a close watch on operations and to verify the accuracy of all communications. In many situations, however, it tends to be slow and ponderous. The manager must devote a great deal of time to relaying messages to workers. True group action is unlikely to be achieved with a restricted communications network.

The **open,** or **web, network** encourages direct communications among every member of the group. In this network, the manager acts more like a facilitator and verifier of information, rather than as an exchange agent and controller. This system encourages joint group action. It is fast. It allows individual initiative and responsibility. However, it has the disadvantage of promoting rumors and false information. Managers also have less direct control of both work and communications.

Key Concepts

1. Important social, economic, and political developments in the United States have led managers to try to increase the effectiveness and satisfaction of the work force. This trend has resulted from the influences of legal pressures and the growth of labor unions, as well as changes in human attitudes and behavior.

2. Managers have begun to interpret human behavior in organizations as an expression of personal needs and motivations. Individual behavior on the job is also shaped in various ways by interactions within work groups.

3. A number of descriptions of the factors that motivate people to work effectively help managers to increase worker productivity and job satisfaction. These theories point to the value of praise, respect, recognition, and opportunities for responsibility and self-fulfillment as positive motivators.

4. To be effective leaders, managers must possess personal traits such as intelligence, social skills, and self-motivation. They must be able to shift from an autocratic to a participative management style to suit specific situations.

5. Making changes in the work itself—through job enlargement and enrichment—is one way to increase worker productivity and job satisfaction. These changes increase the variety and scope of work and provide more opportunities for personal responsibility, recognition, and involvement in decision making.

6. Managers must consciously strive to communicate with employees, giving them complete and accurate information on how to do assigned work and general information about the organization which may affect workers.

Review Questions

1. Define, explain, or identify each of the following key terms or phrases found on the pages indicated.

   autocratic manager   (p. 315)
   flexitime   (p. 310)
   group dynamics   (p. 312)
   hierarchy of human needs   (p. 311)
   human resources accounting   (p. 308)
   job enlargement   (p. 318)
   job enrichment   (p. 318)
   maintenance (hygiene) factors   (p. 314)
   management by objectives   (p. 316)
   morale   (p. 312)
   motivating (satisfying) factors   (p. 314)
   open (web) network   (p. 321)
   participative manager   (p. 315)
   restricted (satellite) network   (p. 321)
   System 4   (p. 314)
   Theory X   (p. 313)
   Theory Y   (p. 313)

2. How has the affluence of society forced business managers to stress human resources management?

3. What important prediction about human motivation derived from Maslow's theory has important applications to business management?

4. What are some factors that partially control the amount of influence a group will have on an individual member's behavior?

5. What are some important benefits of high employee morale?

6. Describe some of the beliefs about work and workers held by Theory X managers and by Theory Y managers.

7. What kind of management is used in Likert's System 4? What kind of motivators does it provide employees?

8. What are some ways in which jobs can be redesigned to make them more satisfying?

9. Why is the quality of work life movement so deeply related to participatory management?

10. Distinguish between a web and a wheel communications network.

Case Critique 17-1
The Apathetic Insurance Clerks

Sam Spates, manager of the records department in a major insurance company, was puzzled by the apathy of his work force. When the firm had moved to its rural location a couple of decades ago, employees had appeared to be careful, energetic, and compliant. Gradually, however, their attitudes and work behavior had changed. Or so it seemed to Sam. Whereas in the past a simple order to move an employee from one work station to another was never questioned, it now seemed to induce endless arguments. The pay scale, which was once regarded by local people as unbelievably high, was now the subject of bitter complaints. Then there was the matter of misfilings. Ten years ago, more than 1 percent of misfiled records was considered intolerable. Now, no matter how hard Sam stayed on the back of his clerical crew, their apparent carelessness and indifference resulted in a misfiling rate of more than 3 percent.

Sam reviewed the situation this way: "These employees have better than average working conditions. Their pay, if not exceptional, is more than adequate. The employment record here at the company shows them that they have secure jobs. What more could they possibly want?" Finally, at clock-out time after a particularly discouraging day, Sam came to this conclusion. "This situation has gotten out of hand. If ever I'm going to correct it, I'll have to really crack down on this bunch of malcontents. Tomorrow, I'll begin putting it to them."

1. What do you think of Sam's conclusion about what he should do?
2. What are some of the influences outside the company that may have caused the changes in employee attitude and behavior?
3. If you were Sam, how would you approach this problem?

Case Critique 17-2
The Factory That Turned Itself Around

In 1979, Ford Motor Company was about to shut down its stamping plant in suburban Cleveland. The plant was at the bottom of the productivity pile among nine plants in the division. Communications between management people and hourly employees was almost nil. Production departments were quarreling endlessly with the staff support departments. Then a near miracle occurred. By 1981, the plant improved its productivity dramatically. It established a reputation for management and employee cooperation. And Ford decided to keep the 3,000-employee plant open.

Credit for the progress goes to a process known at Ford as Employee Involvement, or simply EI. Ford does not call it a program, but simply a process. The change in employee attitudes was preceded, says Ford, by a new attitude on the part of the Ford Motor Company—and of the plant's management. Three words describe the new management attitude: respect, trust, and confidence. With that attitude in place, the EI operates on the basis of employee participation in identifying and in solving problems associated with their work. The EI process was spearheaded by appointing new plant management which met with work groups throughout the factory. The meetings provided factual information about the critical productivity problems. The new managers acknowledged the mistakes that had been made "by a totally autocratic, production-driven Ford management." Under EI, 36 voluntary groups of employees and supervisors were created. They met regularly on company time to uncover and dig into problems of all sorts. There was no game playing. Nor were these gripe sessions. The focus was always on accepting mutual responsibility for a problem and solving it. As one example, the daily rate of rejection for dash panel stampings had been 150. An EI suggestion for changes in the stamping tools reduced the rejection rate to 40.

Typical employee comments sounded like these: "There's only one thing wrong with EI. It's 25 years late. It's had a tremendous impact on attitudes here." "When guys on the line see something going wrong, they want it fixed right away. Before EI, they let it happen so that they could take an extra rest break." "Three or four years ago when a boss came down on the floor, nobody would really talk to him. Now, if we have something to say, we spit it out. And he's listening."

1. What kind of leadership would you say is now being used at this plant?
2. In terms of Maslow's hierarchy of needs, what kinds of motivational attractions does the EI process have for employees?
3. Why didn't the workers do something about the productivity problem earlier by themselves?
4. What is the implication of calling EI a "process" rather than a "program?"

Source: Howard C. Tuttle, "Employee Involvement Turns a Plant Around," *Production*, April 1982, p. 74.

Chapter 18

Labor-Management Relations

1 THE MAKEUP OF THE UNITED STATES LABOR FORCE

changes as business needs change:

More service and clerical workers

More skilled and professional workers

Fewer industrial and farm workers

2 THE LABOR MOVEMENT,

throughout its history, has attempted to satisfy employee needs:

Improved working conditions   Better wages   Job security

3 LABOR UNIONS

are classified according to type and structure:

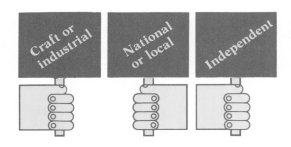

4 COLLECTIVE BARGAINING

addresses itself to these issues:

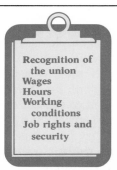

Recognition of the union
Wages
Hours
Working conditions
Job rights and security

5 LABOR DISPUTES
typically involve these tactics:

By Union:
  Strike
  Slowdown
  Picket
  Boycott

By Management:
  Lockout
  Strike-breaking
  Injunction
  Lobbying

By Both:
  Grievance
  procedures
  Mediation
  Arbitration
  Government action

6 LANDMARKS OF LABOR-MANAGEMENT LEGISLATION
include these laws:

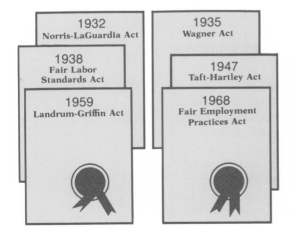

1932
Norris-LaGuardia Act

1938
Fair Labor
Standards Act

1959
Landrum-Griffin Act

1935
Wagner Act

1947
Taft-Hartley Act

1968
Fair Employment
Practices Act

Learning Objectives

The purpose of this chapter is to describe the role of labor-management relations and collective bargaining and specifically to illustrate the occupational makeup of the labor force, describe briefly the history of organized labor and the different types of unions, explain the collective bargaining process, and discuss the principal legislative guidelines for labor-management relations.

As evidence of general comprehension, after studying this chapter, you should be able to:

1. Analyze the occupational trends in the U.S. labor force.
2. Identify the main factors leading to the development of trade unionism in the United States.
3. Distinguish between the various types of labor unions.
4. Identify issues that are negotiable between management and labor and explain the collective bargaining process.
5. Recognize the principal bargaining tactics of labor and management and distinguish between mediation and arbitration.
6. Explain the main points of labor legislation.

If your class is using SSweetco: Business Model and Activity File for Business in Action, see Chapter 18 in that book after you complete this chapter. There you will find exercises and activities to help you apply your learning to typical business situations.

From 1880 to 1923, a legendary woman in a black dress led an unrelenting struggle in the mines and mills of America to advance the rights of the working people. Her name was Mother Jones, and this is her description of what she saw in one textile mill:

Little girls and boys, barefooted, walked up and down between endless rows of spindles reaching thin little hands into the machinery to repair snapped threads. They crawled under machinery to oil it. They replaced spindles all day long, all night through. Tiny babies of six years old with faces of sixty did an eight-hour day for ten cents a day. If they fell asleep, cold water was dashed in their faces, and the voice of the manager yelled above the ceaseless racket and whir of the machines.

Child labor and the exploitation of working people by owners and management made Mrs. Jones a furious avenger. She became the symbol of the organized labor movement in America. She was jailed in a half dozen cities for her efforts. She was at the bloody battle between police and labor supporters in Chicago's Haymarket Square, the Cripple Creek coal strike in Colorado, and the steel strikes in Pennsylvania. Her efforts, however, were rational as well as militant. They set a pattern for labor-management relations that is followed today. As Mrs. Jones observed in the last days of her life: "Both employer and employee have become wiser. Both have learned the value of compromise. Both sides have learned that they gain when they get together and talk things out in reason rather than standing apart and slinging bricks, angry words, and bullets."

A strike by the workers in a company or industry is only one dramatic phase of a continuing complex interaction between labor and management. Although over three-quarters of the workers in the United States are not members of labor unions, organized labor is a strong and specialized influence in business, especially in manufacturing, construction, transportation, and mining. Collective bargaining and the settlement of labor disputes are important to both labor and management.

1   MAKEUP OF THE LABOR FORCE

More skilled and white-collar workers

Human labor is the most powerful resource that businesses possess. Like other resources, it has been exploited from time to time. The rise of the trade union movement, coupled with laws that protect labor's rights has served to make today's management more enlightened in its treatment of this valued resource. At the same time, the makeup of the labor force changes constantly. Some occupations (like farm laborers) diminish in number and value while other new ones (like data processing machine mechanics) are created and are in short supply. These changes in makeup of the labor force affect the role of labor unions and the way in which management and unions quarrel over their respective roles in dealing with employees.

Figure 18-1 illustrates four major changes that are taking place in the U.S. labor force today:

■   The number of white-collar jobs has increased substantially in proportion to other jobs. These are generally more attractive, cleaner,

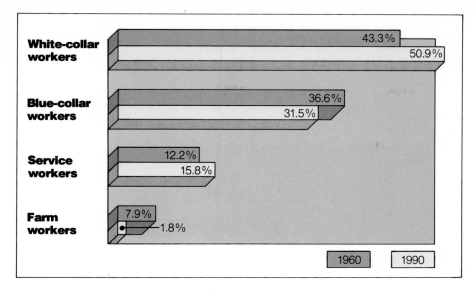

White-collar workers — 43.3%, 50.9%

Blue-collar workers — 36.6%, 31.5%

Service workers — 12.2%, 15.8%

Farm workers — 7.9%, 1.8%

1960   1990

Source: Max L. Cary, "Occupational Employment Growth through 1990," *Monthly Labor Review*, April 1982, p. 42.

Figure 18-1
Occupational forecast by major kinds of employment.

higher-paying jobs with more status. This group includes professional and technical workers (about 17 percent of all men and women), managers (15.4 percent of the men and 7.7 percent of the women), salespeople (about 6 percent of both men and women), and a great mass of clerical workers (6.3 of the men and 35.2 of the women).

■   The number of blue-collar jobs continues to decrease in proportion to other jobs. These are the jobs that are traditionally factory and industrial jobs represented by trade unions. So-called craft workers make up, for men, 21.2 percent of the labor force and for women, only 1.8 percent. The less-skilled operative jobs are populated by 16.5 percent of the men and 10.3 percent of the women. Blue-collar jobs also include a grouping of nonfarm laborers, or 6.0 percent of men and 1.1 percent of women.

■   Service workers continue to increase in numbers and in their proportion to other workers. This reflects the growth in airlines (although this is moderating), fast-food establishments, office personnel, and computer-related service industries. The increase, at least up until 1980, is also partly due to the growth of government employment.

■   Farmers and farm workers have decreased in numbers to such an extent that agricultural production work is no longer an important source of employment. Farm work, as a percent of all employment was at 7.9 percent in 1960, but it is forecast to drop to only 1.8 percent in 1990.

In general, more workers are employed in higher level, more rewarding jobs than ever before. More and more of the undesirable, repetitive, and dangerous production jobs are now being performed by machines.

Projections of the makeup of the labor force in the near future show that this trend is likely to continue. The U.S. Department of Labor expects that workers will be needed most in industrial research and technology, educational and health services, office "paperwork" jobs—all of which can be classified as skilled or white-collar positions. See Table 18-1 for a list of "high-growth" occupations.

TABLE 18-1
Occupations Forecast to Grow Most Rapidly

Occupation	Percent Growth in Employment, 1978–1990
Data processing machine mechanics	147.6
Paralegal personnel	132.4
Computer systems analysts	107.8
Computer operators	87.9
Office machine and cash register servicers	80.8
Computer programmers	73.6
Aero-astronautic engineers	70.4
Food preparation and service workers, fast food restaurants	68.8
Employment interviewers	66.6
Tax preparers	64.5
Correction officials and jailers	60.3
Architects	60.2
Dental hygienists	57.9
Physical therapists	57.6
Dental assistants	57.5
Peripheral EDP equipment operators	57.3
Child-care attendants	56.3
Veterinarians	56.1
Travel agents and accommodations appraisers	55.6
Nurse's aides and orderlies	54.6

Source: May L. Carey, "Occupational Employment Growth Through 1990," *Monthly Labor Review*, April 1982, p. 42.

Unemployment, however, remains a severe threat to job security for everyone. Some economists believe that because of basic changes in the economy, society must accept a higher level of unemployment than has been the case in the past. Unemployment continues to be especially severe for minorities and for young people. Despite government intervention in business cycles, layoffs and cutbacks are still a reality in many industries and promise to continue.

Against this economic backdrop, organized labor has come to play an important role in business. The economic status of workers in the United States today is the standard for most industrialized nations. Organized labor has made an important contribution to fostering these favorable conditions. Still, threats remain to the security and standard of living of workers. Unemployment, layoffs, inflation, and sweeping economic changes cause uncertainty and the desire for even greater security.

2 HISTORY OF U.S. ORGANIZED LABOR

A struggle for recognition

When artisans during the Middle Ages performed the entire production process, from buying raw materials to selling finished products, there was virtually no distinction between labor and management. The establishment of the factory system during the Industrial Revolution changed all this. It created a clear separation between the people who owned the factories and the people who worked in them. At the same time, working conditions—which had been poor all along—grew even more unpleasant and dangerous. Workers had no security and received poor wages. Most owners regarded workers as simply another production expense, like iron or coal, and had no reservations about exploiting their employees.

These conditions led to the labor union movement. Long ago it was recognized that an individual worker could achieve very little by complaining about unfair conditions. If many workers banded together, however, they would have a strong voice. By withholding their labor, they could take away a basic necessity of production, forcing the factories to close and keeping the owners from making their profits.

The influence of labor unions has increased since the eighteenth century. Local craft unions flourished in the United States in the nineteenth century. The Knights of Labor, however, was the first national labor organization and had its greatest impact in the 1880s. The Knights of Labor were later succeeded in national importance by the American Federation of Labor (AFL), which was founded in 1881. The AFL continued to organize only skilled workers. The increase of mechanized production, however, created tens of thousands of unskilled jobs, most of them with no union representation. The Congress of Industrial Organizations (CIO) was created in the mid-1930s largely to organize these unskilled workers. The AFL and CIO continued their side-by-side growth until 1955. In that year, the two organizations merged to create a very strong union force. Independent national and local unions not associated with the AFL-CIO have also developed in many fields.

All union organizations have had the same aim: to increase the power, influence, and rewards of workers. They have pushed for higher wages, better hours and working conditions, job security, and for protection from discrimination.

UNION MEMBERSHIP

A diminishing appeal

Labor unions do for their members collectively what they cannot accomplish separately. The power that an individual can bring to bear in an organization to assert his or her rights or to protect against discrimination is limited. Collectively, and given the legal status granted by an employer's recognition of the union, union members can approach management as equals. Membership in a union also offers social benefits, a sense of belonging to a respected organization. It provides an opportunity to fraternize with people who have similar interests and aggravations.

Despite the obvious advantages of belonging to a labor union, only a quarter of all American workers belong to unions. In fact, this percentage

ACTION BRIEF

In the Beginning. Item in the *Pittsburgh Commercial Gazette, November 16, 1881:* "Mr. Samuel Gompers, the representative of the International Cigar Makers' Union, said he had come to Pittsburgh, not to air his opinions, but to work, 'not to build a bubble, but to lay the foundation for a super-structure that would be solid, and that would be a true federation of trade unions.' He was in favor of progressing slowly, and wanted the organization to be emphatically a workingman's organization; one that is not defiled by money, but which will in itself contain the elements of strength." This was on the occasion of the founding of what was to become the American Federation of Labor, to which the AFL-CIO traces its origin.

Source: Stuart Bruce Kaufman, "Birth of a Federation," *Monthly Labor Review, November 1981, p. 23.*

has been declining since its peak in the late 1950s. In 1970, 30.8 percent of all nonfarm workers belonged to unions; by 1980 this figure had dropped to 25.2 percent. There are several reasons for this decline. The most important may have been the steady decline in the growth of blue-collar employment (as seen in Figure 18-1), the major stronghold of trade unionism. The other important factors cluster around the general improvement in wages and working conditions, a more enlightened management approach in dealing with employees and with union organizers, and the protection assured most workers by federal laws.

This is not to say that labor union membership has not grown in certain fields. It has. Between 1977 and 1980, for example, the number of white-collar union members grew from 7.3 to 8.5 million. The United States Bureau of Labor Statistics expects this figure to reach 9.5 million members by 1990. This growth has been in spite of the fact that white-collar workers tend to identify more closely with management than do blue-collar workers. Nearly 6 million public employees are union members. Some 65 percent of all supermarket chain employees are unionized as are 33 percent of grocery wholesaler warehouse personnel.

Union membership figures do not accurately represent the influence of organized labor. Many workers in unionized companies and industries receive the benefits of higher wages and better working conditions negotiated by labor unions without being union members. Even in nonunionized companies and industries, management usually provides benefits that would probably not be offered were it not for organized labor. Knowledge of union gains elsewhere, or the threat of unionization of their own companies, induces management to more liberal practices.

3 TYPES OF LABOR UNIONS

Size and extent predominate

The historical development of labor unions is still reflected in their organization today. Unions vary (a) as to whether they are organized by crafts or by industries, (b) in the extent and level of representation, and (c) as to whether they are independent or affiliated with the AFL-CIO.

CRAFT AND INDUSTRIAL UNIONS

Specialization versus conglomeration

Skilled workers were the first to organize. Many of their unions remain influential today. Unions like the United Brotherhood of Carpenters and Joiners of America are *craft unions.* They are organized according to the craft or skill performed by member workers, regardless of the kind of company or industry for which the work is done.

Industrial unions are organized around a particular industry, such as automobile manufacturing, steelworking, or coal production. In theory, all workers in the industry—skilled and unskilled and workers in every craft and trade—belong to the same union when it is organized this way. A few of the largest and best known are the United Steelworkers of America, the Transport Workers Union of America, the United Mine Workers, and the International Union of United Automobile, Aerospace and Agricultural Implement Workers of America (UAW).

NATIONAL AND LOCAL UNIONS
Power stems from the grass roots

Local unions are the foundation of organized labor. They are made up of craftworkers in a restricted geographical area or of the industrial workers of one or more local plants. Some locals are independent and have as their only goal the representation of local workers. They have the complete authority and responsibility for negotiating local contracts. Other locals are parts of national or international unions.

National unions represent the interests of members all over the U.S. and even the world. They may be craft or industrial unions. The national organization gains its financing and authority from local unions. Some national unions are the primary bargaining agents for all member workers. They negotiate contracts for entire industries. Locals may then further negotiate local conditions. Other nationals operate mainly to assist locals, which retain the primary bargaining role. For example, the nationals may assist locals in their organizing efforts or in handling grievances.

INDEPENDENT UNIONS
They avoid the AFL-CIO

About three-quarters of the unions in the country are members of the AFL-CIO. Those that are not members are said to be *independent unions.* Some of the largest independents are the International Brotherhood of Teamsters, the United Auto Workers, the National Association of Government Employees, the United Electrical, Radio, and Machine Workers of America, and the United Mine Workers of America. The largest of these are the Teamsters and the Auto Workers, together representing about 3.25 million workers.

4   THE COLLECTIVE BARGAINING PROCESS
Give and take between management and unions

Labor unions often provide many services to their members: job placement, training, day-care for children, and many others. Despite the importance of these, the essential role of the union is to carry on collective bargaining with management. *Collective bargaining* is a process of negotiation. It is "collective" because union negotiators represent all the member workers as a group. The issues that are negotiated revolve around the rights and responsibilities of labor and management.

ISSUES FOR NEGOTIATION
Recognition comes first, then wages, hours, working conditions, and job security

The first bargaining issue must always be the recognition of a union as an agent of the workers in a company or industry. Management, in general, does not encourage the organization of workers. Managers often delay and attempt to avoid recognizing unions. Initial goals sought by unions are the right to represent workers, the right to collect dues, the right to exchange information about union activities, and others. Once recognition is achieved, negotiations are aimed at four basic issues:

- *Wages and wage policies*—Virtually every aspect of compensation is fair game for negotiation: pay rates for types and levels of jobs, determination of pay increases and promotions, payment of trainees and apprentices, benefits, pensions, and insurance.
- *Hours of work*—Shorter work weeks for the same pay are of obvious benefit to workers. In times of high unemployment, such changes may also put more people to work. With each worker putting in fewer hours, the work can be spread out over more employees.
- *Working conditions*—These include safety measures, plant temperatures, operating procedures, rest breaks, work rules, job assignments, and many other factors.
- *Job security and related rights*—Many union contracts (a) prohibit dismissal without good cause, (b) include controls over layoffs and rehiring, (c) specify how promotions will be decided, (d) spell out disciplinary procedures that may be used against workers, and (e) define a grievance procedure for workers who have been unfairly treated.

ESTABLISHING THE BARGAINING PROCESS

Union recognition is the most difficult step

Historically, the most difficult and dangerous step in establishing the bargaining process has been gaining management's recognition of a union as a bargaining agent. In the past, the use of violence was common when union leaders were determined to represent workers, and company owners and managers were equally determined to keep the unions out. Armed battles actually erupted at Carnegie Steel's Homestead plant, at the Toledo Auto-Lite plant, and elsewhere.

Among the first important actions taken to prevent such hostility and violence were the government's recognition of the legality of unions and the establishment of the National Labor Relations Board (NLRB) in 1935. The NLRB supervises elections in which workers decide whether they wish to be represented by a union and, if so, by which one. If a majority of the workers vote for union representation, management is obliged to begin negotiations. The NLRB helps to establish the initial collective bargaining procedure.

DEGREES OF UNION RECOGNITION

Open, union, and agency shops

One issue that arises early in negotiations is the extent to which the union is protected and its authority to impose membership on employees. Companies and industries vary in their degree of unionization:

- An *open shop* has no officially recognized union, although individual workers may belong to unions of their choice. In a true open shop, managers make no formal efforts to avoid unionization. Workers are free to make their own choices.

■   A *union shop* requires all employees to join a recognized union by a specified time after they have been hired. They need not be members before being hired. A union shop gives considerable strength and security to union representation. A *closed shop* is an even stronger agreement— now outlawed—which forbids companies to hire employees who are not union members.

■   An *agency shop* allows employees to belong to the recognized union if they choose, but they are not required to do so. However, all workers must pay union dues.

CONTRACT NEGOTIATION

A labor contract is the outcome

Once the extent of union representation has been established, collective bargaining focuses on negotiating and administering periodic *labor contracts.* These are written agreements between the union and company management specifying wages, worker and union rights, work conditions, management rights, and other provisions. A labor contract usually is in force for a period of one, two, or three years. At the end of the period, it may be renewed or renegotiated.

There are a number of steps in routine contract negotiations:

■   Union and management representatives gather information relevant to the issues likely to be discussed. This may include data on the general economy and surveys of other plants and working conditions.

■   Representatives meet to establish the rules that will govern the negotiation process.

■   Union negotiators usually present their demands for contract changes first.

■   Management studies labor's proposals and makes counterproposals. Table 18-2 illustrates some of the bargaining tactics used by management during negotiations.

■   In ensuing meetings, both sides argue in favor of their positions and negotiate a compromise agreement acceptable to both the union representatives and to management.

■   Union members then vote on the agreement. If they accept it, it is ratified and becomes effective. If they reject it, the negotiation process must begin again to try to draft a contract that they will approve.

ADMINISTERING THE LABOR CONTRACT

Grievance procedures provide relief

Arriving at an acceptable labor contract is only the first step. For collective bargaining to be truly effective, the contract must be administered in a way that is fair to workers and to the company. In practice, this administration must result from a cooperative effort by the company's personnel and line managers (especially supervisors) and union officials and shop stewards.

ACTION BRIEF

Backward Moves.   In the economic crunch that hammered the auto industry in the early 1980s, the United Auto Workers (UAW) reversed direction. For the first time in their history, the UAW agreed to "give-backs." These were concessions the union made to the automakers in which previously negotiated wage increases and other benefits would be passed up, at least for a period of time. The UAW estimated that a reduction of $1 an hour in the union's negotiated compensation package of $18.75 could yield enough to cut car prices by $150. The union insisted, however, that the auto companies also make some sacrifice through cuts in management and manager's salaries. That way, the total reduction in car costs would be $300.

Source: "A Deal That Could Put a Brake on Car Costs," Business Week, *January 25, 1982.*

TABLE 18-2
Bargaining Tips From a Management Point of View

1. Never give a false signal.

2. Never indicate you will consider a demand on which you do not intend to move.

3. Spend plenty of time listening.

4. Be sincere about your motives—do not attempt to conceal the fact that you are in business to make money.

5. Do not indicate you cannot afford or cannot compete if a demand is given unless you are willing to show your books or are sure they will not be demanded.

6. Do not index economic items on a percentage base; negotiate on fixed cost so that you can negotiate on the item in the future, and both company and union gain credit for improvements.

7. Do not indicate you will not negotiate on a subject unless you are sure that you have no legal duty to negotiate on it.

8. Let the union drop its demands gracefully.

9. Do not lose self-control or attack any member of the union committee personally.

10. Do not take or give abuse; adjourn the meeting until tempers have cooled.

11. Work from the company's language.

12. Make sessions last as long as necessary to obtain satisfactory understanding.

Source: Paul W. Bockley, "Labor-Management Relations," in *Encyclopedia of Professional Management*, McGraw-Hill Book Company, New York, 1979, p. 592.

The company supervisors who have direct contact with unionized employees are especially important. They must often make the final detailed interpretation of work rules and other matters in the actual work situation. **Work rules** refer generally to contract clauses that affect working conditions. Work rules may involve such procedures and precedents as to how many machines an operator may tend at one time or who among a list of employees will get the first choice of overtime.

The union shop steward has a similar role as an on-site union official. He or she must make the first moves in protecting workers' day-to-day interests. Cooperation between stewards and supervisors can often prevent disputes from breaking out.

When a dispute does occur, especially over unfair treatment of workers, a grievance procedure is set up. Most contracts spell out an orderly manner in which claims of ill-treatment can be appealed through various levels of union and company management until they are settled. This **grievance procedure** is meant to make sure that all complaints will receive a fair and full hearing. It is probably the single most important guarantee that collective bargaining will actually result in fair treatment of individual workers. Complaints and grievances are usually handled

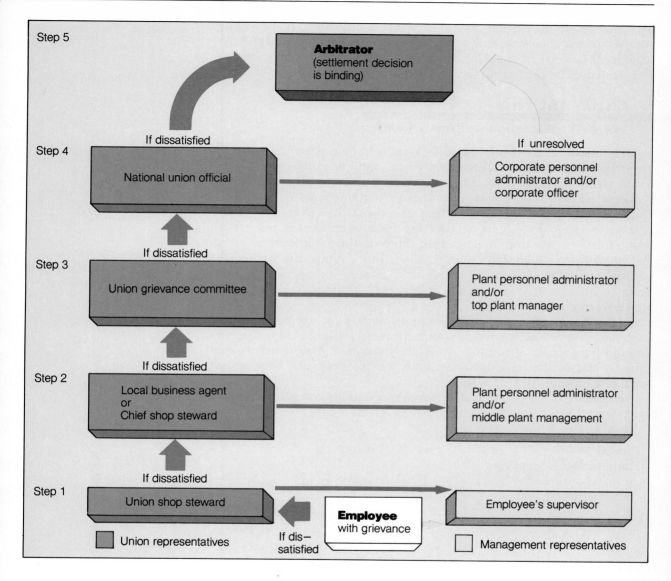

first at the shop steward-supervisor level. They then move up by designated steps to higher levels if their resolution continues to be unsatisfactory to the aggrieved party. Figure 18-2 illustrates the grievance procedure in a large corporation.

Figure 18-2
How the settlement level moves upward in a typical grievance procedure.

5   LABOR DISPUTES AND THEIR SETTLEMENT

Both parties employ power tactics

Labor disputes do occur, despite procedures and efforts to avoid them. The most likely time for unresolved disagreements to develop is when new contracts are being negotiated. Labor and management are often unwilling or unable to reach compromises acceptable to both. Negotiations can be emotional and may lead to severe disputes. The day-to-day administration of contracts also can cause disputes that are not settled by organized, rational means. Unions and managers use a variety of tactics and strategies for furthering their own cause when disputes arise.

UNION TACTICS

The strike is a union's ultimate weapon

The methods most often used by unions to help achieve their goals are strikes, slowdowns, picketing, boycotts, and lobbying.

A *strike* attempts to force management to give in to union demands. Workers refuse to work and thus damage the company financially by shutting down production and cutting off income. Strikes are most effective when sales are highest and inventories lowest. Strikes may result from efforts to gain union recognition, from on-the-job grievances, from the breakdown of contract negotiations, from sympathy with other unions engaged in disputes, and from other causes. Recent historical data seem to indicate that unions are increasingly hesitant to resort to the strike weapon. (See Table 18-3.)

A work *slowdown* is another union method for exerting force on companies. Slowdowns have the same effects as strikes, except that production is reduced rather than completely stopped. Also, workers continue to be paid during a slowdown, unless employers take some action, such as a lockout, to stop wages.

Picketing is the practice of advertising a union's complaints against

TABLE 18-3
Trend in Work Stoppages

Year	Number	Workers Involved
1970	5,716	3,305,000
1971	5,138	3,280,000
1972	5,010	1,714,000
1973	5,353	2,251,000
1974	6,074	2,788,000
1975	5,031	1,748,000
1976	5,648	2,420,000
1977	5,508	2,040,000
1978	4,230	1,623,000
1979	4,827	1,727,000
1980	3,885	1,368,000
1981	2,577	1,082,000
1982	1,701	714,000

Source: *Monthly Labor Review*, March 1983.

The Right
to Work
or a
Free Ride?

The Taft-Hartley Act of 1947 enabled the separate states to pass laws that prohibit employers and labor unions from negotiating contracts that require membership or nonmembership in labor unions as a condition of employment. Subsequently, 20 of the 50 states (mainly in the southern and plain states) have passed these "right-to-work" laws. Labor unions dub people who would support these laws "free riders." They contend that benefits won by labor unions are enjoyed by other workers, and they should pay their share by joining the union and paying dues. Such "free riders," the unions claim, weaken unions and eventually cause lower wage and salary levels. On the other hand, opponents of right-to-work laws maintain that those who don't wish to join unions become "captive passengers" when obliged to do so. They claim that to force a person to join a union is an abridgement of a person's freedom and that, further, only a voluntary union membership will make union leadership responsive and responsible to members' interests.

Source: Marc G. Singer, H. L. Durrett, and K. L. Shannon, "An Empirical Investigation of Comprehension of the Right-to-Work Law Among Residents of the State of Virginia," Journal of Collective Negotiations, Vol. 12, No. 3, 1983.

Why do you suppose that so many of the states that have passed right-to-work laws are not in traditionally urban or industrialized areas? Where do you stand on this issue? Should a person be compelled to belong to a union in order to hold his or her job? Would you become a "free rider" if you had a choice whether or not to join a union at your place of employment?

management by walking around with signs near the entrances of a company's facilities. Picketing usually accompanies strikes and may be used when major grievances remain unresolved. Picketing is effective because it helps publicize the union's position and because it may cut off services and supplies that the company needs or prevent it from shipping goods from its inventory.

A *boycott* is an organized refusal to buy the products of a company or industry. A large union with many members can sometimes significantly reduce a company's sales with a boycott.

Unions use lobbying in local, state, and national governments to protect their long-term interests. *Lobbying* is any effort by a group to influence legislators and government administrators to pass laws and interpret them to the advantage of that group.

MANAGEMENT TACTICS

Lobbying seems to be most effective

The chief methods management uses to combat union demands and to strengthen its position are lockouts, strikebreaking, injunctions, industry associations, and lobbying.

In a *lockout,* management refuses to allow workers into the plant to work. The company forces economic hardship on workers by cutting off wages. Lockouts can work only when the company is in a strong financial position and can endure a period of reduced or lost production. Lockouts have grown less common as a management tactic in recent years.

Strikebreaking is the practice of hiring replacement workers to continue production while union workers are on strike. This has been the cause of much violence in the past and is less common now.

Court injunctions can sometimes be obtained against strikes in industries that are critical to the national defense or welfare. These injunctions forbid workers to strike while negotiations continue.

Industry associations may help strengthen management's position by providing bargaining information, appealing to public opinion, and increasing companies' solidarity to offset that of the union.

Companies and industries also use lobbying to influence legislators to pass laws favorable to business and management. Lobbying has proved to be management's most effective tactic in the long run, as management is usually better able to subsidize lobbying efforts than are unions.

RECONCILIATION OF LABOR-MANAGEMENT DISPUTES

Outside parties intervene

Often no compromise agreement can be reached because of the interplay of pressure tactics used by labor and management. Grievance procedures at the management level may be exhausted without an acceptable settlement. Contract negotiations may drag on for months without effective compromises. In these situations, two procedures are available to help bring about settlements: mediation and arbitration.

Mediation is a process in which a third party not directly involved in a dispute attempts to facilitate a settlement by clarifying issues, bringing in new information, and generally influencing the negotiators to compromise. Compliance with a mediator's suggestions is entirely voluntary.

Arbitration is similar, except that negotiating parties agree to be bound by the decisions of an arbitrator. Arbitrators may attempt to achieve a voluntary settlement but are empowered to impose a settlement. Many labor contracts specify that when an agreement cannot be reached in other ways, a dispute should be subject to arbitration.

In general, any person or agency acceptable to both sides may serve as a mediator or arbitrator. Some industries have industrial relations organizations to help in negotiations. Many state and city governments use effective mediation and arbitration boards. The Federal Mediation and Conciliation Service provides assistance with negotiating and can even provide mediators or arbitrators. The National Labor Relations Board also provides information and aid in the resolution of labor disputes, particularly when union representation is first being sought.

Labor unions also have disagreements among themselves. In such *jurisdictional disputes* they may differ as to which union has the right to represent a particular group of employees or as to which union's employees have the right to certain kinds of work. When jurisdictional disputes occur, labor unions have the same options as management in seeking relief or in using bargaining tactics. Often, however, management, employees, and the public are caught in between the adversary unions.

6 LANDMARKS OF LABOR-MANAGEMENT LEGISLATION

The law tries to equalize the distribution of power

The important labor legislation enacted in the twentieth century evolved as a result of centuries of struggle. Up until the 1930s, court cases in labor-management disputes were regularly decided in favor of management. Since then, stronger feelings nationwide in favor of unions have resulted in legislation that has diverted the pro-management trend.

MILESTONE LEGISLATION OF THE 1930s

Includes labor's "Magna Carta"

The Norris-La Guardia Act, passed in 1932, sharply reduced the ease with which companies could get court injunctions to stop union activity. Up until this time, courts had been unfailingly cooperative in stopping strikes, picketing, and membership drives. This law gave considerable legal legitimacy to these activities.

The National Labor Relations Act of 1935 was hailed as labor's "Magna Carta," since it provided the legal foundation for the rights of unions and workers. This act, which is commonly called the Wagner Act after its main sponsor (a) guaranteed the right to collective bargaining and union membership, (b) outlawed employer interference in labor organization and administration, (c) outlawed company discrimination against union members, (d) required companies to bargain with legally elected unions, and (e) created the National Labor Relations Board to administer the act. The Wagner Act was followed by the Fair Labor Standards Act of 1938, which deals in a general way with the rights of workers. It established the minimum wage, prohibited hiring children in certain occupations and circumstances, and required companies engaged in interstate commerce to pay higher wages for overtime work.

LAWS LIMITING UNION POWER AND PROTECTING WORKERS' RIGHTS

Prevent abuses by unions as well as management

Many businesses and other interest groups believed that the legislation of the 1930s gave unions too much power. By the end of World War II, union membership had greatly increased. There were numerous strikes once the wartime restraints on wages were ended, and there were some unions that actually did abuse their freedom and power. Public sentiment moved somewhat away from unions and influenced the passage of two bills limiting the unions' freedom.

The Taft-Hartley Act (the Labor-Management Relations Act of 1947) amended the Wagner Act. Most of the restrictions on management interference in union activities were retained, and new restrictions were placed on unions. Unions were prohibited from coercing members or prospective members, from discriminating against workers who were not union members, and from refusing to take part in collective bargaining. The Taft-Hartley Act also gave the states the option of passing *right-to-work laws* (see Issues & Highlights on page 337).

The Landrum-Griffin Act (the Labor-Management Reporting and Disclosure Act), passed in 1959, protects union members from possible misuse of power by their own union's leadership. It enforces the use of democratic procedures in union efforts to expand membership and requires fuller disclosure of unions' financial affairs.

More recently, legislators have been concerned with protecting the rights of the individual worker. The Civil Rights Act of 1968 contains a group of provisions referred to as the Fair Employment Practices Act. They prohibit employers from discriminating against job applicants because of race, color, religion, national origin, or sex.

Key Concepts

1. Changes in the U.S. labor force today include an increase in the number of professional, technical, clerical, and service workers but fewer farm workers. Unemployment and layoffs remain a threat to workers' job security.

2. The main goals of the organized labor movement in the United States have been fairer wages, better hours and working conditions, more job security, and protection from discrimination.

3. Labor unions may be organized according to the skills performed by members or by the industries in which members work. Unions

may be local, national, independent or affiliated with the AFL-CIO.

4. Collective bargaining is a process of negotiating work-related issues. Workers are represented collectively by negotiators who are chosen by election. Issues negotiated include union recognition, wages and wage policy, work hours, working conditions, job rights, job security, and others.

5. Labor and management both use tactics to further their positions and to try to force the other to give in or compromise. Union tactics include strikes, slowdowns, picketing, boycotts

and lobbying. Management tactics include lockouts, strikebreaking, injunctions, industry associations, and lobbying. When pressure and negotiation do not produce a settlement, mediation or arbitration of disputes may be used.

6. Government legislation has partially directed the growth of organized labor. In the 1930s, several bills gave labor union activities legal protection and gave unions great freedom. Later laws have restricted their freedom somewhat in an effort to reestablish the power balance between unions and management.

Review Questions

1. Define, explain or identify the following key terms and phrases found on the pages indicated.

   agency shop (p. 333)
   arbitration (p. 339)
   boycott (p. 338)
   closed shop (p. 333)
   collective bargaining (p. 331)
   court injunction (p. 338)
   craft union (p. 330)
   grievance procedure (p. 334)
   independent union (p. 331)
   industrial union (p. 330)
   industry associations (p. 338)
   jurisdictional disputes (p. 339)
   labor contract (p. 333)
   lobbying (p. 338)
   local union (p. 331)
   lockout (p. 338)
   mediation (p. 338)
   national union (p. 331)
   open shop (p. 332)
   picketing (p. 336)
   right-to-work laws (p. 340)
   slowdown (p. 336)
   strike (p. 336)
   strikebreaking (p. 338)
   union shop (p. 333)
   work rules (p. 334)

2. What changes have already occurred and will continue to occur in the makeup of the United States labor force?
3. What have been the main goals of organized labor in the United States?
4. Do membership figures for labor unions truly represent the influence of organized labor? Why, or why not?
5. What is the difference between a craft union and an industrial union? Give some examples of each.
6. What are the most common issues that are subject to collective bargaining?
7. Describe the process of routine labor contract negotiation.
8. Why is the establishment of a grievance procedure important to the unions?
9. Explain the difference between a strike and a lockout.
10. What was the aim of the Taft-Hartley Act?

Case Critique 18-1
Who Should Lay the Bricks?

A construction company employing members of Local 2 of the International Union of Bricklayers got a contract with the United States' Steel Company to rebuild its coke ovens at Clairton, Pennsylvania. The company chose to have these repairs made at that time because the steel plant was temporarily shut down for lack of orders. This meant that some 300 company maintenance workers who belonged to the United Steel Workers' union (USW), which represented all kinds of employees at the company, were laid off. The president of USW Local 1557 said this was unfair. The company replied that for years their agreement with USW gave the company an unrestricted right to bring in outside contractors for new construction work and major rehabilitations, such as the coke oven building. In fact, when times were good and employment high in the steel mill, the USW local tended to allow even routine maintenance jobs to slip away from their members. Now, the Steel Workers wanted to put a halt to these practices. But the business manager of the Bricklayers' union said: "This kind of work rightfully belongs to us. Bricklaying is our livelihood."

1. From the information in the case, which of the two unions involved appears to be primarily a craft union and which an industrial union?
2. What is the term applied to disputes of this kind between two unions?

3. Which union seems to have the better argument? Why?
4. If the Steel Workers do not like what is going on, what recourse do they have?
5. Under the circumstances, what choices are open to the management of the steel plant?

Source: "A Quarrel Over Fixing the Plant," *Business Week,* October 13, 1980, p. 50.

Case Critique 18-2
Your Money or Your Work Rules

A few years ago, retail clerks shut down Safeway Stores, Inc.'s San Francisco supermarkets when 7,000 members of the United Food & Commercial Workers (UFCW) went out on strike. Another 6,000 retail clerks were then put out of work temporarily when four other supermarkets, who were members of the Northern California Food Employers' Council, closed their stores in support of Safeway. The supermarkets defended their actions by pointing to the average clerk's wage of $24,500 a year (including fringe benefits). The UFCW union was bargaining for a wage and benefit package that would total 33 percent in increases over the next three years. The companies were ready to settle if the union would agree to certain concessions in the way the stores were operated. The supermarkets wanted to convert some full-time jobs to part-time, relax some seniority provisions in moving employees between stores and jobs, and the right to assign lower-paid food clerks to work in other areas such as housekeeping and parking lot cleanup.

"We are less willing than ever to tolerate restrictions in our contracts that tie the hands of our management," said a supermarket officer. "Profits are down, there is stiff competition from the no-frills box stores, and wages and benefits are 60 percent of operating costs."

"It's just an attempt to flood the stores with cheap labor," retaliated the spokesperson for the union.

1. Besides wages and benefits, what is the main issue in this dispute?
2. Why have the issues in this dispute become so important to both parties?
3. What is the term applied to the action taken by the Food Employers' Council? Do you think the action was justified or not? Why?

Source: "Why Retail Clerks Hit Safeway With a Strike," *Business Week,* February 11, 1980, p. 34.

Unit 7

Basic Business Operations— Information and Controls

Unit 7 covers the essentials of information analysis and planning, formal accounting procedures and financial reporting, and the use of forecasts and budgets to control business operations.

Because decision making in business is a science as well as an art, it must be based on reliable information. Management information systems collect and process data to fill this need.

The accounting process, which should provide a careful record of business transactions that involve money, allows managers to better direct and control and owners and investors to judge the financial worth of a business.

Budgets help managers to control business operations. They are prepared from business forecasts, which estimate future sales, expenses, and profits. Managers compare the budget to actual company performance in order to determine how their businesses can function at maximum efficiency and lowest cost.

Chapter 19

Information Systems, Decision Making, and Planning

1 A MANAGEMENT INFORMATION SYSTEM (MIS) is an orderly procedure for collecting, analyzing, and reporting past, present, and projected information about internal and external influences. It is used by managers in

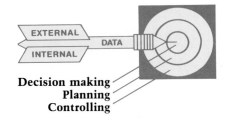

Decision making
Planning
Controlling

2 A DATA PROCESSING SYSTEM —whether manual, mechanical, or electronic—is chosen on the basis of usefulness, speed, and cost.

Manual

Mechanical

Electronic

3 DECISION MAKING involves choosing a specific plan of action from among several alternatives.

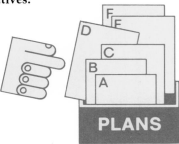

PLANS

4 GOOD DECISIONS
depend on the quality of

| Quantitative estimates | and | Personal judgments |

5 PLANNING BUSINESS ACTIVITIES
involves answering these questions:

6 PLANS INCLUDE STRATEGIES AND TACTICS
and can be short-term or long-term.

The most effective plans are

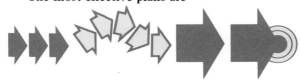

Specific   Flexible   Feasible

Learning Objectives

The purpose of this chapter is to define information and describe a management information system and its relationship to data processing systems, explain factors that affect decisions and outline the classic decision-making process, and show why good planning is essential to a business and describe the planning process.

As evidence of general comprehension, after studying Chapter 19, you should be able to do the following:

1. *Define information and recognize its sources.*
2. *Differentiate between various types of data processing.*
3. *Understand the relationship between decision making and risk.*
4. *Explain the factors that influence decisions and describe the decision-making process.*
5. *Recognize how various planning dimensions are utilized.*
6. *Outline the six steps of a business plan and carry out a prescribed planning procedure.*

If your class is using SSweetco: Business Model and Activity File for Business in Action, see Chapter 19 in that book after you complete this chapter. There you will find for exercises and activities to help you apply your learning to typical business situations.

Every year, private and government organizations publish over 30,000 books, tens of thousands of magazine and journal articles, and hundreds of thousands of pages of statistical data on labor, business, the economy, research and technology, and government activities. Companies and government agencies prepare countless reports for internal use. Billions of individual business and financial transactions take place, every one having some effect on the economy.

Every manager knows that effective decisions and effective business plans must be based on reliable, complete, and well-organized information. However, to select the useful information from the tremendous mountain of facts that confronts a manager is not an easy task. A systematic effort is essential in order to summarize and organize the data, filter out what is irrelevant, and put the valuable information to work. This is the goal of Management Information Systems. They are meant to provide up-to-date, organized information on markets and sales, financing, production and overhead costs, materials, personnel, and other concerns so that managers can make better decisions and plans.

1   MANAGEMENT INFORMATION SYSTEMS (MIS)

The mainspring of planning and control

A *Management Information System (MIS)* is a set of interrelated procedures. The procedures include collecting, analyzing and reporting past, present, and projected information from within and outside of an organization. The information is organized so that it is directly usable by managers for decision making, planning, and controlling.

INFORMATION AND DATA

All the facts and circumstances

Information, in the business world, is defined as the knowledge of facts or circumstances. "Data," though often implying numerical information, is interchangeable with "information." Information has different levels of usefulness. The manager of a large retail store could be presented with thousands of individual sales slips at the end of a day. The slips, however, are only raw data. Analyzing and summarizing them can make them far more informative. A brief report showing total sales, sales by departments, sales by product type, and sales by cash or credit payments would be far more effective in helping with most decisions than would be the individual sales slips. An important purpose of MIS is to make data more useful and more informative. (See Figure 19-1.)

COLLECTION OF DATA

Selectivity is required

The precise information needed for planning and decision making depends on the careful, consistent collection of data. Managers need knowledge of what is going on within their own organizations. This information about internal affairs is used to monitor and control current oper-

ACTION BRIEF

Up the Ladder.   Starting out in business on the information data processing side gives a person a good leg up the career ladder. That's the conclusion drawn from a survey of data processing people who made the transition into general business management. The advantages of the information systems background most often mentioned were: (a) a first-hand knowledge of the full range of a company's operations, (b) the ability to communicate with coworkers and managers, and (c) the ability to analyze problems and plan efficiently for their solution. Said Robert A. Breakstone, president of Health-Tex (a subsidiary of Cheseborough-Pond's, Inc.), "DP is an excellent route to the top."

Source: "Room at the Top," Management Information Systems Week, *October 7, 1981, p. 6.*

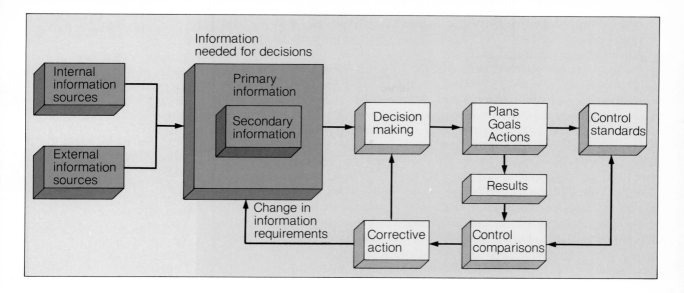

Information needed for decisions

Internal information sources

External information sources

Primary information

Secondary information

Change in information requirements

Decision making

Corrective action

Plans Goals Actions

Results

Control comparisons

Control standards

Figure 19-1
Components of a management information system.

ations and is used for planning. Information about developments external to the organization is also important. Government action, impending price changes by competitors or suppliers, shifts in population, and scores of other issues may affect management decisions.

Internal Sources   Tallies of the amount of goods or services produced, the number of working hours spent on each unit of production, the time spent on maintenance, the amount of materials used, the amount of materials wasted, the number of products rejected by inspectors, and the amount of utilities used are only a few kinds of data resulting directly from the production process. The accounting system yields data about the sales of various products, the costs of financing and operating, changes in personnel costs, the profits and losses of particular divisions or product lines, and so on. The purchasing department, the shipping department, and the warehouses all have information about inventory levels and changes. Data on absenteeism, injuries and accidents, and employee turnover is available from the personnel department.

External Sources   Companies also need information from external sources to anticipate important changes in the business environment. Among the most important sources of data are government agencies. The federal government publishes a huge quantity of data, analyses, and regulations that may be of interest to business managers, including the censuses, or numerical estimates, of the population, housing, business, agriculture, labor and the work force, manufacturing minerals, and government organizations. State and local governments often maintain and publish similar information for their own jurisdictions.

Information useful for business management is also available from many private sources. One of the main functions of trade and professional associations is the collection and publication of statistics, new technical developments, new product information, new legislation, and other information. Many private companies are in the business of providing information. Scores of commercial newsletters and journals meet special needs. Some companies carry out sophisticated surveys of retail sales, buying power, building construction, and other important fields. They then sell the results to subscribers.

Data that is collected and published by others is called *secondary data.* It was not compiled specifically to help solve a specific problem of an individual company. *Primary data* is gathered to meet particular needs and has not been published before in a usable form. Some companies have sufficient need and resources to collect primary data for their own use. They may survey customers to find out their product preferences or their response to a new credit plan. They may observe buyers' behavior in stores to get information on the effects of a certain package design or point-of-purchase display. They may use highway traffic counts to help pick a location for a new store. Gathering primary data on business problems can be quite expensive. In many large projects, however, it is unavoidable because other relevant and reliable information is unavailable.

A recent trend in data processing has been to collect interrelated data in computer files for easy access, retrieval, and updating. Such a file, or system of files is called a *database.* It is, in effect, an electronic library. The database may be developed and maintained by a company for its internal use, or the database may be one jointly developed by companies with a mutual interest (such as a hotel trade association) from which all parties may draw information. Many databases are put together by independent firms which offer access to the files to any organization for a fee.

2   DATA PROCESSING SYSTEMS

Integrated methods and machinery

It is obvious that a great deal of internal and external data is potentially available to managers. To be useful, however, the data must be organized so that relationships among facts are apparent. It must usually be presented in summary form. It often must be subjected to statistical analysis to find trends and changes. All of these operations of collecting, organizing, and analyzing data are called *data processing.* The methods and equipment used are integrated into data processing systems. Data processing today is often associated with the use of computers, but manual, mechanical, and electronic methods are all widely used.

In a small organization, a manual data processing system may be used effectively. Hand tallies of production and quality control results, abstracts of payroll and bookkeeping records, tabulations of purchasing, inventory counts, and sales totals can provide fundamental management information. In order to work, procedures must be well thought out, simple, and consistently applied. Even a very large MIS in a major corporation is at least partly manual, especially in the original recording of data and in checking accuracy and completeness.

Mechanical data processing equipment is often used to produce simple reports from moderate amounts of data. Most of this equipment uses punched cards. These familiar IBM or Hollerith cards can record 80 single numbers or letters. They can be sorted, alphabetized, added together, and manipulated in other ways by relatively inexpensive electromechanical equipment. Reports are easier to make with these methods than with entirely manual methods. Punching and sorting cards is still a common means of preparing data for computer analysis.

Electronic data processing mainly involves the manipulation of numbers and letters by computers. Computers are able to perform so many different arithmetic operations, comparisons, and data transformations that they allow great flexibility in arranging data for maximum usefulness. Some of the capabilities and contributions of computer systems are discussed in Chapter 24.

Manual, mechanical, and electronic data processing merely helps in gathering the information. They are by no means sufficient in themselves. The really important aspect of a data processing system is the extent to which it reliably collects data and quickly provides it in the most usable form to those who need it. To achieve a system like this, clear and relevant objectives, thoughtful planning, and careful attention to daily operation are almost always more important than the use of a particular method or machine.

System Guidelines   In devising or improving a Management Information System, the users must constantly focus on clarifying and meeting organization objectives. In deciding what information their system will provide, they must judge the usefulness, timeliness, and affordability of every proposed kind of information:

■   The *usefulness* of output is a prime criterion of the effectiveness of MIS. A production manager wishing to reduce costs must know where the total costs originate, how much comes from worker wages, how much from waste materials, how much from utility charges, and so forth. The manager needs that information presented in a clear and simple report, free of all extraneous and useless data.

■   To be of real help in making decisions, information must be *timely*. Reports must be produced quickly or the information they contain will not help with current decisions. Some companies have even placed **on line** data collectors that record transactions and operations as they take place and keep current the available results when they are needed.

■   An effective MIS must be *affordable*. Large data collection and processing systems often cost hundreds of thousands or even millions of dollars a year to operate. The system must be designed so that the information gathered is worth its cost. Systems must be scaled to match the size and needs of the company that uses them.

Figure 19-2 on page 350 shows how data processing links up information sources with information users in an MIS.

Figure 19-2 on page 350 shows how data processing links up information sources with information users in an MIS.

ACTION BRIEF

Everyone's Database.
Remember how your Aunt Emma used to save old magazines in her attic? And what fun it was to read them on a rainy afternoon? Now, The New York Times saves on computer tape the abstracts (or summaries) of all the articles published in 55 important magazines and newspapers. This periodical database carries over two million abstracts, with articles going back to 1969 and current within five days of publication. Subscribers to this database of external information can retrieve articles within 24 hours. Articles can be located by a combination of descriptors, such as a particular subject, geographical location, person, and organization. For example, the index will locate all articles referring to the President of the United States' comments about monetary policy as it affects the European Economic Community while visiting France.

Source: *"N.Y. Times Offers Abstracts of 55 Major Periodicals," Desktop Computing, April 1982, p. 80.*

3   MANAGERIAL DECISION MAKING

The courage and insight to choose

Managers want information because they need it to make decisions. The proper use of information is an important part of decision making,

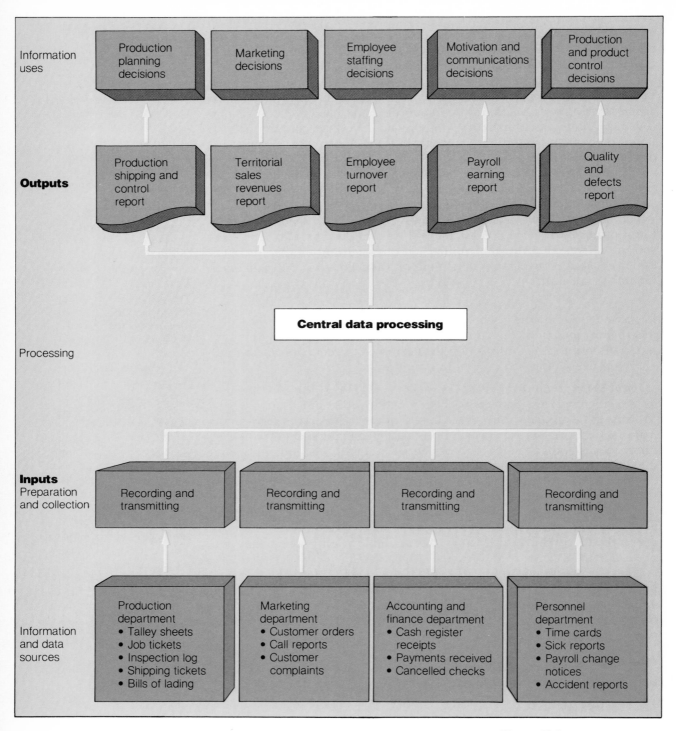

Figure 19-2
How a data processing
system links up input source
with output users in a
management information
system.

but it is only one aspect of a complex creative process. *Decision making* is the selection of one course of action from among a number of possible courses of action. The alternatives may be immediately obvious or they may be purposely developed as part of the process of deciding.

Decision making is difficult and often requires a good deal of courage. The reason is that the outcome of choosing a particular course of action is not certain. It involves risk. The decision maker may be right or wrong. If a manager knew for sure that the company will make a $50 million profit by introducing a new product, the decision would be easy. However, a manager almost never knows that. The actual result of bringing out the new product may be a $5 million loss followed by the firing of the manager by the board of directors. Uncertainty about the future always exists and causes risks to decision makers.

In making a decision, managers must have expectations about the results of actions and about what will happen in the future. These expectations are always tested against actual events. The closer the expectations are to reality, the better the decisions that can be made. Considerable attention is now being given to techniques that will improve projections of the future.

4   DECISION-MAKING TECHNIQUES

Information and logic are the foundation stones

A manager's ability to make decisions is an important part of what makes him or her valuable to an organization. Decisions range in scope and difficulty from whether to spend $100 for a new file cabinet to whether to merge with another corporation in a multibillion-dollar transaction. For any kind of decision, managers can increase the likelihood of success by systematically using the resources available to them.

TOOLS FOR DECISION MAKING

Quantitative techniques are on the rise

Making good decisions is like most management skills: it is both an art and a science. Good managers have an intuition about what the effects of actions will be even when all the facts are not available. They may accurately judge, for example, that a new advertising campaign will not work, even without being exactly sure why. Experience truly is a good teacher. Watching the effects of many varied decisions and efforts over the years can improve judgment, even when the process is not rationally analyzed.

Managers strengthen their personal judgments by using various techniques to analyze numerical and factual data so that future activities can be planned. These methods range from the simple analysis of figures to discover sales or cost trends to computer simulations using hundreds of variables. The basis of nearly all of these techniques is the use of past experience and data to try to predict the future. A few of these statistical methods are discussed in detail in Chapter 24.

When it comes to making decisions, people tend to fall into two classes: those who will consider only hard facts and those who are greatly influenced by their feelings. Robert McNamara, once president of Ford Motor Company and noted for his service as U.S. Secretary of Defense during the Cuban Missile Crisis and the Vietnam War, represented the hard-facts school. Before attacking problems, he demanded that they be reduced to a detailed range of alternatives with facts and figures to support each option. McNamara said, "As long as I can make decisions through analysis of the problem and thus base them on the greatest evidence on hand, the decisions are not difficult." People who rely upon emotional judgments, however, are in the great majority. Two psychological researchers sum up popular decision-making this way: "We persevere in our judgments even when the evidence is overwhelming that they are wrong." The researchers' experiments showed time and again that once a person has formed a judgment, the resistance to change it is monumental.

Source: **Mort La Brecque, "On Making Sounder Judgments," Psychology Today, June 1980, p. 33.**

How do you make your judgments? Do you lean more to the factual, rational side or more to the emotional, intuitive side?

FACTORS AFFECTING DECISIONS

Costs, benefits, and circumstances

How does a manager determine whether a course of action is desirable, even after good estimates of its results are available? In most cases, the important issues are costs versus expected returns and suitability to projected business situations.

Many business situations can be defined by expected costs and returns. A retail store manager may wish to begin advertising on the local radio station. He or she can easily get an accurate estimate of the costs by adding together the station's time charges, the costs of writing and recording the advertisements, administrative costs, and other expenses. A fairly good idea of how much advertisements will increase sales may be had by looking at the experience of other stores, by judging the suitability of the store's products to the station's listeners, and by other means. If the expected return is greater than the estimated cost, the manager will probably decide to begin advertising. This seems to be a very basic process, but many bad business decisions have come from not following it. Either the comparison of costs with returns has been omitted, or the projections of costs and returns have been grossly inaccurate because of lack of information, carelessness, or wishful thinking.

Many proposed courses of action are basically good ideas, but they come at the wrong time. All decisions must be evaluated in light of present and expected conditions within the company and in the economy. A corporation must think twice about a major expansion if borrowed money is needed and interest rates are very high. A new production process may be very efficient but may fail in the future if a needed material is expected to be unavailable.

THE DECISION-MAKING PROCESS

As ancient as Aristotle

Most people can make better decisions in complex situations if they approach problems systematically. Although different paths may be used to reach the same goals, a good approach to decision making involves six important steps first suggested by the ancient Greek philosopher Aristotle:

■ *Identify and define the problem.* Answer the questions: Why is a decision needed? What is the exact problem to be solved or issue to be settled?

■ *Establish objectives.* Decide what outcome is desired once the decision is made. How will the success of the chosen course of action be determined? Business objectives may be defined monetarily, by improved personnel morale, by better company reputation, and in countless other ways.

■ *Gather, classify, and study information.* Become well-informed about every possible aspect of the problem. Try to understand the relationships among different forces and factors.

■ *Develop possible alternate courses of action.* Creatively work out a number of possible courses of action that might help you reach the desired objectives.

■ *Evaluate each alternative.* Determine the advantages and disadvantages of each possible action. Decide whether returns will exceed costs, whether each action is suitable to expected business situations, and how successful each will be in meeting objectives.

■ *Make a choice.* Use the results of the evaluations to pick the best alternative.

5   BUSINESS PLANNING

Should leave little to chance

Planning is an extension of decision making. **Planning** is a process of systematically making decisions about what will be done in the future and how it will be done. Managers must decide *what* their organization will do, *where* and *when* it will be done, *how* to do it, and *who* will do it.

ADVANTAGES OF PLANNING

Minimizes risks and optimizes resources

Planning of some sort must take place or all other activities must stop. A production shop can do nothing, for example, unless someone has decided what product to make, has ordered the materials, and has decided on the production method. Whenever there is business activity, there is some kind of planning. Planning methods mainly differ in the extent to which they are systematic, thorough, adequately long-range, and based on sound information and methods. There are important advantages to systematic planning:

■ Good planning minimizes risk and uncertainty. Although neither can be eliminated, both risk and uncertainty can be reduced by making estimates of future events and problems and by systematically making changes to improve future performance.

■ Planning focuses attention on goals. Successful planning forces managers to decide what an organization's goals are. It helps eliminate irrelevant activities.

■ Planning helps to make organizations operate economically. It can eliminate expensive mistakes. It allows enough time to develop the most efficient designs and work methods. It allows managers to anticipate—and take advantage of—economic and social changes.

■ Planning is essential to effective control. Plans, and the information on which they are based, provide the measure of success by which a company's actual operations may be judged.

OUTPUTS FROM PLANNING

A framework for operations

Plans that are well thought out form the basis of most of the operational guidelines used in a business.

The development of objectives is a critical part of the planning process. Without them, a business would not know where it was headed.

Objectives (the term may be used synonymously with goals and is closely related to the term mission) are the targets, or end-point results toward which an organization or business moves. A company's objectives become fundamental to nearly every management decision. A decision that advances a business toward its objectives will be judged as a good one. A decision that diverts a business from its objectives is a poor decision.

Organization objectives exist in a hierarchy. The overall goal of a business might be to make a profit on investors' capital. Other specific goals should support this main goal—and others on the same level. The company may establish a goal of generating $25 million in income. This will require lower-level goals of a specified amount of production and sales during the year. Lower-level goals, such as keeping machinery in operation 80 percent of the time or making sales calls on five customers a day, help to meet the production and sales goals.

Planning helps establish policies; in fact, policies *are* a kind of plan. A *policy* is a general guide as to how managers and workers should make decisions on issues that may come up in future situations. A company may have a policy of always buying from the lowest of three bidders. The policy does not specify from whom, but it does guide the decision. Policies do not absolutely specify what decision is to be made; they direct the process, but the ultimate choice is made by the decision maker. Policies help make decisions consistent from person to person and department to department so that a difficult decision process does not have to be repeated every time there is a recurring problem.

Planning also develops the lower-level guides as to how a company operates. Workable procedures result from planning. A *procedure* is a defined way of performing an activity. A procedure, for example, might specify how incoming materials are to be checked for quality.

Rules are even more specific than procedures. A *rule* prescribes a particular action that ought to be taken—or not taken—by employees. Rules allow no room for decision making. Examples are the prohibition of personal calls on company phones or the requirement that all incoming mail be immediately stamped with the date and time.

A *program* is another kind of operating plan. Programs combine all of the goals, methods, work assignments, budgets, and other guides and resources needed to complete a segment of work. For instance, a company might institute a program to automate its production facilities.

A budget is an operating plan that is expressed in concrete numbers. The most common kinds of budgets are financial. These show expected or allowable expenditures. Many other kinds are possible, however. Budgets may show working hours, materials, shipping time, or almost any other factors that can be expressed numerically. Budgets and budgeting are further discussed in Chapter 21.

6   PLANS AND THE PLANNING PROCESS

General plans lead to specific ones

The objectives of an organization exist in a hierarchy. Plans to meet the objectives also have different levels. Two in particular are generally recognized: strategies and tactics. *Strategies* are overall guides to courses of action taken to meet long-range objectives. Strategies serve as long-range guides and are determined by high-level management. A paper manufacturer might decide that it could best maintain high sales by providing faster delivery than its competitors. It might then adopt the strategy of always delivering sooner than the other paper companies.

Tactics are specific planned actions needed to support strategies. Tactics usually concentrate more on short-term goals and are often developed by lower-level managers. The paper manufacturer might make changes in its shipping room, use different shipping methods for certain orders, change package sizes or shapes, or make any number of other moves to support its strategy of quick delivery.

Most organizations maintain overall plans for three-month and one-year periods. Companies also need long-range plans to guide development for four-year periods, ten-year periods, or longer. In spite of how difficult it is to make accurate projections about the future, long-range planning helps to establish objectives that aid in decision making.

THE PLANNING PROCESS

Five steps to a business plan

Plans at any level can be developed effectively by following a process that brings together relevant information and uses careful analysis to set goals and find ways of meeting the goals. The use of the following specific planning steps is often helpful:

■ *Determine objectives.* Discovering and setting goals is the main step in the planning process. A company's goals depend partly on the philosophy and general attitudes of its owners and managers.

■ *Establish strategies and tactics.* Once goals have been established, the means for achieving them are developed in much the same way that any other decisions are made. Managers study relevant information, propose and evaluate alternative courses of action, and choose a specific set of actions to take.

■ *Set a timetable.* The scheduling and coordination of planned activities are essential to success. Timing should be influenced by (a) the availability of funds, (b) the work force and other resources, (c) the urgency of the planned actions, (d) how fast plans can be implemented, and (e) the extent and kind of social or economic changes.

■ *Check plans for specificity, flexibility, and feasibility.* Specificity insures that planned actions are defined clearly enough to be put into operation and that results are measurable in some way for success to be judged. Flexibility insures that plans serve as carefully examined guides for managers. Plans should never lock managers into certain patterns and roles and rob them of their ability to react to changing conditions. Feasibility is the extent to which plans are practical and attainable, given the resources an organization has to work with. The best plans for new marketing or production methods, for example, are worthless if a company cannot afford to pay for them.

■ *Integrate with reporting and control system.* This final step is critical to success. The whole purpose of planning—and of management in general—is to reach objectives. Success can be judged only by comparing actual results with planned, desired results. Methods must be used that will clearly show the outcome of plans that have been put into effect. This information will help to make sure that plans are in fact being carried out and also serves as fundamental data for the continuation of the planning process.

FIVE VITAL QUESTIONS

Plans must provide an answer for each

Stripped down to their essentials, plans contain five key elements. Each element responds to a vital question:

- **What?** What are the objectives of the plan? What is it that must be accomplished?
- **Where?** At what particular place must the plan be carried out, the resources obtained, or the results delivered?
- **When?** What is the deadline date? When must the plan be initiated and completed? How much time will be allowed?
- **How?** What strategy or tactics should be employed? What are the prescribed policies, procedures, sequence, and rules that must be followed?
- **Who?** Who will be responsible for the plans' implementation? Who has the authority to command the necessary resources, make personnel assignments, and exercise control?

Key Concepts

1. A Management Information System is a set of procedures for collecting, analyzing, and reporting past, present, and projected information from within and outside of an organization. Managers use this information in planning, decision making, and controlling operations.
2. Management Information Systems use manual, mechanical, and electronic methods to process data so that it is readily available in a usable form. The information provided should be useful, timely, and affordable.
3. Decision making uses estimates of projected conditions to help choose a specific course of action for the future from among a number of possible alternatives.
4. Decision makers combine personal judgment with formal projection methods. They may use a systematic process which involves (a) defining the problem, (b) setting objectives, (c) studying information, (d) creating possible solutions, (e) evaluating solutions, and (f) choosing the best alternative.
5. Planning is a process of deciding in advance what an organization will do, where and when it will be done, how it will be done, and who will do it.
6. Plans may be strategic, tactical, short-term, or long-range. The quality of plans may be improved using an orderly procedure consisting of (a) setting objectives, (b) establishing strategies and tactics, (c) setting a timetable, (d) checking for specificity, flexibility, and feasibility, and (e) integrating planning with reporting and control procedures.

Review Questions

1. Define, explain or identify each of the following key terms and phrases found on the pages indicated.

   database (p. 348)
   data processing (p. 348)
   decision making (p. 351)

information   (p. 346)
Management Information System   (p. 346)
objectives   (p. 355)
on line   (p. 349)
planning   (p. 354)
policy   (p. 355)
primary data   (p. 348)
procedure   (p. 355)
program   (p. 355)
rule   (p. 355)
secondary data   (p. 348)
strategies   (p. 355)
tactics   (p. 356)

2. What is a Management Information System?
3. Give some examples of internal sources of information that could be useful in business planning and decision making.

4. What is data processing and why is it important to the management of an organization?
5. Name the three main factors a manager must consider when planning what information should be derived from a Management Information System.
6. The text discusses two important ways to evaluate alternate courses of action when making decisions. Describe them.
7. What are the six steps in the decision-making process described in the text?
8. What are some of the advantages of systematic planning?
9. Distinguish between a policy, procedure, program, and rule.
10. What is the difference between strategies and tactics?

Case Critique 19-1
Monitoring $50 Million in Candy

Revco Discount Drug Centers have 1,560 outlets spread around the country. In addition to drugs and cosmetics, Revco sells a lot of candy. About 4 percent of its sales, or $50 million, come from that source, and the chain ranks fourth in the country in total candy sold. For Revco's store managers and central purchasing managers, keeping the right amount in stock is a gargantuan task. The stores draw their supplies from eight warehouses which must be ready to ship stock when requested.

Each store manager makes his or her own decision on how much to order each normal week and how much to order in advance for the major holidays like Halloween and Valentine's Day. Revco has decided that its central information system need not know exactly what each store has in its regular weekly inventory, but it does keep track of holiday store inventories. If a store orders what appears to be too much for a holiday, the central buyer reduces the amount of that order.

Much more control is exercised of stock shipments into and out of the central depots. The purchasing managers receive daily information of shipments into the warehouse and weekly data for outgoing shipments. The weekly computer printouts reporting warehouse inventories provide the following information:

a. Inventory on hand at end of week.
b. Amount shipped to stores during the week.
c. Amount shipped for each of previous six weeks.
d. Total shipped for the previous 13-week period.
e. Amount on order but not received.
f. Date and amount of last shipment received at warehouse.
g. Items that are out of stock.
h. For out of stock items, amount that could have been shipped if item had been in stock.
i. For all items, comparable shipments for 13-week period one year ago.

All purchases to suppliers are issued on a weekly basis. Data about what is held in the stores is calculated from shipment records and periodic hand-posted inventory reports from store managers.

1. Upon what kinds of information does the Revco management information system for candy purchases and control depend?
2. Is Revco's information system a manual, mechanical, or electronic system? Why?

3. What would be needed to make Revco's an online inventory control system, so far as its stores were concerned?
4. What is the reason that Revco wants to know what items are out of stock in its warehouses (items g and h)?
5. What is the importance of knowing how much was shipped during the past 13 weeks (item d) and for one year ago (item i)?

Source: "Revco Drug's Candy Sales Soar Under Chain's Discount Policy," *Candy Marketer Quarterly,* Vol. 1, No. 2, 1982, p. 40.

■ Case Critique 19-2 ■
Open a Store a Year—Forever!

When Chuck Sims, chief executive officer of Remco Enterprises, Inc., a Houston-based television, stereo, and appliance rental chain, was starting up he had big ideas for the future. Growth was what he had in mind. His basic plan was simple: "Let's open one rental store a year—forever!" How did he decide where that store would be? "We used to say—that's a big city; let's go there. There's got to be a lot of business there; look at all those folks." Following this plan, Remco exploded from a hole in the wall to a company with 20 stores doing $3.6 million annually. The problem was that Chuck Sims no longer had a good idea of where the company was going. He asked himself, "How far into the future should we plan? Two years? Three years? Five? Maybe we should flip a coin," says Sims, "I still had only vague goals in the back of my head, nothing I ever communicated to anyone. I wanted things like a store everywhere in the country, a nice office—all that ego stuff."

1. What was wrong with Chuck Sims' planning process?
2. What was a prime missing ingredient in Sims' plans and planning process?
3. When Sims tried to decide how far he should look ahead, what kind of plan was he concerned about? What kind of a plan was the one for opening a store a year?
4. What do you think of the way in which Sims picked new store locations? How would you improve the process?

Source: Lucien Rhodes, "He Learned You Can't Do It All Alone," *INC,* March 1980, p. 41.

Chapter 20

Accounting
for Managerial
and Financial
Control

1 ACCOUNTING IS A NUMERICAL INFORMATION SYSTEM that

Records
Classifies
Summarizes
Interprets
a company's transactions

2 ACCOUNTING IS USED TWO WAYS:

internally by a company's managers and externally by investors, bankers, creditors, and the government.

Managerial accounting   Financial accounting

3 ACCOUNTING PRINCIPLES

provide standardized ways of recording and classifying financial data. All accounting procedures are based on the accounting equation:

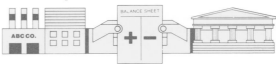

4 COST ACCOUNTING

analyzes expenses, labor, materials, and overhead to find actual and standard costs and per unit costs of goods or services produced.

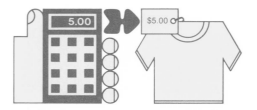

5 A BALANCE SHEET

summarizes a firm's financial position on a particular date.

Assets   DEC. 31   Liabilities + Equity

6 AN INCOME STATEMENT

summarizes what has happened financially to a firm over a period of time.

Income   Expenses   Profit or Loss

7 A STATEMENT OF CHANGES IN FINANCIAL POSITION

explains changes in working capital that take place from one year to another.

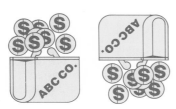

Start   Finish

8 THE INTERPRETATION OF FINANCIAL STATEMENTS

is essential in assessing a company's financial position, its liquidity and profitability, and the quality of its management.

ABC CO.	
Financial position	✔
Liquidity/Profitability	✔
Management	✔

Learning Objectives

The purpose of this chapter is to describe the accounting process and its uses, explain standard accounting principles and practices, show how cost accounting contributes to good management, and explain, illustrate, and interpret the basic financial statements of a business.

As evidence of general comprehension, after studying Chapter 20, you should be able to:

1. *Describe the accounting system and relate it to a management information system.*
2. *Distinguish between managerial and financial accounting.*
3. *Recognize the basic language and procedures of the accounting process and identify and apply the accounting equation.*
4. *Distinguish between variable and fixed expenses, actual and standard costs, and explain how a unit cost is determined.*
5. *Understand the purpose and explain the distinctive features of a balance sheet.*
6. *Understand the purpose and explain the distinctive features of a statement of income and retained earnings.*
7. *Explain the purpose of the statement of changes in financial position.*
8. *Read and interpret selected data from financial statements.*

If your class is using SSweetco: Business Model and Activity File for Business in Action, see Chapter 20 in that book after you complete this chapter. There you will find exercises and activities to help you apply your learning to typical business situations.

Of all the information that is transmitted within a business and between a business and its environment, none is ultimately more important than information about money. Businesses are established for the purpose of making profits. After all the costs are added up and subtracted from income, the resulting profit or loss—the "bottom line" on an income statement—will be the final measure of whether a business succeeds or fails.

The accounting system provides this information about money. It is absolutely fundamental to management because every function and activity of the business depends on adequate funds. (The accounting system is often the central source in the Management Information System. In many companies, the accounting system and MIS are united.) Many of the business's dealings with the outside world also depend on information from the accounting system: paying taxes, borrowing and repaying money, reporting to government agencies, and many others.

The basic purposes of accounting, then, are to allow managers to (a) remain constantly aware of the financial condition of their companies, (b) maintain or improve the financial condition, and (c) carry out and control financial transactions with people and organizations outside the company.

1   THE ACCOUNTING PROCESS

A numerical information system

Like so many other business functions, accounting incorporates various methods for meeting goals. **Accounting** is a numerical information system designed to record, classify, summarize, and interpret an organization's day-to-day business transactions. Basic accounting information is about money. Accounting monitors the flow of cash and the continuing changes in financial obligations. The accounting system's function of supplying financial information is entirely interdependent with a company's other activities and resources. Personnel, equipment, material, and everything else a business uses or produces are reflected in its accounting information.

The sources and nature of accounting information make it necessary to include two kinds of activities in an accounting system: recordkeeping and true accounting. **Recordkeeping** records and classifies raw data that is used in the accounting function. A recordkeeping system keeps track of all transactions in which money changes hands, whether in the form of cash, credit, or some other kind of financial obligation. The main responsibility of recordkeeping is to make sure that there is an accurate written record of every transaction. The records may be classified or summarized in many different ways, as required by the accounting system.

True accounting focuses on the analytical requirements of keeping and using financial records. Accountants work out the methods used by recordkeepers. They determine the classifications in which records must be placed. They summarize the data to make it usable for decision making. They interpret the information to clarify its true meaning for the current and future operations of the business.

ACTION BRIEF

From Ticket to Journal to Ledger, Automatically. Lois Brozey, who runs a small accounting firm, tells the story of a laundry whose books she straightened out. Before her arrival, not only the shirts were misplaced, so were the customers' bills. She started with a fundamental change in the laundry ticket itself. A three-part ticket was chosen. The lower part is the customer's receipt and is returned with the bundle. The two other parts contain identical information: customer's name and address, mark, route number, date, and total amount of the job. One part goes to the driver in place of a weekly summary sheet. The other part goes to the accounting department. To simplify sales analysis, a different colored ticket is used for each class of work—laundry, rugs, etc. The accounting ticket goes to a distribution machine that automatically sorts and records the data in a sales journal. A standard bookkeeping machine then posts the data on a ledger card to a customer's account and also prepares the customer's monthly statement. Accounts receivable are no longer scrambled, and customer's bills are mailed on time.

Source: Lois A. Brozey, "Modernizing a Laundry's Accounting System," Management Accounting, May 1982, p. 55.

In a small retail store, for instance, the distinction between accounting and recordkeeping is clear. The recordkeeper actually writes records of business transactions: sales, rent payments, payroll, inventory purchases and so forth. An accountant decides how the records are to be organized and how they are to be grouped together and interpreted. The accountant puts the data into useful form for deciding what price to set on new merchandise, when to undertake business expansion or reduction, and how to pay for new display racks. All of the information will be extracted so that any necessary reports may be made, and income taxes and payroll taxes may be filed.

The accounting process actually encompasses six phases (as shown in Figure 20-1). Each financial transaction—sales, purchase, payment and so on—is first recorded in a sort of business diary, called a journal. Periodically, the journal entries are sorted out and transferred, or posted, to a record book, or ledger, according to various kinds of accounts. At the end of a month, the total of all income accounts is matched against the total of all outgo accounts to be sure that no monies have been lost or are unaccounted for. In Step 4 (work sheet analyses), the various accounts are broken down or combined to analyze and explain where the money has gone during the month. From this analysis, accounts are arranged to subtract the costs of doing business from a company's sales receipts; the difference represents what accountants call "income", commonly called either profit or loss. In the final step, accounts are sorted and analyzed to

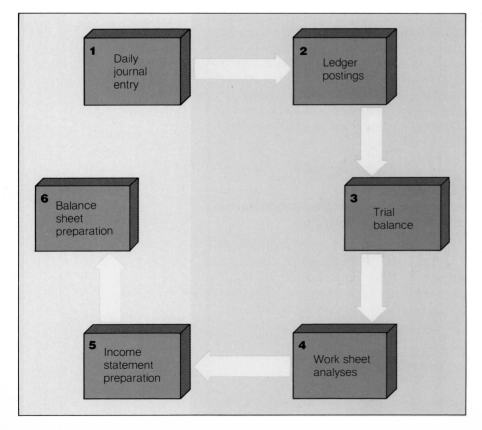

Figure 20-1
The accounting process.

show what is owned by the company (assets), what is owed by the company (liabilities), and what might remain for the owners (equity) of the assets if the liabilities were paid off. These figures appear on the balance sheet. An analysis of what appears on the income statement and the balance sheet provides data for the preparation of the statement of changes in financial position now required by the Securities and Exchange Commission (SEC) for all firms listed on organized stock exchanges. (The statement of changes in financial positions is also required for all companies audited by public accounting firms.)

2 USES OF ACCOUNTING INFORMATION

Managerial and financial

The information produced by the accounting system must meet internal and external needs:

■ Accounting must provide information for managers to use for running their company. This function is usually called *managerial accounting.* It provides information on costs and revenues that managers use for controlling operations and in their efforts to make a profit. Accounting information on sales income, production results, personnel, cost of equipment and materials, size and value of inventory, and other data are used for planning, budgeting, and controlling.

■ Financial information must also be gathered for reporting to and dealing with the world outside the organization. This external *financial accounting* reports financial conditions to stockholders, employees, banks and other financial institutions, and to the government, when required. External reporting is especially important to corporations that must send financial statements to owners, potential investors, brokers, stock exchanges, regulatory agencies, and others. All companies need accurate and complete accounting information to pay income taxes and payroll taxes, such as social security, and to deal with creditors, banks, and government agencies.

3 ACCOUNTING PRINCIPLES

A standardized language and procedure

Accounting methods used today are often complex and sophisticated. The goal of accounting remains fairly simple: to maintain a complete and accurate record of every transaction and organize and summarize the records so that they are useful to management. Accounting is so important to every aspect of operations that it has become a standard means for expressing business results.

THE ACCOUNTING EQUATION

Assets equals liabilities plus equity

Accounting methods are based on an understanding of the general financial makeup of an organization. Every company has control of certain things of value: land, equipment, cash, accounts receivable, and others. These are the company's assets. Assets may be acquired in two ways. They may be acquired through *equity,* or money invested by owners. They may also be borrowed or bought on credit. In either case, when money is owed by the company, it has a *liability.*

Since liabilities and equity are the only two sources of assets, together they must equal assets. This is the *accounting equation:*

Assets = Liabilities + Equity

This equation is basic to modern accounting methods and to understanding the reports accountants use to reflect the financial conditions of businesses.

RECORDING TRANSACTIONS

Two balancing entries every time

To help insure that accounting records are correct, recordkeepers and accountants use a *double-entry method* of recordkeeping. This is a technique for entering every transaction twice in such a way that the sum of all of the first entries will equal the sum of all the second entries if the records are complete and accurate. This provides a built-in check.

An accountant will develop categories of sources for a business's funds and for the uses of these funds. The most basic of the categories are assets, liabilities, and equity. Each of these is broken down further, into specific accounts to maintain more detailed records. Assets might include separate accounts for real estate, equipment, and checking and savings accounts. Liabilities might include notes payable and accounts payable. Equity includes the actual values owned by investors. For a proprietorship, equity would usually be in the form of a single account belonging to one owner. A large corporation might keep a number of different accounts for different types and classes of stock.

For further controls, separate accounts are maintained for specific *expenses* and *revenues.* Expense accounts will include payroll costs, purchase of supplies, rents paid, and other similar operations expenditures. Revenue accounts will include income from sales, interest received, rents received, and so forth.

An accounting system, even for a small business, may be quite complex. A greatly simplified example illustrates the general principle of double-entry accounting. Someone who has recently become a licensed accountant might begin a business to provide computerized recordkeeping and accounting services for small retail stores. Figure 20-2 shows four accounts that might be established for such a business and demonstrates how transactions are recorded in these accounts.

Figure 20-2
Example of double-entry account records.

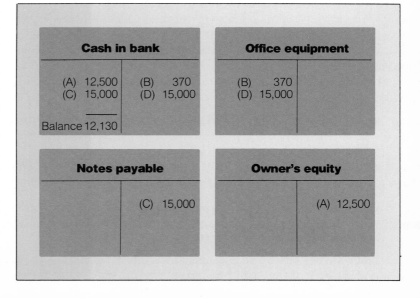

Cash in bank	
(A) 12,500	(B) 370
(C) 15,000	(D) 15,000
Balance 12,130	

Office equipment	
(B) 370	
(D) 15,000	

Notes payable	
	(C) 15,000

Owner's equity	
	(A) 12,500

Each account (sometimes called a T-account because of the T-shape formed by the rulings) has space for two columns of entries below the account title. The left-hand column is always called **debits** and the right-hand column **credits.** Some general rules for entries are:

■ For expense and asset accounts, enter a transaction on the *left* if it *increases* the account and on the *right* if it *decreases* the account.

■ For revenue, liability, or equity accounts, enter a transaction on the *right* if it *increases* the account and on the *left* if it *decreases* the account.

These rules are necessary to make the built-in checking mechanism work. It is always possible to check for accuracy by comparing the sum of the left-hand entries with the sum of the right-hand entries. It is also easy to check that assets really do equal liabilities plus equity.

In the first transaction in Figure 20-2, the proprietor takes $12,500 and deposits it in the business checking account (A). This increases the account (an asset) and is entered in the left column of "cash in bank." It also increases equity, since it is the owner's investment and is entered in the right column of "owner's equity." The owner then writes a check for $370 to buy a new desk. This decreases "cash in bank" and is placed in the right column. It increases "office equipment," also an asset, and is placed on the left (B). Note that this purchase makes no change to liabilities or equity. Assets have not been increased but have only changed in form from cash to a desk.

The proprietor then borrows $15,000 from a bank to buy a small office computer. The loan increases liabilities (it is a note payable) and increases "cash in bank" (C). The owner writes a $15,000 check for the computer, decreases "cash in bank," and increases "office equipment" (D). In a real accounting system, complications such as depreciation and interest payable would have to be considered.

The "cash in bank" account has been increased by $27,500 and decreased by $15,370. Its present balance is $12,130. The "office equipment" account—the only other asset shown—has been increased by $15,370. Total assets are the sum of the asset accounts: $12,130 + $15,370 = $27,500. This equals the total liabilities ("notes payable") plus equity ("owner's equity"): $15,000 + $12,500 = $27,500. In an actual system with many accounts and entries, numerous other checks are also possible.

Double-entry accounting serves three especially important functions when appropriate accounts are set up:

■ It keeps track of assets and liabilities, showing what form they are in.

■ It keeps accurate records of revenue and expenses.

■ It allows the financial condition of a company to be determined by adding up all account balances for assets, liabilities, and equity.

ACCOUNTING AND RECORDKEEPING PRACTICES

Standardization is required

To be successful, an accounting system must include a large number of standard procedures. Methods must insure that every transaction is recorded. Accounts must be established to accurately reflect the financial activities and condition of the business. Standard practices must be developed controlling how and how often records will be balanced and summarized. The length of time between the preparation of summaries of income, expenses, and profit or loss is called the **accounting period.** Accounting periods may be monthly, quarterly, yearly, or over any other length of time desired by management.

For a number of reasons—including the requirement to pay income taxes and for corporations to report to stockholders—nearly all companies do an annual summary of accounting information in addition to any other summaries they prepare. These annual accounting periods may coincide with the calendar year and end on December 31. They may also end on any other day that is convenient for the organization. A year set up for accounting purposes is called a **fiscal year.** The most common fiscal year—other than the calendar year—begins on July 1. The federal government begins its fiscal year on October 1.

PUBLIC ACCOUNTANTS
They certify accounting accuracy

Many companies—especially corporations—must make statements of their financial condition to the public, to organizations such as stock exchanges, and to the government. Such statements must usually be examined for accuracy by independent accountants. These public accountants are licensed by the states after meeting rigorous requirements. An accountant who is licensed to express an opinion on the completeness and accuracy of a company's financial reports is a Certified Public Accountant (CPA). Most states require a college degree in accounting, passing scores on a series of accounting tests, and a minimum period of accounting experience before granting certification.

AUDITS
A means of verifying accuracy

An **audit** is a careful examination of accounting methods and of financial records and reports to insure that the financial activities and condition of a company are being truly and completely reported. When they are required for presentation to the public, to the government or to lending institutions, audits are most commonly performed by independent CPA's. Companies also often have internal auditors for their own assurance of accuracy. The government may also perform audits, especially when tax disputes exist.

ACCOUNTING STANDARDS
For consistency and credibility

Accountants adhere to what are known as generally accepted accounting practices, or GAAP. Since 1973, however, the Financial Accounting Standards Board (FASB) has been designated by the SEC and the Institute of Certified Public Accountants to establish rules governing the preparation of financial reports. The intention of GAAP and of FASB is to establish methods of reporting that are consistent and comparable

TABLE 20-1
How LIFO Accounting Changes the Valuation of Inventories*

Inventory Accounts	1983	1982	1981
Finished goods	$18,750,128	$14,260,256	$13,783,625
Goods in process	9,179,649	9,553,797	9,879,875
Raw materials and manufacturing supplies	18,928,563	17,825,964	20,107,876
Total	$46,858,340	$41,640,017	$43,771,376
LIFO adjustment	4,429,179	1,547,347	—0—
Total	$42,429,161	$40,092,670	$43,771,376

*XYZ Furniture Industries, Inc., changed from FIFO to LIFO method of pricing its inventories on December 31, 1981. This had the effect of lowering the value of the inventories shown on its balance sheet while adding to its cost of goods sold and reducing its net income.

between companies and that reflect honestly the financial transactions and conditions of a business, especially one that is publicly owned.

Two areas of accounting practices have, in recent years, gotten considerable attention. These involve the valuation of inventories and the adjustment for the effects of inflation.

Inventory accounting offers a choice of two methods: FIFO or LIFO. **FIFO** means first in, first out. Under this system, the accountant assumes that the cost at which an inventory was accumulated will be charged to the finished goods made from them when sold. As a result, in times of rising prices, this system makes profits look better than they may really be. **LIFO,** on the otherhand, means last in, first out. Under this system, the accountant charges the latest costs of accumulating inventories against the cost of goods sold. In times of rising prices, this system makes profits look worse than they may really be. There are arguments for either method, but many major firms have chosen the LIFO system because they feel that this approach is more realistic and offers tax benefits. Table 20-1 shows the effect of LIFO on one hypothetical company's earnings.

Rising prices affect much more than inventories. Most importantly price inflation also affects the cost of replacing other assets such as land, building, and equipment. Accordingly, many firms add a note to their financial statements (they are encouraged to do so by the SEC) showing a comparison between actual values and what they might have been if inflation had not taken place. Table 20–2 shows how a hypothetical company reports this comparison.

4   COST ACCOUNTING PRACTICES

Invaluable for managerial control

A specialized form of accounting—cost accounting—is particularly important to managerial control of operations. **Cost accounting** consists of a set of procedures used to determine the total costs of performing a business activity and to find out in detail the many different sources of the total cost. Cost accounting usually has three main purposes:

TABLE 20-2
How Rising Prices Might Affect Data Reported on Financial Statements

	1983*	1982*	1981*	1980*	1979*
Net Sales					
As reported	$5,446.7	$5,469.8	$4,933.1	$4,155.0	$3,604.0
In constant 1983 dollars	5,446.7	6,066.3	6,215.6	5,792.3	5,388.0
Net Income					
As reported	$ 251.0	$ 228.3	$ 310.6	$ 264.8	$ 255.6
In constant 1983 dollars	145.5	152.9	330.2	307.2	338.4
In current cost 1983 dollars	130.5	157.1			
Net Assets at Year End					
As reported	$2,449.6	$2,133.4	$1,966.7	$1,748.2	$1,563.4
In constant 1983 dollars	3,663.2	3,471.2	3,419.6	3,230.6	3,054.7
In current cost 1983 dollars	3,950.4	3,968.4			
Average Consumer Price Index					
Yearly	268.5	242.1	213.1	192.6	179.6

*All figures are in millions of dollars (except for the Consumer Price Index).

■ It provides information about expenses so as to determine whether a profit has been made. This is a part of the normal accounting process.

■ It finds out the exact sources of expenses to help with efforts to reduce costs and increase profits.

■ It reassembles detailed cost information needed in setting sales prices of goods or services produced.

Generally speaking, the costs of business activities may be classified as either variable or fixed.

VARIABLE EXPENSES

Rise and fall with changes in activity

Variable expenses include materials and labor directly used in the production of goods and services. Also covered by this category are other resources for which consumption varies with the amount of production carried out. Starting materials and labor, power for running equipment, and freight costs are variable. A plant that manufactures light bulbs, for instance, will have far greater expenses for materials and labor if it makes ten million light bulbs than if it makes only one million.

FIXED EXPENSES
Remain stable regardless of activity levels

In addition to variable costs resulting from the amount of production, companies have to pay for the unavoidable costs of simply staying in business. These *fixed expenses* include administrative, secretarial, clerical, and other salaries, insurance and taxes on real estate and equipment, rent, and utilities, in addition to other expenses. These costs are often called "burden" or "overhead."

ACTUAL COST ACCOUNTING
Finds out what costs really were

A common goal of cost accounting is to find out what portion of total dollars spent by a firm results from a particular activity. For instance, a company might want to know the total amount spent for shipping during the past year. Accountants would first bring together all of the direct costs of shipping: postage, freight charges, wages of packers and shippers, cost of packing materials, reduction in value of wrapping and shipping equipment caused by depreciation, and others. To the sum of these costs, they would add a portion of the company's overhead costs. How much of the overhead is added may be determined in different ways. Accountants may, for instance, determine that of the total hours worked by all of the firm's employees, 14 percent were devoted to the shipping function. They might then apportion 14 percent of the overhead to shipping.

The cost of a particular product can be calculated in the same way. Adding up all variable costs of a product and apportioning part of the total fixed costs will give the total production costs for that product during an accounting period. This figure can be made more useful for many purposes by turning it into a *unit cost.* This is derived by dividing the total production cost by the number of units produced. If a manufacturer finds that $1 million was spent on producing a particular kind of valve during the year and 25,000 valves were made, the unit cost for the valve would be $40.

STANDARD COSTS
Specify what costs ought to be

Actual cost accounting is intended to show what it actually cost to produce a unit of output. *Standard costs* try to show what is *should* cost to produce the output. Accountants, engineers, and managers usually work together to set cost standards. They analyze the materials, labor, and overhead required for a production unit. They decide on the minimum amount of expected waste and plan efficient work methods. They then assign dollar values to everything that goes into this ideal production method and determine what a product would cost when everything works as planned. Actual costs can then be compared with the standard costs. Any serious differences should be investigated because ways of reducing actual costs may be discovered.

5 BALANCE SHEET

Balances the accounting equation on a particular date

The information that is collected and organized in the accounting system is presented and used in many ways. Three summary reports show the financial position and performance of a company: the balance sheet, the income statement, and the statement of changes in financial position.

The *balance sheet* is the main report of overall financial condition. It shows the assets, liabilities, and equity of a company at a particular time, usually on the last day of a fiscal year. The balance sheet shows what a company owns or controls and what the sources of the assets are.

Figure 20-3 shows the balance sheet for Abaco Industries (a hypothetical company) on December 31, of 198X. The statement is arranged according to the accounting equation. Assets are entered in the top section, liabilities in the center, and equity at the bottom. It can be seen that the total assets are equal to, or in balance with, the combined liabilities and equity.

Current Assets   The assets section of the statement is divided into current assets (expected to be turned into cash in less than a year) and long-term assets. The current assets of Abaco Industries include (a) cash and temporary investments that can be easily turned into cash, (b) accounts receivable, (c) inventories, including finished products, work in process, and materials and supplies, and (d) prepaid items, like leases and insurance policies, that have been paid for but have not expired.

Fixed Assets   Fixed, or long-term, assets typically consist of land, buildings, and equipment owned by the company. These fixed assets, especially those of buildings and equipment, are usually listed at the price that was paid for them, minus their accumulated depreciation. As a delivery truck grows older, for example, its value decreases—or depreciates—due to wear and tear. Federal tax laws allow a company to charge a depreciation expense each year against the original cost of the truck. If it cost $40,000, the company might be allowed to charge one-fifth of the cost (or $8,000) each year as depreciation. The balance sheet after the third year would show for the truck $40,000 less accumulated depreciation of $24,000 for a net asset of $16,000.

When one company buys another and pays more money than the concrete assets of the purchased company, goodwill may be included as an asset. The excess payment is in return for the good reputation, customer relations, work methods, and other intangible assets of the purchased company. Those intangibles are called goodwill.

Liabilities   The Abaco Industries balance sheet also divided liabilities into current and long-term. Current liabilities include short-term debts, long-term debts due for repayment during the current year, and accounts payable to suppliers and other creditors. Accrued liabilities are obligations that have built up but that are not yet due for payment. Examples are interest owed on debts or money owed to employees for their

Figure 20-3
Example of a balance sheet.

ABACO INDUSTRIES INC.

Consolidated Balance Sheet
December 31, 198X

ASSETS

Current Assets

Cash, certificates of deposit, and marketable securities	$68,000	
Accounts receivable	44,000	
Inventories	40,000	
Prepaid expenses	2,000	
Total current assets		$154,000

Property, Plant, and Equipment

Buildings	$40,000		
Machinery and equipment	68,000		
	108,000		
Less accumulated depreciation	60,000	48,000	
Land		14,000	
Goodwill		2,000	64,000
Total assets			$218,000

LIABILITIES AND STOCKHOLDERS' EQUITY

Current Liabilities

Accounts payable	$16,000	
Accrued liabilities	6,000	
Current maturities of long-term debt	1,000	
Accrued income taxes payable	5,000	
Total current liabilities		28,000
Long-Term Debt		4,000
Total liabilities		$32,000

Stockholders' Equity

Common stock: 10,000 shares outstanding	38,000	
Retained earnings	148,000	186,000
Total liabilities and stockholders' equity		$218,000

work during the current pay period. Income tax is another accrued expense. The amount owed increases every day income is earned, but the taxes only have to be paid quarterly or annually.

Long-term liabilities consist mainly of bonds, notes, and mortgages that do not have to be repaid during the year. Abaco Industries has a relatively small long-term debt of $4,000. It is the unpaid portion of the mortgage on its building. Large corporations frequently have several entries under long-term liabilities, such as mortgages, bonds of various types, and long-term notes.

Equity   The remaining section of the balance sheet shows the monetary value of owners' equity. Earnings the company has generated but not paid out to investors still belong to the owners and are listed in the equity section under "Retained Earnings."

The point of a balance sheet is to show the financial condition of a company. Abaco Industries, on the date of the statement, had $218,000 worth of assets. The balance sheet shows what form the assets were in, how much money the company owes, and where the capital that produced the assets came from.

6 INCOME STATEMENT

Reports profit or loss over a period of time

An *income statement*—technically a "statement of earnings and retained earnings"—is an accounting report that shows the revenue received and expenses paid during a certain period of operations. One of its main purposes is to show the profit or loss resulting from operations. The income statement is often called a "profit and loss statement," or an "operating statement." It shows income and its sources and expenses and their sources. It reports the financial results of a period of operations, usually a month, a quarter, a half-year, or a year. The income statement for Abaco Industries, for the 52 weeks ending December 31, 198X is shown in Figure 20-4.

Revenues   Abaco Industries' revenues of $310,000 come from two sources. Net sales equal the total income from the sale of goods and services after refunds, discounts, and other similar adjustments have been deducted. Other income includes interest earned on investments, savings accounts, loans, and rental from properties.

Expenses   Expenses are divided into four major categories, plus taxes. *Cost of sales* (also called "cost of goods or products sold") includes all expenses that were necessary for producing the goods and services sold. Production materials and labor, direct supervision of production, utilities for production facilities, equipment maintenance, and other similar costs are placed in this category. Depreciation of production facilities is also included. *Depreciation* is an expense resulting from the loss in value of equipment, buildings, or other fairly permanent assets caused by normal wear and tear and age.

The overhead costs of marketing, selling, and distributing products and of generally administering operations are shown as a second separate

Figure 20-4
Example of income statement
(statement of earnings and
retained earnings).

ABACO INDUSTRIES INC.

Statement of Consolidated Income and Retained Earnings
For the 52 weeks ended December 31, 198X

Revenues

Net sales	$300,000	
Other income	10,000	
Total revenues		$310,000

Costs and expenses

Cost of products sold	$230,000	
Marketing, administrative, and general expenses	29,000	
Interest expense	1,000	
Total costs and expenses		260,000
Earnings before income taxes		50,000
Less income taxes		20,000
Net income		$30,000

Retained earnings

At beginning of the year (from last year's balance sheet)	118,000
Retained earnings before dividends	$148,000
Deduct cash dividends declared	10,000
Retained earnings at end of year	$138,000
Net income (or earnings) per share	$3.00
Dividends per share	$1.00

expense category. A third expense category is interest paid on borrowed money used in the business. Subtracting the total of these three kinds of expense from total revenues shows the company's earnings before income taxes. The fourth major expense, income taxes, is then deducted.

Income   Subtracting income taxes paid produces the final earnings—or profit—for the year. Abaco Industries paid $20,000 in federal and state income taxes, leaving a net profit of $30,000.

Retained Earnings   The income statement also gives additional information on retained earnings. Companies usually keep part of their earnings in the business and use them to expand, to improve or buy new facilities, or in other ways. Abaco Industries up to the beginning of the period shown in the income statement had reinvested $118,000 this way. Of the latest year's earnings, $10,000 was paid to the stockholders as dividends and $20,000 was retained. This left a new balance of $138,000 for retained earnings. Earnings per share is calculated by dividing the $30,000 profit by the 10,000 shares of stock outstanding listed in Figure 20-3, which is equal to $3.00 per share. Dividends per share is smaller than this. It is found by dividing the $10,000 declared in dividends by the number of shares, or $1.00 per share.

7   STATEMENT OF CHANGES IN FINANCIAL POSITION

Reveals where the money came from and how it was used

The last of the major accounting reports is the *statement of changes in financial position,* also called a "funds statement." This statement explains the overall changes in the balance sheet from one year to the next. It shows the sources of funds the business used during the accounting period and the uses to which the funds were put. It shows how ongoing operations are financed and gives an idea of a company's ability to finance future operations.

The sources and uses of funds in a funds statement are described in Chapters 13 and 14. Sources include earnings from operations, depreciation, revenue from selling property, and money gained from debt financing.

Funds are used for adding capital assets, such as buildings and machinery, paying dividends, paying off part of a loss on a discontinued operation, and repaying borrowed money.

A statement of changes in financial position deals with current funds and current uses of funds. If the funds received are greater than the funds used, the difference can be added to working capital. Working capital is discussed in Chapter 13. It is important in a financial statement because it shows a company's capabilities for meeting upcoming financial obligations and for financing operations.

8   INTERPRETATION OF FINANCIAL STATEMENTS

Analyzes a firm's financial position and the quality of its management

Financial statements reveal a great deal of information about the assets, liabilities, ownership, and operating success of companies. More information can be derived from the statements by analyzing and interpreting them. This is also the job of accountants, and it is one of their greatest contributions to successful business operation.

Most small firms fail because of poor management. But that is only the outward sign. Internally, the fault often lies with an abysmal ignorance of basic recordkeeping and accounting practices on the part of the owner. When Frank Taylor, for instance, bought a faltering screw manufacturing business in Rockford, Illinois, he found that he not only had to change what was happening on the factory floor, he had to transform the entire bookkeeping system. "The previous owners had no idea what their costs were," he said. "In addition, accounts receivable were allowed to run 50 days late." Taylor installed a standardized accounting system so that he could keep track of revenues and expenses. Then he put in a simple cost accounting system to assess variable and fixed costs so that he could know what his unit costs were and price his products accordingly. This knowledge led Taylor to drop low-profit, standard screws and to concentrate on high markup custom-made screws for industrial use.

Source: Sanford L. Jacobs, "How an Enterprise Revived Faltering Firm Despite Slump," The Wall Street Journal, June 7, 1982, p. 23.

If accounting is so important to a business, why do so many people shy away from accounting responsibilities? What might be done to help managers become more aware of the need to know about generally accepted accounting practices and terminology?

RATIO ANALYSIS

Selected comparisons of financial report data

Accountants and managers use a technique called *ratio analysis* to help interpret financial statements. This technique compares certain categories of assets, earnings, expenses, liabilities, and equity to make statements more informative. By computing ratios, the performance and condition of one company can be compared with that of other companies and with standards of performance established by analysts. Data on financial ratios in companies and industries is available from Dun & Bradstreet, Inc., from other business publishers, from trade associations, and, in some cases, from government publications. Individual analysts often use information provided by corporations in their annual or quarterly reports. All figures used below are extracted from either the balance sheet or the statement of earnings and retained earnings for Abaco Industries.

LIQUIDITY INDICATORS

Measures the ability of a firm to pay its debts

Several of the most important ratios indicate the extent to which a firm has sufficient liquid assets to meet its financial obligations. These are called measures of *liquidity.* Other closely related indicators show how effectively current funds are being used to create income for the company.

■ The *current ratio* is a measure of a company's ability to pay current debts and other financial obligations. The current ratio equals current assets divided by current liabilities. Although factors specific to the condition of an individual company should be considered, many analysts believe that the current ratio should be two or higher. A company with twice as much in current assets as current liabilities should have no difficulty making payments as they are due. A company with a current ratio of one is likely to have recurring problems of coming up with cash in time to pay bills. A current ratio of less than one is a clear indication that more funds will have to be located to keep the company operating.

$$\frac{\text{Current}}{\text{ratio}} = \frac{\text{current assets}}{\text{current liabilities}} = \frac{\$154,000}{\$\ 28,000} = 5.5$$

■ The *quick ratio,* or *acid-test ratio,* is a more sensitive indicator of the ability to meet current obligations. It includes as current assets only those assets that can very quickly be used to pay bills: cash, marketable securities, and accounts receivable. These are called quick assets. Other current assets, like inventory or prepaid expenses, may sometimes be difficult or impossible to convert to cash and are eliminated from this ratio.

The acid-test ratio equals quick assets divided by current liabilities. An acid-test ratio of one is usually considered a comfortable minimum.

$$\frac{\text{Quick}}{\text{ratio}} = \frac{\text{current assets} - \text{inventory}}{\text{current liabilities}} = \frac{\$154,000 - \$40,000}{\$28,000} = 4.1$$

■ *Inventory turnover* measures the number of times the average inventory of merchandise is sold, or turned over, during a year. It is computed by dividing the cost of goods sold by the average inventory. The average inventory is usually approximated by adding the inventory level at the beginning of the year with the level at the end of the year and dividing by 2. A similar figure can be computed by using net sales and retail value of inventories which is illustrated below. The meaning of inventory turnover can only be determined by comparing similar companies with one another because it varies considerably. In general, however, a higher inventory turnover will indicate higher sales and a greater potential for creating profit.

$$\frac{\text{Inventory}}{\text{turnover}} = \frac{\text{net sales}}{\text{inventories}} = \frac{\$300,000}{\$\ 40,000} = 7.5 \text{ times}$$

■   Receivables turnover and collection period are also of value since they show how diligent a company is in collecting its bills. **Receivables turnover** is found by dividing net sales by accounts receivable.

$$\frac{\text{Receivables}}{\text{turnover}} = \frac{\text{net sales}}{\text{accounts receivable}} = \frac{\$300,000}{\$\ 44,000} = 6.8 \text{ times}$$

Collection period simply converts the number of times that receivables are turned over into a figure that shows, on average, how long it took the company to collect its bills—the average number of days a bill is left unpaid.

$$\frac{\text{Collection}}{\text{period}} = \frac{365 \text{ days}}{\text{receivables turnover}} = \frac{365 \text{ days}}{6.8} = 53.7 \text{ days}$$

Both the receivables turnover and collection period figures must be compared with industry norms to judge whether they are favorable or not.

PROFITABILITY INDICATORS

Measure how good the firm is at making money

A number of other measures and ratios indicate how profitable a business is, how well it is using its funds, and what kinds of funds are contributing to profits:

■   Comparing a company's **markup** with other similar companies shows the degree of success at generating gross profits from sales. Markup varies greatly among different industries. The markup may be determined by subtracting the cost of goods sold from net sales and dividing the result by the cost of goods sold. Abaco Industries with net sales of $300,000 and a cost of goods of $230,000 has an average markup of 30.4 percent. (Markup for pricing purposes is often calculated by dividing the "difference" figure by the net sales figure. In the previous example, the markup calculated by comparing with sales would be 23.3 percent. Obviously, it is important to determine exactly what markup calculation is used.)

■   **Return on sales,** one of the most common ratios, is also called "ratio of net income to sales," or the "net profit margin." It is calculated by dividing net income (or "net earnings") by net sales. When used as a means of comparing different companies, it is a clear indication of a company's ability to derive profits from sales. For most businesses, this figure is surprisingly low. For supermarkets, for example, this ratio is likely to be less than 3 percent.

$$\text{Return on sales} = \frac{\text{net income}}{\text{net sales}} = \frac{\$\ 30{,}000}{\$300{,}000} = 10.0\%$$

■ *Return on investment* is a measure of how much income was produced from the capital invested in the business by owners. To many analysts, this is the true test of a business's success, since the whole purpose of investing capital in a business is to earn profits. Return on investment can be determined a number of ways. The most commonly used formulas are shown here.

$$\frac{\text{Return on}}{\text{assets}} = \frac{\text{net income}}{\text{total assets}} = \frac{\$\ 30{,}000}{\$218{,}000} = 13.8\%$$

$$\frac{\text{Return on}}{\text{equity}} = \frac{\text{net income}}{\text{stockholders' equity}} = \frac{\$\ 30{,}000}{\$186{,}000} = 16.1\%$$

■ *Capitalization ratios* show the proportions of funds used by a business that come from certain sources. They indicate the extent to which a company is relying on borrowed funds or permanent owners' investment to carry on operations. The debt-to-equity ratio is calculated by dividing total liabilities by stockholders' equity. This ratio will be less than one for a company with more equity than debt financing, more than one when debt financing exceeds equity, and equal to one when the two sources of funds are equal. A similar measure, known as debt-to-assets ratio, is derived by dividing stockholders' equity by total assets. This index shows the proportion of the assets that resulted from permanent owners' investment.

$$\frac{\text{Debt-to-equity}}{\text{ratio}} = \frac{\text{total liabilities}}{\text{stockholders' equity}} = \frac{\$\ 34{,}000}{\$186{,}000} = 17.2\%$$

A similar measure is derived by dividing stockholders' equity by total assets.

$$\frac{\text{Debt-to-assets}}{\text{ratio}} = \frac{\text{stockholders' equity}}{\text{total assets}} = \frac{\$186{,}000}{\$218{,}000} = 85.3\%$$

This ratio, or percentage, shows the proportion of a company's assets that have been acquired or developed from permanent investment by the owners or stockholders. As discussed earlier in Chapter 13, the greater the dependency of a company's financing of its assets on debt, as opposed to equity, the greater the leverage the company has. The use of some leverage is usually considered good business. Too much leverage, however, is considered dangerous. Too little or too much can be judged by comparing the two ratios above with the norms for the industry to which the business belongs.

Key Concepts

1. Accounting is a numerical information system designed to record, classify, summarize, and interpret business transactions.
2. Accounting provides information (*a*) for inter-nal use (managerial accounting) in planning, budgeting, cost estimating, and controlling activities and (*b*) for external use (financial accounting) in paying taxes and reporting busi-

ness results to interested outside parties.

3. Accountants establish double-entry record-keeping systems in which every transaction is entered twice so that the records can be easily checked for accuracy and completeness. The records are organized according to the accounting equation.

4. Cost accounting is a specialized accounting process for determining the actual or standard costs of activities or products.

5. A balance sheet is a statement of financial condition on a particular date. It shows the amount and type of firm's assets, amounts and types of liabilities, and owner's equity.

6. An income statement is a summary of revenues and expenses over a period of operation. It shows profit or loss for the period.

7. A statement of changes in financial position shows the amounts and sources of funds acquired during an operating period and how the funds were used.

8. Accountants use comparisons between different categories of assets, revenues, expenses, liabilities, and equity to help interpret financial statements. The comparisons are often expressed as ratios which are useful for comparisons with similar companies and trends within the same company.

Review Questions

1. Define, explain or identify each of the following key terms and phrases found on the pages indicated.

   accounting   (p. 362)
   accounting equation   (p. 365)
   accounting period   (p. 367)
   audit   (p. 367)
   balance sheet   (p. 371)
   capitalization ratios   (p. 379)
   collection period   (p. 378)
   cost accounting   (p. 368)
   cost of sales   (p. 373)
   credits   (p. 366)
   current ratio   (p. 377)
   debits   (p. 366)
   depreciation   (p. 373)
   double-entry method   (p. 365)
   equity   (p. 365)
   expenses   (p. 365)
   FIFO   (p. 368)
   financial accounting   (p. 364)
   fiscal year   (p. 367)
   fixed expenses   (p. 370)
   income statement   (p. 373)
   inventory turnover   (p. 377)
   liability   (p. 365)
   LIFO   (p. 368)
   liquidity   (p. 377)
   managerial accounting   (p. 364)
   markup   (p. 378)
   quick ratio (acid-test ratio)   (p. 377)

   ratio analysis   (p. 377)
   receivables turnover   (p. 378)
   recordkeeping   (p. 362)
   return on investment   (p. 379)
   return on sales   (p. 378)
   revenues   (p. 365)
   standard costs   (p. 370)
   statement of changes in financial position   (p. 375)
   true accounting   (p. 362)
   unit cost   (p. 370)
   variable expenses   (p. 369)

2. Describe the four basic activities that must be performed by an accounting system.

3. What is the difference between recordkeeping and true accounting?

4. How does managerial accounting differ from financial accounting?

5. What is the accounting equation? Why must both sides of the equation be equal?

6. Why is double-entry recordkeeping in accounting so widely used?

7. What are actual costs and standard costs? Why would many managers want to use both in decision making and control?

8. Why does a company prepare a balance sheet?

9. What is an income statement? How is it different from a balance sheet?

10. What is the purpose of the statement of changes in financial position?

Case Critique 20-1
Cooking the Books

Investors who bought shares publicly in Mc-Cormick & Co., the spice company, discovered one day that the profits the company had been reporting were lower than they actually were. McCormick's management conceded that some of its managers had been fooling the company's accountants in order to make their performances look good. For example, sales in the grocery products division were inflated by counting as "sold" goods that had been taken off the shelves in the warehouses but not shipped. In some instances, shipping documents were backdated in January to give the appearance of earlier sales in December. Inventories of black pepper were manipulated at the end of the year by postdating shipments or by simply not counting pepper as inventory when it should have been. The company president and treasurer said they knew that false records were being kept. They did not feel that this was wrong, however, since they were reporting more, rather than less, profits so far as income taxes were con-cerned. The Securities and Exchange Commission, however, was not pleased with the explanation of why the company had "cooked the books."

1. Which form of accounting used by the company, managerial or financial, was especially unacceptable to the shareholders? Why?
2. What accounting procedure should have caught the juggling of the true records?
3. On what financial statement in particular would the misrepresented profits appear? On which would the misstated inventories appear?
4. Why should it be any concern of the SEC that the company used unacceptable accounting practices to report its profits? (Review Chapter 14, if necessary.)

Source: Jerry Knight, "McCormick Has a Need for All Its Spices," *The Washington Post,* June 7, 1982, p. 1.

Case Critique 20–2
It's OK Only if the Financial Shoe Fits

The chances are pretty good that at one time or another you have bought a pair of shoes from Melville Corporation. It operates 1,261 Thom McAn outlet stores. Melville isn't too happy about its shoe business, since it doesn't really make money very fast. Melville is more enthusiastic about its Marshall men's clothing stores, its Mack Drugs chain, and its Kay-Bee's toys and hobbies shops. When Melville gets unhappy with the results of one of its businesses, it closes it down or sells it. In recent years, the company got rid of Clothes Bin, a network of off-price women's apparel shops and Metro, a men's pants manufacturer. What kind of results does it take a particular business to make Melville happy? It's simple, says the company's president: "Just give us a 20 percent return on equity and a five percent return on sales." On average, the company does far better than that.

1. Which kind of financial indicator, in general, and financial ratios, in particular, appear to be most important to Melville Corporation?
2. Why might Melville wish to get rid of businesses that do not come up to the ratio levels the company prescribes?
3. According to the information in the case, would Melville be likely to acquire a business that made a profit of $100,000 on an equity investment of $1,000,000 and sales of $2,000,000? Why?
4. If Melville were only concerned with the two ratios mentioned in the case, overlooking what other key indicators might lead to financial trouble? Why?

Source: Howard Rudnitsky, "Fancy Footwork," *Forbes,* March 29, 1982, p. 74.

Chapter 21

Business Forecasts and Budgets

1 BUSINESS FORECASTS are projections of future business conditions.

Background forecasts

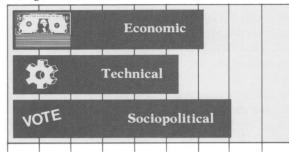

Business forecasts

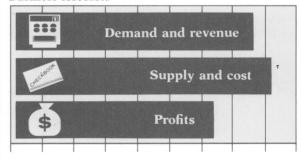

2 FORECASTING TECHNIQUES include

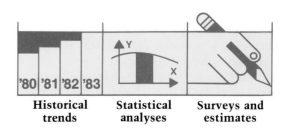

Historical trends

Statistical analyses

Surveys and estimates

3 BUDGETS SERVE AS GUIDES FOR PLANNING AND CONTROL

They are specific financial plans that anticipate overall company income and outlay and establish controls for departmental expenditures.

DEPT. A   DEPT. B   DEPT. C

4 THE MAJOR KINDS OF BUDGETS are

Sales
Cash
Expense
Capital expenditures

5 BUDGETS MAY BE EITHER FIXED OR FLEXIBLE

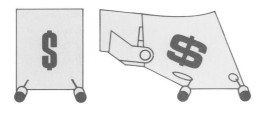

6 THE VARIANCE REPORT

is the principal form of budgetary control.

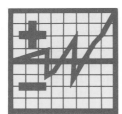

Learning Objectives

The purpose of this chapter is to explain the uses of business forecasts and describe some of the techniques for making them, describe and illustrate various kinds of budgets, and explain a flexible budget and show how it is used for managerial control.

As evidence of general comprehension, after studying Chapter 21, you should be able to:

1. *Distinguish between background forecasts and business forecasts and identify the sources of data for each.*
2. *Identify the three basic forecasting techniques.*
3. *Define a budget and explain its purpose.*
4. *Explain the purposes and uses of the sales, expense, cash, and capital expenditure budgets.*
5. *Distinguish between a fixed budget and a flexible budget and explain how the latter may be used for managerial control purposes.*
6. *Describe a typical variance report and justify its importance as an instrument for budgetary control.*

If your class is using SSweetco: Business Model and Activity File for Business in Action, see Chapter 21 in that book after you complete this chapter. There you will find exercises and activities to help you apply your learning to typical business situations.

If business managers could really see into the future, their fortunes would be made. If they knew for sure that demand for their products would increase in three years, they could plan now to increase facilities and inventory and beat the competition. If they knew that a material they needed was about to become scarce, they could make production changes to decrease their dependence on that material. If they knew that the government was going to pass a law that would make their products significantly easier or harder to sell, they could take action now to anticipate the change.

Managers cannot, of course, really predict the future, but they can try. Business forecasting is a management activity that uses orderly methods to try to determine what future conditions important to the business will be. Managers use these estimates during the planning process and as an aid to decision making.

Forecasts are routinely translated into formal, numerical plans that help a business to guide and control future operations. The most common of these plans appears in the form of a financial budget. Such budgets help managers to decide in advance how much and in what way money should be spent to keep the business operating and profitable during the time periods immediately ahead.

1   BUSINESS FORECASTS

Numerical expressions of business plans

Most decisions are made with the future in mind. The decision to buy new production machinery may have been made with a view to avoiding the anticipated failure of present equipment or to increase production to meet expected demand. Some of the information needed for this kind of decision comes from forecasts.

A *forecast* is a projection of future business conditions both within a particular company and in the social, political, and economic environment in which the company operates. Forecasts contribute to setting organization objectives. A description of what a company is trying to achieve can have no relevance without some idea of what the future holds. For instance, a goal of increasing sales by 15 percent a year for five years is useless to management unless there is some reason to believe that customer demand will be adequate. Forecasts are also of help in making plans to meet objectives. Having estimates of future costs, for instance, will help managers decide whether to plan for certain activities.

Good forecasts result from well-planned and well-operated management information systems and accounting information systems. The entire collection of organized facts and summaries in these systems may be useful for forecasting future events and conditions. Many forecasts, especially projected sales and costs, will be routinely produced by an accounting system. In other cases, the MIS and accounting information will provide a basis for special studies used in forecasting. Projecting the effects on the profitability of a proposed change in production methods is an example of an analysis of this type.

In general, forecasts may fall into two classes. Some provide a preview of the conditions in the environment outside the company. These are called *background forecasts.* Others forecast the future operations of the company itself. These are called *business forecasts.*

BACKGROUND FORECASTS

Readings of the environment

Plans are the specific guides managers use to control operations. All plans are based on assumptions or beliefs about what the future may hold. If, for example, a company plans to expand its production facilities within the next three years, many factors external to the company will affect the success of that plan. Will the financial markets be in a position to lend money at an affordable rate? Will adequate raw materials be available to support the new production? What will the price of the raw materials be? Will workers be available in sufficient numbers? Will consumers have enough money to buy the goods? Will the government impose any regulations that would make the production more difficult or less profitable?

Obviously, none of these questions can be answered with certainty. Risk is involved in any business decision. The purpose of background forecasting, however, is to gather as much information as possible about projected conditions in the company's environment to reduce uncertainty. The sources of data used in background forecasting are generally the ones used in management information systems: government statistical publications, private abstracts and periodicals, trade associations, government censuses, annual reports, and so forth.

Background forecasts usually try to predict changes in economic and financial conditions, in technological resources, and in the social and political environment.

Economic conditions affect nearly every aspect of a business. Managers and analysts use measures of economic activity called *economic indicators* to try to judge the direction in which the economy is moving. Many indicators may be used: employment statistics, measures of worker productivity, consumer spending, capital investments by businesses, the money supply, interest rates, prices on major stock exchanges, the inflation rate, measures of imports and exports, the gross national product, and many others. As well as giving the general outlook for the economy, many of these measures directly affect the operations of an individual business. Figure 21-1 shows graphs of several commonly used economic indicators.

Forecasts of expected technological changes can have an important effect on the success or failure of a business. Managers must always consider technology for possible application in the company. An equally important consideration is the anticipation of technological changes employed by competitors. Technology makes new products possible. A clearly superior or more desirable product can make an existing product obsolete in months. Technological changes can also increase profitability or allow companies to reduce prices and improve their competitive position. Manufacturing methods, storage and transportation systems, and the use of new materials can all help to reduce production costs.

Social and political changes are often the most difficult to forecast. Changing tastes and expectations among consumers can create important changes in the demand for specific products. Even the public's attitudes

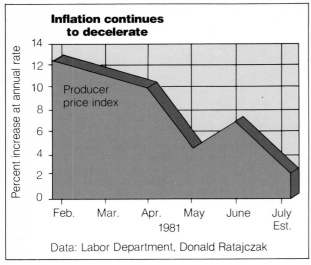

Inflation continues to decelerate

Producer price index

Data: Labor Department, Donald Ratajczak

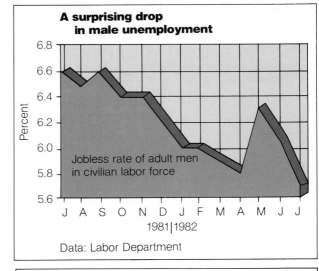

A surprising drop in male unemployment

Jobless rate of adult men in civilian labor force

Data: Labor Department

Wholesale and retail inventories pile up

Inventory-sales ratios*

Wholesale

Retail

Data: Commerce Department, *Business Week* estimates

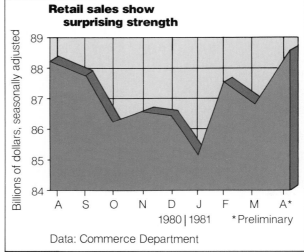

Retail sales show surprising strength

Data: Commerce Department

Source: Adopted from "Economic Diary," edited by Gene Koertz, *Business Week,* with permission of the copyright holder, McGraw-Hill Publications Company, 1981–1982.

Figure 21-1 Economic indicators.

toward manufacturers can affect success. Government regulations can increase costs by requiring expenditures to improve product safety or to reduce pollution. Some products or business activities may be restricted or prohibited. The best defense against such environmental changes is to be well informed and to attempt to devise plans that are flexible enough to be adapted to changing conditions.

BUSINESS FORECASTS

Specific expectations

Much of the information used in managing and planning business operations results from activities within the company itself. Although it is somewhat easier to forecast these internal developments than it is to predict changes in the business environment, uncertainty still remains.

The three most common classifications of forecasts used by individual businesses are demand and revenue, supply and costs, and profits.

■ *Demand and revenue forecasts* of customer demand for products and of sales are used primarily to predict the amount of revenue a company will have to work with in the future. Although sales forecasts are one kind of internal prediction, they depend heavily on background forecasts for their accuracy. General economic conditions, consumer spending, interest rates, and inflation have a strong effect on sales in almost any industry.

Sales forecasts are useful for more than predicting revenues. Many expenses, including direct selling, advertising, and promotion costs, will depend to a great extent on anticipating sales. Expected sales also control plans for production quantities and help to determine a company's breakeven point as discussed in Chapter 12.

■ *Supply and cost forecasts* aim first at getting an accurate idea of what it will cost to operate the company at some future time. This estimate is obviously useful in financial and general management. Forecasts of this kind are also useful for highly detailed planning and management. Projections of the labor supply and of the cost of hiring workers may result in efforts to help workers to be more productive or in more efficient production methods. Forecasts of the availability and costs of starting materials may force managers to use alternate materials or to make other adjustments to reduce waste. Similarly, a retailer's plans will be affected by forecasts of price changes of merchandise.

■ *Profit forecasts* are arrived at through the other projections of revenues and costs. Profit estimates are important because they provide a standard with which to evaluate income and costs. Profit forecasts show whether the company will be able to realize its goals and expectations.

In projecting profits, managers want to be able to use some of the same analyses that are applied to income statements for past operating periods. They want to know the projected profits in dollars, sometimes adjusted to offset the effects of inflation. They also use the ratios of profits to sales and profits to investment. Other standard ratios, such as the current ratio, can be used on projected financial information to estimate the financial condition of the company at some future time. Since growth is one of the most common objectives of businesses, these kinds of projections can be especially important. By assessing the prospects for future resources and obligations, managers are better able to stimulate growth in a controlled setting.

2   FORECASTING TECHNIQUES

More than a crystal ball is needed

Many forecasting techniques in common use today are highly sophisticated and require specialized technical knowledge. The main overall approaches, however, are usually the same, even for complex mathematical analyses. The most common forecasting methods include projecting trends from historical data, analyzing relationships, and using surveys and other specific data-gathering techniques.

HISTORICAL TRENDS

The past predicts the future

Historical trend forecasts reveal the consistent patterns that have occurred in the past and assumes that these will continue in the future. Figure 21-2 shows a historical trend forecast plotted on a graph. If, for example, a company's sales have increased by about 10 percent a year for each of the last five years a forecast would project that sales of a particular product will continue to increase by 10 percent a year. A similar analysis of trends could be based on the historical relationship between two or more variables. A large home-building company might find that in the past sales have increased by 5 percent every time mortgage interest rates have decreased by 0.05 percent. This relationship might be assumed to continue in the future.

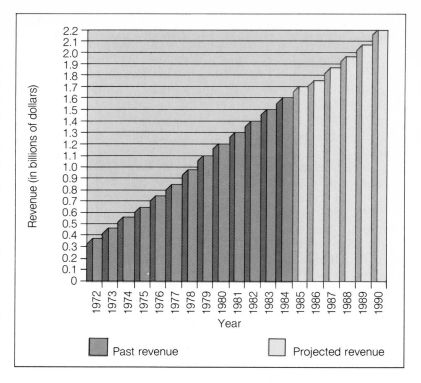

Sometimes, forecasts based on the continuation of past trends can be dangerously inaccurate. They usually do not take fully into account what *causes* the changes. As general economic and social changes occur, the relationships may become unreliable for predicting the future without the forecasters' realizing it.

Figure 21-2
Example of a historical trend. Blue bars show past revenue. Yellow bars project revenue will continue.

STATISTICAL ANALYSIS OF RELATIONSHIPS

Cause relates to effect

Forecasts may be based on assumptions or theories about what really causes changes in the economy, business, costs, sales, or profits. *Statistical relationship forecasts* bring together many different kinds of data on factors believed to affect sales volume, for example. Analysts may decide that the advertising budget, the number of sales calls made, the money supply in the economy, consumer credit interest rates, the sales volume of competitors, and many other factors actually control a company's sales volume. They will assign numerical values to each factor identified and describe mathematically the effect those factors taken together have on sales. The method allows sales projections to be successively updated as the predictive factors change.

SURVEYS AND ESTIMATES

Put an ear to the ground

A number of specific data-gathering methods are used to make forecasts of future conditions. One method uses the opinions and estimates of people within the organization. This is especially common in cost and sales volume forecasting. *Survey and estimate forecasts* may use the opinions of a group of informed executives. Sales predictions, in particular, may be based on estimates made by the people who actually do the selling. This grass-roots approach has often been successful. Salespeople maintain constant contact with customers and get to know their likes and dislikes, their plans, and their current moods and expectations.

More formal methods are used to determine the buying behavior of consumers. Direct surveys may be made of customer buying plans and expectations for the future. When new products are introduced, test marketings are commonly used to estimate future demand. A trial introduction of the product is made in a limited geographic area. The results are then applied to the entire final sales area to get a rough idea of the sales volume when the product is fully introduced.

3   BUDGETS

Financial guides for planning and control

A *budget* is a specific type of plan in which data are presented in numerical form, often in dollars, for a specified period of time, usually a year or less. Budgets are derived from goals and forecasts, as illustrated in Figure 21-3. For most businesses, the sales budget (stated in dollars and numbers of units to be produced and sold) becomes the fountainhead for all other budgets. Typically, the budgeted revenues are apportioned into two major classes of expense budgets. One class covers expenses that vary with the amount of sales or production volume. The other class covers expenses that are relatively constant, or fixed overhead, with respect to sales or volume. Out of these two classes of expense, dozens or more budgets are prepared for various functions, departments, and activities of a business.

Budgets allow managers to be specific in anticipating revenues and uses of funds. This is indispensable for good financial planning. When managers do not look ahead and determine in detail how much money

**Figure 21-3
How budgets are derived from forecasts.**

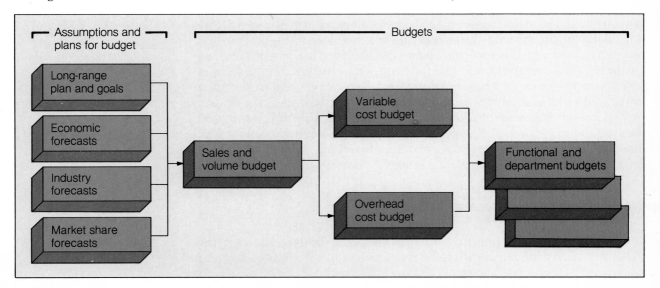

will be needed and where it will come from, they must continually react to unexpected needs that will arise. Budgets also help in evaluating the usefulness of various activities carried on within the organization.

Budgets also set limits on how much will be spent on each business activity and provide a means of controlling those expenditures. A shipping department, for instance, may be given a maximum amount of money to use for wages, materials, repairs, freight and postage, and other controllable costs of operation. If the costs are exceeded, managers have a basis for evaluating the sources and causes of the excess and for making future improvements if needed.

Actual dollar values or other units are used in stating expected costs, income, production quantities, and other forecasts. Stating these objectives precisely makes them easier to achieve.

Finally, budgets provide a convenient time frame within which operations can be controlled and evaluated. Budgets are usually annual, often with quarterly or monthly reviews. They provide short-range goals within consistent time periods that are useful for comparative analysis.

4   TYPES OF BUDGETS

One for every purpose

In practice, a company usually has a group of budgets that are designed to work together. If properly planned and coordinated, the different budgets will function collectively to meet the company's goal of guiding and controlling operations and expenditures. Most companies have sales, expense, cash, and capital expenditure budgets.

SALES BUDGETS

Fountainhead for expenses

The sales or revenue budget is usually the first one to be prepared. The amount of revenue expected to be received sets the upper limit for the total of the expense budgets. If income from all sources is expected to be $1 million, a company cannot plan to spend $2 million without running into debt or into trouble. *Sales budgets* are forecasts of income anticipated from sales in an upcoming budget period. They are prepared by one or more of the methods mentioned in the section in this chapter labeled "Business Forecasts." Often, the opinions of executives and of the sales force will be used to modify a projection made by a statistical technique. A *revenue budget* usually shows total income from all sources that will be available during the budget period. It starts with sales revenue and adds income from interest on savings accounts, dividends, additional capital investment (if any is planned), and from any other source.

EXPENSE BUDGETS

Limits on spending

Managers usually prepare an overall *expense budget* showing the total amounts that are planned to be spent for specified purposes during a

ACTION BRIEF

Everyone for Budgets.
U.S. citizens, most of whom have trouble balancing their own budgets, have been increasingly irritated with the federal government's failure to do so. It looks easy: just make revenues meet or exceed expenses. Businesses must do it all the time, or they fail. So must householders and individuals. Nevertheless, the trick keeps eluding the people in Washington. President Reagan, who once derided the budgeting process as "the most irresponsible Mickey Mouse arrangement that any government body has ever practiced," learned something more soon on his arrival in the nation's capital. He found that another old adage still applied: "Expensive appetites cannot be fed from small paychecks." When revenues are forecast to decline, spending must be controlled accordingly. Ask anyone who operates a business.

Source: *Tom Morganthau and Gloria Borger, "Anyone for a Budget?,"* Newsweek, *June 7, 1982, p. 31.*

Historical trends forecasting is still the most popular technique for making a business projection. It works because it is based upon a fairly good assumption: what has happened in the past is likely to keep on happening in the future. In fact, weather forecasters rely heavily upon this assumption. In effect, they say, "Yesterday's weather will persist until today or tomorrow." The problem, of course, is when something unanticipated comes into the picture to throw off the trend. That's when people talk about needing a crystal ball. For this reason, some companies—General Motors (GM) is one of them—are employing risk analysts who make qualitative assessments of the future instead of purely numerical or statistical ones. When General Motors was considering whether or not to open an assembly plant in Argentina in 1981, GM's political-risk analysts warned of impending economic collapse and labor unrest. They didn't predict the war in the Falkland Islands, but GM had heard enough to give up that plan for its future.

Source: Michael Reese and Hope Lampert, "The Risk Analysts," Newsweek, June 7, 1982, p. 59.

Do you think that too much business forecasting is based upon numerical or technical analysis and not enough on general knowledge, common sense, or intuition? Why? What future conditions can you think of that might be aided by the use of risk analysts?

budget period. This general expense budget may show, for instance, total amounts for direct production expenses, administrative costs, distribution costs, and other general categories. There are several ways of breaking down overall costs into more detailed operating budgets.

Production expenses usually show specific dollar amounts for materials, wages, equipment maintenance, and other costs directly related to creating products for sale. Depending on how the budget is to be used, overhead costs may or may not be allocated to operating activities at this point. Administrative cost budgets include management salaries, part or all of the general overhead costs, and other expenses such as employee training, legal fees, and accounting charges. Distribution expenses include costs such as advertising, maintaining a sales force, shipping, storing, and promoting products. Expenses shown in this manner give one a good idea of the detailed purposes for which money will be spent in the budget period. Such expense budgets often are not arranged in a way to give good operations control, however.

For administrative control of day-to-day operations, another kind of expense budget is often required. The internal organization usually does not match general expense categories. There may be any number of separate departments that will have some production expenses and will use different amounts and types of materials, labor, supplies, and equipment. The same is true of administrative and distribution expenses. For effective control, each of these operating departments usually has its own budget with specific cost categories related to the work it does.

CASH BUDGET
Watches the bank balance

It is not only essential that a business have more money coming in each year than going out, it is also important that the flow of cash coming in be timed so that it is available to make purchases and pay bills as they come due. Many businesses use a cash budget to insure that this will happen. A *cash budget* shows the expected receipts of incoming cash from every source, including from bank loans, and the expected payments to be made each month for a given period of time, typically a year. (See Figure 21-4.) It shows when there will be an excess of cash, which might be moved from a checking account to a savings certificate or a money market fund for greater interest earnings. It also shows when there will be a deficiency of cash (a negative cash flow), which will usually require borrowing to pay bills. Even the largest and wealthiest of companies, like IBM and DuPont, must constantly juggle their cash flow and use a cash budget to guide them in doing so.

CAPITAL EXPENDITURE BUDGET
Provides for equipment purchases

The buildings, machinery, offices, and business's other fixed assets are an indispensable resource. But these assets are not truly fixed. They wear out and must be replaced. They must be expanded as a company grows. Spending money on these fixed or long-term assets is a capital expenditure. Companies must carefully control capital expenditures.

ACTION BRIEF

The Capital Spending Cycle. *One of the most reliable economic indicators of all is the extent of money that private firms invest in new buildings and equipment. Annually, McGraw-Hill surveys the capital spending plans of 500 U.S. companies. When companies are ready to make long-term investments, the economy is assumed to be ready to move upward. When companies pinch their pennies, the economy is forecast to turn down. Why do companies decide to hold back on their spending? Because their forecasts of sales revenues and profits are not encouraging. Unfortunately, when companies do not spend heavily on new plants and equipment, this tends to deflate the economy still further. The economy then continues to spiral slowly downward until businesses, one by one, discover the sun shining through somewhere and begin to make optimistic forecasts about their sales. This improves their willingness to spend money on capital equipment, which tends to stimulate the economy which spirals slowly upward again.*

Source: "Capital Spending Takes a Dive," Business Week, March 22, 1982, p. 24.

Month	J	F	M	A	M	J	J	A	S	O	N	D
Sales budget in cash revenues	40*	40	40	40	80	100	50	20	30	50	60	100
Expense budget in cash payments	30	30	80	70	60	50	20	30	80	60	40	50
Cash excess (+) or shortage (−) each month	+10	+10	−40	−30	+20	+50	+30	−10	−50	−10	+20	+50
Cumulative cash excess (+) or shortage (−)	+10	+20	−20	−50	−30	+20	+50	+40	−10	−20	0	+50

Cumulative excess cash

Cumulative cash shortage to be filled by short-term borrowing

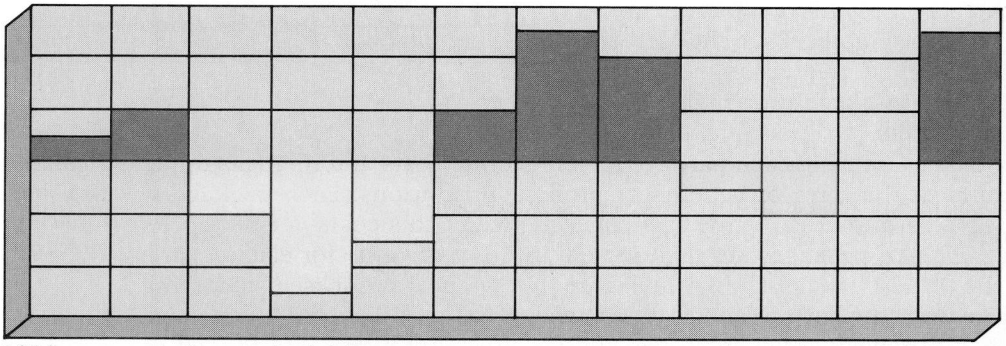

*All figures are in thousands of dollars.

Companies must make sure they always have adequate facilities without dangerously straining their financial resources. *Capital expenditure budgets* help to accomplish this.

These budgets are based on analyses of future needs for the replacement or expansion of facilities. Since costs for machinery, factories, and office buildings are very high, it is especially important to plan for them in advance. A capital expenditure budget shows what kind of capital expenditures will be made, when they will be made, and where the funds will come from. Decisions to make capital expenditures are often based upon whether or not the earnings from a proposed investment will meet a company's criteria for a capitalization ratio. For example, if a plastics factory wanted to purchase an extruding machine for $20,000 and it was calculated to save money at the rate of $1,000, or 10 percent, a year, it would not be placed on the capital expenditures budget if the company's requirement was that it wanted a 15 percent return on assets.

The time value of money (as discussed in Chapter 14) also plays an important role in deciding on the capital budget. Since capital expenditures are long-term investments they involve long-term assets and often long-term liabilities as well. Accordingly, when interest rates are high and forecast to remain that way, a projected return on assets must also be very high.

Figure 21-4
Example of a cash budget showing cumulative monthly excess or shortage.

ZERO-BASED BUDGETING

Starts each year from scratch

Another approach to budgeting challenges the traditional approach, which is often based upon historical trends. The traditional budget assumes that if a function or activity had a budget last year, it should be given budget monies this year. The main decision is usually how much money. *Zero-based budgeting* requires, instead, that every year each manager justify his or her entire budget from scratch. Each budget request is then treated as a separate decision "package" for higher-level management to examine. This is done by examining each package in terms of its costs and its measurable results in the form of benefits or profit contributions. Each package is assigned a numerical value as a consequence of this costs-versus-profits analysis. All packages are then ranked in order of value for each department or activity, as shown in Figure 21-5. Since zero-based budgeting starts from the bottom and works its way upward, in Figure 21-5 package A-1 in purchasing, B-1 in stores, and C-1 in maintenance are ranked as most valuable. These are then stacked in the righthand column, and the budget is built package-by-package until it reaches the cutoff line. This is the point at which the total of all packages reaches the total amount of money approved by the company. The packages above that point lose out and get no budget money.

Zero-based budgeting is widely used in government, but it is also used by many large companies, most notably Texas Instruments Corp., and for the budgeting of industrial research programs.

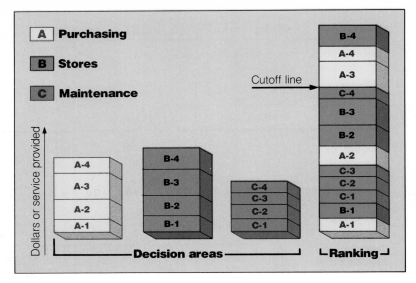

Figure 21-5
How budget packages are ranked in a zero-based budgeting system.

5   FIXED OR FLEXIBLE BUDGETS

Room for adjustments

At the beginning of a fiscal year, the manager of a billing department, for instance, may receive a budget showing how much he or she will be allowed to spend for certain things during the year. There may be amounts allotted for payroll, supplies, equipment rental and maintenance, and part of the company's overhead cost apportioned to the department. The budget shows anticipated maximum amounts and the manager is expected to spend no more. This is a *fixed budget.*

But what happens if sales unexpectedly double during the year? The existing staff will not be able to handle that volume of billing, certainly not without a lot of overtime. More equipment or office space may be needed. In instances like this, *flexible budgets* provide adequate control even when conditions change. A number of techniques permit this flexibility to be built into the budgeting process.

Several budgets may be prepared for a single department, each based on a different level of output. A production department may have four budgets, one for 3,500 tons produced, one for 4,000, one for 4,500, and one for 5,000. A budget of this type is shown in Table 21-1. The actual budget to be used is selected according to the amount of output actually required.

A company may also reduce the budgeting period to take into account changing conditions. For example, a new budget may be prepared every month. Then, as sales or production increase or decrease, expense budgets can be adjusted to match. The same kind of adjusting may be done at the end of a budget period. Budgets are recalculated to show what costs should have been for the output levels actually achieved. These methods provide

TABLE 21-1
Example of a Flexible Budget

Account Title	Monthly Allowances Based Upon Four Operating Levels in Terms of Tons Produced			
	3,500 Tons	4,000 Tons	4,500 Tons	5,000 Tons
Direct labor	$ 7,000	$ 8,000	$ 9,000	$10,000
Indirect labor				
Material handling	600	600	900	1,200
Shop clerical	500	500	500	500
Supervision	1,200	1,200	1,200	1,200
Overtime premium	0	0	450	450
Shift premiums (2d and 3d)	0	0	0	100
Operating supplies	350	400	450	500
Maintenance and repairs	1,200	1,400	2,000	2,800
Gas, water, steam, compressed air	1,500	1,800	2,100	2,400
Electrical power	700	800	900	1,000
Total controllable costs	$13,050	$14,700	$17,500	$20,150
Insurance	$ 120	$ 120	$ 120	$ 120
Taxes	80	80	80	80
Depreciation of equipment	400	400	400	400
Building occupancy	800	850	900	950
Total allocated costs	$ 1,400	$ 1,450	$ 1,500	$ 1,550
Total allowable costs	$14,450	$16,150	$19,000	$21,700

flexible budgets that can respond to changing conditions while still fulfilling their purpose.

6 BUDGET VARIANCE REPORTS

An investigative tool

The control function of a budget is directly provided by a **budget variance,** or **cost variance, report.** This is a listing, similar to that shown in Table 21-2, of all proposed expenditures compared with the actual costs that were incurred for each item. Its primary purpose is to identify which expenses were higher than planned so that efforts can be made in the future to bring excessive costs back in line. This exactly fits the definition of the control function: comparing actual performance with a standard for the purpose of identifying areas where improvements can be made. (Figure 24-1 in Chapter 24 shows a computer printout of a variance report.)

TABLE 21-2
Example of Cost Variance Report

Account Title	Actual	Budget	Variance*
Direct labor	$ 8,000	$ 8,000	0
Indirect labor			
Material handling	900	600	+300
Shop clerical	500	500	0
Supervision	1,200	1,200	0
Overtime	100	0	+100
Shift premium	0	0	0
Operating supplies	500	400	+100
Maintenance and repairs	1,900	1,400	+500
Gas, water, steam, air	1,600	1,800	−200
Electrical power	800	800	0
Total controllable budget	$15,500	$14,700	+$800

Department: Assembly **Dept. no.:** 707 **Month:** July
No. of units scheduled for production: 4,000.
No. of units actually produced: 4,020.
Production variance: +20 units

*(+) indicates over; (−) indicates under.

When properly used, the cost variance report is an investigative tool. Its purpose is to locate the specific sources of excessive costs so that corrective action can be taken. Many times, unexpectedly high costs may be unavoidable. Moving up a production deadline may require extra overtime. Increased production and sales will raise expenses and will not be reflected in a fixed budget. In any case, the variance report should be useful in identifying the sources of costs and should point the way to improvements.

Key Concepts

1. Forecasts are projections of future business conditions. They are used for developing and carrying out business plans in order to meet organization objectives. There are two types of forecasts: (a) background projections of conditions in the environment of a company, such as economic, technological, social, and political influences and (b) business forecasts specific to an individual company, including estimates of future demand and revenue, supply and costs, and profits.

2. The most common forecasting techniques are (a) assuming that significant trends in past performance will continue in the future, (b) statistically analyzing the interrelationships among the causes of business changes, and (c) using surveys, collecting opinions and estimates, and other data-gathering methods.

3. Budgets are specific forecasts or plans expressed in numbers. Financial budgets are most common. They (a) help to anticipate company revenues and expenditures, (b) help

to control the use of company funds by departments and activities, (c) force plans to be specific by requiring the use of dollar values or other units, and (d) provide a convenient time-frame—the budget period—for the evaluation and control of operations.

4. Most companies use a group of coordinated budgets. Common types are sales and revenues, expense, cash, and capital expenditure budgets.

5. Budgets may be fixed or flexible. Flexible budgets are capable of responding to changing conditions while still guiding and controlling operations.

6. The budget variance report is the direct means by which budgets are used for controlling. The report compares actual expenses with budgeted amounts to locate sources of excess costs and to allow corrective action to be taken if needed.

Review Questions

1. Define, identify, or explain each of the following key terms or phrases found on the pages indicated.

   background forecast   (p. 385)
   budget   (p. 389)
   budget variance (cost variance) report (p. 396)
   business forecast   (p. 385)
   capital expenditure budget   (p. 393)
   cash budget   (p. 392)
   demand and revenue forecast   (p. 387)
   economic indicator   (p. 385)
   expense budget   (p. 390)
   fixed budget   (p. 394)
   flexible budget   (p. 395)
   forecast   (p. 384)
   historical trend forecast   (p. 388)
   profit forecast   (p. 387)
   revenue budget   (p. 390)
   sales budget   (p. 390)
   statistical relationship forecast   (p. 388)

   supply and cost forecast   (p. 387)
   survey and estimate forecast   (p. 389)
   zero-based budgeting   (p. 394)

2. Why do businesses make forecasts?
3. What are the two general classes of forecasts? Give some examples of the kinds of questions each of the two might try to answer.
4. What are some techniques a company might use to forecast sales volume for the coming year?
5. What makes the sales budget so important to the budgeting process?
6. Why must forecasts based on the projection of historical trends be used with caution?
7. Name four important ways in which budgets contribute to better management.
8. What is the purpose of a cash budget?
9. Upon what key variable does a flexible budget depend?
10. What is a budget variance report, and what is it used for?

Case Critique 21-1
Forecasting the High Cost of Electricity

Detroit Edison serves nearly 2 million customers in southeastern Michigan. Like most public utilities, it has been under fire from the public for the continuing rise in electrical power costs. Detroit Edison, however, is determined to do something to keep power costs in line. Beginning in 1974, it initiated a productivity planning program that systematically asked three probing questions about the future of the company:

Where are we today?
Where will we be 5 years from now?
How are we going to get there?

To answer the first question and to suggest an answer to the second one, Detroit Edison engineers carefully examined the company's past records. One set of records was particularly significant. It showed that from 1969 to 1979, there had been a slow but steady increase in the total investment (land, buildings, and equipment assets) made by the company in relation to the number of company employees. In 1969, for example, there was a plant investment of $200,000 per operating employee. In 1979, the figure had risen to about $700,000. Based upon these figures, the company was convinced that investment costs would keep rising for the next 5 years at least. Detroit Edison decided upon two approaches to deal with this seeming inevitability. First, it would try to make its plant and engineering employees more productive so that the same number of employees could, in effect, provide service for a greater number of customers each year. Second, the company examined its entire system of producing and distributing energy and then developed a more efficient method of meeting its power demands. The results haven't dramatically reduced rates, but Detroit Edison has been exemplary in keeping them in line with fuel costs. It is now able to project two important trends affecting future productivity. Based upon extrapolating progress from 1960 to 1979, the Detroit Edison can forecast an increase of 150,000 kilowatt hours of electricity generated

per employee each year for the next 5 years. In terms of customers served by each employee, the forecast growth will be about 60 customers a year.

1. What method of forecasting does Detroit Edison apparently depend upon?
2. Using Detroit Edison's forecasting method, how much will the investment cost per employee be 5 years after 1979?
3. What technique might Detroit Edison use to show the relationship between investment required per employee, electricity generated per employee, and customers served by employee?
4. In order to supplement its forecasts based upon internal records, what other forecasting method might Detroit Edison use to estimate future customer demand for energy?

Source: Lloyd W. Coombe and Robert R. Densmore, "How Detroit Edison Improves Its Productivity," *Management Accounting,* May 1982, p. 50.

Case Critique 21-2
The Tightened Budget

In 1982, Swift & Company (a subsidiary of Esmark, Inc.) raised its sales revenues only 2 percent over the year before, but it increased its net income by 35 percent. The actual figures were about like this: sales in 1981—$1.50 billion, in 1982—$1.53 billion; profits in 1981—$38.4 million, in 1982—$51.8 million. The improvements were not an accident. Swift's president was running the company on a tight budget. His forecast for an increase in sales was dim because of the condition of the U.S. economy. But, the president figured, if sales remained about the same, he could reestablish some critical budget limits that would create greater profits from the same amount of business. Some of his key budget targets included a decrease in inventories of 25 percent and a reduction of working capital requirements of 23 percent. Other budgets trimmed corporate overhead in staff personnel by 50 percent, or 340 people. The sales, profit, and expense budgets were all

related to a budget imposed by Esmark on Swift that required the company to reach a return on assets of 15 percent by 1984. By the end of fiscal 1982, Swift was close to the target with a 14 percent return.

1. What background forecast influenced Swift's acceptance of only a small budgeted increase in sales?
2. Since sales remained almost the same in 1982 as they were in 1981, what enabled Swift to increase its earnings so dramatically?
3. If Swift were working under a flexible budgeting system and sales dropped to $1.0 billion in 1983, about how much profit would the company budget for that year?

Source: "Swift: Cutting Costs and Adding Products to Beat a Profit Deadline," *Business Week,* June 21, 1982, p. 65.

Unit 8

Advanced Business Operations

Unit 8 examines the nature of the expansion and growth of American business.

In the United States, the economy is presently dominated by large corporations. They offer economies of scale to the owners, generate a major portion of the national income, provide employment to a substantial sector of the work force, and are a major source of taxes. At the same time, the corporate structure exhibits certain flaws that disturb the public, the government, and owners.

For many companies, establishment in the international market represents the final opportunity for growth. Some multinational companies have so much power that they are not welcome in other countries. However, most nations demonstrate cooperation in business matters.

Technological advances, such as the computer, also contribute to growth. Businesses are now able to apply and control scientific developments and utilize statistical techniques in coping with their problems.

Chapter 22

Formation and Management of Corporations

1 CORPORATIONS DOMINATE THE BUSINESS SCENE IN THE UNITED STATES

because of their size, productive output, number of employees, and high profits.

2 THE FORMATION OF CORPORATIONS

is regulated by state or federal laws. The internal operations of corporations are guided by corporate bylaws.

ARTICLES OF INCORPORATION
NAME
PURPOSE
CAPITAL STOCK

BYLAWS
OFFICERS
BOARD OF DIRECTORS
STOCKHOLDERS

3 A CORPORATION GOES PUBLIC

when it offers its capital stock for sale to the general public.

STOCK CERTIFICATE
FOR SALE

4 STOCKHOLDERS ARE THE OWNERS OF A CORPORATION, BUT THEIR CONTROL IS LIMITED

Decisions on the use of resources are made by the corporate management with authority delegated by stockholders through elections.

ABC
MANAGEMENT
STOCK STOCK STOCK

5 CORPORATIONS EXPAND AND DIVERSIFY

Internally by plowing back profits

Externally by combining with other companies

6 BIGNESS OF CORPORATIONS

is a growing concern to owners, the public, and the government.

Owners:
Sluggishness
Waste
Impersonality

The Public:
Corruption
Monopoly

Government:
Competition
Illegal practices

Learning Objectives

The purpose of this chapter is to explore more fully the implications corporations have with respect to management and to the public, explain the way in which a corporation is formed and makes its stock available to the public, assess the role of the stockholder, and examine the advantages and disadvantages of corporate size.

As evidence of general comprehension, after studying Chapter 22, you should be able to:

1. Discuss the contributions of U.S. corporations to the nation's prosperity and growth.
2. Explain the procedures for incorporating and establishing the structure of a corporation.
3. Explain the process of "going public," the role of the Securities and Exchange Commission in that process, and the purpose of a prospectus.
4. Discuss stockholders' rights and the relationship between stockholders and management.
5. Explain the principal ways a corporation diversifies.
6. Assess the value of corporate size to the corporation itself, to the public, and to the government.

If your class is using SSweetco: Business Model and Activity File for Business in Action, see Chapter 22 in that book after you complete this chapter. There you will find exercises and activities to help you apply your learning to typical business situations.

Humorist and social observer Art Buchwald once imagined a future in which all companies west of the Mississippi River had merged into one giant corporation called Samson Securities. All companies east of the Mississippi River had similarly merged to form the Delilah Company, the only other company in the nation. When the two corporate giants apply to the Antitrust Division of the Federal Trade Commission for clearance to merge into one corporation embracing all of the business activities in the country, the antitrust lawyers give the proposal long study. They finally decide that, "While we find drawbacks to only one company being left in the United States, we feel the advantages to the public far outweigh the disadvantages." The merged Samson and Delilah Company later negotiates with the President for the purchase of the United States.

Business has not reached the point where only one huge company produces all the goods and services for the entire country. Great size, rapid growth, mergers, and the corporate form of ownership do characterize modern business, however. General Motors Corporation, created from the merger of 17 small automobile makers early in this century, now produces sales of over $100 billion. In the nineteenth century, William Procter made and delivered candles; James Gamble made soap. The company they formed, now known as Procter & Gamble, has more than $7 billion of assets.

Corporations have brought immense capabilities to American business. It would be nearly impossible to construct and run a giant refinery or steel mill with any other form of private ownership. At the same time, problems have arisen that are unique to companies that have grown to corporate dimensions.

1   THE CORPORATE FORM OF BUSINESS

A unique role in American business

A corporation was defined in Chapter 4 as an association of individuals, created under the authority of the law that exists and has powers and liabilities independent of its members. The corporate form of ownership is appropriate for most large, profit-making enterprises because, among other reasons, corporations (a) are able to raise large amounts of capital from their many stockholders, (b) can attract numerous investors because owners are protected from personal liability, (c) can have a continuous existence independent of any individual employees or owners, (d) are easy to invest in and withdraw investment from, and (e) can attract managers who are specialists in the varied duties involved in running a large company.

Before the explosive growth of corporations in the nineteenth century, businesses that needed large amounts of capital either had to depend on personal or family fortunes or organize themselves as joint stock companies. However, steel production, the railroads, the development of oil supplies, and the swift growth in popularity of the automobile called for resources on a scale that could not be provided through any form of ownership except the corporation. The fact that many modern industries need to be backed by investments of millions of dollars for large-scale operations has led to the development of corporations that can only be described as enormous. Today, corporations dominate the American economy not only because of their size, but also because of the products and services they offer, the work force they employ, and the profits they earn. Some of the top corporations have grown so large that their annual sales are now greater than the gross national products (GNPs) of many countries.

2 FORMATION OF CORPORATIONS

A routine legality open to any group

A corporation is an artificial "proprietor" created by law. It has the right to carry on business in its own name, to own property, and to incur debts. These rights are usually granted to corporations by state governments, but sometimes by the federal government. Forming a corporation requires a **charter,** or **articles of incorporation.** This is a state-issued document legally recognizing the existence of a new corporation. It is based on information provided by the people who establish the company.

Charters include the legal name and present address of the corporation. They describe the purpose for which the corporation has been formed. The type of business and its purpose are usually defined in terms as general as possible to avoid severely limiting the future activities the company may undertake. Detailed information on the maximum amounts and types of stock the corporation is authorized to issue is usually included in the charter. Provisions for the length of time the corporation is allowed to exist, the adoption of bylaws, and other administrative matters may also be included.

A corporation that carries on business in the state in which it is chartered is called a **domestic corporation.** A corporation that does business in a state other than the state of its incorporation is a **foreign corporation.** A corporation doing business in Iowa, for instance, but chartered in Delaware is known as a foreign corporation in Iowa. Many states have extensive licensing and taxation measures for foreign corporations. It is increasingly common for corporations formed in other countries to trade in the United States. These are called **alien corporations.**

STRUCTURE OF CORPORATIONS

Operations are delegated to management

Corporations are owned by stockholders. In theory, at least, the stockholders retain final control over how the corporation will be operated. However, except in corporations with very few owners, it is not practical for stockholders to perform day-to-day management tasks. When a corporation is formed, the owners decide on rules, stated in the corporate **bylaws,** describing how stockholders should go about delegating management control to achieve effective organization and operation.

The delegation of management authority usually is a two-step process. Stockholders first elect a board of directors. The board then appoints corporate officers who directly run the company. The board of directors usually elect from among its members a chairperson, a vice-chairperson, a

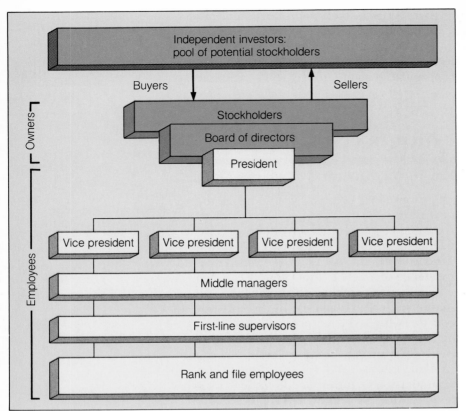

**Figure 22-1
Relationship among
stockholders, managers, and
employees in a typical
corporate structure.**

secretary, and a treasurer. All board members are obliged to remain informed about company operations and to represent the interests of stockholders. The boards of different companies vary in the extent to which they make actual operating decisions. Boards often establish committees to do detailed studies and provide guidance in certain areas, such as finance or corporate development. Figure 22-1 shows an example of the corporate structure.

One important function of all corporate boards is to select the officers who will actually run the corporation. Most corporations have a president and one or more vice-presidents. Final operating responsibility does not always rest with the president, however. In many large companies, the person who chairs the board of directors may be a fulltime operating executive and may act as chief executive officer. Other board members may also assume direct operating control of certain functions, such as when the corporate treasurer acts as the highest financial officer and directly manages financial affairs.

Boards of directors meet periodically—usually monthly or quarterly—to review company operations and to make the decisions required of them. Corporations with numerous stockholders have, in addition, a special annual meeting at which stockholders with voting privileges select members of the board. Annual stockholders' meetings in the past have been largely routine affairs where a slate of board members proposed by existing directors or managers was rubber-stamped by the stockholders. Today, however, more and more annual meetings are marked by lively discussions of operating issues, especially those related to social concerns and stockholders' influence on operations. The treatment of unions, consumer issues, pollution, bribery, and illegal contributions are beginning to take their place along with profitability as subjects of concern for some stockholders. Stockholders' concerns may even extend to the morality of doing business in countries where alleged violations of human rights exist. For example, stockholders at some firms have heatedly debated the ethics of carrying on business in South Africa because of its policy of apartheid, or racial separatism, with respect to blacks.

3 GOING PUBLIC

Sale of stock to the general public

Many corporations, especially small ones, do not offer their stock for sale to the general public. These are called *close corporations* because ownership is closely held and not generally traded. Such companies often have a limited number of owners, sometimes as few as three. The owners are usually directly involved in the management and operation of the business. The reason for creating a close corporation is not to obtain large amounts of capital but to gain other advantages such as limited liability.

Open corporations are also called "public" corporations because they offer their stock for sale to the general public. Anyone who has the money may buy shares of ownership from present stockholders or from company issues of stock. Nearly all large corporations are open. They use the sale of stock to the public to acquire the capital assets needed for major enterprises.

OFFERING AND SALE OF STOCK

A task for the underwriters

Corporations may sell their stock directly to investors. A company wishing to sell 100,000 shares of its stock can contact private investors and others known to buy stock, negotiate a sales price, and directly sell its own offering. This method of selling stock is the exception, however.

Most stock offerings are sold through an intermediary, often called an *underwriter,* who buys all or a large portion of an issue and resells it to actual investors, thereby guaranteeing its sale. Underwriters receive a commission for their services. Investment bankers commonly act as underwriters for corporations.

Although underwriters handle stock offerings even for the best known and most stable large corporations, they are especially important when a new corporation sells stock to the public for the first time. For new or unknown companies, the reputation of the underwriter is often very important in making stock salable to investors. The act of making the first public offering of stock is called *going public.* A close corporation may go public and become an open corporation in order to raise expansion capital. A proprietorship or partnership may incorporate and go public for the same reason.

REGISTRATION AND PROSPECTUS
A closely regulated procedure

When issuing stock, corporations must comply with the legal regulations mentioned in Chapters 13 and 14. All public offerings must be registered with the Securities and Exchange Commission (SEC). The SEC must compile and make available extensive information on the company's financial position, operations, and management. The SEC must summarize this information in a *prospectus* (a written statement) given to every potential investor before an attempt can be made to sell shares.

4   STOCKHOLDERS AND THE CORPORATION
Owners but not managers

Anyone who has excess money to invest may buy stocks. All kinds of people hold stocks as investments, as indicated in Table 22-1. These figures from the New York Stock Exchange indicate that stockholders have diverse occupations, life-styles, and income levels. Stock is also bought by large institutional investors such as banks, insurance companies, investment funds, and similar institutions with large amounts of capital to invest. In the United States about 35 percent of the stock in public hands is owned by institutions and 65 percent by individuals.

REASONS FOR BUYING AND OWNING STOCK
A share of profit and hope for capital gain

With rare exceptions, investors buy stock for one or both of two reasons:

■   Corporate stock permits owners to share in the profits created by the company. Many companies have been extremely reliable in producing and distributing profits. Some have not missed a dividend in decades. Such companies provide secure, regular incomes for investors.

■   Stocks are an attractive investment because the stocks themselves may increase in value. Many people buy stocks with the hope of being able to sell them later at a price higher than they paid. This increase is a *capital gain,* a profit made from buying and reselling capital assets. The increasing value of stock is especially important in offsetting the long-term effects of inflation. Stock prices and dividends are likely to keep pace with other prices in the economy, whereas many other assets, particularly cash, will lose value as the prices of goods and services rise.

THE RIGHTS OF STOCKHOLDERS
Their influence is limited

Stockholders' rights stem from their ownership. They may receive shares of profits. They can claim a share of assets if the corporation dissolves. They are entitled to annual reports on the financial status of the company. They may inspect company records. They may receive prefer-

ACTION BRIEF

A Race Among the Rich.   *When you buy a bottle of shampoo, you are contributing to an industry that generates over $1 billion in sales each year. In fact, the shampoo business keeps on growing at 10 percent a year. Growth industries like this attract crowds. If a product really catches on, profits can be enormous. The problem is that it takes a lot of cash to get into the game. Says Gillette Company's personal care division president, W. J. Ryan, "Shampoo is not an area where you can play on the cheap." Procter & Gamble Company, for example, spent $50 million to establish its Pert shampoo. Other nationally known companies that strive for the business include Helene Curtis, Lever Brothers Company, Noxell, and S. C. Johnson & Son, Inc. Small companies have very little chance. Not only is the money required staggering, the risk is just as large. In fact, Procter & Gamble's advertising campaign for Pert enabled the company to get just 5 percent of the market.*

Source: "A Free-for-All on the Shampoo Shelf," Business Week, September 28, 1981, p. 32.

TABLE 22-1
Ownership of Corporate Stocks

Individual Shareowners	1975	1981
Number of individual shareowners in the United States	25,270,000	32,260,000
Incidence of adult shareowners in the population	1 in 6	1 in 5
Median household income of shareowners	$19,000	$29,200
Adult shareowners with household income under $10,000	3,420,000	2,164,000
Number of adult female shareowners	11,750,000	14,154,000
Number of adult male shareowners	11,630,000	15,785,000
Median age of individual shareowners	53	46
Estimated Holdings of Institutions* (in billions of dollars)		**1980**
Insurance companies		65.0
Investment companies		43.2
Pension funds		219.0
Nonprofit institutions: foundations and educational endowments		44.5
Other: mutual savings banks and private trusts		11.0
Foreign investors		57.5
Total market value of NYSE held by institutions		440.2
Total market value of all NYSE listed stocks		1,242.8
Percent of total held by individuals		64.6%
Percent of total held by institutions		35.4%

*New York Stock Exchange (NYSE) only

Source: Surveys of stockholders conducted by the New York Stock Exchange, *1982 Fact Book*, The New York Stock Exchange, New York, June 1982, p. 47, p. 50.

ence for buying future stock or bond issues. At the same time, stockholders cannot individually seize their share of the assets unless the company dissolves and there are assets left after all liabilities are paid. Nor can a stockholder individually direct the corporation as to how to use his or her share of the assets. Decisions on the use of resources are made by the corporate management with authority delegated by all stockholders collectively through elections.

Owners of common stock and of some kinds of preferred stocks have voting privileges. They elect members of the board of directors. They may amend the bylaws or request changes in the articles of incorporation. They may vote directly on company policies. Such voting takes place at the annual meeting. Since many stockholders cannot attend these meetings, there is a way for them legally to allow another person to vote in their place. This is called voting by **proxy.** Since current officers or directors of the company are usually chosen as the ones to cast the proxy votes, the system usually has the effect of concentrating more company control with the management.

Direct control of a company by stockholders clearly has definite limits. At times it has been difficult for stockholders to exert any control at all over management. When present managers and directors have extensive proxy rights, they may perpetuate their own positions and make decisions with little influence from stockholders. One or two stockholders who own a large portion of the company's shares may be able to elect all the board members, even against the desires and best interests of other stockholders. A related problem occurs when representation is not granted to minority interests, even when ownership is equal and widespread.

One procedure that helps achieve fairer representation of minority ownership and more democratic elections of directors is **cumulative voting.** Each stockholder may cast all of his or her votes for a single director if desired. If a company were electing eleven directors, for example, and a stockholder owned 100 shares of stock, the stockholder could cast 1,100 votes for a single candidate, 550 for each of two candidates, or any other combination desired. Under **noncumulative voting,** the stockholder would only be allowed to cast 100 votes for each position open. Cumulative voting does permit representation of small groups of stockholders.

5   GROWTH OF LARGE CORPORATIONS

Expansion has become nearly uncontrollable

Growth and bigness are fundamental to today's business world. How well do large-sized corporations function? The merger, or joining together, of the New York Central Railroad and the Pennsylvania Railroad in the late 1960s is one example of the failure of bigness. The merger of the two inefficient companies into one giant corporation did not produce a more effective operation. Within two years, the merged Penn-Central was bankrupt. W. T. Grant Co., after a spurt of rapid growth and expansion into a retailing giant, also went bankrupt in 1976.

Far more companies have found success in great size, however. General Electric Co. has acquired some of its best-selling products by buying out smaller companies that actually carried out the technical development for those goods. The pop-up toaster is one example. Eastman Kodak's success has at least partly resulted from truly dominating its markets. The same is true of IBM. IBM holds a major share of the computer market in the United States and in most parts of the world. Its tremendous revenues and profits have made the huge development costs of new computers and related equipment relatively easy for the corporation to handle. Hundreds of other examples exist. *Forbes* magazine, in 1983, listed over 500 companies with annual sales of $1 billion or more. Some 109 of these companies had sales of more than $5 billion. Twelve of them had profits of over $1 billion. Leading the list were AT&T with $6,992,000,000 profits, followed by such notables as IBM, Exxon, Mobil, four major oil companies, General Electric and Eastman Kodak. The total employment represented by the top 808 large corporations was some 21.6 million. AT&T again headed the list with 1,015,900 employees. General

Motors had 657,000; General Electric 367,000; Sears Roebuck 401,800; Safeway Stores 156,900; McDonald's 130,700; Johnson & Johnson 78,400; and Procter & Gamble 62,400. More than half of these 808 very large companies employed more than 2,000 people.

ADVANTAGES OF BIGNESS TO CORPORATIONS

Economies of production, purchasing, and resources

Despite the fact that great size sometimes leads to great waste and inefficiency, it does have certain advantages. Large companies are often able to achieve economies of scale. One large assembly line can usually produce 100,000 automobiles faster and at a lower cost than can 100 smaller operations, each making 1,000 cars.

Large companies can buy materials in huge quantities, and pay lower unit prices than can small companies. Large companies inspire confidence in suppliers because they usually have a longer history and are believed to be more stable. In practice, consumers also seem to demonstrate confidence in large companies. Despite many legitimate complaints about product quality or service, most buyers select well-known brands from large companies even when given the alternative of buying a similar, lesser-known brand.

Large companies are better able to diversify. *Diversification* is the extension of a business's product, service, or markets beyond a dependence upon a single one. Economic cycles can be hard on companies with only one or two products. A large company with many products and services is partially protected from business slumps. If sales are off in their retail stores, income from insurance sales or grain exporting, for example, may offset the retail losses. Diversification helps to provide income stability. This is one important reason why so many companies have merged or formed business ties with other companies.

TYPES OF BUSINESS COMBINATIONS

A three-way stretch is possible

One way companies grow to a large size is by successfully producing profits and reinvesting the profits in expansion to produce even greater profits. Another way to grow is by joining a number of smaller companies together into one large company. Many U.S. businesses have expanded through this latter method.

There are three main types of business combinations: vertical, horizontal, and conglomerate.

Vertical combinations bring together some or all of the processes that contribute to producing and selling a single product. Gasoline is a well-known example of a vertical combination. A company that combines oil exploration, drilling, refining, shipping and retailing companies is one example. Vertical combinations are created by joining different levels of the same general production process. These companies either advance their operations toward the customer (forward integration) or bring their operations backwards toward the supplier (backward integration).

Horizontal combinations join more than one company operating at the same level of production or distribution of the same kind of goods or services. If one hardware store buys out another hardware store in town, a horizontal combination will be formed. When Warner-Lambert merged with Parke, Davis & Company, this was a horizontal combination. Both firms manufactured pharmaceutical supplies and were formerly direct competitors in many of their service areas. Horizontal combinations typically eliminate a competitor producing the same goods or services.

Conglomerate combinations join together companies that produce different, generally unrelated goods and services. If, for example, a wool manufacturer buys a copper mine, a conglomerate combination is the result. Conglomeration is one of the main sources of diversification in this country. Notable conglomerates include ITT, Norton Simon Inc., Greyhound Corp., Gulf & Western Industries, W. R. Grace, Esmark Inc., and Walter Kidde.

Means of Joining Companies Together   Two or more companies that join together so that only one company remains are said to undergo a **merger.** Mergers may occur in two general ways: (a) firms may decide to pool their resources and assets and create a new, larger company, or (b) one firm may buy another by paying its present owners (stockholders, partners, or proprietor) for the value of the assets acquired.

The organization of merged companies may also vary. Often, a completely new organization is created so that the original companies are no longer recognizable as separate units. Sometimes, an acquired company may be continued as a recognizably different company with its own management as in the case of Parke, Davis & Company under Warner-Lambert and Swift & Co. under Esmark Inc. Such a company, whose assets are mainly or entirely owned by another company, is called a **subsidiary.** Though subsidiaries retain corporate identity, they run their own operations but report their financial conditions with the parent company. Some companies buy most or all of the stock of other companies without taking a direct role in their management. The buying company operates as a holding company in these instances. A **holding company** receives income in the form of dividends on the stock it owns. Sometimes, companies will join for a short-term purpose, such as underwriting a large stock offering of a corporation. These combinations are called **syndicates** and exist only for as long as needed to accomplish their single, specific purpose. Another kind of temporary combination, called a **joint venture,** is very similar to a syndicate but is usually longer lasting. For example, two real estate companies may wish to pool their resources and technical skills to subdivide and resell a piece of land for residential building lots. They could undertake a joint venture that would be dissolved when the lots are sold.

HOW BIGNESS CONTRIBUTES TO SOCIETY

Provides revenues and achieves economies of scale

Many products—automobiles, steel, aluminum, oil, and gas—could only be produced at very high prices without the huge facilities and resources of major corporations. Some could probably not be produced at all. Large corporations provide a relatively secure investment opportunity for everyone. Without them, it would be difficult for ordinary citizens to take part in the profit-making process of private enterprise.

ACTION BRIEF

Merger's Children.   Can you match up the corporate parents with the well-known companies that came into their folds through merger and acquisition?

Corporate Parents
1. *Ralston Purina Company*
2. *Heublein, Inc.*
3. *Borden, Inc.*
4. *Reynold's Tobacco*
5. *Phillip Morris, Inc.*
6. *Gillette Company*
7. *Mars, Inc.*
8. *Colgate-Palmolive Company*
9. *Quaker Oats Company*
10. *CBS, Inc.*

Children
A. *Steinway pianos*
B. *Cracker Jacks*
C. *Del Monte Foods*
D. *Chicken of the Sea tuna*
E. *Fisher-Price toys*
F. *Paper-Mate pens*
G. *Kentucky Fried Chicken*
H. *Uncle Ben's Rice*
I. *Seven-Up*
J. *Baggies*

Answers
1-D   3-B   5-I   7-H   9-E
2-G   4-C   6-F   8-J   10-A

Issues & Highlights

An End to Bailouts?

As the economy of major industries has shifted, many seemingly invincible companies have found themselves in trouble. Lockheed, Chrysler, A&P, the major steelmakers and tiremakers, to name a few. Some companies, like Chrysler, approached the government for, and obtained, loan guarantees. That is, if the company borrowed money from banks and couldn't pay it back, the U.S. government would. The steel corporations sought, and obtained from Congress, the establishment of "trigger-price mechanisms" to protect them from low-priced imports. Similar legislation protects the textile industries. Even some states and cities have offered to put up money to try to keep ailing plants of major corporations (like International Harvester) operating in their communities.

Such supports and bailouts have been criticized on the basis that they allow unfit corporations to survive. Critics argue that the United States should not be trying to protect companies in industries that are now being challenged by more productive foreign companies, regardless of the immediate damage this might do to stockholders, employees, and local communities. It is better, these critics say, for the United States to devote its energies toward ensuring the creation of a new generation of profitable industries (like computers, sea mining, and solar energy) and innovative, new companies, even if we all suffer a little in the meantime.

Source: David Vogel, "A Funny Thing Happened to the Down-With-Big-Business Movement," Across the Board, December 1980, p. 45.

Would you vote to use federal funds to prevent the failure of a large corporation employing thousands of people? How would your vote be affected according to whether or not you were an employee of that company, a stockholder, a person who owned one of its products, or a resident in a town where the company was a major employer and tax-payer?

To the extent that large companies are able to achieve economy of scale, lower prices are passed on to consumers. This is particularly true in industries where considerable competition still exists. Large corporations in general make a tremendous contribution to the gross national product, to employment, and definitely to the tax revenues needed by governments to provide services.

EMPLOYMENT IN LARGE CORPORATIONS

Advantages outweigh disadvantages

Just as some people are attracted to employment in small businesses, the great majority of people not only work for large corporations, but they also find it more desirable. They do so for a number of reasons. Large companies usually pay better wages and salaries. They offer more benefits in the way of health care and life insurance and pension plans. Working conditions are generally better, too. Since large companies are so visible to the law and to the public, there is greater pressure put upon them to create and maintain clean, safe work environments. The law also pays greater attention to the way in which large firms comply with legislation that affects employment. In enforcing the Equal Employment Opportunity laws, for example, the federal government chose to initiate its investigations against the largest corporations first, even those, like AT&T, whose reputation for fairness was exemplary at the time.

Large corporations usually offer more opportunities for training and advancement. Cost of developmental programs that would represent an unbearable overhead cost to small businesses are considered routine in larger ones where these costs can be spread over thousands of people. The sheer size of employment in large companies also creates larger numbers of opportunities for individuals to move from one occupation to another and to be promoted to positions of increasing responsibility.

The major drawbacks of working for large corporations are probably the pressures to conform to prescribed behavior and procedures and the tendency for many jobs to be narrowly specialized, routinized, and —as a consequence—boring.

The simple conveniences that are present when working for a small business are often not possible in large ones. An employee working for a small manufacturer, for example, may be able to park her car next to the shop door and step outside for some fresh air during a coffee break, or walk home for lunch. In a larger company, she might have to leave her car in a gigantic parking lot and take a shuttle bus to the plant door, remain indoors all day long, and eat in a cafeteria that seats 500 people. The food and the atmosphere may be better than a vending corner of a small plant, but the intimacy and chance to relax may be less.

6   ARE BIG CORPORATIONS GOOD FOR THE UNITED STATES?

Their values are being challenged

While large corporations are very much a part of the American business scene, their values—which affect the internal organization as well as the public—can be challenged.

INTERNAL CORPORATE PROBLEMS

Sluggishness, waste, and impersonality

Huge corporations are difficult to manage. Errors of judgment are magnified when output is measured in millions of units. A company with hundreds of thousands of employees and thousands of managers is especially subject to loss of control, lack of accurate communications, and disorganization. Large companies have struggled for years with the question of decentralizing versus centralizing. In theory, a centralized organization gives top management more direct control over operations. Often, however, it creates a huge and expensive bureaucracy that is unresponsive to changing conditions and opportunities. Decentralized management gives more control to local, regional, or division managers. It allows greater flexibility but may result in poor communications and conflicting policies and actions.

Another problem with corporations is that corporate boards are often given important responsibilities without having the information or direct involvement needed to fulfill them. In large corporations, maintaining even a casual contact with actual operations requires many long hours of study and familiarity with thousands of pages of data. Many board members are unable to keep this contact.

The ability to assemble large amounts of capital has not always solved the financial problems of corporations. The huge amounts needed to continue operations and expansion sometimes are not available. Periodically, for instance, new stock issues have often been difficult to sell. Debt financing through bonds or loans may also be unavailable in the amounts needed. The very size of corporate enterprises is part of the problem. Whereas hundreds of thousands of dollars might be easy to find, hundreds of millions are sometimes unobtainable.

Large organizations often encourage conformity among their members. The conformity results partly from a competitive urge to get ahead in the organization by imitating those who are in the upper levels of the hierarchy. Conformity is also often encouraged by management as one means of achieving consistency and of keeping control over large numbers of employees. Many authorities believe that this atmosphere seriously interferes with the inventive and innovative creativity required for progress.

One thing seems certain. Bigness, alone, does not insure corporate efficiency or survival. The bellwether industries of the United States have not had a good record in adapting to changing market and competitive environments. The steel and auto companies, in particular, have been slow to accommodate change. In both industries, the major corporations failed to modernize their production facilities as rapidly as overseas competitors did. The auto companies were slow to react to consumer demands for smaller, more reliable cars. Not only did foreign carmakers capture a large share of the American and international market, U.S. automakers set records for operating losses during the early 1980s. Only with the threat of failure staring them in the face did the U.S. car builders adopt modern styling and convert their plants to modern technology. Their resources had been enormous; their operations were sluggish and inefficient. Similar shortcomings of operation and responsiveness plagued the tire makers and the machine tool builders. Even IBM, with its tremendous resources, lagged behind in its field when change was imminent. It was the newer, smaller companies—not IBM—that triggered the development and proliferation of mini, micro, and personal computers.

PROBLEMS FOR SOCIETY

Monopoly, corruption, and irresponsibility

Many large corporations have achieved true dominance over their markets. Often, competing goods or services are simply not widely available. This has, in many cases, significantly reduced the variety of products. In the long run, higher prices and lower quality may result from the reduced competition as well. Even where competition exists, rival corporations show a tendency to set the same prices so as to share the market.

Large corporations have frequently shown irresponsibility by causing severe pollution, using unsafe work methods, producing low-quality or dangerous products, and engaging in political corruption and accepting bribes. It may be true that corporations are no more guilty of these practices than other organizations or individuals. The size and power of major corporations, however, make the effects of their irresponsibility much more severe.

Because corporate business activities may be far removed from top management, corporations often show a disregard for local interests. If an oil company wishes to tear down a local historical landmark to build a gas station, executives in New York or Philadelphia or Houston cannot see it from their office windows. They may not even know anything about it. Locally based companies are more subject to local pressures, needs, and interests. Some companies have begun to respond positively to these failings of social responsibility. Some have appointed **ombudsmen,** whose duty it is to discover and solve problems resulting from the company's products. These and other consumer departments and committees, along with government pressure for quality and pollution control, have begun to exert an influence on corporations.

GOVERNMENT ACTIVITY AGAINST RESTRAINT OF TRADE

Federal antitrust legislation

The extreme power of large corporations in the United States has been a continuing topic of political debate, especially in the last decade. The financial and management capabilities of the giant companies make them competitors even of national governments. Federal antitrust laws are designed to prevent business combinations that cause an unfair reduction of competition. These laws generally have had little effect on recent business combinations, especially conglomerate combinations. Creating a monopoly—by joining all steel manufacturers, for example—can be prevented by the antitrust laws. A large and effective company that wishes to gain dominance of a market is not prevented from doing so, nor is a huge conglomerate prevented from acquiring great financial power. Both of these situations can be damaging to the economy and to customers. Lawmakers and the public will be challenged in the future to find effective ways of eliminating the negative effects of corporations without also destroying the advantages offered to society.

Key Concepts

1. The corporation is the dominant form of business ownership in the United States in terms of size, assets, number of employees, amount of goods and services produced, and profits generated.

2. Corporations are formed when a charter is issued by the state or federal government. The charter states the corporation's name, purpose, stock authorization, and other information. Corporations are managed by officers appointed by a board of directors elected by stockholders according to procedures in the corporation's bylaws.

3. Corporations may be "close" if they do not offer stock for sale to the public or "open" if they do. Open corporations raise equity financing by selling issues of stock to investors, using investment bankers or other underwriters as sales agents.

4. Investors usually buy stock as a source of income, capital gain, or both. Stockholders have the right to obtain information about the corporation and usually the right to elect board members. The actual supervision of a large corporation is undertaken by paid professional managers.

5. Many corporations have grown to large size through internal growth financed from profits and through mergers and other business combinations. Combinations may be horizontal, vertical, or conglomerate and may be carried out in various ways. Large size has a number of advantages: economy of scale, the confidence of suppliers and consumers, and a stable income resulting from diversification. Large corporations make major contributions to the national economy.

6. The large size of corporations has also created problems. Large companies are difficult and expensive to manage, may have trouble raising the huge amounts of money they need, and may foster conformity and stifle innovation. Large companies can also have negative effects on society as with pollution, unsafe work methods and products, and dominance of markets, for example.

Review Questions

1. Define, identify, or explain each of the following key terms and phrases found on the pages indicated.

   alien corporation   (p. 403)
   bylaws   (p. 403)
   capital gain   (p. 406)
   charter (articles of incorporation)   (p. 403)
   close corporation   (p. 405)
   conglomerate combination   (p. 410)
   cumulative voting   (p. 408)
   diversification   (p. 409)
   domestic corporation   (p. 403)
   foreign corporation   (p. 403)
   going public   (p. 405)
   holding company   (p. 410)
   horizontal combination   (p. 409)
   joint venture   (p. 410)
   merger   (p. 410)
   noncumulative voting   (p. 408)
   ombudsman   (p. 414)
   open corporation   (p. 405)
   prospectus   (p. 406)
   proxy   (p. 407)
   subsidiary   (p. 410)
   syndicate   (p. 410)
   underwriter   (p. 405)
   vertical combination   (p. 409)

2. What five factors have allowed corporations to achieve their present size and dominance?

3. What is included in a corporate charter?

4. What role do stockholders play in managing a large open corporation?

5. What is the difference between a close corporation and an open corporation? In which category do large corporations like General Motors fall?

6. To what extent are stockholders able to control the assets of the corporation in which they share ownership? What does their ownership mean?

7. Why do people and organizations invest in stock?
8. How can diversification benefit a corporation?
9. Distinguish between internal methods of diversification and those used by combining with other companies.
10. Briefly describe some of the problems that great size can present to a large corporation.

Case Critique 22-1
The High Cost of Staying Private

The world's largest maker of bobby pins ($125 million in sales) is found in the small industrial town of Kearny, New Jersey. Up until 1980, the company was privately owned by the Goodman family. Henry Goodman founded Goody Products in 1907 when he noticed that the peddler with the pushcart next to his was making more money selling ornamental combs than Henry was selling groceries. That night Henry went home and, together with his wife and sons, began making combs in the back room of their apartment. They drilled and set rhinestones into blank combs they bought. One thing led to another and soon Goody was the leader in women's hair care items, especially bobby pins.

The trouble with being a closely held family company, even if incorporated, was that whenever Goody needed money to buy new equipment, it had to go to the bank to borrow it. For 20 years, Goody saw other small, family-owned competitors fall into debt and eventually fail. Goody, too, went constantly to the banks. Each time, Goody would put up all the assets it owned as collateral. "We were never out of debt," says Goody's president, the grandson of Henry. "We were adding equipment in all the buildings, borrowing as we went. At no time did we have a good balance sheet. Things were getting tighter and tighter."

Finally, in 1980, with the company heavily saddled with debt, Goody went public. It raised $4.4 million by selling 500,000 shares of stock, retaining about 1,500,000 shares for the family. (Goody Products is sold "over the counter.") For the first time in its history, the firm became adequately capitalized. It quickly spent some of the proceeds of the public offering to automate its production line. This enabled Goody to become the lowest-cost producer in its field, able to undersell imports from Hong Kong and Korea. Goody also broadened its product line and launched a television campaign. "We should reach $200 million in sales by 1985, possibly $400 million by 1990," says Goody's president.

1. Before going public, what form of ownership did Goody's have?
2. What advantages did Goody gain by selling shares of its ownership to the public?
3. What were the disadvantages of Goody's going public?

Source: Steven Flax, "The Cost of Staying Private," *Forbes,* February 15, 1982, p. 102.

Case Critique 22-2
When You're Big in Parking Lots

Parking lot operators have had a roller-coaster ride of boom and bust in the past three decades. As population and shoppers switched to the suburbs in the 1960s, inner-city parking lot owners took it on the chin. Then as air travel zoomed in the 1970s, operators of airport parking lots made it very big. As air travel leveled out in the 1980s, however, airport franchises declined in profitability. At the same time, office building complexes began to replace retail trade downtown in the cities. So, once again, inner city parking facilities became profitable.

Market cycles that swing wildly like those in the parking lot industry take their toll on the operators. A great many small owners failed or sold out to corporations. Today, the largest parking lot operator by far is APCOA, a corporation that is nearly twice as large as its nearest competitors. What has been the secret of its survival? Good management that timed its moves with the switches, first to the airports, and then back to the city. More importantly, APCOA uses its size— and resultant financial resources—to minimize its risks. It carefully avoids owning the land under its parking lots or the buildings on them. That keeps APCOA from becoming saddled with high interest rates on mortgages. Instead, APCOA uses its funds to lend money to real estate developers, who buy and own the land and build the parking facilities. APCOA then leases the lots back from the owners it has financed. APCOA has the money to do it this way. It makes its profits two ways—from financing the real estate developer and from operating the lots.

1. What is a major financial problem that usually faces parking lot owners?
2. What is it that APCOA does differently from most small operators? What advantage does it gain by doing so?
3. Why should a small company have difficulty in doing what APCOA does?
4. Would you restrict, by law, the number of parking lots a corporation can operate? Why? Would it make any difference if the corporation owned them outright or simply leased them?

Source: "APCOA: A Parking Lot Operator Uses Its Big Size to Advantage," *Business Week,* March 22, 1982, p. 107.

Chapter 23
International Business

1 IMPORT AND EXPORT TRADE AND OPERATIONS
make business an international activity.

2 A NATION'S NATURAL, HUMAN, AND ECONOMIC RESOURCES INFLUENCE ITS ABILITY TO TRADE

Some countries have more to offer than others.

3 UNITED STATES COMPANIES
do business abroad directly without a broker or indirectly through a broker.

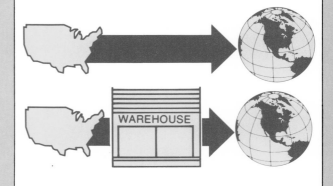

4 THERE ARE MANY OBSTACLES TO CARRYING OUT INTERNATIONAL BUSINESS

Cultural   Financial   Trade   Operational

5 MULTINATIONAL CORPORATIONS

may own, produce, or market in many nations.

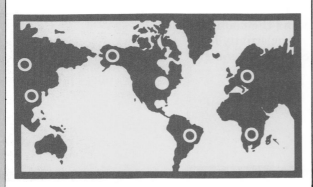

6 BUSINESSES ARE AIDED BY INTERNATIONAL COOPERATION

in the form of:

 Multinational economic communities (Common Market)

 International laws and treaties

 International banks

 International trade associations

Learning Objectives

The purpose of this chapter is to provide insight into the factors that help or hinder a nation's ability to trade and conduct international business operations, describe how companies do business on an international basis and what obstacles they must overcome, discuss the impact of multinational companies on world affairs, and explain some of the ways in which international trade is encouraged.

As evidence of general comprehension, after studying Chapter 23, you should be able to:

1. *Define international trade and operations.*
2. *Evaluate the various influences on a nation's ability to trade, and distinguish between absolute advantage and comparative advantage.*
3. *Explain various methods of international trade participation and business operations and their relationship to direct and indirect distribution.*
4. *Outline some of the principal obstacles to international business.*
5. *Evaluate the impact of multinational operations on international and domestic affairs.*
6. *Identify the various vehicles of international cooperation in trade.*

If your class is using SSweetco: Business Model and Activity File for Business in Action, see Chapter 23 in that book after you complete this chapter. There you will find exercises and activities to help you apply your learning to typical business situations.

A clerk in Hong Kong fills in a sales slip with a ball-point pen man-ufactured in New England. In Omaha, a family watches a television news story about the demands made by U.S. growers to reduce sugar imports. Their television was manufactured in Japan, partly from raw materials bought from the United States. At the same moment a student in Los Angeles buys a soft drink, thousands of people all over the world are buy-ing the same product.

International trade and production are a way of life for business man-agers today. A product like an automobile may contain materials and parts directly or indirectly contributed by a hundred different nations. Completed automobiles may themselves be exported to scores of coun-tries.

International business makes available a range of materials and pro-cesses that could not conceivably exist in one restricted area. It would be practically impossible to make a fruit salad in any area of the world which included locally grown apples and bananas. The two fruits do not nor-mally flourish in the same climate. The same situation exists with met-als, oil, timber, and many other products.

International business also opens vast, diverse markets that do not exist in any single area. The world population is a huge assembly of people with needs that range from basic grains for subsistence to multimillion dollar computer systems.

Commercial interdependence and cooperation among the countries of the world are necessary to the success of businesses. The strictly local development of local resources for local markets is becoming as much a relic of the past as the frontier subsistence farm.

1   WHAT MAKES BUSINESS INTERNATIONAL?

When they buy from, sell to, or operate in foreign lands

Companies may be involved in international business in two main ways:

■   They may buy from or sell to companies or governments in other countries. This *importing* and *exporting* activity is called *international trade.*

■   They may directly engage in *international operations,* that is, marketing or producing goods and services in another country.

Many large corporations carry on both kinds of international business with and in many different countries. Although any particular interna-tional business may result from a variety of particular needs, there is a general need that stimulates trade between nations. The resources of every region or country are limited to some extent. Every country needs materials or products that are only available in other countries. The United States is unusually rich in resources. Still, we import all our tin,

TABLE 23-1
Corporate Involvement in International Business

Corporation	Extent of Participation in Foreign Markets in 1982
Texaco, Inc.	Net income of $833 million, or 65 percent of all income, from overseas, mainly in the eastern hemisphere. Similarly, $13 billion, or 48 percent, of its assets were held outside the United States.
Warner-Lambert Company	Introduced a dietetic food product in Germany and a new package for Trident gum in Japan, opened a manufacturing plant in Egypt, and stepped up gum production in Portugal by 500 percent. Sales of $1.35 billion overseas or about 46 percent of total.
Central Soya Company, Inc.	Sales of $373 million abroad, mainly of cattle feeds. Company operates 14 manufacturing plants in Europe and South America. Lost $900,000 on exchange rates.
Amerada Hess Corporation	International sales of $977 million (or 12 percent) of total revenues with $1.8 billion (or 29 percent) of its assets overseas. Continued to explore for, or operate, oil wells in Canada, Norway, Abu Dhabi, Ireland, and the United Kingdom.
Fluor Corporation	This construction firm derived 5 percent of its revenues of $7,866 million from Africa and 7 percent from the Middle East, where it constructed a major industrial complex and drilled oil wells.
Stauffer Chemical Company	Exports to more than 75 companies through 35 foreign manufacturing and marketing subsidiaries. Foreign sales declined from $267 million in 1980 to $214 million in 1982 due principally to adverse economic conditions in Eastern Europe.
MCA, Inc.	This film, TV, and music publishing company had revenues of $273 million, or about 17 percent of its total, from international business. This was divided about equally between foreign operations and exports, mainly to Europe and Asia.

Source: 1982 Annual Reports from the seven corporations listed above.

industrial diamonds, natural rubber, coffee, tea, cobalt, platinum, tungsten, manganese, nickel, antimony, bauxite, chrome, and many other goods and materials.

Even when a country may be able to produce certain kinds of goods, those goods can often be produced more inexpensively and more efficiently elsewhere. Countries specialize in making the goods for which their resources are best suited. When free trade exists, the effect of this specialization is greater efficiency and lower prices for everyone.

International business makes a huge contribution to the economy of nearly every country. In the United States, exporting accounts for 8 percent of the gross national product. We import about the same amount. Many American-based companies depend on overseas sales and operations for significant parts of their revenues and profits. Table 23-1 shows a few of these companies. The entire economy is becoming more and more intertwined with that of other countries. Manufactured goods of all kinds—chemicals, steel, sulfur, cotton, wheat, corn, and hundreds of other products—flow out to buyers in other countries. Zinc, tin, copper, silk, tea, bananas, and other materials and goods flow in.

2   INFLUENCES ON A NATION'S ABILITY TO TRADE

Many have more to offer than others

Since international trade arises partly because of the unequal distribution of specific resources, countries and regions differ in the extent and nature of their involvement in world trade. The conditions and resources in any country control how much it imports and exports and determines the kinds of products traded.

NATURAL RESOURCES

Unevenly distributed advantages

Natural resources are a vital part of every country's economy. They determine, among other things, what a country can sell to other countries and what it must buy. For example, a country with great wealth in the form of mineral deposits is in a very favorable position. If it has the skilled labor, facilities, technology, and capital to do so, it may manufacture and export finished metal products, or it may use the minerals directly for export. Oil is probably the best example of a pure natural resource dominating international trade. Nations that export oil have reaped tremendous profits. Importing nations have been so strained by the need to pay for oil that, in some cases, their economies have suffered.

As for agricultural products, the kinds and amounts that a country can export or must import depend on the country's climate, terrain, and soil, as well as on its technology. The United States is so favored on all these counts that in recent years, over 30 percent of our exports have been agricultural products.

HUMAN RESOURCES

Skilled or specialized labor

In the modern world, skilled labor is usually a necessity of production. Fewer jobs than ever before require only brute strength or thoughtless repetition. Any country with a trained, capable work force will have an advantage in producing goods for trade. Unlike climate and other natural resources, an outstanding work force can be created through good education systems and company training and incentive programs.

Some developing countries view the low wages paid workers as a resource giving their nation a competitive advantage. Some goods can be effectively produced at a lower total cost where wages are low. However, the advantage can only be temporary. If the competitive strategy is successful, the country will gain in international trade. Its standard of living will rise and workers may no longer be willing to accept low wages.

CAPITAL, TECHNOLOGY, AND TRANSPORTATION

Money and modern methods

Trying to assemble capital resources can be one of the most frustrating aspects of producing goods for international trade. Even abundant natural resources cannot be adequately exploited without production facilities. Production facilities are difficult or impossible to build without the revenue from the natural resources. However, that revenue is unavailable without the facilities. A country with a large stock of production plants and equipment in operation is at a tremendous advantage, even if the facilities are outmoded.

The same problem must be faced with technology. Profitable finished products cannot be created without it, but it is difficult to develop technology without sufficient revenue. A lack of high-level technology is likely to prevent a country from participating in world trade. Even countries that exploit pure natural resources, such as oil or nitrogen fertilizers, need access to modern methods of extraction in order to remain competitive.

Countries also need a modern system of transportation to get their goods to market. Minerals that lie deep in a jungle are inaccessible until a railroad or a good system of roads is built. This is one of the factors that puts developing countries at a disadvantage in world trade. However, even under the best of circumstances, transportation is expensive. Modern transportation methods have made the world one big marketplace, but this situation can continue only if importers are willing to pay higher prices for the goods.

TRADE ADVANTAGES

These determine specialization

A country has an *absolute advantage* in the production of a product when it (*a*) is the only country that makes the product, or (*b*) can make the product at a lower cost than another country. A country with a much needed mineral product found nowhere else in the world would obviously devote its effort to producing and exporting that mineral. The country would profit from its monopoly position. A country that can make a particular product at a lower cost than another country also has an absolute advantage. In this case, however, a country may do well to import that product and concentrate on producing some other product. Such a decision will be based on comparative advantage.

The theory of *comparative advantage* embraces two related concepts: (*a*) a country with absolute advantages in a number of different products should concentrate on the products which bring the greatest advantage, and (*b*) a country with no absolute advantages should concentrate on products which bring the least disadvantage.

The production and trade of agricultural products is a simple example of how trade advantages operate. Country X has an absolute advantage in wheat and corn production. Country Y is at a disadvantage in growing both products but has a much greater disadvantage with corn than with wheat. According to the theory of comparative advantage, it would ben-

efit Country X to specialize in growing corn and import wheat from Country Y. Similarly, Country Y should concentrate on growing wheat and
should import its corn.

3   HOW COMPANIES TRADE AND OPERATE INTERNATIONALLY

Degree of participation varies broadly

Just about any company can enter international trade. They can do so
in many ways. Some methods of entry are more risky than others, as
demonstrated in Figure 23-1. Despite the fact that risk can be held to a
minimum, less than 10 percent of U.S. firms make an attempt to sell their
products overseas. Only a very small minority of companies actually operate overseas. This reluctance stems from a feeling of uncertainty about
international trade and from a difficulty in obtaining specific and reliable
information about opportunities and operating methods for any given
type of business.

Companies engage in international business in any of six principal
ways:

■ *Casual* exporting occurs when goods are produced and sold locally but also exported or resold overseas by the local buyer. Many companies engage in this kind of international trade without even being aware
of it.

■ Many companies produce goods with the specific intention of
exporting them. *Active* participation in export trade may be achieved
through different distribution channels. A manufacturer may sell and
ship directly to an import firm abroad. The import firm may sell to a
domestic export firm, which in turn resells to a foreign importer. In many
cases, as with the sale of component parts, for instance, companies sell
directly to a user firm abroad.

■ *Foreign licensing* is a transitional stage between exporting and
international operations. Under this procedure, a domestic manufacturer
of a particular product grants a company in a foreign country a license to
make the product there. In return for the production rights, the foreign
firm pays the domestic manufacturer a fee or a portion of its revenues.
This arrangement allows the domestic company to take at least partial
advantage of the foreign market. It saves transportation costs and may
avoid high tariffs or other trade barriers. At the same time, it is far simpler
than creating a new overseas operation to produce and sell the product.

■ *Marketing abroad* is the first way in which most companies
become involved with overseas operations. Production facilities remain
in the company's home country. By maintaining a marketing subsidiary
or affiliate abroad, a company gains far greater control of sales operations
and can aggressively and creatively promote its products to foreign markets.

■ A company strongly committed to international business will
often *manufacture and sell* its own goods abroad, sometimes in several
countries. This makes selling easier. It saves transportation costs, eli-

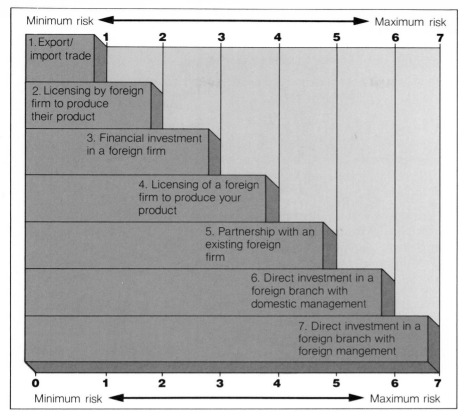

Figure 23-1
Degree of risk associated with different methods of entering international trade.

Minimum risk ←——————————————→ Maximum risk

1   2   3   4   5   6   7

1. Export/import trade

2. Licensing by foreign firm to produce their product

3. Financial investment in a foreign firm

4. Licensing of a foreign firm to produce your product

5. Partnership with an existing foreign firm

6. Direct investment in a foreign branch with domestic management

7. Direct investment in a foreign branch with foreign mangement

0   1   2   3   4   5   6   7

Minimum risk ←——————————————→ Maximum risk

Source: David Kollat, Roger Blackwell, and James Robeson, *Strategic Marketing*, Holt, Rinehart and Winston, New York, 1972, p. 173. Copyright © 1972 by Holt, Rinehart and Winston, Inc.

minates unnecessary intermediaries, and avoids trade restrictions and tariffs. Normally, this option is available only to relatively large companies capable of decentralizing their organizations to some extent.

■ *Joint ownership* of an enterprise with a company or government in the foreign country sometimes has unique advantages. The foreign co-owner's specialized knowledge of local conditions often contributes to success. Such an arrangement has a preferred legal status in some countries. For large ventures, more capital may be available and the risk is shared.

DIRECT AND INDIRECT DISTRIBUTION

Resembles marketing channels

Many of the methods of engaging in international business correspond to direct and indirect distribution in domestic trade. Companies with international operations—marketing, manufacturing, or both—use a direct channel. They may establish a branch or subsidiary abroad to handle the marketing or manufacturing activities. Often, the foreign operation is established by acquiring an existing foreign company. A domestic company with its own export company to sell directly to foreign customers is also using a direct channel.

Indirect channels involve intermediaries. Much of the import-export trade of any country is handled by import or export merchants, agents, brokers, or buyers.

4   OBSTACLES TO INTERNATIONAL BUSINESS

The hurdles are many, but they are not insurmountable

Engaging in international business is a very sophisticated activity. It requires great personal and business skill, experience, and knowledge. Even the best international business manager will encounter political, legal, social, and financial obstacles that may be difficult to overcome.

CULTURAL BARRIERS

Language, attitudes, and customs

Dealing with a country that uses a different language creates many problems. It is often difficult to find top managers who speak more than one language fluently. Advertising written in one language often cannot be translated into another and retain its meaning and force. Even product names can be troublesome. Chevrolet's Nova automobile would seem oddly named to the world's 200 million Spanish-speaking people for whom "no va" means "doesn't go."

Language difficulties can often be solved. On the other hand, deep cultural differences—social expectations, manners, and methods of doing business—can be persistent problems to a salesperson or manager doing business in a foreign country. Countries differ in their preferred meeting times, the formality or informality of discussion, the length and styles of negotiation, and in scores of other subtle approaches to business.

Consumers also differ in their preferences from country to country. Color, shape, packaging, and advertising may have different effects in different nations. Marketers in Japan, for example, have found all of these cultural barriers. Western instructional manuals seem cold and impersonal to Japanese buyers accustomed to the cordial, personal, explanatory tone of their own manuals. Japanese buyers expect to find their goods packed in containers that are clean, unmarked, and unbent. Western marketers sometimes have to double-pack goods being sent to Japan, with an attractive display box packed inside another box for shipping. Men's toiletries cannot be displayed near women's cosmetics in Japan because the men usually will not approach the women's counter. Cultural differences like these can make marketing a challenging undertaking in a foreign country.

American children eat candy as a treat between meals. Italian children are likely to put a bar of chocolate between two slices of bread for a snack. French cooks routinely use bar chocolate in their cooking.

People in France and West Germany eat more packaged spaghetti than Italians do. The catch is that Italians buy theirs loose. German and

Dutch businesspeople take their spouses with them on business trips. This is less likely to occur with the British and is almost unheard of in Asia.

FINANCIAL TRANSACTIONS
Much can be lost in conversion

Trading between sovereign nations creates financial complications because currencies are not of equal value and the rates of exchange between currencies are not fixed. An *exchange rate* is the amount of one currency that exactly equals a given amount of another currency at a given time. In May 1983, for example, one U.S. dollar equaled 2.45 West German marks. A U.S. company in Germany could exchange 1,000,000 marks for about $408,160 (minus the exchange fee). However, if the exchange rate rose to three marks to the dollar, the company's marks would only be worth $333,000. The shifting rates complicate transactions and can cause a significant loss of value to a company's currency assets.

TRADE BARRIERS
Protection for domestic industries

Countries often limit international trade by legal means. The most common methods are tariffs and quotas. A *tariff* is a tax collected on imported goods. Many tariffs, called *revenue tariffs,* are levied only to raise money for the government. Others are *protective tariffs,* established to discourage importation of certain products or to raise their price so as to reduce competition with domestic goods of the same type. A *quota* is a legal limit on the quantity of specific goods that may be imported. An *embargo* is a final extreme quota. It actually prohibits trade in certain goods or with certain countries. The United States has prohibited trade with certain communist countries, partly in an effort to weaken their economies. Most Arab nations have a trade embargo on Israeli shipments resulting from their political and religious differences.

The underlying reason for imposing protective tariffs and quotas is to encourage the growth of domestic industries and to protect them from price competition from foreign companies. This is considered to be especially important for those industries that are essential for the national defense.

Tariffs are also used to maintain a favorable balance of payments. A nation's *balance of trade* may be defined as the total value of its exports minus the total value of its imports. The balance of trade closely affects another figure, the *balance of payments,* which is the total of all payments made to foreign countries minus total receipts from abroad. This figure includes trade plus other factors, like international loans and spending by tourists. The balance of trade is said to be favorable, or positive, when exports exceed imports. It is unfavorable when imports exceed exports because the country is not receiving adequate revenue from selling exports to pay for needed imports. For that reason, governments may impose tariffs or quotas to limit imports, thereby making the balance of payments more favorable.

For 50 years or more, the American style of management was emulated all over the world. After all, U.S. industries set the pace for technology and productivity. This must stem from a superior form of management, was the reasoning. Within the last decade or so, however, the rest of the world hasn't been so sure about the American way of doing business. Nor have some U.S. companies. A great many have begun to copy other international styles, most notably the Japanese style of management.

In its simplest form, Japanese management can be characterized, says Jay Hall, Ph.D., "by several practices solely lacking in American managers." For example: The Japanese have a great sense of civility, good manners, and a genuine concern for personal dignity. The Japanese managerial system does not pit management against labor, or in fact, one person against another. It promotes collaboration so that the organizational and cultural structure is not damaged. The Japanese routinely appeal to a higher purpose than making money, the satisfaction an individual gets from performing well. As a consequence, Japanese businesses try to involve the whole person at every level and seek a consensus in making decisions. Dr. Hall contends that the reason Japanese products compete so effectively with American ones, not only in the United States, but elsewhere in the world, is because of the "wholeness" of the Japanese approach.

Americans need not reinvent the "management wheel," concludes Dr. Hall. We should, however, recall or adopt from the Japanese many of the features now forgotten or missing in U.S. business practice. It would, he believes, make us more effective in international markets.

Source: Jay Hall, "In Search of the Japanese Wheel," Datapoint (Teleometrics International, The Woodlands, Texas), Vol. 1, No. 1, Spring 1981, p. 1.

Do you think the Japanese system of management would work as well in the United States as it does in Japan? Should U.S. companies adopt the Japanese style of management when doing business abroad, or is just "being ourselves" likely to be more effective?

OPERATIONAL PROBLEMS

Delays and uncertainty

Complex problems arise in international business. Transportation between countries is more difficult than domestic transportation because goods must pass through customs each time they cross a national border. A great deal of paperwork is usually needed to get import and export licenses. Delay and outright harrassment are not unusual. Transportation is also more expensive in international trade when distances are great.

Foreign political climates are often unpredictable. Production facilities have been expropriated by unfriendly governments. Terrorism and kidnapping have been directed against U.S. companies operating abroad. Foreign tax structures may be unfavorable in some cases.

Foreign business climates and methods may create ethical problems. In some parts of the world, bribery is more widely accepted than in the United States, although it is practiced here, too. In major sales efforts abroad, many U.S. firms have offered and paid large "commissions" to government officials, company officers, and others in return for sales orders or for help in getting orders. This is illegal in the United States but has been commonly practiced by U.S. companies trading in other countries.

5 MULTINATIONAL COMPANIES

The ultimate international involvement

The expansion of international business, particularly since the end of World War II, has resulted in the creation of a unique structure: the multinational corporation. A *multinational corporation* is one that carries on operations in a number of different countries. Its international operations contribute significantly to overall revenues and size. In recent years, differences among countries have decreased. Markets in the Philippines, Hungary, Zaire, Indonesia, and in every other country have grown in similarity. Demands exist nearly everywhere for the same general kinds of consumer goods. This, combined with the advantages of producing goods in the country where they will be sold, has greatly encouraged the growth of multinationals.

Many people think of Avon Products, Inc., the cosmetics firm, as an exclusively American company. Surprisingly, Avon has 900,000 ladies "calling" outside of the United States. Avon representatives sell in 35 countries including Nigeria, Peru, Portugal, and Taiwan. The company operates a major printing operation in London, one that produces 93 million promotional brochures in eight languages each year. All told, Avon generated 41 percent of its sales revenues, or $1.22 billion from international markets in 1982. Avon is truly multinational in that 31 percent of its assets are overseas.

IBM, General Motors Corporation, General Electric Co., Exxon, Texaco, Deere, International Telephone and Telegraph Co., and scores of other giant companies are true multinationals. Table 23-1 on page 421 lists several multinational corporations and shows the extent of their involvement in foreign trade.

A company usually evolves into a multinational over a period of time. First, it places more and more emphasis on exporting goods produced by its home factories. Then, it opens one or more foreign offices to allow for more aggressive marketing efforts. The offices may expand to include the production of goods. The company often buys foreign companies already in business producing the same or different kinds of products. Soon, full-fledged multinational operations are under way.

The countries in which multinationals operate often are not enthusiastic about their presence there. The citizens of those countries tend to regard the companies as basically foreign rather than multinational. This view is justified to the extent that the company's profits from international operations are returned to its home country for distribution to owners. The multinationals are becoming more truly international, however, and it is likely that this feeling will fade. Big corporations are now concentrating on hiring natives of the countries in which they operate. Multinationals are also encouraging their other employees to learn more about foreign cultures and languages. Management is becoming more decentralized and actual ownership of many companies is becoming more and more international.

IMPACT ON WORLD AFFAIRS

Companies bigger than countries

The great size and true international character of multinational corporations is bound to give them intentional and unintentional influence in the political and economic affairs of the countries in which they operate. The most famous example has probably been that of International Telephone and Telegraph Co. (ITT) in Chile. The traditional business of ITT had been constructing and operating telephone and telegraph companies in foreign countries, but it has diversified into many other lines, from cosmetics to hams. In one of a succession of scandals concerning the company, it was alleged that ITT had made serious efforts in the early 1970s to block the election of presidential candidate Salvador Allende and later to encourage his overthrow.

Regardless of the legality of ITT's efforts, it is clear that the large multinationals are capable of exerting decisive power in the countries in which they operate. Chile's entire GNP in 1972, the year of Allende's election, was only $7.7 billion. For that year, ITT's sales were $8.6 billion. Effective and fair means of controlling this kind of influence have not been developed. The corporate executives of the top multinationals can wield as much power internationally as most heads of state.

6   INTERNATIONAL COOPERATION IN TRADE

An easing of restraints

Nations erect trade barriers. The political decisions of individual countries often complicate and interfere with international business. Still, there are many instances of multination cooperation, making trade easier, fairer, and more beneficial for all involved.

MULTINATIONAL ECONOMIC COMMUNITIES

Success in the common market

Countries with close mutual interests often join to create trade communities. The best known and most successful is the European Economic Community, often called the **Common Market.** The Common Market currently includes nine European nations. Its most notable contribution has been to completely eliminate tariffs among member nations and to establish a uniform tariff for all goods shipped to the Common Market nations from nonmember nations. The cooperative effort appears to be enjoying considerable success in encouraging the free movement of labor, capital, technology, goods, and services among members. In addition, the Common Market's share of world trade has increased substantially.

Economic agreements elsewhere have been less successful, but progress is being made. Honduras, El Salvador, Nicaragua, Guatemala, and Costa Rica, despite recent political differences among these nations, have formed the Central American Common Market. Its purpose is to promote the economic integration of member nations, including the elimination of tariffs among members and the establishment of a uniform currency. The Latin American Free Trade Association is working toward creating a cooperative economic community similar to the European Common Market. Its members are ten South American countries and Mexico. Progress has been slow, but some members have succeeded in reducing trade barriers. A number of other trade associations exist but are generally not so close-knit as the Common Market and the other economic communities mentioned. However, they also encourage communication and cooperation in business matters.

INTERNATIONAL TREATIES

Toward fewer trade barriers

The General Agreement on Tariffs and Trade (GATT) is a treaty pledging that all subscribing nations will work for freer trade with fewer barriers. The agreement has the practical effect of bringing nations together periodically to discuss their trade differences. Some progress has been made in reducing trade barriers. Individual nations may also establish treaties spelling out terms of trade. The United States, for instance, gives preferred status to certain favored trading partners.

INTERNATIONAL BANKING INSTITUTIONS

Sponsored by the United Nations

An institution called the World Bank has been established to provide financial assistance for international development and trade. In recent years it has been engaged in a major effort to help debt-ridden countries, such as Mexico, Brazil, and Argentina, avoid default on their international loan obligations. The World Bank includes three subsidiary institutions, all associated with the United Nations:

■   The International Bank for Reconstruction and Development was formed after World War II to borrow money to relend to countries needing financial assistance to recover from the effects of war.

■ The International Finance Corporation makes loans to help finance projects that will contribute to economic development.

■ The International Development Association makes long-term, low-interest loans, mainly to developing nations. The association provides these nations with funds so that they can build or acquire production facilities that will enable them to participate in world trade.

The United States maintains its own federally operated Export-Import Bank. Backed by the U.S. Treasury, this bank makes loans for U.S. international trade ventures when private sources of funds are unavailable.

THE UNITED STATES DEPARTMENT OF COMMERCE

Numerous assistance programs

For companies engaging in or planning to engage in international business, the United States Department of Commerce has numerous assistance programs. The Bureau of International Commerce, in particular, is a source of information and aid useful for the planning and management of exporting, importing, and overseas operation. The Department of Commerce also compiles information on the U.S. balance of payments and other overall indicators of world trade performance.

Key Concepts

1. International business includes (a) international trade—importing and exporting of goods among nations—and (b) international operations—carrying on marketing and production in foreign countries.
2. Resources control a nation's ability to engage in international business. Countries specialize in producing certain products for international trade based on their absolute advantages or comparative advantages over other countries.
3. Companies engaging in international business may undertake casual or active exporting, foreign licensing, overseas marketing and production, or joint ownership of foreign production facilities.
4. There are many obstacles to easy, free trade among nations. Among these are different languages and customs, varied currencies with shifting exchange rates, tariffs, quotas, embargoes and other trade barriers, and operational problems such as transportation costs and unfavorable tax policies.
5. Multinational corporations do business in a number of different countries and view their international operations as an essential part of their business. Some multinationals are so large and powerful that they exert an uncontrolled influence on some of the nations in which they operate.
6. Common markets, trade agreements, treaties, and international banks and lending institutions are methods countries use to encourage and regulate international business.

Review Questions

1. Define, identify, or explain each of the following key terms or phrases found on the pages indicated.

absolute advantage   (p. 423)
balance of payments   (p. 427)
balance of trade   (p. 427)

Common Market (p. 432)
comparative advantage (p. 423)
embargo (p. 427)
exchange rate (p. 427)
exporting (p. 420)
importing (p. 420)
international operations (p. 420)
international trade (p. 420)
multinational corporation (p. 430)
protective tariff (p. 427)
quota (p. 427)
revenue tariff (p. 427)
tariff (p. 427)

2. International business includes two different kinds of activities. Name and define them.
3. Why is it difficult for a developing nation to acquire the capital resources needed to successfully take part in world trade?

4. The concepts of absolute advantage and comparative advantage include three ways a country may decide on which goods to specialize in for foreign trade. Describe them.
5. Define casual exporting and active exporting. How do they differ?
6. Distinguish between direct and indirect distribution methods in international trade.
7. Why are fluctuating exchange rates an obstacle to international business?
8. What is the underlying reason for imposing protective tariffs and quotas?
9. What distinguishes a multinational company from others that do business overseas?
10. What is the European Economic Community? How has it affected international trade?

Case Critique 23-1
The Case of the Missing Agent

Dayco Corporation, a major manufacturer of industrial V belts, mostly sold its products inside the United States. The company only sold an occasional small order to the Soviet Union. Then, in 1978, there came a chance to expand the company's export business. An international trade agent, or broker, based in New York City, told Dayco that she had good connections with European importers and especially in the U.S.S.R. First, the agent said, Dayco would have to prove that it could manufacture a specially designed belt for the Russians. Proper papers for this transaction were signed with Tractorexport, a Soviet trade organization. Dayco made the goods, shipped them to the U.S.S.R. and got paid $1 million dollars for the order. The agent got a typical 10 percent, or $100,000 commission. Now, said the agent, there was another $120 million in Soviet orders awaiting Dayco. In fact, the Soviets were so pleased with the company's products that Dayco could set a profit margin of 50 percent more than usual. The only hitch, said the agent, was that her commission as a trade broker would have to be paid to her in advance. It was needed to make the proper "connections" with European agents and others dealing with the Soviet Union.

Dayco paid the agent $14 million and then began making the special V belts as fast as it could.

At the agent's direction, the belts were packed in wooden crates marked "European Exports" and shipped off to a port in West Germany where they were supposed to be picked up by Soviet freighters. Then a hitch developed. The problem, it appeared to Dayco, was that the Soviets were very slow paying customers. The company waited and waited. It pressed the agent, and periodically she was able to get a small payment of $100,000 or so. Finally, in desperation, the company went to the United States' Department of Commerce. Were the Russians typically slow to pay up? Why, no, said the Commerce Department officials. But it is important that you have an irrevocable letter of credit from them before you ship the merchandise. Do you have one? Dayco management did not. Dayco then contacted Tractorexport. The Soviets knew nothing about the second order, had never heard about it. In turn, Dayco tried to hunt up the agent to find out what happened. Not surprisingly, the agent had disappeared.

In Dayco's annual report of 1980, there appeared this statement: ". . . an outside sales agent made substantial misrepresentations in connection with orders submitted for certain export customers. This determination was made because of discrepancies discovered between orders presented by the agent and actual orders verified by the customers." The "discrepancy" cost Dayco about $12 million in agent's fees and $25 million or more in inventories of custom-made belts gathering dust in a German warehouse.

1. Would you call Dayco a multinational company? Why? Was its foreign trade with the U.S.S.R. active or casual?
2. In carrying on trade with the Soviet Union, what channel did the company use?
3. Why would the Soviet Union have wanted to buy the V belts from Dayco in the first place?

Source: Dean Rotbart, "Trade Fiasco," *The Wall Street Journal*, April 5, 1982, p. 1.

Case Critique 23-2
China Trade in a Van

Rosemary Trible got the idea of setting up an import firm after visiting China. She was intrigued with the exquisite porcelain produced there. Together with two other women from her hometown—one of whom could speak Chinese—Trible declared themselves in the importing business. They went to a bank, explained what they wanted to do and were assured of a loan. Then, the fledgling firm (Friendship Imports) discovered the real problem in trying to do business with the People's Republic of China: good, old-fashioned red tape. There are restrictions on both sides, but especially in China, which means, said Trible, "You have to be very persistent." Nearly every aspect of business represents a delay, from initiating a purchase to transportation of shipments.

One of the first hurdles a company faces is obtaining an invitation to visit China so that orders can be placed. A principal occasion to visit is the Canton Trade Fair, a semiannual event where all sorts of Chinese export items are displayed and sold. To attend that fair, Trible approached the Chinese Embassy in the United States. The embassy requested detailed financial information and background files on all of Friendship's partners. Then the partners waited for approval. It took several weeks, but it was granted in time to visit the fair.

Trible's congressional connections—she was married to a member of Congress—seemed to have helped. But the key to the invitation of

Friendship Importers to do business with China lay primarily in the unique way in which the firm proposed to operate. Friendship first imports merchandise to its warehouse. It then takes a representative selection of items in its "showcase van" on the road to display them directly to buyers at department stores and specialty shops throughout the middle Atlantic states. Among the most popular merchandise is jewelry, lacquerware, cloisonné, and decorative porcelain objects. A Department of Commerce trade expert says that China's trade companies are more interested in selling goods than in making friends. Friendship will succeed as an importer, the expert said, strictly on its ability to demonstrate effectiveness to the Chinese.

1. Why would articles imported from China represent merchandise that might be bought by Americans?
2. What particular international obstacles did Friendship Imports have to overcome in order to start up their business?
3. So far as risk is concerned, where would Friendship Imports' method of entering international trade stand on a scale of low to high risk?

Source: Marsha Blakemore, "Mrs. Trible Makes Go of Venture," *Wilmington* (North Carolina) *Morning Star*, July 20, 1981, p. 1.

Chapter 24

Use of Technology, Statistics, and Computers in Business

1 TECHNOLOGY REPRESENTS ADVANCES IN THE PHYSICAL, BIOLOGICAL, AND MATHEMATICAL SCIENCES

In applying technology, businesses must balance human values against material gains.

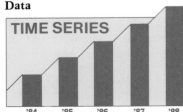

2 STATISTICS MAKES NUMBERS MEANINGFUL AND USEFUL

This is accomplished through

Measurement	Analysis	Interpretation

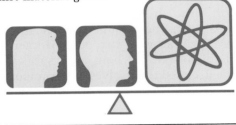  

3 DESCRIPTIVE STATISTICS

Summarize and Present Data Data

MEDIAN
201
263
292
329
358

TIME SERIES

'84 '85 '86 '87 '88

4 INFERENTIAL STATISTICS
help managers draw conclusions about

Cause   and   Effect

5 A COMPUTER IS A SYSTEM
of incredibly fast electronic data processing devices (hardware) and programmed instructions (software).

6 COMPUTERS PERFORM A VARIETY OF FUNCTIONS

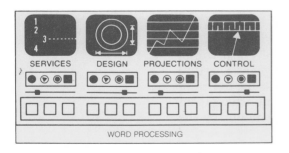

Learning Objectives

The purpose of this chapter is to show how technology and its application present both an opportunity and a problem to business management, to define and illustrate certain basic, useful statistical terms and techniques, to define computer components, and to describe how computer systems assist managers in planning and operating a business.

As evidence of general comprehension, after studying this chapter, you should be able to:

1. Identify the major disciplines from which technology develops and differentiate between scientific research and applied engineering.

2. Explain how a statistical sample might represent a numerical population, or universe.

3. Calculate the mean, median, and mode and understand the way in which index numbers and time series are used.

4. Comprehend the significance of correlation and identify applications for linear programming and mathematical models.

5. Describe the nomenclature of computer hardware and software and of computer operations.

6. Recognize the functions performed by computers and discuss the advantages and disadvantages of business' use of computers.

If your class is using SSweetco: Business Model and Activity File for Business in Action, see Chapter 24 in that book after you complete this chapter. There you will find exercises and activities to help you apply your learning to typical business situations.

Everyone knows that business is no longer carried on by individuals seated at rolltop desks, keeping books with a quill pen. However, it may still be difficult to conceive of the true extent to which modern technology has revolutionized business.

No other change has so fundamentally affected the capabilities of business as the tremendous growth of sophisticated technology. The basic resources of land, methods of accumulating capital, and the willingness and ability of labor to produce goods and services still constitute the foundations of production. However, the explosion of knowledge about methods of carrying out production and distribution has profoundly affected the way the basic resources are being used now and will be used in the future.

1   TECHNOLOGY

A scientific storehouse of methods and techniques

Technology is the collection of methods a society uses to provide itself with material needs and wants. It embraces all the specific ways people obtain food, clothing, shelter, security, transportation, warmth, and the other things they desire. In a primitive society, technology may encompass a body of knowledge about hunting, gathering roots, herbs and other naturally occurring plants, and about how to make and use a few simple tools. In a society such as ours, technology includes an incredible range of methods for discovering and extracting natural resources, converting them to useful products, and distributing the products to end users. The more a society exploits its resources, the more technology must stress the proper management, conservation, and allocation of those resources. In our society, most advances in technology stem from engineering and the applications of formal research in the physical, biological, social, and mathematical sciences to management.

GROWTH OF TECHNICAL KNOWLEDGE

A virtual explosion

The total fund of knowledge, particularly about the physical world, has been increasing at a breathtaking pace for the past 25 years. Every 10 years, the total amount of technical knowledge doubles. By the mid-1970s, there were already over 100,000 different journals publishing technical information. There will be more than double that amount by the time you read this book.

This increase in information and knowledge represents an unparalleled absorption in the physical reality—that which can be measured, counted, or reported. At the same time, it has produced a wide range of products. The attraction these goods hold for consumers has probably led to an ever greater reliance on material goods for personal satisfaction. Many observers have felt that this strong emphasis on material goods interferes with the satisfaction of true human needs. They point out a person's capacity of psychic and spiritual knowledge and growth and argue that materialistic values do not contribute to achieving this full human potential. Others, like Dr. Howard Johnson, chairperson of the Massachusetts Institute of Technology, argue that material progress may be a necessary foundation for the ultimate development of sound spiritual values.

APPLICATION OF TECHNOLOGY

Converting theory to practice

Genuine concern over the ultimate utility of material investigation and development has in no way slowed its progress. Scientific study is a major priority in colleges and universities, in private business, and in the government. Basic research and applied research in the physical sciences, biology, mathematics, and the social sciences have had a profound effect on what our society does and how it does it.

The physical sciences generally include physics, chemistry, geology, astronomy, and other fields having to do with the concrete, nonliving materials and processes of the world and universe. The effects of developments in the physical sciences are found everywhere. The discovery and design of new products, materials, conversion processes, and energy sources often grow from new basic knowledge of the physical world. Comfort, mobility, safety, and nutrition have all been improved by physical science.

The biological sciences focus mainly on the life processes and the behavior of living things, although much biological research is based on physics, chemistry, or some other strictly physical science. Biological research has contributed to nutrition and many other needs of human life and has resulted in striking gains in health care and the extension of the human life span.

Psychology, sociology, anthropology, and related disciplines concentrate on the behavior and interactions of human beings and are called the social sciences. These studies have affected our understanding of what people want, why they work, and under what conditions they work best. The influence of the social sciences on management methods and on the structure of organizations has been especially significant.

Mathematics is essential to all scientific study. In recent years, with the further development of statistics and logic and the systematic study of information exchange, mathematics has had even broader applications. Statistical and mathematical methods have important uses in business management. Some of these will be described later in this chapter.

Scientific research normally concentrates on gaining knowledge. Scientists seek to understand how and why things work without stressing how the knowledge can be used. Engineering emphasizes the practical application of scientific knowledge. Engineers have special skill in designing products and mechanisms and selecting materials and production methods. Many business organizations carry on their own research and development, combining the activities of science and engineering. *Industrial research and development (R&D)* aims ultimately at creating new products that can be produced and sold. In the process, R&D often engages in rigorous and creative scientific work, sometimes uncovering important theoretical principles.

The application of technology to modern business creates some difficult requirements for business managers:

■   They must keep informed about a huge number of scientific and engineering developments, which may be of potential use to their companies in the future.

■   They must find ways to select the technical developments that would be economically useful to their companies. They must then incorporate these technological developments in the production process.

■   They must deal with the human problems that accompany high technology in industry. They need to be able to help men and women work effectively with increasingly sophisticated machines. They need to approach the social problems that result partly from changing technology: unemployment, job changes, employees with skills that are no longer usable, demeaning and meaningless routine jobs, and others.

2   STATISTICS IN BUSINESS

Making numbers meaningful and useful

The results of most research efforts can only be made useful by submitting the findings to statistical analysis. *Statistics* makes any kind of numerical data useful and meaningful. On the one hand, the term, statistics, is often used to refer to a collection of numerical data. On the other hand, and in its more important sense, statistics can better be understood by dividing the definition into three parts. Statistics embraces (a) methods of collecting data, (b) the art of summarizing and presenting data, and (c) the art and science of interpreting and drawing inferences from data. Methods of collecting data will be discussed immediately below. The second part of the definition—summarizing and presenting data—is called descriptive statistics and its explanation will be treated separately. The third part of the definition—interpreting and drawing inferences—is called inferential statistics, and it will also be treated separately.

Regardless of terminology, the use of statistics has become invaluable in business. It provides the keys that unlock the wealth of information that businesses depend upon. Statistics has become especially important since the advent of the computer. Up until then, the use of statistics was sharply limited because old-fashioned ways of manipulating and computing numbers were very slow and cumbersome. Nowadays, almost anyone with a basic knowledge of statistics can, with the aid of a computer, accomplish what only gifted mathematicians could do only a quarter century ago.

MEASUREMENT AND SAMPLING

The means for collecting data

Statistics begins with measurement. The measurements may be as simple as counting. The United States Bureau of the Census, for example, counts all of the people in the country every ten years. The measurements may be physical, as when a quality control inspector weighs products from a manufacturing process. The measurements may be answers to questionnaires, tallied results of observations, scores on tests, or any other measure that gives a consistent numerical result. One of the basic rules of statistics is that if measurements are not accurate, consistent, and truly pertinent to the information desired, no amount of mathematical analysis will make them mean anything.

Statistical methods are most often used when large quantities of data must be interpreted. Many times, the potential number of measurements is so great that it is not possible to measure every single item or event. A researcher who wants to compare the average height of individuals in the United States with the average height of individuals in the People's Republic of China cannot possibly measure every person in both countries. In such situations, it is necessary to take a sample. A *sample* is a subgroup chosen for measurement which has characteristics similar to the larger group that is the researcher's real interest. The larger group being investigated by the study of a sample is called the *population,* or *universe.*

One of the most common failings of statistical analysis is making interpretations based on unrepresentative samples. A sample that gives results significantly different from the universe it is meant to represent is a *biased sample.* Great care is required in order to avoid biased sampling. Business methods analysts might, for example, want to learn the opinions of top executives on a new law that has just been passed. The analysts prepare a detailed questionnaire and mail it to 1,000 executives. Five hundred questionnaires are returned, and the analysts based their conclusions on those 500. However, there is always reason to believe that the executives who returned the questionnaires are different from the entire population of executives. They may be the less successful businessmen with time on their hands to fill out questionnaires. The questionnaires may have actually been completed by aides or secretaries. The executives who took the time to respond may have been especially opposed to the law and viewed the questionnaire as an opportunity to protest. It takes extremely skillful research to weed out such misleading data.

3   DESCRIPTIVE STATISTICS

Classifying and summarizing data

Collecting meaningful mesurements is the first major aim of statistics. The second is to classify and summarize the measurements to make their practical meaning apparent. *Descriptive statistics* is used to summarize quantities of current numerical data and give an overall picture of their meaning. For example, a manager of a telephone ordering service may want to make a statistical analysis of the length of time it takes a clerk to handle a call. The first step would be either to time all the calls received, or, if that were not practical, to time a representative sampling of the calls. An *array* is then made of the number of minutes that each call lasted. An array is a group of numbers placed in order according to size. Table 24-1 illustrates such an array. The next step is to describe this array in terms of its central value and/or its dispersion.

CENTRAL TENDENCIES

Finding the averages

All sports fans know the value of finding a central tendency, or average. That's the best way to compare the typical performance of one player or team with another. The same kind of information is useful to companies that want to find the average sales performance of various products and dozens of other indicators of progress and control.

The **central value** of a group of numbers is the number chosen, or calculated, to be typical of the whole group. This may be the mean, median, or mode. The **mean** is calculated by adding all of the measurements and dividing by the number of measurements taken. (A in Table 24-1.) The **median** is the point that divides an array in half: 50 percent of the measurements are greater than the median and 50 percent are smaller. (B in Table 24-1.) The **mode** is the measurement which is observed most frequently in a set of data. (See Figure 24-1.) For example, if the number 12 occurs most frequently

TABLE 24-1

Finding Central Tendencies From an Array
(Sample of times required by an airlines clerk to process reservation requests by telephone)

Array		
Call Number		Duration in Seconds
8		63
3		64
2		65
9		66
13		68
11		79
5		92
1		111 Median (B)
12		116
15		129
14		130
7		132
4		280
6		360
10		364
Total	15 calls	2,119 seconds

Range: 63 to 364 seconds = 301 seconds (C)

Arithmetic mean = $\dfrac{2,119}{15}$ = 141.3 seconds (A)

in an array of numbers, 12 is the mode. Using only one of these three ways of measuring the central value may give a distorted picture. For example, if several of the calls to the telephone ordering service were excessively long, the mean would be off. The median and the mode would be needed to give added information.

DISPERSION

The range from high to low

Even outstanding baseball players have good and bad months. In evaluating a batter's performance for the season, a manager finds it helpful to know what the range from best to poorest was. For example, a player may average .310 in April, the player's best month, and .205 in August, the worst month. For the season, the player's average may be calculated as a mean of .265. It helps to know that this mean ranged from .205 to .310. Another player may also have a mean batting average of .265 for the season, but that player's range might be from .255 to .280. This would indicate that the second player was the more consistent batter of the two.

The **dispersion** of a group of numbers is an indication of how widely varied the measures are. The simplest indication of dispersion is the **range,** calculated by subtracting the smallest value from the largest. (C in Table 24-1.) Another statistic, the mean absolute deviation, can be used in some cases. The *mean absolute deviation* is the average amount by which individual measures deviate from the mean of all the measures. The number is large when there is much variability and small when all of the measures are relatively similar.

The advantages of the knowledge of central tendencies and dispersion in business are to summarize large sets of data. Such statistics give managers a much clearer idea of the meaning and implications of 1,000 quality control measures or of 20,000 measures of production times than could be gained from looking at lists of individual measures.

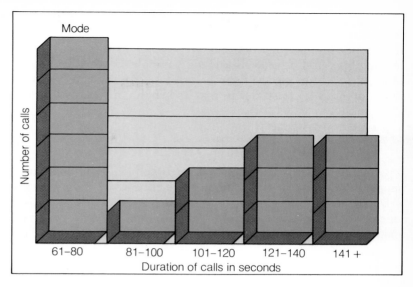

INDEX NUMBERS

A base for comparison

Companies and consumers regularly like to know what has been happening to the prices of a particular product over a period of time. A common question is "How does the price of milk, or bread, or coffee today compare with what it was, say, ten years ago?" Index numbers provide a simple way of making such comparisons. *Index numbers* provide a measure of changes over a period of time by expressing increases or decreases as additions to or subtractions from 100. (Occasionally, numbers other than 100 are used.) A manager who wanted to keep comparisons of the price changes in bread and milk would be likely to use index numbers. See Table 24-2. On some starting date, the price of each product would be taken as the equivalent of 100, the index benchmark. For example, if January 1, 1970, were the starting date, prices on that date would equal an index of 100. Index changes are calculated by dividing the current price by the benchmark price and multiplying the result by 100.

Figure 24-1
Illustration of a mode. When data gathered from Table 24-1 are plotted in 20-second intervals, the most number of occurrences, or largest concentration of data, occurs in the interval from 61 to 80 seconds. The mode could be estimated as 70 seconds.

TABLE 24-2
Hypothetical Indexes for Milk and Bread

| Year | Bread | | Milk | |
	Price per Loaf	Index	Price per Gallon	Index
1970	$0.38	100	$1.20	100
1975	0.43	113	1.55	129
1980	0.59	155	1.75	146
1985	0.72	189	2.10	175

Such indexes represent percent increases or decreases and are very convenient for studying relative changes in prices, production quantities, and other economic factors that can be expressed in numbers. The Consumer Price Index, a well-known example of this technique, shows changes in composite consumer prices, that is, data collected on the prices of various consumer items. Its benchmark year is 1967.

TIME SERIES

Past, present, and future

Managers study time-series data to help them understand what has happened in the past and to help make educated predictions about what will happen in the future. A *time series* is a collection of measures made repeatedly of the same variable. The measures are arranged in chronological order. A list of monthly factory production quantities, for instance, is a time series.

Three major kinds of variations are often used to help interpret time series. The simplest is *seasonal variation,* or the normal changes that are to be expected in each season. For example, sales of garden furniture are expected to be slow in the winter. *Secular trends* are genuinely long-term changes over a period of 30 or 40 years like population growth or shifts in a product's popularity. *Cyclical fluctuations* are shorter-term changes in a business time series caused by unpredictable—and often unknown—factors. These are changes that result from business cycles: overall swings in economic activity, employment, prices, interest rates, capital expenditures, and many other indicators. The actual measures taken by managers for a time series will often reflect all three of these variations.

Time series statistics help managers to use past experience in making judgments about the future. Suppose that in the past, a company has introduced 100 new products and 10 of them have been truly successful. Its managers might then estimate that another new product would have a 10 percent chance (10 chances in 100) of succeeding. Experience and judgment that can be numerically expressed like this can be used as a formal aid to decision making.

Time series statistics are often presented graphically. Data may be plotted on charts that show variations as the months or years progress. A most common type of graphical presentation of time series data is the bar chart, which was illustrated in Figure 21-2 in Chapter 21.

4   INFERENTIAL STATISTICS AND OTHER QUANTITATIVE METHODS

Analyzing and interpreting data

It is one thing to be able to describe a condition by means of various statistical measures. In many instances, however, that is only the beginning of statistical analysis. Businesspeople then want to know how to interpret the data so that they can make use of it. *Inferential statistics* provides methods for drawing inferences, or conclusions, from one sample and applying these conclusions to the populations. It also helps man-

Issues & Highlights

The idea of spotting a new technology and with it beating out the competition certainly seems like a good one. Yet a number of companies have discovered the risks in this game. AM International lost $245 million and plunged into bankruptcy trying to switch from its traditional electromechanical copiers to electronic ones. A decade earlier, National Cash Register dropped $139 million trying to do the same thing with cash registers. These were companies that had been technological leaders in their field. Then, when they stopped protecting their traditional technology and tried to enter the new technology, they became losers.

The cords used for automobile tires are another case in point. Originally, they were made of cotton. Rayon supplanted cotton. Next, nylon came to the fore. Finally, polyester filaments took over the market. At each stage of substitution, the company that had the most technical know-how in the present material spent most of its R&D dollars on perfecting it even further. No matter what they did in the way of improvement, however, they could not block the path of the oncoming technology.

Research into the unknown is highly speculative and risky. Who knows what will or will not turn up? Research and development of proven products and processes usually assures their improvement. The former strategy is an offensive one; the latter, a defensive one.

Source: Richard N. Foster, "A Call for Vision in Managing Technology," Business Week, May 24, 1982, p. 24.

If you were running a successful business with a proven product, which research strategy would you choose to emphasize—an offensive one looking for products that would replace the ones you now have, or a defensive strategy trying to make your product invulnerable from competitive products?

agers to make estimates about the future and to test out ideas, or hypotheses, not only about future happenings but about how various conditions can affect a business operation.

CORRELATION STATISTICS

Verifying relationships

Researchers and businesses regularly turn to statistical methods when they seek cause-and-effect relationships. A marketing manager, for example, may want to know whether or not spending more money on advertising a product will cause increased sales. A laboratory scientist may want to know whether the medicine that was statistically shown to work on rabbits will also work on human beings. The type of statistical analysis, called correlation analysis, helps to answer these questions. *Correlation analysis* shows how closely two or more sets of measurements are related. Two variables are very closely related when a change in one is consistently accompanied by a change in the other. The relationship shows a *positive correlation* when an increase in one variable is accompanied by an increase in the other. A *negative correlation* exists when an increase in one variable is accompanied by an decrease in the other.

Correlation analyses are useful to business managers and planners because they can help to predict future trends and events. A construction manager who knows that an increase in interest rates is often followed by a decrease in home-building can plan more intelligently. A sales manager can adjust sales projections knowing that consumer purchases are positively correlated with personal income.

QUANTITATIVE METHODS

Practical applications of statistics

An entire body of statistical methods and mathematical techniques have been developed to help businesses make estimates of a hypothesis about future conditions and happenings. These enable a specialist or manager to learn by trial and error on paper, or in a computer, as opposed to learning by experience. Two methods, in particular, are widely used to provide an organized approach to planning and decision making.

Linear programming is a quantitative method for deciding the best ways of allocating resources to accomplish a certain aim. It is most often used when many different resources must be combined. The resources may be materials, like minerals or component parts, or labor, equipment and facilities, money, and anything else needed to meet a production goal. The usual purpose of linear programming is to decide which resources and how much of each will produce the greatest revenue or the lowest cost. Linear programming is widely used in production and contract planning, in preparing maintenance schedules for airplanes, in transportation scheduling, and in the selection of warehouse locations.

Managers are becoming increasingly aware of the value of theoretical understanding of the workings of markets, production methods, organizational structures, and other factors affecting business operations. Understanding how different elements interact and influence each other allows analysts to make better projections of the effects of management decisions. They use simulation models to test their ideas, or hypotheses, about the changes that will result if certain factors are altered. A *model* is a mathematical description of the way variables interact in a system. (A model may also be verbal, geographical, or three-dimensional, such as a scale model of a store layout.) A simulation is a model that imitates the behavior of a particular process, situation, or system.

A mathematical model may be constructed, for example, of all the known factors affecting the sales volume of a particular product. The model would show mathematically how sales are affected by the number of salespeople, advertising budget, inflation rates, product price, disposable consumer income, and scores of other factors. Managers can then introduce a change on paper—such as an increase in the advertising budget—and have the model show what result the change can be expected to have on sales.

5 COMPUTER SYSTEMS

Devices that extend human capabilities

A prime example of the impact of new technology on business practices and capabilities is the growing use of computers. Computers have reshaped methods of obtaining, recording, and applying information in nearly every company of any size. The increasing use of statistics and formal management control and decision methods has largely resulted from the availability of general purpose computers. Such methods were nearly inconceivable in the past.

A *computer* is a system of electromechanical devices (symbolized in Figure 24-2) that receives data from its environment, processes the data arithmetically or logically, and transmits the converted data back to the environment in some way. The data read by the system usually includes instructions for its own operations. This broad definition covers a wide range of different devices and applications.

DIGITAL COMPUTERS

Manipulate numbers

A large class of computers work by turning all the data received into numerical form and performing operations on these numbers. These are *digital computers.* A typical use for a digital computer is reading a set of customer orders, adding up the total dollar amount ordered, and printing a report showing the total sales. Computers are able to perform thousands of different tasks of this type with huge quantities of data—often billions of different numbers—at extremely high speeds. To operate, computers require appropriate hardware and software.

Modern digital computers use the binary number system, where all numbers are combinations of ones and zeros. Electrical switches open and close in various sequences, to represent on for one and off for zero. The sequences are determined by the numbers being added, subtracted, multiplied and so on. The original computers used mechanical switches, later ones vacuum tubes. All of today's computers use some form of transistors that act as on-off switches capable of performing at incredible speeds. The

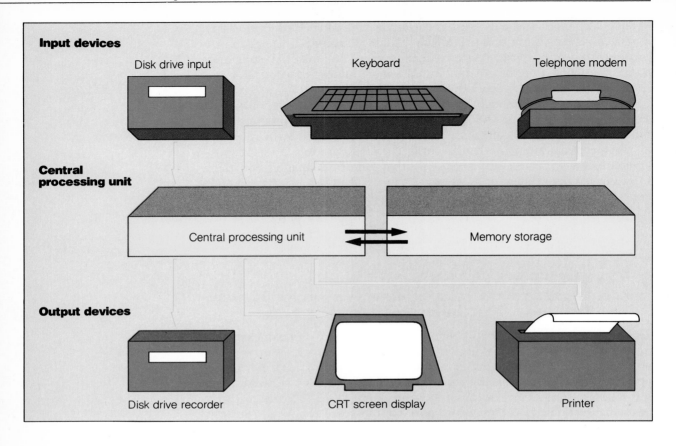

Figure 24-2
Hardware components of a small computer.

operation of these switches is dictated by a system that combines the appropriate computer equipment and instructions that give the computer the capability to perform its operations.

COMPUTER HARDWARE

Receives, manipulates, and transmits data

The most visible components of a computer system are the various devices that function in combination to receive data, process or manipulate it, and transmit the processed data on to whomever will be using it at the next step. In many instances, this will be the same person who put the data into the computer in the first place. This occurs when a salesperson, for example, checks a customer's creditworthiness when using a charge card. The salesperson inserts the card into a device that reads, or receives, that data and relays it into a computer. The computer processes the data to find out if the customer's credit balance has not been exceeded. Then the computer transmits this information back to a screen that the salesperson can read. The card reader, the computer, the readout screen, and even the electric wires that connect them are all part of the hardware.

Computer *hardware* is the term applied to the physical devices that send and receive data and perform operations on it. Every functioning digital computer must have one or more pieces of equipment capable of reading data in the form of numbers, symbols, or letters and converting them into electrical codes that can be used by an electronic processing unit. This data is called **input.** The most common input units are magnetic tape similar to that used for sound recording, and magnetic disks much like those used for "instant replays" on television. An optical scanning device (something like an electronic wand that is moved over printed figures, symbols, or letters) is also an important source of input. It is seen at grocery checkout counters and in schools for grading test questionnaires. Another device increasingly in use, especially for smaller computers, is the "floppy disk drive." It is the receptacle and transmitter into which the magnetic tape or disk is inserted. It operates in somewhat the same way as the device into which the cassette is placed in a home video game.

Computers must also have devices for sending **output,** or processed information back to users. These devices record information on media similar to those used for transmitting input. Output is commonly seen on a video display tube (also called a cathode ray tube, or CRT) or simply in printed form, as illustrated in Figure 24-3. When output is printed, this is popularly known as hard copy.

A *central processing unit (CPU)* operates between the input device and the output device. The CPU is the heart of the computer because it actually operates on the input, changing it in some way to create useful output. Most CPUs are able to perform only very simple operations, such as adding, subtracting, or comparing one number with another to determine which is larger. However, when performed in the right sequence on the numbers and letters read by the input devices, these operations can create very complex, highly structured, and useful output.

An essential component of the central processing unit is its **memory unit.** These memories are capable of storing vast amounts of information for further use and/or examination. The memory may be an integral part of a computer or a separate unit connected to it electrically.

Other terms for particular units of hardware are often encountered. Very large computers, with which smaller computers may interact, are called "mainframe computers." The proliferation of much smaller computers that are seen almost everywhere, in small businesses and in homes, are variously called "minicomputers," "microcomputers," or "personal computers." In 1976, only a few thousand small computers were made. By 1982 there were more than 1.5 million. The forecast is for over 4 million computers of all sizes to be in place by 1985.

COMPUTER SOFTWARE

Provides the instructions

In the restricted sense, *software* is a collection of instructions read by a computer that tell it where to read input, what specific operations to carry out on the data, and where to write the resulting output. (All of the procedures used to gather and verify the data, prepare it for input, locate and correct errors, and check and distribute output are sometimes also included in software.) Software is composed of a group of computer programs. A *program* lists extremely detailed instructions to the computer telling it how to carry out a specific step in a job.

Software and hardware must work together to produce the output. If a company wishes to use its computer to add up total sales every day, a number of steps are needed to enable the computer to do so. Analysts must find a way to make individual sales records readable by the computer. They might decide to collect handwritten sales slips at the end of each day and have a trained operator record the data by keypunching it into a computer input terminal. Then, a program is needed. A program even for such a simple task would have to specify the following instructions in details:

- The form in which data is recorded and how to read the input.
- How to record the data to be operated on.
- What should be added and where.
- In what form to describe the output.

TABLE 24-3
Selected Glossary of Computer Terms

Bit. The smallest unit of information that the computer recognizes, a bit is represented by the presence or absence of an electronic pulse, 0 or 1.

Byte. A byte is to a bit what a word is to a letter. Usually, one byte is eight bits long.

Compatibility. A characteristic of some computers that allows a program developed for one system to run on another system.

Database. A collection of interrelated data that is organized for ease of update and retrieval. For example, a personnel database would include information such as employee names and Social Security numbers.

Disk. A revolving plate upon which data and programs are stored.

Documentation. The printed material accompanying a program that describes what the program does and how to use it.

File. A collection of related records; an inventory file, for example.

Machine language. A program—consisting of a string of 1's and 0's—that the computer understands directly.

Memory. The section of the computer where instructions and data are stored.

Memory capacity. The maximum number of storage positions in a computer's memory. Typically, a microcomputer can have up to 64K (64,000) bytes of memory.

Menu. A list of alternative actions displayed on the video display screen for selection by the user; for example, ADD A CUSTOMER might be one option on a menu.

Microcomputer. A small computer in which the CPU is an integrated circuit deposited on a silicon chip.

Modem. A telephone hookup device that converts computer signals so that they can be sent over telephone lines; this allows microcomputers to communicate with larger systems, such as timesharing networks.

Packaged software. Sometimes referred to as "off-the-shelf" software, this is usually used as is but can be modified to fit a business's particular needs.

Peripheral. A device—for example, a video display screen or a printer—used for storing data, or for entering it into or retrieving it from the computer system.

Prompt. A request for action that is presented to a user on a video display screen.

Terminal. A peripheral device through which information is entered into or extracted from the computer.

User-friendly (user-oriented). This describes software that is designed to be easily understood by the user.

The software then has to be tested extensively. The new application can then be put in operation to produce reports of total sales.

As the computer industry matures, it introduces a number of new terms into the English language. A sampling of some of these unusual terms are shown in the computer glossary of Table 24-3.

COMPUTER LANGUAGE

Converts numbers into English

Computer programmers not only write the instructions for a computer, they also must find a way to communicate this information to the computer. They accomplish this with special languages that convert English and algebra into the binary number system the computer can understand. Three computer languages are commonly used by programmers.

COBOL (COmmon Business-Oriented Language) is designed especially for business applications. It employs English words and sentences almost exclusively.

FORTRAN (FORmula TRANslation) may be used for business, but its principal application is for scientific work where mathematical equations are solved.

BASIC (Beginners Algebraic Symbol Interpreter Compiler) is especially adaptable for input and output users, which is making its application common in business.

In addition, there have been a number of "user-friendly" programs developed for people who have no training in any of the formal computer languages. These conversational programs allow a clerk or a manager to use the computer by following the computer's instructions. For example, here's how an inexperienced person might proceed.

You turn on the terminal.

Terminal: Hello. What do you want?

You: I want to find a customer's account balance.

Terminal: Do you need instructions?

You: Yes.

Terminal: Type in customer's account number.

You: 312 5719

Terminal: Balance is $258.57 on January 15, 1984.

You: Thank you.

Terminal: Do you want anything else?

You: No.

Terminal: Turn me off. Bye.

The trick, of course, is that the computer has been programmed to recognize and respond only to the exact words that the operator has been told to use when conversing with the computer. If the operator were to say, in answer to the first query, "I want a customer's account balance," the computer would reply, "I don't understand you. Will you check your instructions and ask me again?"

COMPUTER ACCESS
Near or far, now or later

Most companies that have their own computers operate them by physically sending data to the computer, scheduling time to run each job, running the jobs, and distributing output back to users. Today, *remote access* is becoming more common. Under this operating plan, much of the data preparation—and sometimes the program writing—is done in or near the user's department, away from where the computer is located. A device is then used to read the data and transmit it over a telephone line or other connection to the computer. The data (and programs) are then either processed immediately or stored for later processing. Output may either be transmitted back over the telephone line or printed at the computer and delivered to the user.

Some computers are operated to provide *real-time service.* This means that data is processed as soon as it is fed and results are made available immediately or when requested. A good example is an automatic cash register system. As sales are entered on a cash register in a store, details about the sale may be immediately sent to a central computer. The computer can keep a running tally of sales activity and up-to-date reports may be obtained whenever requested.

COMPUTER SERVICES
From time sharing to networking

Originally, computers were so expensive to own and operate that a special kind of company was formed to provide computer services for small companies. Even today, these computer centers sell $20 billion of data processing services, computer systems analysis, and software programs. Many user companies not only purchase computer time—time sharing—but also access to "banks" of certain kinds of information held by the service company. A newer development establishes networks of cooperating computer owners who have common information needs. Members of the network, through remote access devices, may add to or manipulate data in the network's bank. Several industry associations have created computer networks for their member companies. Some states operate such networks for farmers.

ANALOG COMPUTERS
Operate on nonnumerical inputs

Digital computers operate by manipulating numbers and letters and symbols represented by numbers. *Analog computers* operate on information that is not represented numerically. They might record and respond to changes in the strength of an electrical current, in the pressure in a steam valve, in furnace temperature, in the amount of light reaching a receptor, or in any number of other kinds of non-numerical data.

ACTION BRIEF

Goodbye Postal Delivery, Hello Electronic Mail? Instead of mailing letters and memos between its 100 affiliate radio stations, RKO Networks does it by computer. It uses an electronic mail system to distribute scheduling changes, program notes, talk show biographies, and a weekly bulletin. Each station is equipped with an electronic "mailbox" and must keyboard a receipt for each message received. That way RKO is assured that the correspondence has been received and read. Merck, Sharpe and Dohme, the pharmaceutical giant uses a similar electronic mail system to keep its chain of service representatives abreast of developments to be brought to the attention of the physicians they call on. Merck used to communicate by phone, but found the home office swamped with calls. Now representatives get the information on their personal computers, which they can tap into the home office by a telephone terminal.

Source: Jeffrey Rothfelder, "Electronic Mail Delivers the Executive Message," Personal Computing, *June 1982, p. 32.*

Many combinations of analog computers and digital computers also exist. Input may be a physical process and output numerical, or input may be numerical and output physical. Such devices have obvious applications in controlling manufacturing processes.

6 COMPUTER APPLICATIONS

They serve many purposes

The ability of computers to process huge masses of data rapidly and accurately has resulted in widespread use of computers in nearly every aspect of business operations. Computers have many drawbacks, however. Even though virtually fool-proof internally, they are at the continual mercy of human error at the input stage. Nevertheless, their applications seem limitless at this time.

BASIC APPLICATIONS

Service, analysis, design, and control

One of the earliest and most thoroughly explored applications of computers has been to provide support for the activities of an organization. This has been particularly true in the area of financial recordkeeping, so that today even small companies use computers to carry out major parts of their accounting processes.

Computers are also widely used for statistical analysis services, which require complex calculations with large bodies of data. Information on the quantity and quality of production, material storage and use, inventories, sales, and hundreds of other areas of concern to management is easier to gather and use with a well-designed computer system. In large companies, the huge amounts of data could not be processed quickly and inexpensively by hand. Figure 24-3 shows a computer-prepared cost variance report.

Another increasingly important use for computers is for developing new products and procedures. The automobile industry has computer programs that display part or all of the structure of an automobile on a device similar to a television screen. Technicians can make changes in design by drawing on the screen with a beam of light. Computers store and print the drawings. They perform the complex mathematical analyses needed for determining the shapes and materials of mechanical products.

Computers also play a direct role in production control. Complex production scheduling, inventory controls, and resource allocation schemes are easier to use with computers. Automation requires digital and analog systems to control production equipment and processes.

WORD PROCESSING

Automates the modern office

Computers have had their biggest impact upon clerical operations involving numbers. In recent years, however, combinations of computers

```
MFG DIVISION      600      600                        PAGE 1
PERIOD 13 19--
```

	Period expense			Year-to-date expense		
	Planned	Actual	-Over* Under	Planned	Actual	-Over* Under
DIRECT LABOR	59,758	51,502	8,256	693,389	622,754	70,635
01 INDIRECT LABOR	42,224	30,844	11,380	497,953	468,998	28,955
07 SUPERVISION	14,622	15,804	-1,182	186,842	184,942	1,900
09 CLERICAL SALARIES	11,771	9,083	2,688	141,646	134,530	7,116
PAYROLL WORK DONE	128,375	107,233	21,142	1,519,830	1,411,224	108,606
06 ALLOWED TIME	1,136	577	559	13,868	15,321	-1,453
12 VACATIONS	—	3,024	-3,024	78,543	77,339	1,204
13 HOLIDAYS	6,882	13,588	-6,706	62,402	57,861	4,541
33 TAXABLE SICK ACCDE	1,494	846	648	18,239	17,534	705
34 NONTAXABLE SICK AC	1,513	2,283	-770	18,435	34,691	-16,256
PAYROLL BENEFITS	11,025	20,318	-9,293	191,487	202,746	-11,259
TOTAL PAYROLL COST	139,400	127,551	11,849	1,711,317	1,613,970	97,347
14 IND LAB POT	1,699	5	1,694	12,222	1,645	10,577
16 DIRECT LAB POT	1,855	6	1,849	12,731	2,125	10,606
18 PAYROLL TAXES	7,490	9,316	-1,826	99,482	94,090	5,392
19 INS WK MENS COMPEN	1,045	9,921	-8,876	13,736	22,857	-9,121
46 INSURANCE ALL OTHE	522	3,009	-2,487	6,786	9,273	-2,487
47 TAX PROPERTY MISCE	4,257	2,489	1,768	55,341	45,371	9,970
52 TRANSPORTATION	2,768	3,303	-535	32,358	35,960	-3,602
53 SUPPLIES	3,678	5,803	-2,125	44,545	41,137	3,408
54 HEAT	1,281	2,069	-788	19,400	19,367	33
55 WATER	600	—	600	7,936	5,353	2,583
56 POWER LIGHT	3,026	2,783	243	32,585	35,896	-3,311
57 PERISHABLE TOOLS	119	—	119	1,175	86	1,089
62 MACHINE RENTAL	10,769	376	10,393	140,357	64,376	75,981
64 TRAVEL	189	38	151	1,904	744	1,160
65 REPAIR MAINT	1,375	2,105	-730	14,833	13,591	1,242
67 DEPRECIATION	16,722	14,894	1,828	217,386	215,570	1,816
68 MISCELLANEOUS	198	204	-6	1,834	942	892
70 PATTERNS OUTSIDE	1,848	2,358	-510	23,708	16,478	7,230
71 SEVERANCE PAY	—	—	—	—	2,103	-2,103
80 PERISHABLE TOOLS M	5,437	5,653	-216	63,478	47,449	16,029
81 REPLACEMENT GAGES	412	186	226	4,306	2,106	2,200
82 TEMP AGENCY EMPLOY						
84 OUTSIDE DP SER	174	1,023	-849	1,953	1,921	32
85 RENT EXPENSE	5,505	5,506	-1	71,565	71,566	-1
86 REPLACE TIP TOOLS	197	197	—	1,958	2,253	-295
87 SERVICE CONTRACTS	26		26	730	661	69
89 EXPENDABLE EQUIPME	323	561	-238	1,890	891	999
90 MACH SHOP OIL	895	618	277	10,283	8,192	2,091
95 MACH SHOP SUPPLIES	235	75	160	2,347	3,099	-752
99 OVT BILLED	—	—	—		10,510	10,510
TOTAL OTHER EXPENS	72,645	72,498	147	896,829	754,592	142,237
GRAND TOTAL	212,045	200,049	11,996	2,608,146	2,368,562	239,584

*Accounting practice here identifies expenses that exceed plans (over budget) with a minus (–) sign, since these figures deduct from planned profit. Figures without minus signs indicate that actual expenses are under budget.

Figure 24-3
Example of hard copy from a computer printout.

and other devices have made major changes in the traditional office activities of stenography and secretarial work. This kind of automation has had its most dramatic effect in the introduction of word processing. **Word processing** is the production of written communications through the combined use of systems management procedures, automated technology (primarily computer-related), and skilled personnel. The least sophisticated word-processing equipment is the automatic typewriter. The most complex are literally small computer systems (like the schematic one shown in Figure 24-2) with an ability to set type and compose charts and other illustrations for printing into hardcopy records or other publications.

ADVANTAGES AND DISADVANTAGES
Computers are a mixed blessing

To a great extent, the introduction of computer methods to business operations has been a positive step. However, like nearly all technological innovations, computer use has its advantages and disadvantages.

The main *advantages* of computers are as follows:

- They are extremely fast, sometimes performing millions of simple operations every second.
- Computers can store and rapidly locate and organize tremendous amounts of information.
- They are very accurate. With well-written and thoroughly tested software, computers are virtually error-free.
- Computers can relieve employees of some of the routine clerical and mechanical work that accompanies all production activity.
- Because of their speed, memory, and ability to handle so much data, computers have made possible the use of complex statistical and analytical methods that could never be used with manual processing.

The chief *disadvantages* are as follows:

- Mainframe computers are very expensive to own and operate. Many larger mainframe models cost several hundred thousand dollars a month to rent, plus the cost of highly trained analysts, programmers, and operators.
- All computer systems require accuracy and detail in their operating software. To create an effective application is a demanding and expensive undertaking. Extensive program testing is needed.
- Software preparation or modification is still a major problem for computer users. While there is a multitude of proprietary programs that can be purchased from software companies and service centers, a great many of these programs must be modified at considerable cost to accommodate the characteristics of the user's computer system.
- Computers are only tools. The real requirement for success is an outstanding human organization surrounding the computer to decide on its use, accurately prepare input, and usefully interpret output.

Key Concepts

1. Technology is the collection of production methods used by society. Advances in technology stem mainly from research in the physical, biological, social, and mathematical sciences. Managers must remain aware of potentially beneficial technological developments, manage their introduction into their companies, and find ways to deal with problems that result from technology.

2. Statistics is a technology used for gathering, analyzing, and presenting data to give it practical value. Sampling of a large population is a technique for minimizing the time and cost of gathering data.

3. Descriptive statistics are used to summarize and present masses of numerical data. The principal methods used include measures of central tendencies and dispersion, index numbers, and time series.

4. Inferential statistics help managers to draw conclusions about the data that has been described and to project it into the future by testing ideas about possible outcomes. Numerical methods like linear programming and modeling help in planning and decision making.

5. Computers are systems of electronic devices that greatly enlarge human capability due to their incredible accuracy and speed in handling numbers and related information. These systems consist of physical devices, or hardware, and operating programs, or software.

6. Computers provide a wide variety of operational and planning services as well as process and product design and control. They have important advantages due to their speed and accuracy but require a complex, well-trained human organization in order to be used effectively.

Review Questions

1. Define, identify, or explain each of the following key terms or phrases found on the pages indicated.

analog computer   (p. 452)
array   (p. 441)
BASIC   (p. 451)
biased sample   (p. 441)
central processing unit   (p. 449)
central value   (p. 442)
COBOL   (p. 451)
computer   (p. 447)
correlation analysis   (p. 446)
cyclical fluctuations   (p. 444)
descriptive statistics   (p. 441)
digital computer   (p. 447)
dispersion   (p. 442)
FORTRAN   (p. 451)
hardware   (p. 448)
index numbers   (p. 443)
industrial research and development (p. 439)
inferential statistics   (p. 444)
input   (p. 449)

linear programming   (p. 446)
mean   (p. 442)
mean absolute deviation   (p. 443)
median   (p. 442)
memory unit   (p. 449)
mode   (p. 442)
model   (p. 447)
negative correlation   (p. 446)
output   (p. 449)
population (universe)   (p. 441)
positive correlation   (p. 446)
program   (p. 449)
range   (p. 442)
real-time service   (p. 452)
remote access   (p. 452)
sample   (p. 441)
seasonal variation   (p. 444)
secular trends   (p. 444)
software   (p. 449)
statistics   (p. 440)
technology   (p. 438)
time series   (p. 444)
time series statistics   (p. 444)
word processing   (p. 455)

2. What is technology? How does today's technology differ from that of the past? In what way does scientific research differ from engineering?

3. Why are statistical methods so concerned with measurements? What is a sample and how is it used?

4. Distinguish between an arithmetic mean, a median, and a mode.

5. Describe three types of variations that may be observed in a time series.

6. Define hardware and software. Why are they both needed for a computer system?

7. Which computer language is likely to be most commonly used for business? Give the reason for your answer.

8. Where might you actually see a remote access to a computer?

9. In what ways is word processing related to computer technology?

10. Explain some of the disadvantages of using computers.

Case Critique 24-1
The Computer Gathering Dust in a Corner

Wobco Hardware store's owner, Carla Wobble, bought a computer a couple of months ago. At the moment, it's gathering dust in a corner of the office. The computer is a beauty. It can do just about everything, including complex scientific calculations. And, along with the purchase, Carla also bought a stack of floppy disks with standard, or canned programs, that ought to be able to handle her inventories, payroll, accounts receivable, as well as her checking account balance. When the computer salesperson had come along, Carla was intrigued with what she saw. The salesperson could type perfect letters from it, draw charts and graphs, and even showed Carla how it could handle a direct mail list that Carla had been thinking about for years.

When the computer arrived at the store along with its ancillary equipment—disk drives, CRT screen display, separate memory unit, and printer, Carla was wildly enthused. She called Leon Smith, her veteran jack-of-all-clerical-trades, to take a look at it. "What are we ever going to do with that stuff?," asked Leon.

"It's going to be all yours," said Carla. "Life in this office will be easy for you from now on."

"Electrical thingamajigs like that scare me half to death," said Leon.

"You'll get used to it in no time at all," replied Carla. That was two months ago and the computer is still idle.

1. Why do you think that the computer hasn't been used?

2. What might Carla have done beforehand to assure its use?

3. What do you think of the computer system that Carla bought?

4. How might Carla have gone about buying a computer system that was more appropriate for her business?

Source: Leslie R. Schmetz, "Surviving the Computer Revolution," *Desktop Computing*, March 1982, p. 36.

Case Critique 24-2
The Electronic Boss

"Sally, will you get a copy of the SynCo report," asked Ms. Brown.

"You don't need me to get that report," said Sally. "Just call for it by using the keyboard of your management computer."

"Really! I thought that preparing and filing reports was your job."

"That's the way it used to be," said Sally, "before the main office installed this word-processing and computerized management information system. Now, my time is better spent preparing letters and reports for the word processing equipment than in retrieving material from the files for you. I don't mean to seem impertinent, Ms.

Brown, but that's the way it's supposed to work. In fact, I find myself spending more and more time supervising the people who are preparing routine letters and reports for the central word processor."

Sally smiled and left Ms. Brown's office.

Ms. Brown looked warily at the computer terminal on her desk. She touched a couple of keys rather gingerly. Then she checked her instruction manual and found the method for calling up reports. Carefully, she typed the proper call letters on the keyboard. Sure enough, right on the green screen in front of her the report began to appear, line by line. With a sigh of resignation, Ms. Brown studied the report and copied from it the information she was seeking.

At lunch later that day with a colleague, Ms. Brown commented, "Say hello to the new secretary in my office."

1. What does this case tell you about the potential impact of computers and word processing on a secretary's job?
2. What do you think Ms. Brown believes that the computer system is doing to her job?
3. What justification might there be for Ms. Brown to devote more of her time performing "secretarial work" than in the past?

Source: "Will the Boss Go Electronic, Too?," *Business Week*, May 11, 1981 p. 106.

Unit 9
Societal Influences on Business

Unit 9 shows how the American public guides and controls business activity. It enacts laws that regulate business and tries to raise ethical standards of business through persuasion and the exercise of social and economic power of consumers, employees, and concerned citizens.

The American legal system strives to ensure competition and to protect property rights, consumer interests, and the general welfare of the public. Various federal, state, and local governments tax business heavily and have established a body of law that is particularly applicable to business and commerce.

Some businesses seek to make a profit in almost any way they can to stay alive. In so doing, such enterprises may damage human lives and spoil the environment. Some people believe that business as a whole will improve ethically only when under pressure from power groups or by order of law. There is growing evidence, however, of more responsible behavior on the part of business collectively and of individual companies in particular. As to the future, it would appear that the conduct of business will continue to be no better or worse than the ethical standards exhibited by the society in which it operates.

Chapter 25

Government Regulation, Taxation, and Law

1 GOVERNMENT PROTECTS BOTH BUSINESSES AND CONSUMERS

It insures competition, protects property rights and human rights, licenses certain businesses, and regulates utilities.

2 BUSINESSES IN THE UNITED STATES ARE TAXED

so that the government can collect operating revenue and regulate or restrict certain business practices.

Revenue taxes   Restrictive taxes

3 CERTAIN LAWS APPLY PARTICULARLY TO BUSINESS

These laws may be enforced
on a federal, state, or local level.

UNIFORM
COMMERCIAL
CODE

Contract law
Sales and property law
Agency law
Negotiable instruments
Warranties
Bankruptcy law

4 THE RELATIONSHIP BETWEEN BUSINESS AND GOVERNMENT

may be that of adversaries
or partners.

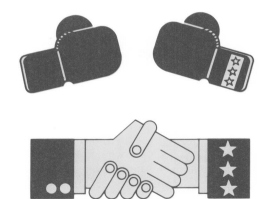

Learning Objectives

The purpose of this chapter is to explain why and how the federal government regulates business, describe the reasons for taxation and specific business taxes, and outline and interpret certain laws that apply particularly to businesses in the United States.

As evidence of general comprehension, after studying this chapter you should be able to:

1. Explain the underlying reasons for and aims of government regulation of business and identify certain regulatory agencies and their functions.
2. Recognize the two basic reasons for taxation and identify various revenue and regulatory taxes.
3. Distinguish between business law and other kinds of law; identify the basic rules of law of contracts, sales, agency, and negotiable instruments; differentiate between express and implied warranty; explain the purpose of bankruptcy, the Uniform Commercial Code, and trademark and copyright protection.
4. Discuss certain aspects of business-government relations and describe the principal kinds of government assistance to business.

If your class is using SSweetco: Business Model and Activity File for Business in Action, see Chapter 25 in that book after you complete this chapter. There you will find exercises and activities to help you apply your learning to typical business situations.

Both business and government have been created and developed by society to meet certain needs. In the United States, the main goal of business is to produce goods and services and make a profit on them. The main goal of government is to provide society with stability and to protect the rights and property of individuals and organizations. The interests of business and the interests of government are not always in harmony, even though both ultimately serve society. Considerable conflict has existed, especially in the last 50 years, between business owners and managers and government representatives.

It is important to remember, however, that even though friction between business and government is highly publicized, the two institutions are mutually supportive. The areas in which they agree and the benefits they share far outnumber their conflicts.

1   GOVERNMENT REGULATION OF BUSINESS

Protects business as well as consumer interests

As protector of the rights of individuals and organizations against harm caused by others, government has assumed an active role in regulating many business practices. This is accomplished through a variety of agencies. The most important of those are shown in Table 25-1. Basically, the goals of the federal government have centered on protecting fair competition, promoting property rights, consumer interests, and the general welfare, and overseeing certain essential industries. State governments also engage in regulation of certain business and professional activities.

PROTECTING COMPETITION

Curtails monopoly and price fixing

Chapter 1 points out that even though free enterprise is partly based on the operation of free competition, actual conditions in the marketplace and the activities of certain companies often limit competition. During the nineteenth century particularly, it became clear to some business owners and managers that competition in the marketplace was limiting the prices they could charge for their goods and was thus lowering profits. The period was one of *laissez-faire* business management, a French phrase meaning nearly complete freedom of operation. Given this freedom, many businesses set out to systematically destroy the competition that was reducing profits. Frequently, the goal was to create a business organization that was the sole source of a needed commodity. With such a monopoly position, prices—and profits—could be raised almost as high as desired, causing great hardship to consumers.

Businesses that reached a monopoly position combined two approaches: (a) driving competitors out of business, or (b) buying up or merging with them. The most common method for driving competitors out of business was for a large company to charge unreasonably low prices in one area while supporting its losses with income from other products or from other parts of the country. A small local competitor could not match the artificially low prices and would be forced to sell out or close down.

ACTION BRIEF

"Moneyball" Exempt From Antitrust. *Professional baseball, whose players average more than $200,000 a year and whose franchises are traded for millions, is still a sport. That's the federal point of view, and it leaves the "moneyball" game exempt from antitrust laws. That decision was handed down by the Supreme Court in 1922. It still stands today, although Curt Flood's suit in 1972 gave the owners a scare. [In his suit, Flood, then a player for the St. Louis Cardinals, challenged the baseball rule that said a player could not negotiate freely with another team for a trade even after the expiration of that player's contract.] The owners were happy when the Supreme Court refused to hear Flood's complaint. The Court, however, did let the sport know that it should put its house in order. In 1976, another complaint went to arbitration with a ruling that established the free agent status, wherein contracts had specified concluding dates rather than being open-ended. For the owners it became a nightmare; for the players, it was a dream come true.*

Source: Randall Poe, "Moneyball," Across the Board, September 1981, p. 12.

TABLE 25-1
Important Federal Agencies With Regulatory Powers

Agency	Regulatory Function
Environmental Protection Agency (EPA)	Enforces federal legislation controlling the environmental effects of business and government activities.
Federal Aviation Administration (FAA)	Regulates air transportation, including navigation, safety rules, and airports.
Federal Communications Commission (FCC)	Regulates rates and service of interstate telephone, telegraph, and cable companies. Allocates radio frequencies and oversees operations of radio and television stations.
Federal Power Commission (FPC)	Regulates interstate portion of electric power and natural gas industries, including site selection, wholesale rates and services, financial management, and other aspects.
Federal Reserve System (FED)	Influences and regulates the operations of its member banks. Controls certain kinds of securities transactions.
Federal Trade Commission (FTC)	Enforces antitrust laws and regulates advertising to prevent deceptive practices and promote free and fair competition.
Food and Drug Administration (FDA)	Regulates the introduction and prescribed use of new drugs, pesticides, additives, and colorings in food and cosmetics. Oversees the contents and processing of food products, drugs, and cosmetics.
Interstate Commerce Commission (ICC)	Regulates rates and services of companies providing interstate land or water transportation of passengers or freight.
Occupational Safety and Health Administration (OSHA)	Regulates business processes and workplaces to protect worker safety and health.
Securities and Exchange Commission (SEC)	Regulates the issuing, promoting, and trading of stocks, bonds, and certain other securities to protect the interests of investors and of the general public.

Many former competitors simply merged, to their mutual benefit. Many large companies bought out their competitors, often having first beaten them down in a price war. Combinations other than formal mergers were also common. Standard Oil Company devised a scheme whereby they gave dividend-paying trust certificates in return for voting control of the stock of other companies. This method of controlling competitors without actually owning them was called a *trust.* That term soon came to be used for any business combination that limited or eliminated competition. Another scheme was *interlocking directorates.* Under this plan, different companies had the same, or some of the same, people on their boards of directors. Thus companies that were supposed to be competitors were actually run by the same people.

The end result of these efforts were manipulated markets that caused high prices and loss of choice for buyers. Trusts ended forever the laissez-faire business climate. The federal government stepped in to protect the public from trusts, and regulation has been the rule ever since. A number of important acts have been passed specifically to combat monopoly and encourage competition. See Table 25-2 for a list of these acts and the specific activities which they outlaw.

The general effect of all these laws has been to promote competition and retard the development of monopolies. Another more general goal of providing consumers with a wide range of goods at prices determined by the market has been met to a lesser degree. Unwritten pricing agreements among competitors still interfere with the operation of the market in some industries. Outright price fixing has been uncovered from time to time and prosecuted.

Competition is also lessened in many cases by the high technology common today. It is so expensive and difficult to enter many industries that potential new competitors are discouraged from the start. Entrenched producers may then sometimes enjoy relative freedom from effective competition. On the other hand, the burgeoning of electronic technology, which often requires more creative inputs than capital, has stimulated competition. The proliferation of computer hardware, software, and peripheral equipment manufacturers are testimony to this. Still, in one of the most significant antitrust cases of all times, American Telephone & Telegraph Company agreed to voluntarily break up its vast network of interlocking telephone companies. The government's argument was that AT&T, with its enormous resources in technology, would simply overwhelm competing information companies if it were allowed to retain all the advantages of its size.

PROTECTION OF RIGHTS AND WELFARE

Safeguards the public interest

Another major area of government regulation concerns the protection of property rights and human rights and the promotion of the general welfare. The right to own property is basic to private enterprise. The ultimate responsibility to enforce that right lies with the government and its justice systems. The government also helps to define property, as in the case of patents, copyrights, and trademarks. As explained in Chapter 3, protection of such intangibles is an important characteristic of the American business system.

There are limitations on property rights which are also enforced by the government. The requirement to pay taxes is an important one. In times of war or when special needs, such as building public facilities, arise, the government can actually seize private property. This power is called *eminent domain*. The government must, however, show that the seizure will benefit the public, and it must pay the owner a fair price. The government may also prevent private property from being used in a way that harms others.

A number of regulations to protect the rights of consumers, such as laws that regulate credit practices, have been presented in earlier chapters. There are also many regulations designed to protect the public's health and safety. Some examples of the agencies that administer these kinds of regulations are the Food and Drug Administration, the Consumer Product Safety Commission, and the Occupational Safety and Health Administration. The effects of business activity on the environment are surveyed by the Environmental Protection Agency. The Department of

Table 25-2
Federal Antitrust Laws

Act	Activities Prohibited	Significance
Sherman Antitrust Act of 1890	Outlaws contracts, combinations, and conspiracies in restraint of trade.	First statute to combat monopolies and trusts. Labor unions included in definition of combinations in restraint of trade.
Clayton Antitrust Act of 1914	Outlaws anticompetitive sales contracts, price cutting to force competitors out of business, interlocking directorates for larger corporations, and certain anticompetitive stock acquisitions and mergers.	Labor unions now given limited protection by not being included in definition of combinations in restraint of trade.
Federal Trade Commission Act of 1914	Outlaws unfair competitive practices harmful to business competitors.	Created the Federal Trade Commission (FTC) to enforce this and other laws and regulations protecting competition.
Robinson-Patman Act of 1936	Outlaws *price discrimination* (charging different buyers of the same goods different prices) if such practice tends to lessen competition.	Designed, in part, to protect independent retail stores from unfair competition from chain stores.
Wheeler-Lea Act of 1938	Outlaws any unfair competitive practice harmful to the public.	Broadened the definition of what constitutes an unfair competitive practice (see the Federal Trade Commission Act above).
Celler-Kefauver Act of 1950	Outlaws formal mergers of two or more companies if the merger creates a monopoly or reduces competition.	Significantly strengthened the provisions of the Clayton Act by outlawing anticompetitive mergers.
Antitrust Procedures and Penalty Act of 1974	Increases fines for individuals and corporations that violate the Sherman Act. Makes violation of that act a felony rather than a misdemeanor.	Put added teeth into the enforcement provisions of the Sherman Act.
Antitrust Improvement Act of 1976	Requires companies planning mergers to give prior notice to appropriate federal agencies. Allows state law officials to bring suit at the state level on behalf of injured parties damaged by violations of this act.	Led to a number of lawsuits intended to prevent anticompetitive mergers between companies in unrelated industries (so-called *conglomerate mergers*).

Labor has a number of regulatory powers regarding employment and management-labor relationships as discussed in Chapter 18.

REGULATED INDUSTRIES

Establishes controlled monopolies

Monopolies are desirable for providing certain kinds of goods and services. Telephone service is one example. A town with five competing telephone companies would not get efficient service. Service lines would be duplicated all over town. Each user would have to have five different telephones, one connected to each company, in order to be able to communicate with everyone else. Governments have avoided this situation by allowing and encouraging the formation of monopolies to provide certain services. These **public utilities** are private companies protected from competition so they can efficiently provide essential public services. Utilities include companies providing electricity, gas, telephone service, mass transportation, and a variety of other products needed by the public. To compensate for their freedom from competition, public utilities are closely regulated by governments. The state, local, or federal government, unlike competitive businesses, can directly control the quality and extent of service a utility gives and the rates it charges.

Direct regulation of many utilities providing service within a state is the responsibility of state governments. Federal regulation of utilities is most important in the areas of interstate power lines and pipelines, transportation, and communications. The Federal Power Commission has broad powers to control rates for electric power transmitted between states and to regulate the operations of interstate power companies. The Interstate Commerce Commission and the Federal Power Commission both have some authority over interstate pipelines, depending on how the lines are used.

The Interstate Commerce Commission regulates surface transportation companies operating between states. Air transportation is regulated by the Civil Aeronautics Board and the Federal Aviation Administration. The Federal Communications Commission can directly control rates and service for interstate telephone and telegraph transmissions. In addition, it licenses and regulates radio and television stations and allocates radio frequencies for specific communications uses.

Significant changes in the public's attitude toward regulation of business, especially transportation, took place during the late 1970s and early 1980s. As a result of this and other factors, both the trucking industry and the airlines have been greatly deregulated. The effect has been to promote vigorous, often cutthroat competition. On the one hand, the public has gained through lower rates. On the other hand, many convenient services required by the regulatory agencies have been discontinued.

OTHER STATE REGULATIONS
Imposition of laws, fees, and licenses

In addition to controlling the operation of utilities, state governments—and, to a lesser extent, local governments—impose detailed regulation on certain other business and professional activities. They grant charters for the formation of corporations. They often have pollution, safety, property rights, and wage and hour laws supplementing or overlapping federal statutes. They may require direct licensing of businesses and nearly always require a license for the practice of medicine, law, and certain other professions. They often regulate specific kinds of businesses, such as the insurance industry or automobile repair shops. They may independently outlaw certain products, such as disposable bottles or cans, for environmental or health reasons. They often regulate interest rates charged by lending institutions. Local zoning, licensing, advertising, and trade regulations also affect businesses. The interaction of local, state, and federal regulation presents a difficult and complex administrative problem for many companies.

2 TAXATION

All businesses pay in some way

Most businesses are influenced to some extent by government regulation. The government's taxation powers are enforced on all businesses. Governments incur expenses by providing public services and promoting the general well-being. They pay these expenses by collecting taxes from individuals and organizations, including businesses, within their jurisdiction. Establishing a tax structure that provides enough revenue and is fair to all taxpayers is a difficult and complex job. Three different policies of taxation are often combined in a tax program:

■ *Proportional taxation* collects the same percent rate of taxes from every taxpayer. A 10 percent proportional income tax would take 10 percent of everyone's income, regardless of whether the individual made $5,000 or $5 million a year. Real estate and personal property taxes are often proportional.

■ *Progressive taxation* charges an increasing tax rate as the amount of income or property being taxed increases. A person with a small income may pay 15 percent in taxes, while someone with a larger income might pay 50 percent.

■ *Regressive taxation* charges a lower percent rate as the amount being taxed increases. Under this scheme, a person with a higher income would pay a lower rate than someone with a smaller income.

In the United States, most income taxes are meant to be progressive and most other taxes proportional. Regressive taxation may still occur, however. Obvious examples of this are the sales taxes charged by many state and local governments. Low-income people contribute a far higher percent of their income to the sales tax than do the wealthy and therefore pay a higher tax rate.

The most important purpose of taxation is to raise revenue for governments. In addition, taxation may be used as a regulatory method.

REVENUE TAXES

Designed to provide government support

Governments gain revenue to support their operations through a variety of taxes. The most important source of revenue for the federal government is a tax on personal and corporate incomes. The general sources of federal revenue are shown in Figure 25-1. Many states and some cities also depend heavily on income taxes.

An *income tax* is a regular payment made to a government. The amount paid is based on how much money an individual earns from employment and investments. *Corporate taxes* are also an income tax based on profits remaining after all costs have been paid.

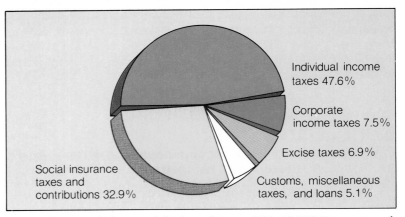

Source: Statistical Abstract of the United States, 1982–83, U.S. Department of Commerce, Bureau of the Census, p. 249.

Figure 25-1
Sources of revenue for the U.S. government in 1982.

For most corporations, federal and state taxes are significant expense items, routinely taking up to 50 percent and more of pretax profits. Since corporations in general have no way to pay the taxes except from revenue generated by sales, the taxes are ultimately paid for by raising the prices of goods. It is the individuals and firms that buy these products who actually pay corporate taxes.

Most states and many smaller governments have sales or property exchange taxes to raise revenue. A *sales tax* is a tax payment for which the amount is determined by the value of products being bought. A property *transfer tax* is similar to a straight sales tax, except that it generally applies only to major purchases like cars or real estate. In certain cases, the transfer tax may be paid in part or wholly by the seller.

Property taxes are paid at regular intervals, their amount being based on a valuation of real or personal property. Property taxes are a major source of operating revenue for towns, cities, and counties.

Payroll taxes are deducted from regular payments of salaries and wages. The most important of these is the social security tax, which is shared by employer and employee. The proceeds are used partly to maintain a retirement and disability fund for U.S. workers. A further payroll tax—unemployment insurance—is paid by employers. It is used by state unemployment commissions to make partial wage payments to workers who are laid off or discharged.

A further source of government revenue is *estate taxes,* paid when property is inherited. The amount of the tax is determined by the value of the assets inherited.

REGULATORY OR RESTRICTIVE TAXES

Imposed to discourage undesirable actions

Though all taxes provide revenue, some are meant to accomplish more than that. A protective tariff, for example, is a tax. Its real purpose, however, is to reduce the amount of goods imported by raising their price relative to domestically produced goods.

Excise Taxes   *Excise taxes* are collected from the manufacturers, or sometimes the retail sellers, of certain kinds of goods. One use of such taxes is to provide revenue for special purposes. Excise taxes on tires and motor vehicles, for instance, contribute to highway construction. Excise taxes may also be imposed in an effort to discourage the use of certain manufactured goods. This is part of the rationale behind taxes on tobacco products and alcoholic beverages.

Tariffs and Customs Duties   *Customs duties* are service taxes collected when goods are imported, either by private travelers or commercially. They provide government revenue and, to some extent, discourage importation. *Tariffs* are sometimes set on certain products to substantially raise the domestic prices of imported goods and protect domestic producers.

Communications and Transportation Taxes   Telephone and teletypewriter services are also taxed. Air travel has a special tax; it is paid directly from airlines and by customers who purchase tickets. Truck transportation companies sometimes must pay a special *use tax* for highway use in addition to general licenses. These taxes are often interpreted as a partial compensation for the government's granting of monopoly status (in the case of telephone service) or partial repayment by private companies for the use of public facilities. However, the taxes are, in fact, all paid by consumers.

Other Business Taxes   All levels of government have imposed a variety of minor taxes that apply to businesses in specific situations. Businesses usually need licenses to operate. A large company may need scores of different licenses from different cities, counties, and states. Each license requires a fee. Charters for corporations are usually taxed, sometimes quite heavily. Utilities pay "franchise fees," or taxes for the right to operate within jurisdictions. When new facilities are built, fees must be paid to obtain building permits. Many areas have *severance taxes* that must be paid when a natural resource like timber or minerals is used. These taxes encourage conservation and provide further revenue.

IMPACT OF TAXES ON BUSINESS DECISIONS
Depreciation and interest are major tax factors

Taxes are of interest to business managers because they represent an important amount of money that must be paid out. They are also important because the specific ways they are assessed can influence the best choice to make in many business decisions.

A simple example is selecting a site for a new manufacturing plant. If the value of the plant is $10 million, annual real estate taxes could be as low as $60,000 or less in many rural areas with low property tax rates. In many highly developed urban areas, property taxes on the same plant could be $250,000 or higher. If the rural area could provide the utilities, transportation facilities, work force, and other requirements, the factory could operate there at a significantly lower total cost.

The decision of whether to back an undertaking with borrowed money or with equity financing is often influenced by the effect of taxes. Interest paid on borrowed money is a deductible expense for income tax, reducing the amount of tax owed. The reduction, for many companies, is substantial enough to make borrowing significantly less expensive in the long run. In this situation, debt financing may be more attractive than equity financing.

Taxes are often involved in decisions about buying new equipment or building facilities. Production facilities depreciate in value as they are used. The average loss in value each year can also be counted as a deductible expense, and thus, reduce income taxes. Tax statutes, however, set limits on the length of time facilities can be depreciated. A 50-year-old factory, for example, may operate perfectly well. If it can no longer be depreciated, however, income earned from its products will, in effect, be subject to higher taxes than income from a new factory with substantial depreciation expense.

Lease Versus Buy   The lease of a building or equipment, rather than buying it outright, often offers attractive tax advantages to businesses. Leasing is a form of renting, although the commitment tends to be longer and more binding than ordinary rental agreements. If a company purchases a warehouse, for example, for $1,000,000 it may be allowed by the Internal Revenue Service to charge the depreciation of this building as a yearly expense for 25 years. Each year, the company could deduct 1/25 of the building's cost (or $40,000) from its income as a depreciation expense. If the company were paying income taxes at the 50 percent rate, this would save the company $20,000 each year. On the other hand, if the company chose to lease the same kind of building from another owner at $100,000 a year, it could deduct this expense from its income before taxes and save $50,000 a year in taxes. That doesn't tell the whole story, of course. In the first instance, the company has to consider the additional yearly loss of interest-earning power of the $1,000,000 it has invested in the building. When interest rates are at 10 percent, this cost would be $100,000 a year. The net cost of owning would then be $80,000 ($100,000 minus the $20,000 saved on taxes). The net cost of leasing the same building would be $50,000 (annual leasing expense of $100,000 minus the $50,000 saved on taxes). In this instance, tax considerations might lead management to choose to lease the building rather than to buy it.

Tax effects such as these are very common. They influence hundreds of decisions such as whether to rent or buy facilities, whether to manufacture components or buy them from suppliers, and whether to expand internally or buy existing operations. Nearly every conceivable business decision can be influenced to some extent by some type of local, state, or federal tax.

3 BUSINESS LAW

Applies mainly to business activities

The main formal institution for providing and enforcing stable relationships among individuals and organizations is the law. *Law* consists of a collection of formal rules and regulations—written or unwritten—that are enforced by the government. What mainly distinguishes laws from other special controls, such as moral obligations, is that the government's formal legal system judges conformity to law and enforces its decisions.

Businesses and business employees are subject to general laws as are all other individuals. Specifically, criminal law and law of torts must regulate their actions in addition to laws concerned directly with the conduct of business. *Criminal law* is a group of laws enforced by the government for the good of the general public. Forgery, embezzlement, the use of violence, and many other actions are subject to punishment under criminal law. It is the government itself that seeks relief in the case of a criminal offense. In the case of a *tort,* which is a civil offense that does not arise out of a contract, it is the person who has been injured who seeks redress. A few examples of torts common in business operations are trespassing, fraud, and copyright and patent infringements.

The body of law that applies specifically to the conduct of business activities is called *business law.* These laws mainly deal with agents, warranties, bankruptcy, the making and enforcing of contracts, and the ownership and sale of property.

CONTRACTS
Make agreements binding

Contracts among individuals and companies are basic to conducting business. A *contract* is a voluntary agreement in which two or more parties (people or corporations) bind themselves to act or not to act in a certain way. A sales agreement is a typical example. A seller might agree to provide a certain quantity of goods by a specified date. The buyer might agree to pay an established price upon receipt of the merchandise.

For a contract to be valid, it must meet certain requirements:

■ There must be an offer by one party and an acceptance by another.

■ The contract must be voluntary. An agreement resulting from force or fraud is not normally enforceable.

■ The parties to the contract must be competent. They must be legally sane and of legal age, although minors can also enter into contracts that have special rules.

■ The parties must exchange a *consideration,* something of value such as money, property, and a promise to perform work.

■ The specified considerations and actions must be legal. A price-fixing contract or one for the sale of illegal drugs would not be legally enforceable because the contracted service is illegal.

If these requirements are met, most contracts are valid, even if they are not written down. An oral contract can be just as enforceable as a written one if the parties involved can later prove the pertinent facts. The law requires, however, that some contracts be written: those lasting longer than a year, for example, and transfers of ownership of real property.

Many contracts include promises of some future actions that will or will not be carried out. Contract performance is the process of actually doing what was promised. For example, a contract to work for a company for one year is not satisfied until the year's work is done. Some contracts have such complex specifications that special legal analysis and interpretation may be needed to determine whether parties have performed adequately. If one or more parties fails to carry out the terms agreed to, the contract is broken. In some situations, such as bankruptcy, death, or serious illness, the nonperforming party may be excused from the contract with no penalty. In other cases, nonperformance may be handled in one of three ways:

■ All the provisions of the contract may be disregarded. If one party does not perform, the other party does not have to perform either. The obligations are said to be "discharged."

■ A court order, backed up by a fine or jail sentence, can be obtained to force the other party to perform.

■ A court may be requested to force a nonperformer to pay damages for the monetary loss that resulted from the nonperformance.

LAW OF SALES

Governs the transfer of property

Governments in the United States protect private property. Property may be *real property*—land or possessions with a long-term attachment to land, such as buildings or uncut timber or *personal property,* such as automobiles, machinery, and furniture. An important aspect of protecting property ownership is defining the terms and procedures by which control passes from one owner to another. Real property may be transferred by deed or lease. A *deed* actually transfers ownership to a new owner. A *lease* gives temporary, partial control of real property. Extensive and complex legal guidelines and traditions surround the writing and interpretation of these legal documents.

Ownership of personal property is transferred by sale. Even such a seemingly simple transaction requires considerable legal definition and regulation. Laws control who is capable of entering into sales agreements, at which exact point the sale has taken place (which is important in deciding who loses if damage occurs), what action can be taken when deceptive practices have been used, and many other issues.

AGENCY LAW

When others act on the company's behalf

An *agent* is a person or company authorized to carry out business and enter into agreements on behalf of another person or company, called the *principal.* This relationship exists when employees of a company—executives, purchasing agents, sales representatives, and others—act on behalf of the company. An agent may also be an outside third party especially skilled at handling certain kinds of business. Lawyers often act as agents, particularly in real estate trading. Actors, writers, professional sports figures, and others use agents to negotiate contracts. The law has quite clearly defined the responsibilities of both principal and agent in these relationships. The agent is obliged to work for the benefit of the principal and to follow his or her instructions, while the principal is required to compensate the agent for his or her performance.

NEGOTIABLE INSTRUMENTS

Checks and promissory notes

Important legal controls exist on the use of *negotiable instruments,* which are written documents that stand for currency in business transactions. The best known negotiable instruments are checks and promissory notes. The law specifies the characteristics a negotiable instrument must have in order to be transferable to a new owner, that is, to circulate much like cash. It must, for example, be written and properly signed. It must contain an unconditional promise to pay, either on demand or at a definite future date. Other requirements must be met in certain situations.

The law also specifies the circumstances in which a person does or does not actually own a negotiable instrument. It must not, for instance, be past due or show any sign of tampering. Transfer from one person to another is controlled. Endorsing a check by signing it on the back, for example, is one way of transferring a negotiable instrument. Specific methods of endorsement such as "for deposit only," "payable to," or "accepted in full settlement of" and their contractual obligations are all defined by law.

WARRANTIES AND PRODUCT LIABILITY
Legal assurance of performance

A *warranty* is a legal assurance that goods or services being sold have certain characteristics. An *express warranty* is a statement, often written, made by the seller that the property being sold is of a specified quality and type. Express warranties often state that the seller will repair any defects or replace the merchandise if defects are found. An *implied warranty* accompanies most sales as a standard part of law, even when the seller does not actually express it. The main provisions of an implied warranty are that (a) the buyer is receiving ownership of the property and that the seller is authorized to sell it, and (b) that the goods are what they were represented to be and can be used for their intended purpose.

Closely related to the law regarding warranties is the law of *product liability.* Under the impetus of the Consumer Product Safety Act, the federal government places a legal responsibility on the manufacturer or seller of a product to compensate a buyer who suffers injury when using that product. Over one million product-liability claims seeking damages in excess of $50 billion were filed in one recent year. The owners of businesses, especially small enterprises, often complain that the high costs of purchasing product liability insurance makes it extremely difficult to continue with their operations.

BANKRUPTCY
Procedure for handling insolvency

Bankruptcy laws are intended to protect as fully as possible both a company or person with not enough assets to pay debts and the creditors to whom the debts are owed. *Bankruptcy* is a legal procedure by which a court divides up the remaining assets of an insolvent person or company among the people and organizations to whom money is owed. Bankruptcy is a way for someone who is in severe financial distress because of debt to get a new start.

When bankruptcy is declared, nearly all of the assets of the debtor are eventually sold for cash. The proceeds are used to pay court costs and other costs, unpaid employee wages up to a maximum limit for each worker, taxes, and secured loans. If any money is left after these charges, it is divided among general creditors according to the percent of total debt each is owed. The creditors then have no further claims. Bankruptcy is handled under federal law in federal courts. Other bankruptcy laws provide businesses with temporary protection from creditors' suits while the company tries to reorganize and make enough money to pay its creditors in full. (For more about bankruptcy, see the section entitled "Commercial Bankruptcy" in Chapter 15.)

TRADEMARKS AND COPYRIGHTS

Provide identification and protection

As consumers, all of us are exposed to trademarks daily. They are on practically every product we use. Even when we turn on television, we may hear the NBC chimes of the "Today" show, a registered trademark. So are "Today" and "NBC," as are "CBS" and its "eye" design. So is the name of your daily newspaper; almost every advertisement features at least one trade or "service" mark. The Patent and Trademark Office of the United States estimates that the average American is exposed to 1,500 trademarks every day.

By its legal definition, a trademark distinguishes goods supplied by a particular manufacturer or merchant from similar goods manufactured or sold by others. It helps consumers to choose between different products or services. For this reason, the entire law of trademarks depends upon how consumers perceive them. Questions as to whether or not a mark can be registered or protected focuses upon what might go on in the buyer's mind.

When a trademark owner sues an infringer, two things are accomplished. First, the monetary interests of the trademark owner are protected from a form of unfair competition. Second, the public is also protected from being deceived or misled. It is in this view that trademarks are not considered a form of monopoly, since they protect the public as well as the proprietor. On the other hand, some consumer groups oppose the use of trademarks. They believe that they give the owner exclusive rights to products that could be manufactured and sold by anyone. Many items such as soap, sugar, coffee, and medicinal drugs, for that matter, are essentially identical except for the mark that a proprietor establishes to make the product distinguishable from those of competitors. In the case of medicinal drugs, the consumer movement has sought for and obtained laws that encourage doctors to prescribe a drug generically rather than by its brand, or trademark. That way, consumers would have a choice to purchase medicine by its chemical name rather than by its brand, and, the hope would be that the medicine would be more inexpensive as a result.

Copyrights are somewhat similar to trademarks in that they provide a legal means of protecting one's ownership. In the case of copyright it involves property created by the mind. The most commonly eligible copyright properties are literary, musical, and dramatic works; pictorial, graphic, sculptural, and choreographic works; motion pictures and sound

More Than

Kicking

the Tires

Periodically, the Federal Trade Commission (FTC) tries to regulate the sale of used cars. The FTC argues that overeager used-car salespeople have a reputation, deserved or otherwise, for dumping lemons on unsuspecting buyers. The FTC wants to offer consumers something more reliable than kicking the tires. Its proposed regulation, should it ever take legal effect, would require the dealer to post a friendly warning on a window sticker in each car. The sticker would read this way: "Ask us to put all promises in writing. You can make a seller keep written promises." The window stickers then would go on to list 14 general categories of possible defects related to 52 specific problems. These would include: "Is there abnormal visible exhaust? Are the shock absorbers functioning? Do the brake linings have a thickness of less than $\frac{1}{32}$ of an inch?" The dealers' lobby, representing some 70,000 small dealers, does not like the proposal. Defending their role as traders, they invoked the ancient admonition of "caveat emptor"—let the buyer beware. Their lobbying efforts so far have proved successful at the federal level, although the effort to put so-called "anti-lemon" laws on the law books has made some limited headway at the state and local levels.

Source: James J. Kilpatrick, "FTC Regulation Is a Lemon," Daily News Record (Harrisonburg, Virginia), April 29, 1982, p. 7.

Would this be a good law? How would it be enforced? If you were a used-car dealer with a good reputation, why might you want to see such a regulation?

recordings. Generally ineligible are ideas, methods, systems, principles, concepts (although some of these might qualify for a patent). Also usually ineligible are names, titles, slogans in which the creative content is slight (although these may qualify for trademark protection). The U.S. Copyright Act has been simplified so that an individual's copyright belongs to him or her immediately upon creation of the work. Registration, for which there is a small fee, is a legal formality and not a condition of copyright protection.

Patents, unlike trademarks, are considered a limited form of monopoly. They give the owners exclusive rights to make and sell a patented product or to use a patented process. To be patentable, a product must consist of an idea or process not known before. It must be a discovery as distinguished from mere mechanical skill or knowledge. In the United States, this privilege lasts for 17 years after a patent is issued. When other persons or companies use the patented product or process without permission, they are trespassing and may be sued for damages.

UNIFORM COMMERCIAL CODE

A guideline for consistency in state laws

Many laws that affect the conduct of business, especially in interstate commerce, are federal. Individual states, however, have the authority to pass laws controlling business practices and transactions within their own boundaries. In addition, state courts interpret existing laws. Interpretations, however, may vary considerably from state to state. Many of the most important legal controls of day-to-day business transactions fall under state laws. When every state had different rules for contracts, sales, agencies, and other significant aspects of business law, great confusion resulted. Regional and national operations were complex and difficult.

To help solve this problem, a commission of legal experts wrote a large body of laws called the *Uniform Commercial Code.* The code itself, first published in 1957, has no legal force. State legislatures, however, have adopted it as a guideline and have made most parts of the code enforceable law. Many provisions of the code have been adopted by nearly every state and are truly uniform nationwide.

The code is a large body of commercial law that includes statutes on sales, negotiable instruments, banking practices, shipping and warehousing, securities, and general business transactions and contracts. Every major area of business law that falls under state jurisdiction is covered. The wide adoption of the Uniform Commercial Code has facilitated regional and national business. In general, what is legal in one state is also legal in others.

The partial standardization of state business laws by the Uniform Commercial Code has made business' job of dealing with its legal environment somewhat simpler than it was 25 years ago. However, the growth during the same period of federal, state, and local regulation has largely offset the gain. State and federal laws, regulation by as many as five separate governments, and regulation by countless agencies at a single business location is not uncommon. Sometimes, there are scores of different taxes to pay. Such regulation makes dealings between business and government an extremely complex management responsibility.

4 GENERAL RELATIONSHIPS

From adversary to aide

From the business manager's point of view, the government often appears to be an enemy. It appropriates large portions of company and personal profits and tells managers how to run their own companies. In reality, however, business and government are mutually supportive. Business provides major financial assistance to governments through tax payments. Government provides business with many of the public facilities it needs. It is very unlikely, for instance, that there would be a trucking industry in the United States without a government-built highway system. The construction of the railroads was heavily government-subsidized in various ways. Government protection makes utilities profitable no matter how high their costs rise. Many businesses are directly dependent on government subsidies. Many others receive tariff protection, which allows them to charge higher prices. Much private borrowing is supported by governments. It would be difficult to carry on business at all without government protection of property ownership and enforcement of contracts or a government-backed money supply.

GOVERNMENT ASSISTANCE

A major source of information

The federal government of the United States vigorously promotes and subsidizes businesses by furnishing financing, insurance against various risks, information and services, and a source of both supply and sales.

Financing   A number of federally sponsored programs provide guarantees of loans made to businesses through commercial lending institutions. Representative loan programs include:

■   The Agricultural Stabilization and Conservation Service, which grants crop loans through county offices.

■   The Overseas Private Investment Corporation, which provides direct loans for United States investors in overseas projects ranging from $50,000 to $2 million and running from five to twenty years.

■   The Small Business Administration (SBA), which provides various types of loans to qualified small business concerns and to disaster victims.

Insurance   Various federal agencies insure against risk that is too great for a firm to bear alone when the venture is part of a specific policy program:

■   The SBA reinsures, or guarantees, surety companies against the major portion of losses on construction bonds issued for minority-owned businesses.

■   The Export-Import Bank guarantees repayment to commercial banks which finance medium-term transactions for exports.

■   The Overseas Private Investment Corporation insures United States lenders against both commercial and political risks by guaranteeing payment of principal and interest.

■   The Federal Crop Insurance Corporation insures crops against unavoidable damage.

Information and Research   The major source of government information and aid is the Department of Commerce. It maintains domestic field offices in more than three dozen cities and provides export data on opportunities, production, and pricing. The Department of Commerce also conducts other programs that provide businesses with information or research through the following agencies: the National Bureau of Standards, the Economic Development Administration, the National Technical Information Service, the Patent and Trademark Office, the Bureau of the Census, and the Office of Minority Business Enterprise. The SBA provides management assistance through conferences and publications and maintains ten regional offices and a number of local offices.

A number of agencies have grant programs that aid businesses. Most such programs are administered by grants to state or local governments or to nonprofit organizations. Industry cooperation with grant recipients, such as universities, is encouraged by agencies such as the National Science Foundation.

Customer and Vendor   The federal government is the largest single customer of business in the United States. In fiscal year 1982, for example, it spent $249 billion for goods and services. It spent another $28 billion on contracts issued by recipients of federal grants, like local governments and universities. The biggest spender, by far, is the Department of Defense. The procurement system is regulated by some 4,000 legislative provisions and implemented by 485 procurement offices. The General Services Administration (GSA), which is the second biggest buyer, maintains Business Service Centers in ten major cities. The centers not only advise about how to sell to the federal government, they also handle the sale of much of the federal surplus goods.

GOVERNMENT RELATIONS

An unbreakable bond of economics and politics

Government and business are difficult to separate in some operations. Some transportation companies, subsidized by local, state, or federal funds, are virtually joint ventures of private industry and the government. The communications satellite system is similar. The banking industry is private enterprise, but it is so closely tied to the Federal Reserve System as to be nearly a mutual undertaking.

Some government activities are competitive with private business. Government old-age and disability insurance, public recreation areas, and energy and electric power development provide services that are also offered by the private sector.

The government can directly intervene in business management through regulation and such activities as the arbitration of labor disputes. It also strongly influences the economy, controlling the money supply and interest rates by selling and redeeming government securities. At the same time, business has a significant influence on government. Lobbying by individual companies and by industry associations is a potent force in the legislative process. Business executives are often selected for important government positions and can directly set government policies.

Key Concepts

1. An important role of the government is regulating business activities to protect the general welfare of society. Regulation is specifically intended to promote free and fair competition, to protect property rights and the interests of consumers, and to improve the general welfare in such areas as health and safety, environmental quality, and working conditions.

2. The main purpose of taxation is to provide the revenue governments need to carry on operations. Some important revenue taxes are those levied on personal income, corporate income, sales, property, and payrolls. Some taxes, while generating revenue, also have the effect of restricting or regulating certain activities. Import tariffs, for example, discourage the importation of certain goods.

3. Law is a collection of formal rules and regulations enforced by the power of government. All business activities must conform to laws that apply to everyone: the law of torts and criminal law. In addition, there are groups of laws that apply specifically to business concerns: for example, contracts, property, sales, agencies, negotiable instruments, warranties, and bankruptcy.

4. The general relationship of business and government is one of interdependence. Business provides major support for government through tax payments. Government provides the legal structure and public facilities business needs to operate. Government also often gives direct aid to business, as in the cases of subsidies and tariffs.

Review Questions

1. Define, identify, or explain each of the following key terms or phrases found on the pages indicated.

   agent (p. 472)
   bankruptcy (p. 473)
   business law (p. 471)
   consideration (p. 471)
   contract (p. 471)
   corporate tax (p. 468)
   criminal law (p. 471)
   customs duties (p. 469)
   deed (p. 472)
   eminent domain (p. 464)
   estate tax (p. 468)
   excise tax (p. 468)
   express warranty (p. 473)
   implied warranty (p. 473)
   income tax (p. 468)
   interlocking directorate (p. 463)
   laissez-faire (p. 462)
   law (p. 470)
   lease (p. 472)
   negotiable instruments (p. 472)
   payroll tax (p. 468)
   personal property (p. 472)

   principal (p. 472)
   product liability (p. 473)
   progressive taxation (p. 467)
   property tax (p. 468)
   proportional taxation (p. 467)
   public utilities (p. 466)
   real property (p. 472)
   regressive taxation (p. 467)
   sales tax (p. 468)
   severance tax (p. 469)
   tariffs (p. 469)
   tort (p. 471)
   transfer tax (p. 468)
   trust (p. 463)
   Uniform Commercial Code (p. 476)
   use tax (p. 469)
   warranty (p. 473)

2. What have been the main goals of government in regulating business?

3. What is a regulated industry? What are some examples? Why are they allowed to exist?

4. What is the difference between a revenue tax and a restrictive tax? Give an example of each.

5. Distinguish between proportional taxation, progressive taxation, and regressive taxation.
6. What are the five main requirements that must be met for a contract to be valid and legally enforceable?
7. What recourse does a contracting party have if another party does not perform as specified?
8. Why has the Uniform Commercial Code been important to business?
9. Identify a number of ways in which the government helps business.
10. In what ways does the government compete with private business?

Case Critique 25-1
Too Big, Too Rough

When giant computers were all the rage, Control Data Corporation beat IBM to the market with the fastest, most capable one of them all. IBM's chairperson, Thomas Watson, Jr., was furious. He said to his executives, "I understand that in the laboratory (of Control Data) developing this system there are only 31 people including the janitor." IBM has a cast of thousands performing such research. Determined that IBM would not be left behind, Watson mounted an all-out effort to bring a bigger, better, faster computer to the market.

In the meanwhile, IBM engaged in a number of competitive practices that displeased Control Data very much. In charges eventually brought before a federal court, it became evident that IBM had played the competitive game very rough. The U.S. Justice Department charged that IBM kept announcing its new, supercomputer before it had left the drawing board. Even after it was ready for sale, the Justice Department said that IBM had priced it below cost and was prepared to sell at a loss. One memorandum circulated within IBM urged that its high-speed computer be introduced as a "competition-stopper" and "should be deliberately done as a money loser."

IBM denied these allegations and fought Control Data and the Justice Department in the courts for 13 years. Finally, the Justice Department gave up its charges and withdrew its case. The Justice Department reasoned that, since IBM had not been able to defeat Control Data with this model, charges of operating a monopoly could not be sustained.

1. What agency of the federal government is most likely to have brought the charges in this case?
2. What American business privilege would the federal government have been trying to promote through this legal action?
3. If the company were willing to price its product below that of its competitors, consumers would have benefitted at the time. Why would the government want to prevent such price-cutting practices?
4. At the time that this case occurred, there were only a few companies making very large computers. How would that have influenced the government's attitude toward the leading company?
5. What impact has the development of the minicomputer and personal computer had on IBM and other large computer manufacturers?

Source: William M. Carley, "Computer Wars," *The Wall Street Journal*, May 19, 1982, p. 1.

Case Critique 25-2
The Leaking Roofs

Not so long ago, a major chemical company developed a unique insulating product to be used in constructing "built-up" roofs. These are the flat roofs that are built up from layers of paper and tar. The new roofing product, made of a plastic foam material, would replace the wooden panels traditionally used as a support for the paper. After thousands of roofs were constructed using the new material, a problem became evident. The plastic expanded and contracted more than wood did. This eventually caused the paper to tear and cracks to appear. When the rains came, water seeped through the roof. In some instances, it poured in and damaged valuable materials stored in roofed-over warehouses.

When hundreds of building owners sued for damages, the maker of the new roofing material denied any responsibility. Its argument was that the company did not build roofs. Roofing contractors do. They should be responsible. Industry records show that about 15 percent of all built-up roofs need repair within five years of installation. For this reason, a great many roofing contractors and roofing materials companies offer a "bond," which is a form of warranty against roof failure within a specified period of time. Typical bonds call for the contractor to provide repairs for a roof up to a certain percentage of its original cost.

The materials manufacturing company, in this instance, did not issue bonds with its materials. It did advertise, however, that its product "does not shrink, resists temperature variations, and never deteriorates." The company settled most law suits out of court, to the tune of hundreds of thousands of dollars. It always denied any failure of the material. Eventually, the product was taken off the market.

1. If the roofing materials company did not offer a bond or guarantee for this faulty product, what kind of a warranty might a purchaser expect anyway?
2. Who might the owner of a building with a faulty roof hold responsible; the roofing contractor, the manufacturer of the materials, or both?
3. Besides having to defend itself against charges of product liability, what other legal charges might the roofing material company expect? From whom?

Source: Victor F. Zonana, "Crack in Strategy," *The Wall Street Journal*, April 24, 1980, p. 1.

Chapter 26

Ethical Behavior and Social Responsibility

1 ETHICAL BEHAVIOR IN BUSINESS

is conduct that is acceptable to those directly involved and to the community at large.

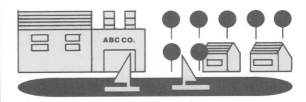

2 BUSINESS MUST RESPOND TO ATTITUDES AND EXPECTATIONS

from many influences.

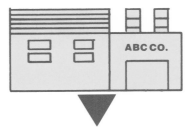

Competitors/Employees/Suppliers/Customers/
Creditors/The community/Investors/.

3 BUSINESS MUST COPE WITH POWER GROUP PRESSURES FROM MANY SOURCES

Public interest groups/Trade associations
The legal system/Labor unions

4 THERE IS EVIDENCE OF BUSINESS'S GROWING SOCIAL RESPONSIBILITY

United Way

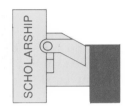
SCHOLARSHIP

5 STILL, PROBLEMS REMAIN
with respect to the environment, economic growth, land use, minorities and women, and multinational operations.

Learning Objectives

The purpose of this chapter is to define ethical behavior as it applies to business conduct, discuss the general trend of business's response to the growing demand for ethical behavior and social responsibility and analyze some of the continuing problems that will affect the future direction of business in the United States.

As evidence of general comprehension, after studying this chapter you should be able to:

1. Distinguish between ethical business practices and legally required business practices.

2. Identify the attitudes and expectations of the various groups that are involved with the business community.

3. Explain some of the ways in which power groups try to influence business practices.

4. Cite evidence of how business, collectively and as individual companies, have responded to the call for social responsibility.

5. Express considered opinions about continuing problems that confront business, such as problems related to the environment, land use, the value of economic growth, multinational operations, and opportunities for minorities and women.

If your class is using SSweetco: Business Model and Activity File for Business in Action, see Chapter 26 in that book after you complete this chapter. There you will find exercises and activities to help you apply your learning to typical business situations.

When managers today need new employees, they do not go to the weekly auction and buy slaves. Instead, they hire people who willingly accept employment in return for wages, salaries, and other benefits. However, only 150 years ago businesses in some parts of the country had the option of using slave labor and in many cases chose that option.

Two important factors keep businesses from using slave labor today. The first is that slavery is now against the law, but the second factor is even more important. Nearly everyone in the United States, including business owners and managers, believes it is *wrong* to own slaves. It is the change in ethics that eliminates the possibility of slavery in the United States today.

Much business activity is indirectly regulated by the values people in our society hold. As society changes, beliefs change, and with them the practices that are deemed acceptable. Also, there is seldom universal agreement about what is right. For instance, some people today do not object to the extinction of certain species of animals or plants caused by business processes or public facilities development. These people reason that the potential economic gain is a greater good than the kind of natural life that will be endangered. Others feel that the destruction of biological diversity is wrong and that a short-term economic gain is not an adequate justification for it. Managers have to deal with thousands of questions like this. They must find ways to operate businesses in a way that will agree with their own often conflicting ethical beliefs. At the same time, they must operate within an environment of social pressure brought about by the beliefs of others.

1   ETHICAL BEHAVIOR

What is good for society should be good for business too

Ethics is a collection of moral principles and rules of conduct accepted by part or all of the members of a society. Ethics guides behavior based on beliefs about what is right and wrong. The source of these beliefs may be tradition, religion, or reasoned judgments about what is best for the individual and society as a whole. *Business ethics* is the group of rules of conduct applied specifically to business activities.

Ethics is not the same as law. Many ethical beliefs are formally reinforced by law, but many are not. Until recently, it was legal to fire almost any employee, regardless of the length of his or her service. Usually the terminated employee was denied any provision for a company pension. Today, this practice is prohibited by federal law.

In practice, ethics is expressed and felt as a combination of pressures that direct one to take or not to take certain actions. Decisions must be acceptable to many different elements of society. First, they must be acceptable to the conscience of the decision maker. A manager may legitimately think, "I could legally take this action, and I could probably get others to accept it, but I ought not do it because it isn't right."

Managers must consider the potential effects of their decisions on the people and companies directly involved with the business operation: customers, suppliers, competitors, employees, investors, and creditors. In addition, managers must consider—and try to control—the possible effects of their decisions on the community at large.

It is only recently that business has become aware of how it affects individuals and the whole society. The laissez-faire business environment of the nineteenth century promoted the belief that almost any practice that increased profits was, in the long run, good for the country. The result was cutthroat competition, fraud, deceptive marketing, price and market manipulation, worthless and dangerous products, exploitation of workers, and other practices that today are generally considered unethical.

At the same time that so many harmful business activities were being carried on, some companies did abide by the fundamentals of good business ethics. At the height of the ruthless development of the nineteenth century, many managers still believed in producing high quality products, honestly sold at a fair price. They felt success could be built on hard work, creativity, and genuine customer satisfaction. It is the belief that high ethical standards are in the long-run good for profits that is stressed in business today.

In spite of improvements, however, there is evidence that managing a business may involve, at every level, a compromise with an individual's ethical standards. In 1975, a major survey asked 238 managers whether they felt "pressured to compromise their personal standards to attain company goals." About 50 percent of the top-level executives said they did. In 1981, 8,000 first-line supervisors nationwide were asked a similar question: "Are you ever asked to carry out orders or policies that are contrary to your moral beliefs about what is right or wrong?" Half of the supervisors said they never were, 45 percent occasionally, and 5 percent frequently.

2   ATTITUDES AND EXPECTATIONS

Business decisions must take into account many influences

If a manager accepts the notion that how decisions affect others should be considered, then decision making becomes even more complex than it ever was. A wide variety of individuals and organizations, as well as society as a whole, may be affected by a given business decision. Each of these groups has its own desires and expectations, which may conflict with those of other groups and may also change as various conditions change.

INDIVIDUALS IMMEDIATELY AFFECTED BY MANAGEMENT DECISIONS

Consideration of their viewpoint

Among those who have a high personal stake in management decisions are employees, customers, suppliers, competitors, investors, and creditors.

Employees   Workers were once viewed as being similar to machines—as standard, interchangeable elements to be used at the lowest possible cost with the highest possible productivity. Modern ethics, however, tends more toward the view that the company has a real obligation to provide its employees not only with good pay and good working conditions, but also with the opportunity to grow and to achieve their full potential.

In three areas, in particular, employee rights and privileges are being advanced by both legal and voluntary means.

■ *Rights to free speech and to privacy.* It used to be that employees, like children, were supposed to be seen but not heard. Currently, most employees expect to be able to say what they think about their jobs and companies without reprisals being taken against them. Then there is the matter of employee records. Employees want to know what is kept in their files and they do not want unauthorized people looking at them. At companies like United Technologies, Smith Kline, and Chase Manhattan Bank, there are formal policies limiting what will be kept in company files and assuring employees access to see that the information is correct.

■ *Greater assurances of job security.* During the wave of factory closings and movement of manufacturing operations overseas in the early 1980s, employees, labor unions, suppliers, and communities made themselves heard. Employees were asking for extensive advance notice before a plant could shut down or move. Furthermore, there is a growing pressure for a company to demonstrate economic justification before such an action.

■ *Improved quality of work life.* Increasingly, employees cannot see why work should necessarily be boring, hazardous, or demeaning. They are asking employers to provide greater opportunities to share in the decisions that affect their work. And some employers are responding to these expectations because they believe that an improved quality of work life will also improve employee productivity.

Customers   The attitude toward customers is changing too. Business has become increasingly conscious of the importance of fair prices, good quality products, and honest merchandising. This has been helped along by **consumerism,** which refers to organized efforts to protect the users of various products from harmful or deceptive business practices.

Many states and municipalities maintain offices of consumer affairs. These agencies provide information services for consumers, act as watchdogs over supermarkets, retail stores, and lending institutions. They also provide an avenue through which to seek redress when a consumer feels wronged. Some corporations have added consumer representatives to their boards of directors.

Suppliers   Ethical considerations also arise in relation to suppliers. The decision of one company to buy from another depends on price, quality, supplier capabilities, shipping costs, and similar factors. The problem is that some unfavorable purchasing decisions can put a supplying company out of business. Opportunites for fraud, illegal payments in return for purchase orders, and other illegal activity may often arise.

Competitors   Even though many business activities that affect competition are strictly controlled by law, ethical questions still abound. The use of industrial espionage to discover trade secrets of competitors is

ACTION BRIEF

Consumerism: Aging But Not Fading.   *Sometimes, it appears that the once vigorous consumer movement might just dry up and fade away. This isn't likely to happen, say Harvard marketing professors Paul Bloom and Stephen Greyser. The aims of consumerism are more mature, however, say the professors. Massive popular appeals are giving way to sharply targeted, local actions. Furthermore, consumerism has been institutionalized in the American system, say the professors. First of all, people have been educated to know that they don't have to accept a product or service that doesn't please them. They know that their complaints will be listened to, if not by the producer, then by the government. Secondly, companies are now so aware of the potential harm done their businesses by a publicized consumer complaint that they try to anticipate such reactions when designing the product or service in the first place.*

Source: "Consumerism—It's Mature, Not Fading," Advertising Age, *December 28, 1981, p. 9.*

an example, as is the hiring away of key employees by competitors. The central problem of ethical competition is how to compete fairly without losing the aggressiveness and will to win needed for success.

Investors and Creditors   The traditional view of business's responsibility is to maximize profits at any price. This places the interests of owners and investors above those of consumers and the public. Managerial decisions are understandably influenced by this priority. It is still clearly a manager's duty to operate businesses in such a way that profits will be created for investors. Creditors also deserve protection from fraud and deception on the part of borrowers who refuse to meet obligations.

THE COMMUNITY AT LARGE

A concern for the greatest good

There has been increasing concern about business' commitments to society as a whole. Business obviously plays a central role in the economy. In the United States, private business is still the primary means of converting resources into goods and services the society needs to function. The question arises of whether a company should temper its business decisions with considerations of what is best for the overall economy. Especially in the case of a very large corporation, a decision could be made that would benefit the corporation but damage the economy. For instance, a decision by a large oil company to limit supplies of oil may help that company to increase prices and profits. However, it may also prove damaging to the economy as a whole since industrial growth is dependent on an ever increasing supply of energy sources such as oil.

Similar conflicts occur in business activities that affect the quality of the environment. Efforts to control air and water pollution, for instance, can be very expensive. They can cost individual companies millions of dollars, which means higher prices and a possible increase in sales volume and profits.

Businesses usually benefit from a stable and well-managed social and political environment. However, it is not always easy to decide how much business should contribute to improving society. Again, expense is the key. If companies devote large amounts of time and money to reducing poverty and improving public education and health-care facilities, the companies may suffer economically. At the same time, both ethical and practical considerations make it important for businesses to make every effort to improve society as a whole. This conflict remains unresolved. The important point is that in recent years, the social and business climate has led to an extended public examination of such issues. It appears likely that in the future, businesses will be more likely to take the community into consideration when making major decisions. Indeed, some progress is already evident. Companies like IBM and the Ford Motor Co. now have board members responsible for promoting sensitivity to community needs.

BUSINESS AS THE BAD GUY

Is the general impression accurate?

Since the time of the first capitalists, it has been a popular theme to portray businesspeople as predatory, greedy, inconsiderate human beings.

As the owners and managers of the very large corporations become farther and farther removed from ordinary citizens, the feeling about them has not diminished. The question arises: How justified is this portrait? Studies have been conducted to find out how people really feel about business. They show that from 1968 to 1977, the general disenchantment intensified. In 1968, for example, a study by Yankelovich, Skelly & White asked a large number of people whether or not they agreed with the statement that "Business tries to strike a fair balance between profits and interests of the public." Some 70 percent agreed in 1968, only 15 percent in 1977. Similarly, a Louis Harris survey asked whether or not you "have a great deal of confidence in the people in charge of running major companies." In 1968, 55 percent said they did; in 1977, only 18 percent said so.

A more recent survey of a cross section of 1,513 adults by Louis Harris in 1979, showed a reversal of the downward trend in attitude toward business. The statement read: "In general, business helps us more than it harms us." Almost uniformly throughout the survey sample (by age, occupation, education), the response was affirmative; 72 percent agreed with the statement. The survey analyst concluded that (a) the American public is highly pragmatic and realistic, and (b) it wants business to step forward with concrete, workable policies and procedures to protect individual citizens in their relationships with business as employees and/or customers.

Business, of course, helps to create its own image. The spectacle of 527 U.S. firms cited in 1978 by the Securities and Exchange Commission for bribes and "questionable payments" to obtain business abroad, for example, did not add to the stature of business. On the other hand, business is fair game for either criticism or satire. In a study conducted by the Media Institute in 1981, it was apparent that television projects a distorted view of business to the public. Some 200 prime-time programs were examined, with 118 businesspeople in important roles. The study concluded that two out of three were portrayed as either foolish, greedy, or criminal. Almost half of the episodes showed businesspeople involved in illegal acts. Typical portrayals ranged from the diabolical J. R. Ewing of "Dallas" to the gracious Mrs. Pynchon, the newspaper publisher in the now canceled "Lou Grant" show. In between, there were the odious Louie, the cab manager of "Taxi;" the familiar proprietor of "Archie Bunker's Place;" and Mel, the tough-talking owner of the diner in "Alice". All told, the survey concluded, television almost never portrays business as a socially useful or economically productive activity. Since half of the working population in the United States is employed in the private sector, this seems like an unfair picture of the work life of a very great many Americans.

3   POWER GROUPS

Business can and must fend for itself

Businesses operate in an environment in which the interests of people and organizations affected by business decisions are aggressively represented by public pressure groups. Business, in turn, has its own organizations representing and working for business interests. It is important to recognize that all of the influences may affect a decision at the same time. The major power groups include:

Labor Unions   Many companies on their own initiative are beginning to demonstrate more concern for the development and satisfaction of their employees. At the same time, labor unions remain a strong force working for the rights of employees. Unions have a great deal of influence on wages and fringe benefits, work hours, working conditions, safety efforts, and other issues that affect the welfare of workers. In some cases, unions have also become involved in consumer protection. From management's point of view, labor unions are an important complicating factor in decisions affecting personnel policies and actions.

Trade Associations   Businesses often create organizations to publicize and promote the concerns of particular industries or of business as a whole. These trade associations influence public opinion on issues affecting the trade, inform businesses involved in a trade of important legal, market or social changes, lobby for favorable legislation, and carry out research and education in order to further the progress of member businesses. The policies of trade associations are an important influence on the decisions made by managers of individual companies.

Government Agencies   Government agencies are the means by which government regulations are carried out. These agencies may actually use legal action when regulations have been violated. They are important in business decisions because managers must try to determine ahead of time whether a proposed action will be a violation.

The Legal System   Apart from the powers of government regulatory agencies, the overall legal system influences the decisions of managers. Competitive pressures sometimes make laws governing business look like obstacles to success. Genuine questions of legality may arise, especially when decisions become very complex as a result of trying to balance other conflicting influences.

Public Interest Groups   Increasingly, formal groups representing the general public are playing an important role in business and government decisions. Ralph Nader's organizations, Common Cause, the Urban League, the Sierra Club, Friends of the Earth and other organizations strive to protect workers, minorities, consumers, and the environment. They inform, educate, lobby, and carry out research. They may actively confront managers with issues they believe are not being properly handled, such as local air pollution. They may use formal or informal boycotts or other pressure tactics.

4 BUSINESS RESPONSE

A growing social awareness

The response of many modern business managers to increasing social pressures has begun to be guided by ***enlightened self-interest.*** This is an ethical concept that calls for acting to further one's own best interests while taking into account the effects of one's behavior on others. The

ACTION BRIEF

Business Power in Numbers.   The oldest trade association in the United States was the Spermaceti Candlers of Rhode Island, created in 1752. Today, there are some 4,700 large trade groups, and more than one-quarter of them have their headquarters in Washington, D.C. In that community alone, these associations employ 40,000 people. They are the fifth largest employers in the country, following government, retailing, tourism, and construction. All told, in the United States, there are an estimated 20,000 national and international associations, some 25,000 regional and state associations, and as many as 400,000 local and county associations, each with a special interest to pursue.

Source: William H. Jones, "Trade Associations Flourish," The Washington Post, July 4, 1976, p. F1.

concept also includes the notion that when one helps others, one also benefits in the long run. Business efforts to support public education, for instance, not only help society as a whole but also provide better educated employees for the future. Social unrest caused by racial prejudice and poverty is harmful to business. Companies that work to overcome these problems are improving the overall climate for business in the long run. There have been important responses to the need for social responsibility by the business community collectively and by individual companies.

COLLECTIVE RESPONSE

Gradual commitment

One way of promoting social responsibility within business and professions has been the adoption of *codes of ethics.* Industry and professional organizations may specify standards for ethical conduct. Doctors, lawyers, public accountants, and managers who are members of the American Management Association, radio and television stations that are members of the National Association of Broadcasters, and many other individuals and companies agree to accept codes of ethics. These codes set standards for dealing with other companies or professionals in the field, for honesty, and for service to the public. The codes vary as to the extent to which they have been defined to guide specific decisions and the extent to which they are enforceable. It is generally true, in any case, that when the members of a trade or professional organization publicly accept a written code of ethics, the occurrence of severe abuses decreases.

Business organizations have made positive efforts to help other groups concerned with social improvement. The Advertising Council Inc., for example, prepares advertisements and solicits free advertising space from its members to publicize the programs of scores of charitable and public service organizations. Businesses collectively make large donations to such groups, and individual businesspeople devote much free time and effort to fund raising and management counseling. The United Fund, for example, is largely supported by the business community.

The National Alliance of Businessmen is a business-based organization. One of its goals is to create training and employment opportunities for the hard-core disadvantaged who have few job skills. These private efforts, partly funded by the federal government, have actually turned many long-term unemployed people into productive workers with permanent jobs.

INDIVIDUAL COMPANY RESPONSE

Taking responsibility for their employees and their products

Individual businesses also often adopt codes of ethics concerning the behavior of their employees. These codes stress honesty and loyalty and sometimes give quite detailed policies on dealing with suppliers, customers, competitors, and employees. They may also prohibit such practices as accepting gifts or entertainment or entering agreements where a conflict of interest might occur.

Some companies have very aggressive hiring and training programs for minorities and women. Some automobile manufacturers, for instance, seek out potential workers in the community, give them complete prejob and on-the-job training and actively provide opportunities for promotion and advancement. Hundreds of other companies have similar programs. In addition, many businesses give advisory and financial support to local training and retraining efforts and to educational institutions in general.

Many companies, such as Johnson Wax, have set up special departments to identify and resolve consumer problems with their products. Other companies have become deeply involved with community efforts at developing parks, recreation facilities, wildlife preserves, and similar public use areas. Certainly, individual businesses have spent many millions of dollars to reduce the extent to which their production facilities or their products lower the quality of the environment.

POLITICAL ACTION COMMITTEES

Financial aid for friendly legislators

A somewhat recent development has been the creation by business of political action committees (PACs). These organizations are formed either within a corporation or by a trade association. A main purpose of them is to provide a legal way of making contributions to the political campaigns of candidates whom they look upon with favor. Individuals within a company, not the corporation, make the donations to the PACs. In 1982, there were more than 2,000 corporate and association PACs, and they made campaign contributions of nearly $50 million. Among the largest PACs are the American Medical Association, the National Association of Realtors, the National Automobile Dealers Association, the Associated General Contractors of America, and the Independent Insurance Agents of America. The maximum PAC contribution to an individual allowed by law is $15,000.

PACs have been criticized, due to their business relationships, for the potential of raising funds far in excess of what groups of ordinary citizens could raise. As such, their critics contend, PACs may be able to exert an influence politically and socially in far greater proportion than the number of their members would warrant.

ACTION BRIEF

"Baggies" for Coal. Environmentalists do not like to see pulverized coal transported by fresh water through pipelines. It's no good for the water, and it invites potential spills. W. R. Grace & Co., a corporate miner, offers a solution. Pack the coal in huge plastic bags, nearly 2 feet in diameter and 10 feet long. The bags would be inserted into a 20-inch pipeline and blown through it by jets of salt water like peas in a peashooter. The line's cost would be astronomical— $2.5 billion—but it would save money on coal hauling over the long run. And it would not pollute the water.

Source. Ann Hughey, "A Coal Company's Way to Pacify Environmentalists: Use 'Baggies,'" The Wall Street Journal, *June 1, 1982, p. 29.*

5   CURRENT AND CONTINUING PROBLEMS

The cost-versus-benefits dilemma stands in the way of solutions

Despite the fact that businesses are willing to take greater responsibility, important and complex problems continue to beset relations between business and the rest of society.

THE ENVIRONMENT

Catching up is costly

Remedying the damage done by industry to the physical environment and protecting it from further destruction is a severe challenge. Pollution from all sources has become such a serious problem today that it threatens life and health.

Air pollution results from the release into the air of gases or solid matter that may be harmful to various kinds of life forms. Automobiles are the largest single source of pollution. They pour hundreds of millions of tons of pollutants into the atmosphere every year. Many industrial processes also cause severe air pollution. Other offenders include public waste treatment plants and trash disposal incinerators.

Water pollution may be caused by a number of sources. Chemicals from industrial processes, chemical fertilizers carried in runoff water from farms, oil spills from offshore wells and tankers, heat from power plants, human waste from inadequate sewage treatment plants, and many other pollutants reach our lakes, rivers, and streams. Many eventually settle in the ocean, threatening the balance of life there.

The land is polluted by pesticides and industrial chemicals that build up in the soil. Billions of beverage containers and millions of tons of paper products litter fields and roadways. Cities and towns create huge mountains of refuse every year which is buried, burned, or simply allowed to pile up.

Pollution is, in fact, seriously threatening life. The problem is made critical by the tremendous expense of creating and applying solutions. In some instances, the technology needed to prevent or control pollution has not even been invented. In addition, nearly every pollution control effort has economic effects beyond its immediate cost. A factory with devices to reduce pollution produces goods that are more expensive than one without the devices. A farm using less effective pesticides has lower yields than one using more damaging sprays. Truly effective sewage treatment usually means higher municipal taxes. Nonpolluting automobile engines use devices that make cars more expensive to operate.

Pollution problems are slowly being solved. The government, business, and private citizens must make a concerted effort if pollution is to be significantly reduced. The cost of creating and maintaining a safe and clean environment must be borne by all.

LAND USE AND QUESTIONS ABOUT GROWTH

The rights of private ownership are at issue

As the United States continues to develop, available land becomes scarce and the uses of private property begin to interfere with each other. The problem of controlling the use of land without distorting the concept of private ownership can only grow worse as population increases and industrialization progresses.

The need to manage land use arises from two principal causes:

■ Many areas of the country have developed to such an extent that there simply is not enough land available for all uses. This creates a need to use land more efficiently and with less waste.

■ Different ways of using land do not always work well together. For example, a metal-stamping plant 50 feet away from a hospital may interfere with the proper operation of the hospital. In order to prevent such interference, specific uses of land must be restricted to certain areas.

Issues & Highlights

Industrial Waste?

You Take It!

A major problem with industrial societies is what to do with the various harmful and polluting wastes it generates. The most spectacular wastes are from nuclear energy plants. But they make up only a small portion of hazardous chemical wastes from normal processes in the manufacture of chrome and other metal platings for autos and appliances, insecticides, and other products. It is no small problem: New York State generates more than 100,000 tons a year. Even the prescribed treatment plants for many pollutants end up with a noxious waste that must be disposed of. The problem is where to put it.

In less sophisticated days, industrial wastes were used in land fills, dumped in abandoned quarries, taken out to sea, shipped to friendly nations abroad, or buried in salt mines. Few people ever asked the question of what ever happened to the waste after it was dumped. We now know that it remains as a hazard for many years, sometimes forever. Most people believe that the benefits from industry far outweigh the disposal problem. But when it comes to finding a place to dump the waste, it's a different matter. New England, for example, does not have a single commercial hazardous waste disposal facility. Everywhere you look, the typical answer today from most countries, states and communities is: "Put it in someone else's backyard."

Source: "Industrial Wastes With Nowhere to Go," Business Week, March 8, 1982, p. 33.

Should each state be required to take care of the hazardous waste its own industries create? Should the federal government act as referee to find the best disposal places for it? Or should we give up products and services whose processes are the main culprits?

Attempts by governments to manage land use decrease the control individual owners have over their property. This is a source of conflict. However, without control, many areas of the country would rapidly become unlivable. The usual response to this issue is for local governments to enact ordinances giving the government limited control of land use. These *zoning ordinances* restrict the use of land within defined areas to specified purposes. For instance, a zone might be created where only single-family houses are allowed and another with only heavy industry. Governments also use their powers of taxation to encourage or discourage certain kinds of land uses. For example, a lower tax rate for agricultural land encourages farming.

The problems of real estate development and land use have grown so severe in some areas that a separate issue has emerged: efforts are being made to prevent further growth altogether. In some areas, citizen groups and governments have made attempts to slow or stop growth. This clearly conflicts with business goals, since growth is nearly always desired by individual companies and by the business community as a whole. However, if the quality of life suffers enough as a result of growth, actions may be taken to restrict such "progress."

MULTINATIONAL OPERATIONS
Cultural differences are narrowing

Many practical and ethical problems that result from international business operations have already been mentioned. Bribery, kickbacks, and other practices have flourished in overseas operations on a greater scale than has been common in domestic operations. Two factors contribute to the problem: (a) the growth of international operations resulting in increased competition and more opportunities for unethical practices and (b) a more widespread acceptance of a common standard of behavior arising from cross-cultural contacts and influences.

In 1977, the United States Congress moved to put a check on bribery by domestic companies abroad by passing the Foreign Corrupt Practices Act of 1977. This makes it a crime for any individual or corporation to make or promise payments to foreign nationals, agencies, governments, officials, or political parties "in order to obtain or retain business." The law is enforced by the Security Exchange Commission, which can impose fines of up to $1,000,000 on corporations and up to $10,000 and/or imprisonment for up to five years on company officials.

MINORITIES AND WOMEN
Progress has been made, but there is still a long way to go

Opportunities for minorities and women have been increasingly promoted in the business community in the past decade. Progress has clearly been made in select occupations.(See Table 26-1.) However, the problem still remains unsolved. Unemployment is much higher among minorities than among other groups. Educational opportunities are still limited. Prejudice and hatred are still commonplace. Most career opportunities are still very restricted for women. Many vocations, particularly those with a high level of responsibility and large salaries, are closed to almost everyone but white males.

TABLE 26-1
Percentage Distribution of Female, Male, and Minority Workers in Select Occupations, 1972 and 1981

	1972	1981
Accountants		
Female	21.7%	38.5%
Male	78.3%	61.5%
Minorities	4.3%	9.9%
Computer Specialists		
Female	16.8%	27.1%
Male	83.2%	72.9%
Minorities	5.5%	9.4%
Lawyers and Judges		
Female	3.8%	14.1%
Male	96.2%	85.9%
Minorities	1.9%	4.6%
Personnel and Labor Relations Workers		
Female	31.0%	49.9%
Male	69.0%	40.1%
Minorities	9.0%	10.9%
Bank Officers and Financial Managers		
Female	17.6%	27.5%
Male	82.4%	72.5%
Minorities	4.0%	5.8%
Buyers (wholesale and retail trade)		
Female	32.9%	43.6%
Male	67.1%	56.4%
Minorities	4.3%	6.7%
Office Managers		
Female	41.9%	70.6%
Male	58.1%	29.4%
Minorities	1.0%	4.0%
Sales Managers		
Female	15.7%	26.5%
Male	84.3%	73.5%
Minorities	1.6%	4.6%

Source: U.S. Bureau of the Census, *Statistical Abstract of the United States, 1982-1983*, 103d ed., Washington, D.C., 1982.

However, progress is in sight. Government-enforced programs, like affirmative action plans, are reducing barriers. Business's growing concern for the development and training of employees is also improving the lot of women and minorities. As managers and other professionals gain experience in working with them, more top-level positions and new occupations are likely to open up for these groups.

CONFLICT OF VALUES

The creation of wealth is still business' greatest responsibility

There are several sides to the issue of what business's responsibility to society should be. One viewpoint is that business must subordinate its objective of creating profits to the general needs and interests of society at large. Another viewpoint is that the creation of wealth is still business' greatest responsibility, and concern about ecology, conservation, and society's well-being should not take priority over this primary objective. Still another viewpoint is expressed by people like the late Harold Smiddy, founder of the General Electric Academy of Management at Croton, New York. He believed that it is unrealistic to make business firms responsible not only for the generation of wealth and all the values it brings, but also for restricting its own efforts in the pursuit of its goals. It is better, he believed, for a nation that advocates free enterprise to employ the same kinds of checks and balances in business that it does in government. In Smiddy's opinion, the community at large should establish laws that regulate business in the best interests of the people, and the government should enforce those regulations. Regardless of the wisdom of this philosophy or its chance of prevailing in the future, at the present time, and probably for a long time to come, people who wish to move ahead in business can be expected to accept the profit motive as its main impetus.

Key Concepts

1. Business ethics is a collection of principles and rules of conduct for carrying on business in a way that is fair both to those who deal directly with a company and to the community.
2. Managers today must consider the diverse, often conflicting, attitudes and expectations of employees, customers, suppliers, competitors, investors, creditors, and society as a whole.
3. Business decisions are made in an environment of pressure brought about by groups representing their own interests. These forces include labor unions, government agencies, the legal system, and public interest groups.

4. Business' response to these pressures and expectations is demonstrated by the establishment of codes of ethics, charitable and community leadership efforts, educational support, programs to develop opportunities for minorities and women, pollution control programs, and in other ways.
5. In spite of business' growing social consciousness, serious problems remain. Difficulties with pollution, land use, opposition to growth, multinational operations, and opportunities for minorities and women are still basically unsolved.

Review Questions

1. Define, identify, or explain each of the following key terms or phrases found on the pages indicated.

   business ethics (p. 484)
   code of ethics (p. 490)
   consumerism (p. 486)
   enlightened self-interest (p. 489)
   ethics (p. 484)
   zoning ordinance (p. 494)

2. What is business ethics? What is its relationship to law?
3. Contrast the general ethical beliefs of nineteenth-century business with an equivalent principle in the twentieth century.
4. What three expectations are especially important to employees now?
5. What is consumerism, and why is it important in many business decisions?
6. What two main factors must be balanced when businesses are deciding how much positive action to take toward improving general social conditions?
7. What role do industry trade associations play in business ethics?
8. In what ways do political action committees (PACs) resemble consumer organizations?
9. Do you think enlightened self-interest is better than any other kind of self-interest? Explain.
10. Why do each of the following present a problem for business and for society?
    a. environmental pollution
    b. land use
    c. economic growth
    d. multinational operations
    e. opportunities for minorities and women

Case Critique 26-1
Profits That Came Naturally

When Morris J. Siegel and his friends founded Celestial Seasonings, Inc., they were judged by family and friends to be bona fide hippies. As "flower children" of the 1970s, they picked herbs in the mountains of Colorado and mixed them together for a healthful tea that they sold to natural food stores. One thing led to another, and before long they were selling a number of now-famous brands like Red Zinger and Mountain Thunder. All they really wanted to do, they said, was to combine some very hard work with a happy sort of love-and-peace approach to capitalism.

By the 1980s, Celestial Seasonings was taking in $16 million a year. Its annual profits topped $1 million. The owner-managers now wear button-down shirts to work and have adopted a typical corporate organization structure. As the business has grown, however, it has caused the owners to regularly examine its substance. For example, customers intensely protested the company's use of a rare herb imported from South Africa, where racial discrimination is practiced. The company

changed its recipe and abandoned that source. Then, there is the matter of caffeine. How would the company reconcile its commitment to people's health and sell teas with caffeine in them? One of its most popular brands contains it. The company is reluctant to eliminate the caffeine. Says the marketing manager, "It sells a lot of the product."

The manner in which Celestial Seasonings conducts business is also a matter of internal conflict. In typical laid-back style, the management used to hold an eight-hour staff meeting each Monday, dwelling on such weighty matters as the philosophical attributes of tea bags. They are more businesslike now. Mr. Siegel, who is very religious, insists that Celestial Seasonings won't be run like just any business. "The company has grown," says his partner, "but, at the same time, it has maintained its goodness." Mr. Siegel confirms this view, "I want the company to be something of a social experiment, as well as a real button-down, top-notch marketing and sales company. But I've learned a lot of lessons in the past five years. I used to promise people the moon. Now I have to come down to the treetops."

1. The owners of Celestial Seasonings apparently try to match their own attitudes and expectations with those of their customers. What problems does this cause?
2. How does the company's reaction to customer pressures differ or resemble that of more traditional companies?

3. What do you think Mr. Siegel means when he says that he's learned not to promise the moon to employees, to settle for the treetops?
4. How well do you think this company is combining ethical behavior with business?

Source: Eric Morgenthaler, "Herb Tea's Pioneer: From Hippie Origins to $16 Million a Year," *The Wall Street Journal*, May 6, 1981, p. 1.

Case Critique 26-2
The Grease Job

You are the head of a multinational corporation. Your company has, for years, operated a chemical plant in a distant republic overseas. You are notified one day that the plant manager has been arrested and is about to be put in jail. The alleged crime is that goods found in the company's warehouse lack the proper customs' stamps and papers of that country.

You know that the truth of the matter is more complicated. The practice of "grease," or making payoffs to local officials, is the basic way of doing business in this country's bureaucracy. Over the years, the plant manager has routinely paid gratuities to the custom officers. Recently, your company, in complying with the laws of the United States, directed all plant managers, wherever their location, to desist from such practices. This plant manager, in following "home office" policy, stopped the payments. The customs' officials "in-spected" the warehouse and found alleged customs' violations. The plant manager is arrested. The price for dropping the charges is relayed to you by a local lawyer who represents your company: "Pay $18,000 of 'grease' to be distributed among local officials, and all charges will be dropped. Otherwise, your plant manager can sit in jail."

1. What would you do if you were the company president?
2. What are some of the alternate ways of dealing with this and similar situations in the future?

Source: Carl B. Kaufman, "A 5-Part Quiz on Corporate Ethics, *The Washington Post*, July 1, 1979, p. C1.

1 TRANSITION INTO BUSINESS

Making your education pay off

There are about 100 million jobs in the United States. More than 70 million of them are involved with some form of business enterprise.

Some of these jobs are very attractive. The work is interesting and challenging. The surroundings are pleasant. The pay and security are good, and there are opportunities for advancement. These are the kinds of jobs that most people seek.

On the other hand, there are many more jobs that are less appealing. They are dull and monotonous. The working conditions are hectic or dirty. The pay is marginal, and the outlook for a career is bleak.

JOBS OR CAREERS?

Goals are important

Many people must take one of the less appealing jobs first if they wish to get a toehold in business. After they have learned the ropes and developed a skill, they can seek jobs with better conditions and greater promise for the future. If they are properly prepared—by education as well as by experience—they are often successful. If they are unsuited for improvement, either by a poor attitude, ineptitude, or lack of relevant learning, they may languish for the rest of their lives in the backwaters of business. The successful employees build careers; the less successful ones seem to work forever at jobs.

STARTING POINTS

Job experience helps

Individuals who leave high school in search of a job are usually at a disadvantage. Typically, one-fifth of the 16- to 19-year-olds who wish to work cannot find employment. If they are black and live in inner cities, the chances are much worse; only one out of two is likely to find a job. Often, this work experience is not particularly valuable, for it emphasizes low-level or entry-level work. Jobs for young women usually focus on white-collar, clerical work. Young men, on the other hand, are likely to move into blue-collar employment. About one-third of all young people employed, men or women, perform some sort of lower-level service work.

Job seekers leaving college have a far better chance. In terms of previous employment, they start from three different bases:

■ *No previous employment.* These persons are at some disadvantage since they have not tested the water. They know little from experience about the "positives" and the "negatives" of business life. The discipline of an eight-hour day and a five-day week may be hard to take. It may be a novelty for some people to forgo free choice for a portion of each day in their lives. On the other hand, those who have never held a job may be pleased with the feeling that comes from a regular paycheck and the independence of earning their own livelihood.

■ *Part-time employment.* Most college students have performed some sort of work on a part-time, or temporary, basis. In general, their main objective has been to earn money, either for tuition or for recreation. Accordingly, their work experience may not have given them a representative view of business. Certainly, most of these jobs have been at the lower end of the attractiveness spectrum. The experience may have been negative. Nevertheless, some business experience is far better than none.

■ *Full-time employment.* A great many students acquire their college education while working full time. They probably have the best base of all for seeking career positions. They now have book learning as well as "hard knocks" experience. Often, they may have served their business apprenticeship in a menial role. But they are now prepared for something better. In general, these people have two choices: (a) they can look toward development and advancement in their present line of work and with their current employer, or (b) they can search elsewhere, to make a fresh start toward a meaningful and rewarding career.

In any case, those without employment experience should strive to capitalize on their formally acquired education.

2 A CHOICE OF TWO DIRECTIONS

Independence or employment

Individuals about to enter business have two choices: they can go to work for someone else, or they can start a business of their own. The first choice is easier; the second is, without question, the harder. So, first, let us examine the hard way.

A BUSINESS OF YOUR OWN

Doing it the hard way

Each year, about 500,000 people in the United States go into business on their own. Half of these new businesses fail within two years. One-quarter of them do not make it to the five-year mark. Every day, 1,000 small businesses fail or quietly close down. That is the bad side. On the good side, more than 8 million people who own and operate their own businesses are successful. They have been able to succeed because they have learned to be good business managers. They have learned, by experience, by education, or both, how to create products and services that people need and how to bring these products and services to market with the least risk.

Businesses succeed because they follow well-thought-out business plans. The owners of successful businesses have checked all the requirements before committing their capital and time, and they routinely operate according to their plan, changing and improving it as they go along. Business owners do make mistakes. This is the risk they take when they are constantly creating. The successful ones, however, learn from their experience so that their knowledge of how to hit the profit targets improves constantly.

Business Plans The previous chapters of this text (especially Chapter 12) have touched on most of the factors that business people must consider and manage if they are to be successful. Some of the most important factors you should consider when developing a plan for establishing your own business are listed in Table A-1.

TABLE A-1
Checklist for Establishing Your Own Business

	Chapter Reference
Product or Service	
Does it satisfy a demonstrable consumer need?	1
Is it commercially feasible? Can you make (or provide) it and make a profit on it? What are the competing or substitute products, and how strong are they?	7
What is the break-even point? Are there enough people willing to pay the price you need to get in order to cover your fixed costs as well as your variable costs?	12
Business Plan	
What are your immediate objectives in terms of sales and profits?	19
How long can you afford to wait to break even?	12, 20, 21
Which legal form of enterprise is most suitable for you?	4
How much and what kind of help can you get from the government, particularly the Small Business Administration?	25
What kinds of licenses or permits are required? What regulations must you conform to?	25
Have you prepared a detailed budget for your first year of operation?	12, 21
Have you made a forecast of income and expenses for the next three years?	12, 21
Resources	
Will you rely upon equity financing or debt financing, and to what degree? What sources can you approach for either form of financing?	13, 14
What kind of equipment and place to operate the equipment are needed? What is the cost of the equipment and the plant? What is needed? What is the cost of operation and maintenance?	10
Should you make or buy your product or its components? Should you subcontract some services? What is the availability and price of critical materials?	11
Have you checked out your pricing policy to be certain that it is competitive and realistic? What distribution channels will you use? Who will do your selling and promotion?	7, 8, 9
How many employees will you need? What skills should they have? How much must you pay them? How will you distribute the work and manage your employees?	16, 17
What trade association can you rely upon for comparative performance standards? Does Dun & Bradstreet provide useful financial ratios? To what extent does the U.S. Department of Commerce collect information relevant to your product or business?	20, 25
Controls	
How will you take care of your accounting needs?	20
How can you minimize risks? Will you carry adequate insurance? What kind of insurance will you carry?	15
What will your credit policy toward customers be?	15

One final word of caution: A business of your own requires long hours of work, a knack for doing many different things, and a willingness to perform your own menial chores.

WORKING FOR OTHERS

The smoother road

This is the way most people enter the business world. It involves the least personal risk and usually offers the greatest security. It does require that individuals relinquish, to some degree, their own desires or goals in exchange for wages or salaries paid by their employers. In the best kind of an arrangement, individuals find an acceptable balance between their goals and those of the company for which they work. Additionally, working for others often provides a wider opportunity for self-development and advancement than do the confines of self-employment.

Range of Jobs and Choice of Industries   The *Dictionary of Occupational Titles,* published by the U.S. Department of Commerce, contains some standard job descriptions ranging from token-taker to tinsmith. But generally speaking, jobs can be classified in a sort of hierarchy, based upon popular attitudes toward the work involved. An arbitrary classification of jobs is given in Table A-2 on page 503 as an example.

Another way to select a job is to look at the range of opportunities available in different industries. Table 1-1 in Chapter 1 shows the range of different industries in which business engages—from agriculture to mining to service businesses, such as hotels and amusement parks. The manufacturing industry has the widest variety of businesses, with about 450 different classifications listed. A look at the *Standard Industrial Classification Manual,* issued by the Office of Management and the Budget, is worthwhile. It is a valuable aid to the career hunter.

An especially valuable source of job and career information is the annual *Occupational Outlook Handbook* published by the U.S. Department of Labor. It can be found in every library. It provides a forecast for jobs in various classifications such as industrial, office, construction, transportation, and services. Within each classification the *Handbook* examines dozens of occupations in detail, describing the nature of the work, working conditions, places of employment, training and qualifications required, employment and advancement opportunities, and typical earnings. An hour or two spent looking through the *Handbook* is time well used.

Nature of the Work   Certain industries tend to be characterized by the general nature of the work available. Much construction work, for example, is seasonal and is performed under harsh weather conditions of extreme heat or cold. Work in a television manufacturing firm probably requires sensitive manual skills and long hours in a confined work place. Work in the transportation industries may be clean and glamorous, as for a flight attendant, or it may be frustrating and repetitious, as for a city bus driver. Working for a public utility might be less exciting than working on an oil drilling rig, but it probably offers far more security.

In seeking and selecting the kind of work you will do, it is helpful to try to rate the particular industry, the department you might work in, and

TABLE A-2
General Classification of Work From a Career Point of View

Least Skilled

The jobs in this category can be learned very quickly by a person with no special skills or education. These jobs typically require heavy physical work. They may, in addition, involve much standing, walking, close attention to work, and a fast pace. They occur in white-collar as well as in blue-collar occupations. They are the so-called "labor grade" or "entry" jobs in both areas.

Semiskilled

These jobs are most typified by factory or office jobs that are above the entry level but fall short of the skilled occupations. The U.S. Department of Labor frequently calls people employed in these jobs "operatives," in that they operate industrial machinery. This category may also include office work such as filing and duplicating.

Skilled

These are the jobs usually requiring considerable training (formal or informal) and long experience. Typically, skilled people are craftspeople like plumbers, toolmakers, carpenters, and electricians. Many technically trained people are included in this category, especially those who require licenses in their jobs, for example, laboratory technicians, dental hygienists, and surveyors.

Specialized

There are a growing number of people who provide specialized services to production and clerical workers. Among these specialized people, like the skilled group of which they may also be a part, are accountants, statisticians, planners, and computer programmers. This group is characterized by the extent of formal education required. Their specialties may not be readily transferable from one employer to another the way those of a skilled craftsperson usually are. Staff positions are often closely associated with management.

Professional

Members of this group usually have followed a carefully prescribed course of extended formal study and have experience related to that study. Usually they adhere to a code of ethical behavior, and are licensed or certified. Doctors, lawyers, and architects are the most visible of this group, but engineers, certified accountants, dentists, nurses, and many others are considered "professionals."

Managers

This is the group of people, employed mainly by owners of proprietorships or corporations, to whom the responsibility and authority for supervising certain business functions have been delegated. These are generally considered white-collar jobs, although they occur regularly in heavy industries like mining and construction. The range of these positions begins with the first-line supervisor, who has direct contact with production employees, and moves up through various levels to the position of paid president.

the job you wish to perform against the ranges of possibilities listed in Table A-3.

Obviously, no single job or company can provide an employee with everything the employee wants. The wise job candidate, however, makes a list of those job characteristics that are most important to him or her and tries to choose a career that matches them.

TABLE A-3
Industry, Job, and Company Assessment Guide

Factor	Extremely Important	Somewhat Important	Unimportant
Instructions: On a separate sheet of paper, indicate for each factor your attitude about the importance of that particular factor in a work situation.			
1. Cleanliness and organization of work area	_____	_____	_____
2. Lighting	_____	_____	_____
3. Work space	_____	_____	_____
4. Pace of work	_____	_____	_____
5. Physical demands of work	_____	_____	_____
6. Amount of attention work requires	_____	_____	_____
7. Amount of supervision	_____	_____	_____
8. Social classification of job (white-collar versus blue-collar)	_____	_____	_____
9. Technology involved in job	_____	_____	_____
10. Financial security	_____	_____	_____
11. Salary or wages	_____	_____	_____
12. Benefits	_____	_____	_____
13. Safety of workplace	_____	_____	_____
14. Size of company	_____	_____	_____
15. Length of time company has been in business	_____	_____	_____
16. Company ethics	_____	_____	_____
17. Job security	_____	_____	_____
18. Stability of company	_____	_____	_____
19. Competitiveness	_____	_____	_____
20. Location	_____	_____	_____
21. Personal contact	_____	_____	_____
22. Mental challenge	_____	_____	_____
23. Advancement opportunities	_____	_____	_____
24. Responsibilities involved in job	_____	_____	_____

3 GETTING A JOB

Marketing your personal values

Wanting the right job for yourself and finding it can make the difference between a meaningful, happy life or one of continual disappointment. Accordingly, it is important to know not only what you want, as outlined earlier, but also what employers may want from you.

EMPLOYER EXPECTATIONS

Assessing your worth

A recent study yielded the information shown in Table A-4. Although the focus of the study was on candidates for managerial positions, the findings are indicative of what is required for business success. Note the emphasis placed on communications skills, personal appearance, previous work experience, personality, the individual's career goals, and recommendations from former employers.

William N. Yeomans, manager of training and development for the J. C. Penney Company, lists 10 attributes that employers want to see in applicants:

A burning desire to learn and grow.

Brute determination to succeed.

Good old common sense.

A natural ability to get along with people.

A talent for selling or persuading.

Good writing and speaking skills.

A sense of urgency.

An affinity for details and accuracy.

Well-defined personal goals.

A love of hard work.

JOB HUNTING

Finding the opportunities

The search for good jobs starts with research. Your business school or college placement counselor is a good source of leads and advice. So, too, are your federal and state employment agencies. Special programs sponsored by federal and/or state departments of labor open other doors. Certainly, you should check with your local chamber of commerce or an equivalent business organization. The help-wanted advertisements in newspapers in communities where you wish to work are a basic reference.

In the appropriate section of the classified advertisements or in telephone books you can find numerous advertisements for private employment agencies. All are in business to make money, but some offer chances for employment that are not found elsewhere.

TABLE A-4
Importance of Factors in Evaluating Candidates for Managerial Positions

Factor	Very Important	Important	Minor Importance	Not Considered
Communication skills	88.3%	11.7%	0.0%	0.0%
College grades	8.0	70.5	18.9	2.7
Prestige of college attended	0.4	18.6	53.4	27.7
Recommendations of teachers	7.2	36.0	47.3	9.5
Major field of study	30.3	58.3	11.4	0.0
Personal appearance	43.4	50.6	6.0	0.0
Degree received or years of college	24.2	57.4	17.0	1.5
Previous work experience	49.1	39.6	10.6	0.8
Impression of personality	50.8	46.6	2.3	0.4
Career goals	49.2	43.9	6.4	0.4
Familiarity with company	14.8	29.5	45.1	10.6
Extracurricular activities	4.2	32.6	49.2	14.0
Recommendations of former employers	43.0	43.8	10.9	2.3

Source: Robert Greenberg, "The Importance of 13 Factors in Evaluating Job Applications," Indiana Commission for Higher Education, 1976.

Experts in job search advise the following:

■ Get in touch with as many employers as you can afford to contact. Do not rely exclusively on the want ads.

■ Answer advertisements promptly. Many opening are filled before the advertisement has stopped running.

■ Do not expect too much from "blind" advertisements; experience shows that the chances of finding a job through them are slim.

■ Be cautious about answering "no experience necessary" ads. It often means that the job is unattractive and hard to fill because of low pay, poor working conditions, or is straight commission work.

■ Look for unsolicited work. Get a list of firms in your neighborhood from a bank, chamber of commerce, or the Yellow Pages. Make application at personnel offices. Let friends, relatives, and others know of your job search. Informal methods like this are often fruitful.

■ Be diligent in making out applications, seeking interviews, and following up. Persistence is a strong tool for prying open job opportunities.

■ Be ready to accept something less than the perfect job in order to get a foothold, especially with a good employer. Most people have to perform work that has its menial, tedious, and unattractive facets so that they can show their potential. Good jobs are obtained by building on a record of sound performance on lesser jobs.

Beyond knowing where to look, it is important to know how to apply for a job. Application forms should be filled out neatly and legibly. Résumés (see Figure A-1) should be prepared ahead of time, with the help of your school or college placement office or another advisor. Résumés should accompany your written job inquiries and should be available to supplement the application form used by the company. Opinions vary as to what should be included in a résumé, but a good rule of thumb is not to overload them with inconsequential details that can detract from your most valuable qualifications.

JOB INTERVIEWING

Putting your best foot forward

Professional interviewers and recruiters not only consider an applicant's basic qualifications, they also are impressed by how well candidates handle themselves during the interview. Typical advice from interviewers stress the following:

■ Read all you can about a potential employer before you go into the interview.

■ Credentials mean little if you do not make a good impression.

■ Be well-groomed and appropriately dressed for the interview.

■ Make a strong effort to stress the skills you have that would help the company meet its goals.

■ Show how whatever work experience you have had has contributed to your business worth.

■ Relate your extracurricular activities to your ability to work with other people or lead groups of people.

■ Let the interviewer establish the interview pattern; follow the interviewer's lead.

■ Listen carefully to the questions. Try to respond without wandering from the point of the question.

■ Acknowledge your weaknesses, but do not dwell on them.

■ Demonstrate maturity by accepting responsibility for your failures as well as your achievements. Do not blame others for your failures.

■ Be prepared to answer questions like these: How did you choose your major or specialty? What personal qualifications would make you valuable to our firm? Would you rather work alone or with others? What kind of boss have you liked best in the past? Least? Which course did you enjoy most? Least? What made you seek an interview with this company? What are your career objectives? What is your single greatest strength? Weakness? How do you spend your spare time?

4 HOLDING A JOB

Capitalizing on your performance

When it comes to holding a job, results count the most of all. Employers recognize the value of diligent, capable performers. People who come to work regularly and on time have won half the battle for job security.

NAME:	Wilma Kaye Nagel
ADDRESS:	106 North Main Street Valleyville, Virginia 22999
TELEPHONE:	(703) 555-9090
CAREER INTERESTS:	Responsible position in some aspect of retail merchandising.
EDUCATION:	**1979 to 1983—** Turner Ashley High School, Valleyville, Virginia. Graduated with diploma in general education; electives in retailing, typing, and Spanish.
	1983 to the present— Blue Ridge Community College, Weyers Cave, Virginia. Have accumulated 64 credits toward Associate degree in applied science with major in merchandising. Expect to graduate in June 1985.
SCHOLASTIC ACHIEVEMENTS:	Graduated in top 25 percent of high school class of 345 students. Achieved grade point average of 3.25 out of possible 4 points.
EXTRACURRICULAR ACTIVITIES:	**High school—**Captain of swim team; vice president of junior class; held part-time job as cashier in department store from 1981 to 1983.
	College—Chairperson of Spring Festival; member of Phi Beta Lambda; worked an average of 15 hours per week since date of enrollment.
WORK EXPERIENCE:	**1975 to 1979—** Self-employed, doing garden and lawn work during the summers.
	1979 to 1983— Part-time checkout cashier during Christmas rush, Mid-Way Department Store, Hainesville, Viginia.
	July 1983 to February 1984—Part-time salesclerk, Rosaline Fashions, Bridgewater, Virginia. Duties included arranging stock, waiting on customers, and taking inventory.
	February 1984 to the present—Part-time assistant merchadise manager, Z-MART Clothing Company, Harrisonburg, Virginia. Duties include checking stock in and out for sportswear department, supervising two salespersons, and displaying merchandise.
OUTSIDE INTERESTS:	Volunteer, 3 hours per week, at Chilton General Hospital, Bridgewater, Virginia. Hobbies include bingo, swimming, interior design, and sewing.
REFERENCES:	Lawrence R. Buxton Instructor, Merchandising Department Blue Ridge Community College Weyers Cave, Virginia
	Rhonda F. Feinberg Store manager, Z-MART Clothing Company Harrisonburg, Virginia
	Marlene H. Duchamp Coordinator of Volunteers, Chilton General Hospital Bridgewater, Virginia

Figure A-1
A sample résumé.

People who regularly get their work done properly and on time usually have the job locked up. Those who contribute other dimensions to their work are valued even more. Employers have difficulty in finding people who take the initiative in solving problems, who look for additional responsibilities, and who can work with others without creating conflicts.

There is also a certain amount of job etiquette that makes a good deal of common sense. It does not mean that you should be a sycophant, but it does imply that the accommodations demanded by most business situations are appreciated when you initiate them rather than expecting them from others. For example, Shirley Sloan Fader, writing in *Working Woman* ("Start Here: What Your Boss Wishes You Knew," *Working Woman*, May 1982, p. 22) suggests these basics on a new job:

■ When in doubt, ask questions rather than proceed in error.

■ Watch for the priorities that matter to your boss and the company. What is most important: neatness, speed, customer relations?

■ Arrive on time; staying late rarely compensates. When you are not available, it interferes with the work of others.

■ Let your boss know where you are. If you have to attend a meeting or carry on business in another department, the boss should be informed ahead of time.

■ Take your time developing permanent lunchtime associates. It does not pay to be locked into a group that may not provide the most appropriate social or professional support.

■ Realize that every job has some duties that are boring, annoying, or seemingly pointless. After you are really established in the organization, you can question their worth. At the beginning, however, accept them. Being inflexible about what you will or will not do can cost you the job. Challenging the "system" before you know what it is all about may only prove to reveal your ignorance.

■ Dress in a way that suits your job. What is right in an advertising agency may be wrong in a bank. When in doubt, dress conservatively until you are sure of what is appropriate.

Learning how to hold a good job is the first step toward advancement. Once you have shown that you can do good work within the business system, you have laid the foundation for obtaining a better job, either with the company you work for or another one. Careers are built by acquiring related experience, job by job. As you start out, your career direction will be understandably broad. As you acquire experience, however, your advancement trail will begin to narrow down to the field (and the specific jobs within that field) that best suit your capabilities, training, and interests.

ACTION BRIEF

Work, Work, Work!
Andy Warhol, one of the most successful people in the creative field, is a businessperson, artist, filmmaker, and publisher. He has parlayed his talents from ownership of an advertising agency, through the creation of his pop art Campbell soup cans, to the establishment of a multimillion dollar private enterprise. When queried at a "Talking Shop" interview at the Overseas Press Club in New York, he was asked what advice he could give to an aspiring artist. Warhol's succinct reply was: "Work!"

Source: "Want to Succeed? Work, Says Warhol," OPC Bulletin, January 1, 1977, p. 2.

Glossary

The number or numbers in parentheses following each definition refer(s) to the chapter or chapters in which the terms are introduced and explained.

Absolute advantage   A term used to describe the position of a country in international trade when it is the only country able to make a certain product or when it can make that product at a lower cost than any other country can. *See also* **Comparative advantage.** (23)

Accountability   The ultimate responsibility for proper completion of a task even if the task has been delegated to a subordinate. (6)

Accounting   A numerical information system whereby the day-to-day monetary transactions of an organization are recorded, classified, summarized, and interpreted. An accounting system monitors the flow of cash and the fluctuations in financial obligations. *See also* **Cost accounting; Financial accounting; Managerial accounting.** (20)

Accounting equation   A basic assumption in modern accounting: Assets = liabilities + equity. Since liabilities and equity are the only two sources of assets, their sum must equal assets. (20)

Accounts receivable   The amounts owed to a company for goods or services provided to customers but not yet paid for by them. (13)

Acid-test ratio   *See* **Quick ratio.**

Advertising   A sales presentation delivered in some way other than personal contact. (9)

Affirmative action plan   A written plan intended to eliminate discrimination in employment policies by spelling out positive steps to increase hiring and promotion of minority groups and women. An affirmative action plan is required by law of federal agencies and private industries contracted by the government. In most other cases, it is voluntary. (16)

Analytical process   An industrial process in which materials are broken down into new and more useful forms. (10)

Arbitration   A process in which a third party not directly involved in a labor-management dispute tries to facilitate a settlement. In arbitration, negotiating parties agree to be bound by the decisions of the arbitrator. *See also* **Mediation.** (18)

Array   In statistics, a group of numbers placed in order according to size.

Articles of incorporation   *See* **Charter.**

Assembler   A wholesaler who specializes in buying farm produce from individual farms and assembling large quantities for processing, resale, and distribution. (8)

Assembly process   An industrial process which creates products by joining together component parts without changing their shape or composition. (10)

Assets   (1) Any valuable property used for or resulting from a business. Examples of assets are cash, money owed by customers, inventory, and real estate. (2) Those things of value which a company controls, such as land, equipment, cash, and accounts receivable. (4, 13)

Audit   A careful examination of the accounting methods and the financial records and reports of a company to determine that its financial activities and condition are being reported accurately and completely. An audit may be performed by either an internal or an independent auditor. (20)

Automation   A collection of methods for controlling machinery and production processes by automatic means, sometimes with electronic equipment. (10)

Balance of payments   The total payments by a nation to foreign countries minus the total receipts of that nation from foreign countries. (23)

Balance sheet   The main report, in summary form, of the overall financial condition of a company, showing assets, liabilities, and equity at a particular time, usually the last day of a fiscal year. (20)

Bank term loan   A direct loan made, usually by a bank, for a period of from one to five years or sometimes longer. (13)

Bankruptcy   A legal procedure in which a court divides up the remaining assets of an insolvent person or company among the people and organizations to whom money is owed; when this procedure is applied, all debts are erased. (25)

Bill of materials   A list of every kind of raw material or semifinished goods needed for a production run, specifying the quantity needed of each. (11)

Bona fide occupational qualification   The legal requirement that a job specification regarding age, sex, or other restrictive characteristics be proven to be undeniably related to job performance. (16)

Bond   A written pledge to a lender or lenders stating the intention of the borrower or borrowers to repay a loan and specifying the principal, the date of maturity, and the rate of interest. (13)

Brand   A combination of words or symbols intended to identify the goods or services of a specific producer and to distinguish them from the products of others. (7)

Break-even analysis   A method of calculating the minimum quantity of a product that can be manufactured at a profit. (11)

Budget   (1) A plan or forecast, often financial in nature, in which data is presented in numerical form. (2) An operating plan expressed in concrete numbers. It, too, is usually financial, showing expected expenditures, but it may also show other factors that can be expressed numerically, such as worker-hours and materials. (18, 20)

Business cycle   A period during which business activity and general employment alternatively rise and fall. (2)

Business enterprise   An activity that satisfies human wants and needs by providing goods or services for private profit. (1)

Business law   A body of laws that applies especially to the conduct of business activities. (25)

By-laws In corporation management, a group of rules, agreed upon by the owners, describing how stockholders will delegate management control. (22)

Capital (1) Any kind of wealth that is available to support the activities of producing goods and services, that is, of creating more wealth. (2) Private money and resources which are used to pay for the cost of setting up and running a business. (1, 2)

Capital gain A profit made from buying and selling capital assets; for example, selling stock at a price higher than was paid for it results in capital gain. (22)

Capital-intensive process A production process in which equipment or materials are of primary importance; the activities of workers have a lesser significance. (10)

Capitalization ratio A profitability indicator which shows the proportion of funds used by a business that come from certain sources, such as borrowed funds or permanent owners' investments. A capitalization ratio may be calculated by dividing (1) total liabilities by the stockholders' equity or (2) stockholders' equity by total assets. (20)

Cash budget A budget showing expected cash receipts and expenditures for a particular planning period. (21)

Centralized organization An organization in which almost all authority is concentrated in a few positions at the top. (6)

Chain of command The downward flow of authority, responsibility, and channels of communications within an organization. *See also* **Scalar principle.** (6)

Chain store One of a group of stores which are associated under a common management or common ownership and follow a common policy. Chain store operation is usually characterized by central purchasing and warehousing of products before they are distributed to local retail outlets. (8)

Charter (Articles of incorporation) A state-issued document legally

recognizing the existence of a new corporation. The charter states the name and purpose of the corporation as well as stock authorization and other fundamental information. (22)

Class rate A railroad shipping rate based on the characteristics of the goods, such as weight, value, and perishability. (8)

Close corporation A corporation, usually small, whose ownership is closely held and not traded or offered as stock to the public. The owners are usually directly involved in the management of the business. (22)

Code of ethics A statement made by an industry or professional organization specifying standards for ethical conduct. Such a code sets high standards for dealing with other companies or professionals, with respect to honesty, service to the public, and so on. (26)

Coinsurance provision A common provision in fire insurance policies which states that if property is insured for less than its total value and it suffers damage that is less than total, the insurance company will pay only a specified portion of the loss. (15)

Collateral Anything of value that a borrower promises to give the lender if the borrower is unable to repay a loan. (13)

Collective bargaining The process of negotiation by a union with the management of a company. This type of bargaining is called "collective" because the negotiators represent all the member-workers as a group. (18)

Command economy An economic system in which the government plans and controls economic activity by assessing available resources and social needs and then directing the manufacturing and distribution facilities of the country toward certain goals. *See also* **Communism; Socialism.** (2)

Commercial bank In the United States, a privately owned business that provides financial services to customers but which must obtain a government charter in order to operate. (13)

Commercial paper A short-term promissory note that does not have any security. (13)

Committee A group of people within an organization formally assigned the responsibility to discuss, or deal directly, with a well-defined matter. (6)

Commodity rate A special, reduced shipping rate offered by railroads for certain basic goods that are regularly shipped in large quantities. (8)

Common Market (European Economic Community) A cooperative trade community of nine European nations acting together to further common interests by promoting the free movement of labor, capital, goods, and so on among members. (23)

Common stock Stock issued by every corporation to its owners in order to provide permanent risk capital. (13)

Communism An economic system in which central government control and planning has almost entirely replaced the free market, eliminating private ownership and profit and competition. Examples: the Soviet Union, the Peoples' Republic of China. *See also* **Command economy; Socialism.** (2)

Comparative advantage A theory for determining which kinds of production will be most advantageous for a country in international trade: (1) a country with multiple absolute advantages should concentrate on the products in which its advantage is greatest; (2) a country with no absolute advantages should concentrate on products in which its disadvantage is the smallest. *See also* **Absolute advantage.** (23)

Conglomerate combination The joining together into one company of various companies that produce different, generally unrelated, goods and services. (22)

Consideration In law, "something of value." Consideration may be money, personal or intangible property, a promise to perform work, and so on. In contract law, consideration is the impelling influence or "thing of value" that causes a contracting party to enter a contract. (25)

Consumer market People who purchase goods and services for their own or their family's use. (7)

Consumerism In the United States, an emerging social force with the aim of protecting individuals from low-quality or unsafe merchandise and from unreasonably high prices and other unfair business practices. The movement is made up largely of consumers to protect their own interests. *Consumerism* also refers to the organized efforts, usually of private consumers, to protect the interests of the users of business products. (3, 26)

Contract In law, a voluntary agreement in which two or more parties (individuals or corporations) bind themselves to act or not to act in a certain way. A contract may be written or oral. (25)

Convenience goods Familiar, frequently used goods and services that consumers select chiefly because of the ease of buying them, for example, razor blades, chewing gum, bread, and milk. (7)

Conversion process In business, the process of creating or adding value or usefulness to available resources by changing them into an end product or service for which there is a demand. (1)

Cooperative A form of business ownership in which production, marketing, or purchasing facilities are jointly owned by a group and are operated mainly to provide a service to members of the group rather than to make a profit. (5, 8)

Corporation An association of individuals, created under the authority of law, which exists and has powers and liabilities independent of its members. (4)

Cost accounting A set of procedures used to determine the total costs of performing a business activity and to find out in detail the many different sources of the total costs. *See also* **Accounting.** (20)

Current assets Working capital, or the assets used to support the day-to-day operations of a company. Typically, current assets are cash, accounts receivable, negotiable securities, and inventories. (13)

Current ratio Current assets of a company divided by current liabilities. Current ratio is a measure of the ability of a

company to pay current debts and other obligations. (20)

Data processing All of the operations involved in collecting, organizing, analyzing, and presenting data, or information. Data processing may be, but need not be, associated with the use of computers. (19)

Database Interrelated data stored in a computer file for easy access, retrieval, and updating. (19)

Debt financing Funds raised by a business through borrowing, principally in the form of a bank loan or the sale of bonds. (13)

Debt ratio The ratio of the total liabilities of a business to its total assets. A debt ratio is a key measure of a firm's leverage. *See also* **Leverage.** (13)

Decentralized organization An organization in which much authority is delegated to managers who are close to the actual operations. In this type of organization, top management does not usually concern itself with lower-level operating decisions. (6)

Decision tree In statistical analysis, a graphic method for displaying the costs and possible returns of various decisions. The method is usually used to organize and simplify decision making in very complex situations. (24)

Deed A legal document which transfers ownership of real property to a new owner. (25)

Demand deposits Money in checking accounts which can be used like cash, that is, exchanged immediately for goods and services. (14)

Demand economy An economy in which the wants and needs of consumers determine the allocation of resources. This type of economy is characteristic of the free enterprise system. (2)

Demography The statistical study of human population, with regard to size, growth, and so on. (7)

Depreciation A loss in value of equipment, buildings, or other fairly permanent assets caused by normal wear and aging. (20)

Differentiation A promotional technique which points out the unique features of a product that will make it appeal to the chosen

market. (9)

Direct distribution channel The path to markets followed by goods which pass directly from producers to ultimate users. (8)

Discount The amount below face value at which a bond must be sold when it becomes less valuable to investors because general interest rates have risen above those paid by the bond. (14)

Discounting Lending money secured by the proceeds of accounts receivable at a percentage less than face value. (13)

Discretionary income The amount of money left over after the basic needs of life have been paid for. (7)

Disposable income Take-home pay, that is, the amount of money available for spending after all taxes and fixed deductions are taken out. The amount of disposable income is a measure of the standard of living. (2, 7)

Distribution All those activities involved in moving goods from their point of production to consumers or from the seller to the buyer. (8)

Distribution channels The routes products follow as they are bought and sold on their way to ultimate markets. (8)

Dividend A portion of the surplus profits of a corporation divided among its owners, or stockholders. (13)

Division of labor (1) Dividing up all activities, tasks, and responsibilities of a business into specific jobs and then grouping them into departments. (2) Breaking down production processes into separate tasks and assigning one or more tasks to individual workers. (6, 11)

Double-entry accounting A recordkeeping technique in which every transaction is entered twice in such a way that the sum of all the first entries equals the sum of all the second entries. The method provides a built-in check. *See also* **Recordkeeping.** (20)

Economic indicator A measure of economic activity which can be used to judge the direction in which the national economy is moving. Examples of economic indicators are employment statistics, consumer spending, the money supply, and interest rates. (21)

Entrepreneur An individual who uses personal initiative to organize a new business. (2)

Equity Money invested in a business. *See also* **Capital.** (20)

Equity financing Funds raised by a business by selling shares in its ownership. (13)

Exchange rate The amount of currency of one country that is equal to a given amount of the currency of another country. (23)

Excise tax A tax collected from the manufacturer (or sometimes the retail seller) of certain goods, with the intent of accumulating revenue for special purposes or of discouraging the use of certain goods. (25)

Executive A manager in the highest level of an organization's hierarchy. (5)

Express warranty A statement made by a seller, often in a written form, that the article being sold is of a specified quality and type. The warranty may also state that the seller will repair or replace the merchandise if defects are found. (25)

Extractive process An industrial process whereby resources are removed from the earth, sea, or air and then used in manufacturing processes or directly by consumers. (10)

Fabrication processes Industrial processes whereby the size or shape of materials is changed or the materials are joined together in various ways to create new products. (10)

Factoring Providing money in return for accounts receivable, either by discounting or by buying the accounts outright. Factoring is performed by a company. (13)

Fair-trade laws State laws which prohibit retailers from selling goods at a price lower than that set by the producer. (7)

Federal Reserve System (the "FED") An agency, partly governmental and partly private, created by Congress to regulate the supply of money and credit in the United States in order to promote a stable and productive economy. (14)

FIFO First in, first out; an inventory accounting system that assumes that the cost at which an inventory was accumulated will be charged to the finished goods when sold. *See also* **LIFO.** (20)

Financial accounting The maintaining by an organization of financial information which must be reported to, and used in dealing with, the "outside world"—investors, banks, regulatory government agencies, and so on. *See also* **Accounting.** (20)

Fixed cost Manufacturing costs which do not vary according to the amount or type of goods produced or services provided, but remain relatively stable, for example, rent and utilities. (11)

Flexible budget A budget that is capable of responding to the changing conditions of a business while still fulfilling its purpose. A flexible budget is usually achieved by the adoption of alternate budgets as conditions require. (21)

Flexitime A personal scheduling system that allows employees to begin or finish work at times different from a rigid time schedule. (17)

FOB (free on board) destination A term applying to the situation when the seller pays transportation costs except for unloading the goods at their destination. (8)

FOB (free on board) factory A term applying to the situation when the buyer pays shipping costs except for loading the goods at their point of origin. (8)

Follow-the-leader pricing Setting prices very close to those already established for similar products of competing firms. (7)

Franchise An independently owned company that pays a parent company a fee for the right to sell a certain product or to use certain methods or brand names; for example, McDonald's is the parent company or franchisor that issues a franchise to a franchisee. (4)

Free market (also referred to as a free market economy or free enterprise system) A term describing an economy in which businesses are allowed to pursue their operations without central government planning or control. (2)

Funds statement *See* **Statement of changes in financial position.**

General partnership Co-ownership of a business by two or more people who contribute their private capital, share all profits, and accept individually and as a group all responsibility for satisfying the debts of the business. (4)

Goals Used interchangeably with objectives; the targets, end points, or results toward which business efforts are directed. *See also* **Objectives.** (5)

Grading and labeling Using standardized terms in packaging to enable buyers to know the quality of a product without inspecting it. (7)

Grievance procedure An orderly procedure spelling out the steps by which claims of wrongful treatment of workers by management can be appealed through various levels of union and company management. A grievance procedure is usually included in a labor contract. (18)

Gross national product (GNP) The total market price of all the goods and services created by an economy, usually measured over a period of one year. (2)

Holding company A company which buys most or all of the stock of another company and receives dividends on the purchased stock but takes no direct role in the management of the subsidiary company. (22)

Horizontal combination The joining together of more than one company operating at the same level of production or distribution of the same kind of goods or services, for example, two pharmaceutical manufacturers. (22)

Implied warranty A warranty, implied by law even when it is not expressed by the seller, that in most sales the buyer is receiving clear ownership of the property and the seller is authorized to sell it, and that the goods are as represented and can be used for their intended purpose. (25)

Income statement (Operating

statement; Profit and loss statement)   An accounting report that shows the revenue received and the expenses paid by a company during a certain period of operations. (20)

Index number   In statistics, a number used to measure changes over a period of time by expressing increases or decreases from a benchmark figure as an index number, for example, an addition to or a subtraction from 100. (24)

Indirect distribution channel   The path to markets followed by goods which pass through intermediaries (wholesalers, distributors, assemblers, brokers, agents, retailers, and so on) to the ultimate consumers of those goods. (8)

Industrial goods   (1) Goods used to make other products. (2) Goods used in the general operation of a business or an institution. (7)

Industry   A collection of all the businesses that perform similar operations to provide the same general kind of goods or services, for example, the steel industry. (1, 3)

Inferential statistics   Mathematical methods for drawing inferences (or conclusions) from one population and applying these conclusions to another population. (24)

Institutional advertising   Advertising which presents messages from a company, a group of companies, or other institutions without the intent to sell specific products but usually to promote a good reputation or goodwill. (9)

Institutional investor   An organization that invests large amounts of money and whose buying and selling activities strongly affect the prices of securities, for example, a pension fund or a foundation. (14)

Instrument   A document of any kind that sets forth the terms of a financial transaction. (13)

Insurance   A means of protecting businesses from various kinds of loss by sharing the risks. Each participant contributes regularly to a fund which is used to reimburse any contributor who suffers a specified type of loss. (15)

Interlocking directorate   A directorate linked to that of

another corporation by placing the same people or some of the same people on the boards of directors of different companies. Establishing an interlocking directorship is a means of controlling competition. (25)

Intermediary   An individual or business that performs some marketing functions in return for discounts from the producer or for markups when the goods are resold. (8)

Intermittent process   A production operation which runs for a short period and is designed to be easy to change. (10)

Inventory turnover   A measure of the number of times the average inventory of merchandise is sold, or turned over, during a year. It is computed by dividing the cost of goods sold (or total sales) by the average inventory level in one year. (11, 20)

Investment bank   A bank which acts as a financial agent for businesses, governments, or other organizations wishing to raise money by selling stocks, bonds, or other securities. (14)

Job enlargement   The process of increasing the number and kinds of activities performed by a single worker in order to make his or her job more interesting. (16)

Job enrichment   The process of making a job more satisfying for a worker by increasing his or her involvement in it through any of a variety of means, such as encouraging the worker to improve job techniques or to train others. (17)

Joint venture   A form of business ownership set up by two or more companies to carry out a one-time, short-lived business project, at the completion of which it ceases to exist. (4, 13)

Labor-intensive process   A production process in which workers make a more significant contribution to the value of the output than does any other element in the production process, such as equipment. (10)

Leverage   The ability of the owners of a business to control and use the profits from the total

amount of capital when part of the capital is borrowed. *See also* **Debt ratio.** (13)

Liabilities   Money owed by a company for any reason, for example, borrowing or purchasing on credit. (20)

LIFO   Last in, first out; an inventory accounting system that charges the latest cost of accumulating inventories to the cost of goods sold. *See also* **FIFO.** (20)

Limited partnership   A form of business ownership in which one or more partners are granted limited liability, provided there is always at least one partner with unlimited liability. (4)

Line of credit   The amount of credit a lender agrees to place at the disposal of a borrower. The maximum amount is specified. (13)

Linear programming   In statistics, a quantitative method for deciding how best to allocate resources to accomplish a certain aim. (24)

Liquidity   The ease with which a possession can be turned into cash. (14, 20)

Make or buy   The decision process of comparing the total cost of manufacturing a product internally with the price of purchasing the product. (12)

Management information system (MIS)   A set of interrelated procedures for collecting, analyzing, and reporting information (past, present, and projected) organized in such a way that the information is directly usable by managers for decision making and planning and controlling operations. The system is closely related to accounting. (19)

Management by objectives (MBO)   An arrangement between superiors and subordinates that enables subordinates to participate in establishing performance goals in such a way as to motivate and guide the subordinates' progress toward these goals. (17)

Manager   A person who performs the unique work of management— planning, organizing, directing, and controlling; an individual who works through the efforts of other people in an organization to enable

the organization to meet its objectives. (5)

Managerial accounting A system which provides managers with information on costs and revenues. This information is used internally in running the company. *See also* **Accounting.** (15)

Manufacturer's agent An intermediary who sells only part of a company's output and whose marketing functions are limited. (8)

Market segmentation The breaking down of a market into subgroups that are homogeneous in some way. (7)

Marketing concept A concept that rests on the belief that profits can be maximized by concentrating on the needs and wants of consumers and by creating products for which there is consumer demand. (7)

Marketing research Systematic research with the goal of identifying and characterizing markets and of forecasting future market trends. (7)

Markup An indicator of a company's profitability. It is the difference between what a retailer pays for merchandise and the price a customer is charged. Computation of markup varies; it is determined by subtracting the cost of goods sold from the net sales and dividing the result by the cost of the goods sold, or by dividing the net sales by the difference between the cost of goods sold and the net sales. (12, 20)

Mediation A process in which a third party not directly involved in a labor-management dispute tries to facilitate a settlement by clarifying issues, bringing in new information, inducing compromise, and so on. Neogitators are not required to comply with a mediator's suggestions. *See also* **Arbitration.** (18)

Mercantile buying Purchasing, carried out by commercial companies, of goods to be resold without further processing. (11)

Merger The joining together of two or more companies, either by the pooling of their resources and assets or by outright purchase, with the result that only one company exists. (22)

Model Usually, a mathematical description of the way variables interact in a system. A model may also be verbal, geographical, or three-dimensional. It is used in decision making to show changes that will result if certain variables are altered. (24)

Modified capitalism A free enterprise system which has been changed, or modified, to a limited degree by government regulation of business practices, for example, the contemporary economic system in the United States. *See also* **Pure capitalism.** (2)

Money A means of exchange which serves as a standard of value and also provides a convenient means of storing value. (14)

Money market mutual funds Speculative investments (from which investors can buy shares) made up exclusively of interest-bearing, short-term borrowing instruments. *See also* **Mutual funds.** (14)

Monopoly A company that operates with no competition in producing or marketing particular goods. (2)

Multinational corporation A corporation that carries on operations in a number of different countries. (23)

Mutual funds Investment companies in which individual investors pool their money to buy stocks, bonds, and other securities. (14)

Mutual insurance company. An insurance company owned exclusively by policyholders (those insured) and, like a cooperative, operated as a nonprofit organization. (15)

Mutual savings bank A cooperative bank which maintains savings accounts for depositors and uses part of the deposits for making mortgage loans and other investments. This type of bank may distribute earnings to depositors. (14)

Negotiable instrument In law, a written document used to represent currency in business transactions, for example, a check or a promissory note. (25)

Net profit margin *See* **Return on sales.**

Objectives *See* **Goals.**

Oligopoly An economic situation in which only a few competitive businesses supply the same goods or services to the same market, usually without strong competition. (2)

Ombudsman A person appointed by a company, generally a firm that has a sense of social responsibility, for the purpose of discovering and solving problems resulting from the products of the company. (22)

On-line data processing Relating to a method of collecting data in which transactions and operations are recorded as they take place, so that up-to-date results are always available when needed. (19)

Open corporation A corporation which offers its stock for sale to the general public. (22)

Open shop A company or industry that has no officially recognized union. Workers are free to join the union of their choice, and management makes no formal effort to avoid unionization. (18)

Operations The term generally used for all business processes except those that create physical goods, which are generally called "production processes." (10)

Organization All the people, their roles, and relationships, that make up the human resources of an enterprise. (6)

Over-the-counter trading (OTC) Trading of stocks and bonds through a network of brokers rather than through a specific city exchange such as the New York Stock Exchange. (14)

Overhead Expenses that do not add visible value to a product or service during its manufacture or provision. (12)

Participative management (System 4) One of four styles of management identified and described by Rensis Likert. Highly motivating, it stresses the active participation of employees in the management process. (17)

Penetration pricing Setting as low a price for a product as possible, with the expectation of achieving profits through volume sales. Penetration pricing is used when new products are introduced. (7)

Plans, strategic Plans, policies, and procedures for attaining the overall, or long-term, goals of a business. (5)

Plans, tactical Plans and procedures for attaining the short-term goals of a business that are a year or less away. (5)

Point-of-purchase (POP) advertising Any kind of sales message presented at the place where the goods are actually bought, especially retail stores. (9)

Policy A general guide as to how managers and workers are to decide issues that may occur in the future. Establishing a policy provides a way of shaping the deciding process while allowing discretion to the decision maker. (15, 19)

Positioning Aiming a product at the specific market segments that would be most likely to buy it. (9)

Preferred stock Stock which has priority over common stock when the profits of a company are distributed to stockholders. (13)

Premium (1) A regular payment made by an insured business into a pool maintained by the insurance company. (2) The extra price investors will pay, beyond the face value of a bond, in order to purchase a bond paying higher interest rates than other investments. (3) Gifts, usually inexpensive, offered free with a purchase of a product as a means of promotion. (9, 14, 15)

Primary data Data, or information, that is compiled specifically to help solve an identified problem of an individual company and that has not been published before in a usable form. (19)

Prime rate The interest charged by major banks for short-term loans to their large commercial customers with the best credit standings. (14)

Principal (1) A person or company who authorizes another person or company (called an "agent") to carry out business and enter into agreements on behalf of the authorizing party. (2) The amount of money that has been borrowed, as specified in a loan or bond (13, 25)

Private nonprofit organization An organization whose primary goal is to meet needs that cannot or are not effectively or fully satisfied by business. Although financed, established, and operated much like a business, it does not intend to make a profit. Examples of private nonprofit organizations are hospitals and museums. (1)

Process In business, the transformation of some sort of resource into an end product, thereby increasing the value of the original material. (10)

Product life cycle The set of stages through which most finished products move, usually identified as introduction, growth, maturity, and decline. (7)

Product line A group of similar or related products that can be sold by using the same kind of distribution and promotion methods. (7)

Production The manufacture of physical materials or goods. Production ranges from basic resource extraction, such as mining, through the use of already manufactured materials to produce other manufactured goods, such as television sets. Production comprises all those activities which create goods or services to be sold, including manufacturing, purchasing of raw materials, and supervising production workers. The term is generally used for business processes in which the physical form of materials is changed. (1, 10)

Productivity The amount of goods or services produced from a given amount of resources. Productivity is a measure of production efficiency. (2)

Profit The amount of money left from income made by selling goods and services after all the costs of producing the goods and services have been paid for. (1)

Promissory note A document formalizing an unsecured loan. The borrower, who signs the note, states that he or she will pay back the money borrowed plus interest at a specified rate by a specified date. (13)

Prospectus A written statement (required by the Securities Exchange Commission) of a company's financial affairs to be given to every potential investor before an attempt can be made to sell shares in a newly formed corporation. (22)

Protective tariff A tax levied on imported goods by a country in order to discourage the importation of certain products or to raise the price of these products so that they compete less effectively with domestic goods of the same type. (23)

Public enterprise An organization, not intended to make a profit, operated by a unit of government and financed by taxes or service charges paid by the public which produces goods or renders services deemed essential for the public good. (1)

Public utility A private company protected by government from competition so that it can provide essential services such as electricity, gas, and telephone in an efficient manner. (25)

Pulling strategy A technique used in promoting a product in which attempts are made to stimulate a strong consumer demand, usually by advertising. (9)

Pure capitalism True free enterprise, based on the private ownership of business capital, in which consumers and producers enjoy unrestrained freedom to buy, sell, compete, and retain profits from invested capital. *See also* **Modified capitalism.** (2)

Pure risk A type of business risk. *Pure risk* refers to the possibility of loss caused by accidental fire, injury, or other damage to property or life. (15)

Pushing strategy A technique used in promoting a product in which strong promotional efforts are directed toward wholesalers and retailers in an attempt to persuade them to sell the product aggressively. (9).

Quality circles Small groups of employees who acknowledge a mutual dependency for quality and productivity and who meet regularly to identify and resolve operating problems. (11)

Quantitative approach A modern theory of management which emphasizes the overall system in which work is done and uses the statistical study of groups of operations, workers, consumers, and so on to permit prediction and to guide decision making. It is derived from systems theory. (5)

Quick ratio (Acid-test ratio) Quick assets (assets that can be used very quickly to pay bills, that is, cash, marketable securities, accounts receivable) divided by current liabilities. The quick ratio is a sensitive indicator of liquidity. (20)

Ratio analysis A technique for interpreting financial statements in which certain categories of assets, earnings, expenses, liabilities, and equity are compared. Ratio analysis permits a comparison of the performance and condition of a company with its own standards or with those of other companies. (20)

Ratio of net income to sales *See* **Return on sales.**

Real property Land or possessions with a long-term attachment to the land, such as buildings or uncut timber. (25)

Real-time service A computer operation in which data is processed as soon as it is created and results are made available immediately or whenever requested. An example is an automatic cash register system that transmits every transaction to a central computer. (24)

Receivables aging schedule An accounting analysis that categorizes the accounts receivable of a company to show how much money owed to the company has been outstanding for specified lengths of time. It reflects the liquidity of a company. (20)

Recordkeeping The recording and classifying of raw data used in the accounting operation, that is, an accurate written record of every transaction in which money, whether it is cash, credit, or any other medium of exchange, changes hands. *See also* **Double-entry accounting.** (20)

Remote access In computer terminology, the process of transmitting data to, and having it processed by, a computer some distance removed from the user. The connection between the computer and the user can be

made by telephone lines or other devices. (24)

Retailer A company or an individual who buys products for resale to ultimate consumers. (8)

Retained earnings Profits from operations that are kept in a business for possible use in expansion and growth. Also called **Owner's equity.** (13)

Return on investment A measure of how much income has been produced from the capital invested in a business by its owners. Return on investment is calculated by dividing net income by owners' equity. (20)

Return on sales (Net profit margin; Ratio of net income to sales) An indicator of the profitability of a company. Return on sales is determined by dividing net income before taxes by net sales. (20)

Revenue budget A budget that attempts to forecast, in numerical form, the total income from all sources that will be available during an upcoming budget period. Among these sources are sales revenues as well as all others, such as dividends and interest from savings accounts. (21)

Risk For a business, the chance of the loss of money or the loss or destruction of other valuable possessions, or of the failure of the business to prosper. (15)

Robotics A form of automation in which mechanical devices duplicate the motions of the human hand. (11)

Safety stock A minimum supply of materials or goods or an inventory, for example, for one-week's use. This stock is kept on hand in case regular deliveries are delayed. (11)

Sales promotion The category of promotion that includes all promotional activities except actual selling and advertising. (9)

Sample (1) In marketing and promotion, quantities of a product which are distributed free, usually during an advertising campaign to introduce that product to the market. (2) In statistics, a subgroup chosen for measurement to estimate the characteristics of the larger group that is the researcher's real interest. (9, 24)

Scalar principle The concept that authority and responsibility should flow in an unbroken line from the top to the bottom of an organization. *See also* **Chain of command.** (6)

Schedule performance report A method for monitoring work progress during production. A series of schedule performance reports can determine how well production activities are keeping within established time limits. (11)

Seasonal variation In the interpretation of time series statistics, the factor of periodic or seasonal change in each calendar year. (24)

Secondary data Data concerning a company that is collected and published by individuals or organizations not associated with the company. (19)

Secular trend In the interpretation of time series statistics, the long-term changes in a variable caused by an underlying factor such as population growth or product obsolescence. (24)

Self-insurance The practice, followed by some businesses (usually large ones), of maintaining a reserve fund to be used if a major loss occurs. (15)

Services Personal, professional, or financial activities that help people or organizations. The creation of a physical product is not a direct outcome of these activities. (1)

Shopping goods Regularly purchased but comparatively expensive goods for which buyers are willing to "shop around" before making a selection. (7)

Single-line store A store that sells only one type of merchandise, such as food, hardware, or drugs. (8)

Sinking fund A fund to which a company contributes annually so that, by the maturity date of a bond issue, the fund will contain enough money to retire the issue. (13)

Skimming The practice of setting the highest price consumers are likely to accept when introducing a new product, with the intent to reduce prices later, when competition is felt. (7)

Socialism An economic system in which the government owns and operates the major industries of production and distribution and plays a heavy regulative role in all other business activity, but permits certain freedoms of capitalism to exist in a modified form. *See also* **Command economy; Communism.** (2)

Software   In computer terminology, (1) the collection of instructions, readable by a computer, that tells the computer what to do, for example, computer programs, or (2) the procedures for gathering, preparing, checking, and distributing data and output. (24)

Sole proprietorship   A form of business ownership in which a single individual assumes the risk of operating the business, owns its assets, and controls and uses its profits. (4)

Sources and uses statement   *See* **Statement of changes in financial position.**

Specialty goods   Products with unique characteristics—especially a brand name—that make consumers willing to exert considerable effort to locate and buy them. (7)

Specialty shop   A type of single-line store which carries a very specialized, narrow line of goods, such as luggage, tobacco products, or cameras. (8)

Standard cost   A figure determined by accountants, engineers, and management to show what the cost of producing an output *should be.* The figure is an evaluative tool when compared with actual costs. (20)

Standard Industrial Classification (SIC)   A numerical system which groups specific industries into comprehensive categories. The system was devised by the Office of Management and the Budget. (1)

Standard Metropolitan Statistical Area (SMSA)   A concentrated population of 50,000 or more people which has been designated a SMSA by the federal government for census and statistical purposes. (7)

Statement of changes in financial position (Funds statement; Sources and uses statement)   An accounting report in summary form showing the sources of funds a business has used during an accounting period and the uses to which the funds were put. (20)

Statistics   A group of methods used to make numerical data more useful and meaningful. The term refers to the collecting, analyzing, and classifying of measurements, as well as to the presenting of these measurements in a way that is easy to understand and difficult to misinterpret. (24)

Stock company   An insurance company that is organized in the same way any other business is organized and whose stockholders invest money with the goal of making a profit and earning dividends. (15)

Stock dividend   A dividend paid to the stockholders of a corporation in the form of new shares of stock rather than cash. (13)

Stock split   The procedure of dividing each share of the existing stock of a corporation into two or more new shares in order to reduce the price of single shares. (13)

Subchapter S corporation   A legal form of small business that combines the limited liability of a corporation with the tax advantages of a single proprietorship. (4)

Subsidiary   A company that has merged with one or more other companies and whose assets are mainly or entirely owned by another company. (22)

Subsidy   Direct financial aid from the government for use in business operations such as agriculture. (3)

Supervisor   A manager at the lowest level of the management hierarchy in an organization. (5)

Synthetic process   An industrial process which creates new materials by physically combining and changing other materials. (10)

System   An organizational form or set of interrelated rules, procedures, and the like. A system can be economic, social, political, physical, and so on. (3)

Systems theory   A group of verbal and mathematical principles that describe how the related parts of a system may be organized. (5)

Time deposit   Money in savings accounts which is considered an investment and cannot be used directly in exchange for goods or services. (14)

Time series statistics   A statistical method for studying changes through time or attempting to predict future events on the basis of current data. (24)

Tort   In law, an injury, harm, or interference with the basic rights of someone else, even if caused by negligence rather than by intention. A tort is a private wrong against an individual. (25)

Trust   (1) Any business combination that limits or eliminates competition. (2) Literally, a scheme by which a company gives dividend-paying trust certificates in return for voting control of the stock of another company. (25)

Turnkey operation   In franchising, the provision by the franchisor of everything needed to set up a franchisee in business. (12)

Underwriter   In business finance, an intermediary (such as an investment bank or banker) that buys all or a large part of an issue of the stock of a corporation and resells it to investors, receiving a commission for services rendered. (22)

Uniform Commercial Code   A large body of commercial laws, written by legal experts, covering every major area of business law that falls under state jurisdiction and designed to make the laws governing business transactions more uniform in application. Of itself, the code has no legal force, but much of it has been made enforceable law by most state legislatures. (25)

Union shop   An industry or company that requires all employees to join a recognized union within a specified time after they are hired. (18)

Unit cost   The cost of one manufactured product, derived by dividing the production cost of all the units by the number of units produced. (20)

Unit pricing   Giving the price of an item in some standard unit such as an ounce or a pound. (7)

Unity of command   The principle that each person in an organization should have only one immediate superior. (6)

Universe (Population)   In

statistics, the larger group being investigated by the study of a sample. *See also* **Sample.** (24)

Value analysis An analysis carried out jointly by the engineers and purchasing agents of a company to examine every part of a product to determine whether less expensive substitutes can be used without impairing its function. Value analysis is a means of reducing the costs of materials and production. (11)

Variable costs or expenses Costs which rise and fall according to changes in production activity or volume of output. Examples are expenses for materials, labor, and other resources whose use depends

on production. (11, 20)

Variety store A type of general store offering a large range of goods and often specializing in inexpensive merchandise. (8)

Vertical combination A method of joining together into one large company a number of smaller companies, all of which contribute at some level to producing and selling a single kind of product, such as gasoline. (22)

Word processing The production of written communications through the combined use of systems management procedures, automated and/or computer technology, and skilled personnel. (24)

Worker's compensation insurance Insurance carried by businesses to compensate employees for losses caused by physical injury or illness suffered because of their jobs. Worker's compensation insurance is required by law in all 50 states. (15)

Zero-based budgeting A budgeting and planning system that requires managers to justify their annual budget requests as if the associated expenses had never occurred before. (21)

Zero defects The concept that everyone in an organization, if properly motivated and instructed, can eliminate all errors or defects before they occur. (11)

Index

Accident prevention, 298
Accountability, defined, 94
Accounting, 363–381 (see also Financial management)
 accounts receivable, 221, 378
 audits, 367
 balance sheet, 371–373
 Certified Public Accountant (CPA), 367
 changes in financial position, 375
 cost accounting, 368–370
 cost of sales, 373
 credits, 366
 debits, 366
 defined, 362
 depreciation, 373
 double-entry recordkeeping, 365–366
 equation, 364–365
 expenses, 365, 373
 FIFO (first in, first out), 368
 financial, 364
 Financial Accounting Standards Board (FASB), 367
 financial ratios, 375–379
 financial statements, 371–379
 GAAP (generally accepted accounting practices), 367
 income statement, 373–375
 LIFO (last in, first out), 368
 managerial, 364
 period, 367
 principles of, 364–368
 process of, 363–364
 recordkeeping, 362, 363–366
 retained earnings, 224, 374–375
 revenues, 365, 373
 and Securities and Exchange Commission (SEC), 368
 standards, 367–368
 trial balance, 362
 true, 362
Accounts receivable, 221, 378
Administration, defined, 76
Advertising (see also Promotion, marketing)
 agencies, 153–154
 classes of, 150–151
 defined, 144
 differentiation, 147
 direct, 150
 indirect, 150
 informative, 146
 institutional, 151
 leading advertisers, 157
 media, 152–154
 objectives of, 149–150
 pervasive, 146
 positioning, 147
 principles of, 149–152
 product, 150
 and product life cycle, 115, 146–147
 regulation of, 155–157

Advertising (continued)
 reminder, 146
 societal implications of, 157–159
Advertising Council, Inc., 490
Aetna Life & Casualty Company, 200
Affirmative action plans, 291
AFL-CIO (American Federation of Labor-Congress of Industrial Organizations), 329, 330
Agency law, 472
Agent
 legal, 472
 manufacturer's, 132
 selling, 132
Agricultural Stabilization and Conservation Service, 477
Agriculture, U.S. Department of (USDA), 44
Amerada Hess Corporation, 421
American Federation of Labor (AFL), 329, 330
American Management Association (AMA), 490
American Stock Exchange (AMEX), 254, 258
American Telephone & Telegraph (see AT&T)
AM International, 72–73, 267
Antitrust laws, 414, 465 (see also Regulation)
Antitrust litigation, 480
A & P (The Great Atlantic & Pacific Tea Company), 411
APCOA (corporation), 417
Apparel Mart, 140
Application forms, 507
Apprenticeship training, 296
Arbitration, 339, 478
Array, statistical, 441, 442
Assembler, wholesale, 132
Assembly process, 169
Assets
 current, 221, 371
 fixed, 221, 371
 and ownership, 58
AT&T (American Telephone & Telegraph), 257, 318, 408, 412, 464
Audits, accounting, 367
Authority, defined, 93
Automated teller machine (ATM), 249
Automation, 171
Avon Products, Inc., 430

Bad debts, 223
Balance of payments, 427
Balance sheets, 371–373
Balance of trade, 427
Bank of America, 200
Banking (see also Money supply)
 automated teller machine (ATM), 249
 checks, 243
 commercial banks, 247, 248
 credit unions, 250
 demand deposit, 242–243
 discount rate, 247
 electronic, 244, 249–250
 electronic funds transfers (EFT), 244

Banking (continued)
 Export-Import Bank, 433, 477
 Federal Deposit Insurance Corporation (FDIC), 252
 Federal Reserve System (FRS), 242–244, 246–248, 463
 Federal Savings and Loan Insurance Corporation (FSLIC), 252
 investment banks, 250
 mutual savings banks, 250
 prime rate, 247
 regulation of, 247, 251–252
 reserves, 247
 savings and loan associations, 250
 system, 247–252
 time deposits, 243
Bankruptcy, 266–268, 500 (see also Credit; Financial management)
 Chapter 7, 267
 Chapter 11, 267
 Chapter 13, 268
 commercial, 267, 474
 insolvency, 266
 liquidation, 266
 personal, 267–268
 receiver in, 266
Barter system, 242
BASIC (computer language), 451
Behavioral school of management, 78
Behavioral theories (see Human relations)
Bill of materials, 186
Boards of directors, 404
 interlocking, 463
Bona fide occupational qualification (BFOQ), 291
Bond(s), 230–232
 bearer, 230
 callable, 231
 convertible, 231
 corporate, 230–231
 coupon, 230
 debenture, 231
 discount rate, 257
 and Federal Reserve System, 247
 indenture, 230
 insurance, 276
 market reports, 258–259
 maturity date, 230
 noncorporate, 231–232
 premium rate, 256
 principal, 230
 redeemable, 231
 registered, 230
 regulation of, 259–260
 retirement of, 231
 securities exchanges, 254–256
 sinking fund, 231
 tax-exempt municipal, 45, 231
 transactions, 256–260
 trustee, 230
 types of, 231–232
Bonuses, 302
Boycott, 338
Brands, 114–115
Braniff International, 267
Break-even point, 210–212
Broker
 stock, 254

Broker *(continued)*
  wholesale, 132
Budget(s)
  capital expenditures, 392–393
  cash, 392, 393
  defined, 389
  expense, 390, 392
  fixed, 394
  flexible, 394–395
  and forecasts, 389 *(see also* Forecasts, business)
  revenue, 390
  sales, 390
  types of, 390–396
  variance reports, 396
  zero-based, 394
Bureau of the Census, U.S., 478
Business
  cycle, 34
  dynamics, 11
  enterprise, 4
  history, 14–15
  plans, 208, 354, 500
  processes, 8 *(see also* Environment; Processes, business)
Buying, 110–111, 117 *(see also* Purchasing)
Bylaws, corporate, 403

Call, stock, 255
Campbell Soup Co., 160, 200
Capital, defined, 20
Capital expense budget, 392–393
Capital gains, 406
Capital supply, 31
Capital-intensive business, 204
Capital-intensive processes, 170
Capitalism
  modified, 27
  pure, 25
Capitalization ratio, 379
Careers, 499–509 *(see also* Employment; Jobs)
  attributes of success, 505
  business plans, 500
  Dictionary of Occupational Titles, 502
  employment agencies, 505
  full-time employment, 500
  interviewing, 507
  job choices, 502–504
  job search, 505–507
  in large corporations, 412
  managerial, 503, 506
  Occupational Outlook Handbook, 502
  part-time employment, 499–500
  professional, 503
  proprietorships, 500–502
  résumé, 507, 508
  starting, 509
Cash budget, 392, 393
Celestial Seasoning, Inc., 497–498
Celler-Kefauver Act of 1950, 465
Census, U.S. Department of the, 440
Central Soya Company, Inc., 421
Centralization, 95–96
Certified Public Accountant (CPA), 367

Chain
  cooperative, 132
  voluntary, 133
Chain of command, 95
Chain store, 132
Channels of distribution *(see* Distribution channels)
Charter, corporate, 63, 403
Checks, 243
Chrysler Corp., 411
Cimino, Michael, 87
Civil Aeronautics Board (CAB), 139, 466
Classical school of management, 78
Clayton Antitrust Act of 1914, 465
Closing, sales, 148
COBOL (computer language), 451
Coinsurance, 272–273
Collateral, 226
Collection period, 378
Command economies, 28
Commerce, U.S. Department of, 45, 502, 478
  Bureau of International Commerce, 433
Commercial paper, 277
Commissions as employee compensation, 302
Committee for Economic Development (CED), 214
Committees, 102
Commodity exchanges, 255–256
Common Cause, 489
Common Market (European Economic Community), 432
Communications, organizational, 320–321
  defined, 85
  closed network, 321
  open network, 321
Communism, 30
Communities
  attitudes of, 166
  and business responsibility, 487
  Common Cause, 489
Compensation plans, 299–302
  benefit programs, 302–303
  bonuses, 302
  commissions, 302
  Federal Wages and Hours Law (Fair Labor Standards Act), 302
  job evaluation, 299–302
  piece rates, 302
  wages, 302
  Walsh-Healy Public Contracts Act, 302
Competition, 486
  free, 26
  from government, 478
Component parts, 115
Computer(s), 447–455
  access, remote, 452
  advantages of, 455
  analog, 452–453
  applications of, 453–456
  BASIC (language), 451
  COBOL (language), 451
  defined, 447
  digital, 447

Computer(s) *(continued)*
  disadvantages of, 455–456
  FORTRAN (language), 451
  hard copy, 454, 455
  hardware, 448–449
  languages, 451–452
  printout, 454
  program, 335, 449, 451–452
  real-time service, 452
  services, 452
  software, 449–452
  terms, 450
  user-friendly language, 451
  word processing, 453–455
Conformity, 413
Conglomerate, 410
Congress of Industrial Organizations (CIO), 329, 330
Consideration in contracts, 471
Consumer, defined, 21
Consumer goods, 109
Consumer markets, 110–113
Consumer Product Safety Commission, 464
Consumer purchasing habits, 110–111
  discretionary income, 111
  disposable income, 111
  emotional motives, 111
  patronage motives, 111
  primary needs, 110
  purchasing power, 111
  rational motives, 110
  selective purchasing, 110
Consumerism, 118, 486
Contests, promotional, 155
Contingency management, 79
Contract
  business, 471–472
  insurance, 278–279
  labor union, 333
Control *(see also* Controlling)
  production, 185–190
    schedule performance report, 190
    scrap report, 190
  span of, 95
Control Data Corporation, 480
Controlling, 81–82 *(see also* Control)
  process of, 82
  standards for, 82
Convenience goods, 112
Coolidge, Calvin, 4
Cooperative
  defined, 66
  marketing, 129
Cooperative chain stores, 132
Copyright, 474, 476
  defined, 44
Corporate citizenship, 48
Corporation(s), 402–414 *(see also* Legal forms of business)
  advantages of, 62, 409
  alien, 403
  articles of incorporation, 403
  boards of directors, 404, 463
  bylaws, 403
  charter, 63, 403
  close, 405
  conformity in, 413
  conglomerate, 410

Corporation(s) *(continued)*
  defined, 61
  disadvantages of, 63, 410
  diversification, 409
  domestic, 403
  employment in, 411
  foreign, 403
  form, 61–63, 402–403
  going public, 405–406
  growth of, 408–412
  holding company, 410
  horizontal combination, 409–410
  internal problems of, 412
  joint venture, 410
  limited liability, 62
  multinational, 430–431, 494
  ombudsman, 414
  open, 405
  prospectus, 260, 406
  proxy, 407
  and society, 414
  stock offerings, 405–406
  stockholders' rights, 406–408
  structure of, 404
  Subchapter S, 63
  subsidiary, 410
  syndicate, 410
  vertical combination, 409
  voting privileges, 407–408
Cost(s)
  fixed, 210
  of sales, 373
  standard, 370
  unit, 370
  variable, 210, 369
Cost accounting, 368–370
  actual, 370
  fixed expenses, 370
  standard costs, 370
  unit costs, 370
  variable expenses, 369
Cost forecasts, 387
Cost-plus pricing, 117
Cost variance report, 396
Coupons
  advertising, 155
  bond, 230
Credit *(see also* Bankruptcy; Financial
      management)
  commercial, 279–280
  consumer, 281–282
  Consumer Credit Protection Act, 281
  Fair Credit Reporting Act, 281–282
  Fair Debt Collection Practices Act, 281
  "four C's" of credit, 279–280
  line of, 226–227
  management, 279–280
Credit unions, 250
Credits and debits, 366
Critical incident appraisal, 295–296
Critical path, 189
Culture, defined, 45
Currency, 242 *(see also* Money supply)
Custom products, 170
Cyclical variations, 444

Data, 346
  on-line, 349

Data *(continued)*
  primary, 348
  secondary, 348
  statistical, 440
Data base, 348
Data processing, 348–349, 350 *(see also*
      Information systems)
Debenture, 231
Debits, 366
Debt ratio, 225
Debt-to-equity ratio, 379
Decentralization, 95–96
Decision making, 83, 349–355
  and data processing, 348–349
  and management information sys-
      tems, 346–348
  and planning, 354–357
  process of, 353–357
  techniques for, 351
  tools of, 351
Deed, property, 472
Deflation, 244
Demand, defined, 22
Demand forecast, 387
Demographics, 121
Department store, 133
Departmentalization, 91–92
  by customer, 92
  by function, 91
  by geography, 92
  by product, 92
Deposits, bank, 242–243
Depreciation, 373
Dictionary of Occupational Titles, 502
Direct mail, 128, 207–208
Directing
  defined, 81
  as part of management cycle, 81
Discounting, financial, 227
Discretionary income, 111
Discrimination in labor relations, 339–
      340
Dispersion, statistical, 442–443
Disposable income, 111
Distribution
  of agricultural products, 131
  direct, 127–128
  indirect, 128–131
  industrial, 131–132
  physical, 134–139
  retailers, 132–134
  transportation modes, 135–139
  warehouse locations, 135
Distribution channels
  international trade, 425–426
  marketing, 127–131
Distribution enterprises, 10
Distribution systems, marketing, 126–
      139
Diversification, 409–410
  conglomerate, 410
  horizontal, 409
  vertical, 409
Dividends, stock, 233 *(see also* Stock,
      corporate)
  cumulative, 233
  defined, 233
  passed, 233
  preferred, 233

Division of labor, 92
Double-entry recording method, 365–
      366
Dow Jones Index, 251–258
Drop shipment, 208
Dun & Bradstreet, Inc., 204
duPont de Nemours, E.I., Co., 200, 257

Eastman Kodak Company, 408
Ecology, defined, 50
Economic Development Association,
      478
Economic forecasts, 386
Economic measurements, 30–32
Economic order quantity (EOQ), 194–
      195
Economic systems, 20–37
  business cycles, 34
  capitalism
      modified, 27
      pure, 25–26
  command economies, 28
  communism, 30
  comparisons between systems, 29
  consumers, 32
  employment in, 32
  exchange systems, 21–22
  flow of income, 21
  free market, 24
  law of supply and demand, 23–24
  measurements of, 30–32
  private enterprise, 24
  producers, 21
  productivity of, 32
  resources, 20–21
  socialism, 28
  trade advantages, 423
Economy
  marketing, 15
  service, 14–15
Electronic fund transfers (EFT), 244
Embargo, trade, 427
Eminent domain, 464
Employee relations *(see* Human rela-
      tions; Labor relations)
Employment, 7–8 *(see also* Careers;
      Jobs)
  application forms, 507
  in corporations, 412
  by franchisors, 69
  full-time, 499
  of minorities, 495–496
  outlook, 499
  part-time, 499–500
  as a proprietor, 500–502
  résumés, 507, 508
  and unemployment, 328
  in various economic systems, 32
Employment agencies, 292, 505
Energy supplies, 49–50
Engineering, 439
Enterprise
  business, 4
  distribution, 10
  private nonprofit, 6
  production, 9
  public, 6
  service, 10

Entrepreneur
  defined, 25
  proprietorship, 500–502
Environment
  business, 40–53
    economic, 41–43
    legal-political, 43–45
    physical, 49–51
    social-cultural, 45
    systems, 40–41
  physical and business, 491–494
    cost-versus-benefits, 491–492
    land use, 492, 494
    regulation agencies, 464
    Sierra Club, 489
  social and political, 487 (see also Social responsibility)
Environmental Protection Agency (EPA), 463, 464
Equal Employment Opportunity Act, 309
Equal Employment Opportunity Commission (EEOC), 289, 291, 293, 295, 299, 412
Equilibrium point, 24
Equity, 373
Ethics, business, 484–485
  codes of, 490
  values, 496
European Economic Community (Common Market), 432
Exchange rate, 427
Executive, 77
Export-Import Bank, 433, 477
Exporting, 421

Facilities
  layout, 173–174
  location, 165–168
Factoring, 228
Fader, Shirley Sloan, 509
Fair Labor Standards Act (Federal Wages and Hours Law), 302, 339
Fair-trade laws, 117
Fayol, Henri, 78
FDA (Food and Drug Administration), 46, 463, 464
Fed (see Federal Reserve System)
Federal antitrust laws, 465
Federal Aviation Administration (FAA), 139, 463, 464
Federal Communications Commission (FCC), 463, 466
Federal Crop Insurance Corporation, 478
Federal Deposit Insurance Corporation (FDIC), 252
Federal Maritime Board, 139
Federal Mediation and Conciliation Service, 339
Federal Power Commission (FPC), 129, 463, 466
Federal Reserve System (Fed; FRS), 242–244, 246–248, 463
  credit regulation, 282
  discount rate, 247
  reserves, 247
Federal Savings and Loan Insurance Corporation (FSLIC), 252

Federal Trade Commission (FTC), 44, 155, 463, 465, 475
Federal Trade Commission Act of 1914, 465
Federal Wages and Hours Law (Fair Labor Standards Act), 302, 339
FIFO (first in, first out), 368
Finance company, 228
Financial Accounting Standards Board (FASB), 367
Financial institutions (see Banking)
Financial management, 220–236
  accounting sytems, 363–381 (see also Accounting)
  accounts receivable, 221, 378
  bad debts, 223
  balance sheet, 371–373
  bank term loans, 230
  bonds
    corporate, 230–231
    noncorporate, 231–232
  changes in financial position, 375
  collateral, 226
  commercial paper, 227
  current assets, 221
  debt financing, 221, 225–232
  debt ratio, 225, 379
  defined, 220
  discounting, 227
  equity financing, 221, 222–223, 233–236
  factoring, 228
  financial ratios, 375–379
  financial statement interpretation, 375–379
  fixed assets, 221
  government assistance, 477–478
  income statement, 373–375
  leverage, 225
  line of credit, 226–227
  long-term financing, 228–236
  mortgages, 230
  planning, 220–223
  promissory note, 226, 227
  retained earnings, 224
  short-term financing, 225–228
  sources of funds, 223–236
    government, 232
  stocks, corporate (see Stocks, corporate)
  trade credit, 226
Financial ratios, 375–379
  acid test, 377
  capitalization ratio, 379
  collection period, 378
  current ratio, 377
  inventory turnover, 377–378
  markup, 378
  quick ratio, 377
  receivables turnover, 378
  return on investment (ROI), 379
  return on sales, 378
Flexitime schedules, 310
Fluor Corporation, 421
FOB destination, 138
FOB factory, 138
Follow-the-leader pricing, 116
Food and Drug Administration (FDA), 46, 463, 464

Forecasts, business
  background, 385–386
  and budgets, 389 (see also Budgets)
  cost, 387
  defined, 384
  demand, 387
  economic, 386
  estimates, 389
  historical trend, 388
  profit, 387
  revenue, 387
  supply, 387
  survey methods, 388–389
  techniques, 387–389
Foreign licensing, 424
Foreign trade (see International trade)
FORTRAN (computer language), 451
Franchise, 66 (see also Franchising)
  advantages and disadvantages of, 69–70
  defined, 66
  kinds of, 67
  operation of, 69–70
Franchisee, 68
Franchising, 66–70, 207
Franchisor, 68
Fringe benefits, 302–303
FRS (see Federal Reserve System)
FTC (Federal Trade Commission), 44, 155, 463, 465, 475
Funds
  money market mutual, 251
  sources of, 223–236

GAAP (generally accepted accounting practices), 367
Gantt, Henry L., 187
Gantt chart, 187–188
General Agreement on Tariffs and Trade (GATT), 432
General Electric Company, 9, 36, 257, 408, 496
General Motors Corporation (GMC), 4, 46, 62, 157–158, 184, 319, 402
  environmental forecasting, 391
General partnership, 60 (see also Partnership)
General Services Administration (GSA), 478
Generally accepted accounting practices (GAAP), 367
Georgia Pacific Corporation, 52
GNP (gross national product), 31, 43
Goal, defined, 80 (see also Objectives)
Goods, defined, 4
Goody Products, 416
Government assistance, 477–478
  financing, 477
  information sources, 478
  insurance, 270, 477–478
  purchase contracts, 478
Government regulations, 27–28, 43–44, 46–47, 462–478 (see also Regulation)
  antitrust laws, 465
  laws, 470–476
  regulated industries, 466–467
  regulatory agencies, 463
  taxes, 467–470

Government relations, 477–478
  competitive activities, 478
  intervention, 478
Grading and labeling, 120
Grant, W. T., Company, 267, 408
Greenberg, Robert, 506
Grievance procedure, 334–335, 338–339
Gross national product (GNP), 31, 43
Growth, business, 11, 14
  corporate, 408–412
  cyclical, 42

Hall, Jay, 428–429
Hardware, computer, 448–449
Health and safety, 44
  employee, 297–299 (see also Occupational Safety and Health Administration)
Heaven's Gate (film), 87
Herzberg, Frederick, 313, 314
Hierarchy of human needs, 4, 311
H. J. Heinz Company, Inc., 122–123
Holding company, 410
Holiday Inn Motel, 68
Human relations, 308–321
  communications, 320–321
  environmental influences, 309
  flexible work schedules, 310
  group dynamics, 312
  hierarchy of needs, 311
  human resources accounting, 308
  hygiene factors, 314
  job enlargement, 318
  job enrichment, 318
  and labor pressure, 309
  leadership approaches, 315–316
  legal aspects of, 309
  management by objectives (MBO), 316
  morale, 312–313
  motivational theories, 311–314
  and productivity, 314, 319
  quality of work life, 318–319, 486
  satisfying factors, 314
  school of management, 314
  System 4, 314
  Theory X and Theory Y, 313, 314
  two-factor theory, 313–314
  work design techniques, 318–319
Human resources (see Personnel Management)
Human resources accounting, 308

IBM (International Business Machines Corp.), 84, 318, 408, 413, 480
Importing, 421
Income
  discretionary, 111
  disposable, 111
  purchasing power, 111
Income statement, 373–375
Index numbers, 443–444
Indexes, stock, 257–258
Industry, defined, 10
Inflation, 244
Information, defined, 346

Information systems, 346–351 (see also Data processing)
  collection systems, 346–348
  management (MIS), 346–348
  on-line, 349
Innovation, 83
Inputs, business, 8
Insolvency, 266
Inspection, 176–178
Institutional advertising, 151
Instrument, negotiable, 472–473
Insurance, 268–279 (see also Risk)
  accident and health, 276
  business interruption, 272
  casualty, 273–274
  coinsurance, 272–273
  companies, 251, 270
  contract language, 278–279
  defined, 268
  fidelity and surety, 276
  fire and allied loss, 271–272
  government, 270, 477, 478
  group, 276, 302
  inland marine, 273
  life, 277–278
  mutual insurance company, 271
  policy, 270
  premium, 268, 277
  private insurers, 270
  public insurers, 270, 477–478
  public liability, 274
  self-insurance, 269
  stock company, 270
  types of, 271–279
  worker's compensation, 274
Intangible property, defined, 44
Interest, 220
  compound, 245
  rates, 244–246
  time value of money, 245
Interlocking directorates, 463
Intermediaries, 127
Internal Revenue Service (IRS), 470
International Bank for Reconstruction and Development, 432
International Brotherhood of Teamsters, 331
International Development Association, 433
International Finance Corporation, 433
International Harvester Company, 411
International Telephone and Telegraph Co. (ITT), 431
International trade, 421–433
  absolute advantage, 423
  active participation, 424
  balance of payments, 427
  balance of trade, 427
  casual participation, 424
  comparative advantage, 423
  cooperation, 431–433
  corporate involvement, 422
  distribution channels, 425–426
  embargoes, 427
  European Economic Community (Common Market), 432
  exchange rate, 427
  Export-Import Bank, 433, 477
  exporting, 421

International trade (continued)
  foreign licensing, 424
  General Agreement on Tariffs and Trade (GATT), 432
  impact on world affairs, 431
  importing, 421
  International Bank for Reconstruction and Development, 432
  International Development Association, 433
  International Finance Corporation, 433
  joint ownership, 425
  methods of operation, 424–425
  multinational companies, 430–431, 494
  obstacles to, 426–430
  operating problems, 430
  operations, 421, 424–425, 430, 494
  political forecasting of, 391
  quotas, 427
  resources for, 422–424
  societal aspects of, 430–433
  tariffs, 45, 427, 469
  taxes, 469
  U.S. Department of Commerce, 433
  World Bank, 432
International Union of United Automobile, Aerospace and Agricultural Implement Workers of America (UAW), 331
Interstate Commerce Commission (ICC), 463, 466
Interview, job, 507
Interviewing, employment, 292
Inventory
  cycle, 194
  defined, 134
  management (see Inventory control)
  periodic, 195
  perpetual, 195
  safety stock, 194
  turnover, 194
  ratio, 368
Inventory control, 193–195 (see also Inventory)
  economic order quantity (EOQ), 194–195
  inventory cycle, 194
  inventory turnover, 194
  ratio, 368
  lead time, 194
  LIFO and FIFO, 368
  material inventory, 193
  merchandise inventory, 193
  periodic inventory, 195
  perpetual inventory, 195
  safety stock, 194
Investors
  bulls and bears, 257
  institutional, 257
  speculators, 257

Japanese management, 428–429
Job analysis, 289
Job description, 289, 290
Job design, 178
Job enlargement, 318

Job enrichment, 318
Job evaluation, 299, 300 (see also Compensation plans)
Job Instruction Training (JIT), 294
Job security, 486
Job specification, 289, 290
Jobs (see also Careers; Employment)
    criteria for selection, 502–504
    managerial, 503
    and minorities, 291, 299, 300, 494–496
    professional, 503
    skilled and unskilled, 503
Howard Johnson Company, 439
Johnson Wax, 491
Joint stock company, 66
Joint venture, 66, 410
Jones, Mother, 326
Justice, U.S. Department of, 480

Kantor, Rosabeth Moss, 319
Knights of Labor, 329

Labeling, 120
Labor, U.S. Department of, 327, 330, 502
Labor force
    defined, 20
    makeup of, 326–328, 495
    occupational opportunities, 328
    trends in, 327
Labor relations, 326–340 (see also Labor unions)
    arbitration, 339, 478
    bargaining tactics, 334, 339
    collective bargaining, 331–339, 489
    grievance procedure, 334–335, 338–339
    history of, 329
    issues, 331–332
    labor contract, 333–334
    labor disputes, 335–339
    legislation, 339–340
    lockout, 338
    mediation, 338–339
    National Labor Relations Board (NLRB), 332
    union recognition, 332–333
    work stoppages, 336
Labor unions, 309 (see also Labor relations)
    boycott, 338
    closed shop, 333
    and collective bargaining, 331–339, 489
    contract administration, 333–334
    craft, 330
    grievance procedures, 334–335
    history of, 329
    independent, 331
    industrial, 330
    jurisdictional disputes, 339, 341–342
    local, 331
    membership in, 329–330
    national, 331
    open shop, 332–333
    slowdown, 336
    strike, 336

Labor-intensive business, 204
Labor-intensive process, 170
Labor-management relations (see Labor relations)
Laissez-faire business management, 462
Land, defined, 20
Landrum-Griffen Act, 346
Law, business, 470–476 (see also Government regulations; Regulation)
    agency, 472
    agent, 472
    bankruptcy, 267, 474
    contracts, 471–472
    copyright, 474, 476
    defined, 471
    negotiable instruments, 472–473
    patents, 476
    principal, 472
    of sales, 472
    trademarks, 115, 474
    Uniform Commercial Code, 476–477
Law, commercial, 471
Law of supply and demand, 23–24
Layouts, 173
    office, 174
    process, 173
    supermarket, 206
Leadership, 83–84, 315–316
    autocratic, 315
    management by objectives (MBO), 316
    participative, 315
    traits, 315
Lease, defined, 472
Lease versus buy, 470–471
Legal forms of business, 56–72
    alternate forms, 65–66
    choices of, 64–65
    conglomerate, 410
    cooperative, 66
    corporation, 61–63, 402–403 (see also Corporation)
    franchise, 66–70, 207
    holding company, 410
    joint stock company, 66
    joint venture, 66, 410
    partnership
        general, 60–61 (see also Partnership)
        limited, 66
    private versus public ownership, 56
    sole proprietorship, 58–59
    Subchapter S corporation, 63
    subsidiary, 410
    syndicate, 410
Leverage, financial, 225
Liabilities, financial, 371–372
Liability
    limited, 62
    product, 473–474
    unlimited
Licensing, 467
Life cycle, product, 115, 146–147
LIFO (last in, first out), 368
Likert, Rensis, 314
Line of credit, 226–227
Line and staff, 97–98 (see also Organization, internal)
Linear programming, 446

Liquidity, 252, 380
Lloyds of London, 278–279
Loans, bank, 230
Lobbying, 338
Lockheed Corporation, 411
Lockout, 338
Louis Harris poll, 488

McCormick & Co., 381
MacDonald's Corp., 68, 69, 175
McGregor, Douglas, 313
Mail order house, 133
Maintenance process, 179
Make-or-buy decisions, 193
Management
    approaches, 77
        behavioral, 78
        classical, 78
        human relations, 78
        quantitative, 78
    as art and science, 77
    characteristics of, 83–86
    contingency, 79
    cycle, 79
    defined, 76
    development, 296
    ethics, 484–496
    financial (see Financial management)
    functions, 79–82
    Japanese, 428–429
    process, 79–80
    situational, 79
    social responsibilities of, 484–496
    span of control, 95
    types and levels, 76–77
Management and the Budget, U.S. Office of (OMB), 10
Management by objectives (MBO), 316
Management information systems (MIS), 346–348
    and accounting, 352
    data processing, 348–350 (see also Data processing)
    database, 348
    and decision making, 349–355
    on-line, 349
    and planning, 362
Manager(s) (see also Management)
    characteristics of, 83–84
    defined, 76
    and ethics, 484–485
    executive, 77
    marketing, 117–120
    middle, 77
    supervisor, 77
Manpower, Inc., 68
Manufacturer's outlets, 128
Market(s), 109–113 (see also Marketing)
    consumer goods
        classified, 111–112
        defined, 109
    consumer markets, 110–113
    consumer purchasing habits, 110–111
    demographics, 121
    dynamics, 31–42
    and facilities location, 165
    free, 24
    industrial goods, 109

Market(s) *(continued)*
 industrial market, 113
 research, 121
 segmentation, 120–121
 Standard Metropolitan Statistical Area
  (SMSA), 110
Marketing, 108–122 *(see also* Markets)
 advertising, 149–159
 brands, 114–115
 concept, 108
 consumer channels, 127–129
 consumer markets, 110–113
 distribution channels, 127–131
 distribution systems, 126–139
 elements of, 108–109
 emphasis upon, 15
 industrial channels, 131–132
 industrial markets, 113
 information, 120
 intermediaries, defined, 127
 managerial functions, 117–120
 mix, 108–109
 personal selling, 147–149
 physical distribution, 134–139, 196
 pricing, 116–117 *(see also* Pricing
  strategies)
 product distribution, 109
 product life cycle, 115, 146–147
 product line, 114
 product placement, 109
 product planning, 109, 114
 product promotion, 109
 production concept, 108
 promotion, 144–159 *(see also* Advertising)
  objectives, 145–147
  pulling strategy, 146
  pushing strategy, 145
  strategies, 146–147
 research, 121
 retailers, 132–134
 segmentation, 120–121
 selling concept, 108
 trademarks, 44, 115, 474
 transportation modes, 135–139, 196
 wholesalers, 131–132
Markup, 205
 accounting method, 378
Maslow, Abraham H., 85, 311, 314
Massachusetts Institute of Technology
 (MIT), 439
Materialism, 45, 309
Materials
 finished goods, 185
 raw materials, 185
 semifinished goods, 185
Materials handling, 135, 195–196
Materials management, 175–176, 184–
 196
 defined, 185
 inventory control, 193–195
 movement and handling, 195–196
 production control, 185–190
 production planning, 185–190
 purchasing management, 190–193
 scheduling, 187–190
 transportation, 134–139, 196 *(see also*
  Distribution)
Matrix organization, 101

MCA, Inc. (Music Corporation of Ameri-
 ca), 421
Mean, statistical, 442
Media, advertising, 152–154
Median, statistical, 442
Melville Corporation, 381
Mergers, corporate, 408–410
Merrill Lynch Pierce Fenner & Smith
 Inc., 250, 251
Methods Improvement, 178–179
Midas-International Corp., 68
Miller, Arjay, 84
Minorities
 affirmative action programs, 291
 bona fide occupational qualification
  (BFOQ), 291
 employment, 291, 299, 300, 494–496
 Equal Employment Opportunity Com-
  mission (EEOC), 289, 291
 job evaluation, 299, 300
 and labor relations, 340
 Office of Minority Business Enterprise,
  214, 478
 testing, 293
Mode, statistical, 442, 443
Models, statistical, 447
Money *(see also* Banking; Money supply)
 currency, 242
 exchange rate, 427
Money market mutual funds, 251
Money supply, 42, 242–252 *(see also*
 Banking)
 banking system, 247–252
 currency, 242
 deflation, 244
 discount rate, 247
 Federal Reserve System (Fed; FRS),
  242–244, 246–248, 463
 inflation, 244
 interest rates, 244–246
 M1 money supply classification, 243
 prime rate, 247
 regulation of, 246–247
 time value of money, 245–246
Monopoly, 462–463
 defined, 26
 regulation of, 43–44 *(see also* Federal
  Trade Commission)
Mortgage, 230
Motivation
 defined, 85
 hierarchy of needs, 85
 theories of, 311–314
Motor Carrier Act of 1981, 139
Mountbatten, Lord Louis, 84
Multinational companies, 430–431
 operation of, 494
Mutual fund, 255
Mutual insurance company, 270

Nader, Ralph, 489
National Alliance of Businessmen, 490
National Association of Government
 Employees, 331
National Association of Securities Deal-
 ers Automated Quotation System
 (NASDAQ), 255, 256

National Bureau of Standards, 478
National Cash Register Company
 (NCR), 445
National Labor Relations Act (NLRA),
 339, 340
National Labor Relations Board (NLRB),
 332, 339
Needs, human, 4, 311
New York Stock Exchange (NYSE), 254
 shares ownership, 406–407
Nike, Inc., 123
No-par-value stock, 233
Norris-LaGuardia Act, 339
Noxell Corporation, 158
Nuclear power, 49

Objective, defined, 80
Objectives
 management by (MBO), 316
 in planning, 356
Occupational Outlook Handbook, 502
Occupational Safety and Health Administration (OSHA), 298–299, 309,
 463, 464
Office of Minority Business Enterprises,
 214, 478
Oligopoly, defined, 27
Ombudsman, 414
Operations
 defined, 167
 management, 174–179
Operations research, 79
Option, stock, 255
Options market, 255
Order, securities
 limit, 256
 market, 256
Organization, internal, 90–98
 accountability, 94
 authority in, 93
 centralization, 95–96
 chain of command, 95
 committees, 102
 communications, 85, 320–321
 corporate structure, 403–405
 decentralization, 95–96
 delegation, 92–94
 departmentalization, 91–92
 division of labor, 91
 formal, defined, 90
 functional, 100–101
 informal, 90–91
 line, 96–97
 line-and-staff, 97–98
 matrix, 101
 organization, defined, 90
 organizing process, 90
 privileges of, 94–96
 responsibility in, 92
 scalar principle, 93
 span of control, 95
 structures, 96–101
 unity of command, 95
Organizing process, 81, 91–94 *(see also*
 Organization, internal)
OSHA (Occupational Safety and Health
 Administration), 298–299, 309,
 463, 464

Outputs, business, 8
Overhead costs, 373
Overseas Private Investment Corporation, 477
Over-the-counter (OTC) trading, 255, 256
Ownership
 joint foreign, 425
 private, 25, 56

PACs (Political Action Committees), 491
Partnership
 advantages and disadvantages of, 60–61
 articles of, 60
 general, 60
 limited, 66
Par-value stock, 233
Patent and Trademark Office, U.S., 478
Patents, 476
 defined, 44
Path, critical, 189
Patronage buying motive, 111
Penney Company, J.C., 104, 505
Pension funds, 251
Pensions, 303
Personnel management, 288–303 (see also Human relations)
 affirmative action plans, 291
 bona fide occupational qualifications (BFOQ), 291
 compensation plans, 299–302
  federal regulation of, 302
 employee benefit programs, 302–303
 employee records, 296–297
 employee turnover, 289
 employment agencies, 292
 Equal Employment Opportunity Commission (EEOC), 289, 291, 293, 295, 299, 412
 human resources planning, 288–291
 interviewing, 293
 job analysis, 289
 job description, 289
 job evaluation, 299, 300
 job specification, 289, 290
 legal aspects of, 289, 291
 Occupational Safety and Health Administration (OSHA), 298–299
 pensions, 303
 profit sharing, 303
 recruiting, 292
 safety and health, 297–299
 selection, 292
 testing, 293
 training and development, 293–295
 work force planning, 288–291
PERT, 188–290
Picketing, 336
Piece rates, 302
Plan(s) (see also Planning; Schedules)
 business, 208, 354, 500
 checklist for, 357
 defined, 80
 and objectives, 356
 operating, 81, 356
 policy, 355

Plan(s) (continued)
 procedure, 355
 program, 355
 rule, 355
 strategies, 80, 355–356
 tactics, 81, 356
Planning, 80, 81 (see also Plan)
 business, 354–357
 checklists, 357
 goals, 80, 356
 objectives, 80, 356
 outputs, 354–355
 plans, 80–81 (see also Plan)
 process, 80–81, 355–357
 production, 185–190
Policy
 business, 355
 insurance, 270
 public, 43
Political Action Committees (PACs), 491
Pollution, 50, 487, 491–492
Population, statistical, 441
Position (see Job)
Positioning, product, 147
Premium price, 256
Price controls, 44
Prices, stock
 ask, 256
 bid, 256
 exercise, 255
Pricing, unit, 117
Pricing strategies, 116–117
 cost-plus, 117
 follow-the-leader, 116
 and the law, 117
 penetration, 116
 skimming, 116
Prime rate, 247
Principal
 in agency law, 472
 bond, 230
Privacy, 486
Private enterprise system, 24–25
Private nonprofit enterprise, 6
Private ownership, 25, 56
Procedure, 355
Processes, business, 167–170
 analytical, 168
 assembly, 169
 automation, 171
 capital-intensive, 170
 continuous, 170
 conversion, 8
 direct service, 169–170
 equipment, 171–172
 extractive, 167
 fabrication, 168
 industrial, 167–169
 inspection of, 176–178
 job design, 178
 labor-intensive, 170
 layout of, 173–174
 maintenance of, 179
 management of, 174–179
 manufacturing, 167–169
 materials management, 175–176
 nonindustrial, 169–170
 operations, defined, 167

Processes (continued)
 process redesign, 179
 production, defined, 167
 and quality control, 176–178
 retailing, 169
 robotics, 171
 synthetic, 169
 technology trends, 170
 terminology, 170
 time and motion studies, 178
 transportation services, 169 (see also Distribution; Transportation)
 warehousing, 169, 205–206 (see also Wholesalers)
 wholesaling, 127, 169, 205–206
 work methods improvement, 178–179
 work simplification, 179
Procter, William, 402
Procter & Gamble Co., 157, 402, 406
Producers, 21
Product advertising, 150
Product classifications, 109–110
Product design, 175
Product differentiation, 147
Product liability, 473–474
Product life cycle, 115, 146–147
Product line, 114
Product planning, 114–115
Product positioning, 147
Product pricing, 115–117
Production, 167
 concept, 108
 enterprise, 9–10
 processes (see Processes, business)
Production management, 174–179
Production materials management, 184–196
Productivity
 of economic systems, 32, 33
 and human relations, 314, 319
Products
 convenience goods, 112
 custom, 170
 shopping goods, 112
 specialty goods, 112–113
 standard, 170
Profit(s), 5–6, 42
 defined, 5
 forecasts, 387
 motive, 5
 private, 26
Profit sharing, 303
Profitability, 3
 indicators, 378
Program, computer, 335, 449, 451–452
 BASIC, 451
 COBOL, 451
 FORTRAN, 451
 user-friendly, 451
Promissory note, 226, 227, 473
Promotion, marketing, 144–159
 advertising, 149–159 (see also Advertising)
 advertising agencies, 153–154
 campaign, 145
 objectives, 145–147
 personal selling, 147–149
 push-pull effect, 144–145

Promotion *(continued)*
  regulation of, 155–157
  sales promotion, 154–155
  and society, 157–158
Property
  intangible, 44
  personal, 472
  real, 472
Proprietorship, 58–59, 500–502
Prospectus, 260, 406
Proxy, 407
Public *(see* Communities; Social responsibility)
Public enterprise, 6
Public ownership, 56
Public utilities, 466–467
Purchasing
  government, 478
  industrial, 190–193
    economic order quantity (EOQ), 194–195
    inventory control, 193–195 *(see also* Inventory control)
    lead time, 195
    make-or-buy decisions, 193
    purchase order, 191
    purchase requisition, 191
    receiving report, 191
    safety stock, 194
    value analysis, 193
  mercantile, 190
Purchasing power, 111
Put, stock price, 255

Quality circles, 178
Quality control, 176–178
  quality circles, 178
  scrap report, 190
  zero defects, 178
Quality of life, 34
Quality of work life, 318–319, 486
Quantitative management, 78–79
  operations research, 79
  systems theory, 79
Quantitative methods *(see also* Statistics)
  linear programming, 446
  models, 447
  simulations, 447
Quotas, trade, 427
Quotation, stock, 256

Radio Shack, 262–263
Rates, freight, 138
Ratios
  debt, 225
  financial *(see* Financial ratios)
Raw materials, 113
Real-time, computer, 452
Receiver in bankruptcy, 266
Receiving department, 191
Recordkeeping
  defined, 362
  double-entry method, 365–366
Regulation(s)
  accounting, 367–368
  advertising, 155–157

Regulation(s) *(continued)*
  banking, 247, 251–252
  compensation, 302
  consumer credit, 282
  corporations, 414
  and ethics, 484–485
  federal antitrust laws, 414, 465
  government, 27–28, 43–44, 46–47, 462–478
    of AT&T, 464
    business law, 470–476
    eminent domain, 464
    licensing, 467
    of monopolies, 462–463
    public utilities, 466
    regulatory agencies, 463
    state, 467
    taxation, 467–470
    of trusts, 463
  government agencies, 489
  of labor relations, 339–340
  social responsibility, 484–496
  of stock and bond sales, 259–260
  of transportation, 138–139
  zoning ordinances, 494
Regulatory agencies, 463, 464, 466
Remco Enterprises, Inc., 359
Research and development, 439, 440, 445
Resources
  defined, 8
  natural, 50
  and site location, 165–166
Responsibility
  defined, 92
  social *(see* Social responsibility)
Résumé, job, 508
Retailers, 132–134
  chain stores, 132
  department stores, 133
  mail order house, 133
  small business, 204–205
  specialty shops, 133
  trends in retailing, 134
  types of goods and services, 133–134
  variety stores, 133
  voluntary chains, 133
Retailing, 213
  financing of, 224
  small business, 204–205
Retained earnings, 224, 374–375
Return on investment (ROI), 379
Revco Discount Drug Centers, 358
Revenue budgets, 390
Revenue forecasts, 387
Revenues
  accounting definition, 365, 373
  tax, 468
Right-to-work laws, 337, 340
Risk, 41, 266–270 *(see also* Insurance)
  bankruptcy, 266–268
  business, 4
  defined, 266
  management, 269–270
  pure, 268
  reduction, 269
  self-insurance, 269
  speculative, 266
Risk-bearing, 120

Robinson-Patman Act of 1936, 465
Robotics, 171
Romney, George, 109
Routing, production, 187
Rule, 355

Safety, 44
  and health, 297–299
    Occupational Safety and Health Administration (OSHA), 298–299, 309, 463, 464
    process, 194
Safety stock, 194
Safeway Stores, Inc., 342
Sales *(see* Selling, personal)
Sales, law of, 472
Sales promotion, 154–155 *(see also* Advertising)
  contests, 155
  coupons, 155
  defined, 144
  point-of-purchase, 155
  premiums, 155
  samples, 155
  trade shows, 155
Sample
  advertising, 155
  statistical, 441
Sanitation, 298
  process, 179
SBA (Small Business Administration), 44, 212–213, 477, 478
Scalar principle, 93
Schedules
  flexitime, 310
  production, 187–190
    critical path, 189
    Gantt chart, 187–188
    PERT, 188–190
Seasonal variations, 444
Securities, 252–260 *(see also* Bonds; Stocks, corporate)
  exchanges, 254–256, 260
  indexes, 257–259
  liquidity, 252
  prospectus, 260
  regulation of, 259–260, 364, 368, 406, 494
  reporting of, 257–259
  Securities and Exchange Commission (SEC), 260, 364, 367, 368, 406, 463, 494
  stock brokers, 254
  transactions, 256–260
Securities Act of 1933, 259
Securities Exchange Act of 1934, 259
Securities and Exchange Commission (SEC), 260, 367, 368, 463
  financial statements, 364, 368
  multinational operations, 494
  stock regulation, 406
Segmentation, market, 120–121
Selling, personal, 117, 147–149
  closing, 148
  defined, 144
  nonselling functions, 148
  process, 148
  profession of, 148–149

Service economy, 14
Service enterprises, 10, 206
Services, 169–170
 defined, 5
 operations, 206
Severance taxes, 409
Sherman Antitrust Act of 1890, 43, 465
Shopping goods, 112
Sierra Club, 489
Simulations, 447
Singer, Marc G., 337
Singer Co., 68
Sinking fund, 231
Site location, 165–168
 and taxes, 469–470
Situational management, 79
Skimming price, 116
Slowdown, labor, 336
Small Business Administration (SBA), 44, 212–213, 477, 478
Small Business Institute (SBI), 213
Small business operation(s), 200–214
 advantages of, 203–204
 break-even point, 210–212
 business plan, 208, 500
 capital-intensive, 204
 Committee for Economic Development, 214
 criteria for, 201, 202, 501
 direct mail, 207–208
 ease of entry, 204
 entrepreneurs, 202–203
 franchising, 207 (see also Franchising)
 government assistance, 212–214
 labor-intensive, 204
 manufacturing, 207
 Office of Minority Business Enterprises, 214
 retailing, 204–205
 scale of, 202, 501
 services, 206
 small business, defined, 201
 Small Business Administration (SBA), 44, 212–213, 477, 478
 Small Business Institute (SBI), 213
 subcontracting, 207
 turnkey arrangement, 207
 venture capital, 212
 wholesaling, 205–206
Smiddy, Harold, 496
Smith, Adam, 99
Social responsibility, 484–496
 Advertising Council, Inc., 490
 competition, 486
 consumerism, 118, 486
 enlightened self-interest, 489
 and environment, 50, 463, 464, 487, 491–494
 ethics, 484–485
  codes of, 490–491
 free speech, 486
 and growth, 492
 industrial wastes, 493
 and international trade, 430–431
 land use, 492, 494
 and minorities, 494–496
 multinational operations, 494
 National Alliance of Businessmen, 490

Social responsibility (continued)
 power groups, 488–489
 privacy, 486
 product liability, 473–474
 quality of work life, 486
 Ralph Nader, 489
 television portrayals, 488
 values, 496
 and women, 494–496
 zoning ordinances, 494
Socialism, 28
Society
 and business, 484–496 (see also Social responsibility)
 and corporations, 414
 and international trade, 430–431
Software, computer, 449–452
Sole proprietorship, 58–59
Span of control, 95
Specialty goods, 112
Standard costs, 370
Standard deviation, mean absolute, 443
Standard Industrial Classification (SIC), 10
Standard Industrial Classification Manual, 502
Standard of living, 31
Standard Metropolitan Statistical Area (SMSA), 110
Standard Oil Company, 463
Standard products, 170
Standardization, 120
Standards, 82
 accounting, 367–368
Statistics, 440–447
 array, 441, 442
 central value, 442–443
 correlation analysis, 446
 cyclical fluctuations, 444
 data, 440
 defined, 440
 descriptive, 441–444
 dispersion, 442–443
 forecasts, 388 (see also Forecasts)
 index numbers, 443–444
 inferential, 444–447
 linear programming, 446–447
 mean, 442
 mean absolute deviation, 443
 measurements, 440–441
 median, 442
 mode, 442, 443
 models, 447
 population, 441
 range, 442
 sample, 441
 sampling, 440–441
 seasonal variations, 444
 simulations, 447
 time series, 444
 universe, 441
Stauffer Chemical Company, 421
Stock, corporate, 232–236
 callable, 235
 capital gains, 406
 cumulative, 233
 cumulative voting, 408
 defined, 232
 dividend, 233, 235–236

Stock (continued)
 going public, 405
 indexes, 257–258
 market reports, 257–259
 noncumulative voting, 408
 no-par-value, 233
 offerings, 405
 participating, 234
 par-value, 233
 preferred, 233
 prospectus, 406
 proxy, 407
 regulation of, 259–260, 364, 368, 406, 494
 and Securities and Exchange Commission (SEC), 260
 securities exchanges, 254–256
 splits, 236
 trading, 236, 256–260
 transactions, 256–260
 underwriter, 405
 voting and nonvoting, 234, 407–408
 voting privileges, 407–408
Stock broker, 254
Stock company, insurance, 270
Storage, 118
Strategies, 355–356
Strike, labor, 336
Subchapter S corporation, 63
Subcontracting, 207
Subsidiary, 410
Subsidy, 44
Supermarket layout, 206
Supply, defined, 22
Syndicate, 410
System, defined, 41
Systems theory, 79

Tactics, 356
Taft-Hartley Act, 337, 340
Tandy, Charles, 262
Tariff(s)
 defined, 45, 427, 469
 embargo, 427
 protective, 427
 quota, 427
 revenue, 427
Taxation, 467–470
 communications, 469
 corporate, 468
 custom duties, 469
 and depreciation, 469
 estate, 469
 excise, 468
 impact on business, 469–470
 income, 468
 lease versus buy, 470–471
 and municipal bonds, 45, 231
 payroll, 468
 progressive, 467
 property, 468
 proportional, 467
 regressive, 467
 regulatory, 468–469
 sales, 468
 severance, 469
 tariffs, 469
 transportation, 469

Taxation (continued)
  use, 469
Taxes (see Taxation)
Taylor, Frederick Winslow, 78
Technology, 439–440, 445
  application, 439–440
  defined, 21, 438
  growth, 438–439
  research and development, 439
  trends, 172
Testing, employment, 293
Texaco, Inc., 257, 421
Texas Instruments, Inc., 318
Theory X and Theory Y, 313, 314
Thomas National Group, 103
Time and motion studies, 78, 178
Time series, statistical, 444
Timetables for plans, 356
Title insurance, 276
Tort, 471
Trade, international (see International
  trade)
Trade associations, 489
Trade credit, 226
Trade shows, 155
Trademark(s), 115, 474
  defined, 44
Traffic manager, 196
Transport Workers Union of America,
  330
Transportation, 118, 196
  modes of, 135–139
    freight rates, 138
    regulation of, 138–139
    terminology, 138
  regulation of, 466
  taxes, 469
Trouble code list, 176
Trust, corporate, 463
Trustee, bond, 230
Truth-in-Packaging Act, 157
Turnkey arrangement, 207
Turnover
  inventory, 194, 368
  receivables, 378

Underwriter, stock, 405
Unemployment and the labor force, 328
Uniform Commercial Code, 476–477
Unions, labor (see Labor unions)
Unit costs, 370
Unit pricing, 117
  defined, 48
United Food and Commercial Workers,
  342
United Mine Workers
United Nations, 433
United States Steel Corporation, 257,
  341
United Steelworkers of America, 330,
  341
Unity of command, 95
Universal Product Code, 172
Universe, statistical, 441
Utilities and site location, 166
Utility
  of form, 9
  of place, 9

Utility (continued)
  of possession, 9
  of time, 9

Value, central statistical, 442–443
Value analysis, 193
Value systems, 6–7
Values, social, 45, 496
Variance report, 396
Variety stores, 133
Venture, joint, 66, 410
Venture capital, 212
Voluntary chain store, 133

Wages, 302
Wagner Act (National Labor Relations
  Act), 339, 340
Walsh-Healey Public Contracts Act,
  302
Warehouse, location of, 135
Warhol, Andy, 509
Warner-Lambert Company, 421
Warranty, 473
Watson, Thomas, Jr., 480
Wealth, defined, 7
Weight Watchers International, 122
Wheeler-Lea Act of 1938, 155, 465
Wholesalers, 131–132
  agents, 131–132
  assemblers, 132
  brokers, 132
  cooperative chain, 132
  full-service, 131
  limited-function, 131
  merchant, 131
Wholesaling, small business, 205–206
Wolverine World Wide, Inc., 17
Women, in business, 494–496, 509
Wool Products Labeling Act, 157
Word processing, 453–455
Work methods improvement, 178–179
Work rules, 335
Work simplification, 179
Worker's compensation insurance, 274
Working Woman, 509

Xerox Corporation, 16

Yankelovich, Daniel, 488
Yellow Pages, 506
Yeomans, William N., 505

Zero-based budget, 394
Zero defects, 178
Zoning ordinance, 494